TABLE OF CONTENTS

RENAISSANCE
AND
REFORMATION

William R. Estep

GRAND RAPIDS, MICHIGAN
WILLIAM B. EERDMANS PUBLISHING COMPANY

To
Professor W. Gordon Ross
of
Berea College
Esteemed teacher and friend
who first introduced me to the
world of the Renaissance and Reformation

Library of Congress Cataloging-in-Publication Data

Estep, William Roscoe, 1920–
  Renaissance and Reformation.

  Bibliography: p. 317
  Includes index.
  1. Renaissance. 2. Reformation. I. Title.
BR280.E87   1985   270.6   85-27431

ISBN 0-8028-0050-5

The author and publisher gratefully acknowledge permission to quote material from the following publications:

Betty Radice's volume of translations of two of Erasmus's works, *"The Praise of Folly" and "Letter to Martin Dorp, 1515."* Copyright ©1971 by Betty Radice. Reprinted with permission of Penguin Books Ltd.

Herbert Workman's *John Wyclif: A Study of the English Medieval Church.* Copyright ©1926 by Oxford University Press.

J. C. Wenger's translation of the Schleitheim Confession, found in *Baptist Confessions of Faith* by William Lumpkin. Copyright ©1959 by Judson Press.

John C. Olin's *Christian Humanism and the Reformation: Selected Writings of Erasmus.* Copyright ©1965 by John C. Olin. Reprinted with permission of Harper & Row.

Lewis Spitz's *The Religious Renaissance of the German Humanists.* Copyright ©1963 by the President and Fellows of Harvard College. Reprinted with permission of Harvard University Press.

Martin Luther's *Three Treatises.* Copyright ©1960 by Fortress Press.

T. H. L. Parker's *John Calvin: A Biography.* Copyright ©1975 by T. H. L. Parker. Published in the United States by Westminster Press, Philadelphia, Pa.

The maps and tables that appear in the text are from the second edition of Henry Lucas's *The Renaissance and the Reformation.* Copyright ©1934 by Harper & Row. Copyright ©1960 by Henry Lucas. Reprinted with permission of Harper & Row.

Unless otherwise noted, all translations are those of the author.

ACKNOWLEDGMENTS

uch a work as this would have been utterly impossible without the labor of others, both past and present. I am indebted to other historians whose works have been available to me in various languages, but I owe a greater debt to those whose intellectual and spiritual legacies make the history of the Renaissance and the Reformation worthy of study. Of these, Martin Luther is the pivotal figure. It was the five-hundredth anniversary of his birth that inspired me to make a fresh attempt to place the Reformation—in which he played such an indispensable role—in its proper historical context.

Neither the Renaissance nor the Reformation took place in a vacuum; neither was a series of unrelated phenomena without antecedents. Each was a cohesive drama with principal players and a vast supporting cast. Thus I am indebted to a myriad of others who constitute a veritable panorama of medieval and Renaissance society: popes and kings, priests and peasants, artists and poets, musicians and reformers, to list only a few from among the nameless multitudes.

But there are those to whom a word of gratitude must be more specifically expressed. Professors Robert Clouse of Indiana State University, W. Gordon Ross of Berea College, and Jarold Knox Zeman of Acadia University read the manuscript in an early stage of its preparation and made valuable suggestions that led to its improvement. Most of all, they encouraged me in my efforts. To those of my students who read an earlier draft and from whose comments I greatly benefited, I wish to say "thank you." Several libraries have made their facilities and their holdings available to me, among them the Zentralbibliothek, Zürich; the Bodleian Library, Oxford; the University Library, Cambridge; the Mennonite Archives, Amsterdam; and the A. Webb Roberts Library, Southwestern Baptist Theological Seminary, Fort Worth. These were indispensable in my research.

Without the generous sabbatical program of Southwestern Baptist Theological Seminary, this book would never have materialized. The three years I was able to spend doing research and traveling outside the United States and the sabbatical year I was able to commit to preparing the manuscript made it all possible. However, this work represents the combined efforts of a number of others to whom I also owe a debt of gratitude. First among these is Miss Dian Roberts, a recent Master of Divinity graduate of Southwestern who during her student days also served as my secretary. Without her conscientious efforts, this work would have been a much more difficult project than was the case. Ms. Mary Hietbrink, my editor, has been both cordial and exacting in the performance of her difficult task. Through her ceaseless efforts to turn my manuscript into the best possible book, I have been constantly reminded of how dependent authors are on both editors and publishers. To Mrs. Cindy Barnett, who typed the final copy of the bibliography and the index, I also owe a word of thanks.

My indebtedness to others who have helped

to make this book a reality is great. As always, I take full responsibility for whatever errors may have escaped me or whatever imbalances have persisted as well as for whatever biases, hidden or apparent, mar the final product. Perhaps I alone recognize how inadequate this work would have been without all the help I received, and can visualize how much more complete it might have been if the limitations of time and the printed page had not imposed their own inescapable dilemmas.

WILLIAM R. ESTEP

LIST OF ILLUSTRATIONS

PROLOGUE

his book is primarily about reform—reform of learning, reform of the church, and reform of society. It could be divided, although unevenly, into three parts: Renaissance, Reformation, and revolution. Admittedly, I give less attention to the Renaissance than to the Reformation and ostensibly still less to revolution. I say "ostensibly" because throughout the book I consider the revolutionary aspects of certain Reformation movements.

Although the attention I give to the Renaissance may appear somewhat sketchy, I have attempted to present the essential features of the movement and to examine its relationship to the Reformation. The perennial question of whether the Reformation could have occurred without the Renaissance may always go unanswered. That which is beyond question, however, is that the Renaissance made its own unique and indispensable contribution to the intellectual and religious development of the age. Not only did the Renaissance go a long way toward freeing medieval man from the shackles of ignorance and superstition, but it introduced him to new worlds of art and literature, inspiring him with the desire to learn from the ancient Greek and Latin sources and providing him the methodology with which to do it.

Without the Reformation of the sixteenth century, I believe that much of the progress achieved by the Renaissance would have been lost. This is a matter of debate, of course, because it appears to be a subjective evaluation that sees in the Reformation the fruition of some of the highest aspirations of Renaissance man. What saves such a judgment from being merely an expression of uninformed bias is the vast body of literature that supports it. Obviously, research does not free one from the presuppositions that undergird and flaw all human undertakings—hence I do not claim to be completely objective or impartial. But my long-standing interest in the Reformation has compelled me to seek to understand with a fresh openness the Renaissance and its humanism that is so much maligned these days. I encourage the reader to attempt to understand the thrust of this remarkable age and to recognize the debt that contemporary society owes to the bold pioneers of the new learning.

The Reformation—with its appeal to "the rabble" and its rejection of art forms in church worship—has frequently been represented as a repudiation of the Renaissance. Although there is evidence to support such a contention, the Reformation did not brusquely turn its back on the Renaissance. Indeed, in its desire to return to the pure fountains of the ancients and its rediscovery of Greek and Latin sources of learning, the Renaissance showed Reformers the way in which they could effect a renaissance in the life of the church. By returning to the New Testament and the best manuscripts of the Greek text, they could once again hear the voice of the apostles—and of God. In a sense, then, it is possible to interpret the entire Reformation in terms of the application of Renaissance principles to medieval Christianity. This was surely a part of the driving power of Erasmus's ceaseless efforts to bring the Roman Church back to its original purity. But there was much more to the Reformation than an attempt to return to the sources of the church's faith.

Like most historical events of its magnitude, the Reformation has been interpreted in a variety of ways. There are those who see it as medieval man's last desperate attempt to find purpose and meaning in life by applying the religious myths of a dying age to the problems of the current age. From this perspective Luther is seen as the last of the species. Others, notably certain Marxist historians—Friedrich Engels, Max Steinmetz, Manfred Bensing, M. M. Smirin, and Gerhard Zschabitz—attempt to interpret the Reformation in terms of Marxist paradigms. They find it meaningful primarily because it involved a class struggle that provides a sixteenth-century prototype for twentieth-century revolution. In their eyes Thomas Müntzer emerges the hero, the farsighted prophet of the new era of the classless society. On the other hand, social historians, although they do not follow a Marxist party-line, seek to understand the Reformation in terms of the economic, political, and social changes of the fifteenth and sixteenth centuries. Consequently, they tend to either ignore or regard as relatively insignificant the religious, theological, and philosophical aspects of the phenomenon.

Once a study of the Reformation is undertaken, it becomes readily apparent that the movement was a complex phenomenon, the result of converging factors that, like the threads in a tapestry, are not always easy to separate or discern. As the Reformation progressed, its complexity increased. Upon occasion the participants in the drama were apparently overwhelmed and confused by the course of swiftly changing events. Their motives were often mixed, and lust and greed sometimes sabotaged what had begun as a high and holy ideal. Nevertheless, the Reformation remains one of the great achievements of the human spirit. Within it were forces that forged the foundations of modern society and that provide a key to understanding the Western world—its government, its ideals, and its religious life. This is particularly true when the Reformation is allowed to tell its own story instead of being turned into a vehicle for a contrived thesis.

In this work, therefore, I have attempted to allow the Reformation to bear witness to itself. The scope of my observations is necessarily limited by the printed page, but I hope that the reader may glimpse something of the pulsating life of this era—with its agony and its ecstasy, its pathos and its grandeur—in which men and women larger than life made superhuman efforts to further a cause that they supported with undying allegiance.

To understand the ethos of the Reformation, one must try to relive its events, much like one immerses oneself in Rachmaninoff's Piano Concerto No. 3 in D Minor or Beethoven's Ninth Symphony or—perhaps a better analogy—Handel's *Messiah*. After reading this narrative history, the student should be better able to discern whatever lasting changes the Renaissance and the Reformation may have wrought in modern man's apprehension of the nature of the Christian faith, the church, and society, and whether these changes were indeed revolutionary. Understanding them is important, but there can and should be more: accepting the challenge of and commitment to that gospel that called forth the best of men and women in the worst of times.

RENAISSANCE
AND
REFORMATION

The Cathedral of Notre Dame in Paris RELIGIOUS NEWS SERVICE

Chapter I

A MEDIEVAL MONTAGE

Very few periods in history are clearly fixed and agreed upon. For every position taken by a historian on the basis of the most solid evidence, there are opposing opinions. This is especially true in regard to the Middle Ages. Both nomenclature and dating are matters in dispute. The slice of history often designated "medieval" has been dated from 500 to 1500 and any number of other dates in between. The bracketing dates selected depend more upon the nature of the era in the eyes of the historian than the pegs upon which the historical narrative is hung. The crowning of Charlemagne by Pope Leo III on Christmas Day in 800 A.D. marks a fairly definite turning point in the history of European civilization. But when the Middle Ages end and a new period begins is not so readily determined.

The term "Middle Ages," although not without ambiguity, does have the merit of objectivity. Other terms often applied to the era, such as "the Age of Faith" and "the Dark Ages," are more descriptive but hardly objective. Perhaps no one term, however appropriate, can provide an adequate umbrella for such a huge block of history—hence the logic of dividing the period into the Low Middle Ages and the High Middle Ages. In this case the Fourth Lateran Council in

1215 provides a natural division. It certainly represents the medieval papacy at the apex of its power under the pontificate of Innocent III.

The intent of this chapter is to develop a picture of medieval Europe before the Renaissance had begun to gain enough momentum to make its impact upon the age. It will take a bit of imagination on the part of the reader to project himself or herself back into an age beginning some twelve centuries ago. But there is no possibility of understanding the revolutionary changes brought about by the Renaissance and Reformation movements without the effort.

FEUDAL EUROPE

The Middle Ages have been described as "a thousand years without bath." While this statement, like most generalizations, is not wholly true, it correctly suggests that Europe, by modern standards, was filthy. This was certainly true of the peasants and of peasant life in general. A walk down a village street was an experience to forget. Every thatch-roofed stone house was graced by its manure pile and stack of firewood. The stench was stifling and varied, dependent upon the predominant odor, the season of the year, and the time of day. Cows and goats—

3

even hogs—frequently lived under the same roof with the peasant family. In a region where the winters were harsh and people were often snowbound for weeks on end, such an arrangement was both necessary and convenient, if somewhat unsanitary. And in an era when all of life was marked by pungent odors, what difference did it make?

But it did make a difference. Because of the lack of sanitation and ventilation typical of the hovels in which whole families frequently shared the same bed of straw, epidemics were frequent, and the infant mortality rate was high. Feeding on such conditions, the Black Plague, the scourge of Europe (which apparently originated in central Asia in about 1338), raced across Europe unchecked. It is estimated that thirty to forty percent of the population in the cities died as a result. And the death toll would have been far greater if more of Europe's populace had lived in towns and cities. As it was, the plague returned with frightening regularity as Europe became increasingly overpopulated toward the end of the era. It is not difficult to understand medieval man's preoccupation with the brevity of life and the certainty of death considering what he faced: famine, the recurring plague, and incessant warfare.

Artists reminded their contemporaries of the inevitable with their gruesomely detailed portrayals of the dance of death and scenes of the last judgment. It is little wonder that peasants lived in a state of perpetual fear and that their only hope lay in the church and its sacraments, of which the priest was the indispensable agent. Their superstitiousness and illiteracy increased both their burden and their dependence upon the church.

Medieval Europe was, for the most part, an agrarian society. With Charlemagne's empire broken and divided up among his quarreling grandsons, feudalism took over to preserve the little law and order that prevailed during most of the Middle Ages. It was a system of government based upon a landed aristocracy. A Carolingian law of 847 made it mandatory for every freeman to place himself under the rule of a lord. Of the estimated sixty million people in-

Page from *The Art of Dying*, which illustrates the fears of the medieval man

habiting Europe by 1300, more than ninety percent lived outside its towns and cities. The vast majority of these lived in villages on the manorial estates of feudal lords, themselves vassals to higher nobility, who generally oversaw the large land holdings (fiefs) of the church or of kings, princes, and noblemen. While life on the manor did not offer a variety of vocational choices or the freedom to follow other pursuits, it did provide stability for a society that felt the roof caving in and the walls crumbling all around it. Its foundation, while it showed some signs of shifting, remained intact. It was, after all, a sacral society in which the church, by its own admission and that of its popes, was supreme. Surely the church, with the support of the faithful, could fend off the Muslims and Jews and infidels. But the ordinary man would not have much say about just how this was done. He was at the mercy of the lord of the manor.

In a sense the peasants were only pawns in a

real-life chess game. They represented the lowest class in medieval society, and they fared no better in the ranking of the church. It has been correctly said that life in the Middle Ages was organized into two hierarchies: that of the church and that of the state. At the top of the state's hierarchy was the king, followed by lords, vassals, knights, freemen, and serfs. The class of serfs was further subdivided, and at the very bottom of the hierarchy was, occasionally, the class of slaves, a division dictated by heredity. Marriage could, upon occasion, change one's status, but a career in the church offered the only sure avenue of escape for the low born. In the church—theoretically at least—a peasant's son could become a pope, or if a converted Jew, a bishop. In practice, however, peasants' sons more often became the parish priests. They lived in somewhat better housing than other peasants on the manor, but sons of the nobility became the princes (bishops) of the church.

The stratification of medieval society was dramatized both by dress and by architecture. The nobility were distinguished from the commoners by their regal trappings: the ermine cape, the bejeweled medallion, the high leather boots. The lord of a manor lived in a manor house, if not a castle, and kings, lords, and vassals as well as knights occupied well-fortified castles. The two most prominent buildings in a manor village, in fact, were the parish church and the manor castle.

As inadequate as the feudal system was, from almost any standpoint it was better than chaos. Besides, it did make some positive contributions to medieval life. It developed the three-field system, which has been called the most important advance in agriculture that the Middle Ages produced. It also created communities in which cooperation in the equitable distribution of the peasants' allotted acreage became a matter of communal decision, thus providing the peasants with some degree of economic security. At the very least, feudalism made possible the bare essentials of government without which civilization could hardly have survived.

THE MEDIEVAL CHURCH

To the eyes of the casual observer, the parish church, the monastery basilica, and the bishop's cathedral were the most prominent features of any medieval skyline. And even if architecture had not conveyed this fact, the constant ringing of the bells from countless church towers surely would have. Every manor had its parish church, and its priest was easily the most important personage in the community. As rapidly as towns and cities began to develop, church steeples and towers rose against the horizon, frequently dwarfing all other buildings in sight. These structures, sometimes splendid, were medieval man's monument to his faith. For whatever else he may have been, he was basically a religious man, intent on saving his soul. It is difficult to escape the impression that the times were, indeed, an "Age of Faith."

Monasticism

Symbolic of the devotional life of the medieval church was the monastic movement. Arising in the East, it was soon adapted by the organizing genius of Western Christianity. The Benedictine order, founded by Saint Benedict of Nursia (ca. 530), provided the prevailing rule upon which numerous orders were established. In some respects monasticism may be viewed as an attempt to reform the church, which was rapidly becoming captive to its culture. But by the tenth century it was painfully evident that monasticism itself was decadent and in need of reform. Revival came in the tenth century when a monastery was founded at Cluny based upon a revised form of the Benedictine rule. Before the Cluniac reform had run its course, more than eleven hundred new monasteries had been founded, and the Cluniacs had become the most aggressive and influential order in the medieval church, placing their members among the upper echelons of the hierarchy, including the papacy itself. Success took its toll, however, and still another monastic order was founded, this time at Cîteaux in 1098. This order sought to improve upon the revised rule of the Cluniacs with yet another revision. Bernard of Clairvaux, the caustic critic of Abelard and author of the hymn "Jesus, the Very Thought of Thee," became the most ardent promoter of the Cistercian movement, organizing sixty-five new houses himself.

However, the monastic ideal found its most famous embodiment in Saint Francis of Assisi (1182-1226). Previous monastic orders had looked inward, concentrating on the cultivation of the devotional life. Saint Francis reversed this emphasis. To some extent his work and the new shape of the mendicant orders had been anticipated in the life and work of Saint Bernard. To the familiar vows of poverty, chastity, and obedience the Franciscans added the vows of preaching and begging. While the older orders remained cloister-bound, the Franciscans were mobile. Saint Francis and his early followers took the vow of poverty seriously. They did not attempt to make a comfortable living; instead they dedicated themselves to the care of the sick and the outcasts of society. The Franciscans also became the first of the mendicant orders to actively engage in mission work. They were given tentative recognition in 1210. They rapidly won other adherents, including women—in fact, a second order was founded as the female counterpart of the original. However, as Pope Innocent had feared, the asceticism of Saint Francis and his most ardent followers was much too severe for most would-be Franciscans. As the order grew more lax, certain Franciscans formed splinter groups in an attempt to keep faith with the ideals of the saint from Assisi. Consequently the Franciscans became so notorious for their schismatic tendencies that they were frequently referred to as the "Franciscan rabble."

Yet Saint Francis had succeeded in setting a new pattern for medieval monasticism. Following the formation of his order, three other major mendicant orders arose: the Dominicans (1216); the Carmelites (1229), an order formed by crusaders on Mt. Carmel, who claimed Elijah as their founder; and the Augustinians (1256), who took the name of the famous bishop of Hippo for their own. Although they shared a similar vision, the orders became quite different, not only in dress but in character. In time the Franciscans, despite their tendency to quarrel, became the most important missionary order. The Dominicans became renowned for both their scholarship and their nose for heresy. And the Carmelites faded into the background as the Augustinians forged ahead, vying with the Dominicans for the most important chairs of theology in the new universities that were being established in every part of Europe.

In the wave of religious enthusiasm that swept over Europe in the High Middle Ages, laymen formed semimonastic orders that also served the church. Closely associated with the Spiritual Franciscans were the Beguines (women) and the Beghards (men). Although they did not take monastic vows, they followed a simple life-style, combining contemplation with service to the sick and needy. They were suspected of heresy.

Mysticism sparked by the preaching of Gerhard Groote (1340-1384) spawned still another semimonastic lay movement known as the Brethren of the Common Life. The Brethren became famous for the Latin schools that they established in the Netherlands and Germany. Their houses were composed of laymen marked by their sincerity and learning. However, most lay people of medieval Europe were both illiterate and credulous, content to express their religious fervor in other less demanding and more entertaining ways—hence the pilgrimage movement.

The Pilgrimage Movement

In his Canterbury Tales Chaucer gives an incisive glimpse into the pilgrimage movement as it had developed in England by the fourteenth century. Here one learns of the worship of both patron saints and often-fraudulent relics such as the Pardoner's "Our True Lady's veil" and his bottle of pig's bones. After mentioning a few of the Pardoner's "relics," Chaucer concludes, "And thus, with flattery and such like japes, / He made the parson and the rest his apes." As Chaucer portrays so vividly in his character sketches of the twenty-nine pilgrims who happened to meet at Tabard Inn while en route to Canterbury to visit the shrine of the famous English saint, Thomas à Becket of Canterbury, the pilgrimage movement held an attraction for all classes of medieval society. The tales told by Chaucer also give the reader a glimpse into the nature of popular piety. Apparently that which was characteristic of England was also—allowing for some regional variations—characteristic of Europe.

At a comparatively early date, relics of the martyrs were becoming objects of veneration and worship. Such practices received unprecedented support during the Cluniac revival. In essence every monastery became a shrine as more and more relics of the saints were gathered for the purpose of encouraging pilgrimages to the various houses. With the rise of the Cistercians there was a rejection of relic worship and a corresponding discouragement of pilgrimages. Despite this temporary setback, however, the pilgrimage movement gained momentum throughout the Middle Ages, culminating in the greatest pilgrimage of them all, the Crusades.

At the height of the pilgrimage movement, hundreds of people were traveling almost constantly from one shrine to another. A major shrine dedicated to Christ, the Virgin Mary, or a patron saint would sometimes (as in Bavaria) be encircled at a convenient distance by as many as twenty-five smaller shrines dedicated to lesser saints. Lionel Rothkrug verified the existence of 1,036 shrines in the Holy Roman Empire, the majority of which were established before the sixteenth century.[1] There were perhaps an equal number in the remainder of Europe. For every country had its own patron saint with numerous other saints exalted to such a position by cities, towns, villages, guilds, armies, and peasants.

The shrines varied from country to country. In France, for example, numerous shrines were dedicated to local saints, while in Germany, where there was a noticeable lack of local saints, the shrines were dedicated to Christ or the Virgin Mary. In some instances shrines were built upon sites where Jews had reportedly desecrated the host or where synagogues had been either abandoned or destroyed during the pogroms carried out against the Jews in the name of the Virgin Mary. Naturally some shrines became much more popular than others. Such was the shrine at Einsiedeln, Switzerland (near Zürich), reportedly dedicated to the Virgin of Meinrod in 800 A.D.

Instead of discouraging pilgrimages, the emergence of the doctrine of purgatory and the subsequent traffic in indulgences may have encouraged such spiritual excursions. And certainly there were other attractions that lured the religious pilgrim to venture far from home. If he was not performing an act of penance, the opportunity to travel, to see the world, to enjoy the company of congenial friends, to meet pilgrims from other places, or simply to escape from the daily grind or responsibility may have been as powerful a motivation as the purely religious one. In fact, the pilgrimage movement was apparently closely related to the anti-Semitism pervasive at the time and had little if anything to do with the betterment of morals. Indeed, the opposite may have been true, if the known instances of sexual orgies (related to "the Beautiful Maria" in Regensburg) and the gross immorality of crusading armies are any indication.

For a people steeped in superstition and ignorance, the worship of relics, saints, and the host helped to dramatize a religion that otherwise could have been too abstract for them to appreciate. Aware of this potential problem, the medieval church became the master of pageantry and ceremony to enable its illiterate followers to comprehend to some degree the majesty, mystery, and authority of the church. Thus there was a sacrament for every significant event in a person's life: birth, puberty, the inescapable recognition of sin, marriage, vocational choice, and death. The heart of the whole sacramental system was the mass, with its miracle of transubstantiation and its reenactment of the crucifixion, which in itself became a fresh sacrifice of Christ's blood upon the altar for the benefit of the communicant. All were expected

---

1. See Rothkrug, "Religious Practices and Collective Perceptions: Hidden Homologies in the Renaissance and Reformation," *Historical Reflections* 7 (Spring 1980): 203ff.

to make their confession at least once a year and partake of the consecrated wafer. It was far better, they were admonished, to confess and partake of the mass three times a year and view its celebration weekly. The opportunities for the baptized to attend mass and to partake were abundant: mass was said at least once a day in every parish church and more often on Sundays and the numerous holy days. People could even make provision for mass to be said for their souls after death, provided relatives or friends could pay for such benefits. After all, who could be sure of heaven? But the anxious could take all possible precautions by seizing every opportunity to gain additional merit from the "treasury of merits" acquired by Christ and the saints. For the medieval Christian nothing could surpass a plenary indulgence granted by the pope himself. Originally the surest way to obtain one of these coveted pardons was to go on a crusade, the pilgrimage of pilgrimages.

THE CRUSADES

For two hundred years or more the Crusades challenged and fired the imagination of the masses of Europe like no other movement or event in the Middle Ages. The side effects of these holy wars were to change Europe in ways that no one could have foreseen in 1095. A hundred years before, the first inkling that trouble was brewing for Christian pilgrims in Moslem lands had surfaced in Spain. Here the Islamic tide had carried all before it. But Christianity had learned to survive even under the Mohammedan caliphs. Disaster struck in 996 when Almanzor sacked Leon and the following year burned the city of St. James de Compostela. The shrine was spared, but pilgrimages became increasingly precarious ventures. Sancho III, king of Navarre, determined to enlist the help of the Cluniacs, who were known for their concern for the welfare of pilgrims visiting the holy shrines of Christendom. This explains the interest of the Cluniacs and the papacy in the possibility of using the armed might of the Normans and Franks to recover access to holy shrines in Spain as well as in the Holy Land itself.

Without Frankish, English, and German knights, the Crusades would have been impossible. However, the knights who observed the code of medieval chivalry must have been a rare breed indeed if the history of the Crusades is any indication. "Truth and honor, freedom and courtesy" were scarce virtues where crusading armies marched under the banner of the cross.

The Council of Clermont

It was at the Council of Clermont in 1095 that Pope Urban II (1088–1099) first suggested that the cross become the symbol of soldiers on crusade. It was to adorn the crusading knight's shoulders, his horse, his shield, and his battle standards. Popes before Urban's time had dreamed of the day when crusading armies pouring out of Christian Europe would march against the infidel and vanquish those who had caused such misery for Christian pilgrims in Moslem lands. But not even Pope Gregory VII had succeeded in mustering an army to do his bidding.

At Clermont it was evident that the time had come. Urban, trained at Cluny and an understudy of Gregory VII, came armed with a plea for help from Emperor Alexius of Constantinople, determined to challenge the council to support a crusade that would aid the Eastern Empire, save the Greek Church, and free Jerusalem from the grasp of the Turks. For the occasion the council, made up of about three hundred men, had been augmented by several hundred laymen and clerics who had been forewarned of the importance of the impending papal pronouncement. Because the cathedral was too small for the crowd, the council convened in an open field just outside the gates of the city. Urban made an eloquent appeal that met the challenge of the occasion. The aroused assembly interrupted his speech numerous times with outbursts of "*Deus vult, Deus vult*" ("God wills it, God wills it"). Adhémar, the bishop of Le Puy, was so moved that he fell on his knees before the papal throne to beg permission to join the army of the Lord. During the next several months, with the backing of the council, the Cluniacs, and such nobles as Count Raymond of Toulouse, Urban crossed and recrossed the Alps in search of recruits. He was joined by Peter the Hermit, who became the most effective preacher of the First Crusade.

The First Crusade

As a result of successful recruitment, no fewer than five separate armies set out for the Holy Land, but they were plagued by mixed motives and poor organization. Of these, two armies managed to get as far as Constantinople. However, the undisciplined hordes did stir up the resentment of the Greeks and succeeded in striking fear into the hearts of those inhabiting the lands through which they passed. They pillaged and plundered, robbed and raped; once engaged in battle they showed no mercy except when mercy promised more profits than cruelty.

The first victims of the Crusaders' swords were the Greek Christians who were tortured and massacred as the crusading armies left Constantinople for Nicea. The first Moslem stronghold of any importance to fall was the castle of Xerigordon, not far from Nicea. It was taken by a German army and held for a short time until it was retaken by the Turks. With its recapture all those who refused to deny the Christian faith were slaughtered.

The superior discipline and military prowess of the Moslems dealt Christian zeal a near-fatal blow at Civetot. An army of twenty thousand Christians was ambushed and virtually annihilated along with thousands of camp followers, including priests, women, and infants; a few children who met with the victors' fancy were taken captive. News of the disaster at Civetot was not long in reaching Constantinople and Rome. Perhaps for the first time the Crusaders were confronted with the harsh realities of the campaign upon which they had embarked.

Progress on the road to Jerusalem was to prove agonizingly slow. One by one the ancient cities of Nicea, Antioch, and Tyre fell. But it was not until July 15, 1099, after endless months of incredible hardship and sacrifice, that Jerusalem was captured. It was taken by an army of less than forty thousand, the remnant of an army that had been ten or more times that size when it had first set out for Jerusalem. When the day of vengeance finally arrived, the Christians showed themselves to be even less merciful than the infidels. Of the inhabitants of the Holy City, only the Moslem defender Iftikhar and his bodyguards were allowed to escape. The rest—men, women, and children, Moslem and Jew—were mercilessly slaughtered.

Soon all of Europe had heard of the fall of Jerusalem and the subsequent massacre. Raymond of Aquilers wrote that the next morning on his way to the temple area he was forced to wade through corpses and blood up to his knees. Among the Moslems the news of the defeat evoked an undying hatred for the Franks and a determination not to rest until the city had been retaken.

Two weeks after the fall of Jerusalem, Urban died in Rome, unaware of the success of the First Crusade. If he had heard about it, he could not have known how empty the victory was, despite the jubilant exultation of the conquerors. Jerusalem remained in Christian hands less than a century before it was retaken by a thoroughly provoked and united Islamic world.

The Last of the Crusades

For more than another century Europe was overrun by successive crusading armies. Despite lofty goals and frequent heroic sacrifice, the Crusades were little more than an unmitigated failure. Symbolic of the death of the crusading spirit was the fiasco of the last crusade proposed by Pope Pius II. Unable to arouse the old enthusiasm, the pope had determined to finance and lead a crusade himself. On July 18, 1464, he set out from Rome for Ancona, from which he hoped to sail with his crusading army. He reached Ancona only to discover that the crews that had been hired to carry his holiness and his retinue on their holy expedition had deserted. Less than a month later, on August 14, the pope died, and with him died the dream of recapturing the Holy Land from the infidel.

The Results of the Crusades

The accomplishments of the Crusades were not what had been hoped for or expected. One of the stated purposes was to defend the Eastern Empire and the Greek Catholic Church against the Islamic threat and possibly reunite Christendom. If the First Crusade did not shatter that hope, the Fourth Crusade certainly did. From the First Crusade it soon became evident that the Crusaders had little respect for the Greek Church. Consequently Greek Christians and Greek towns and villages became the first victims of crusading zeal and greed. The siege and subsequent rape of Constantinople during the Fourth Crusade was one of the most incredible events in the entire history of the Crusades. The desecration of St. Sophia's Basilica and the wanton plunder of the world's most beautiful city, with its unparalleled treasures of art and culture, defies description. Thus the Crusades, instead of becoming an instrument of reconciliation between the two historic Catholic Churches, became a source of further alienation. Instead of strengthening the Byzantine Empire, they weakened it beyond hope. It finally capitulated to the Turks in 1453.

The unscrupulous Venetian merchants, who had largely financed the Fourth Crusade, probably did not foresee that the capture of Constantinople would change the trade routes of the Mediterranean world, but it did exactly that. The East would never again rival the West as the commercial center of the medieval world.

The Crusades also made possible a fusion of cultures that was certainly beyond the vision of Urban II. For one thing, Europeans, who had previously been far too arrogant and self-righteous to think they could learn anything from the infidels, did learn from their enemies—although how much the world of Islam influenced Europe and to what extent the new learning was due directly or indirectly to the Crusades is a matter of debate. The Crusades had essentially run their course when the Renaissance was just beginning. That Spain and other European countries appropriated knowledge and skills borrowed from the Moslem world is rather evident. As a result, life and learning in medieval Europe would never again be quite the same. In addition, the contact with the world of Allah and his prophet brought

Europe into a closer relationship with the Greeks and Greek classical heritage.

The Crusades changed to a considerable extent the way Christians viewed war. Despite previous attempts to establish among the feudal lords and vassals of Europe the "peace of God" or "truce of God," the church embraced war as a means of dealing with the Mohammedan menace. These holy wars legitimized the extension of the Frankish empire, and in the process the Roman Church itself became victimized by a new barbarism. No less a pope than Innocent III (1198–1216) sent a crusading army against the Albigenses and Waldenses with the same promise of spiritual benefits for the warriors as that offered to those fighting the Turks. The Crusades spawned several military orders such as the Knights Templars and the Hospitalers. Three other similar orders were formed in Spain during the twelfth century.[2] This development represented the ultimate capitulation of the church to the warrior syndrome, for these were not knights of some secular lord fighting on behalf of the church—they were the church. Members of these orders took the traditional monastic vows of poverty, chastity, and obedience for the purpose of fighting the battles of the Lord using the weapons of the world. Fortunately for Christianity, the religious fervor of the times was expressed in other ways as well. However, the reorganization of the Inquisition as a part of the Curia under Innocent III was based upon the same philosophical presuppo-

---

2. The military orders founded in Spain were those of Calatrava, Santiago de la Espada, and Alcántara. The Calatravas and Alcántaras followed the Benedictine rule of Cîteaux while the Santiagos adopted the less severe rule of the Augustinians. Originally organized to protect the pilgrims en route to the shrine of St. James of Compostela, the Santiagos were soon engaged in driving the Moors out of their strongholds in Spain. They became the most popular, affluent, and effective of the Spanish military orders. This was due in part to the exemptions from traditional monastic vows—such as permission to marry with certain restrictions—that were granted members of the order from the beginning. See *The Catholic Encyclopedia*, special edition, 1913, s.v. "Saint James of Compostela" and "Calatrava," and for additional information on the Knights Templars (the first military order), "The Knights Templars."

The Florence Cathedral in Italy RELIGIOUS NEWS SERVICE

sitions that gave rise to the Crusades and in some respects can be considered a continuation of that movement.

THE CATHEDRAL

In the thirteenth century medieval Christianity reached a high-water mark of which the Gothic cathedral was the most enduring monument and best-known symbol. In the latter part of the twelfth century Gothic became the prevailing architectural style of the magnificent churches being built. In earlier times churches and cathedrals had been octagonal or, like most Romanesque structures, simply rectangular. But the

Gothic cathedral was cruciform. It was designed primarily for the celebration of the mass, intended to be a visual reminder of the sacrifice of Christ. Besides featuring the awe-inspiring Gothic arch with its transcendental implications, the cathedral was designed to portray scenes from the Bible. Its stained-glass windows often depicted in exquisite colors the crucifixion and resurrection of Christ. Scenes of the nativity carved in stone or portrayed in mosaics reminded the viewer of the birth of Christ and the role of the Virgin Mary in the Incarnation. The statuary both inside and out completed these visual aids to faith.

The Gothic cathedral originated in France—indeed, the French cathedrals, towering over the rooftops of half a dozen French cities, are considered the finest representatives of their kind. Of these, Notre Dame in Paris is the best known and most often pictured—despite the fact that other French cathedrals such as those at Amiens and Chartres are superior to it in some respects. Like many of the French cathedrals, Notre Dame was dedicated to the Virgin Mary and was under construction for some two hundred years. Its flying buttresses and gigantic rose window make it a worthy example of its kind.

Other European countries also adopted the Gothic style and erected enormous structures with some interesting variations. The York Minster, with its huge stained-glass windows and its massive, central Lantern Tower, is a good example of the English version of Gothic style. Begun through the efforts of Archbishop Walter de Grey in 1220, it was not completed until 1472. German cathedrals were less ornate than those of the French, although the cathedral at Cologne, the largest in Germany, does rival the grandeur of its French models. It is perhaps in Spain that the basic Gothic pattern underwent the most change. While the Spanish deliberately tried to avoid the influence of Moorish architecture in their cathedrals, they more often than not ended up with a skillful blending of the Moorish and Gothic styles. An example of this fusion is the cathedral of Toledo. Begun in 1227, it was not finished until 1497. The first architect,

a Frenchman, was followed by a succession of unknown architects whose influence gave the completed structure a touch of the culture that for so long had enveloped Spain. In Italy the stained-glass windows so common in Northern cathedrals were replaced with murals and mosaics.

Thus, in numerous cities of the Holy Roman Empire, the cathedral became a symbol of the times and a reflection of the religious devotion of those who sought to express their faith in glass and stone. But the cathedral was more than a symbol. Originally conceived as the bishop's church, it became a meeting place for large assemblies and a school for training priests. Some of the earliest universities grew out of these cathedral schools.

THE MEDIEVAL UNIVERSITY

Before the first universities were established in the twelfth and thirteenth centuries, schools were rare. Charlemagne had established a palace school at Aix-la-Chapelle and by so doing stimulated learning. However, until late in the twelfth century, cathedral and monastic schools were the only centers of learning. Naturally the curriculum in these schools was quite limited. It consisted of the study of Latin and the classical disciplines divided into the trivium and the quadrivium, which were derived from the old rhetoric schools of Rome. The trivium consisted of grammar, rhetoric, and logic; the quadrivium consisted of arithmetic, music, geometry, and astronomy. This course of study was appropriated by the medieval universities for the basic degree in the arts.

The term university originally referred to a guild of scholars engaged in serious study. Apparently the first two universities were those of Paris and Bologna, established sometime late in the twelfth century. Both soon became popular centers of learning because of teachers who acquired international reputations. Among these were Abelard (1079–1142) at Paris, who taught theology, and Gratian (d. 1179) at Bologna, who taught canon law.

The medieval university was a far cry from its

modern descendants. For one thing, there was no campus. The university—whether one of masters (that is, controlled by the faculty, like the University of Paris) or one of scholars (in which the students set the rules, as they did at the University of Bologna)—had no buildings of its own. What declared the presence of a university in a particular city was the distinctive garb of students and teachers. At first classes were held in the living quarters of the teachers or in rooms rented by them for the purpose. Later, as universities became organized according to nations, this responsibility was assumed by the new organizations. Bursas (residence halls) under the direction of accomplished scholars provided both lodging and instruction and became the prototypes for colleges characteristic of the Universities of Oxford and Cambridge.

While the organization of medieval universities varied, the basic curriculum remained much the same. However, some universities in time became distinguished for their offerings in one of the three classical disciplines: theology, law, or medicine. In theology Peter Lombard's *Books of Sentences* was the major textbook and remained so for centuries, even though the Bible was also studied. Since at that time textbooks were very expensive because the printing press had not yet been invented, the lecture method and the exchange of student notebooks became standard procedure. Even medicine was taught in this manner.

The rediscovery of Aristotle brought about a fresh synthesis of Greek philosophy and Christian thought. It was in the universities that the great systems of theology, under the category of "Scholasticism," developed. Thomas Aquinas (1224–1274) represents the peak of this development. Kenneth Scott Latourette has characterized him as an "Aristotelian-realist" because he used both Aristotelian philosophy and some Platonic presuppositions in developing a system of theology in support of church dogma. His *Summa Theologica* became his most important work. Aquinas is important because he was a man of genius committed to a defense of the medieval dogmas of the church. Utilizing Aris-

totelian concepts on the nature of reality, he developed a rational basis for a theology of the sacraments. For the first time transubstantiation received a thorough theological underpinning. It was also Aquinas who taught "the two sword doctrine" so eloquently enunciated by Pope Boniface VIII (1234–1303) in his bull *Unam sanctam.* Thus the medieval university became the heir of both monastery and cathedral as the guardian of learning and the defender of the faith.

THE MEDIEVAL PAPACY

The history of the papacy in the Middle Ages is to a considerable extent an account of a tug-of-war between popes and kings. The struggle was primarily one in which the popes attempted to assert their authority to make their own appointments to ecclesiastical positions throughout the church or at least to make it impossible for anyone to hold an office in the Roman Catholic Church without their consent. This was the essence of the investiture controversy. The success or failure of the papacy in achieving its goals determined the quality of men who, beginning with Nicholas I (858–867), wore the papal crown.

The seeds of the investiture controversy were inherent in the coronation of Charlemagne. Even though the newly crowned emperor was taken by surprise by the wily Leo III, his acceptance of the imperial crown at the pope's hands was symbolic. In effect, it was a tacit admission that the pope had the authority to bestow the crown and thus the power to take it away. That Charlemagne resented the implications of papal pretensions implicit in Leo's act became apparent when his son was made emperor coregent. Charlemagne instructed him to take the crown with his own hands from the altar of the cathedral in Aix-la-Chapelle (Aachen). Nevertheless, popes continued to assert the right to crown emperors and to make and break kings, as well as the exclusive right of jurisdiction in all ecclesiastical affairs.

TABLE 1. LIST OF POPES, 1294–1605

Boniface VIII, 1294–1303
Benedict XI, 1303–1304

THE AVIGNONESE PAPACY, 1309–1377

Clement V, 1305–1314
John XXII, 1316–1334
Benedict XII, 1334–1342
Clement VI, 1342–1352
Innocent VI, 1352–1362
Urban V, 1362–1370
Gregory XI, 1371–1378

THE PAPAL SCHISM, 1378–1415

POPES IN ROME	POPES IN AVIGNON
Urban VI, 1378–1389	Clement VII, 1378–1394
Boniface IX, 1389–1404	Benedict XIII, 1394–1424
Innocent VII, 1404–1406	
Gregory XII, 1406, resigned in 1415	

COUNCIL OF PISA, 1409

Deposed Gregory XII and Benedict XIII
elected Alexander V, 1409–1410
John XXIII succeeded him, 1410, but was deposed
by the Council of Constance, 1415

Martin V, 1417–1431
Eugenius IV, 1431–1447
(Felix V, 1439–1449, counterpope
elected by Council of Basel)
Nicholas V, 1447–1455
Calixtus III, 1455–1458
Pius II, 1458–1464
Paul II, 1464–1471
Sixtus IV, 1471–1484
Innocent VIII, 1484–1492
Alexander VI, 1492–1503
Pius III, Sept.–Oct., 1503
Julius II, 1503–1513
Leo X, 1513–1521
Adrian VI, 1522–1523
Clement VII, 1523–1534
Paul III, 1534–1549
Julius III, 1550–1555
Marcellus II, April, 1555
Paul IV, 1555–1559
Pius IV, 1559–1565
Pius V, 1566–1572
Gregory XIII, 1572–1585
Sixtus V, 1585–1590
Urban VII, Sept., 1590
Gregory XIV, 1590–1591
Innocent IX, Oct.–Dec., 1591
Clement VIII, 1592–1605

A Decadent Papacy

The stage was set for the dramatic series of episodes involving Nicholas I. He was the first pope to make use of the Pseudo-Isidorian Decretals (ca. 864) to support the exalted claims of the papacy. Unfortunately, the papacy soon became the pawn of certain unscrupulous families in Rome. From 882 to 994, those who occupied the papal see suffered one indignity after another. Perhaps the lowest point reached began with Sergius III; as William Cannon writes, "For approximately sixty years the papacy was tied to a woman's apron strings. Theodora and her two daughters, Theodora the Younger and Marozia, through their charming and enticing harlotry controlled Rome and with it even the church itself in the West."[3] "The Pornocracy," as this period is called, was finally brought to a close by the assassination of Pope John XII, but not before Otto I (936–973), who had been crowned emperor of the Holy Roman Empire by the pope himself, had assembled a synod on November 6, 963, in St. Peter's to hear charges against the pontiff. The synod proceeded to depose Pope John and elect a layman, Leo VII, to take his place. In the struggle that followed, Pope John convoked another synod in the same place on February 26, 964, to undo what Otto's synod had done. As Otto prepared to lay siege to the city, John was assassinated. Subsequent history bestowed upon Otto, as it did upon Charlemagne, the title "the Great."

The successors of Otto the Great were able to maintain control of the papacy until the death of Otto III. During this time first a German, Gregory V, and later a Frenchman, Sylvester II, served as popes—hence the papacy enjoyed some of its better days, even though the foreigners were bitterly resented by the Italian people. With the death of Otto III, a Roman family by the name of Crescentii placed the next three popes on the papal throne. These pontiffs were followed by three others who owed their elevation to the papal see to the counts of

---

3. Cannon, *History of Christianity in the Middle Ages* (Nashville: Abingdon Press, 1960), p. 133.

Tusculum. Once again the pawn of rival Italian families, the papacy sank to a new low of incompetence and degeneracy. The first of the six popes was a boy of twelve who took the name Benedict IX (1032-1045). After an unspeakably profligate youth he sold the papal office to the highest bidder, John Gratian, who became Gregory VI (1045-1046). The papacy was finally rescued from its morass with the election of Leo IX (1049-1054).

Leo IX and Papal Achievements

Leo IX was a reforming prelate. For twenty years he had served as a bishop in Alsace. After he became pope he launched a personal campaign to rid the church of simony and libertinism. He used all the powers of his office to confront heresy, persuade kings to do his bidding, and bolster claims of the Roman Catholic Church. He even led an army against the Normans in southern Italy. There is little doubt that he was the most able man to occupy the papal throne in centuries. Unfortunately, he was unable to find a way to reconcile himself with Michael Cerularius, the ambitious patriarch of Constantinople. Both men were unyielding. The result was that what had been two traditions, Greek and Roman, within one Catholic church became two churches, each one rejecting the other. On July 16, 1054, the papal legates laid on the altar of Saint Sophia an anathema of Cerularius and his supporters; four days later the patriarch replied in kind at the same place. The pope and his followers were excommunicated. The breach seemed irreparable, and so it has proved to be until the present. In spite of the schism, subsequent popes continued to try to find ways to bring the Greeks back into the church. But councils and crusades failed, and the two Catholic churches continued to drift apart.

Despite his failures, Leo IX established a pattern for the medieval church that was to put the papacy on the road to unprecedented achievements. Gregory VII (1073-1085), Innocent III (1198-1216), and Boniface VIII (1294-1303) represent the medieval papacy at its peak. Of these, Innocent III was undoubtedly the most

successful. It was under his leadership that the papacy reached the zenith of its influence, not equaled since. Each of the three had a fateful encounter with a powerful monarch over the perennial problem of the Middle Ages: the right of lay investiture.

In introducing his reform designed to eliminate lay investiture, Gregory found himself in open conflict with Henry IV of Germany. Henry had already made a couple of ecclesiastical appointments in Italy when Gregory called his hand. The king made a promise to stop granting appointments but promptly broke it. He was summoned to Rome to answer for his conduct but refused to appear. The pope responded by excommunicating Henry and putting his country under an interdict. Henry's subjects supported the pope against their king, but the German bishops supported Henry. The pope threatened to take the crown from Henry and give it to a more subservient monarch. Henry was hardly in a position to negotiate. In January 1077 he hastened over the Alps with his family to Canossa, and spent three days in the snow outside the pope's residence there, garbed as a penitent sinner. Gregory took Henry's apparent repentance at face value and forgave him. Thus the king who had refused to answer a summons to Rome and to kiss the pope's foot (an act Gregory now required of all earthly princes) was humiliated before all of Europe. The pope emerged from the conflict completely victorious. True, Henry's repentance was not genuine, and both king and pope were to continue the struggle with disastrous results. But the point had been made, and subsequent popes were to make the most of it.

Innocent III had learned the lessons of history well. Even more completely than his predecessors, Gregory VII and Alexander III (1159-1181), Innocent grasped and implemented the papal ideal of absolute sovereignty over civil and ecclesiastical affairs of the Empire. The most celebrated case (but by no means the only one) in which the pope emerged absolute victor over his royal opponent was that of King John of England. John misjudged the times, his subjects, and the power of Innocent. He attempted to appoint John de Grey as archbishop of Canterbury. The results were catastrophic for John, who was forced to surrender England to the pope and was only too happy to have it returned to him as a fief. In the meantime, the English barons, taking advantage of the king's predicament, forced him to sign the Magna Carta. Innocent's triumph over John was symbolic of his fortune in achieving papal supremacy against all challenges, both secular and religious.

The end of an era was apparent in the attempts of Boniface VIII to duplicate the feats of Innocent III. In a series of altercations with the various princes, Boniface fared the worse for his efforts. He suffered his most celebrated defeat at the hands of Philip the Fair of France. Philip refused to do the pope's bidding in his war with England, and he would not be cowed into submission. Boniface sought to pacify the irate Philip by canonizing his grandfather. But this act failed to save Boniface from a final assault: French partisans broke in upon the eighty-six-year-old man and beat him mercilessly.

A month later Boniface was dead, but the ideal to which he had devoted his energies was not. Aquinas worked out the theological formula that Boniface had incorporated in the papal bull *Unam sanctam* (1302). The pertinent section reads,

> Both swords, the spiritual and the material, therefore, are in the power of the church; the one, indeed, to be wielded for the church, the other by the church; the one by the hand of the priest, the other by the hand of kings and knights, but at the will and sufferance of the priest. One sword, moreover, ought to be under the other, and the temporal authority to be subjected to the spiritual.[4]

The Babylonian Captivity (1305-1376)

Philip was able to manipulate the appointment of Clement V to the papacy. Clement became completely subservient to French interests and

promptly moved the papal residence to Avignon. Here in the walled city on the Rhône the papacy became notorious for its luxury, greed, and immorality. The popes continued to govern the church from Avignon until Gregory XI (1370-1378), even though a Frenchman, returned the papacy to Rome on January 17, 1377. Perhaps Catherine of Siena (1347-1380), mystic and papal critic, was as much responsible for the restoration of the papal residence to Rome as Gregory himself. However, the papacy returned to Rome much weaker than it had been when it forsook the "holy city" some seventy years before. (Historians subsequently labeled this period of the Avignon papacy "the Babylonian Captivity" because it is reminiscent of the seventy-year period during which the children of Israel were held captive in Babylonia.) French interests had succeeded in reducing the Roman Curia to little more than a department of the French government.

The Papal Schism (1378-1417)

The Babylonian Captivity had hardly ended when an even worse catastrophe overtook the Roman Church. Bartolomeo Prignano, cardinal archbishop of Bari, was elected pope on April 7, 1372. But Urban VI, as he called himself, soon alienated a majority of the cardinals. They retaliated by meeting at Anagni on August 9 to declare his election null and void. Six weeks later, on September 20, they elected Robert of Geneva, a Frenchman, as pope. He took the name of Clement VII and moved his papal offices to Avignon. The nations of Europe became almost equally divided between their allegiances to Avignon or to Rome. This was not the first time Europe had witnessed the spectacle of more than one claimant to the papal throne, but it proved the most durable of such schisms and the most difficult to resolve. Before a solution was found, there were three aspirants claiming the title simultaneously: John XXIII, Gregory XII, and Benedict XIII.

The schism was finally healed at the Council of Constance (1414-1418). The council accepted the resignation of Gregory XII and de-

---

4. Cited in *The Papal Encyclicals in Their Historical Context*, ed. Anne Fremantle (New York: Mentor-Omega, 1956), p. 73.

posed John XXIII (after trying him in absentia), reducing the absent pope to a cardinal bishop. It ignored the claims of Benedict XIII, dubbing him an anti-pope. The council then proceeded to elect Otto Colonna—who took the name Martin—to the papacy on November 11, 1417. Thus one of the most confusing episodes in the history of the medieval church was brought to a close, but not until irreparable damage had been done.[5]

HERESY AND DISSENT

In addition to healing the Papal Schism, the Council of Constance concerned itself with the rising tide of heresy, a growing phenomenon during the Middle Ages. The bishops proved ineffective in dealing with the problem. Thus the Holy Office of the Inquisition was incorporated in the Curia by the action of the Fourth Lateran Council. At this point the suppression of heresy became a crusade against heretics.

Although Jews were technically not heretics, because they had never been a part of the church, they became the perennial objects of persecution. Forced baptisms, advocated by no less an intellect than Duns Scotus, were not uncommon.[6] While Jews had been the objects of discrimination and persecution since the Constantinian era, the Crusades unleashed a new flurry of massacres across Europe, especially in the Rhineland. The Fourth Lateran Council decreed that Jews, along with Saracens, were to wear distinctive garb. By the end of the fifteenth century the Jews had been driven out of numerous cities of Europe; they were allowed to live in isolated villages or, in some cases, in certain ghettos in larger towns. It is not surprising that some Jews found life much more to their liking in these places. But even then they often ran afoul of the Inquisition, as did other heretics.

The most insidious form of heresy with which the church had to contend was that of those who remained within the church. One such was Claudius of Turin (ca. 830), who served as both a bishop within the church and a dispenser of evangelical and antipapal propaganda. Others were not so fortunate as he. Rome dealt harshly with Arnold of Brescia (a student of Abelard), Peter de Bruys, Henry of Lausanne, and—still more significant as far as medieval heresy is concerned—Peter Waldo and the Waldenses.[7] The Spiritual Franciscans, who insisted upon wearing a distinctive habit to set themselves apart from the Conventual Franciscans, can be numbered in this category. However, most medieval heretics maintained a low profile in order not to appear different from their Catholic neighbors. Still, they often lived in communities set apart from other population centers, and this made them easy targets for greedy lords and their crusading armies. The Albigenses and the Waldenses became such objects of persecution during the pontificate of Innocent III.

Heresy and its suppression were a part of the medieval montage but phenomena of minor importance when compared with the Crusades and the waves of Crusaders who swept through Europe to wage war against the bastions of the Moslem world. Apparently dissent over and discontent with the structures of medieval society loomed no larger than a small cloud on the horizon, but out of it was to come a gathering storm. Few aspects of European life in the Middle Ages would escape its impact.

---

5. References to the conciliar movement occur in subsequent chapters of this work. It was a movement that theoretically placed supreme authority in general councils of the church to correct abuses and to censure or depose erring pontiffs. Beginning with the Council of Pisa in 1409, the conciliar movement had run its course by the Council of Florence in 1439, through which Eugenius IV was able to outmaneuver his foes and reverse the action of the Council of Basel (1431), which had deposed him.

6. Edward A. Synan, *The Popes and the Jews in the Middle Ages* (New York: Macmillan, 1965), p. 48.

7. After failing to receive recognition as a new order in the Roman Catholic Church, the Waldenses continued to exist with the help of friendly bishops. They acknowledged the Bible as their authority in spiritual matters and made it available in the vernacular that became influential in the formulation of their faith and preaching. They became the most evangelical of the medieval dissenters. They rejected the metaphysical dualism that characterized other medieval protesters such as the Albigenses. By the sixteenth century they were found in France, Italy, Switzerland, and Bohemia.

Chapter II

THE ITALIAN RENAISSANCE

hen did the Middle Ages end and the Renaissance begin? Is this possible to determine, or is the Renaissance a concept superimposed upon history without meaning or justification? Was the period of history known as the Renaissance simply the flowering of the Middle Ages, or did it mark a new era completely unrelated to the past? A further question concerns the modernity of the Renaissance. Was it the beginning of the modern era or the twilight of a dying day—sunrise or sunset? If it was the beginning of the modern world, what specifically made it so? Was it the rise of nationalism, the spirit of the age (*Zeitgeist*), individualism, freedom of inquiry, the rediscovery of the Greek and Latin classics, the rise of technology based upon observation and experimentation, the urbanization of Europe, the Italian genius come of age, a new secularism devoid of any deep commitment to the Christian faith—or none of these? These are some of the questions that this chapter will attempt to answer.

THE PARAMETERS: 1300-1517

It was Jacob Burckhardt (1818–1898) in his pioneering work *The Civilization of the Renais-*sance in Italy (*Die Kultur der Renaissance in Italien*), published in 1860, who popularized the idea that the Renaissance was a uniquely important and identifiable era in the history of Western civilization. In fact, more than one of his critics has accused him of creating the concept without adequate supporting data from the course of historical events. Burckhardt's creation is commonly referred to as "the Burckhardtian synthesis." However, Burckhardt was not the first to see in the Renaissance a separate and distinct era within medieval history. Voltaire used the term to identify the same era and called it one of four golden ages of European history. Before Voltaire the term had been used by both French and Italian writers. And despite the Burckhardtian revisionists and detractors, the concept of the Renaissance as a separate and identifiable era in the history of the Western world still stands.

Even though the Renaissance is identifiable and separate, this does not mean that it had no roots in the Low Middle Ages or no relationship to movements of preceding eras. Edward Hulme makes this point graphically clear when he writes, "In the great development of civilization there is nothing sudden, but rather is the change like that which takes place in a forest—

ITALY
AT THE TIME OF THE
RENAISSANCE

GRAPHIC PRESENTATION SERVICES · Inc

birth, growth, and death go on almost unnoticed side by side."[1]

Nevertheless, while "history does not turn
corners" and there is an undeniable continuity
between one age and the next, the task of the
historian is to discern the differences in the
times and the distinguishing features that set
one era apart from another; otherwise all of
history runs together to form a mass of indistinguishable facts and events. For this reason if for
no other, the Renaissance must be identified as
a distinct movement within the Middle Ages on
the one hand and distinct from the Reformation
on the other.

The Renaissance deserves study for its own
sake. Yet it can never be understood in isolation
from the heritage of medieval Europe, by which
it was both burdened and enriched. It in turn
made certain contributions to the continuance
of civilization without which modern man
could not hope to understand himself or the
Reformation. This study will focus upon the
period from 1300 to 1517, a period bracketed
by Dante on one side and Luther on the other.
This is not to say that the Renaissance began so
abruptly or ended precisely on October 31,
1517. Obviously the Renaissance did not come
to a close with the beginning of the Reformation
or even the death of Erasmus—it lived on. But
it was not unaffected by the revolutionary impact of the new movement that was rapidly
commanding attention on center stage.

THE NATURE OF THE RENAISSANCE

Dissent in the fourteenth century took many
forms—political, religious, economic, and intellectual. All were indications that the Constantinian "symbiosis"[2] that had held Europe together
for a thousand years was falling apart. Its disin-

tegration, like that of an ice floe in a spring
thaw, was an uneven process, embracing simul-
taneous developments of interaction and
change. The intellectual facet, as it found
expression in the literary and artistic revival of
the fourteenth and fifteenth centuries, became
one of the most fruitful and pervasive of these
developments. This is not to say that the Renaissance was only a literary movement. It was, as
Burckhardt and numerous others have shown, a
multifaceted phenomenon. In its early stages,
however, it was primarily a literary movement
that took its guidelines from the ancient Greek
and Latin classics. Accordingly, it was an Italian
phenomenon in which Florence, the fabled city
on the Arno, took the lead.

This characteristic of the Renaissance was
recognized rather early by those involved in the
movement, but the term *rebirth* was not used
until the sixteenth century. As Wallace Ferguson
points out, every other possible metaphor was
employed: "revival," "restoration," "awakening,"
"reflowering," "return to light." In 1546 Paolo
Giovio, a journalistic historian, referred to Boccaccio as having been born "in that happy century in which Latin letters are conceived to have
been reborn [*renatae*]."[3] The humanists themselves were keenly aware that they were living
in the dawn of a new day. They often characterized the age that preceded theirs as one of
darkness and barbarism. However, it was the
French term *renaissance*, signifying the rebirth
of learning, that finally won the day. The word
embraces a much broader concept than the
word *humanism*, even though it includes the
literary phenomenon designated by that term as
well.

THE POLITICAL AND SOCIAL MILIEU

Burckhardt held that the Renaissance had its
beginnings in Italy, where political circumstances and Italian genius combined to give

---

1. Hulme, *The Renaissance, the Protestant Revolution
and the Catholic Reformation in Continental Europe* (New
York: Century, 1915), p. 3.
2. This term is used by John Howard Yoder and others
to refer to the union of the Catholic Church with the Roman
Empire, which eventually resulted in formation of the Holy
Roman Empire.

---

3. Giovio, cited by Wallace K. Ferguson in *The Renaissance in Historical Thought* (New York: Houghton Mifflin,
1948), p. 66.

birth to the first modern man: "In Italy this veil first melted into air; an *objective* treatment and consideration of the State and of all things of this world became possible. The *subjective* side at the same time asserted itself with corresponding emphasis; man became a spiritual *individual,* and recognized himself as such."[4] The resultant conscious individualism was for Burckhardt the *sine qua non* of the Renaissance. For him the birth of man as an individual over against man in community, the hallmark of medieval man, distinguished the new age from the preceding one. Admittedly this is an oversimplification of Burckhardt's thesis, but the emphasis is clear and the *locus* beyond dispute. The question arises, Why did Italy—specifically Florence—become the birthplace of the Renaissance?

In the wake of the breakdown of feudalism, which never had quite the hold in Italy (Naples being the exception) that it enjoyed north of the Alps, city-states arose. The towns that emerged, particularly Genoa and Venice, became exceedingly prosperous with the shift of the Mediterranean trade routes from the East to the West. With the new prosperity arose a new class within the cities that was neither noble nor peasant: the *bourgeoisie,* or burghers. In order to promote their business interests and protect their freedom from the designs of traditional rulers, noble and ecclesiastical, the burghers organized themselves into communes. In the absence of any strong national government, these communes became virtually independent republics. They hired mercenary troops to defend their borders and launched minor conquests to increase their territorial holdings, occasionally at the risk of war with other city-states.

With the rise of the city-states came the need for men of expertise in law and banking. Thus law took its place alongside the traditional disciplines of theology and medicine in the new universities. The University of Bologna became

Italy's most famous center for the study of law. But medieval universities offered no degree in business administration, so banking could be learned only on the job. By the fourteenth century Florence had become the leading banking center of Europe, and it maintained that position despite stiff competition from Genoa until Augsburg took over the lead in the sixteenth century.

The rise of capitalism brought the growing urban society into conflict with the church's prohibition against the loaning of money for interest, a practice it had traditionally regarded as usury. The entrepreneurs of this economic development avoided direct confrontation with ecclesiastical authority by simply ignoring the traditional stance. There was no way the financial enterprises of the vigorous Italian city-states could survive, much less prosper, without borrowed money. The limited success of the Crusades was dependent upon it as well. Consequently the church simply overlooked any infraction. Later, with the help of Dr. Johann Eck of Ingolstadt and other theologians, Rome changed its position as gracefully as possible to conform to the realities of a changing world. It became increasingly evident that the new age of commerce and industry simply would not permit the calendar to be turned back to the days of the barter economy of feudal agrarian society. Economics played such an important role in ushering in the Renaissance that George Sellery suggests, "It was the bourgeois, not St. Francis or Dante, who was the first medieval man to recognize this life as good."[5]

"THE FIRST MODERN MAN"

To mention Dante and Saint Francis raises the question afresh: Who was "the first modern man"? Was he the anonymous burgher who in his obsession with wealth disregarded the traditions and strictures of the church, Dante of the *Divine Comedy,* or Saint Francis of Assisi,

4. Jacob Burckhardt, *The Civilization of the Renaissance in Italy,* trans. S. G. C. Middlemore (New York: Albert & Charles Boni, 1935), p. 143.

5. Sellery, *The Renaissance: Its Nature and Origins* (Madison: University of Wisconsin Press, 1962), pp. 18–19.

the gentle friar? Perhaps the devout founder of
the Franciscan order can be eliminated most
easily. Surely the pilgrim of Portiuncula, even
with his love of nature, represents the flowering
of medieval monasticism rather than the dawn
of a new age. But Dante is not so easily dismissed.

Dante Alighieri (1265-1321)

Where does Dante belong—in the Middle Ages
or the Renaissance? This question has been answered both ways. Edward Hulme writes,

> Deep as was the sympathy of Dante with the
> Middle Ages, he was nevertheless a child of the
> new birth. In his poetry individuality is supreme.
> One of the most striking characteristics of the
> Divine Comedy is its autobiographical element.
> His concern with the secular problems of his day
> is not that of a medievalist. And in religion he
> held that virtue and inner peace are to be attained
> by ethical rather than by supernatural means.[6]

For other Renaissance scholars such as J. W.
Allen and George Sellery, Dante represents the
last and best of the Middle Ages. Allen writes,
"Dante's book was a piece of imaginative construction; but it was off the point. It was not,
really, what it has been said to be, the swansong
of something dying: it was, rather, an attempt to
resuscitate the dead."[7] It appears that while
Dante was a medieval man in his philosophical
and theological presuppositions, he was a Renaissance man in his literary style. Both Petrarch
and Boccaccio betray an indebtedness to Dante
when they write in the Italian vernacular. Yet
their spirit was different from his, and in that
difference lies the distinction between the medieval man and the Renaissance man.

Dante's masterpiece was the *Divine Comedy*,
which he had entitled simply *Commedia*. In
1555 a Venetian editor added the word *Divina*
to the title, and so it has remained. H. O. Taylor
places the *Divine Comedy* within the context of

the Middle Ages, the era to which it belongs,
while recognizing the beauty and grandeur of
its style:

> Emotionally as well as intellectually, the final
> *Summa*, and a supreme expression, of the Middle
> Ages was the *Divina Commedia.* It was composed
> in the most stately and potent of the vernaculars.
> Beautified and vibrant with the quintessence of
> the gathering religious emotion of the centuries,
> it also brought to expression much that had hith-
> erto had its exclusive home in Latin. For it reset in
> *terza rima* the heart of Aquinas's *Summa Theolo-
> giae;* it held the natural knowledge of the time,
> hitherto kept in Latin; and it was intended to carry
> such fulness of spiritual allegory as Holy Scrip-
> ture:—symbolism was inwoven in it. On the other
> hand, it rendered the very vernacular incidents
> and hates and loves of Dante's time, of Dante's
> self; it bore, as in a greater vessel, the matter of
> Trouvere and Troubadour, already told and sung
> in French and German and Italian. In fine, it ex-
> pressed what had grown up in the vernacular, and
> belonged to the spontaneous thinking and open
> speech of men, while it also translated and re-
> expressed the loftier matters of theology and
> thought, which hitherto had been confined to
> Latin. Not merely from the fact that the *Commedia*
> was written in Italian, but from the nature of its
> translated Latin matter, it represents the turn of
> the noblest forms of expression from the Latin to
> the vernacular.[8]

Florence, the Athens on the Arno

If Dante is not the first modern man, who is?
That title has been claimed for Francesco Petrarch by many scholars of the Italian Renaissance, past and present. This may be true, for it
was Florence that became the cradle of the Italian Renaissance, remaining its center for the
better part of two centuries. Before taking a
closer look at Petrarch, then, it is first necessary
to visit Florence.

By the thirteenth century Florence had established its independence and become a republic.
After a prolonged struggle between two factions

---

6. Hulme, *The Renaissance, the Protestant Revolution
and the Catholic Reformation,* p. 78.

7. Allen, cited by Sellery in *The Renaissance,* p. 36.

8. Taylor, cited by Sellery in *The Renaissance,* pp. 54-
55.

that fought for control of the strife-torn city, a second republic was established. The Florentines were convinced that a republican form of government was best suited to their rapidly developing commercial urban society, in which the new rich were becoming the social elite. However, the second republic did not end its internal strife or guarantee peace with neighboring states. Despite such problems and numerous setbacks, Florence clung tenaciously to its republican ideals.

The success or failure of the city government rested upon an intricate organization that was based upon the city's guilds. The city was ruled by a council called the *signoria*, made up initially of six *priori*, who were chosen by lot from nominations by the guilds. A nominee was required to be a guild member over thirty years old whose taxes were paid up who had never been bankrupt. When chosen, a *prior* served for six months, and then was ineligible to serve again for three years. In spite of the built-in safeguards of the system, Florence experienced more than its share of tempest and tumult. Indeed, its love of representative government did not keep it from being ruled by the Medici family from 1434 to 1494.

Fortunately for the humanists, the Medicis were patrons of the Renaissance—and they were wealthy. They controlled the banking business of Florence and were engaged in the silk and wool trade as well. The "reign" of the Medicis began with Cosimo, who founded the Platonic Academy, and was brought to an ignominious close by his grandson, Piero, the oldest son of Lorenzo the Magnificent. The occasion was the invasion of Italy by the French king Charles VIII, who had designs upon Florence. Piero was frightened into surrendering the city without a fight in exchange for Charles's promise to spare it from the French army. In a violent reaction the citizens of the city forced Piero to flee in disgrace. The Florentines had expected better from a Medici; Lorenzo was made of sterner stuff than his son.

Florence had been threatened before and by no less a personage than Pope Sixtus IV, who had grown increasingly envious of the city and its power under the Medicis. He had joined a conspiracy against them in the hopes of securing Tuscan territory for the Papal States and his nephews. The power-hungry Pazzi family was only too happy to seize the opportunity to advance their own interests while pleasing the pope at the same time. A plot to murder Lorenzo and his brother Giuliano while they were attending mass in the cathedral was hatched and botched. Even though Giuliano was killed, Lorenzo, the real target of the assassins, was able to barricade himself in the vestry. The Pazzis paid a high price for their treachery, and they retaliated. Lorenzo found himself faced with excommunication by Sixtus IV, and Florence was invaded by the armies of the pope in alliance with those of King Ferrante of Naples.

King and pope finally defeated the forces of Florence in 1480. But with the support of Milan, Lorenzo, who was an able diplomat, succeeded in turning the tables on the pope. After two months of feverish negotiations, Milan and Naples formed an alliance with Florence that further frustrated the papal designs on independent Italian states. However, papal intrigue did not keep Lorenzo from using the church for his own ends in true Machiavellian fashion. Due to his machinations, the illegitimate son of his murdered brother became Pope Clement VII, and his own son, Giovanni, was made a member of the College of Cardinals at fourteen years of age. Later he became Pope Leo X.

The Medicis could never have assumed the role of power brokers on the strength of their noble lineage alone. Without the great wealth generated by their banking and commercial interests, they would have been just another family among the impoverished nobility. The wealth of Florence that made possible their rise to power also made possible a life of leisure and study for those intellectuals fortunate enough to find a patron in the church or the state. It is surprising how many humanists found support from one or the other. The truly urban life of Florence tended to be preoccupied with the realities of this world. For the elite, politics and literature became twin obsessions. Politics and commerce made literature and the arts possible, and literature and the arts made politics and commerce complete. Edward Hulme's memorable summary deserves to be quoted on this point: "The oil of commerce filled the lamp of culture. The wealth of the city made possible a high standard of comfort and produced a luxury and a sense of refinement that called into activity the energies of artisans and of artists."[9]

Where did the church fit into this scheme of things? Some were openly skeptical of its claims; others sought to reconcile Christianity with the pagan philosophy of the ancients. But for a good many the impression remained that the church really did not matter. It could, however, be useful in providing benefices for those who longed for the life of a humanist scholar. And why fight so useful an institution? Petrarch was one of those gifted humanists who found the church an unfailing source of financial security.

Francesco Petrarch (1304-1374)

Though a son of Florence, Petrarch was much more than that. He has repeatedly been called "the first modern man" and "the first humanist." Morris Bishop expresses a contemporary view when he claims that "Petrarch was the first modern scholar, the first modern literary man (for Dante we must call medieval)."[10] How did Petrarch see himself? Perhaps Bishop's rendering of Petrarch's answer to this question will give us a more valid glimpse of the man and his times than some modern character sketches do:

> "What am I?" he has asked himself, a few years before. "A scholar? No, hardly that; a lover of woodlands, a solitary, in the habit of uttering disjointed words in the shadow of beech trees, and used to scribbling presumptuously under an immature laurel tree; fervent in toil, but not happy with the results; a lover of letters, but not fully

versed in them; an adherent of no sect, but very eager for truth; and because I am a clumsy searcher, often, out of self-distrust, I flee error and fall into doubt, which I hold in lieu of truth. Thus I have finally joined that humble band that knows nothing, holds nothing as certain, doubts everything—outside of the things that it is sacrilege to doubt."[11]

Petrarch's father had been banished from Florence two years before Francesco's birth. An attorney, his father found himself on the losing side of a struggle between the Blacks and the Whites (the opposing political parties). He sought asylum in Arezzo, but when he failed to find employment there, he was forced to move back to Incisa, which belonged to Florence. But it was in Carpentras, fifteen miles from Avignon, that Francesco spent his boyhood and attended Latin school. In 1326, after his father's death, he and his brother Gherardo moved to Avignon. It was here that Francesco first caught a glimpse of Laura, the Beatrice of his life about whom he fantasized and wrote reams of poetry. Even though he never married, he fathered two children, a son and a daughter. A vain, proud, and immoral man, he was also pragmatic. For this reason he allowed himself to be tonsured in order to become eligible for church benefices and pensions. His income from various sources allowed him to buy a house at Vaucluse and to travel.

Religion for Petrarch was never a serious pursuit. One does get a glimpse of the more earnest side of the poet in his *Secretum,* but his acknowledgment of his sins is little more than attrition. Haunted by thoughts of the inescapable death that stalks every man, a typical medieval obsession, his reaction was hardly that of a Bernard of Clairvaux. The prospect of death caused him to value life in the here and now all the more. He grasped every fleeting moment to write. When Boccaccio urged him to rest from his labors, he replied, "Nothing weighs less than a pen, and nothing gives more pleasure: it is useful not only to the writer but to others far away, perhaps even to those who will be born a

---

9. Hulme, *The Renaissance, the Protestant Revolution and the Catholic Reformation,* p. 91.

10. Bishop, "Petrarch," in Garrett Mattingly et al., *Renaissance Profiles,* ed. J. H. Plumb (New York: Harper & Row, 1965), p. 12.

11. Petrarch, cited by Bishop in "Petrarch," p. 8.

thousand years from now."[12] Like the humanists who followed him, Petrarch was primarily a man of letters. It was for this that he desired fame and fortune, both of which he achieved. In Rome on April 8, 1341, he was crowned with a laurel wreath and declared the poet laureate of Italy.

While he continued to write a variety of poems in the Italian vernacular, he wrote his greatest epic poetry in classical Latin verse. Increasingly he found his models in the ancient authors. He referred to Cicero as his father and Virgil as his brother. Although he never became proficient in Greek, he studied the language with two different teachers. And he and Boccaccio underwrote the translation of Homer into Latin. His appreciation for the ancients, however, was not, like his love for Laura, uncritical. He became an able textual critic, carefully examining and analyzing style to expose forgeries and works falsely attributed to certain authors. Perhaps his education in law at Bologna had not been "seven wasted years," as he thought. Petrarch had no interest in Scholasticism, but, like so many others in Florence, he had a deep appreciation for Plato and at the same time manifested almost no interest in Aristotle.

When Petrarch died in 1374, he was the most widely heralded poet of his age. In his love of life, nature, beauty, books, and authors of antiquity, in his skepticism, vanity, pride, and sensuality, and in his adaptation to the Italian religious milieu, Petrarch established a pattern and expressed attitudes that other Italian humanists would share in time.

Giovanni Boccaccio (1313-1375)

Giovanni Boccaccio was a close friend of Petrarch's and one who shared Petrarch's love of the ancient Latin classics. He was an illegitimate son of a Florentine businessman and a French woman.

Boccaccio survived Petrarch by only a year, but that was enough to become his heir. In his will Petrarch left Boccaccio money to buy himself a warm dressing gown for "winter study and lucubrations by night."[13] Apparently Boccaccio was not as affluent as he might have been. He spurned a career in banking that his father had planned for him, just as Petrarch had turned his back upon a law career years before. Like his friend and confidant, he too became obsessed with the beauty of another man's wife. Boccaccio's Laura was Maria d' Agrino, said to be an illegitimate daughter of King Robert of Naples. However, Boccaccio's affair was no "chaste love from afar." Maria became his mistress for a time and the subject of his poetic tribute in *Fiammetta* for all time. (Toward the end of his career, however, Boccaccio tended to denigrate rather than romanticize the fairer sex.)

While Boccaccio shared Petrarch's love of the Latin classics and even wrote some of his works in Latin, his fame rests upon the risqué *Decameron*, a collection of one hundred short stories in Italian. The setting for the stories is a country villa somewhere in the vicinity of Florence, where ten people—three men and seven women—have fled to escape the plague of 1348. To while away the time, they tell ten tales a day. The stories turn out to be, for the most part, earthy and licentious accounts of the immoral escapades of monks and nuns, courtiers, and clerics. Hulme says of the collection, "It bubbles with merriment, and its style is one of exceptional beauty. But its lack of nobility of thought prevents it from being a great book."[14] Even though he lacked the serious purpose and incisive introspection of Petrarch, Boccaccio revealed a characteristic aspect of the Italian Renaissance—its light regard for conventional morality.

A RETURN TO GREEK

Fortunately, there was a more serious side to Boccaccio than that portrayed in the *Decame-*

---

12. Petrarch, cited by Bishop in "Petrarch," p. 7.

13. Bishop, "Petrarch," p. 7.
14. Hulme, *The Renaissance, the Protestant Revolution and the Catholic Reformation*, p. 83.

ron. Following the lead of Petrarch, he began to study Greek in order to read the ancient authors for himself. Through his efforts a chair of Greek was established at the University of Florence, and Pilato, a native of Calabria who had lived in Constantinople, became its first occupant. However, it was Manuel Chrysoloras (1350-1415) of Constantinople who succeeded in making the study of Greek a going concern.

Almost from the beginning of his career in 1397, Chrysoloras's lectures on the ancient Greek classics were well attended; he was a superbly qualified teacher. Through him and the teachers who followed him with the advance of the Moslems, Italian students were introduced to the new world of the ancients. Among these was the metropolitan of Nicea, John (Basilius) Bessarion (1403-1472), who had first come to Florence to attend the Council of Ferrara-Florence (1438-39). After the failure of the council to reunite a divided Christendom, the archbishop remained in Italy, becoming a cardinal in the Roman Church. His house soon became a refuge for an increasing number of Greek exiles.

The study of Greek began to attract aspiring young scholars from all over Europe. Johannes Reuchlin, John Colet, and Desiderius Erasmus were among those who journeyed to Italy to partake of the new learning. Reuchlin had just arrived in Rome to begin his schooling when he was asked to read a page or two from Thucydides and translate it into Latin. He did it with such elegance that the teacher, John Argyropoulos (1415-1487), in whose home he was staying at the time, is said to have remarked, "Lo! Through our exile, Greece has flown across the Alps." After the fall of Constantinople the trickle of Greek scholars became a flood tide, and if Greek teachers were not "a dime a dozen" there were indeed enough of them so that every university with the interest and the funds could hire one. "The Greek revival" was to have far-reaching consequences—far beyond the hopes and dreams of Petrarch and Boccaccio.

The revival of Greek learning led to new interest in Plato. Aristotle had fallen into disre-

pute among the humanists since his philosophy had been appropriated by Thomas Aquinas and the Nominalists. By the fourteenth century Scholasticism and Aristotelianism were almost synonymous. The Florentine humanists thought they had discovered in Plato the philosophy that would give the Renaissance acceptable metaphysical support. Thus Cosimo de Medici founded and endowed the Platonic Academy at Florence. The academy encouraged the study of Plato by a coterie of brilliant and gifted young humanist scholars. Among them were men as diverse as Poggio (1380-1459), who served eight successive popes yet expressed little else but contempt for Christianity; Traversari (1386-1439), general of the Camaldolese order, who attempted to synthesize Christian teachings with pagan culture; and the irascible Filelfo (1398-1481).

In the rivalry between Filelfo and Poggio the seamy side of Renaissance learning was laid bare. Filelfo was ambitious, greedy, and unscrupulous. Brilliant but lacking in judgment, he attacked Cosimo de Medici, Poggio's patron and benefactor. When Cosimo lost out in a power struggle and was imprisoned in the Palazzo Vecchio, Filelfo suggested that Cosimo should be executed, but his advice was not followed. When Cosimo returned to power, Filelfo went into exile. He expressed his hatred for Poggio in a satirical poem of a hundred verses, one of which reads as follows:

Poggio! ere long thy babbling tongue shall feel
The keen impression of the trenchant steel;
That tongue, the herald of malicious lies,
That sheds its venom on the good and wise.
What mighty master in detraction's school,
Thus into knavery has matured a fool?[15]

This diatribe provoked Poggio to respond in kind:

---

15. Filelfo, cited by M. W. Shepherd in *The Life of Poggio Bracciolini,* 2nd ed. (Liverpool, 1837), p. 250.

Thou stinking he-goat! Thou horned
  monster!
Thou malevolent detractor! Thou father of
lies and author of discord! May the divine
vengeance destroy thee as an enemy of the
virtuous, a parricide who endeavorest to
ruin the wise and good by lies and
  slanders,
and most false and foul imputations. If thou
must be contumelious, write thy satires
against the suitors of thy wife—discharge
the putridity of thy stomach upon those
who adorn thy forehead with horns![16]

As popular as the study of the Greek language, the ancient classical Greek authors, and
Greek culture appeared to have been in Italy,
their impact upon the Renaissance is seriously
questioned by George Sellery. In support of his
position he quotes Samuel Lee Wolff:

The literature of the Renaissance, both in and out
of Italy, is four-fifths of it Latinistic—Virgilian,
Ciceronian, Senecan, occasionally Horatian, very
heavily Ovidian. It springs not immediately, often
not mediately, from Homer, Demosthenes, Pindar,
Aeschylus, Sophocles, or even Euripides. The
other fifth, which does draw nourishment from
Greek literature, draws it from the Greek literature
not of the golden but of the silver and the pinch-
beck ages.[17]

Admittedly it is difficult to measure influence, but to so completely write off the impact
of the ancient Greeks on Renaissance humanism seems unwarranted. While it is true that the
Greek revival stimulated a return to Latin classical authors such as Virgil, Cicero, Seneca, and
others, it helped the humanists to recover the
true Aristotle and Plato. Even though the more
superficial among the Italian elite did no more
than attempt to imitate the style of the Greek
and Latin masters, the impact of Platonic and
Neoplatonic thought was widespread. This obsession with Plato was due in part to the Platonic Academy, to which Lorenzo de Medici was
devoted.

The humanists' appropriation of Plato was
characteristically Italian—that is, it was both se-
lective and individual. This is illustrated by two
very different devotees: Lorenzo de Medici, who
never let his Platonism interfere with his morals,
and Marsilio Ficino (1433–1499), who labored
most of his life to reconcile Platonism and
Christianity. Nevertheless, the devotion to Plato
was genuine, and it found expression in literature and art. "And if the Florentines have been
surpassed in their knowledge of Plato by more
recent scholars," Hulme suggests, "no others
have loved him better."[18]

Giovanni Pico della Mirandola (1463–1494)
died when he was thirty-one. He shared with
Ficino the dream of reconciling Neoplatonism
of the Florentine variety with Christianity. Pico's
contribution lay in his attempt to reconcile Plato
and Aristotle. Beyond this he sought to demonstrate the commonality of all religions and phi-
losophies. To this end he interpreted the
Hebrew Cabala, which he believed established
the deity of Christ.

Florence's leadership in the world of humanist scholarship was largely due to such teachers
as Angelo Ambrogini Poliziano (1454–1494).
Young Poliziano was writing Greek poems by
the time he was seventeen years old. When only
twenty-six he was appointed professor of classical languages at the University of Florence. In
Hulme's estimate he was the first Italian whose
"mastery of Greek was equal to that of the contemporary Greek scholars."[19] Although he became famous for his translations of Homer, he,
like his patron Lorenzo, wrote in Italian. Poliziano's *Orfeo,* written in Italian but patterned
after a classical model, marked the triumph "of
the mother tongue as the vehicle of the new
culture of the bourgeoisie."[20]

---

16. Poggio, cited by Shepherd in *The Life of Poggio Bracciolini,* p. 250.

17. Wolff, cited by Sellery in *The Renaissance,* p. 128.

18. Hulme, *The Renaissance, the Protestant Revolution and the Catholic Reformation,* p. 97.

19. Hulme, *The Renaissance, the Protestant Revolution and the Catholic Reformation,* p. 98.

20. Henry Lucas, *The Renaissance and the Reformation* (New York: Harper & Row, 1960), p. 265.

A RETURN TO THE VERNACULAR

By the turn of the century, when critical editions of Greek and Latin classics had begun to appear, the pendulum had already swung back to the Italian vernacular. Leading the host of humanists was Leon Battista Alberti (1404–1472). A well-rounded Renaissance scholar, Alberti saw the need for a national language to express contemporary thoughts and ideals, and so tried his hand at writing Italian prose. He led the charge, but it was Lorenzo de Medici who popularized and vulgarized the movement with his poems and songs in Italian. Through his work secularized and pagan humanism became the common possession of the Florentines who could neither read nor appreciate Latin verse. His poetry reflected a realism born of keen observation of life around him. Strangely out of character are his religious poems, but they exist quite as much as Petrarch's dialogues with the ghost of Saint Augustine, as if to taunt the boldest of the Renaissance libertines with the inescapable religious dimension of human existence.

THE CHURCH AND THE RENAISSANCE

From the earliest days of the Renaissance the church was one of the movement's most generous patrons. Petrarch, father of the Italian Renaissance, succeeded in living the life of a man of letters because of the good graces of the Avignonese papacy. The Roman Church discovered numerous ways to support and reward Renaissance humanists, both scholars and artists. Benefices always seemed available for the gifted person. Some, like Poggio Bracciolini, one of the secretaries of Nicholas V, used the church as a means of furthering their own careers. The church's patronage of the arts was not without its benefits. While the papacy eventually became captive to the more superficial and pagan aspects of the Renaissance, at the same time it unwittingly encouraged a scholarship that would eventually question the Vatican's traditional claims and undermine its very foundation.

THE POPES AND THE RENAISSANCE

Nicholas V (1447-1455)

Nicholas V represented the finer features of the Renaissance. A faithful patron of the humanists, he sought to reform the church and enrich it at the same time. In most ways the reform fizzled, but he did succeed in organizing the Vatican library and began rebuilding and refurbishing the churches of Rome.

Pius II (1458-1464)

Pius II was an enigma. A scholar in his own right, he died attempting to lead a crusade. Thus Piccolomini proved a disappointment to his former compatriots. It seems that, once on the papal throne, he forsook literary pursuits except for the writing of his memoirs, and failed to share the church's wealth with his former friends. Instead, he used the proceeds from the mines of the Papal States to underwrite his proposed crusade against the Turks.

Sixtus IV (1471-1484)

The successor of Paul II, who had aroused the wrath of Roman humanists by suppressing the Roman Academy, was Francesco della Rovere. Francesco had served as general of the Franciscan order. Dubbed an evil genius by some, he besmirched his reputation in his attempt to hand over a chunk of the Papal States to his nephew Girolamo Riario. He was also implicated in his nephew's plot to murder Lorenzo de Medici in 1478. Nevertheless, he too was a patron of the arts; he is perhaps best known for constructing the Sistine Chapel.

Alexander VI (1492-1503)

Rodrigo Borgia succeeded Innocent VIII through no virtue of his own. It is difficult to determine which of the two was the more unworthy. According to Lewis Spitz, Alexander had been able "to bribe enough cardinals to insure himself of two-thirds of the votes necessary" for

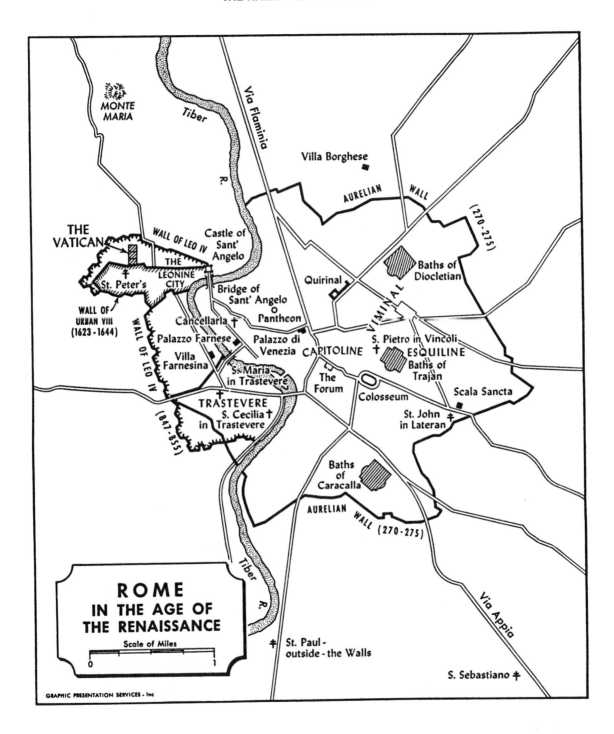

MONTE MARIA

Tiber

Via Flaminia

R.

Villa Borghese

AURELIAN WALL

(270-275)

THE VATICAN

WALL OF LEO IV

Castle of Sant' Angelo

THE LEONINE CITY

Baths of Diocletian

St. Peter's

WALL OF URBAN VIII (1623-1644)

Bridge of Sant' Angelo

Quirinal

Cancellaria

Pantheon

WALL OF LEO IV

Palazzo Farnese

Palazzo di Venezia

CAPITOLINE

VIMINAL

S. Pietro in Vincoli

ESQUILINE

Baths of Trajan

Villa Farnesina

S. Maria in Trastevere

The Forum

Colosseum

Scala Sancta

(847-855)

TRASTEVERE

S. Cecilia in Trastevere

St. John in Lateran

Baths of Caracalla

AURELIAN WALL (270-275)

Tiber R.

Via Appia

ROME
IN THE AGE OF
THE RENAISSANCE

Scale of Miles

0   1

St. Paul - outside - the Walls

S. Sebastiano

GRAPHIC PRESENTATION SERVICES · Inc

election to the papacy.[21] His court was corrupt beyond description. An enthusiastic advocate of Torquemada and the Spanish Inquisition, he attempted to exterminate the Waldenses. He had sixteen children; their marriages were openly celebrated in the Vatican, and they were notorious for their escapades. His son Cesare, who was made a cardinal and archbishop of Valencia, was a murderer, but Alexander was only a shade less contemptible. He was held responsible by some of his contemporaries for the burning of Savonarola, the reformer of Florence. As a patron of the Renaissance, Alexander saw to it that the Borgo was rebuilt and that the Borgian apartments were enlarged and redecorated with frescoes painted by Pinturicchio.

Julius II (1503-1513)

Giuliano della Rovere, who took the name Julius II, was the nephew of Sixtus IV. Known in history as the warrior pope, he was also an ardent patron of the Renaissance. It was he who was responsible for initiating the building of St. Peter's Basilica. Donato Bramante was charged with the responsibility of razing the old basilica and building the new St. Peter's in its place. The genius of Raphael was tapped to paint the frescoes in the Julian apartments. The incomparable Michelangelo was called upon to paint the frescoes on the ceiling of the Sistine Chapel, a task that took him four years, from 1508 to 1512. He was also chosen to build the Tomb of Julius.

However, it was the gifted Erasmus, not Michelangelo, who succeeded in perpetuating the memory of Julius. Erasmus personally witnessed Julius's triumphant entry into Bologna at the head of the papal army. He never forgot it nor forgave Julius for it. To Erasmus it was the supreme prostitution of the papal office. But for Julius it was a moment of triumph for Italy and the church over barbaric invaders. So proud was he of the accomplishment that he commis-

sioned Michelangelo to create a statue of him to be placed over the entrance of the Church of San Petronio in Bologna. It did not last. When they got the chance, the city's irate citizens, who despised Julius with a passion, pulled down the ill-fated image and had it melted down and recast into a cannon.

Leo X (1513-1521)

The son of Lorenzo the Magnificent, Leo X represents the papacy's captivity to the darker side of the Renaissance. He was on the papal throne when the indignant Augustinian monk penned his Ninety-five Theses against the indulgence traffic. A greater contrast between antagonists would be difficult to imagine. On the one side was Luther, the German monk, the son of Hans Luther, a hardworking German peasant. On the other was Giovanni, the son of Lorenzo de Medici, the wealthy and sophisticated banker of Florence. Thanks to his father's mastery of Italian ecclesiastical politics, Giovanni was made a cardinal at the age of fourteen. By 1513, upon the death of Julius II, he was elevated to the papacy. It is difficult to conceive of a pope more ill-equipped to handle the burning issues of the emerging Reformation. Nothing in his background had prepared him for such a career or for such an hour of crisis in Christendom. Not in a thousand years could this son of Lorenzo understand the son of Hans. How could religion ever mean that much to any man?

Leo was above all a patron of the Renaissance. He called upon Raphael to paint additional frescoes. Raphael repaid his patron by depicting Leo X as Leo the Great confronting Attila and the Huns. Bramante and Michelangelo were also beneficiaries of his patronage. Michelangelo's painting of Leo is perhaps his best-known portrait. However, it was Luther, not Michelangelo, who immortalized Leo. Without Luther the superficial pontiff would have become simply a fading part of the church's memory.

SHAKING THE FOUNDATIONS

Although the church supported the Renaissance, the movement undermined the church's

---

21. Spitz, *The Renaissance and Reformation Movements* (Chicago: Rand McNally, 1971), p. 54.

authority in a number of ways, some subtle and some not so subtle. The science of textual criticism was a by-product of the new interest in the Greek and Latin classics. The same linguistic tools that made possible critical editions of the Greek text brought about an improved Vulgate and called into question the medieval forgeries, the Donation of Constantine and the Pseudo-Isidorian Decretals.

Lorenzo Valla (1407-1457)

Valla was not the first to challenge the authenticity of the Donation of Constantine—which the popes had used for centuries and upon which they had founded their claims to the Lateran Palace and the adjoining countryside—but he was the first to base the challenge upon a critical-historical method and linguistic analysis. He specifically called attention to the use of the terms *satraps* and *papal crown,* neither of which, he pointed out, had been used by the Romans in the time of Constantine. His argument was the more telling because of its incisive analysis of the document in question.

Even after Valla's exposé, Pope Nicholas V invited him to Rome, where he spent the last ten years of his life as a notary in the apostolic chancery. The invitation indicates that Nicholas V either appreciated Valla's work (because of his own dedication to Renaissance learning) in spite of its implications, or felt that the papacy's territorial claims were not irreparably damaged by the exposé. However, if Eugenius IV had had his way, the Inquisition would have put an end to Valla's work in 1444.

While Valla's *Declamation on the False Donation of Constantine* is his best-known work, he had other claims to fame. He was an accomplished Greek scholar who also dabbled in philosophy and theology. In addition, he was an excellent Latinist, and he demonstrated his brilliance as a linguist in his *Elegances of the Latin Language.* He also attempted to correct Jerome's translation with his *Annotations to the New Testament.* Two German scholars were to benefit especially from Valla's works: Nicholas Cusanus and Martin Luther.

Nicholas Cusanus (1401-1464)

Nicholas Cusanus is also known as Nicholas of Cusa. Educated in Deventer and Padua, he was identified with the conciliarists at the Council of Basel but switched sides in 1437. Even though he was made a cardinal in 1448, he manifested a more open attitude toward the Moslem and other non-Christian religions than most other highly placed ecclesiastics. He was a true Renaissance scholar with a penchant for theology. True to his Italian humanist leanings, his philosophical frame of reference was medieval Neoplatonism.

He made a number of contributions in widely different fields of knowledge. Upon the basis of the evidence, he rejected the Donation of Constantine and the Pseudo-Isidorian Decretals as forgeries. He also rejected Aristotle's cosmology and with it the concept that the earth was the centerpiece of the universe. Instead he insisted that the earth turned upon its axis. In spite of these revolutionary concepts, Cusanus spent the last four years of his life in Rome in the good graces of pope and church.

WINDS OF CHANGE

The Italian Renaissance, despite its close alliance with the church in almost every period of its development, unleashed a number of pent-up desires that finally found expression in unchristian ways. In the process it revealed how slightly the Christian faith had penetrated the thinking of a number of brilliant and gifted men. The movement's darker side—sensual, pagan, and immoral—revealed its spiritual bankruptcy. At the same time, its search for a norm in the ancient Greek and Latin classics suggested a pattern that the Protestant Reformers would eventually follow. In addition, its emphasis upon Greek and its first halting steps into the realm of textual criticism were destined to have far-reaching consequences for Erasmus and the Protestant Reformation.

The recovery of the ancient Greek classics precipitated a new era of Aristotelian studies. It also stimulated a new appreciation for history and a desire to learn from its pages. In what was initially a literary renaissance there came a rebirth of art.

Although the Renaissance meant different things to different people, it is abundantly clear that the movement brought with it the winds of change.

Chapter III

RENAISSANCE ART AND ARTISTS

or most contemporary students the mention of the Renaissance calls to mind not the literary works of the period but visions of cracked frescoes, vivid—sometimes lewd—paintings, and a variety of sculptures, mostly those of Michelangelo. For such people the epitome of the Renaissance is represented in its works of art. While it is debatable whether even the most astute art critic can learn as much about the nature of the Renaissance from a study of its art as from its literature, there is no question that its painting, sculpture, architecture, and music provide incomparable illustrations of one of the most creative eras in the history of mankind.

Even though the subject matter of so many of the Italian artists' brushes and chisels was religious, its execution on canvas or in plaster or stone was something else. For example, Michelangelo's *David,* even if given another name, would still convey the glorification of the human body. It was not so much a monument to David as to mankind. At times the Renaissance artist would lay aside all pretense of a Christian theme to create what can hardly be called anything other than a pagan production. Such is Giovanni Bellini's *The Feast of the Gods.* It is difficult to imagine a more suggestive, sensual portrayal of men and women satisfying their sexual appetites with complete abandon, although Titian's *Bacchanal* approaches it. The "gods" turn out to be quite human. For the most part they are neither given mythological forms nor represented stylistically. Instead the action is focused on real people, seductive women and aggressive men satisfying very human appetites. The elements characteristic of Italian painting since Giotto are present. What, then, makes Renaissance art different from medieval art? That question can best be answered by taking a look at some representative artists and their work.

PAINTING

Giotto (1266-1336)

As Petrarch is generally acknowledged as the father of Renaissance literature, so Giotto is generally recognized as the father of Renaissance art. Even though Giotto's entire artistic output revolved around religious themes, he treated them with a new realism. Caught up in the Franciscan piety of his day, he painted twenty-eight frescoes depicting various scenes from the life of Saint Francis in the Church of St. Francis

The Lamentation of Christ by Giotto ALINARI/ART RESOURCE, N.Y.

in Assisi. However, his most famous fresco of Saint Francis is that entitled *The Death of St. Francis* in the Bardi Chapel in Florence. *The Lamentation of Christ*, in which he depicts the inexpressible sorrow of Mary and the disciples at the death of Christ, is considered his master-piece. It adorns the Arena Chapel in Padua.

Even though his paintings are religious and to a certain extent express medieval themes, Giotto treats his subjects with a fresh naturalism. He sought to portray Christ, Mary, and the saints as real people capable of very human emotions. It was Giorgio Vasari who first suggested that Giotto was the father of Renaissance art. He was certainly considered such by Boccaccio, but there were no immediate successors capable of perpetuating his new technique, much less using it for innovation. A century passed before

the beginning made by Giotto found a worthy successor.

Masaccio (1401-1428)

Tommaso Guidi, which was Masaccio's actual name, died before he was thirty, virtually un-known. Today he is heralded as the "second Prometheus" who carried Renaissance painting into a new phase in the fifteenth century.[1] Like Giotto, he was a painter of frescoes depicting religious scenes. And he too made his figures lifelike, expressing the variety and vibrancy of life. He surpassed Giotto in his mastery of com-

---

1. Lewis W. Spitz, *The Renaissance and Reformation Movements* (Chicago: Rand McNally, 1971), p. 200.

position and perspective. His genius was recognized by the greatest artists of the *Quattrocento*—Leonardo da Vinci, Michelangelo, and Raphael—who carefully studied his frescoes in the Church of Santa Maria del Carmine in Florence.

Leonardo da Vinci (1452-1519)

When the name of Leonardo da Vinci is mentioned today, the *Last Supper* or the *Mona Lisa* immediately comes to mind, for it is through these two paintings and the lesser-known *Virgin of the Rocks* that the genius of da Vinci is best known. However, Leonardo was more than an artist. He was an inventor, scientist, sculptor, engineer, poet, musician, and above all an intellectual. He may have studied the work of Masaccio, as Vasari relates, but his purpose was not to duplicate Masaccio's paintings but to learn from them in order to improve upon them. Nothing was more abhorrent to Leonardo than imitation. Leonardo himself has left us his feelings on the subject, which constitute his philosophy of knowledge, his epistemology, if you will:

> The painter will produce pictures of little merit if he takes the works of others as his standard; but, if he will apply himself to learn from the objects of nature he will produce good results. This we see was the case with the painters who came after the time of the Romans, for they continually imitated each other, and from age to age their art steadily declined. . . . It is safer to go direct to the works of nature than to those which have been imitated from her originals with great deterioration and thereby to acquire a bad method, for he who has access to the fountain does not go to the water-pot.[2]

Although often regarded as the quintessence of the Renaissance, Leonardo did not learn Latin until late in life and had little respect for those whose knowledge consisted in simply quoting the ancient classical authors. For him experi-

ence and observation of life around him were far better teachers than ancient authors, and the human body was a better model than those of the ancient Greeks. The superficiality of much in humanist learning did not escape him. In fact, Leonardo had some well-chosen words for those who disparaged his work because he knew neither Greek nor Latin:

> I am fully aware that the fact of my not being a man of letters may cause certain arrogant persons to think that they may with reason censure me, alleging that I am a man ignorant of book-learning. Foolish folk! Do they not know that I might retort by saying, as did Marius to the Roman patricians, "They who themselves go about adorned in the labor of others will not permit me my own." They will say that because of my lack of book-learning I cannot properly express what I desire to treat of. Do they not know that my subjects require for their exposition experience rather than the words of others? And since experience has been the mistress of whoever has written well, I take her as my mistress, and to her in all points make my appeal.[3]

Leonardo's father, a lawyer of Florence, took him to Verrocchio when he was fourteen years old, the usual age for those entering the university. For six years Leonardo studied and worked with Verrocchio; according to legend, when he witnessed the exquisite beauty of an angel painted by his young apprentice, he vowed never to paint again. While here Leonardo met and doubtless worked with Perugino and Botticelli. When he entered the painter's guild of Florence, Lorenzo de Medici became his patron for six or seven years. Perhaps it was during this period that Leonardo developed a distaste for the facade of Renaissance learning. During this time he also turned to dissecting the human body over and over again to discover how it was structured, not only to learn best how to paint and sculpture it but to understand its functions and discern the differences between individuals.

Perhaps his distaste for Florentine humanism

2. Da Vinci, cited by Bronowski in "Leonardo da Vinci," in Garrett Mattingly et al., *Renaissance Profiles*, ed. J. H. Plumb (New York: Harper & Row, 1965), p. 77.

3. Da Vinci, cited by Bronowski in "Leonardo da Vinci," p. 76.

prompted him to seek to attach himself to the court of Ludovico Sforza, the ruler of Milan. He left Florence for Milan in 1483 to serve his new patron, performing a multitude of functions until the French invaded the city in 1499. After some years of wandering he was employed by Francis I and spent his last years in France. However, it was in Milan that he produced his paintings and his notebooks; of these, the latter were to enshrine his memory in the annals of time.

It is ironic that one who seemed devoid of any vital faith of his own would be remembered for the *Last Supper*. This famous fresco adorns a wall in the refectory of the Convent of Santa Maria delle Grazie. When the prior tried to prod Leonardo into finishing the work, the artist threatened to paint the prior's face on the body of Judas for all the world to see. Despite his preoccupation with other things, Leonardo did finish the work, and it became the most famous painting of the Last Supper ever done. For one thing, Leonardo so mastered the three-dimensional effect that the viewer feels that he is standing in the room depicted. While the robes of the disciples and Jesus merge into one, giving unity to the painting, each figure is distinct. The expression on each face in reaction to Christ's statement that one of his disciples would betray him reflects a tense moment caught at just the right instant by the artist's imagination. And Judas is pictured on the same side of the table as Jesus, a reversal of the positions envisioned by medieval artists. If Leonardo had done no other painting, this one would have insured his fame. Perhaps in the end, an embittered and frustrated genius, he came to realize that his paintings alone had value, for when he left Italy for France, he took several with him: the *Christ Child, John the Baptist, Anne, Mary,* and probably the *Mona Lisa.*

Raphael Sanzio (1483-1520)

Raphael, acclaimed by a host of critics as the greatest painter of all time, represents Renaissance art at the pinnacle of its development. Raphael's father was also a painter, but he died when his son was only eleven years old. Yet before his father's death the young boy had already embarked upon his lifelong career. For five years he studied with Pietro Perugino, who, upon seeing the youngster's drawings, is reported to have said, "Let him be my pupil! He will soon become my master." The next four years Raphael spent studying with the Florentine masters, Leonardo da Vinci and Michelangelo, while perfecting his own technique. Julius II, who was always on the lookout for promising young artists, invited Raphael to come to Rome in the service of the church. It was here that he produced his greatest works of art.

Raphael was known for his ability to combine pagan and religious elements into a most pleasing and popular art form. Symbolic of his style are the Madonna compositions, which may be seen in some of the world's great art museums. His mistress, in true Renaissance fashion, became the model for these pictures. Of these, the *Sistine Madonna* is generally recog-

The *Sistine Madonna* by Raphael ALINARI/ART RESOURCE, N.Y.

nized as his masterpiece. That which has been lauded as the most perfect example of Renaissance art is his painting *School of Athens* in the *Stanza della Segnatura* of the Vatican palace. Here Raphael's mastery of composition is clearly demonstrated.

That one man could produce so much in such a brief lifetime is still a source of amazement. Unlike Leonardo da Vinci or Michelangelo, Raphael could apparently work steadily and consistently, applying himself to his task until it was completed. His genius was recognized by his peers in his own lifetime. Bramante, nearing death, requested that Raphael be asked to take over his responsibility of designing St. Peter's Basilica. Raphael hardly had time to take up the challenge, however, because he died only twelve years after moving to Rome.

SCULPTURE

Sculpture and painting were very closely related in the Renaissance. Often the painter was also a sculptor with a preference for one of the two art forms. Verrocchio is a case in point. While he was a painter of great repute, an engraver, and a sculptor, he preferred chiseling stone to painting; in fact, it is said that when he could he enlisted the services of gifted students to share in the painting chores so that he might turn his attention to sculpture. Both Leonardo da Vinci and Michelangelo were masters of both art forms. Most of the numerous designs that Leonardo presented to his patron were never implemented. The fame of Michelangelo the sculptor, however, is as great as that of Michelangelo the painter. Actually Michelangelo considered himself a sculptor rather than a painter. In fact, the world might never have come to know Michelangelo as a painter if the pompous Julius II had not interrupted the work that he had commissioned the artist to begin on his grandiose tomb and pressured him into decorating the ceiling of the Sistine Chapel with frescoes.

Verrocchio (1435-1488)

There was Renaissance sculpture before Michelangelo, but he so overshadowed his predeces-

sors that the tendency is to overlook the fact. However, Verrocchio, Leonardo da Vinci's teacher, created a classic illustration of Renaissance sculpture forty years before Michelangelo created his *David*. Verrocchio's *David* (1465) was cast in bronze. His is a youthful figure of the not-quite-mature man that is strikingly realistic. In its workmanship the artist demonstrates his very accurate knowledge of human anatomy. His figure more readily calls to mind the biblical story because he placed the head of Goliath at the feet of the young David, who stands with a sword still in his right hand. His countenance reflects a cool confidence, and his left hand, as if to accent the moment of triumph, rests upon his hip.

Michelangelo Buonarroti (1475-1564)

It was the High Renaissance that witnessed the flowering of Italian art, and Michelangelo was in the center of it all. This peerless artist was born near Florence on his family's estate. His father could barely make a living there, and the family lived on the verge of poverty. But his father was a proud man—in fact, his pride made him unable to come to terms with the son who wished to become an artist. In his eyes an artist was no more than an artisan, holding a station in life unfit for a nobleman's son. Nevertheless, Michelangelo was apprenticed to a Florentine artist, Domenico Ghirlandaio. During these years the students visited the gardens of the Medicis near San Marco to study the antique statuary. Upon one such occasion Lorenzo de Medici noticed the gifted youth at work and invited him to become a part of his household. The association with the Medicis was to leave an indelible impression upon the budding artist. From this period may be dated his introduction to Plato and his fascination with the ancient's works, which became a lifelong obsession. The patronage of Lorenzo made possible all the advantages of study that Florence, at its zenith, could afford.

Even though from 1496 onward Michelangelo's fortunes were dependent upon his relationship to Pope Julius II, for whom he created a number of his greatest works, his was a typical humanist understanding of art undergirded by Platonic philosophy. It was this philosophy that enabled him to glorify and glory in a realistic portrayal of the human body in stone or pigment—hence we see in the works of Michelangelo religious themes treated in a "secular" manner. For him the figures were already in the stone, simply waiting for release. He could also portray God in human form without any sense of impropriety because, he reasoned, the ancients had always portrayed their gods in human form, and besides, if Plato were right, then the material was only a reflection of reality, not the thing itself.

In each of his greatest sculptures—the *Pietà*, *David*, and *Moses*—can be seen the blend of his humanist concept of man and a religious theme. The figure of Mary in the *Pietà* is young and

Moses by Michelangelo ALINARI/ART RESOURCE. N.Y.

beautiful, leaving the impression that the mother was younger than her crucified son. *David* is the portrayal of the perfection of young manhood, with only the slightest hint, symbolized by the sling, that he is the David of the Bible. *Moses*, which was originally created for Julius II's magnificent tomb, reflects Michelangelo's attempt to fashion his statue after the biblical Moses. To authenticate the figure, he included the tablets of stone and also the horns that Jerome's mistranslation of the Hebrew in the Vulgate placed on his head. Here again, Michelangelo's intimate knowledge of human anatomy is evident. With his taut muscles, protruding veins, and intense gaze, the stone Moses looks alive. This work shows Michelangelo at his best. As Henry Lucas points out,

> Michelangelo believed that the highest art consisted in thought wrought in stone. He subordinated all nature to his ideas. It may be said, therefore, that his art transcends nature herself. It exalts human thought above everything material and physical and is therefore the highest expression of man in the Renaissance.[4]

If it had not been for Bramante's jealousy, according to Michelangelo, he would not have been persuaded against his wishes to undertake the frescoes that adorn the ceiling of the Sistine Chapel. Whether or not Michelangelo was justified in his suspicions, the overpowering personality of Julius II was responsible for Michelangelo's ceasing work on the vain pope's tomb and subsequently beginning the frescoes.

There is more to Michelangelo's involvement with Julius II than meets the eye. According to Michelangelo, he left Rome in complete disillusionment when, after five days of repeated attempts to see the pontiff, he was refused the money he had requested to continue the project. This rebuff occurred after Michelangelo had spent eight months supervising the extraction of the marble from the Carrara quarry in preparation for beginning the work on Julius's tomb. However, after the papal army had successfully

4. Lucas, *The Renaissance and the Reformation*, 2nd ed. (New York: Harper & Row, 1960), p. 302.

taken Perugia and Bologna, Michelangelo rushed to Bologna to make peace with his former patron. Julius then asked him to create a statue of him to celebrate his victory. Michelangelo complied, devoting a year of his life to the project. The monument was cast in bronze and placed over the door of San Petronio in Bologna. Three years later it was pulled down by the irate citizens of the city and recast into a cannon. Thus the year Michelangelo had spent on the statue was in a sense wasted, although the work did endear him to the humanist pope, who then persuaded him to return to Rome to resume work on the tomb.

Michelangelo had been asked to design the most magnificent monument ever built to man, and to cap it all off, Julius had originally intended it to be placed over the traditional site of Saint Peter's grave. Thus Michelangelo was understandably perturbed when he was asked to suspend the work already begun in order to take up his brush again, after so many years away from painting, and do the Sistine frescoes. In fact, Michelangelo thought Bramante was behind this bit of "intrigue," attempting to embarrass him since he believed the great sculptor incapable of fulfilling the new assignment. Whatever the actual circumstances, Michelangelo undertook the awesome task. For four years he lay on his back on the scaffolding, painting the entire work himself, enlisting the help of artisans only to prepare the plaster and mix the paint. On the ceiling of 6,000 square feet he painted 145 pictures, including 394 figures.

Michelangelo was given the freedom to determine the subject matter of the frescoes as well as their execution. This he did by dividing the center ceiling into nine panels depicting the creation and fall of man. If one uses the altar as a starting point, the panels in sequence are *God Dividing the Light from Darkness, God Creating the Earth, Creation of the Waters, Creation of Adam, Creation of Eve, Fall of Man, Sacrifice of Noah, Deluge,* and *Fall of Noah.* In the corners of each of these pictures are nude male figures, "athletes," in every conceivable pose. Prophets, sibyls, and the ancestors of Christ complete the

Sistine frescoes. A question arises about how Michelangelo intended his frescoes to be viewed— from the altar in sequence or in reverse? Art historians such as Kenneth Clark suggest that the clue is found in Michelangelo's Neoplatonism. Clark claims that Michelangelo turned the creation narrative of the Bible into a profound philosophy:

> He did so by compelling us to read his "histories" in a reverse order. Over our head, as we enter the chapel, is the *Drunkenness of Noah;* at the far end, over the altar, is the *Creation.* Thus the ceiling illustrates the Neoplatonic doctrine, so dear to Michelangelo, and so often expressed in his sonnets, that life must be a progression from the servitude of the body to the liberation of the soul. It begins with the inert figure of Noah, where the body has taken complete possession, and ends with the figure of the Almighty dividing light from darkness, in which the body has been completely transformed into a symbol of the spirit, and even the head, with its too evident human associations, has become indistinct.[5]

Admittedly there are problems in attempting to interpret the panels as a pictorial presentation of the biblical account of creation and the fall of man because the last three panels are out of sequence, yet this may have been the way Michelangelo intended his work to be viewed. Perhaps the key to how to view the work lies in whether the frescoes were designed to portray God's work of creation or redemption.

But such varying interpretations do not alter the significance of the work. Once the frescoes were unveiled on October 31, 1512, it was clear that Renaissance art had reached a high point, and Michelangelo's work was the standard by which the work of other artists would be measured for at least a century. Michelangelo was only thirty-seven years old at the time. He was still to finish Julius's tomb, the main ornament of which was *Moses,* and to paint *The Last Judgment.*

Pope Paul III commissioned Michelangelo to paint *The Last Judgment* on the front wall of the

5. Clark, "The Young Michelangelo," in *Renaissance Profiles,* p. 49.

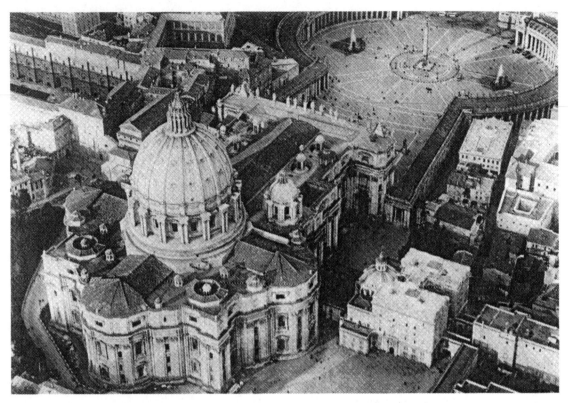

Sistine Chapel. It is an enormous fresco with more than three hundred separate figures. The work is reminiscent of Dante's *Divine Comedy*, a copy of which became Michelangelo's constant companion during the years he devoted to this masterwork. Like the "athletes" on the ceiling, it portrays the human body in every imaginable position (although many of the figures are not completely naked).

The multitalented Michelangelo met his most awesome challenge when Pope Paul III commissioned him to become the chief architect of St. Peter's Basilica. He reworked the designs of his predecessors to conform to his own vision—hence the St. Peter's that tourists visit today is the result of his inspired genius, and remains his greatest monument.

Though he is best known for his artistic triumphs, in his later years Michelangelo became a literary figure as well. Two friends became the objects of his impassioned sonnets: Tommaso dei Cavalieri, a young Roman noble-

man, and Vittoria Colonna, a devout and intelligent young widow. Of the sonnets written to Vittoria, Lewis Spitz writes, "The poetry he poured out in her honor reflected his Christian faith, his Neoplatonic mystical bent, and the tender affection of his heart."[6]

The death of Vittoria in 1547 left Michelangelo a sad and lonely man. Of all the works the great sculptor completed in his later years, that which is most autobiographical is the *Pietà* he fashioned for his own tomb in Florence. Michaelangelo represents himself as Nicodemus, who helped take Christ down from the cross. The figure of Mary in this *Pietà* is more realistic than the one he had created twenty-five years before, yet he was so displeased with his work that he attempted to destroy it. However, someone thoughtfully gathered up the pieces and

6. Spitz, *The Renaissance and Reformation Movements*, p. 223.

An exterior view of St. Peter's Basilica (opposite), and an interior picture, taken during a canonization ceremony. St. Peter's is the largest church in Christendom, able to accommodate 50,000 people. RELIGIOUS NEWS SERVICE

cemented them back together, and today the sculpture may be seen in the cathedral of Florence.

Michelangelo died in 1564 at the age of eighty-nine, after having outlived his closest friends and patrons. His influence was to affect the art of many subsequent generations. Perhaps it is no exaggeration to say that in Michelangelo the Italian Renaissance produced its most representative—if not its greatest—genius.

ARCHITECTURE

The same high regard—even reverence—for antiquity that stimulated study of the ancient classical models in literature and art also provided the stimulus for Renaissance architecture. Architects of the *Quattrocento* were unimpressed by the Gothic styles of the North and the Moorish structures of Spain. Instead, they were ena-

mored with the ancient classical buildings of Greece and Rome. These ancient models, designed to take advantage of the perennial sunshine of the Mediterranean world, were ideal for the mosaics and frescoes that became such popular forms of church decoration during the Renaissance.

Filippo Brunelleschi (1377-1446)

Brunelleschi, like so many of his peers, was a versatile artist. He was first an apprentice in a goldsmith's shop in Florence; he was also admitted to the guild. Becoming interested in geometry, he applied its principles to painting, but his greatest achievement was in architecture.

He began his study of architecture by measuring the ancient Roman structures to determine exactly how they had been built to withstand the stress and support their superstructures through the centuries. Combining his knowledge of geometry with his new understanding of the ancient classical models, he was prepared to improvise in the creation of a new classical Renaissance design.

The dome of the cathedral of Florence is the best-known example of Brunelleschi's work. It is a magnificent structure, reminiscent of ancient classical domes but with a touch of the Gothic in its final execution. Brunelleschi erected the vault without a scaffolding, a then unheard-of accomplishment. Building upon the vault, he raised the dome to a height of ninety feet. He also designed the Pitti Palace and a number of other buildings and churches in Florence. But his greatest architectural triumph remained the dome of the cathedral.

Leon Battista Alberti (1404-1472)

A contemporary of Brunelleschi, Alberti has been designated the "first universal genius" by Jacob Burckhardt. Similar in interests and ability to Leonardo da Vinci, Alberti was a musician, artist, architect, man of letters, and inventor. He is said to have invented a printing press on his own in 1457, one similar to that of Gutenberg. He was associated with the Platonic Academy in Florence, and authored a Latin play and a book on painting. His family was originally from Florence, but they, like so many others, had been banned from the city. When Alberti was twenty-four, he and other family members were allowed to return.

Like Brunelleschi, Alberti studied architecture in Rome by examining the ancient structures. Nicholas V called upon him to restore the papal palace. He also had a hand in renovating and decorating a number of structures, from the Trevi Fountain to the Church of Santa Maria Novella.

More important than his architectural accomplishments, however, were the books he wrote on architecture, painting, and society. He believed that buildings ought to be designed in keeping with their surroundings and that cities should have open spaces conveniently located. Lewis Spitz holds that the modern social planning of cities such as Washington, D.C., and Paris, with their large squares and open space, "was influenced by a tradition of urban design going back to Alberti."[7]

Donato Bramante (1444-1514)

Bramante was selected by Julius II to draw up the original plans for St. Peter's Basilica. A native of Urbino, he was first a painter and later an architect. In 1500 he moved to Rome from Milan to enter the service of the papacy. Like others before him who had pursued careers in Rome, he had an opportunity to study the ancient ruins and buildings of the classical era. He drew up the plans for joining the two corridors linking the Belvedere courtyard with the papal palace. But he did not live long enough to see his plans for St. Peter's materialize. Instead, Michelangelo (his chief rival, of whom he was apparently extremely jealous) took what Bramante and Raphael had done and completely reworked their designs to conform to his own enlarged vision of the new structure.

MUSIC

Of the fine arts, music seems to have lagged far behind in the Renaissance era. Johannes Tinctoris, a Flemish musician who spent most of his life in Naples, dated the beginning of modern music around the year 1435. However, it was the Netherlands, not Italy, that became the center of Renaissance music. Tinctoris held that the English had set the pattern for the modern musical era but had fallen by the wayside. On the other hand, the Dutch composers led all of Europe in developing polyphonic compositions in which various melodic lines were brought together in a pleasing harmony. However, the most notable pioneer of the new art of music (*Ars Nova*) was Guillaume de Machaut (1300-1377), onetime canon of the cathedral of Reims.

That the church did not look kindly upon the

---

7. Spitz, *The Renaissance and Reformation Movements*, p. 199.

innovations in the new art is reflected in the prohibition and rules that Pope John XXII issued to govern church music. John went so far as to prohibit new musical devices and issued rules regulating the use of harmony in the liturgy of the Roman Church. In spite of this, Machaut's *Masse de Nostre Dame* (*Mass of Our Lady*) became the most famous and influential musical composition of the fourteenth century. It was a four-part setting of the Ordinary of the mass with the dismissal formula *Ite missa est.* Through the musical innovation of Machaut and others, the *Ars Nova* was introduced in Italy and soon became characteristic of its music as well as that of France.

The advent of printing made possible the production of musical scores and "partbooks" in numbers that had been impossible before. The first collection of polyphonic music printed on the new presses was published in 1501 by Ottaviano dei Petrucci in Venice. During the next two years Petrucci brought out fifty-nine volumes of vocal and instrumental music. Sheets of instrumental music were run through the presses twice—first to print the staff lines, then the notes; sheets of vocal music were run through a third time for printing of the lyrics. Although Petrucci's collection featured the work of Dutch composers, the Italian Renaissance could lay some claim to Josquin des Prez (1440–1521), the most renowned musician of his time. Like Jean d' Okeghem and a number of other truly great composers, he was born in the Netherlands; his contemporaries recognized him as the greatest of them all. Luther wrote, "He is the master of the notes. They must do as he wills; as for the other composers, they have to do as the notes will."[8] In 1567 Cosimo Bartoli of Florence wrote that Josquin was without a peer in music, even as Michelangelo was peerless in architecture, painting, and sculpture.[9]

Josquin first sang as a choirboy at St. Quen-

tin. Later he joined the Sforza court in Milan and served in the papal chapel from 1486 to 1494. After spending most of his remaining years in Italy and France, he returned to his native land, dying at Conde in 1521. His output was enormous. He composed twenty masses, a hundred motets, and seventy chansons and other secular works. Of his contribution Donald Grout writes, "The early Netherlands chanson reached the climax of its development at Josquin's hand. He was unmatched in the skill of combining the hearty, colorful quality of secular popular song with the intricacies of counterpoint."[10] He is also known to have incorporated secular melodies such as *My Mistress* into his mass compositions—hence the worldly and even the obscene became a part of the solemn celebration of the mass. Why? It may be that Josquin simply liked the secular tunes and thought they would make listening to the complicated compositions more enjoyable, or he may simply have been saying "humbug" to it all in the tradition of the Italian Renaissance. Many of the secular tunes of the period did ridicule the clergy and denounced their immorality. Thus the complaint of the church against the *Ars Nova* may have involved much more than a failure to accept new musical forms.

IN RETROSPECT

From this relatively brief survey of Renaissance art several conclusions can be drawn. The art of the Italian Renaissance may be seen as the flowering of that creative era. This period covered approximately two hundred years. Even though Venice, Bologna, Milan, and Rome, as well as other cities, contributed to and shared in the productivity of the Italian masters, it was Florence that became and remained the center of this age of genius. In the light of this study, Jacob Burckhardt's comment appears to contain more truth than exaggeration: "It was not the revival of antiquity alone, but its union with the

---

8. See Gustave Reese, *Music in the Renaissance* (New York: Norton, 1959), p. 674, for a delightfully different translation of Luther's comment on Josquin.

9. See Donald J. Grout, *A History of Western Music* (New York: Norton, 1960), p. 173.

10. Grout, *A History of Western Music*, p. 173.

genius of the Italian people, which achieved the conquest of the Western world."[11]

------

11. Burckhardt, *The Civilization of the Renaissance in Italy,* trans. S. G. C. Middlemore (New York: Albert & Charles Boni, 1935), p. 175.

The role of Neoplatonism must not be overlooked—it provided a stimulus in this burst of creativity—but it must also be remembered that Neoplatonism was unable to provide a morally uplifting and soul-satisfying philosophy of life for those who embraced its teachings.

Chapter IV

THE NORTHERN RENAISSANCE

he Northern Renaissance was something other than its Italian counterpart. In fact, there are scholars who hold that the Renaissance that emerged in Northern Europe was an indigenous movement. Even though those who advocate this "revisionist" viewpoint have called attention to certain "native" contributions, they have not carried the day. However, there is no denying the fact that the Renaissance in Northern Europe took on quite a different character than its Italian origins would suggest. The major difference lay in its religious orientation. While some Italian humanists such as Pico and Ficino were undeniably concerned with certain aspects of the Christian faith, they were the exceptions. One of the most striking characteristics of the Italian Renaissance was its careless and superficial attitude toward all things religious. In contrast, northern humanism from its earliest days was wedded to a deep religious quest. There were other differences as well, but the preoccupation with religion was by far the most important one.

How does one account for this striking contrast between southern humanism and northern humanism? Was it a matter of climate, geography, or ethnicity? Was it the result of an urban mentality versus a rural mentality, or of a medieval north still preoccupied with medieval questions? The answer probably lies not in any one of these possible contributing factors but in a combination peculiar to the Germanic lands and people. The presence of the Brethren of the Common Life here may provide the key to help answer the questions raised. The Brethren certainly became the transmission lines of both humanist learning and deep religious devotion. Many of the early German Renaissance scholars came under their influence. Thus it appears that some understanding of this semimonastic group, made up predominantly of laypersons, is necessary for a more complete understanding of the Northern Renaissance.

THE BRETHREN OF THE COMMON LIFE

Some of the most influential leaders of the Northern Renaissance came under the influence of the Brethren. The roll call is nothing short of astounding. It includes Cusanus, Hegius, Agricola, Wessel, Reuchlin, Celtis, Mutian, Erasmus, and Luther. Two of the most popular and influential devotional booklets of the fourteenth and fifteenth centuries—*Imitation of Christ* by Thomas à Kempis (directly out of Brethren circles), and *Theologia Germanica*, containing thoughts derived from Meister Eckhart, Johannes Tauler, and the Friends of God—convey the spirit characteristic of the Brethren of the Common Life. The Brethren represent a grass-roots attempt at spiritual renewal within the Roman Church. They were not schismatics but individuals deeply concerned about the abuses, ignorance, and immorality that had become symptomatic of a decadent institution. They did not so much launch a frontal attack upon the church and its theology as bypass it in seeking to promote vital Christianity within its structure.

The formation of the Brethren of the Common Life was the result of the life and work of Gerhard Groote (1340-1384), who founded a semimonastic order of Sisters of the Common Life in his own home in Deventer. Like Saint Francis before him, Groote was the son of a prominent businessman and a profligate playboy in his youth. Interested in astrology, magic, and more earthy pursuits, he became so notorious that during an illness the local priest refused to give him communion. At the same time, his political ties with the church were such that the papacy had increased his income by providing him with two prebends. Finally, after a long period during which he experienced deepening conviction and feelings of guilt, Groote determined to change his way of living. In 1374 he turned his house over to some poor women, reserving two small rooms for himself. His severe struggle for mastery over the temptations that constantly assailed him began with his renunciation of his two prebends and ended five years later in a Carthusian monastery, where he had spent two years attempting to subdue the flesh. The five years that remained to him became by far his most productive. Ordained a deacon by the bishop of Utrecht, he became a wandering preacher proclaiming a gospel of repentance to both laypersons and clergy. In Deventer he soon attracted a band of twelve disciples. They frequently gathered in the home of the vicar of St. Lebwin. From the banding together of this enthusiastic group of dedicated followers—which included the vicar, Florentius Radewyns—the Brethren dated their beginnings.

Groote's preaching against the sins of the clergy and mendicant monks was not without its consequences. Complaints lodged with the bishop of Utrecht prompted his ruling that no deacon could preach. Groote was thus silenced, but he appealed to Urban VI, who eventually overruled the bishop. During the last two years of his life, Groote worked feverishly to translate portions of the Scriptures and some hymns into the vernacular so that the movement he had launched might have the necessary resources for its spiritual sustenance. His emphasis upon an educated clergy led to the involvement of the Brethren in the cathedral school in Deventer. This venture into the education of schoolboys opened up a whole new world of influence through which the *devotio moderna* (as the devotional teachings of the Brethren were known) would in turn shape the course of the Renaissance in North Europe.

After the death of its founder the movement continued to attract some very able men. Among these were Gerard Zerbolt of Zutphen (1367-1398), John Cele (ca. 1360-1419), and Alexander Hegius (1433-1498). Each of these men made a significant contribution to the ongoing work of the Brethren of the Common Life. It was Zerbolt who utilized his university training to defend the Brethren's right to exist. After Groote's death the antipathy of the opposition, which had been smoldering for some time, burst into flame. But Zerbolt, scholarly and devout, was equal to the task. Almost from the beginning of his association with the Brethren until he died, he was engrossed in the struggle with the ecclesiastical enemies who argued that the Brethren constituted a new monastic order contrary to church law. His arguments were drawn up and published in a book entitled *On the Common Life,* in which he argued not only for the right of the Brethren to live in community under certain rules but also for the use of the Scriptures translated into the vernacular. Chapter seven of this work was translated by a monk in Brabant and widely distributed. This work and other writings of Zerbolt were known and read far beyond Brethren communities.

The success of Brethren schools was largely

due to the efforts of John Cele. Under his direction the school at Zwolle attracted as many as twelve hundred students at one time. Dormitories were built to house the burgeoning number of students. The school in Zwolle became, along with those in Deventer and Münster, among the best the Brethren ever developed. In these schools knowledge of the Bible was given fresh emphasis. Although Groote had also emphasized Bible study, Cele implemented it in a systematic fashion for the first time in Zwolle. He dictated appropriate selections to his students three times a day—from the epistles in the morning, from the Gospels in the afternoon, and from some other book in the evening.[1] He constantly encouraged the students to follow Christ's example.

Learning for Cele was a means to an end, not an end in itself—hence all subjects were not of equal value to every student. Under Cele's direction the Latin school in Zwolle was divided into eight grades—apparently the first time such divisions had been made in secondary-school education. He taught his students to pray in both Latin and Dutch. Thus Cele established a pattern that was duplicated not only in the schools of the Brethren elsewhere but also in cathedral and monastic schools from Saxony to Spain.

Perhaps an even more significant development was that the *devotio moderna* became the underlying curriculum for countless schoolboys on the eve of the Reformation. Its spirit and substance were best captured in print by Thomas à Kempis (1380-1471), who used the greater number of his ninety-one years to transmit the concepts of the *devotio moderna* to his and subsequent generations by writing biographies of Groote and others and by copying and editing works embodying their teachings. His success is evident in the enormous popularity of the *Imitation of Christ,* more copies of which have been printed than any other book except the Bible. The *devotio moderna* had a certain attraction for the Augustinian Canons Regular,

who befriended the Brethren and joined Groote, Radewyns, and Zerbolt in their defense. It was through communities of the Brethren and kindred spirits among the Augustinians—as well as through Brethren schools and literary works—that the *devotio moderna* left its mark upon the Renaissance in the Netherlands and Lower Germany.

The fact that the Brethren studiously avoided the taint of heresy by not openly questioning traditional Roman Catholic dogmas and sacraments kept them immune from persecution. Having received permission from Urban VI to follow their own insights, they gained some freedom to expand their operation due to the Papal Schism. In fact, they organized a monastery at Windesheim patterned after the Augustinian Canons Regular that furthered the impression of the orthodox and medieval nature of the movement. Yet their emphasis upon the Scriptures in the vernacular and their commitment to lay education set them apart from the mendicant orders. It was their identity as loyal Catholics that made the penetration of the *devotio moderna* much more pervasive than it could ever have been otherwise.

ALEXANDER HEGIUS (1433-1498)

In Alexander Hegius there was a fusion of humanism and the *devotio moderna* that was to become characteristic of the Northern Renaissance. Albert Hyma calls him—and with good reason—"the greatest educator of Transalpine Europe in the fifteenth century."[2] Hegius shared with Rudolf Agricola and Wessel Gansfort a love for the ancient classics and Greek. However, two things set him apart from some humanists: he did not hesitate to write in the vernacular, and he believed that learning was to be shared, since it was not the sole possession of the elite. His appreciation for humanist learning, however, was apparently genuine. In fact, he studied Greek with Agricola. His faith in combining the best of humanist thought with the ideals of the

---

1. Albert Hyma, *The Brethren of the Common Life* (Grand Rapids: Eerdmans, 1950), p. 91.

2. Hyma, *The Brethren of the Common Life,* p. 119.

Brethren was well-founded; he was very successful as an educator. His school in Emmerich enrolled as many as fifteen hundred students before he transferred to Deventer. In 1483 Hegius was appointed rector of St. Lebwin's School in Deventer, the first school managed by the Brethren. Here he remained until his death. Under his direction the school reportedly reached an enrollment of around twenty-two hundred students.

It was during this period of his life that Hegius's humanist leanings became most apparent, evident in his interest in the ancient authors, poetry, and Greek. In fact, he recommended "in his *Farrago* that one should appropriate the diction of Cicero, Virgil, and Sallust, and imitate the Italian humanists."[3] He also passed critical judgment on contemporary textbooks. On the last page of his *Invecta* he listed grammars that should be altered. His rejection of certain medieval textbooks as no longer worthy of serious study evidenced a definite turning away from Scholasticism to humanism. On this point Hyma's judgment of Hegius's contribution to the Northern Renaissance seems quite valid:

> During the rectorate of Hegius, then, Deventer was one of the chief centers of the movement usually referred to as the German Renaissance. . . . An index of how strong an intellectual movement this was, is the fact that many classics were issued from the presses at Deventer before 1500: more than four hundred and fifty works.[4]

Perhaps an excerpt from a letter of Hegius to Wessel can best reveal the mix of humanist interests and devotion to biblical studies characteristic of the educator:

> I have been, as you know, in the Cusan library. There I found many Hebrew books, altogether unknown to me; but fewer of the Greek. . . . But I brought with me Basil on the Hexaemeron and his Homilies on the Psalms; the Epistles of Paul together with the Acts of the Apostles; the Lives of certain Romans and Greeks written by Plutarch and also his Symposium; some grammars; some

mathematical works; some songs of deepest feeling concerning the Christian religion, composed as I believe by Gregory Naziansen; some prayers, *eúkái.*

> If you want any of these, let me know; they shall go to you. For it is not right that I should have anything that I would not share with you. If it will not inconvenience you to be without the Greek gospels, I beg you to lend them to me. You ask to be informed about my tutoring. I have followed your counsel. For all learning is pernicious that is attended with loss of honesty. Farewell, and if you want me to do anything, signify it to me and consider it done.[5]

TWO MEN FROM GRONINGEN

In Alexander Hegius various aspects of humanism and the *devotio moderna* formed a harmonious synthesis. However, in two men from Groningen, Agricola and Wessel, both sometime students of the Brethren of the Common Life, these elements found very different expressions. Although Wessel Gansfort (1419–1489) was born some twenty-five years before Rudolf (Rodolphus) Agricola (1444–1485), the latter became the most effective transmitter of Italian humanism in Germany and so will be given prior attention.

Agricola was not the first German (Dutch) to embrace Italian humanism. Through his writings Cusanus had already introduced certain aspects of the movement to his fellow countrymen. Yet it is Agricola who is often referred to as "the Father of German Humanism." While both Cusanus and Agricola spent much time in Italy engaged in humanist studies, Agricola became the peripatetic advocate of humanism in the North. Erasmus praised him as one "who first brought with him from Italy some gleam of a better literature." In a letter to the Strasbourg publisher Matthias Schürer, Erasmus wrote, "Whenever I read anything he wrote, I feel fresh admiration and affection for that inspired and

3. Hyma, *The Brethren of the Common Life,* p. 120.
4. Hyma, *The Brethren of the Common Life,* p. 121.

5. Hegius, cited in *Wessel Gansfort: Life and Writings,* 2 vols., ed. Edward Waite Miller, trans. Jared W. Scudder (New York: Knickerbocker Press, 1917), 1: 332–33.

soaring mind."[6] Erasmus may have offered such generous praise because he saw in Agricola something of a prototype. Agricola's disdain for any position or responsibility that would tie him down or rob him of precious time from his studies was well known. For example, when his services were sought for a Latin school in Antwerp, he wrote to a friend,

> To take over a school is a bitter, difficult, joyless affair, viewed merely from the outside, a very hard and sad thing: for I must think of blows, tears and howling, a perpetual prison life. . . . I should take over a school? Where would I find the time for progress in learning? Where would be the quiet and the cheerful frame of mind for my own research and thought?[7]

Agricola preferred the life of a wandering scholar, lecturing upon occasion as it suited him. In Ferrara he supported himself as an organist at the de'Este ducal chapel. He was finally persuaded by the Elector Philip, a patron of humanism, to settle in Heidelberg, with little obligation to do anything other than study. Thus he spent the last three years of his life at the university there, where he lectured occasionally on a variety of subjects, including eloquence (dear to the heart of all humanists), Latin and Greek literature, logic, physics, astronomy, Pliny, and Aristotle's *De anima*.[8]

Agricola apparently saw no conflict between his humanist learning and Christian faith. He was never openly critical of the church or its teachings, yet he held, true to his early education by the Brethren of the Common Life, that "above all others, the Holy Scriptures are the most dependable guide in life."[9] In his denigration of Scholasticism he received support and guidance from the Italian humanists. Like Valla,

he shifted the emphasis from the dialectics of Aristotle to the rhetoric of Cicero, but he did not completely discard the "Angelic Doctor." He emphasized rhetoric rather than scholastic speculation, but not to the exclusion of reason and knowledge:

> It is necessary to disregard all that one has learned and turn to the classic authors, especially those whose knowledge of rhetoric enabled them to put the best light on worthwhile things. It is necessary for the student to master rhetoric in turn, an essential condition of the utility of truth. The skill of the rhetorician, if combined with training in logic and knowledge in a given field, enables one to handle almost any problem presented, like the masters of style, the sophists of ancient Greece, Gorgias, Prodicus, Protagoras, and Hippias.[10]

His letters reveal a great deal more about his thinking than do his formal writings. In a letter to his brother he disclosed that, for him, virtue was the chief end of life. The examples and ethical precepts he found in abundance in the lives of the ancients, especially Seneca. In another letter to his friend Jacob Barbirianus he called his kind of humanism the *philosophia Christi*, a term that was later popularized by Erasmus.

Among Agricola's few formal writings is his *Life of Petrarch*, in which he pointed out that in his later years Petrarch began to devote himself to the study of Scripture. His most popular work was *On Dialectic Invention*, a book on dialectics and rhetoric subsumed under the term *logic*. According to Lewis Spitz, "Agricola's logic took Paris by storm, where Johann Sturm made it popular while teaching there from 1529 to 1536."[11] Its popularity was evident in its numerous printings: at least fifteen editions appeared between 1538 and 1543. However, Agricola's forte was not his literary output but his personal advocacy of the ideals of the *devotio moderna* in a humanist context. He spent

6. *The Correspondence of Erasmus*, vol. 3, trans. R. A. B. Mynors and D. F. S. Thomson, ed. Beatrice Corrigan (Toronto: University of Toronto Press, 1976), p. 43.

7. Agricola, cited by Lewis W. Spitz in *The Religious Renaissance of the German Humanists* (Cambridge: Harvard University Press, 1963), p. 24.

8. Spitz, *The Religious Renaissance of the German Humanists*, p. 24.

9. Spitz, *The Religious Renaissance of the German Humanists*, p. 27.

10. Spitz, *The Religious Renaissance of the German Humanists*, p. 27.

11. Spitz, *The Religious Renaissance of the German Humanists*, p. 30.

much of his time translating Greek and Latin works of rhetoric with appropriate commentaries. He composed a few notable orations, the last of which he wrote for his friend Bishop Dalberg to deliver before Innocent VIII upon his assumption of the papal throne. In these orations and in his letters two themes are paramount: his insistence upon an ethical and moral life, and his fidelity to Rome. Shortly after his return from Rome in 1485, he died in the arms of Dalberg.

Agricola is reported to have been critical of the church only once—in conversation with his close friend Wessel. Wessel may have induced this criticism, for it was he who became known for his reforming tendencies and sharp criticism of the Roman Church, its clergy, and its teachings.

Like Agricola, Wessel was born in Groningen (ca. 1419); he was given the name Johann but was sometimes called Herman after his father. Gansfort (Goesevort), however, became a common designation, apparently derived from a village in Westphalia from which the family originally came. Wessel received his early education in schools of the Brethren in Groningen and Zwolle. During this time he distinguished himself as an earnest student. He also came under the influence of Thomas à Kempis. Further education followed at Cologne and Paris. After his days at Cologne he was invited to accept the chair of theology at Heidelberg, but he turned down the offer in order to continue his studies at Louvain, and a year later he moved on to Paris. For the next fifteen years he pursued his studies at the Sorbonne while lecturing informally, presumably on Greek and Hebrew. While there he made many friends among the humanists, two of whom were Agricola and Reuchlin. It was during these years that his independent bent of mind won him the title "Master of Contradictions."

After his years of study at the University of Paris, Wessel traveled extensively, first in France and later in Italy. His journeys took him to Rome during the pontificate of Paul II, who, even though a patron of the Renaissance, had dissolved the Roman Academy and imprisoned its

leaders for their crass paganism. Upon Pope Paul's death in 1481, one of Wessel's close friends from his student days in Paris, Francesco della Rovere, was elected to succeed him, taking the name of Sixtus IV. It is reported that for a time Wessel served as the personal physician of the new pontiff, who rapidly became known for his political intrigue and nepotism. It is reported that when Wessel called upon Sixtus to offer his congratulations, his holiness asked what favors he would like granted him, whereupon Wessel replied,

> "Most holy father, my kind and just patron, there is nothing with which I would greatly burden your Holiness. I have never sought great honors, as you know; but since you now sustain the character of the Supreme Priest and Shepherd upon earth, I pray that your reputation may correspond with your name; and that you may so administer your high office that when the great Shepherd of the sheep, whose chief servant on earth you are, shall come, he may say: 'Well done, good and faithful servant; enter thou into the joy of thy Lord.' And you fearlessly may say: 'Lord, thou deliveredst unto me five talents: lo, I have gained other five talents.'" Sixtus replied; "This shall be my concern; do you ask something for yourself." "Well then," said Wessel, "I beg you to give me a Greek and a Hebrew Bible from the Vatican library." "These shall be given to you," said Sixtus. "But, you foolish man, why do you not ask for a bishopric or something similar?" Wessel answered: "Because I do not need it."[12]

Eventually Wessel returned to Paris—and controversy. His critique of the Roman Church and its practices was apparently becoming sharper. Thus he left Paris for Basel, where, after a brief stay, Philip, the elector of the Palatinate, invited him to accept a chair of theology at the University of Heidelberg. Problems arose because Wessel had no doctor's degree. He agreed to take an examination, but the faculty insisted that rules dictated ordination to the priesthood as a prerequisite for the doctorate in theology, a necessity for teaching. However, for about three years he taught Greek and Hebrew as a member

---

12. Wessel, cited in *Wessel Gansfort,* 1: 85.

of the faculty of philosophy. After this period of time Wessel longed for his native land and a less demanding schedule, so he returned home.

His return to Groningen was celebrated with fanfare, including a Latin ode composed in his honor. It seems ironic that the man who had rejected the call of the cowl and even priestly ordination would spend the last ten years of his life dividing his time between the monks of Aduard and the nuns of Saint Clara, a convent of the Spiritual Virgins in Groningen. It was among the nuns of Saint Clara that he suffered his last illness and died. Goswin, at that time a younger monk of the Aduard monastery, provides a glimpse into Wessel's life there. It is he who reports that Agricola and Wessel expressed their criticism of the church's teachings on indulgences and the sacramental system.

The differences apparent between Agricola and Wessel were the result of a number of factors. Agricola seems to have made friends easily and to have been just as easily influenced by them. In the company of Bishop Dalberg he appeared to be a good Catholic who harbored no disturbing views concerning the church, but with Wessel he was apparently very critical of the Roman Church, its morals and its theology. A theme that runs through his life is his sincere devotion to virtue and what may be termed "Sermon on the Mount" morality. For this heritage of the *devotio moderna* he found ample support in his selected use of Italian humanist writings. Whatever misgivings he may have had regarding the Roman Church he suppressed in the interest of peace and harmony.

Wessel, on the other hand, showed little appreciation for humanism in either its literary or its artistic expressions. He did, however, appropriate the linguistic developments in Greek and Hebrew and early on made the mastery of these biblical languages a major goal of his career. His independent mind seems to have compelled him to live dangerously. While his friendship with Sixtus IV and the bishop of Utrecht may have saved him from the Inquisition, it did not save his books from the irate monks who burned them or from the *Index* in 1529. In his criticism of indulgences, the teachings on the

mass, and the belief in justification by faith, he seems to have anticipated Luther and Zwingli. Edward Miller even holds that the Heidelberg Catechism owes its uniqueness to the legacy of Wessel. Whether or not this assertion is tenable, there is no question regarding Wessel's final critical stance. He was not a humanist, nor was he a typical medieval Catholic; he was a layman with serious questions about the Roman Church, its morals, and its teachings. Within that church, however, he found many like-minded people who were well along the road to the Reformation.[13]

HUMANISM IN GERMANY

After Agricola and Wessel, humanism in Germany continued to manifest both its Italian heritage and the influence of the *devotio moderna*. However, with the rise of the Reformation in the first decades of the sixteenth century, humanism found itself at the crossroads of history, and humanists were forced to make a choice. The critical stance that German humanists had taken in regard to the Roman Church did not mean that they were ready to leave the church for some sectarian option. For many if not most, a pluralistic alternative to the medieval *corpus christianum* was unthinkable. Papal suspicions of heresy harbored by German humanists were the result of both misinformation and misunderstanding. With few exceptions German humanist scholars were careful to conform—if not in the bloom of life, then certainly in the throes of death. Yet humanism of the fifteenth century, particularly in its expression in Northern Europe, helped to prepare the Continent for the Reformation of the sixteenth century. Perhaps Jacob Wimpfeling in his encounter with Jacob Sturm illustrates both humanism's contributions and its limitations. Lewis Spitz writes,

Whatever contribution Wimpfeling made to the historic Reformation was completely unin-

13. See R. R. Post, *The Modern Devotion: Confrontation with Reformation and Humanism* (Leiden: E. J. Brill, 1968), pp. 536–550, for an analysis of Wessel's writings.

tended. . . . How it must have hurt him to see his prize student and future city councilor, Jacob Sturm, turn Protestant and help win Strassburg for the Reformation. . . . How it must have shocked him, when in answer to his remonstrances, Sturm replied: "If I am a heretic, you have made me one."[14]

Jacob Wimpfeling (1450-1528)

Jacob Wimpfeling was the preacher at Speyer Cathedral and a member of the Rhenish Sodality of humanists in Heidelberg. He was one of half a dozen German humanists who launched broadsides against various abuses of the medieval church up to the very eve of the Reformation but refused to join the new crusade headed by "the German Hercules," Martin Luther. Wimpfeling was more the heir of Wessel than of Agricola. Educated at the Universities of Freiburg and Heidelberg, he took time out from an academic career to serve as cathedral preacher at Speyer from 1498 to 1501. By that time he had become the rector of the University of Heidelberg and a well-known humanist.

Wimpfeling had a love-hate relationship with humanism. He valued its services in the interest of clerical reform and Christian morality, but he was careful to distinguish between good and bad humanists on the basis of a criterion apparently derived from the *devotio moderna*. To his mind humanism was of little value if it did not serve the cause of Christian morality. In some ways Wimpfeling was an enigma. He did not know Greek or act consistently in favor of reform when he had the opportunity to do so. Unlike most humanists, he recommended Aristotle and denounced Plato. He was strictly medieval in his acceptance of the basic structure and dogmas of the Roman Church. That he was suspected of heresy and summoned to Rome upon two different occasions to give an account of himself indicates the church's confusion; as Spitz so inimitably says, "Rome's vision was so

blurred that she could scarcely distinguish too ardent friend from foe."[15]

Wimpfeling was a prolific writer who never seemed to tire of inveighing against the sins of the clergy, especially clerical concubinage. His most important work on the subject was *De integritate*. When forced to declare himself for or against Luther, he left no doubt: he had cast his lot with Rome. As his last years in Strasbourg conclusively demonstrated, he still favored humanist learning and the reformation of morals among the clergy, but he was no proto-Lutheran or crypto-evangelical. As an earnest ethicist he waged many attacks upon loose living and clerical abuses that did help to create a climate of discontent with the medieval status quo.

Conrad Celtis (1459-1508)

Celtis was a humanist but with a temperament quite different from that of Wimpfeling; his affinity for Italian humanism was also much more evident than Wimpfeling's. He was a close friend and student of Agricola and, like his mentor, reflected a genuine appreciation for Italian humanism but little for Italians. Although he traveled extensively in Italy and adopted a lifestyle reminiscent of that of some of the more prominent humanists, he was above all a German patriot. Unfortunately, his feeling of German superiority led him to denigrate other nations and races.

On April 18, 1487, in Nuremberg, Emperor Frederick III crowned Celtis the first German poet laureate of the Empire. His accomplishments, though significant at the time, hardly justified such recognition. His poetry was preoccupied with his illicit love life (*Amores*) and his otherwise private concerns. However, through his writings, self-centered as they were, he managed to launch a major attack on the medieval church, with targets ranging from the ignorance and immorality of its clergy to the pride and haughtiness of its pontiff, Innocent VIII, whose

---

14. Spitz, *The Religious Renaissance of the German Humanists*, p. 60.

15. Spitz, *The Religious Renaissance of the German Humanists*, p. 59.

foot he had stooped to kiss. The sting of his criticism was felt as far away as Spain, where his *Odes* was placed on the *Index librorum prohibitorum* (*Index of Prohibited Books*).

Celtis embraced a number of paradoxical concepts and attitudes. Although convinced of the truth of astrology, he entertained serious doubts about the nature of God and the immortality of the soul. He attacked Scholasticism even though he had a great appreciation for Albertus Magnus. He wrote Latin poetry modeled after that of Horace, yet he idolized German primitive culture. When he sensed that death was near, he made his peace with the church. Lewis Spitz characterizes him well: "He was a complex bundle of conflicting characteristics, for he was at the same time critical and credulous, skeptical and believing, enlightened and superstitious, religious and secular, spiritual and earthy, a natural philosopher much concerned with the supernatural."[16]

Even though Celtis has been called "the best lyric poet among the German humanists,"[17] his contribution to humanism lay more in his activities as its spokesman and promoter than in his work as an author. He was a vagabond student whose wanderings took him from Italy to Poland and back again in 1497 to Vienna via Ingolstadt. In the Universities of Ingolstadt and Vienna, where he introduced aspiring young students to the world of the ancients, he also organized humanist sodalities.

Although Celtis died nine years before Luther startled Europe with his Ninety-five Theses, there is little indication that he would have sided with the Reformer any more than did Reuchlin or Erasmus. In this regard a summary paragraph from Lewis Spitz's *Religious Renaissance of the German Humanists* weighs both the limitations of and the contributions made by German humanism to the Reformation:

Humanism did much to make the Reformation possible, and Celtis added his contribution. He promoted classic learning and the drive to the sources which was important also for the Reformation. He added fuel to the fires of nationalism which were to give a certain direction to the movement later in the century. He helped to shake confidence in the old authorities. Many of his students were prominent leaders in the Reformation movement. Laurentius Corvinus led the reform in Breslau and was a close coworker of Luther and Melanchthon. Andreas Althamer, who read Celtis's odes with enthusiasm, won fame as the Lutheran reformer of the Hohenzollern Frankish lands. Aventine's histories with their antipapal and anticlerical bias were standard reading for two centuries. Zwingli became the Swiss reformer much under Erasmian influence. And Vadian, another student of Celtis in Vienna, led the reform in St. Gallen. But at the very center, in the theological concern for a renewed Christian faith, Celtis was a stranger to the basic impulses which gave birth to the Reformation. Because it answered the deepest need of man in that century, not humanism but the Reformation became the decisive event for German history.[18]

It is difficult to assess personal influence because it is often undocumented; nevertheless, it is perhaps in this dimension that Celtis's most lasting importance is seen. Vadianus (Joachim von Watt), once a student of Celtis, also taught at Vienna. One of his students was Conrad Grebel. It was Grebel, also a disciple of Zwingli, who became one of the early leaders in the emerging Anabaptist movement, a development Celtis could hardly have foreseen.

Johannes Reuchlin (1455-1522)

Reuchlin, a contemporary of Celtis, lacked the flamboyance of his younger friend, but in the area of solid scholarship Reuchlin was clearly his superior. Both Celtis and Reuchlin were at Agricola's bedside when he died, and they were both indebted to him. Perhaps it was Wessel who first started Reuchlin on the road to He-

---

16. Spitz, *The Religious Renaissance of the German Humanists*, p. 107.

17. Spitz, *The Religious Renaissance of the German Humanists*, p. 82.

18. Spitz, *The Religious Renaissance of the German Humanists*, p. 109.

brew studies. But even if this were the case, three men of the past inspired him far more and to a considerable extent shaped his career as a Hebraist: Nicholas de Lyra, a Franciscan monk with a sincere desire to convert the Jews; Nicholas Cusanus, the German cardinal and textual critic; and Pico della Mirandola, the Florentine humanist. Of these, Pico had the most profound influence upon Reuchlin's subsequent intellectual development and devotion to the study of Hebrew and the Cabala.

Like Petrarch before him, Reuchlin began his graduate studies in law, but unlike Petrarch, he actually practiced law for a number of years before his overwhelming interest in humanist studies—particularly the recovery of a correct knowledge of Hebrew—forever turned him away from the profession. He began his academic career at the age of fifteen at the University of Freiburg. Like many a German student in those days, he continued his studies at a number of different universities, including the Universities of Basel, Paris, Orleans, and Poitiers. During his first visit to Florence in 1482, he met Ficino. During a return visit in 1490, he met the gifted and devout Pico. By this time Reuchlin had established his own reputation as a linguist. While he may have begun his study of Hebrew as early as 1486, he made little progress until 1492. In 1506, however, he brought out his Hebrew grammar, *De rudimentis hebraicis.* This was followed by a number of other books designed to aid the student in his mastery of the Hebrew language and to introduce Christians and Jews to the Cabala. For this latter purpose Reuchlin published *De arte cabbalistica,* which he dedicated to Pope Leo X. Reuchlin soon found himself at the center of a controversy in which, because of his love of Hebrew and Hebrew literature, he was accused of heresy.

Reuchlin's position was opposed by a recent convert from Judaism named Johannes Pfefferkorn. It was Pfefferkorn's conviction that the only effective way to win Jews for Catholicism was to destroy all of their sacred writings in Hebrew with the exception of the Old Testament. In 1519 he succeeded in persuading the emperor to issue an imperial order confiscating

all such books. Pfefferkorn's fanatical campaign was opposed by the archbishop of Mainz, who demanded that other scholars versed in Hebrew be consulted before more books were burned. Pfefferkorn himself suggested that Reuchlin's opinion should be sought, a decision he was to regret. Much to Pfefferkorn's consternation, Reuchlin wrote that most Jewish books were not directed against the Christian faith but were intended for the edification of the Jewish people and therefore quite harmless. In his opinion they certainly should not be destroyed. Bitterly disappointed, Pfefferkorn wrote a fiery pamphlet against Reuchlin entitled *Handspiegel* (*Hand Mirror*), in which he questioned Reuchlin's competence and judgment. Reuchlin, now known as the *Phoenix Germaniae* (the "German Phoenix"), did not meekly submit to this insult. He answered with his *Augenspiegel* (*Eye Mirror*). The monks and professors of Cologne rallied to defend Pfefferkorn's position, while the humanist sodalities organized by Celtis, the Mutian circle at Erfurt, and the students and humanists of Heidelberg sided with their champion, Reuchlin. Several universities condemned *Augenspiegel,* however, and Jakob von Hochstraten—Dominican and inquisitor general for the dioceses of Cologne, Trier, and Mainz—summoned Reuchlin to appear before him to answer charges of heresy.

Even though Leo X was reluctant to support Hochstraten against Reuchlin and so many learned humanists, he finally declared Reuchlin's *Augenspiegel* a dangerous book, and the author was condemned as a heretic in 1520. But Reuchlin took special pains to distinguish himself from Luther and his cause. This was not really difficult for him to do—despite Ulrich von Hutten's bitter disappointment at what he considered Reuchlin's betrayal—because Luther and Reuchlin were operating according to fundamentally different sets of presuppositions. Reuchlin spent the last two years of his life teaching at Ingolstadt and Tübingen. While in Ingolstadt, he lived in the home of Dr. Johann Eck, Luther's antagonist. Shortly before he died, Reuchlin, like so many others who had faced death before him, was ordained a priest.

Melanchthon (a great-nephew of Reuchlin) and Luther were genuinely grateful for Reuchlin's efforts in unraveling the mysteries of the Hebrew language; however, they did not share his fascination with the Cabala. Despite his early indictment of the Roman Church and some of its practices and his unfortunate controversy with Pfefferkorn, Reuchlin was a son of the Renaissance, not the Reformation. It is significant, however, that many of Reuchlin's students became followers of Luther and co-laborers in the cause of reform.

Reuchlin's Supporters

At the height of the Reuchlin controversy, humanists, almost to a man, supported their embattled leader. Among these were three prominent representative humanists who took up the cudgels from quite different positions. From the University of Erfurt, Conrad Mutianus Rufus (1471–1526) led the charge aided by his colleagues and students. Willibald Pirckheimer (1470–1530), a Nuremberg patrician, added considerable prominence and some erudition to the quarrel. Ulrich von Hutten (1488–1523), crowned poet laureate of the Empire on July 12, 1517, was the activist of the protest who attempted to weld all the humanist forces into a united front in defense of Reuchlin. The togetherness of the humanists in the Reuchlin affair was only temporary, however, because the various strands in German humanism ultimately failed to mesh in support of another German patriot who came preaching a new gospel.

Mutian (Mutianus) was the leader of the Erfurt humanists. He had studied at Deventer, where he was thoroughly indoctrinated with the *devotio moderna* by the Brethren of the Common Life. In Erfurt he was introduced to the *via moderna*, which was the preferred form of Scholasticism in that citadel of learning. (This term is associated with William of Ockham, who taught his own brand of Nominalism.) After teaching two years there, Mutian left Erfurt for Italy and Florence. It was here that his theology underwent a thorough revision. In a sense he forsook the Scholastic theology of his Erfurt

days for the Neoplatonism of the Florentine humanists. The result was a synthesis of his earlier pietism and his new study of the Pauline epistles through Platonic eyes. While these two strains within German humanism were sometimes antithetical, in Mutian they became perfectly compatible. Lewis Spitz strikes the right chord when he writes of Mutian's new interest in the Greek text:

> The return to original sources was in a sense the heart of Renaissance humanism. The stress on the return to Christian sources was the heart of the new humanism of the Florentine Platonists. Particularly Pico and Ficino were interested in a *renascens pietas*, the *restitutio Christianismi*, and in *Christum ex fontibus praedicare*. The drive to the sources led them to a renewed appreciation of the writings of the Fathers, and most significant of all, to a renewed study of the New Testament, and especially of the epistles of Paul. In urging the study of the Scriptures and Fathers, Mutian held up Pico himself as an example of respect and devotion to this type of study. Ficino directed much of his study to Paul's epistles. He tried by referring to the Greek text of the New Testament to grasp the meaning of the epistle to the Romans, for example, in terms of its own historical setting and its specific concepts. It remained more noteworthy as an attempt than as an achievement, for his interpretation was so full of Plato that he failed to overcome either his own philosophical preconceptions or the dogmatic tradition by a discovery of the true historical context or of the unique religious insight of Paul.[19]

Like other German humanists, Mutian was sharply critical of the Roman Church, but when pressed he refused to break with it and chided Reuchlin for his boldness. However, in both his spiritualizing of the sacraments and his universalism, he transcended his inherited medieval theology.

A far less fickle supporter of Reuchlin and a far more complicated intellect than Mutian was Willibald Pirckheimer. Pirckheimer was the heir to culture and fortune. When he was born, his father was a lawyer in the service of the bishop

---

19. Spitz, *The Religious Renaissance of the German Humanists*, p. 148.

at Eichstatt. He had received his doctorate in both civil and canon law from the University of Padua in 1465. He was also a friend of Peter Luder and an admirer of Ficino, whose books, along with other humanist works, he avidly read. It was this kind of father who introduced his son, a would-be soldier, to the world of humanist learning. Subsequently Willibald spent seven years in Italy, where he became thoroughly captivated by Italian humanism. He studied law for three years at Padua, continuing his studies at Pavia and Rome. He returned to Nuremberg without a degree but with a sound knowledge of Greek. Apparently his study of Greek and the classics had left him little time for his law course, which had never been of compelling interest to him.

Pirckheimer was an atypical German humanist. For one thing, he was a member of the city council of Nuremberg for almost thirty years, and unlike most German humanist scholars, he was not a member of a university community or a humanist sodality, nor had he come under the direct influence of the *devotio moderna.* But his family seems to have been devoted to the church. Seven of his sisters became nuns, as did three of his daughters. As for Pirckheimer himself, religion apparently was not a personal matter but a purely intellectual affair. It is true, however, that he held to a rather strict moral code for the clergy and worked and wrote vigorously for the reform of the church. He seems to have embraced many of Luther's teachings, at least to the extent that he understood them. But it was Reuchlin's cause that called forth his best-known writing. In 1517, in answer to an aspersion cast upon him—he was called "unknown Willibald" by a member of the theological faculty of the University of Cologne—he published his *Piscator,* which contained a letter to the Cologne Scholastics known as *epistola apologetica* or *defensio Reuchlimi* (*Apology* or *In Defense of Reuchlin*). This work constituted a scathing attack on Pfefferkorn and the "obscurantists." The evangelical tones of the Apology make Pirckheimer sound like a pilgrim on the road to the Reformation. But when he was named in the papal bull *Exsurge Domine,* along

with Lazarus Spengler, city secretary of Nuremberg (the only other layperson so designated), he and Spengler left no stone unturned in seeking absolution. Spengler, however, went on to declare himself on the side of the Protestant Reformation; Pirckheimer never did.[20] In his decision not to break with the Roman Church—or rather his inability to do so—Pirckheimer was not unique among German humanists. This was the pattern of the better-known humanists. In this respect Ulrich von Hutten stands quite alone, for he was one of the few who linked their fortunes with those of Luther and the Reformation—probably for the wrong reasons.

Hutten (1488–1523) was born of a noble Franckonian family in the ancestral castle at Steckelberg. He was frail in his boyhood, so his father prepared him for the life of a monk. For this purpose he was sent to an ancient monastery at Fulda when he was only eleven. Rebelling against the strictures of monastic life, he fled Fulda and became a vagabond student. In the process he sampled the offerings at more than half a dozen universities in Germany and Italy. He did manage to pass his examinations for the bachelor's degree in 1506. His introduction into the world of humanism at Erfurt whetted his appetite to further his humanist studies. Following a reconciliation of sorts with his father, he was sent to Italy to study law. But law proved as distasteful to him as theology, so he abandoned formal studies to become a freelance writer, dedicating his facile pen to a variety of interests. Life had not been kind to Hutten, and he began to write about the experiences that had embittered him in an ever-increasing torrent of poetry and prose.

After his Italian sojourn, he found a way to earn a living in the service of the elector of Mainz, who was also the archbishop. By this time two compelling interests were evident in

---

20. For more detailed information on Pirckheimer, see Spitz, *The Religious Renaissance of the German Humanists,* pp. 185–196, and for more information on Lazarus Spengler, see Harold Grimm, *Lazarus Spengler: A Lay Leader of the Reformation* (Columbus: Ohio State University Press, 1978).

his own personal crusade: the reformation of the German Empire and the reform of the church. In Hutten's mind one could not take place without the other. He became convinced that an apostate church with the Antichrist at its head had contributed to the demise of the Empire and the fading glory of the German people. He had seen the warrior pope, Julius II, on one of his military exploits, and his worst suspicions had been confirmed. To hasten the demise of the papacy, he published a new edition of Lorenzo Valla's *De donatione Constantiniana* in 1517 with a dedication to the new pontiff, Leo X. He also seized the opportunity the Reuchlin affair afforded him to defend a fellow humanist from the attacks of Pfefferkorn, Hochstraten, and the Scholastics of Cologne. For this purpose he seized upon ridicule, the weapon Erasmus had begun to use so effectively. In this effort he could count on the support of fellow humanists, including Erasmus.

At the height of the controversy, Reuchlin issued in his own defense *The Epistles of Famous Men* (1514), a collection of letters of commendation from Erasmus and forty-two other prominent scholars from all over Europe. A group of Erfurt humanists, of whom Crotus Rubeanus was the chief, were inspired to produce a collection of false letters, purported to have been written by earnest souls from Rome to their revered professors at the University of Cologne, concerning certain traditional teachings of the church. The volume, entitled, in parody, *Epistolae obscurorum virorum* (*Letters of Obscure Men*), was an instant success. It is now generally acknowledged that Hutten was responsible for the last half of the book; he may even have enlisted Pirckheimer to contribute one of the letters. At any rate, it illustrates how Hutten used ridicule in his efforts to refute the Scholastics in his ongoing war with the church.

When Luther published his three Reformation treatises in 1520, Hutten felt he had found a new champion for his cause. For here was one whose patriotism was unquestionable and who apparently sought freedom of conscience as ardently as did the errant knight. That Hutten understood the theological grounds upon which Luther was building his case is doubtful. However, there is no question regarding Erasmus's attitude toward both Hutten and Luther: "the prince of humanists" and lover of peace saw nothing but disaster awaiting both men. It came to Hutten much sooner than to Luther. He was summoned to Rome in 1520; Leo had had quite enough of this Don Quixote who persisted in calling even him, a patron of the humanists, the Antichrist. With this turn of events the elector of Mainz dismissed Hutten. He rode off to join Franz von Sickingen in an abortive attempt of the knights to restore Germany's glory at the point of the sword. After this failure, when every other refuge failed, he turned for shelter to Zwingli, known for his humanist leanings. He was not disappointed. From his island retreat in Lake Zürich Hutten fired a final blast against Erasmus for his cowardice and treachery, for in Hutten's eyes the man who had been so bold in the Reuchlin affair and so clever in denouncing the ignorance, hypocrisy, greed, and immorality of the clergy in *The Praise of Folly* had become a Judas. As a result, the unity of the German humanist phalanx was permanently shattered. In 1523, when he was only thirty-five, Hutten lay dying of syphilis, a lonely and frustrated man who in his own way demonstrated the inability of militant humanism to invoke any lasting change in the church or society.

Chapter V

ATTEMPTS AT REFORM: WYCLIFFE AND HUSS

By the time of Luther reform was in the air. Attempts at reforming the Roman Church and medieval society, born within the church itself, became increasingly common during the fourteenth and fifteenth centuries. Northern humanism, of which Erasmus became the most prominent exponent, was one of those attempts. It was the result of the synthesis of the *devotio moderna* and humanism, while the protests of John Wycliffe and John Huss arose within the ranks of the secular clergy in which the radical concepts of Marsiglio of Padua (1280–1343) had begun to assume such a significant role. Yet these earlier reformatory efforts largely faded, lingering on in underground movements—that of the Lollards in England and the Hussites (the Utraquists, the Taborites, and finally the *Unitas Fratrum*) in Bohemia. As such they penetrated the fabric of European social and political life long before Erasmus stirred up discontent within the religious establishment among the literate elite. Yet the teachings and writings of Wycliffe and Huss failed to spark a reformation. The reasons for this failure are, on the surface of things, somewhat elusive. Perhaps Wycliffe was too radical for his times. He lost much of his earlier support when he concluded that the pope was the An-

tichrist. In spite of the Babylonian Captivity of the papacy (1304–1377) and the Papal Schism, which had just begun (1378–1417), most Englishmen were not quite ready to make the church subservient to the state.

The burning of Huss (in 1415) and Jerome of Prague (in 1416), decreed by the Council of Constance (1414–1418), publicized dissent as few other events could have, but it also effectively blocked further reform efforts, since the council was under the direction of those who also sought to reform the Roman Church. The conciliarists, with the help of Emperor Sigismund, determined to keep the reform within safe limits under the control of a general council. In this way they distinguished themselves from Huss while at the same time putting a damper on any grass-roots efforts to support the martyred reformer. The Reformation was still a century away.

While the Reformation probably would not have occurred sooner than it did because of the lack of an effective medium for the dissemination of its cause, when it did come its success was due in part to the work of those who preached reform before Luther. Thus the work of Wycliffe and Huss and those who continued to propagate their ideas was not without a certain significance for events that were to follow.

JOHN WYCLIFFE (ca. 1328-1384)

Wycliffe's birth and early life are difficult to discuss with any historical certainty. He rarely referred to himself in his works, and thus next to nothing is known about his parents, his family, or his birthplace. His one autobiographical reference indicates that he was born in 1324. However, Herbert Workman, author of a two-volume study of Wycliffe, thinks this inaccurate, preferring 1328. There is no question that Wycliffe was a Yorkshireman, probably born on the manor of Wycliffe near the town of Richmond. His family, like most of those living in the diocese of York, was staunchly Roman Catholic—so much so, in fact, that Yorkshire relatives attempted to erase all references to him from the family history after he was declared a heretic at the Council of Constance.

Probably sometime in September of 1340 Wycliffe left his home for Oxford. In those days the Michaelmas term began on October 9, the Feast of Saint Denis. The Oxford of Wycliffe's day bore only a slight resemblance to the Oxford of today. There was no Bodleian Library, no Radcliffe Camera, and no Sheldonian Theatre, and there were only six colleges. The city, like York, was enclosed by a wall. There was also a prison tower in which students were imprisoned occasionally and which later housed the Marian martyrs— Thomas Cranmer, Hugh Latimer, and Nicholas Ridley. Gowned students and clerics of one sort or another were much in evidence. Indeed, the monks and priests frequently outnumbered the students. Many a student was tonsured although not yet an ordained priest or a member of an order. In fact, as Herbert Workman suggests,

> Wyclif would marvel greatly at the number of wandering clergy. Some were broken down vagabonds who complained that they could neither study nor find employment, and were in consequence destitute. Here is the pardoner selling relics of the saints, his bulls commonly forged and always useless. He would note also the friars, carrying little portable altars, with which they entered into competition with the secular clergy. But the lad could not fail to see how the crowds listened to their homely if sometimes vulgar preaching. And when all the wanderers foregathered at night in the inn the rustics or townsfolk would come to hear the news, for the friars and pedlars were the postal service and newspaper of the age.[1]

Onto such a scene Wycliffe came to begin his student career, which he would pursue on and off for the next fifteen years. If he was born in 1324, as he believed he was, he was possibly sixteen, a year or two older than the usual age for beginning students, when he first entered Balliol College. Two other colleges, Queen's and Merton, each claim that Wycliffe was one of their students. The claims may have some substance, since during Wycliffe's time in Oxford, two other John Wycliffes were also there. However, Workman has shown rather conclusively that while our John Wycliffe rented rooms during 1362–63 from Queen's College, he nevertheless was enrolled at Balliol, from which he received his master of arts degree in 1361. By this time Wycliffe had become the master of Balliol College, a position he probably had held since 1356. The usual course of study leading to the master's degree took eight years and that for the doctorate an additional eight.

Apparently Wycliffe's slow progress in obtaining both degrees was due to a number of extenuating factors. For one thing, the Black Plague was particularly devastating in Oxford during the thirteen-forties. Subsequently the plague seems to have been a recurring phenomenon, doubtless because of the uncommonly poor sanitary conditions of the city. Pigs and horses shared the relatively small area within its walls; open sewers further polluted the atmosphere. Wycliffe's studies were also interrupted by his father's death in 1353, upon which occasion he became the lord of the manor of Wycliffe, his ancestral estate. He returned to Oxford, but he had hardly had time to pick up the loose ends

---

1. Workman, *John Wyclif: A Study of the English Medieval Church,* 2 vols. (Oxford: Clarendon Press, 1926), 1: 55.

of his studies when in 1355 a student riot over poor wine turned into a full-scale war between "town" and "gown." Several residence halls were pillaged and burned by rampaging towns-men. By the time the fighting had stopped, sixty-three students lay dead. For some time studies were further disrupted, because most of the students and professors had fled the city when the trouble began (a wise move, since students and friars were hopelessly outnum-bered). Wycliffe's academic progress was further delayed by his other interests. He seems to have taken a lively interest in the study of law, math-ematics, and astronomy, the pursuit of which may have sidetracked him occasionally from his other studies. Then too, Wycliffe was an or-dained priest, and he became rector of Fil-lingham in 1361, warden of Canterbury Hall in 1365, and rector of Ludgershall in 1368. Even though he resided in Oxford during most of this time, these positions entailed responsibilities that required his presence elsewhere and un-doubtedly continued to hamper his academic career.

With Wycliffe's appointment as warden of Canterbury Hall in 1365, the monks were re-placed by secular priests by Islip, bishop of Ely. Canterbury Hall had only recently been estab-lished for the purpose of providing a residence hall in which both regulars (monks) and secu-lars (parish priests) could live and study to-gether as fellows in the university. The change instituted by Islip was not allowed to stand. Upon the bishop's death his successor, Simon Langham, attempted to reverse matters in re-sponse to an appeal by the ousted monks. Upon this occasion Wycliffe appealed to Pope Urban V but lost the case. The whole episode can best be seen as a brief glimpse of an ongoing tug-of-war between monks and seculars characteristic of Oxford at the time.

For seven years Wycliffe served as rector of Fillingham, which he visited only rarely, during the long vacations from Oxford. Perhaps be-cause of a pang of conscience or a fear of closer scrutiny by Archbishop Langham, he exchanged the rectorship of Fillingham in Lincolnshire for that of Ludgershall in Buckinghamshire, only

sixteen miles from Oxford. Ludgershall paid considerably less—in fact, only a third as much as Fillingham. It was a poor parish, but it was much more accessible than his former charge, and he could be present for certain holy days and festive occasions. However distracting his altercation with Langham and the monks may have been, a year later he became the vicar of Ludgershall, and in 1369, the year of his final expulsion as warden of Canterbury Hall, he re-ceived a reservation of a prebend at Lincoln. Workman believes it was a sop from Urban V to placate Wycliffe in the loss of his lawsuit. However, Wycliffe never received the promised benefice.

In the next year Wycliffe began his formal lectures on the *Books of Sentences* by Peter Lombard, the standard medieval theological textbook. This was one of the requirements leading to the doctorate in theology at Oxford. Workman gives an interesting description of the complicated requirements that followed the completion of the lectures by the successful candidate:

> After finishing the *Sentences* the candidate, now called a "baccalarius formatus," was required within a year to preach a Latin sermon at St. Mary's—limited to not more than an hour and a half, or at most two hours—and to give a conference ("col-latio") in the afternoon "either by himself or an-other." At last, after all these toils the candidate received his reward. At Oxford all the doctors were required to testify as to his fitness, and a single adverse vote was fatal, a proof that when Wyclif took his doctorate in 1372 the great quarrel had not yet begun. An elaborate and ceremonious disputation called "Vespers" was held in St. Mary's on the eve of inception. Eight days' notice to all regents and bachelors of the two questions to be discussed had to be given by the candidate, who was also expected to solicit attendance by a per-sonal canvass. After the candidate and presiding master had finished, all the bachelors present brought forward their arguments in return. Ves-pers ended with a speech of the president in praise of the inceptor. . . . Vespers over, the can-didate regaled his friends with cakes and wine, who then went round to the great and learned

John Wycliffe, a forerunner of the Reformation whose ideas may have been too radical for his times
RELIGIOUS NEWS SERVICE

inviting their attendance at the final ceremony on the morrow.[2]

Thus, about nine years after beginning his theological studies, Wycliffe was awarded the doctorate. Upon this occasion he was made a canon at Lincoln, and Gregory XI, the successor of Urban V, renewed the reservation of a prebend. Apparently Wycliffe, who seems to have been always short of funds, was anxiously awaiting a substantial income to provide him with the necessary leisure to study and write. It was not forthcoming, however: two benefices became available at Lincoln, but he lost out in both instances. Losing the bid for this income may have been due not so much to his suspect orthodoxy or his alleged refusal to pay the firstfruits to his holiness but rather to the favoritism Gregory showed another. It is probable that Wycliffe never had a chance to pay the firstfruits. And if rumors of his somewhat heretical views on the Eucharist had reached Gregory, it gave

2. Workman, *John Wyclif,* 1: 97–98.

the pope all the more reason to offer the prebend to another.

The problems Wycliffe had encountered with Urban over Canterbury Hall and later with Gregory over the promised prebend, even though they doubtless did not serve to endear the papacy to Wycliffe, would not in themselves have caused him to turn against the church. After all, others before him had been disappointed by unfulfilled papal promises without becoming heretics. Admittedly, before 1370 there was little in Wycliffe's life that set him apart from the average Oxford theological student living off a number of benefices provided by a system that permitted pluralism *in absentia.* In 1370 Wycliffe set forth his views on the Eucharist, apparently taking his interpretative key from Realist philosophy. But this development was little more than a hint of his future protest.

Theological Roots

The question arises, what was Wycliffe's theological stance when he received his master of theology degree (as the doctorate was then called at Oxford)? Even though Wycliffe did not absorb everything he encountered, his own theology reflected the ferment characteristic of fourteenth-century Oxford. The influence of Duns Scotus and William of Ockham was pervasive. While their teachings led many to embrace post-Thomistic Nominalism, the end result was the destruction of Scholasticism. Wycliffe never followed the neo-Nominalists into Nominalism even though he showed some appreciation for Aristotle (whom he read only in translation), and a certain affinity for Aquinas; philosophically he was a Realist. He seems not to have known Plato, however, except through the writings of others, particularly Augustine.

Wycliffe himself acknowledged an indebtedness to certain Oxford lecturers. Among these was Robert Grosseteste, a thirteenth-century bishop of Lincoln who gained international fame with his sharp rebuke of Innocent IV in 1253. Two other aspects of Grosseteste's legacy left a lasting impression upon Wycliffe: his great erudition and his reliance upon biblical authority. However, another Oxford don, Thomas Bradwardine, proved even more influential in Wycliffe's theological development. He referred to Bradwardine as "Doctor Profundus" and considered him his chief mentor. Since Wycliffe maintained a lively interest in mathematics, Bradwardine must have impressed him with his brilliance as a mathematician as well as his competence as a theologian. Though he had only a bachelor's degree, Bradwardine lectured at Merton on the doctrines of grace. His views on the sovereignty of God and the absolute necessity of grace for good works, which contrasted with those of the Pelagians and the Manichaeans, became a formative influence in the rigid predestinarian views Wycliffe developed later. Bradwardine died on August 29, 1349, after a trip to Avignon, where he was consecrated archbishop of Canterbury.

Richard FitzRalph, a graduate of Balliol and later chancellor of the university, also had a considerable influence upon Wycliffe. He was a favorite at the Avignon papal court—so much so that he was made archbishop of Armagh in July 1346 by Clement VI. His main claim to fame and that which endeared him to Wycliffe was his continual battle against the mendicants. He did not believe that friars should be allowed to hear confessions or bury the dead. His major attack on the Franciscans was published under the title of *De pauperie Salvadoris* (*The Poverty of the Savior*). Wycliffe depended greatly upon FitzRalph's ideas in two of his books, *Of Divine Dominion* and *Of Civil Dominion*.

In 1377 Gregory XI wrote that Wycliffe was attempting "to overthrow the status of the whole Church" by teaching the "opinions and ignorant doctrine of Marsiglio of Padua and John of Jandun of cursed memory."[3] There are indeed many striking parallels between Marsiglio's views and Wycliffe's views on the limitations of papal authority and the relationship of church and state—parallels that seem more than coincidental. What is the explanation for Wycliffe's apparent dependence upon Marsiglio? Al-

though Herbert Workman argues that there was no known copy of Marsiglio's *Defensor pacis* (*Defender of the Peace*) in Oxford until after Wycliffe's time, this does not mean that Wycliffe was unaware of its contents or Marsiglio's theories. The fact that he never mentions Marsiglio or his famous work may be a more convincing argument, but even this is not conclusive, for Marsiglio was indeed, as Gregory said, "of cursed memory." And Wycliffe would have prejudiced his case if he had cited Marsiglio in support of his opinions. But it may well have been, as Workman contends, that Wycliffe learned of Marsiglio's position by reading the works of William of Ockham. Whatever the case, it seems rather evident that Wycliffe was restating ideas that Marsiglio had written down half a century before.

By the time Wycliffe began to lead the attack against the Roman Church and its two popes, he had emerged as the most vocal critic of papal policies in Oxford. Obviously one does not explain Wycliffe's thought by citing the sources to which many of his arguments can be traced— the movement he initiated shows that his contribution was much more than simply a compilation of that which others had thought before him. Wycliffe's reformatory work derived much of its force from his two basic sources, the Bible and Augustine. Because he tied his work so closely to Scripture, it was to have lasting significance. But what was it in Wycliffe's experience that turned the Oxford don into a radical reformer? This question demands investigation.

In the Service of the King

Wycliffe probably entered the service of Edward III before he had received his doctor's degree in 1372. Doubtless his staunch support of the crown's interests, as opposed to papal designs upon England, was common knowledge. By 1374 Edward was desperate for help. He found himself in serious financial straits. His war with France was not going well under the incompetent leadership of his son, Duke John of Gaunt. In addition, the English royal court was operating on borrowed money. To relieve

---

3. Gregory XI, cited by Workman in *John Wyclif*, 1: 297.

the situation, the king cast greedy eyes upon a wealthy church and decided to exact a tithe from the income of the clergy to support the war effort. At the same time, Gregory XI was involved in a war against Milan, using mercenaries who had to be paid. Thus, in addition to the annual tribute England had to pay as a vassal state to the papacy required since the humiliation of King John, Gregory demanded that the English clergy send him a supplement of 100,000 florins. Neither king nor clergy took kindly to this demand. To resolve the problem, Edward sent a delegation to Avignon, but the delegates returned empty-handed. Consequently Edward proposed that representatives from both sides meet at Calais or Bruges to iron out their differences. The pope replied that he was sending three nuncios who would arrive in Bruges on June 24. In Edward's eyes Wycliffe seemed an ideal delegate to represent the crown's interests in this affair—hence he was appointed a member of the commission that was to meet with the nuncios.

Prior to the proposed meeting the king called a convocation on May 21 to insure that the English delegation would present a united front with the solid backing of the English prelates. After some disagreement on the first day between the friars who were present and Archbishop Uhtred, the convocation rejected both the subsidy to help finance the papal war and the tribute referred to as "John's gift," since it was pledged without the approval of the realm and the barons. The delegation had all the ammunition it needed to defend the crown's case before the nuncios. Wycliffe could not have agreed with the position more and doubtless took an uncompromising stand on the platform hammered out at Westminster. He was the only theologian among the English delegates. But his stance was too unyielding. The first meeting came to naught. When the English delegation returned to finally work out an agreement, Wycliffe was left out. By the middle of September he was back in Oxford, where he remained. But the experience left an indelible impression upon him. He was astute enough to discern that principle would be sacrificed for harmony.

In the end the wily nuncios outmatched the English, who proved far too vulnerable to temptation to successfully champion their cause. Their own personal ambitions and greed conditioned them to seek a settlement on terms most favorable to Gregory. While it is true that the papacy made certain superficial concessions, England came off second-best. Those who had the power to veto the English surrender—John of Gaunt and Bishop Sudbury—did not. However, the biggest losers were the English people, who were quick to recognize the fact. Even the dullest observer could have drawn this conclusion upon learning, after an agreement had been reached, that several men—Adam Houghton, Ralph Erghum, John Gilbert, and Simon Sudbury (who was made archbishop of Canterbury on May 12, 1375)—were provided with prestigious and lucrative offices in the English Church. Gregory paid his debts. The Concordat was finally affirmed and published by Edward III on February 15, 1377.

With this act Wycliffe's disillusionment with ecclesiastical intrigue and papal politics was complete. Apparently the would-be reformer had already decided to launch his reform from Oxford through his writings. By the time the Concordat with the Vatican was signed and sealed, Wycliffe had published three works dealing with lordship and stewardship. With each book his audience and his popularity with the rank and file increased. John of Gaunt was not slow to recognize the fact. In Wycliffe's attack upon the wealth and worldliness of the bishops he saw a powerful weapon that he could use to advance his own designs upon the estates of the prelates. Thus began an alliance between the high-minded Oxford theologian and the unscrupulous duke of Lancaster. The duke had also enlisted the mendicant orders that he had befriended in his campaign to strip the bishops of their wealth and power. This unholy alliance was eventually to tarnish Wycliffe's image and blunt the duke's efforts. It is not difficult to understand why John of Gaunt sought to enlist Wycliffe's services for his program of disendowment. But it is much more difficult to see why Wycliffe, being the idealist that he was, allowed himself to be used. Perhaps his abhorrence at insensitive prelates living in luxury at the expense of the poor, coupled with his fervent English patriotism, blinded him to the problems inherent in the new alliance.

However, Wycliffe did become a national figure in the service of John of Gaunt, and with the condemnation of eighteen of his conclusions by Gregory XI he became internationally known. Three times the attempt was made to bring Wycliffe to trial, but the procedures were constantly frustrated by John of Gaunt, who was his patron, or by the common people, whose champion he was. One suspects that Archbishop Sudbury really had no stomach for conducting heresy trials of Englishmen. Finally Archbishop Courtenay (who had been made Archbishop of Canterbury on July 30, 1381, upon the murder of Archbishop Sudbury), long Wycliffe's implacable foe, called a convocation in 1382 at the Black Friars' Convent, where he condemned ten of Wycliffe's conclusions. (The condemned articles included Wycliffe's teachings on the Eucharist, the papacy, confession, dominion, and endowments.) By this time Wycliffe had lost much of his former support.

With the election of Robert of Geneva, who took the name of Clement VII, the Papal Schism developed, and the Roman Church found itself with two popes, Urban VI in Rome and Clement VII in Avignon. Thus Wycliffe, who with Urban's election had entertained the greatest expectations for reform of the church, labeled the pope the Antichrist. As a result, the friars who had been his staunch defenders against the machination of the bishops deserted him; so did his royal patron and many of his Oxford colleagues. However, he was allowed to live out the last two years of his life at Lutterworth, the parish church that Edward III had awarded him in 1374. Wycliffe died on December 31, 1384—but the movement he had launched did not die with him. His teachings were destined to live on not only in those of the Lollards but also in the preaching and teaching of John Huss. But what did Wycliffe really teach? This question can be answered only by examining his voluminous works.

Major Theological Concepts

Lordship

Upon his return from Bruges, Wycliffe delivered a series of lectures at Oxford in which he set forth his concept of lordship. They were incorporated in three works: *Determinatio* (1374), *De dominio divino* (*On Divine Lordship*, 1375) and *De civilio dominio* (*On Civil Lordship*, 1376). In these works Wycliffe sets forth the concept that God alone is Lord. No man can be lord in the ultimate sense of the word but only a steward of that over which the Supreme Lord has given him, by divine grace, a temporary lordship, which is not unconditional. Wycliffe taught that "all power, civil and ecclesiastical, [is] held righteously only as long as [its] possessors remain in grace."[4] Thus it follows, according to Wycliffe, that if "lords" of the church are not in grace, "they are not righteous possessors of property and may—nay—should be deprived of it by secular power."[5] He also held with Marsiglio of Padua and William Ockham that Christ gave the church authority only in spiritual matters and not in temporal affairs. He believed that the fall of the church had occurred when Constantine endowed it with wealth and power. He advocated taxation of the clergy by the state; it was his firm conviction that the clergy needed nothing more than enough for the necessities of life. He admired the Franciscan emphasis upon poverty while at the same time denying the scriptural basis of monasticism. He maintained that it was the king's responsibility to dispossess the "Caesarian clergy" and disendow the "delinquent church," thus restoring a priesthood of grace. It is not difficult to see why John of Gaunt would take an interest in Wycliffe and his teachings: the practical effect of such an interest would make the crown head of the church, exalting the state over the church. Such a radical reordering of the structures of

---

4. Matthew Spinka, ed., *Advocates of Reform: From Wyclif to Erasmus*, Library of Christian Classics, vol. 14 (Philadelphia: Westminster Press, 1953), p. 22.

5. Spinka, *Advocates of Reform*, p. 23.

medieval society was abhorrent to many Englishmen.

The Bible

In 1378, the year the Papal Schism began, Wycliffe brought out *De veritate sacrae scripturae* (*On the Truthfulness of Holy Scripture*). This was the Magna Carta of Wycliffe's reform. For Wycliffe the authority of the Bible was supreme. Grosseteste, the bishop of Lincoln, who greatly influenced the early development of Wycliffe's thought, had made much of the importance of Scripture and sought to impress it upon the priests in his diocese. In a sense Wycliffe was but following a trail blazed by Grosseteste and William Ockham, but, as Herbert Workman points out, there was a fundamental difference. For Wycliffe the Bible was not just one authority among many—i.e., tradition and the church; it alone stood above all other authorities. "Neither the testimony of Augustine nor Jerome, nor any other saint," he wrote, "should be accepted except in so far as it was based upon Scripture." Further, he referred to Scripture as Christ's law: "Christ's law is best and enough, and other laws men should not take but as branches of God's law."[6]

Along with Wycliffe's principle of sola scriptura went the conviction that the Bible was intended for everyone. To the objection that laypersons could not understand the Bible, Wycliffe answered that the Holy Spirit is able to give understanding:

> The New Testament is of full authority, and open to the understanding of simple men, as to the points that be most needful to salvation. . . . He that keepeth meekness and charity hath the true understanding and perfection of all Holy Writ, [for] Christ did not write His laws on tables, or on skins of animals, but in the hearts of men. . . . The Holy Ghost teaches us the meaning of Scripture as Christ opened its sense to His Apostles.[7]

Since most Englishmen, like most Europeans, could not read Latin, Wycliffe realized that if the Bible's message was ever to penetrate the English mind and influence the church, the Bible would have to be put into the language of the people. Thus in 1380 he and some trusted colleagues began to do exactly this. Just how much of the Wycliffe Bible was actually the work of the reformer is debatable, but his efforts combined with those of his fellow scholars resulted in the first English translation of the entire Bible. It wasn't long until Wycliffe's followers, with the help of the English Bible, were far more knowledgeable about the Scriptures and its teachings than most priests and not a few bishops besides. Workman considers this a revolutionary development: "All the evidence shows that Wycliffe's plea for the reading of the Bible by the laity was a revolution, not an extension of an existing practice."[8]

The Church

Toward the end of 1378, Wycliffe completed his *De ecclesia* (*On the Church*). In this work he makes a distinction between the Roman Catholic Church and the true church. The visible church, Wycliffe claims, is the institutional church, which contains both saints and sinners, both the saved and the reprobate. The invisible church, on the other hand, is known only to God, for it is made up of those who were predestined to be saved before the foundations of the universe were laid. Outside the body of the predestinate there is no salvation. Borrowing from Augustine, Wycliffe taught that this universal church consists of three parts: the church triumphant, made up of the saints in heaven; the church militant, made up of the predestined who are still alive; and the sleeping church, made up of those who have died and are in purgatory. His Realist philosophy led him to hold that the church existed before the Incarnation because it had always existed in the mind of God. Since virtually all of humanity is embraced by the visible church, how can one distinguish between those who are truly predestinate and therefore members of the true church, and those who are not and therefore reprobate? Wycliffe's answer was that those pre-

---

6. Wycliffe, cited by Workman in *John Wyclif*, 2: 150.
7. Wycliffe, cited by Workman in *John Wyclif*, 2: 151.

8. Workman, *John Wyclif*, 2: 155.

destined will invariably demonstrate their standing in grace before God by the life they lead. That life will be characterized by piety and obedience evident in a selfless devotion to Christ and the welfare of others. Although no one can be absolutely sure that he is among the elect, everyone should act upon the assumption that he is. Certainly ecclesiastical offices—even the highest, that of the papacy itself—cannot guarantee salvation and are no evidence that one is among the elect. The implications of Wycliffe's teachings for the church were far-reaching, as Workman has observed:

> By finding the test of the predestinate in their living in conformity with the teaching of God, Wycliffe sweeps away much of the Catholic system as then practised. Absolution must depend wholly upon worthiness in God's sight; only in so far as this is attained will the absolution of priest or pope benefit at all. Apart from this even the pope has no right to grant absolution, for every sin has its assigned punishment which none can remit. The whole system of indulgences therefore rests upon the false basis of an inexhaustible store of supererogatory merit at the disposal of the pope. Even God himself, Who alone can grant indulgences, cannot remit sin without satisfaction. Moreover if the pope possessed such power he should use it freely and so restore the golden age, or he would be guilty of the death of those whom he might have saved.[9]

As radical as Wycliffe's concept of the church appeared, it was not wholly derived from the teachings of the New Testament but reflected his indebtedness to Augustine, Realist philosophy, and the legacy of medieval Catholicism. Thus his ecclesiology embraced conflicting concepts that were never completely harmonized.

The Eucharist

The same kind of ambivalence was characteristic of Wycliffe's concept of the Eucharist. Three of the fifteen conclusions condemned by Gregory XI were concerned with Wycliffe's denial of the dogma of transubstantiation. Two works of his deal with the Eucharist: *De apostasia* (*On*

Apostasy) and *De eucharistia* (*On the Eucharist*). Both probably date from 1379 and were written in the order given; they contain a rather full exposition of Wycliffe's mature views on the subject.

In the early years of Wycliffe's student days at Oxford, he apparently accepted without question the prevailing interpretation of transubstantiation as taught by Thomas Aquinas. This view held that with the consecration of the bread and the wine in the celebration of mass, a miracle occurred in which the bread was transformed into the flesh of Christ and the wine changed into his blood. The accidents remained the same—that is, the appearance of the consecrated host was that of bread and the appearance of wine, that of wine—but in reality these substances had been annihilated and in their place were the actual flesh and blood of Christ. But Wycliffe's Realist philosophy rejected the concept of annihilation. At first he sought to explain the presence of the accidents by a concept of a "mathematical body," but his opponents at Oxford had considerable difficulty with this, and he could not answer them to his own satisfaction. By 1379, however, he was so sure of his grounds that for the first time he openly attacked the dogma as defined by the Fourth Lateran Council (1215) under the direction of Innocent III.

Wycliffe claimed that his reconstruction of the theology of the sacrament was in harmony with the primitive church of which Augustine was the chief example, and that the modern church erred in following doctors such as Aquinas. He rejected the miracle of transubstantiation but not the "real presence" of Christ. He held that the bread remained bread and the wine remained wine, but also that Christ is in the sacrament and can be perceived by faith. Therefore, the bread and wine are sacramental signs of Christ; he is figuratively present, and yet his presence is more than symbolic—it is spiritual and real. For Wycliffe it was idolatrous to believe that the host was the identical body of Christ. Neither should one partake of the mass at the hands of an ungodly priest. In such instances, he taught, it would be better not to

---

9. Workman, *John Wyclif*, 2: 15.

partake. For Wycliffe Christ's "sacramental presence" in the Eucharist did not depend upon the words of a priest but upon the faith of the recipient:

It is not therefore a matter of concern in what sort of vessel (when his morals are preserved) the priest may consecrate [the Eucharist]. But (as has been said) the custom appropriate to the country should be kept, and—with probity preserved—uprightly to meditate upon Christ. This is infinitely better than to celebrate the sacrament. Nor is it out of keeping that Christ be sacramentally in the wine mixed with water or other liquid, nay, in the midst of the air, but preeminently in the soul, since the end of the sacrament is for Christ to dwell in the soul through virtues. In this way the layman, mindful of the body of Christ in heaven, more efficaciously and in a better manner than this priest who performs the sacrament, yet with equal truth (but in another manner), causes the body of Christ to be with him.[10]

Of Priests and Popes

Perhaps Wycliffe's polemics reached their most strident tone when he spoke out on the various priestly offices of the church. Writing in 1378 in his work *On the Pastoral Office,* he urged priests to fulfill their responsibility before God "by purging the church of all moral stain and feeding Christ's sheep on his Word."[11] Since he was convinced that the love of money was the root of the Roman Church's deplorable moral weakness, he stressed the necessity of clergy living simply and frugally, depending solely upon the support of the parish. When a priest neglected his duties and failed to live an exemplary life before his flock, the members would be justified in withdrawing their support from him. He directed his severest criticism at the friars, whose preaching, he held, was neither biblical nor sincere but done simply for "temporal gain." He urged the preaching of the whole gospel and the dissolution of the monasteries because God never intended "the religious to hide in cloisters."[12]

---

10. Wycliffe, cited in *Advocates of Reform*, p. 85.
11. Wycliffe, cited in *Advocates of Reform*, p. 25.
12. Wycliffe, cited in *Advocates of Reform*, p. 26.

In 1379 Wycliffe renewed his attack upon the papacy in his *De poteste pape* (*On the Power of the Pope*). It is clear that for some time Wycliffe had entertained serious misgivings regarding the papal office, dating from the time that Gregory XI had given the benefice Wycliffe had expected to another. The Papal Schism, which began in 1378, thoroughly disillusioned him. He now denied that the papal office had any divine foundation; rather, it was of human origin—it might even become demonic. Wycliffe declared that the pope who failed to follow Christ in simplicity and poverty was the Antichrist. Before the end of his literary career Wycliffe advocated dispensing with the papal office entirely, something he had not done before. Although the uncompromising Oxford theologian was obviously beyond reconciliation, he was not without influence.

THE LOLLARDS

Wycliffe's influence and teachings lived on in his followers. It was at Lutterworth that he began to prepare a small group of Oxford priests to carry on his reformatory efforts after his death. Chief among these was Nicholas Hereford, who is often credited with making the first translation of the Latin Vulgate into English. Hereford was forced into exile by Archbishop Courtenay, and the movement was suppressed. From this time on Wycliffe's followers were called "Lollards," a term taken from Dutch meaning "mumblers or mutterers of prayers." Despite strenuous attempts to stamp out the heresy, it continued to spread. Wycliffe's secretary, John Purvey, brought out an improved version of the English Bible that became the basis of numerous manuscript copies that were in circulation as late as 1527, when some Lollards were persuaded to purchase a copy of Tyndale's New Testament by Robert Barnes.

By 1395 the Lollards had gained sufficient strength in Parliament to present "Twelve Conclusions," a summary of their major demands for reform of the Roman Catholic Church in England. A. G. Dickens summarizes the points of this document:

It condemns the subordination of the English Church to Rome, together with transubstantiation, clerical celibacy and its untoward moral consequences, the consecration of physical objects (as akin to necromancy), prayers for the dead, pilgrimages, images and the excessive preoccupation of the Church with the arts and crafts. In addition it denounces the work of prelates as temporal rulers and judges, declares all forms of warfare contrary to the teaching of the New Testament and denies that confession to a priest is necessary for salvation.[13]

Dickens suggests that the "Twelve Conclusions" did not emphasize the Lollard insistence upon preaching and putting the English Bible into the hands of the people because of the nature of the document. It called for reform and therefore limited itself to those practices of the church most in need of change. It might also indicate that by this time the strength of the movement was found largely among laypersons. Although Wycliffe and his followers seemed to have overlooked the central truth of the Reformation so fervently preached by Luther and other Reformers, as Dickens points out, "a certain strength shines alongside [the movement's] weakness":

It zealously sought to recover from the Scriptures an authentic sense of the person and spirit of Jesus. It argued with force that the materialism, the pride, the elaborate ritual and coercive jurisdiction of the Church found no justification in the lives of Christ and his disciples as recorded in the New Testament. It made a special appeal to the underdogs of feudal and ecclesiastical society by permitting them a far more active role in the management of their religious lives. In short, it had many of the lively features which characterized the English sects of the Stuart period.[14]

Unfortunately, the Lollards became involved in an armed rebellion led by Sir John Oldcastle, who had been imprisoned for his faith. Once released, he determined to set things right by taking over the seat of government. His ill-ad-

vised march on London was quickly crushed. From that time on the movement went underground, cropping up here and there in populous sections of England. It produced a great deal of unrest for the established clergy and not a few martyrs for the faith, even into the Reformation era. While the reformation it attempted to generate was stillborn, it did provide the seeds of dissent that prepared the masses for the more dynamic movements of reform that arose out of the Reformation of the sixteenth century. While Dickens's evaluation of Lollardy may indeed constitute a classic understatement, it is worthy of serious thought:

As for Lollardy, the prime mover of this shifting world, it boasted its congregations, its preachers, even its heroes, yet in general it was an evasive unheroic and underground affair. It lay far too low in society to achieve a Reformation unaided, yet through this very fact it could avoid obliteration by the judicial machinery of Church and State.[15]

JOHN HUSS AND JOHN WYCLIFFE

Wycliffe's influence was by no means confined to England, though the pervasiveness of that influence varied widely. Lollards carried his message into Scotland only to suffer martyrdom; it was Bohemia that was destined to feel the most lasting impact of Wycliffe's teachings through the writings and preaching of John Huss. Very soon after the invention of the printing press, Huss's writings became well known through the new medium, while Wycliffe's remained in poorly transcribed manuscripts in university libraries, gathering dust. But once historians rediscovered Wycliffe, they tended to make Huss little more than a ventriloquist's dummy who only parroted what he borrowed from his English mentor.[16] However, as Matthew Spinka has pointed out in his book *John Hus' Concept of the Church,*[17] this was hardly the

13. Dickens, *The English Reformation* (New York: Schocken Books, 1964), p. 4.

14. Dickens, *The English Reformation,* p. 25.

15. Dickens, *The English Reformation,* p. 32.

16. See Johann Loserth, *Hus und Wyclif: zur Genesis der Husitischen Lehre* (Munich, 1925).

17. Spinka, *John Hus' Concept of the Church* (Princeton: Princeton University Press, 1966), pp. 4-7.

case. There is no question that Huss, along with Jerome of Prague, was one of the most dedicated disciples of Wycliffe, but he was far more than that. Although Huss did not possess Wycliffe's abstract and speculative bent of mind, he, like Wycliffe, preached with moral earnestness and a desire to see what he considered a decadent church cleansed and reformed.

Wycliffe seems to have backed into the role of reformer after considering the political implications of a church that insisted upon operating upon the basis of Boniface VIII's *Unam sanctam*. As noted earlier, the crisis came when Urban V attempted to impose a subsidy upon the English clergy in addition to collecting the annual payment of "John's gift" to the papacy. In true Marsiglio of Padua fashion, Wycliffe rejected the temporal authority of the popes and sought to severely limit the church's involvement in affairs of the state. However, once his critical eye had begun to scrutinize the medieval church, he began to detect other flaws that needed attention. At this point his philosophical presuppositions and theological understanding led to his questioning the church's teachings as well as its performance. Huss became a reformer through quite a different process, the varied dimensions of which become evident only when his life and times are examined.

JOHN HUSS AND THE EARLY REFORM MOVEMENT

Little is known of John Huss before the time he became a student at the University of Prague in 1390. He was born about 1373 in a town in south Bohemia called Husinec (Goosetown), which name he took for his own. Although nothing certain is known about his parents, his mother was apparently very devout. It was probably due to her efforts that he received the required Latin-school education that was a prerequisite for university studies everywhere. By 1394 Huss had earned his bachelor's degree, and two years later, his master of arts degree. By 1396 he was teaching as a member of the faculty of arts. Five years later he served as dean of the faculty. While retaining membership in the faculty of arts, he began studies in theology and received his bachelor of divinity degree in 1404. Three years later he began lecturing on the *Books of Sentences* by Peter Lombard as a part of the process of earning his doctorate, which he never received. His academic career had become sidetracked because of his opposition to John XXIII's "crusading bull"; with it the pope was attempting, by the sale of indulgences, to raise the funds necessary to wage war on King Ladislas. By this time Huss had become the most popular preacher among the Czech people but was increasingly suspect in the eyes of the German members of the faculty and the archbishop.

In 1402 Huss was appointed preacher at Bethlehem Chapel, which had been the center of the Bohemian reform movement since 1391. Huss was already acquainted with the writings of Wycliffe, having read his works during his early student years at the university. Wycliffe's books had been known in Bohemia since the 1380s, if not before, because of the special relationship of the ruling houses of Bohemia and England. Richard II of England married Anne of Luxembourg, who was the sister of the king of Bohemia. As a result, students from Bohemia were educated at Oxford in increasing numbers. Wycliffe's writings were probably introduced to the students and faculty of the University of Prague by some of these returning students. In 1406 Jerome of Prague, an enthusiastic exponent of Wycliffe's reformatory works, returned from studies in England with a load of Wycliffe's books. At this point it is evident that the old sentiments of reform, dating from the work of the Augustinian monk Conrad Waldhauser (d. 1369), were enjoying something of a revival fortified by the teachings of Wycliffe in the earnest preaching of the young Prague professor John Huss.

However, it was Milíč of Kroměříž (d. 1374) who is considered the father of the Czech reform movement. In addition to calling the clergy to a renewed commitment to ethical living with an emphasis upon poverty, he appealed to the Scriptures as the highest source of authority and attempted to call the church away

from the subtleties of philosophy and back to
the simple gospel of Christ. His work was carried on after his death by Matthew of Janov (ca.
1355–1393).

Matthew went even further than Milič in his
call to reform. He had studied at the University
of Paris, from which he had received his master
of arts degree. While there he must have read
Wycliffe and become aware of the thought current among the conciliarists at the university,
who were anxious to see the church cleansed
of its impurities and unified under one head.
The remedy that Matthew offered for the
church's ills paralleled that of Wycliffe. Of the
four reasons he listed for the decadent condition of the church, three cited the sins of the
clergy, prelates, secular priests, and monks. His
characterization of the priests contained a severe indictment:

> [They are] worldly, proud, mercenary, pleasure-
> loving, and hypocritical; they are the synagogue
> of sinners, the great Whore, serpents and young
> adders, a snare, the apocalyptic locusts, adulterous
> women, worse than public prostitutes. They form
> spiritually the Great Babylon which is the Great
> Whore and the mother of adultery and abomina-
> tion of the earth. They do not regard their sins as
> such, do not allow themselves to be reproved,
> and persecute the saintly preachers. There is no
> doubt that if Jesus lived among such people, they
> would be the first to put him to death.[18]

In Huss the native reform movement and the
teachings of Wycliffe coalesced to produce Bohemia's most effective spokesman for reform. For
a number of years Huss pursued the work of
reform both from his pulpit and in the university. He preached in the Czech language for the
common people, even though he wrote his sermons in Latin at the university. In both his
teaching and his preaching he enjoyed the support of his Czech colleagues, the common people, and the young archbishop Zbyněk. His
influence was enormous. Even the archbishop,
following his lead, had declared fornicating
priests to be heretics. Apparently Huss was in the

good graces of the archbishop until some parish
priests lodged the charge of heresy against Huss
himself in 1408. Five years before, the Germans,
who had never trusted Huss, had begun to take
actions designed to undermine his teachings. A
German master named John Hübner had precipitated a crisis in the university by adding
twenty-one more charges to the twenty-four
charges of heresy brought against Wycliffe in
1382.[19] In a meeting in which the Germans on
the faculty outnumbered the Czechs by three to
one, the university prohibited the teaching of
any of the articles. Nevertheless, Wycliffe's
books continued to be read and taught.

A University Divided

It appears that the situation was exceedingly
complicated, involving intense nationalistic rivalry as well as conflicting philosophical presuppositions. The Czechs, who made up one-
fourth of the faculty, were committed to Realist
philosophy, whereas the Germans, who made
up the other three-fourths of the faculty, were
committed for the most part to Nominalism.
The Czech masters reacted vigorously to the
condemnation of Wycliffe's teachings. Stanislav
of Znojmo, the leader of the Czech masters,
defended the forty-five articles as true and orthodox. Huss wrote Hübner a letter in which he
defended the memory of Wycliffe and his teachings from the charge of heresy. Wycliffe's doctrine of "remanence"—in which he taught that
after consecration the bread and wine remained
bread and wine, even though he affirmed the
real presence of Christ—became the focal point
of the controversy. Stanislav wrote a treatise entitled *De corpore Christi* (*On the Body of
Christ*), in which he defended Wycliffe's teaching. In a work by the same title Huss attempted
to affirm both the doctrine of transubstantiation
and the presence of the bread and wine after
consecration, but he failed to convince his an-

---

18. Matthew of Janov, cited by Spinka in *John Hus' Concept of the Church*, p. 21.

19. See volume 2 of Workman's *John Wyclif* (pp. 416–
17) for the original twenty-four conclusions condemned by
Gregory XI.

tagonists that he did not believe in remanence also.

Not only did Huss's Realist position and his views regarding the nature of transubstantiation come under fire, but his forthright preaching against the sins of the clergy evoked an undying hatred from those whose sensibilities were sorely wounded. He denounced as deceptive the works of wicked priests, the sale of "false indulgences," false miracles such as the bleeding host at Wilsnack, and relic worship. Further, in preaching on 1 Corinthians 15:1, he exhorted the priests "to preach the gospel, not some entertainment, or fables, or plundering lies, so that the people with attentive minds will accept the gospel and both the preacher and the hearer will be grounded by faith in the gospel; . . . that they both, living well in accordance with the gospel, will be saved."[20] It is not surprising that such tactless preaching provoked controversy among the stalwart preacher's peers. In fact, it would have been remarkable if it had not.

The prelates felt themselves to be the chief targets of the uncompromising Czech. However, as long as he could command the support of King Wenceslas and Archbishop Zbyněk, Huss was untouchable. The popular support he received from the common people "who heard him gladly" was both a help and a hindrance—a help because such a favorite of the Czech people had to be handled most carefully, and a hindrance because such a following presented a threat to the archbishop's authority and aroused the jealousy of parish priests as well as the animosity of the German masters of the university. The first Czech master to be brought to trial before the archbishop was the youngest of the group, Matthew of Knín. On May 15, 1408, he was accused of holding to the condemned doctrine of remanence and of having referred to Wycliffe as "the evangelical doctor." At first he refused to recant, asking to be spared the embarrassment of having to do so in the presence of the German masters. However, after the Ger-

mans were dismissed, he submitted. This was the first serious setback for the reform movement. Huss himself now came under increasing fire. The charges of heresy were hurled back and forth between the accused and the accusers. The Papal Schism, which presented the spectacle of as many as three popes claiming the title at the same time, further complicated matters. Alexander V (June 1409–May 1410) was elected at the Council of Pisa (1409) to replace the deposed claimants, Gregory XII and Benedict XIII.

The Germans of the university refused to recognize Alexander V as the duly elected pope and continued to give their allegiance to Gregory XII. When the Germans persisted against the wishes of the king, he unilaterally changed the constitution of the university, giving each Czech master three votes to every one of each German master. The Czechs, who had previously declared their neutrality in the conflict between Gregory XII and Benedict XIII, were elated over this development; the king was obviously supporting the council's solution to the Papal Schism. But the archbishop did not and steadfastly refused to recognize Alexander V as the legitimate pope. As a result, the already strained relationship between the archbishop and Huss, who was elected rector of the reorganized university, further deteriorated. When the Germans failed to reverse the decision of King Wenceslas, they left Prague and its university for Leipzig, where they established a new university in 1409. They never forgave Huss for his part in their exodus nor ceased to accuse him of heresy. The situation in Prague was further aggravated when the embarrassed archbishop switched his allegiance from Gregory XII to Alexander V under pressure from Wenceslas.

Huss Suppressed

Archbishop Zbyněk suspended Huss's right to preach and ordered the confiscation of Wycliff's books. By forsaking Gregory XII and submitting to Alexander, the archbishop secured a papal bull backing his efforts to suppress the reform

---

20. Huss, cited by Spinka in *John Hus' Concept of the Church*, p. 60.

movement in Bohemia. In addition to censuring Wycliffe's books, the bull forbade preaching anywhere except in the cathedral, parish churches, and monasteries. The bull, obviously directed against Huss, whose congregations were said sometimes to number ten thousand, failed to silence the reformer. Instead he put out a tract, *De libris haereticorum legendis,* in which he quoted Scripture and the early church fathers in support of his position. He also repeated Augustine's definition that "heresy is an erroneous doctrine, contrary to the Holy Scriptures, stubbornly defended."[21] Zbyněk retaliated by building a bonfire in which two hundred copies of Wycliffe's books went up in flames to the accompaniment of the ringing of church bells and the singing of the *Te Deum.* Huss and several of his friends were excommunicated as rebels and saboteurs of the Catholic faith. The bold preacher ignored the action, however, and continued to preach in Bethlehem Chapel and to teach in the university. Moral support for Huss was forthcoming from Lollards in both England and Scotland. In reply to a letter of Richard Wyche, a prominent English Lollard, Huss wrote, "Our king with his whole court, the queen, the nobles, and the common people are for the word of Jesus Christ. The Church of Christ in Bohemia sends greetings to the Church of Christ in England, desiring to participate in the confession of the holy faith in the grace of the Lord Jesus Christ."[22]

The sympathies of both the Bohemian king and people were with Huss. After the book-burning episode, Zbyněk, fearing for his life, fled to his country estate at Roudnice, from which he continued to campaign against Huss and his followers. From his retreat he placed the city under an interdict that Wenceslas forbade the clergy to obey. The king tried to end the conflict by asking the archbishop to withdraw his charges of heresy in a letter to the new pontiff at Bologna. He also asked Huss to write

letters of submission to the pope and cardinals, affirming his orthodoxy. Huss complied but Zbyněk refused. Instead he decided to appeal to the king's brother, Sigismund, king of Hungary, soon to be crowned emperor of the Holy Roman Empire. However, en route to Hungary the archbishop died at Bratislav on September 28, 1411.

Huss had now become the major symbol of the reform movement in Bohemia. (Stanislav of Znojmo and Stephen Páleč, two of his former colleagues who had at one time defended Wycliffe, defected.) He had survived the attacks of the archbishop because of the support of Wenceslas, but a new crisis brought a parting of the ways. The crisis was precipitated by a move made by John XXIII, who had succeeded Alexander V upon his death. He was still having a great deal of difficulty in maintaining his papal prerogatives in the face of the counterclaims of Gregory XII, and he decided to settle the dispute by launching a war against the king of Naples, Gregory's protector. In order to finance the war effort, his holiness issued a papal bull authorizing the sale of indulgences for the purpose. Friends advised Huss to ignore the proclamation of the new indulgence, but in good conscience he could not, and he denounced the bull at a university gathering in June 1412, during the course of which he called the pope the Antichrist. At that point he lost the support and protection of King Wenceslas. The city was placed under a new interdict, and Bethlehem Chapel was closed. The Germans launched an attack against it but were beaten back by Czech defenders. Huss left Prague in October in order to spare the city the ill effects of the interdict. He found refuge among the nobility who had been his unflinching supporters through the long and involved struggle. It was during this time of exile from his beloved chapel that Huss carried on the reform with his pen.

The embattled reformer seized his freedom from preaching and teaching responsibilities to put basic materials into the Czech language to help his followers understand the Christian faith as he taught it. Among these treatises were *An Exposition of the Faith, An Exposition of the*

---

21. Huss, cited by Spinka in *John Hus' Concept of the Church,* p. 97.

22. Huss, cited by Spinka in *John Hus' Concept of the Church,* p. 99.

Decalogue, and *An Exposition of the Lord's Prayer.* He also published in Czech a number of the sermons he had preached at Bethlehem Chapel. A polemical work, *De simonia* (*On Simony*), and a theological work, *De ecclesia* (*On the Church*), date from this period. The two Latin works reflect Huss's mature thoughts on the subjects and as such are of major importance in determining just how original Huss's thinking was and to what degree he was dependent upon Wycliffe's works by the same titles.

Huss—a Wycliffite?

As one might suspect, scholars differ widely in their judgments of how heavily Huss depended upon Wycliffe. However, as Matthew Spinka admits, "There is no doubt of his verbal and ideological dependency on Wycliffe's *De simonia.*"[23] Huss also depended heavily on Wycliffe's *De ecclesia.* In fact, Huss lifted selections from Wycliffe's works by the same titles, and although he rearranged and edited them, they reappeared word for word in Huss's books. Huss had made the writings and thoughts of Wycliffe so much his own that he failed to indicate what was from Wycliffe and what was his own. Perhaps at times even he could not distinguish between the two.[24]

Even though Huss was in substantial agreement with Wycliffe both philosophically and theologically, he was much more than an echo of Wycliffe. His doctrine of transubstantiation is a case in point. Huss steadfastly refused to subscribe to Wycliffe's doctrine of remanence even though he held that the consecrated bread and wine, although transubstantiated, remained bread and wine. His adversaries at Constance did not understand his position on this point but accused him of holding to Wycliffe's view, which had been repeatedly condemned as heretical. In regard to a number of doctrines, Huss seems to have been closer to the position of the traditional medieval church than that of Wycliffe. For example, he refused to say that the sacraments were invalid when administered by a priest in mortal sin. Neither did he reject the papal office altogether, even though he did say that the pope could become the Antichrist in instances in which failure of faith or conduct had reached an unacceptable level. Shortly before he went to Constance, however, he apparently concurred with his close friend Jakoubek of Stříbro, who held that both the bread and the wine should be given to the laity in the mass. Another significant difference between the works of Wycliffe and those of Huss is a matter of style. While Wycliffe's works are often ponderous, repetitive, and loaded with intricate theological arguments, Huss presents essentially the same concepts in a much more popular style along with pointed references to local events. This is one of the reasons why Huss's works early found their way into print while Wycliffe's remained virtually unknown. Perhaps an even more significant factor was Huss's execution for heresy at the Council of Constance.

The Council of Constance (1414-1418)

Although excommunicated and under an interdict, Huss continued to find patrons among the Czech nobility who befriended him. Their financial support gave him ample time to write and the freedom to preach—but not for long. This situation was not to the pontiff's liking, as few situations were at the time. Under fire from the conciliarists to call a council to end the Papal Schism, Pope John felt increasing pressure from several quarters to rid the church of the Wycliffite heresy in Bohemia. A trade-off was in the making. Pope John agreed to call a council to convene on November 1, 1414, if Sigismund,

---

23. Spinka, *Advocates of Reform,* p. 194.

24. Workman makes this point: "Important as the *de Ecclesia* is in itself, it is even greater if account is taken of its influence in Bohemia. When in 1413 Hus brought out his own *de Ecclesia,* in reality a mere abridgement of this treatise made, unfortunately, from an inferior manuscript, the historian, Dietrich of Niem, remarked at Constance that it [the abridgement] 'attacks the papal power and the plenitude of his authority as much as the Alcoran the Catholic faith.' . . . Again in his treatise of *Adversus Indulgencias Papales* written in 1412, the Czech reformer followed word for word the twenty-third chapter of Wyclif's *de Ecclesia*" (*John Wyclif,* 2: 7).

who was apparently convinced of Huss's innocence, would see that Huss was brought to
Constance for trial. Wenceslas, who was anxious
to rid Bohemia of the ignominy it had suffered
because of the Wycliffite heresy, encouraged the
move.

Three years before, Wenceslas had agreed
that his brother, Sigismund, could become the
king of the Empire if he were not crowned
while he, Wenceslas, was still living. (Sigismund
was crowned emperor of the Holy Roman Empire in 1433 by Pope Eugenius IV.) However,
since King Wenceslas had withdrawn his support from Huss, he was willing to have Sigismund crowned in exchange for assurances that
Huss would be surrendered to conciliar authorities. Thereupon Sigismund sent two personal
envoys to Huss with the promise of safe conduct
to and from the council even if Huss were found
guilty of heresy. Huss accepted the promise at
face value and resolved to go to Constance to
defend his faith before the highest tribunal of
the Roman Church and the pope himself. While
he may have suspected that a fair trial was impossible, there is no way he could have known
what was about to transpire.

In a sense the Council of Constance was a
reforming council. Its most pressing problem
was the Papal Schism, which Peter d'Ailly and
the conciliarists were determined to end regardless of the wishes of John XXIII. They also came
to the council with equal determination to
strike a heavy blow against heresy as personified
by Huss. There was some concern that the decadent life of the church should not escape the
scrutiny of the council fathers. It was also apparent that action should be taken to demonstrate
the seriousness with which the church looked
upon the moral lapses among the religious and
secular priests. But before much could be done,
the council had to establish its right to act.

For almost a month after arriving in Constance, Huss remained in a private residence
awaiting a hearing before the council. A few
days before the end of the month, however, he
was arrested, and after another eight days he
was imprisoned in a dungeon of the Dominican
monastery in a cell next to the latrine. His secret

interrogation and his imprisonment infuriated
Sigismund, who left Constance in an attempt to
free him. Thereupon the council sent word to
the emperor, asking him if he intended to let
the council do its work or if he intended to do
it. This was the beginning of the final capitulation on the part of the emperor, who on April 8
revoked his promise of safe conduct for all to
whom it had been given. Apparently by this
time Sigismund realized that the cardinals led
by Peter d'Ailly, John Gerson, and Francesco
Zabarella had garnered enough support to assure the continuation of the council even in the
absence of the pope.

After having convened the council, Pope
John announced that he was willing to resign if
the other two popes would. However, on March
21 he left the city disguised as a knight. He sent
word for the cardinals to join him at Schaffhausen, but they refused. He had expected the
council to collapse in his absence, but Emperor
Sigismund let it be known that the council
would, for the sake of a unified church, continue. Thus, on April 6 the council issued the
Sacrosancta, which declared that "it has its authority immediately from Christ; and that all
men, of every rank and condition, including the
Pope himself, is bound to obey it in matters
concerning the Faith, the abolition of the
schism, and the reformation of the Church of
God in its head and its members."[25] This was a
clear statement of the conciliarists' concept of
the authority of a general council and evidence
that the French were in firm control of the council. Furthermore, the conciliarists were bent on
reforming the church while at the same time
distinguishing their movement from that of
Wycliffe and Huss.

The results were as Huss at this point could
have predicted—condemnation and execution.
In the absence of the pope, Sigismund could
have released Huss, but he did not. Instead
Huss was transferred from the Dominican monastery to a castle at Gottlieben belonging to the

---

25. Henry Bettenson, ed., *Documents of the Christian
Church*, 2nd ed. (Oxford: Oxford University Press, 1982),
p. 135.

John Huss before the Council of Constance. His work was influenced by both the teachings of Wycliffe and the native reform movement. RELIGIOUS NEWS SERVICE

bishop of Constance. In the meantime he must have followed with an unusual interest the fortunes of John XXIII. The council brought seventy-two charges against his holiness. They were soon reduced to fifty-four, however, and on May 29 he was deposed and demoted to a cardinal bishop. Gregory XII, realizing that this council meant business, resigned; Benedict XIII was also deposed but ignored the action of the council, claiming to be the only legitimate successor to the papal throne until his death in 1423. Huss wrote to friends in Bohemia, registering his feelings regarding John's fall.[26]

Finally the council turned its attention to Huss, who had been imprisoned upon orders of the deposed pontiff. Since his imprisonment he had been accused repeatedly of holding to the forty-five errors of Wycliffe, first compiled by John Hübner and subsequently condemned. Since Huss protested that these articles were drawn from Wycliffe's works and that it obviously constituted a miscarriage of justice to try him on a garbled version of Wycliffe's teachings, the judges then asked Stephen Páleč, Huss's former colleague and now his relentless enemy, to draw up a list of errors from Huss's own writings. The result was a compilation of forty-two alleged errors. When John Gerson arrived from Paris, he brought with him twenty-one more articles drawn from extracts of Huss's *De*

---

26. See Spinka, *John Hus' Concept of the Church*, p. 377.

ecclesia sent to him by Archbishop Conrad of Prague. The final series of hearings began on June 3. In the process the articles against Huss from all sources were reworked and reduced to thirty-nine charges of error. Through it all Huss repeatedly asked to be instructed by Scripture and shown his error:

> I pray, however, for God's sake, that a hearing be granted me for the explanation of my meaning of the articles brought against me and of the writings of the holy doctors. And if my reasons and scripture will not suffice, I wish to submit humbly to the instruction of the Council.[27]

Huss's appeal to Scripture was to go unanswered. The council considered his request both evasive and obstinate. Huss's Realist philosophy condemned him in the eyes of Cardinal d'Ailly and the Parisian doctors, who were Nominalists. D'Ailly argued that Huss must necessarily hold to Wycliffe's doctrine of remanence because he, like Wycliffe, was a Realist. Huss's denial was rejected. The charges against him were finally reduced to thirty errors that the commission in charge of the trial wished Huss to deny. It appears that in deference to Sigismund the council would have preferred not to burn Huss but rather to sentence him to perpetual imprisonment, which would have been done if he had recanted. But Huss, unaware of the secret provision, could not bring himself to do this. For him it would have been the undoing of his life's work and the ultimate act of hypocrisy. Thus, the day before he was executed, he wrote,

> I, John Hus, in hope a servant of Jesus Christ, am not willing to declare that every article drawn from my books is erroneous. . . . Secondly, concerning the articles ascribed to me by false witnesses, I am not willing to confess that I have asserted, preached, and held them. Thirdly, I am not willing to recant lest I commit perjury.[28]

---

27. Huss, cited by Spinka in *John Hus' Concept of the Church*, p. 367.

28. Huss, cited by Spinka, *John Hus' Concept of the Church*, p. 379.

The next day Huss was led to the cathedral, where the sentence was read. He was condemned to death for being a stubborn disciple of Wycliffe and a rebel against ecclesiastical authority, and for unlawfully appealing his case before Jesus Christ. After being ceremonially debased, he was led outside the city gates past a cemetery, where his books were being burned, to the stake. Here straw and wood awaited the executioner's torch. A last attempt to secure his recantation failed. As the flames engulfed his body, he cried out, "Christ, Thou son of the living God, have mercy on me." The third time he uttered the prayer, the wind shifted, and his voice was heard no more. Thus he died a reformer who never felt himself to be a heretic but only a priest whose earnest desire was to see the church cleansed of iniquity and once again obedient to her Lord.

THE TRAGEDY AND THE TRIUMPH

In the midst of so much greed and hypocrisy, both Huss and Wycliffe longed to see a rebirth of discipleship in terms of life lived in single-minded devotion to Jesus Christ motivated by the love of God above money or self. The tragedy was that the conciliarists, who shared so many of the same goals, could not see that in condemning Huss they were contributing to the demise of that which they were attempting to save. The evidence of this development was not long in appearing. The nobility of Bohemia, the University of Prague, and the Czech people condemned the council's actions. It soon became apparent that the reform movement of which Huss was the chief spokesman did not die with him. Even while Huss was in Constance some of his followers began to offer the laity the cup in the mass. More radical changes were also afoot. At Mount Tabor a communal colony was formed with fervent eschatological expectations that gave rise to a party of Hussites known as Taborites. Under their military leader, John Žižka, they were able to turn back every army sent against them from 1420 to 1431. The Taborites even attempted to advance their cause with forays into neighboring countries. They were finally defeated by their own countrymen, the Utraquists, in 1434.

The Utraquists arose simultaneously with the Taborites and became in essence the state church of Bohemia. Though they represented a more moderate form of the Hussite tradition than did the Taborites, they were separate from the Roman Catholic Church. They were also known as Calixtines because they gave the chalice to the laity. In time they replaced the Roman Catholic Church throughout Bohemia and Moravia. Of their theological latitude Jarold Knox Zeman writes, "With considerable justification, one might describe the Utraquist Church as a proto-Anglican Church, with uniformity in worship and breadth of doctrine."[29] Even though a state church, it did tolerate dissent after 1485.

In Bohemia there arose out of the Hussite milieu still another group that drew its followers from the more conservative Utraquists. These Hussites, who called themselves simply Brethren, became known as *Unitas Fratrum* (United Brethren). They first came into historical focus in 1457, when Gregory of Prague left the Utraquists to establish a new church in Kunvald in eastern Bohemia. They were the spiritual heirs not only of Huss but of Peter Chelčický and the Waldenses.

Peter Chelčický (ca. 1380–1460), who has been described as Bohemia's most original thinker,[30] is credited with synthesizing the divergent strains of Hussite teachings with Waldensian concepts that became the body out of which the United Brethren developed their own faith and practice. At a number of points this devout reformer anticipated the Radical Reformation. Zeman regards the United Brethren as the first Free Church. In this development lies the triumph in the tragedy of Huss's martyrdom. Reformation was on the way, and all the forces of Rome and Avignon could no more stop its advance than sand castles can stop the tide.

---

29. Zeman, "Restitution and Dissent in the Late Medieval Renewal Movements: The Waldensians, the Hussites and the Bohemian Brethren," *Journal of the American Academy of Religion* 44 (Mar. 1976): 16.

30. Zeman, "Restitution and Dissent," p. 20.

Chapter VI

ERASMUS AND HIS DISCIPLES

hen Andrew Zebrzydowski, bishop of Krakow, died in 1560, engraved on his tomb were the words *magni illius Erasmi discipulus et auditor*. The bishop had studied with Erasmus in 1528, spending a few months in his home. From that time on he counted himself among the many disciples of Erasmus. By 1518 this was true of a large segment of literate Europe, for those who were not his disciples were certainly his auditors. By 1518 his *Adages, The Praise of Folly*, and his Greek New Testament had made Desiderius Erasmus the best-known humanist of all time. In fact, John Colet, dean of St. Paul's Cathedral in London, wrote upon receiving a copy of the 1516 edition of Erasmus's Greek New Testament, "The name of Erasmus will never perish."[1]

As Erasmus's enormous output swamped the presses in Venice, Basel, and Paris, the high and mighty—including the pope, cardinals, kings, and princes—vied with one another for his presence—and his dedications. Erasmus, whose early years had been stalked by poverty, found it necessary in later life to turn down the most

alluring endowments in order to maintain his freedom and independence. Although he was acutely conscious of the transitory nature of worldly applause, even he could not have foreseen that the church that he so strenuously attempted to reform and from which he steadfastly refused to separate would place his books on more than one *Index*. Scorned by Protestants for his lack of courage and by Catholics for his treasonous assaults on the divine citadel, his image in the minds of those who give him a second thought today is somewhat tarnished to say the least. However, regardless of how one may feel about Erasmus, he is inescapable. In spite of his disclaimers and studied attempts to disassociate himself from Luther and the Reformation, he and the *Erasmiani*, as his humanist followers were called, helped to create a climate that made possible the Reformation of the sixteenth century.

YOUTH AND EDUCATION, 1467-1499

"Erasmus was born in Rotterdam on October 27 or 28 probably in the year 1467," concludes Albert Rabil.[2] The date of Erasmus's birth has

---

1. Colet, cited in *Christian Humanism and the Reformation: Selected Writings of Erasmus*, ed. John C. Olin (New York: Harper & Row, 1965), p. 1.

2. Rabil, *Erasmus and the New Testament: The Mind of a Christian Humanist* (San Antonio: Trinity University Press, 1972), p. 2.

long been the subject of debate among scholars. Erasmus was not an altogether reliable witness in this regard. He was notoriously poor at personal chronology and for various reasons seemed intent upon falsifying his age. Preserved Smith thought that Erasmus used this ploy to escape the implications of his illegitimate birth. However, more recently A. C. F. Koch has come up with a more plausible explanation and sets Erasmus's birth in the year 1467.[3] Previously the years 1466 and 1469 were the most likely candidates. Regardless of the date of birth, there is no question regarding its nature. Erasmus concocted an elaborate story to hide the fact that he was born out of wedlock and that his father was a priest in orders at the time.

But Erasmus's father was no ordinary priest. Johan Huizinga points out that he was a man of education who knew Greek, the ancient authors, and contemporary humanist scholars. Apparently he had studied in Italy.[4] According to Erasmus, his father's name was Gerard. Margaret, his mother, was the daughter of a physician. They named their second son Herasmus; Erasmus had added "Desiderius" by 1497 and had changed "Herasmus" to "Erasmus" by 1503. By the time the second edition of the *Adages* appeared, the evolution of his name was complete: in this work it appears as Desiderius Erasmus Roterodamus. Like his name, his life was to undergo a number of changes before his vocation was finally determined.

Erasmus, along with his brother, was first sent to school in Gouda, perhaps because his father was from Gouda. However, from 1475 to 1484 he attended the famous school of St. Lebwin's in Deventer, the earliest and one of the better schools operated by the Brethren of the Common Life. His school days in Deventer were interrupted by a period of about two years, during which Erasmus served as a choirboy at the cathedral in Utrecht. It was apparently during his second stay at Deventer that Alexander

Hegius became the headmaster of the school. Erasmus remembered that upon one occasion the famous humanist Rudolf Agricola visited the school and lectured there. Although in retrospect Erasmus felt that the school was more a detriment than a help, it fared much better in his memory than did Hertogenbosch (Bois-le-Duc).

It was here that Erasmus and his brother were sent when their father died. This school was also run by the Brethren, in whose cloister Peter and Erasmus lived while there. The two or more years spent at Hertogenbosch were a disaster in the estimation of Erasmus, whose taste for humanist learning had been whetted at Deventer. Even though there had been little appreciation for the Latin and Greek classics at Deventer, according to Erasmus there was none at Hertogenbosch. In his eyes the teachers were incompetent instructors and harsh disciplinarians intent only upon preparing their young charges for the monastery, which Erasmus suspected was the reason his guardians had sent him and his brother there in the first place. Whether this perception was right or wrong, the unhappy student at Hertogenbosch eventually found himself persuaded to become a monk.

Monastic life was not his first choice. He would have much preferred to attend the university, but now both he and his brother had absolutely no money and so were at the mercy of their guardians, whose motives—and honesty—they suspected. Peter yielded to pressure and entered the Augustinian monastery (order of regular canons) at Sion near Delft. Erasmus held out longer but was finally persuaded to join the Augustinians as well. Instead of joining his brother at Sion, however, Erasmus entered a cloister of the same order at Steyn.

William Herman, a boyhood friend of Erasmus from his Deventer days, is credited with pointing out to the reluctant candidate the advantages monastic life offered for contemplation and study, especially at Steyn. The library must have impressed Erasmus, because he was soon carting off to his room works of his favorite authors. Among these he named Lorenzo Valla as foremost in a list of recommended authors

---

3. Koch, cited by Rabil in *Erasmus and the New Testament*, pp. 2, 3.

4. Huizinga, *Erasmus and the Age of Reformation* (New York: Harper & Row, 1957), p. 7.

he sent to his friend Cornelius of Gouda: "Then for the observation of elegances, there is no one in whom I have so much confidence as Lorenzo Valla, who is unrivalled both in the sharpness of his intelligence and the tenacity of his memory. Whatever has not been committed to writing by those I have named, I confess I dare not bring into use."[5] The early years in Steyn apparently gave Erasmus comparatively free reign to pursue his humanist studies. It was here that he also began to develop his skills as a poet.

His correspondence with two friends at the time also reflects his varying moods and intellectual development. Servatius Roger, who later became prior at Steyn, was not only a fellow monk but also Erasmus's closest friend. As the ardor of their friendship cooled, their letters and poems reflect their deepening intellectual concerns. Erasmus frequently admonished his friend to make a more serious study of the ancients and to cultivate a better Latin style. Erasmus's friendship with a certain Cornelius Gerard, a monk from a nearby monastery, was to point his humanist studies in a new direction. From the beginning the correspondence between the two young Augustinian canons constituted an intellectual fencing match. Up to this point Erasmus had not met anyone among his peers who came anywhere near his level of learning. Cornelius Gerard not only provided an intellectual challenge for Erasmus but was also responsible for helping Erasmus to see, apparently for the first time, that humanist learning was not an end in itself but the means by which literature, especially classical poetry, could serve Christ. It was during this period that Erasmus, who had already discovered Jerome, began to emphasize Jerome's importance for classical studies. For this insight he was apparently indebted to his friend Cornelius. The words of Jerome were to attract and challenge him for the rest of his life. The new seriousness with which Erasmus the humanist began to view all of life is reflected in a work dating from this

period (ca. 1498), *De contemptu mundi* (*The Contempt of the World*), and may be attributed to Cornelius Roger's influence upon Erasmus. This new earnestness in regard to Christian discipleship also reflected the major thrust of the *devotio moderna* under which Erasmus had been educated from his earliest days at Gouda to his years at Steyn. Up to this time, however, that line of thought had not emerged in his writing.[6]

That Erasmus still envisioned himself a humanist is evident from his treatise *Antibarbari* (*Against the Barbarians*), which he began while he was still at Steyn. In this work all the familiar themes of the humanists are resoundingly echoed. While Erasmus cites Jerome and Augustine, he does so very selectively. He does not cite them for their theological content but in support of the humanist emphasis upon languages and the ancient classics. Although Erasmus began *Antibarbari* in Steyn, he did not complete it until he had left the monastery in the service of the bishop of Cambrai.

Possibly in 1492 Erasmus was ordained to the priesthood after being tapped as secretary to the bishop. The bishop had hopes of receiving a cardinal's hat, which would necessitate a visit to Rome. For some time Erasmus had longed to compare notes with Italian scholars in the cradle of humanism; thus he gladly joined the bishop's entourage with prospects of visiting Italy. When the bishop's hopes proved illusory, Erasmus was allowed to leave the monastery to pursue theological studies at the University of Paris with the bishop's blessings and promises of financial support.

Arrangements were made for Erasmus to enter the College of Montaigu, where Jan Standonck was the headmaster. Standonck had been educated in his early years at Gouda under the auspices of the Brethren of the Common Life. An earnest advocate of the *devotio moderna*, he attempted to instill in the students the high moral standards of the Brethren by precept and

---

5. Erasmus, cited by Rabil in *Erasmus and the New Testament*, p. 9.

6. See Rabil, pp. 17–18, footnote 46, for a discussion of this apparent change in Erasmus's thought.

example. Discipline was harsh—in fact, so harsh during Lent in 1496 that Erasmus became ill and retreated to Steyn to recuperate. Upon his return to Paris, he took up lodging elsewhere and attempted to support himself by tutoring in rhetoric several young English noblemen, among whom were Thomas Grey and William Mountjoy. It was Mountjoy who sponsored Erasmus's first visit to England in 1499.

Although Erasmus was permitted to leave the bishop's service to study theology and for a whole year attended Standonck's lectures on Peter Lombard's *Sentences,* his interests lay elsewhere. He soon began to enjoy the company of a small circle of gifted humanists. It was in the home of Robert Gaguin, the leading French humanist, that he met Faustus Andrelinus, a famous Italian humanist. When Gaguin's history of France was published on September 30, 1495, it contained a prefatory letter by Erasmus commending the work—Erasmus's first published piece of writing. The poems of William Herman that Erasmus edited, along with a prefatory letter by Gaguin, soon followed.

Erasmus's correspondence at the time reflects his growing discrimination in the use of the ancient pagan authors. The influence of the *devotio moderna* on him is increasingly evident. But his devotion to a study of the ancient classics still took precedence over theology and the Bible. This is reflected in a model letter Erasmus composed for Heinrich Northoff, one of his students, to send to his brother Christian Northoff—a letter in which Erasmus expressed feelings that he must have entertained himself: "Dearest Christian, are you anxious to hear what the news is here? I am dreaming, 'Dreaming of what?' you ask. Dreaming of what I love—literature, my chief joy in life, and next to literature, of Christian, the beloved part of my soul. . . ."[7] Although this letter, written from Paris in August 1497, is quite revealing of Erasmus's love of the ancient authors, another letter that he wrote in Novem-

ber 1496 leaves the impression that at that time he preferred Christian writers to the pagan among the ancients. This letter, published along with the poems of William Herman, was addressed to Hendrick von Bergen, bishop of Cambrai and Erasmus's patron. It is a superb example of Erasmus's style and may indeed reflect a sincere desire on his part to harmonize humanist learning with a virtuous lifestyle:

> . . . I have decided to dedicate all my studies to you, my unrivalled patron, partly because I could easily foretell that these poems would earn your lordship's kind approval, inasmuch as they plainly embrace in union two things, both of which I know you have much at heart, distinguished learning and an exceptionally high moral tone, qualities which, when they are combined, are as peerless in beauty and perfection as their combination itself is rare. For in most cases we respect men's morals, but what we find to be missing is learning, without which virtue appears somehow defective. On the other hand, it usually happens that men endowed with intellectual gifts are either cursed with a foolish liking for vain display or else, worse still, disposed to vice and indifferent to the goodness and simplicity which belong to the Christian faith. For this reason I tend to be privately indignant from time to time with the poets of modern times (even Christian poets) because in choosing models they prefer to set before themselves Catullus, Tibullus, Propertius, and Ovid, rather than St. Ambrose or Paulinus of Nola or Prudentius or Iuvencus or Moses or David or Solomon, as though their Christianity were forced and not spontaneous.
>
> However, I shall check myself before I go too far, especially in regard to my former "darlings," as people call them to discredit me. I am myself happy to be of my friend Gaguin's opinion in thinking that even ecclesiastical subjects can be treated brilliantly in vernacular works provided the style is pure. And I would not reprehend anyone for applying Egyptian trimmings, but I am against the appropriation of Egypt in its entirety.[8]

ENGLAND AND JOHN COLET, 1499-1500

In the summer of 1499, upon the invitation of William Mountjoy, one of his students, Erasmus

---

7. *The Correspondence of Erasmus,* 6 vols., trans. R. A. B. Mynors and D. F. S. Thomson, ed. Beatrice Corrigan (Toronto: University of Toronto Press, 1974-81), 1: 124.

8. *The Correspondence of Erasmus,* 1: 103.

found himself in England and thrust into a circle of English humanists of whom he had hardly heard. But his reputation had preceded him. From the moment of his arrival he was treated with the utmost respect, as an erudite man of letters. His reception was both gracious and stimulating. His new English friends included Thomas More (1478–1535), William Grocyn (1446–1519), Thomas Linacre (1460–1524), and John Colet (1467–1519). More's home became Erasmus's English home. More was a thoroughgoing humanist who delighted in matching wits with Erasmus and whose highly cultured family provided him with a most congenial audience for his stories and satires. For both More and Erasmus, Lucian of Samosata became a source of many a delightful hour of enjoyable exchange. Born in Syria, Lucian was among the last of the great Hellenists and a master of satire and dialogue. His works appealed to Erasmus because his skepticism and his humor were so akin to Erasmus's own. But it was John Colet who was to influence Erasmus and his subsequent career more than any other person, ancient or contemporary.

In October Erasmus moved on to Oxford for the Michaelmas term; there he discovered that Colet was lecturing on Paul's Epistle to the Romans. Contrary to a long-held opinion, Colet, as W. Robert Godfrey has shown, received both his bachelor of arts and his master of arts degrees at Cambridge. Subsequently he had studied in Italy, and upon his return he was invited to lecture at Oxford, probably as a part of the requirements for his doctor's degree.[9] Whether Colet had been led to adapt the new approach to biblical hermeneutics by a Cambridge don or through his own studies, his lectures were a subtle but definite departure from the traditional medieval treatment. Although Erasmus and Colet conducted a running debate upon certain difficult matters of interpretation such as the reason for Christ's agony in the Garden of Gethsemane, the fact remains that the ground

rules that Erasmus embraced were those established by Colet. Richard McKeon pinpoints the difference between the old approach and the one Colet had embraced:

> The medieval theologian had tried to organize a body of doctrine, point by point, based on a body of texts derived from Scripture and Church Fathers; the new theologian returned to the text of the Scripture itself and its direct interpretation. The new emphasis, therefore, was upon the document and the writer, rather than upon the doctrine and the tradition.[10]

As much as Erasmus admired the new grammatico-historical method of interpreting the Scriptures employed by Colet, he detected a serious flaw in Colet's methodology. Colet lectured entirely from the Vulgate without making any references at all to the Greek text. Thus, when Colet suggested that Erasmus use his approach to lecture upon Isaiah or the books of Moses, Erasmus replied that he was ill-equipped for such an awesome undertaking. He could not be persuaded to change his mind. "How could I ever be so brazen as to teach what I myself have not learned?" he wrote to John Colet in October 1499. "How can I fire the cool hearts of others, when I myself am trembling and shivering all over?"[11] Nevertheless, the Michaelmas term at Oxford with John Colet left an indelible stamp upon Erasmus. Whether he was willing to admit it or not, the entire course of his life was beginning to change.

Although he wrote a poem in honor of the royal children (one of whom was the future Henry VIII), Erasmus claimed in a letter to Colet that he had not come to England to teach poetry or rhetoric. In the same letter he went on to assert for the first time that his life had a plan that precluded classical studies for their own sake:

> I did not come hither to teach poetry or rhetoric, which ceased to be agreeable to me after they had ceased to be indispensable. That sort of teaching

---

9. See W. Robert Godfrey, "John Colet of Cambridge," in *Archiv für Reformationsgeschichte* (Stuttgart: Gütersloher Verlagshaus Gerd Mohn, 1974), 65:6–18.

10. McKeon, cited by Rabil in *Erasmus and the New Testament*, pp. 43–44.

11. *The Correspondence of Erasmus,* 1: 205.

I refuse, because it bears only a slight relation to my plan of life; your sort of teaching I must decline as beyond my capacity. In the case of the former you blame me undeservedly, dear Colet, since I have never proposed to myself the cultivation of what they call secular literature as a profession; to the latter task you exhort me vainly, since I know my exceeding inability for such an undertaking.[12]

Even though Erasmus turned down Colet's invitation and the challenge it presented, there was a delayed reaction. From this time on, Erasmus's mind and heart were turned in a new direction. His longing to see Italy was greatly diminished because he had discovered in England such scholarship as he had expected to find only on the other side of the Alps. His own aversion to Scholasticism had been strongly reinforced by Colet. In a letter Colet wrote to Erasmus in October 1499, Colet even addressed Erasmus as "the Eloquent Theologian." Indeed, Erasmus had used the term "theologian" to refer to himself in a letter he had sent to young Henry with the poem he had hastily written in his honor. While Erasmus had found it difficult to stomach either the food or the intellectual fare at Montaigu, the experience had not turned him completely away from theology. But it was in England that he glimpsed a new vision of how theology could be done with integrity and vitality. With this new awareness of the dynamics of a biblical theology came his resolve not to abandon humanist literature but to use it in the service of the church. From this point on his studies and his writing were to follow this dual track. But first he felt it necessary to study and master Greek.

Perhaps it was both Colet's inability to use Greek in his lectures on Romans and Grocyn's superb mastery of the language that made Erasmus realize that his credibility as a theologian depended upon a knowledge of the biblical languages. According to Erasmus's own testimony in a letter he wrote to Colet in 1504, he did attempt to write about St. Paul's Epistle to

the Romans but was hindered from completing the work because he did not know Greek. This is further evidence that shortly after his return from England Erasmus had embarked upon a project in response to Colet's challenge but had discovered, as he had anticipated, his own inadequacies for the task. For the next three years he studied the Greek language intensively; during this time he also maintained his correspondence and published two major works, the *Enchiridion militis Christiani* (*Dagger of the Christian Soldier*) and *Adagia collectanea* (*Adages*).

The close of this period did not mark the end of Erasmus's Greek studies but only the end of the first phase of them. While in Italy Erasmus lived in the home of Paolo Bombassius, a professor of Greek at the University of Bologna, from whom he must have learned much. In Venice, while living in the home of the famous printer Aldus Manutius, who had founded a Greek academy in which the participants conversed only in Greek, Erasmus, with his quick and acquisitive mind, profited greatly. The second edition of the *Adagia* reveals how much Erasmus's knowledge of Greek had increased. Although he had not begun studying Greek until he was thirty-three years old, his progress was rapid. By 1505, during a second visit to England, he was working on his own Latin translation of the Greek New Testament. However, it was not published until the second edition of his Greek New Testament appeared in 1519. It is Albert Rabil's opinion that in 1505 Erasmus had not yet thought of bringing out a critical edition of the Greek New Testament. Perhaps it was only a matter of time before the idea occurred to him, for as the *Enchiridion* indicates, Erasmus had seen a vision of the reform of Christendom that would be accomplished by calling the church back to the sourcebook of its faith—the Bible.

THE VISION IN PRINT, 1501-1519

Upon leaving England after his first visit there, Erasmus was relieved by English customs agents of all the money he had received from patrons

---

12. Erasmus, cited by Rabil in *Erasmus and the New Testament*, p. 45.

and students during his stay. His subsequent poverty was only partially relieved by his publications. He was still almost completely dependent upon patrons for the necessities of life, which for Erasmus meant books as well as food and lodging. In the light of the circumstances under which he was forced to labor, his literary output was simply amazing. Besides poverty, he had to contend with two other limitations for most of his life: the restraints placed upon him by his order and his own frail body. As if these were not enough hurdles to cross, Erasmus seems to have been constantly on the move. The fear of the plague, his desire to see Italy, the opportunity to become a part of a theological faculty (at Louvain), a congenial environment in which to work—all prompted him to change his residence frequently, sometimes quite suddenly. What is evident is that, in the midst of so many factors that would have constantly frustrated a man of lesser resolve, Erasmus worked as a man possessed, as indeed he was—possessed by a vision of reform. John Olin summarizes it well:

> Erasmus thus emerges, as he begins those labors which thereafter will engage him as a reformer—a reformer of theology, a reformer of morals, a reformer of society. The three spheres are intimately connected. The advance of humanist scholarship and the expansion of Christian knowledge are the means whereby the needed reforms will come. He is aware of the limitations of human learning yet it is knowledge, not ignorance, that will reveal God's truth and God's way. His lifelong efforts are posited on that belief.[13]

The term "philosophy of Christ" first occurs in the writings of Rudolf Agricola, but it was Erasmus who gave it new meaning. This term was symbolic of Christian humanism's approach to reform. The church, it was admitted on all sides, was in desperate need of reform. But there was no consensus on how this could best be carried out. For Erasmus the answer was education. Apparently he reasoned, as Socrates

Desiderius Erasmus, the great humanist scholar, after the painting by Hans Holbein, the Younger
RELIGIOUS NEWS SERVICE

did, that if only men knew right, they would do right. Knowledge, he implied, leads to virtue. Thus the way of reform is the way of Christ. However, Erasmus, the master of Latin prose, failed to recognize that a program of reform "veiled in Latin" could never reach the masses. He was still enough of a humanist that he did not believe in making the masses, in their ignorance and squalor, the primary object of his concern; he felt that they were beneath it. However, the *Enchiridion* does represent his attempt to articulate the philosophy of Christ on the level of one not too far removed from the rabble—an armor maker—and through him bring his message to Europe's literate masses.

Enchiridion militis Christiani (1501)

Erasmus wrote the *Enchiridion* at the request of the wife of Johann Poppenruyter of Nuremberg for the benefit of her wayward husband. Poppenruyter was an armor maker who would have understood the term *enchiridion* as meaning "dagger" rather than "handbook," as it is often

---

13. Olin, *Christian Humanism and the Reformation,* p. 11.

translated. In fact, he was so pleased to receive this book from the pen of Erasmus that he presented the author with his own dagger. However, as Roland Bainton suggests, "neither made any use of the weapon of the other."[14]

Even though the book was written ostensibly for Poppenruyter's benefit, Erasmus had another audience in mind—namely, Europe, the Europe of prelates and priests, outwardly religious but morally corrupt. Herein lies Erasmus's program of reform. Erasmus had never before written a book like this; it is a clarion call to reform. The means by which reform will come, Erasmus says, are spiritual. First Erasmus recommends prayer, not liturgical prayer but personal prayer that comes directly from the heart. Then he recommends knowledge, in which he includes above all, knowledge of the Scriptures. While he does not reject the ancient classics of the pagan Greek and Latin authors, he advocates that they be used discriminatingly. A paragraph or two will illustrate how Erasmus's humanism had become a part of his program of reform:

> However, just as divine Scripture bears no great fruit if you persist in clinging only to the literal sense, so the poetry of Homer and Vergil is of no small benefit if you remember that this is all allegorical, a fact which no one who has but touched his lips to the wisdom of the ancients will deny. I would advise you, though, not to handle the lewd poets at all, or at least not to study them too closely—unless you perhaps learn how to better avoid the vices described in their works and through the antithesis of immorality attain to love of virtue. I should prefer, too, that you follow the Platonists among the philosophers, because in most of their ideas and in their very manner of speaking they come nearest to the beauty of the prophets and the gospels.
>
> In short, it will be profitable to study all pagan literature, provided you do it, as I have already said, at a suitable age and with discrimination—not only warily and judiciously, but also rapidly, like someone just traveling through rather than taking up residence there.[15]

After recommending the judicious reading of pagan authors, Erasmus insists that "everything be related to Christ."[16] All truth, wherever found, belongs to Christ. Here the major features of his philosophy of Christ are beginning to take shape. Christ is supreme, not the Christ of the Scholastics but the Christ of Scripture. He particularly scorns the Scotists because they erect a whole system of theology without any reference to the Scriptures. But, he notes, the Scriptures must be interpreted in an allegorical or spiritual way. Plato is of greater use in understanding the great spiritual truths of the Bible than any of the other ancients, including Aristotle.

The *Enchiridion* makes it quite clear that at this point there was a new seriousness about Erasmus. He no longer believed in pursuing the study of the ancient classics for the sheer delight of the chase. Now he was guided by a far greater purpose: the cause of Christ. The *Enchiridion* shows Erasmus effecting for what is surely the first time "a synthesis between his Christianity and his humanism," to use Rabil's phrase.[17]

Erasmus's reputation as a leading humanist scholar was further enhanced by other publications. In 1504 he was working in a Premonstratensian monastery near Louvain when he discovered Lorenzo Valla's *Notes on the New Testament,* which he took to Paris and published in 1505. In the process it apparently occurred to Erasmus for the first time to follow Valla's lead. Thus on a second trip to England in the same year, he set to work on his own Latin translation of the Greek New Testament. (It was not published until the second edition of his Greek text was published in 1519.) By 1507 Erasmus was entertaining the thought of printing a new corrected text of the Greek New Testament. However, before he even began work on this awesome task, he began to revise his *Adagia.*

Adagia collectanea (1500)

Erasmus continued to revise the *Adagia* again and again until there was little similarity be-

---

14. Bainton, *Erasmus of Christendom* (New York: Scribner's, 1969), p. 66.

15. *The "Enchiridion" of Erasmus,* trans. and ed. Raymond Himelick (Bloomington: Indiana University Press, 1963), p. 51.

16. *The "Enchiridion" of Erasmus,* p. 51.

17. Rabil, *Erasmus and the New Testament,* p. 58.

tween the last edition published in 1535 and the first edition published in 1500. The subsequent editions reflected Erasmus's growing proficiency in the Greek language as well as his spiritual pilgrimage. The first edition of the *Adagia* contained 818 proverbs taken from ancient Latin authors; anyone who wished to improve his knowledge and use of Latin could study the excerpts from the classics with which Erasmus was so familiar. Before leaving Paris for Italy in 1506, Erasmus enlarged the first edition to include twenty-three additional proverbs. Most of the additions were from Greek authors.

While in Italy Erasmus was invited to reside in the home of Aldus Manutius, the famous Venetian printer. Aldus possessed a splendid library of manuscripts of both Greek and Latin classics that served Erasmus's purpose as few other libraries could have. Erasmus's study was reflected in the new edition of the *Adagia*, which was in reality a new book. The title was changed from *Adagia collectanea* to *Adagia chiliades*. The Paris edition of 1507 contained 841 adages; the Aldine edition contained 3,260. "Of these," says Rabil, "about four-fifths are either new or substantially altered in form. And 2734 contain Greek passages of two to six lines or more in length."[18] Other editions of the *Adagia*, which included more and more adages, were to swell the final edition—published a year before Erasmus's death—to more than 4,000 adages. But it was the Aldine edition more than any other that established Erasmus as the undisputed crown prince of humanism.

While staying with Aldus, Erasmus for the first time actually worked with Greek manuscripts, comparing and collating them in order to arrive at the best text. This was as difficult as it was necessary to prepare him for production of the Greek New Testament. We get a glimpse of something of the difficulties involved in an excerpt from the *Adagia* in which Erasmus comments on "The Labors of Hercules":

> And now, shall I mention another thing—the bad state of the books themselves, whether Latin or Greek MSS, so corrupt that when you want to quote a passage you hardly ever find one which does not show an obvious error, or make one suspect a hidden one? Here is another labor, to examine and correct the different MSS . . . and a great many of them, so as to detect one which has a better reading, or by collating a number of them to make a guess at the true and authentic version. This must be done, if not all the time, at least whenever you quote, and quotations occur everywhere.[19]

Erasmus's trip to Italy was crowned with success. If he had done nothing other than revise his *Adagia*, it would have been sufficient cause for rejoicing. But in addition to accomplishing that feat he received a doctor's degree in theology, which he had long sought, from the University of Turin. In Bologna his knowledge of the Greek language was greatly increased, as was his dissatisfaction with the Roman Church. It was there that he witnessed the triumphal entry of the "warrior pope," Julius II, into the city at the head of the papal army after the victory (with the help of the French) over the Bentivogli. After his *Adagia chiliades* came off the press in Venice, Erasmus visited Rome, where he was graciously received. In fact, his visit was such a pleasant experience that he returned to the city two more times before leaving Italy. While in Rome he made valuable friends in high places, including the future pope, Leo X, whose friendship was to stand him in good stead in the turbulent years ahead.

Encomium moriae—The Praise of Folly (1509)

On the long trip back to England from Italy Erasmus had the leisure to mull over events of the past three years. His destination was the home of Thomas More, the man with whom he had spent so many enjoyable hours discussing and translating Lucian of Samosata, the greatest of the Greek satirists. As he thought of More, Lucian, and Rome, he conceived the ultimate

---

18. Rabil, *Erasmus and the New Testament*, p. 68.

19. Erasmus, cited by Rabil in *Erasmus and the New Testament*, p. 69.

satire, a book that would praise foolishness in an entertaining fashion but with a very serious purpose. The fact that in Latin More's name means "folly" may have been the catalyst of the project. Erasmus as much as admits this in a letter to More dated June 8, 1509.

The idea took on flesh in More's home during the brief span of a week while Erasmus was recuperating from an attack of kidney stones. He read selections of his new brainchild to admiring friends, who encouraged him to publish it. Two years later, in 1511, it appeared in print and became an instant success. After more than six hundred editions, it is still the best known and most frequently read of all of Erasmus's voluminous works.[20] It was not well received by all, however. Some thought Erasmus irreverent to approach holy subjects such as transubstantiation and the doctrine of the trinity with unwashed hands. Martin Dorp, professor of theology and later rector of the University of Louvain, wrote an open letter to Erasmus criticizing the work, a letter that Erasmus saw for the first time after it appeared in print. Erasmus's answer is a classic and reveals, perhaps better than anything else he wrote, both the way in which *The Praise of Folly* came to be and his purpose in writing it.[21]

Erasmus explained that he was playing the part of a fool or court jester in praising folly. But unlike Lucian, who apparently delighted in ridiculing the foibles and sacred beliefs of men—even immortality of the soul—for the sheer joy of the process, Erasmus had a serious purpose in mind and quoted Horace to make the point: "What is the matter in saying truth with a smile." It was Erasmus's conviction that humor could make the truth more palatable. He even cited a certain physician who coated the cup with honey in order to administer the dose of medicine to children, and admitted to employing a similar device: "I observed continually how the common mass of humanity in every walk of life was being seduced by the most stupid opinions, and that the desire of a remedy was more genuine than the hope thereof. So it seemed to me justifiable to use a little deceit, as it were, on these pleasure-loving souls and give them this medicine disguised as pleasure."[22]

Even though *The Praise of Folly* provokes mirth, its barbs are rather evident. The point of it all, as Erasmus explained to Dorp, was the same as that of the *Enchiridion*:

> Nor did I have any intentions in the *Folly* different from those in my other works, although the method may have differed. In the *Enchiridion* I simply set down a design for Christian living. In the pamphlet, *The Education of a Prince*, I publicly advised in what subjects a prince ought to be instructed. In the *Panegyric*, using the form of a eulogy of the prince, I did in an oblique manner the very same thing that in the other book I did openly and directly. So for the *Folly*, the same thing was done there under the semblance of a jest as was done in the *Enchiridion*.[23]

More also wrote Dorp in defense of *The Praise of Folly* and seems to have been able to do what Erasmus himself had failed to do—reconcile the two friends. Perhaps the reason More succeeded is that Dorp had yet another grievance against Erasmus. Since it was widely known that Erasmus was at work on a corrected Greek text of the New Testament, Dorp publicly set himself against the project. Erasmus did not endear himself to Dorp with the following reply:

> You do not want to change anything except where there might be, perhaps, a little clearer meaning in the Greek. You deny that there are faults in the edition we commonly use, and think that we are forbidden to alter in any way something approved by the agreement of so many ages and so many synods. I ask you, most learned Dorp, if what you write is true, why is it that Jerome, Augustine, and Ambrose had different readings from the ones that

---

20. See *"The Praise of Folly" and "Letter to Martin Dorp, 1515,"* trans. Betty Radice (New York: Penguin Books, 1971).

21. Translated in Olin, *Christian Humanism and the Reformation*, pp. 55-91.

22. Erasmus, cited by Olin in *Christian Humanism and the Reformation*, p. 60.

23. Erasmus, cited by Olin in *Christian Humanism and the Reformation*, pp. 59–60.

we have? Why did Jerome expressly censure and correct many readings which are still contained in this edition? What will you do in the face of such converging testimony. . . . The solution to the problem almost stares us in the face, for it would be clear even to a blind man, as they say, that the Greek was often poorly translated because of the ignorance or laziness of a translator, that often the authentic and true text has been corrupted by ignorant copyists (something we see happening every day) or even changed by unskilled or inattentive ones. Who is more indulgent to error: the one who corrects and restores the mistakes, or the one who would sooner see a blunder added than removed?[24]

In his rebuttal to Dorp's obscurantism Erasmus attacked ignorance and its attendant evils— a criticism that was characteristic of humanism and particularly dear to the heart of Erasmus. Despite Erasmus's most courteous—even flattering—references to Dorp and his learning, Dorp might have taken this assault personally:

As it is well known, men of this high calling have in their ranks a certain few who have such poor talent and judgment that they are not capable of any kind of learning, much less theological learning. They learned by heart a few little rules from Alexander of Gaul; in addition they mastered a little bit of silly sophistry; next they memorized ten propositions from Aristotle, I dare say without understanding them; then, from Scotus or Occam they learned a like number of chapters; and whatever else they need to know they rest content to draw it from the *Catholicon* or *Mammotrepton* or a similar dictionary, as if from some horn of plenty. Yet how they toss their heads in pride! Nothing is more arrogant than ignorance! These are the ones who condemn St. Jerome as a grammarian obviously because they do not understand him. Such men deride Greek, Hebrew, even Latin; and even though they are more stupid than any pig and lack common sense, they think they themselves occupy the whole citadel of learning. They bring everyone to task; they condemn; they pontificate; they are never in doubt; they have no hesitations; they know everything. And yet few in number as they are, these people are causing

tremendous commotion. What is more impudent, more obstinate than ignorance! Such people are in one great conspiracy against genuine learning.[25]

Erasmus's conciliatory letter to Dorp turned out to be less than placatory. Yet it was not unlike some of the more sober indictments in *The Praise of Folly*. This magnificent satirical work has had many interpreters and various interpretations, some more confusing than the book itself. Perhaps the best clues to understanding it are those given by Erasmus himself. When these clues are followed, three more or less distinct divisions may be discerned within its pages. Erasmus first praises folly because life without foolishness is unbearable. Those who are born fools have the best time because they are oblivious to reality. Erasmus then moves on to consider another class of fools, those who have deceived themselves into thinking that they alone are the Lord's elite. Beginning with merchants and ending with cardinals, Erasmus spares no significant class from his lampooning pen. All this is simply the prologue Erasmus uses to reach his "punch line": recommending what appears to the world to be the height of folly—authentic Christianity. For Erasmus, Christianity, rightly understood and sincerely embraced in life, is truly the highest wisdom, but it neither spurns reason nor is bound by it.

It is clear, as John Olin says, that Erasmus was interested in the reformation of all society. He believed that those who have the greatest power in state and church are the most accountable. He would reform both by calling the power brokers to repentance and to a new standard of morality, the goal of which is to be like Christ. Among the victims of Erasmus's biting sarcasm were "the new breed of theologians" (Schoolmen) and the "religious" (monks). His ridicule of the Scholastics is merciless. It is in this section that Erasmus drops the mask of folly and the reader catches a glimpse of Erasmus the Christian philosopher. The following excerpt

---

24. Erasmus, cited by Olin in *Christian Humanism and the Reformation*, pp. 84–85.

25. Erasmus, cited by Olin in *Christian Humanism and the Reformation*, pp. 68–69.

graphically illustrates the shift from the role of jester to that of reformer:

> In addition, they interpret hidden mysteries to suit themselves: how the world was created and designed; through what channels the stain of sin filtered down to posterity; by what means, in what measure and how long Christ was formed in the Virgin's womb; how, in the Eucharist, accidents can subsist without substance. But this sort of question has been discussed threadbare.[26]

He continues by highlighting some of the more irrelevant speculations making the rounds: "Could God have taken on the form of a woman, a devil, a donkey, a gourd or a flint-stone? If so, how could a gourd have preached sermons, performed miracles, and been nailed to the cross? And what would Peter have consecrated if he had performed the sacrament at a time when the body of Christ still hung on the cross?"[27] Summing it up, he denounces such endless trivial speculations and then moves rapidly to appeal to an apostolic pattern that in his opinion was far superior to that of the Scholastics:

> These subtle refinements of subtleties are made still more subtle by all the different lines of scholastic argument, so that you'd extricate yourself faster from a labyrinth than from the tortuous obscurities of realists, nominalists, Thomists, Albertists, Ockhamists and Scotists—and I've not mentioned all the sects, only the main ones. Such is the erudition and complexity they all display that I fancy the apostles themselves would need the help of another holy spirit if they were obliged to join issue on these topics with our new breed of theologian.
>
> Paul could exhibit faith, but when he says "Faith is the substance of things hoped for, the evidence of things not seen", his definition is quite unscholastic. And though he provides the finest example of charity, in his first letter to the Corinthians, chapter thirteen, he neither divides nor defines it according to the rules of dialectic. The apostles consecrated the Eucharist with due piety, but had they been questioned about the *terminus a quo* and the *terminus ad quem*, about

transubstantiation, and how the same body can be in different places, about the difference between the body of Christ in heaven, on the cross, and at the sacrament of the Eucharist, about the exact moment when transubstantiation takes place, seeing that the prayer which effects it is a distinct quantity extended in time, they wouldn't, in my opinion, have shown the same subtlety in their reply as the Scotists do in their dissertations and definitions. . . . They worshipped, that is true, but in spirit, in accordance only with the words of the gospel "God is a spirit: and they that worship him must worship in spirit and truth." Apparently it had never been revealed to them that a mediocre drawing sketched in charcoal on a wall should be worshipped in the same manner as Christ himself, provided it had two fingers outstretched, long hair, and three rays sticking out from the halo fastened to the back of its head. Who *could* understand all this unless he has frittered away thirty-six whole years over the physics and metaphysics of Aristotle and Scotus?[28]

In his scathing denunciation of monasticism, we see how Erasmus uses his humanist learning to critique the spurious apologetics of an aged monk:

> I've heard another one, an octogenarian and still an active theologian, whom you'd take for a reincarnation of Scotus himself, set out to explain the mystery of the name of Jesus. He proved with remarkable subtlety how anything that could be said about this lay hidden in the actual letters of his name. For the fact that it is declinable in three different cases is clearly symbolic of the threefold nature of the divine. Thus, the first case (*Jesus*) ends in *s*, the second (*Jesum*) in *m*, the third (*Jesu*) in *u*, and herein lies an "inexpressible" mystery; for the three letters indicate that he is the sum, the middle and the ultimate. They also concealed a still more recondite mystery, this time according to mathematical analysis. He divided Jesus into two equal halves, leaving the letter *s*, in the middle. Then he showed that this was the letter *w* in Hebrew, pronounced *syn*, and *syn* sounds like the word I believe the Scots use for the Latin *peccatum*, that is, sin. Here there is clear proof that it is Jesus who takes away the sins of the world. This novel introduction left his audi-

---

26. Erasmus, *"Praise of Folly,"* p. 154.
27. Erasmus, *"Praise of Folly,"* p. 154.

28. Erasmus, *"Praise of Folly,"* pp. 156–58.

ence open-mouthed in admiration, especially the theologians present, who very nearly suffered the same fate as Niobe. As for me, I nearly split my sides like the figwood Priapus who had the misfortune to witness the nocturnal rites of Canidia and Sagana, and with good reason; for when did Demosthenes in Greek or Cicero in Latin think up an "exordium" like that?[29]

As Albert Rabil suggests, it is doubtful that Erasmus could have written *The Praise of Folly*—being the product of an aroused genius that it is—before his trip to Italy. When Julius II was still alive, Erasmus had not been able to express in print the repugnance he felt at the sight of his holiness riding in a victory parade through the streets of Bologna at the head of his triumphant army. Upon that occasion he is reported to have asked, "Whose successor is this Julius, Julius Caesar or Jesus Christ?"

In his cunning satire *Julius II exclusus,* there is no doubt about the answer Erasmus gave to that question. In the publication of this cry of indignation, Erasmus—for all his disgust with the "warrior pope"—displayed his characteristic caution. Written sometime between 1509 and 1513, it was not published until Julius's death in 1513, and even then it was anonymous and undated. But there is no question about the authorship even though Erasmus neither acknowledged nor categorically denied writing it. His disillusionment with Julius was matched only by his high hopes for the papacy with the elevation of Giovanni de Medici to the papal throne. It is a safe conjecture, however, that Erasmus lost little time thinking about Julius or Leo, for he had far more important projects on his mind.

The Greek New Testament (1516)

From 1509 to 1514, Erasmus seems to have been constantly translating and editing ancient classical authors for the pure enjoyment of such work, or for money, or both. His needs still outreached his income—hence his constant ap-

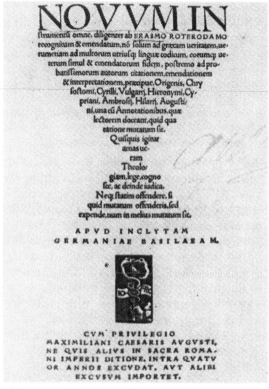

Title page of the 1516 edition of Erasmus's *Novum instrumentum*

peal for additional funds. But Erasmus did not consider the translation of the Greek classics serious work. His "serious work" involved a new edition of his *Adagia,* the editing of a new edition of Jerome, and above all the Greek New Testament. In each of these, Erasmus's obsession with the reform of Christendom became increasingly evident. The commentaries he added to the *Adagia* not only reinforced his ridicule of an insensitive, immoral, and corrupt clergy but launched a fresh attack upon war, which he viewed with horror. Erasmus was one of the first humanists to raise the battle cry against war. "On no subject did Erasmus speak so often and with such passion," writes Roland Bainton.[30] In this regard both his impartiality and his sincerity have been questioned. Yet as early as 1504 Erasmus wrote against that which

29. Erasmus, *"Praise of Folly,"* pp. 169–70.

30. Bainton, *Erasmus of Christendom,* p. 119.

Christian princes and governments had advocated for centuries. The 1515 edition of the *Adagia* includes four outbursts against war, the best known of which is entitled *Dulce bellum inexpertis* ("War is sweet to those who have not experienced it"). In 1517 Erasmus penned his most famous attack on medieval warfare, *Querela pacis* (*Complaint of Peace*), in which he destroys the contemporary arguments for a just war, even against the Turks, for "Is not the Turk also a man and a brother?"[31] In the place of war he suggests arbitration and compromise. An impartial judiciary made up of bishops and magistrates would provide the final court of appeals. Perhaps no teaching of Erasmus has proved more pervasive.

Jerome came into the forefront once again while teaching at Cambridge. For more than two years Erasmus lectured on various subjects, which probably included Jerome, his favorite among the early church fathers. He also found time to write for St. Paul's School for Boys (founded by John Colet) a treatise on education, *De copia verborum as rerum* (*A Treasure of Words and Ideas*). By the end of July 1513 he had completed his collation of the Greek manuscripts of the New Testament and, as he reported to Servatius Roger, "annotated over a thousand places, with some benefit to theologians."[32] He turned his attention to doing the same with Jerome. A year later he had completed his initial project on Jerome's letters and wrote to his friend Servatius Roger that it was ready for the publisher. Because Francis Berckman, a book retailer, had carried Erasmus's revised manuscript of the *Adagia* to the Froben Press in Basel rather than to Josse Badius in Paris, as he had been instructed to do, Erasmus soon found himself in Basel seeing the 1515 edition through the press. He had intended for Aldus to publish his Greek New Testament, but before he could carry out his plan, the famous printer died (in February 1515). By that time, however, Erasmus had established a good working relationship with John Froben and his editors, and Froben was anxious to get the job. By September type was being set, and the first copies came off the press in February 1516. The "Annotations" followed on March 1, 1516. The whole process of printing the first edition of the *Novum instrumentum,* as it was called—including all of its several parts, numbering about a thousand pages—was completed in less than six months. This would be a rather remarkable accomplishment for any publisher today, and was just short of the miraculous at the time. Only the prodigious efforts of Erasmus and the splendid cooperation of the publisher made such a feat possible.

Never was a man better matched with his times. Erasmus set up shop in the publishing house itself, just as he had done some eight years before while working with Aldus. It is a little incongruous picturing this quiet scholar working amidst the din of grinding presses and sweating men. But this must have been how it was as he prepared his precious manuscript, page by page, for the cumbersome machines, correcting proofs on the spot. In the process his "Annotations" grew from thirty to eighty-three pages. But in the end the pace was too rapid even for Erasmus. Mistakes crept in, and problems of interpretation were overlooked. Even during the operation he was determined, as he said, "to get clear of that treadmill before Easter."[33] The New Testament came off the press in February, and the nine volumes of Jerome were completed the following summer. His excuses for putting out something far less than a perfect edition were the rapid pace of the whole process and the fact that he was seeing his work on Jerome through the press at the same time. Writing three months after the first edition was completed, Erasmus indicated his resolve to put out a new edition in order to correct the mistakes of the first and to include his Latin translation made in England years before. This version was an even greater departure from the

---

31. Erasmus, cited by Bainton in *Erasmus of Christendom,* p. 123.

32. *The Correspondence of Erasmus,* 2: 300.

33. Erasmus, cited by Rabil in *Erasmus and the New Testament,* p. 92.

Vulgate than that included in the 1516 edition. By 1519 the new edition, consisting of more than 3,000 pages, was published. Three other editions followed, the last of which came out in 1535, the year before Erasmus's death.

Before 1516 another Greek New Testament had appeared as Volume V of the *Complutensian Polyglot*. It was actually printed in 1514 under the direction of Cardinal Jiménez (Ximénez) de Cisneros, but it was not published until 1522, when the other five volumes containing the Septuagint, the Vulgate, Hebrew texts of the Old Testament, and another volume (VI) of notes and aids to biblical studies were published. This University of Alcalá edition was also dedicated to Leo X.

PEACE AND CONFLICT, 1519-1536

The Greek New Testament was Erasmus's crowning achievement, the most enduring monument to his knowledge and skill. When the first edition came off the press, however, it was subject to both praise and blame. The controversy that had developed in the wake of *The Praise of Folly* now intensified. Even though the volume was dedicated to Leo X, who was obviously pleased with such recognition by Europe's greatest scholar, this fact did not save it from the champions of the Vulgate. From that time on, much of Erasmus's time was occupied with defending his Greek New Testament, especially his new Latin translation included in the 1519 edition. But this time Erasmus was not standing alone. A veritable host of humanists, churchmen, and would-be reformers sprang to his defense.

With the publication of his *Novum Testamentum*, as the second edition was entitled, Erasmus had completed editing the sources necessary for the reform of the church, which he had for so long sought. But when the Reformation did come, Erasmus failed to welcome it, fearing the consequences of the inevitable dissension and division it would bring. Yet during the next seventeen years he continued to work for reform guided by his own insights—that is, to reform without restructuring the Roman Church. It was a difficult role he had designed for himself. While he refused to become Luther's disciple, he steadfastly defended him, even after the bull of excommunication, *Exsurge Domine,* had been issued. Finally, in 1526, pressured by those within the church who demanded that he take a stand, he was persuaded to write against Luther, attacking him on the point on which he least understood him: the freedom of the will.[34] In the meantime he turned his attention to editing the writings of Origen, whom he had grown to appreciate almost as much as Jerome. Augustine, whom he had never ranked as highly as Jerome and Origen, also received a share of his attention. At the time of his last illness Erasmus was living in Froben's home and working—as much as his waning strength permitted—on a new edition of Origen's works, a task that his death interrupted.

In the midst of the fray Erasmus turned down alluring offers from Rome in order to remain his own man, as intolerance and hostility continued to mount on both sides. How well he succeeded is a matter of debate. But what is beyond dispute is Erasmus's conception of the nature of Christianity as basically personal discipleship that he taught and attempted to personify. Above all, Erasmus wanted to be a disciple of Christ; he wanted to love the Lord with all his mind—and his heart. This concept runs through his writings like the recurring theme of a symphony with all its differing movements. In the 1515 edition of the *Adagia*, while pointing out the futility and questionable morality of the Crusades, Erasmus calls Christians to a life of discipleship conceived of as both sane and moral:

> The end and aim of the faith of the Gospel is conduct worthy of Christ. Why do we insist on those things which have nothing to do with morality, and neglect the things which are like pillars of the structure—once you take them away, the whole edifice will crumble at once? Finally, who will believe us, when we take as our device the Cross of Christ and the name of the Gospel, if our

---

34. The differences that emerged between Luther and Erasmus will be discussed in a later chapter.

whole life obviously speaks of nothing but the world?[35]

Again in the same commentary Erasmus weaves his concern for peace in a turbulent age with his call to Christian discipleship:

If Christ is a figment, why do we not frankly reject him? Why do we glory in his name? If he is really the way, the truth and the life why is there such a great contrast between our way of living and this example? If we acknowledge Christ as our authority, Christ who is Love, and who taught nothing, handed down nothing that is not love and peace, come, let us follow him, not only in name, not by wearing his badge, but in our actions, in our lives. Let us embrace the cause of peace, so that Christ in return may acknowledge us for his own. It is for this end that Popes, princes and states should take counsel together. There has been enough shedding of Christian blood.[36]

THE LEGACY

In October of 1533 Erasmus sold his house in Freiburg and moved back to Basel. He had discovered the German stronghold of traditionalism to be somewhat uncongenial despite his hopes to the contrary. Once back in Froben's home, he was cared for by some of his steadfast friends. He was also close to the presses that had made possible the first four editions of his Greek New Testament and that—because death stayed its hand—produced yet another edition of his beloved *Novum Testamentum* with further corrections of text and additional changes in the "Annotations." Once this task was completed, he turned his attention to editing a new edition of Origen.

The last formal piece of writing that Erasmus worked on was an interpretation of Psalm 14 entitled *On the Purity of the Christian Church.* The reason for this last strenuous effort on Erasmus's part was the request of Christopher Eschenfelder, a customs officer at Boppard on the Rhine. During a trip in 1518 Erasmus had met Eschenfelder and discovered that Eschenfelder had read some of his works. The friendship thus formed was a lasting one. Eschenfelder had asked Erasmus to dedicate one of his interpretations of a Psalm to him. Characteristically, Erasmus was honoring the request of a friend and simultaneously writing a tract for the times. But intellectual Europe, the Europe of prelates and Schoolmen, was no longer listening to Erasmus. The center of the action had long since shifted to Wittenberg. Only in England was Erasmus's voice still heard with some appreciation and respect. Paul III had hoped to use him in defense of the beleaguered Roman fortress, but the Protestants had left him standing beside the road with his hat in his hand. Subsequent generations have discovered that Erasmus of Rotterdam, who would be neither used nor ignored, must still be reckoned with, for his legacy is with us yet.

On July 12, 1536, Erasmus breathed his last, surrounded by close friends, among whom was his first biographer, Beatus Rhenanus. As the end approached, they heard him pray in Latin, "*O Jesu, misericordia; Domine libera me; Domine miserere mei!*" ("Oh Jesus, have mercy; Lord deliver me; Lord have mercy upon me!") At last he prayed in his native Dutch, "*Lieve God*" ("Dear God"). A few hours later his frail body was carried to a Reformed Church—which had once been a cathedral—for burial. Is there not something more than an enigma here? Could it be that the death and burial of Erasmus constitute a symbol of his legacy—a legacy that is both Roman Catholic and Protestant?

---

35. Margaret Mann Phillips, *The "Adages" of Erasmus: A Study with Translations* (Cambridge: Cambridge University Press, 1964), p. 346.

36. Phillips, *The "Adages" of Erasmus,* p. 352.

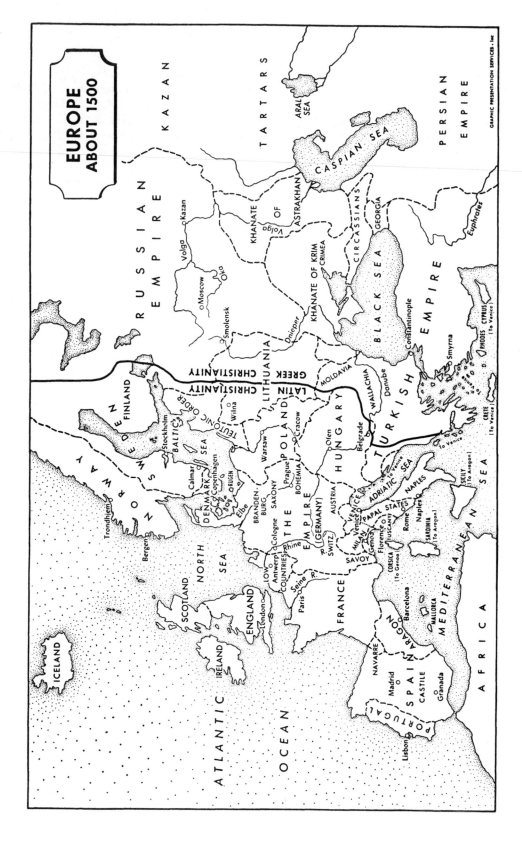

EUROPE
ABOUT 1500

Chapter VII

EUROPE ON THE THRESHOLD

t the dawn of the sixteenth century Europe stood on the threshold of the Reformation and a new age. Both Erasmus and Luther recognized that enormous changes were in the making, although neither could comprehend clearly the nature of the shifts in the currents of time. Luther crossed the threshold, but Erasmus did not. Yet there are those who see personified in Luther the medieval man with the religious concerns and fears of the Middle Ages, and in Erasmus the herald of a new age of reason and tolerance. There is an element of truth in this contrast, but it is far too simple to be accurate. From an altogether different perspective Erasmus is pictured as a John the Baptist who heralded the coming kingdom that he refused to enter. However one views Erasmus and the "changing of the guard," he was a man with feet in two different worlds. Born in one (in 1467), he died in the other (in 1536). Few times have been as convulsive or witnessed events so fraught with lasting significance as those in which Erasmus lived.

No analysis of Europe on the threshold of the Reformation can be completely accurate or objective. Yet the essence of the historian's task, as Leopold Von Ranke reminds us, is to make the attempt. For purposes of analysis, the fabric of society in sixteenth-century Europe will be examined piece by piece as we attempt to understand those momentous developments that alternately threatened and challenged medieval man at the turn of the century.

AN AGE OF DISCOVERY

The last half of the fifteenth century gave birth to a number of remarkable inventions and discoveries. Among these was the final successful production of a printed book, the Latin Bible, by Johannes Gutenberg (1456). A psalter followed the next year and bears the distinction of being the first dated printed book in Europe. This was the beginning of what Elizabeth Eisenstein in *The Printing Press as an Agent of Change* calls "book culture" as distinct from "scribal culture," which preceded the invention of printing. Although there were books before those of Gutenberg, they were hand-produced by scribes in a scriptorium. Each copy was unique in both its fine points and its flaws. (Erasmus grew exasperated in working with inadequate manuscripts containing both errors and omissions.) The invention of the letterpress thus constituted something of a revolution, as Myron Gilmore suggests: "The invention and development of printing with movable type brought about the most radical transformation in the conditions of intellectual life in the history of western civilization. It opened new horizons in education and in the communication of ideas. Its effects were sooner or later felt in every department of human activity."[1]

It takes a vivid historical imagination to picture what the world must have been like without printed books. The illegibility of manuscripts and the cost and inaccuracy of manuscript copies made learning almost exclusively the province of the elite, who had both leisure and a Latin education. Printing began to change all of that. For example, only a hundred editions of the Bible were printed before 1500. Perhaps as many as forty thousand other books were included in this period of the *incunabula*. While it is debatable whether or not the Renaissance gave birth to the printing press, it is beyond dispute that the spread of printing and the emergence of print shops in the major cities of Europe not only enabled the revival of learning to endure but disseminated its message and ideas in ways never thought possible before.[2] One need look no further than Erasmus for proof of this statement. The Reformation is also inconceivable apart from the new process of printing. Luther was quick to affirm this when he told his students that printing was "God's latest and best work to spread the true religion throughout the world."[3] As Lewis Spitz points out in *The Renaissance and Reformation Movements*, from 1500 to the beginning of the Reformation, German printers were turning out only forty books a year, but once the Reformation was launched, the figure "rocketed to five

hundred titles" annually.[4] Beatus Rhenanus wrote to Zwingli that "Luther's books were not so much sold as snatched from the hands of the booksellers."[5]

As important as the polemical pamphlets were in the progress of the Reformation, the translation and publication of the Bible was more so. Before Luther's *September Bibel* of 1522, fourteen versions of the Bible in High German and four in Low German had appeared. Luther's New Testament was an immediate success. It was soon followed by the Froschauer Bible printed in Zürich (in 1529). Shortly thereafter Luther and Melanchthon completed their translation of the Old Testament and began a revision of Luther's New Testament. In Zürich alone ninety editions of the Bible came off the presses before the close of the sixteenth century. Simultaneously, paperback versions of the New Testament, sermons, and tracts in the language of the people poured forth in a steady stream from both well-known and little-known presses from Wittenberg to Geneva and from Antwerp to Nikolsburg, Moravia. Never before had printer's ink spread ideas with such contagious enthusiasm or with such signal success.

From almost the beginning of the fifteenth century, exploration parties of courageous Italian, Portuguese, and Spanish sailors had discovered new trade routes to offset the losses inflicted upon Europe by the encroaching Moors. The fall of Constantinople became the stimulus that led to further exploration along the African coast and increased trade in ivory, gold, and slaves. Bartholomew Diaz, with two Portuguese ships, sailed round the Cape of Good Hope—so named by the Portuguese monarch—in 1487. However, it was the young Vasco da Gama who succeeded in sailing around the Cape and on to India, a trip from which he returned with a wealth of spices. Fired with a crusading zeal, the tiny country of Portugal led the way a full half-century before Spain em-

---

1. Gilmore, cited by Elizabeth Eisenstein in *The Printing Press as an Agent of Change*, 2 vols. (New York: Cambridge University Press, 1979), 1: 28.

2. The relationship of the printing press to the Renaissance is a very complicated matter. See vol. 1 of Eisenstein's *The Printing Press as an Agent of Change*, pp. 181-225 for a discussion of the interrelatedness of the Renaissance and book culture.

3. Luther, cited by Roland H. Bainton in *Here I Stand: A Life of Martin Luther* (New York: Abingdon Press, 1950), p. 295.

4. Spitz, *The Renaissance and Reformation Movements* (Chicago: Rand McNally, 1971), p. 306.

5. Rhenanus, cited by Spitz in *The Renaissance and Reformation Movements*, p. 306.

barked upon its great century of adventure and expansion inspired by a similar religious fervor.

The very year in which Columbus discovered the islands of the West Indies, the Spanish were finally able to rid themselves of the last of the Mohammedan caliphs in the Alhambra. For the first time in more than half a century the Iberian peninsula was free of Moorish banners and rulers. And suddenly Europe, which had been steadily shrinking as both its east and west flanks were curbed by Moslem armies, found breathing room and new worlds to conquer. Pedro Cabral claimed Brazil for Portugal in 1500, and the very year in which Luther debated Dr. Johann Eck at Leipzig (1519), Magellan began his famed voyage around the world. The French and English, although somewhat tardy, were to find their places in the Western sun as each laid claim to vast territories in North America.

The discovery of the New World not only ushered in Spain's "Golden Age"; it changed the shape of European commerce and, hand in hand with the rise of capitalism, created a whole new class of enterprising entrepreneurs who in turn upset the stratification of medieval society that had existed for centuries. Trading companies were formed to raise money for ventures that few families or banking institutions could undertake alone. Some became fabulously wealthy in relatively few years. Such were the Welsers of Antwerp, Lisbon, and Madeira. Equally powerful and much more wealthy was the banking family of Augsburg, the Fuggers, whose combined wealth in 1546 was estimated at sixty-three million gulden. With the increased trade within both Europe and the New World, Antwerp surpassed the Italian trade centers to become Europe's most important commercial center. It was from this city that Protestant literature, polemical tracts, and Bibles were shipped to both Spain and England. Thus increased trade coupled with the avalanche of religious books and Bibles gave both men and ideas more mobility than they had ever had before.

Man's insatiable curiosity for knowledge of himself and his universe was not limited to a desire to learn about the earth. The heavens as well as the earth became the object of exploration and discovery in this stirring age. Although the Mohammedans had introduced astronomy to Europe, it was far from an exact science. In fact, astronomy and astrology were so interrelated that they were almost indistinguishable from each other. Despite hints from Pythagoras that the world revolved around the sun, Ptolemy's theory remained unchallenged until Nicolaus Copernicus (1473–1543) discovered from his own observation and research that the earth turns upon its own axis and, indeed, revolves around the sun. He refrained from publishing his findings, however, until he was near death. This saved him from the hands of the Inquisition, which sought to silence Galileo, who seventy years later confirmed Copernicus's theory with his own careful studies aided by his newly invented telescope. The new discoveries were upsetting. Medieval man had never imagined the earth to be so large or populated with so many unknown aborigines and at the same time to be such an infinitesimal speck in an unfathomable universe. The old assumptions and concepts formulated in an unscientific age were shattered. With their demolition came a considerable loss of confidence in the church, which now found its credibility seriously questioned on a number of fronts.

NATIONS IN THE MAKING

By the end of the fifteenth century and the beginning of the sixteenth, the heady spirit of nationalism was in the air. It was to have far-reaching consequences for both church and state. In Spain it would snuff out the fires of reform almost before they could begin to burn. In Germany, Luther would successfully appeal to the rising tide of German nationalism in his battle with Rome. In England the Reformation would be embraced; in France it would be rejected. Only a closer look at this phenomenon will help the modern student to understand how such contradictory effects were possible.

Spain

Spain became the most powerful nation in sixteenth-century Europe. Its history and that of

Portugal help to explain how these two countries manifested so early such fervent patriotic feelings. For centuries the Arabic masters of the Iberian peninsula had governed and kept in check the Christian element, which had been reduced to tiny enclaves in what was otherwise a Moslem world. However, from the successful siege of Toledo in Castile by El Cid in the eleventh century to the final ouster of the last of the caliphs from Granada in 1492, Spain developed a crusading zeal that welded the fortunes of church and state together in an indissoluble union. The same was true of Portugal, which had rid itself of Mohammedans more than half a century before. The voyages of discovery and conquest added immeasurably to its national pride. But it was the marriage of Ferdinand of Aragon and Isabella of Castile in 1469 that paved the way for the unification of the two most powerful states in Iberia and eventually for the unification of the entire peninsula, with the exception of Portugal. With the successful expulsion of the last of the Mohammedan rulers, the Spanish turned their attention to the conversion of the remaining Jews and Moors in their midst.

In 1478 Pope Sixtus IV authorized the establishment of the Inquisition in Spain at the request of the "Catholic sovereigns." This institution, under the complete control of the crown, was to prove a valuable instrument in ridding Spain of both Jews and Moors. Hostility against the Jews had been growing for some time. The revival of Spain's religious zeal, coupled with the fact that the Jewish people had enjoyed—despite ugly episodes of persecution—enormous prosperity, made them the objects of envy and suspicion. By the time of their expulsion, they virtually controlled the financial nerve-centers of the country. Doubtless their great wealth fueled the covetousness of those who stood to profit from a new exodus. Thus in 1492 the zealous monarchs ordered all Jews to become Christians or leave the country. It is estimated that more than 150,000 Jews left as a result. But 50,000 others submitted to baptism. The *Conversos* or *Marranos,* as Christians of Jewish descent were called, were suspected of insincerity or heresy even if they succeeded in

rising to the highest offices of the church. It became one of the major tasks of the Inquisition to keep an eye on suspected heretics. It is not surprising, therefore, that the first victims were four Jews who were burned at the stake in Seville in 1481. The Moors who remained in Spain with the assurance that they would not be so dealt with were soon subjected to the same kind of treatment. Most became unwilling converts (*Moriscos*) to the Christian faith. Thus Spain assured itself of a degree of religious uniformity unknown to the rest of Europe.

In this way religion became, indeed, the "cement" of the newly formed nation that helped Ferdinand and Isabella overcome the unruly sectionalism that would have been completely unmanageable with any lesser cohesive force. Spanish nationalism and Spanish Catholicism made common cause and to a considerable extent were indistinguishable from one another. Spain's determination to become the most formidable nation in Europe was fired by a religious zeal that saw its goals almost completely achieved under Charles V. Its empire stretched from Peru to Naples and from Africa to the Netherlands. In between lay France.

France

To the French, Spain was an upstart nation lacking both a rich cultural heritage and a stable monarchy. However, France soon learned to respect the military prowess of its neighbor across the Pyrenees. The French also possessed an overweening national ambition. This was due in part to their prolonged conflict with England, the Hundred Years' War. Their designs upon Naples were first encouraged and then frustrated by the Spanish, led by their Machiavellian monarch, Ferdinand. Nevertheless, the French considered themselves the greatest nation in Europe. This feeling was partly due to the legacy of the Crusades. Even though England and Germany as well as other nations had provided soldiers and even "generals" for the crusading armies, from the beginning the Crusades had been largely inspired and led by the French.

Up until the Reformation France had been

deeply involved in the life of the medieval church. The Avignon papacy and the conciliar movement were both expressions of the French spirit. French control of the papacy at Avignon gave way to the embodiment of the concepts of conciliar reform in the Pragmatic Sanction. At Bourges in 1438 the French king, Charles VII, embraced these reforms and imposed them upon the French clergy in the presence of papal legates. According to Thomas Lindsay,

This Pragmatic Sanction embodied most of the cherished conciliar plans of reform. It asserted the ecclesiastical supremacy of Councils over Popes. It demanded a meeting of a Council every ten years. It declared that the selection of the higher ecclesiastics was to be left to the Chapters and to the Convents. It denied the Pope's general claim to the reservation of benefices, and greatly limited its use in special cases. It did away with the Pope's right to act as Ordinary, and insisted that no ecclesiastical cases should be appealed to Rome without first having exhausted the lower courts of jurisdiction. It abolished the *Annates,* with some exceptions in favour of the present Pope. It also made some attempts to provide the churches with an educated ministry. All these declarations simply carried out the proposals of the Council of Basel; but they had an important influence on the position of the French clergy towards the king. The Pragmatic Sanction, though issued by an assembly of the French clergy, was nevertheless a royal ordinance, and thereby gave the king indefinite rights over the Church within France. The right to elect bishops and abbots was placed in the hands of Chapters and Convents, but the king and nobles were expressly permitted to bring forward and recommend candidates, and this might easily be extended to enforcing the election of those recommended. Indefinite rights of patronage on the part of the king and of the nobles over benefices in France could not fail to be the result, and the French Church could scarcely avoid assuming the appearance of a national Church controlled by the king as the head of the State. The abolition of the Pragmatic Sanction was always a bait which the French king could dangle before the eyes of the Pope, and the promise to maintain the Pragmatic Sanction was always a bribe to secure the support of the clergy and the *Parlements* of France.[6]

The adoption of the Pragmatic Sanction against the protests of Pope Eugenius IV meant that the French church became virtually autonomous. Like Spain, France was most devoted to the Roman Catholic Church—that is, as long as it could be made to serve national interests. Consequently, nowhere in Europe was the church more subservient to the crown than in France. On the threshold of the sixteenth century the French monarchs had subdued all rivals to their authority within France, and France was a proud nation unified around the French king, Francis I (1494-1547).

England

England, the third of the three most developed nations of Europe at the time, was in some respects the most fortunate. It had not been invaded by Arabs or devastated by wars of foreign invaders. This does not mean that Henry VII's reign was free of strife. For centuries York had manifested a separatist spirit that occasionally would flare up in armed rebellion. Lambert Simnel, who claimed to be a son or nephew of Edward IV, raised an army in Ireland that invaded England with the help of soldiers from Yorkshire. With the greatest of difficulty Simnel's army was defeated at Stoke-on-Trent in 1487. Subsequent uprisings were successfully put down by 1497, and by 1500 England enjoyed internal peace.

A unique feature of English society was its vigorous and growing middle class. This new and increasingly important element in English society was fed from two sources—the nobility and the merchant or artisan class. In England only the oldest son of a noble family retained the title and the land; the younger sons were considered commoners. This arrangement made for a more literate and aggressive middle class than was true elsewhere. Although the English people did not constitute a completely classless society, the middle class became an increasingly significant element in English life. The result was that "England was the first land to become a compact nationality."[7] In addition,

---

6. Lindsay, *A History of the Reformation,* 2 vols. (New York: Scribner's, 1907, 1928), 1: 24-25.

7. Lindsay, *A History of the Reformation,* 1: 25.

a rapidly rising merchant and artisan segment added a new dimension to the character of the middle class. Serfdom had been abolished, and those who had been virtually slaves tied to the soil had become wage earners. Some by their industry and native ability rose above their peers to a middle-class status.

Henry VII, following the example of Ferdinand, attempted to do by marriage what he was not willing to attempt by armed aggression. He arranged for his daughter Margaret to marry James IV of Scotland, which led to the unification of the two countries a century or so later. His son Arthur dutifully married Catherine, the third daughter of Ferdinand and Isabella of Spain, and when Arthur died five months later, Henry VII, reluctant to lose the advantage of an alliance with Spain—and the dowry—persuaded his younger son, Henry, to marry her. Thus at the beginning of the sixteenth century England found itself a nation poised for future exploration and conquest. Although not yet the equal of Spain or Portugal as a maritime power, the island kingdom had the potential that by the end of the century was to push it to the forefront of discovery and colonization in the New World.

Germany

Germany was not, strictly speaking, a nation. Nevertheless, a strong spirit of nationalism was abroad within the Holy Roman Empire, which was in essence a federation of German states. Since 1356 the selection of the emperor had rested in the hands of seven electors—"three on the Elbe and four on the Rhine. On the Elbe were the King of Bohemia, the Elector of Saxony, and the Elector of Brandenburg; on the Rhine, the Count Palatine of the Rhine and the Archbishops of Mainz, Trier, and Köln."[8] In addition to these rather large political entities extending from the western part of Hungary to the Lowlands, there were innumerable smaller states. Each prince was

sovereign in his own realm. The larger of these held assemblies of the lesser nobility, administered justice in accordance with their own laws, and even minted their own coins. Despite a strong Germanic sense of ethnic togetherness and countless expressions of the desire for a unified Germany, the princes were apparently determined not to sacrifice their independence for unity. Thus attempts to make the emperor supreme were constantly frustrated. For their part the emperors—Frederick III, Maximilian, and Charles V—were not above impoverishing the Empire in the interest of augmenting their own fortunes and those of their families.

Upon the death of Maximilian in 1519, Charles V, his grandson, was chosen emperor. The German people and the electors thought on that fateful day in June that they had chosen one of themselves, a German. They could not have been more mistaken. Although a Hapsburg, the son of Ferdinand and the grandson of Maximilian, Charles was, by his education and in his sympathies, a Spaniard. He was ill-equipped to understand the depth of German religious devotion that welled up in the soul of the monk who stood before him at Worms. However, he did understand the longing of the German people for a united Germany. Thus he agreed to accept a *Reichsregiment,* which was the last attempt to give the German Empire a constitutional unity. But the taxation necessary for its support was to come from the cities that were not represented at the diet. When the merchants of the cities upon which the taxes were to be levied learned of the scheme, they protested. Representatives of the cities met in Valladolid with the emperor, who agreed to veto the plan and rule alone. At the turn of the century, despite the rising tide of German nationalism, Germany as a nation existed only in the dreams of the German people.

Switzerland

Technically the Swiss Confederation was a part of the Holy Roman Empire until 1521. However, by 1499 the Swiss had effectively thrown off the

---

8. Lindsay, *A History of the Reformation,* 1: 35.

rule of the Hapsburgs and the yoke of the Empire. The Confederation, which originally consisted of three cantons—Uri, Schwyz, and Unterwalden—now included Lucerne, Glarus, Zug, Zürich, and Bern. Together they could muster a formidable fighting force. In fact, Swiss mercenary troops were much in demand by both Roman pontiffs and French kings. To the Swiss, war became a lucrative business, and the export of young Swiss men became the Confederation's "cash crop."

Until the Reformation divided Swiss from Swiss and the forest cantons from the city cantons, these states—even though they were not, strictly speaking, a unified nation—managed to work together and fight together. Ethnicity, similar needs, and common enemies had brought them together, but religion drove a wedge between these little democratic provinces. The Protestant Reformation, therefore, both divided and united them. While it divided the German-speaking cantons from one another, the Reformed Church brought a new sense of unity to the French-speaking cantons.

Italy

Perhaps the most hopelessly fragmented country in Europe was Italy. It consisted of five major states as well as a large number of small principalities ruled by lesser nobles. These were Venice, Milan, Florence in the north, and Naples in the south, which were separated from the northern regions by the Papal States in the middle of the peninsula. Venice and Florence were rival commercial centers and independent city-states. Maximilian claimed Milan as a fief of the Holy Roman Empire, but France also claimed Milan as a heritage of the dukes of Orleans. By 1494 Alfonso was able to turn the kingdom of Naples over to his son as a united state embracing both Sicily and Naples. The Papal States were subdued and unified, with the help of the Franks, by a series of politically minded and ambitious pontiffs, of whom Julius II was the most celebrated. The popes were not above using their spiritual authority to extend their temporal power. They resorted to all kinds of unholy

alliances, first with Naples and later with France, to enlarge their personal holdings on behalf of their families and the interests of the church. Consequently, feudalism died hard in Italy; its last stronghold was the kingdom of Naples. Thus Italy remained a collection of independent states throughout the Reformation era.

Scandinavia and Eastern Europe

The heartland of the Reformation was Germany. During the Middle Ages the German states exerted a great deal of influence upon the Scandinavian countries, and even though the Scandinavians developed their own languages, never becoming a part of the Holy Roman Empire, they continued to feel a kinship with the German people. The same was true of Poland, Bohemia, and Hungary. All of these countries, however, were sorely divided by ambitious monarchs who, in the eyes of the merchants and the nobility, acted contrary to the best interests of their realms. While the current of nationalism coursed through them, none of the three could be considered a unified national state.

In Bohemia, whose king was one of the electors of the Holy Roman Empire, the nationalistic spirit suffered a severe blow with the defeat of the native reform party and the execution of John Huss at Constance. But Bohemia's sense of destiny did not die. Rather, with the rise of the Utraquist Church as well as the smaller Taborite reform party, the Bohemians in effect separated themselves from the *corpus christianum*. Eventually the rise of the United Brethren would keep alive the more evangelical expression of the Hussite movement. By the sixteenth century the Taborites had been reduced to a few isolated groups after suffering defeat at the hands of the Utraquists. Poland and Hungary could hardly escape the repercussions of the religious upheavals among the Czech people.

SOCIETY IN FERMENT

At the dawn of the sixteenth century momentous changes in the structure of medieval society were afoot. The change from a barter economy to a monetary system and the advent of capitalism were only two such developments that were to have far-reaching effects in the sixteenth century and subsequent centuries. The disintegration of feudalism, which had held Europe together for more than a thousand years, was rapidly accelerated by what has been termed the commercial revolution. A part of the total picture included the development of towns and cities as centers of industry and commerce, and with them a new burgher class (bourgeoisie) made up of artisans, merchants, and unskilled laborers. The commercial revolution threatened the craft guilds, which found it no longer possible to control the marketing of their products. With the rise of the new middle class, there were those who by the nature of the changes were left out. They were at the extremes of the social hierarchy, which included both peasants and nobility. The tensions and bitterness engendered by the struggle for survival made for mounting discontent, which was frighteningly expressed: robber barons, marauding knights, and rampaging peasants roamed the land. While these conditions lacked the dynamic to bring forth the Reformation, they certainly helped to create a climate in which Luther's attacks on a money-hungry hierarchy met with widespread approval.

The Rise of the Towns

That Europe would be urbanized by the end of the fifteenth century was a foregone conclusion. But the towns and cities of this time could not begin to compare with their modern counterparts. In addition, their development was uneven. Paris, the largest city in Europe, had only 300,000 inhabitants. Köln (Cologne) and Erfurt could boast of only 30,000 each. Little Wittenberg on the Elbe, the cradle of the Reformation, would have been hard-pressed to find 2,500 souls. Of Europe's 70,000,000 people, seven million or less lived in towns and cities. Europe, then, was still largely rural, but the new towns, despite poorly ventilated houses, open sewers, and polluted rivers, constituted an irresistible attraction for the restless and impoverished

peasants. Towns offered an alluring escape from the increasingly harsh conditions on the manors. They also promised a degree of freedom, the rewards for labor in hard cash, and the possibility of becoming a journeyman. Protection by the guilds provided security against the feudal lords, who found themselves unable to compete with the growing power of the cities. In the cities new religious ideas found an eager audience. It is not surprising, therefore, that the cities of the Empire early became supporters of the Reformation.

The Commercial Revolution

The rise of capitalism and the commercial revolution went hand in hand: the one demanded the other. Trading ventures, which prior to the discoveries of the last decades of the fifteenth century had often been local enterprises or family affairs, had grown too large and demanding for such simple arrangements. Now corporations were organized to raise the capital for a variety of business ventures, from a mining company to a printing firm that provided ledgers, bank drafts, and books on bookkeeping. Banking houses like that of Jacob Fugger (II) of Augsburg loaned money for such enterprises and for all kinds of enterprises by individuals—even those of monarchs as well as of city governments—provided there was the promise of profit or a substantial rate of interest. The laws against usury were circumvented to suit the realities of the new economics, which demanded capital that in turn involved loans and interest. The need for cash drove the church to resort to questionable methods of finance, including traffic in indulgences. Large landowners were under pressure to exchange the products of their farms for cash. The result was that what had been a heavy burden for the peasants became intolerable.

Peasant Uprisings

Even though a nobleman may have owned as much as three thousand acres, the new economic conditions that prevailed from the last half of the fifteenth century on, particularly in Germany, frequently left him impoverished. In the search for ways to make up the deficit, traditional rights of the peasants to hunt in forests and fish the lakes and streams belonging to the nobility were revoked. In addition, the community grazing lands became off-limits for the peasants' sheep and cows. And peasants could no longer cut firewood as they had done for centuries. Whether serfs or peasants, the people increasingly resented being used as property by the lords. The most galling of burdens the peasants were forced to bear was the death tax, which was levied upon a peasant when there was a death in his family. The eleventh article of "The Twelve Articles of the Peasants" (1525)—in which the South German peasants listed their grievances—underscores this fact:

> The Eleventh Article.—In the eleventh place we will entirely abolish the due called Todfall [i.e., heriot], and will no longer endure it, nor allow widows and orphans to be thus shamefully robbed against God's will, and in violation of justice and right, as has been done in many places, and by those who should shield and protect them. These have disgraced and despoiled us, and although they had little authority, they assumed it. God will suffer this no more, but it shall be wholly done away with, and for the future no man shall be bound to give little or much.[9]

While conditions for peasants were not good anywhere in Europe, they were most deplorable in Germany, where feudalism held on with a tenacity hardly equaled elsewhere. The repeated failure of the harvests in much of Europe from 1490 to 1503 exacerbated the situation. The unrest of the German peasants gave rise to a number of peasant movements, from the one in 1475 to their final bloody suppression at the battle of Frankenhausen in 1525. The peasants had virtually no way to legally redress the increasing oppression of the nobility, and not every serf or peasant could flee to the cities. To desperate men concerted armed rebellion appeared the only way out. When the Swiss defeated Charles the Bold of Burgundy at Nancy, the German peasants took heart.

The earlier peasant uprisings, stimulated by Lollard and Hussite beliefs, were basically religious movements. But, as Thomas Lindsay points out, this was not true after 1476.[10] From this point on into the sixteenth century the revolts were primarily socioeconomic movements that used religion to justify rebellion. They were also generally German and—although this was not always the case—anticlerical as well. Peasants resented financial exploitation by the church quite as much as, if not more than, that by the nobility.

The first of these movements was that led by Hans Böhm of Helmstedt, an illiterate vagabond minstrel. Böhm launched his movement by publicly announcing that he had received a vision from the Virgin Mary to preach at Niklashausen on the Tauber during Lent on March 24, 1476. Subsequently the Chapel of Our Lady at Niklashausen, a popular shrine, became the center of his activities. In his preaching he denounced the nobility for oppressing the peasants, denied purgatory, and declared all men equal before God. When he called for his followers to arm themselves, he was arrested by the bishop of Würzburg, condemned for heresy, and burned at the stake. He died singing a hymn of praise to the Virgin Mary. After his death his ideas spread, and peasant protests became characteristic of German society.

By 1490 the German peasants along the Rhine and Neckar rivers succeeded in organizing themselves into a more permanent organization under the banner of the peasant's shoe, *Bundschuh*. This symbol was meant to strike fear in the heart of the young emperor Charles V at Worms as late as 1521. Despite its anticlerical stance the movement had certain religious overtones, symbolized by its painting of the crucified Christ. A *Bundschuh* adorned one side, and a peasant kneeling in prayer adorned the other. Their motto was "Only what

9. Cited in *Documents Illustrative of the Continental Reformation,* ed. B. J. Kidd (Oxford: Clarendon Press, 1911), p. 179.

10. Lindsay, *A History of the Reformation,* 1: 97.

is just before God." The members were required to repeat five times a day the Lord's Prayer and the *Ave Maria*. Under the leadership of Joss Fritz, a former *Landsknecht* (soldier), the movement seems to have won the confidence of some parish priests, who were often as destitute as the peasants themselves. The organization honeycombed the Alsace, including the towns of Weissenburg and Hagenou, where authorities uncovered a conspiracy between the peasants and the townsmen "to slay the civic councillors and judges and all the inhabitants of noble descent."[11] They had also agreed not to pay any imperial or ecclesiastical taxes. Fritz, who fled for refuge among the Swiss, had assured his followers that the Swiss would come to their aid.

While it is too much to say that the peasants contributed directly to the rise of the Reformation of the sixteenth century, their discontent with the structures of medieval society did make them receptive to the gospel as preached by Luther and other Reformers. From the time of Böhm they had demonstrated a tendency to go their own way in religion, seeking a faith that spoke directly to their needs. The peasant uprisings in Germany in 1525, by Thomas Müntzer in the north and Hans Müller in the south, may be seen as a continuation of the peasant unrest of the fifteenth century, only at this point appealing to the rising evangelical movement for justification of their cause.

CRISIS IN THE CLASSROOM

A world apart from the grim realities of peasant life were the concerns of the university classroom. This does not mean that the students were well off in the sense that they came exclusively from the ranks of the nobility or the cloister; life was often difficult for them as well. The biographies of Luther and Erasmus testify to this fact. Among the disciplines most remote from Europe's masses was that of theology. Theology was strictly for professionals, and it was the

exclusive province of the medieval university, the entrance to which was guarded by Latin. This theology was known as Scholasticism, the theology of the Schoolmen, a system by which the church had sought to support its dogmas by deductive reasoning. Frequently torn by warring factions by the end of the fifteenth century, it appeared to many to have turned upon itself.

The *via antiqua* was the term applied to the teachings of Augustine, Anselm, and Aquinas. In effect it was Scholasticism as expounded by Thomas Aquinas, the Angelic Doctor. His system of theology was a synthesis of Aristotelian philosophy and Christian thought. Eugene Fairweather suggests that the whole history of medieval Christian thought can be organized around the rediscovery of Aristotle.[12] Aquinas took his cue from what Arab thinkers had already done in attempting to synthesize Moslem teachings with Aristotelian philosophy. He was indebted to them for the Latin translations of Aristotle's works. In Aquinas Scholasticism reached its high-water mark, but it was not without its critics. Both Bonaventure (1221–1274) and Duns Scotus (1265–1308) attacked Aquinas's teachings from an Augustinian position and Neoplatonic presuppositions. For example, Duns Scotus held, contrary to Aquinas, that the sacraments were not efficacious in themselves but derived their efficacy from a prior covenant with God "in which God has agreed to be present with his grace."[13] The conflict between Thomists and Scotists constituted one of the major crises in Scholasticism. It was continued by another Franciscan, William of Ockham, who retained a critical stance while rejecting Realism.

William of Ockham (ca. 1280–1349) was the most influential Scholastic thinker this side of Aquinas. It is he whose ideas gave rise to the *via moderna* (the modern way). An Aristotelian,

---

11. Lindsay, *A History of the Reformation*, 1: 106.

12. Fairweather, ed. and trans., *A Scholastic Miscellany: Anselm to Ockham*, vol. 10 of the Library of Christian Classics (Philadelphia: Westminster Press, 1956), p. 27.

13. Steven Ozment, *The Age of Reform, 1250–1550: An Intellectual and Religious History of Late Medieval and Reformation Europe* (New Haven: Yale University Press, 1980), p. 35.

he used Nominalist philosophy to destroy the rational supports of Scholasticism. He also denied the existence of universals. Reality exists, he taught, only in individual objects that can be known only by observation and intuition. Thus he rejected the traditional Scholastic arguments for the existence of God. Man must accept the existence of God by faith, since revelation, not reason, is the basis of Christian theology. In an attempt to force his contemporaries to abandon what he considered fallacious reasoning, he insisted, much like Duns Scotus, that God's will was absolute. God can will that which appears to be unethical, unreasonable, or even immoral. Furthermore, Ockham held that God is not obligated by man's conduct to reward him or withhold reward. This God does upon the basis of his own inscrutable will. In his attempt to make man utterly dependent upon revelation and tradition, which are accepted by faith, Ockham destroyed Scholasticism's fusion of reason and faith, which was a prelude to its death. He insisted that "what can be done with fewer assumptions is done in vain with more." This principle became known as Ockham's razor.[14]

However, the end for Scholasticism did not come with Ockham and his "razor" but with the advent of the Reformation, which was indebted through Luther to Ockham. In fact, Heiko Oberman rejects the concept of a decline in medieval theology—the traditional interpretation—for a new understanding that sees in Ockham the flowering of Scholasticism. Instead of considering Gabriel Biel the redactor who salvaged Ockham for the church, he holds that Biel was a faithful disciple of Ockham and as such shows the rich mine of pastoral theology available in Ockham for a truly catholic church: "Biel's pastoral works provide us with the evidence that the Occamistic system, preserved with full integrity, is perfectly suited for explicitly theological and pastoral application."[15] Even though

Oberman admits the Nominalist concept of justification was unable to avoid a Pelagian position, he insists that this "should not obscure the fact that Nominalism was involved in the ongoing medieval search for proper interpretation of Augustine."[16] While Oberman's reinterpretation of the "crisis" in medieval theology may indeed be the correct one, it did not appear so to many of Ockham's contemporaries but precipitated a conflict in Nominalism that existed into the Reformation era.

THE RELIGIOUS SITUATION

Religion was so much a part of all aspects of life in medieval Europe that it is difficult to view it as a separate element in itself. Then, too, the fact that it involved institutional religion as well as personal religious life makes it a complex and elusive subject to analyze. However, this much is clear: religious life at the beginning of the sixteenth century was in ferment. Not only was the Constantinian symbiosis failing, but the Thomistic synthesis was under serious attack by both Realists and Nominalists. The uncertain sound of the Scholastic trumpet was an ominous sign for the church's future.

The Conciliar Movement

The conciliar movement was the church's longest sustained attempt to reform itself. It was long on promise but short on fulfillment. At the heart of the conciliar idea was the conviction that a general council of the church was the supreme judicature over prelates and popes. Ockham was the major theoretician of the conciliar idea. In his *Dialogues* (1343) Ockham made a distinction between the Roman Church and the universal church. He asserted that when a pope fell into heresy, it was the responsibility of a general council to depose him. In such situations the council might be called by bishops, secular princes, or even the faithful members of the church. Ockham was not alone in his view of

14. Robert G. Clouse, "William of Ockham," in *The New International Dictionary of the Christian Church*, ed. J. D. Douglas (Grand Rapids: Zondervan, 1978), p. 1052.

15. Oberman, *The Harvest of Medieval Theology: Gabriel Biel and Late Medieval Nominalism* (Cambridge: Harvard University Press, 1963), p. 424.

16. Oberman, *The Harvest of Medieval Theology*, p. 427.

the necessity and authority of a general council. Marsiglio of Padua in his *Defensor pacis* (1324) taught essentially the same thing. A general council, he held, had authority over all ecclesiastical matters provided it adhered to Scripture.

The movement to bring an end to the Papal Schism through the convening of a general council was initiated by a group of theologians and canon lawyers teaching at the University of Paris, the most prominent of whom were Conrad of Gelnhausen and Henry of Langenstein. However, when their efforts, which had won the full support of the university, were frustrated because of the timidity of the French court, they left the university for more fertile fields. With the exodus of the Germans, the burden of leadership fell upon two Frenchmen, John Gerson and Peter d'Ailly. The persistence of the Parisian professors finally paid off. Because of the aggressive action of the French court, the Council of Pisa convened in 1409. The council apparently succeeded only in adding another pope to an already overcrowded field.

But the handwriting was on the wall. The Council of Constance succeeded where the Council of Pisa had failed. In this action the conciliarists were the chief architects. They outwitted the first John XXIII by prearranging the voting by nations, which completely frustrated the pope's feverish attempts to "stuff the ballot box" by adding to his entourage newly consecrated bishops by the dozens.

The triumph of the conciliarist movement at Constance illustrated both its strengths and its weaknesses. While the council did indeed rid the church of three popes, it did little to reform the morals of the clergy, one of its primary objectives. Instead we see Cardinal d'Ailly acting as the judge at the trial of the saintly Huss. Both Gerson and d'Ailly were determined to distinguish their movement from that of Wycliffe and Huss; they viewed these reformers as outside the pale of the Roman Church. Yet the inability of the conciliarists to effect any lasting meaningful reforms became increasingly apparent at the Council of Basel (1431–1438). Because Pope Eugenius IV (1431–1447) refused to appear be-

fore the tribunal of the council when summoned, the council deposed him and elected Amadeus of Savoy as Felix V. But as a result of the diplomatic triumph of Eugenius at the Council of Florence/Ferrara—his council—Felix V was forsaken and with him the conciliar movement as well. The final blow to the conciliar movement was delivered by Pius II in the papal bull *Execrabilis*, issued in January 1460, in which he forbade all appeals to a future council.

That the would-be reformers had lost control of the general councils was evident with the convening of the Fifth Lateran Council on the eve of the Reformation (1512–1517). At the opening session Egidio da Viterbo, the general of the Augustinian order, called for a spiritual reform expressed in outward reforms. But the council seemed oblivious to this plea and all other calls for reform. Instead it called for financial assistance of the nations of Europe in order to launch a new crusade against the Turks. In its last session the council reaffirmed the *Unam sanctam,* the papal bull of Boniface VIII, which affirmed the supreme authority of the papacy over all states and temporal rulers. Clearly the pope and the Curia had their minds and hearts set on other things—precisely what other things, a brief glimpse of the papacy at the time will likely reveal.

The Papacy

Leo X (1475–1521) was the pope guiding the decisions of the Fifth Lateran Council. He had assumed the papal crown in 1513 after a long period in ecclesiastical service. He was tonsured before he was eight years old, becoming a cardinal-deacon at thirteen and a member of the College of Cardinals at seventeen. As a member of that body he took part in the elections of both Alexander VI and Julius II, neither of whom provided an adequate model for the aspiring Giovanni de Medici. Since he was a Florentine humanist, educated in the enlightened circle of his father, Lorenzo the Magnificent, many a sincere soul looked to his elevation with the greatest expectations for reform and renewal. In fact, Erasmus dedicated the first edition of his Greek New Testament to him. But Leo's humanism was far different from Erasmus's philosophy of Christ. Once in the papal chair he proved a bitter disappointment. The Medici pontiff turned out to be a big spender with an insatiable appetite for money with which to finance his carnivals, his art collection, and the hunt. Roland Bainton characterized him as "elegant and as indolent as a Persian cat."[17] He is reported to have said of the papacy, "God has given it to us—let us enjoy it." He thought nothing of squandering papal revenues on himself and his personal pleasures to enhance his family's fortunes. When he attempted to raise money at the Fifth Lateran Council for a crusade against the Turks, the Venetians were skeptical of the announced purpose of the assessment, suggesting that the funds would be used to finance his war against Urbino on behalf of his family. It is not surprising that Leo would dismiss Luther's attack on the traffic in indulgences that he was using to raise money as simply a quarrel between the Dominicans and the Augustinians. He was hardly able to understand the issues, much less deal with them.

Unfortunately, Leo was not unique in his incompetence or in his avarice. He was preceded by a string of unworthy men beginning with Innocent VIII, who was the father of sixteen illegitimate children whom he acknowledged openly. "Cynicism and corruption," writes Lewis Spitz, "corroded the moral fiber of the whole curia. The pope's vice-chamberlain was quoted as saying, 'The Lord desireth not the death of a sinner, but that he live and pay.'"[18] With or without Innocent's consent, some cardinals inaugurated a profitable enterprise by forging bulls to sell. At the same time Innocent proclaimed a papal bull calling for the extermination of the Waldenses.

Upon the death of Innocent VIII in 1492, Rodrigo Borgia (Alexander VI) bribed enough cardinals to insure his election, although he was living with his fourth concubine at the time.

While he was a man of few if any principles, his children brought the family further disgrace and ultimate ruin. His son Cesare apparently murdered Alexander's favorite son, Giovanni. Despite the fact that Cesare was a notorious criminal suspected of murder and assassination, he was archbishop of Valencia and a cardinal until 1498. His sister Lucretia became famous for her immoral escapades. Perhaps Alexander's greatest sin was his part in the excommunication and execution of the saintly Florentine reformer Girolamo Savonarola.

Julius II was Leo X's immediate predecessor. He followed Pius III, who lived to serve as the vicar of Christ for less than a year in 1503. Both Raphael and Erasmus immortalized the warrior pope—Raphael with his brush and Erasmus with his pen. As we have seen, Julius was a lover of art and a patron of artists. It was he whose vision of St. Peter's Basilica resulted in the St. Peter's of today. It was also he who convened the Fifth Lateran Council, but he died soon after, leaving the council in the hands of Leo X.

It is not surprising that with such pontiffs at the helm of Saint Peter's bark, thoughtful people began to view the church as perilously off-course, if not completely shipwrecked. In fact, Sebastian Brant says as much in *The Ship of Fools*. This was not the first time the church had suffered under the profligate leadership of the bishops of Rome, but now two things made a difference—the printing press and Erasmus. In his enormously popular *Praise of Folly* Erasmus articulated what multitudes must have been feeling about the popes:

> The only weapons they have left are the fine-sounding benedictions to which Paul refers (and these they certainly scatter around with a lavish hand) along with interdicts, suspensions, repeated excommunications and anathemas, painted scenes of judgement, and that dreaded thunderbolt whereby at a mere nod they can dispatch the souls of mortal men to deepest Tartarus. This the holy fathers in Christ, who are in fact the vicars of Christ, launch against none so savagely as those who at the devil's prompting seek to nibble away and reduce the patrimony of Peter. Lands, cities, taxes, imposts and sovereignties are all called Pe-

17. Bainton, *Here I Stand*, p. 74.

18. Cited in Spitz, *The Renaissance and Reformation Movements*, p. 53.

ter's patrimony, despite the words in the gospel "We have forsaken all and followed thee". Fired with zeal for Christ they will fight to preserve them with fire and sword, and Christian blood flows freely while they believe they are the defenders, in the manner of the apostles, of the Church, the bride of Christ, through having boldly routed those whom they call her foes. As if indeed the deadliest enemies of the Church were not these impious pontiffs who allow Christ to be forgotten through their silence, fetter him with their mercenary laws, misrepresent him with their forced interpretations of his teaching, and slay him with their noxious way of life![19]

Sources of Discontent

The rising tide of discontent was swollen from many sources. Erasmus's reformatory works stimulated others to express in print their suspicions of Rome and criticisms of its clergy. Among these works were Sebastian Brant's *The Ship of Fools,* Simon Fish's *A Supplication for the Beggars,* and the *Epistolae obscurorum virorum* (*Letters of Obscure Men*), written and edited at Erfurt by a group of humanists led by Crotus Rubianus. This work, designed as was *The Praise of Folly* to publicize the need of reform by pointing up the sins and foibles of the clergy, proved greatly inferior to Erasmus's work. However, the charges of ignorance, immorality, avarice, drunkenness, concubinage, simony, and nepotism brought against the priests, friars, and prelates—although sometimes grossly exaggerated—are quite well documented by ecclesiastical and legal records. For example, most of the vices delineated in *Letters of Obscure Men* were catalogued by Chancellor William Melton in a Latin sermon addressed to newly ordained priests in the diocese of York and later published (in 1510). His description of the clergy of his day constituted both a sharp rebuke of those who were guilty and a severe warning to the newly ordained:

For it is from this stupidity and from this darkness of ignorance that there arises that great and deplorable evil throughout the whole Church of God, that everywhere throughout town and countryside there exists a crop of oafish and boorish priests, some of whom are engaged on ignoble and servile tasks, while others abandon themselves to tavernhaunting, swilling and drunkenness. Some cannot get along without their wenches; others pursue their amusement in dice and gambling and other such trifling all day long.[20]

Other preachers such as Huss, Savonarola, and Johann Geiler von Kaysersberg denounced the ecclesiastics from the popes down. Such preaching had its effect—and its cost. By this means a grass-roots protest merged with a protest of the humanist elite in a growing demand for reform.

Perhaps the greatest source of scandal and resentment was the avarice characteristic of all ranks of clergy. Some cases, of course, were more notorious than others. One of the most celebrated was that of Richard Hunne, who was sued by his priest for the shroud of his deceased infant. Hunne had refused to surrender the burying sheet as a mortuary tax due the priest. When summoned by the ecclesiastical court, he refused to appear. Instead he countersued the priest in premunire for having taken him to a foreign court, whereupon Fitzjames, the bishop of London, accused Hunne of heresy. He was arrested and imprisoned in the Lollard's Tower. A short time later he was found dead in his cell, an apparent suicide. But an inquest determined that he had been murdered. His murder was traced to the bishop's bellringer and Dr. Horsey, the chancellor. Due to Wolsey's intercession, Horsey was allowed to plead not guilty and leave the city. According to John Foxe, "The mangled remains of the poor man Hunne were adjudged to be burned at Smithfield. To the disgrace of the church, the bishops of Lincoln and Durham, and many doctors of divinity and

---

19. Erasmus, *"The Praise of Folly" and "Letter to Martin Dorp, 1515,"* trans. Betty Radice (New York: Penguin Books, 1971), pp. 180–81.

20. Melton, cited in *The Reformation in England: To the Accession of Elizabeth I,* ed. A. G. Dickens and Dorothy Carr, Documents of Modern History Series (London: Edward Arnold, 1967), p. 15.

of the common law sat with the bishop of London on this case, so that the sentence was considered as the unanimous act of the clergy."[21]

The two aspects of the Hunne affair that Foxe thought made it a particularly despicable episode were the crude greed of the priest and the support of the English hierarchy. Although such incidents may not have been as common as sometimes supposed, the alienating effect of the practice of collecting mortuaries—*Todfall* in Germany and heriot in England—was undeniable.[22]

The length to which some priests would go to collect a mortuary is seen in the actions of Edward Molyneux, a parish priest at Sefton who in 1514 enlisted the help of armed henchmen to seize an ox belonging to John Cokeson, whose wife had recently died. Molyneux had the ox slaughtered. The following year, when Cokeson was taking his cattle to market, the priest seized thirty-eight of them and kept them for a month, during the course of which five died. Peter Heath continues the tale:

> By this means Molyneux extracted from Cokeson 40s. in cash and a bond that he would not sue at law under pain of another 20s. This wanton slaughter of Cokeson's ox and the rustling of his cattle was thus capped by a speciously legal agreement to deprive him of the right of complaint. Molyneux argued that Cokeson's wife and family had resort to the Sefton tenement and that when his wife died seven years before, the ox was surrendered by some of her family as the mortuary;

Cokeson, moreover, owed Molyneux and another as feoffees *L*3, but by the advice of the plaintiff's friends the rector had contented himself with 40s. The plaintiff argued that his wife did not die in Sefton but in Warrington, sixteen miles away and that in any case no mortuary was due for a covert woman in Sefton.[23]

The financial burden on parish priests may have driven them to all kinds of reprehensible acts, but the prelates were not immune from the same kind of greed. In order to increase their incomes they held multiple bishoprics, some *in absentia* which they rarely if ever visited. They were frequently guilty of simony and nepotism. Some, such as Thomas Wolsey, provided their illegitimate sons with various sources of ecclesiastical revenue, including bishoprics. There were surprisingly few protests against such practices until the Reformation. But as the Bible became available in the language of the people and literacy increased, the new literate laity and the Christian humanists began to differentiate between the divine right of kings and the divine right of prelates and priests.

It appears that with few exceptions (such as the Carthusians), the church everywhere had attracted to itself more than its share of unworthy, ignorant, and immoral priests, both secular and religious. If they were not a calloused and indifferent lot who sought the priestly office out of laziness or any number of less than commendable motives, they ceased to be challenged to improve themselves for the sake of their calling or the service of their flocks. Their ignorance may not have been as obvious as clerical concubinage, but it merely lay beneath the surface. Most priests had no university training. They had memorized enough Latin to say mass and perform other priestly functions, but they were severely lacking in any true knowledge of the Bible. Bishop Hooper's visitation records, made well after the Reformation had begun (in 1551), are illustrative of the point. Hooper's findings of 311 clergy in the diocese of Gloucester indicated that 168 were unable to repeat the Ten Commandments, 9 were unable

21. *Foxe's Book of Martyrs: Acts and Monuments of the Christian Church,* ed. A. Clarke (London: London Printing and Publishing Co., n.d.), p. 106.

22. Peter Heath describes the situation: "What items were due as mortuaries varied with local custom: the best beast usually in country parishes, often the best gown in towns, but not infrequently a sum of money. Although mortuaries formed a small, if significant, proportion of the clergy's income, they were usually a substantial expense for the person concerned. . . . No wonder parishioners, to preserve family wealth from clerical depredations, sometimes sold the best beast or chattel just before death. Trouble also arose when the incumbent preferred to take a cow, albeit the best beast, when the deceased left abundant horses or sheep, but few cows" (*English Parish Clergy on the Eve of the Reformation,* Studies in Social History Series [Toronto: University of Toronto Press, 1969], pp. 153–54).

23. Heath, *English Parish Clergy,* pp. 155–56.

to count them, and 33 could not locate them; 10 were unable to repeat the Articles of Faith, and 216 could not cite biblical references to support them; 10 could not repeat the Lord's Prayer, 39 failed to locate it in the Bible, and 34 did not know who the author was.[24]

Peter Heath's studied evaluation of the parish clergy in the early sixteenth century is revealing:

> Basically they were men who, if they read at all, read the wrong books; they were totally unaware of the New Learning even where it touched upon the very core of their faith, the life and values of Christ. Not only did they lack the modern guides to Christianity, the works of Erasmus foremost, they were rarely in possession of the very source of inspiration and contemplation, the Bible. Third unfamiliarity with this central work, the very Word itself, was emphasized by the evidence of their wills as well as by Hooper's findings.[25]

It is Heath's opinion that the situation of the clergy was no worse in England than in Europe in general but possibly much worse in Ireland, Scotland, and Wales. As Heath points out, bishops had a "myopic tendency" to regard any anticlericalism as heretical regardless of the justification. He continues, "Unfortunately for the bishops Lollardy was about to be supplanted by a far more dynamic challenge and the clergy were to be embarrassed by new circumstances and judged by more exacting standards."[26] An obvious reference to the Reformation, this statement brings to mind the dependence of the Reformation upon the Bible in the vernacular, a development for which the printing press was the indispensable agent.

Revival

On the Continent and particularly in Germany, a crude revival of religious enthusiasm was in progress. It was sparked by fear and characterized by credulity. As Lionel Rothkrug has shown, during the growing pilgrimage movement the Jews were the scapegoats and objects of perse-

cution more often than the Turks. The Turks were somewhat inaccessible but nevertheless feared as the scourge of Europe. The frenzied crowds went from one shrine to another. Those with sufficient funds could visit the shrine of Saint James at Compostela and Saint Michael at Monte Gargano as well as the holy places of Rome. On their return they would be tempted to stop first at the shrine dedicated to the Virgin of Meinrod at Einsiedeln in Switzerland and (after 1520) the shrine dedicated to the *Shöne Maria* (beautiful Mary) in Regensburg, Germany. However, most of the shrines were located in Germany, and most of the pilgrims were Germans. The shrines featuring the worship of the Virgin Mary were the most popular. Of these, the one dedicated to the *Shöne Maria* in Regensburg topped the list. It was here that the Jews had been driven out, and in the place of the dismantled synagogue a chapel had been erected. The worship of the Virgin Mary was a prominent part of this rather superficial revival of the Christian faith in its most superstitious and pagan aspects.

In the meantime the Bible was beginning to be read as never before. By the time of Luther's translation, fourteen Bibles had appeared in High German and four in Low German. With the appearance of Erasmus's Greek New Testament, the New Testament and shortly thereafter the entire Bible began to be translated into various European tongues. By the end of the sixteenth century the Bible had been translated into several different and successively improved versions in every major language in Europe. Thus the dream of Erasmus had come true. In his preface to the Greek New Testament (1516), Erasmus set forth the claims of the New Testament against those of Plato, Pythagoras, Aristotle, and Zeno. But if the New Testament is to be understood, Erasmus admonished, it must be approached with a devout and open heart. The New Testament can be understood by the weakest woman, he noted, but it also challenges the mind of the most profound philosopher. He expressed a longing for the Scriptures to be translated into all languages so that they might be read and understood not only by Scots and

---

24. Cited in Heath, *English Parish Clergy*, p. 74.
25. Heath, *English Parish Clergy*, p. 91.
26. Heath, *English Parish Clergy*, p. 191.

Irishmen but also by Turks and Saracens. "Would that, as a result, the farmer sing some portion of them at the plow, the weaver hum some parts of them to the movement of his shuttle, the traveller lighten the weariness of the journey with stories of this kind! Let all the conversations of every Christian be drawn from this source."[27]

In the process of exalting a knowledge of the Scriptures, Erasmus attacked Scholasticism and its dependence upon the subtleties of medieval theologians in contrast to the plain and simple words of Christ. He commended the worship of the living Christ that one may encounter in Scripture rather than the worship of places

where Christ may have been or the worthless relics associated with him. One should spend time studying the biblical languages rather than a "mongrel tongue under ignorant teachers." He also gave some instructions about how the Scriptures should be studied along with the principles of hermeneutics that he had long ago adopted.

Even though Erasmus was permitted to witness only the beginning of the Reformation, to a considerable extent it carried out his fondest hopes for such scriptural knowledge. Subsequently a new force had entered the world. What Wycliffe and Huss—and the Bohemian wars and the religious enthusiasm of the credulous masses—had failed to do, Luther and the Reformers did. Out of a society in ferment, because an Augustinian monk would not accept a substitute for God, a revolution began.

27. *Christian Humanism and the Reformation: Selected Writings of Erasmus*, ed. John C. Olin (New York: Harper & Row, 1965), p. 97.

Chapter VIII

MARTIN LUTHER: THE STRATEGY OF CONFRONTATION

For centuries before Luther, reform movements had flared up only to sputter and die or to linger on in beleaguered enclaves of harassed dissenters. After the eclipse of Wycliffe and Huss, the conciliarists, following the guidelines of their mentor, William Ockham, offered some hopes of reform, but these soon faded amid the hard realities of papal politics. In the writings of Erasmus, however, the smoldering sentiment of reform broke out once again into open flame. Yet the Reformation of the sixteenth century was ignited not by Erasmus but by Luther. Inevitably the question arises—Why? A part of the answer is fairly obvious. Erasmus was still committed to the Roman Church, which he longed to see cleansed but not destroyed. He feared the demolition squad that he saw closing ranks around Luther after 1520. Then, too, his solution to the problems of the church was that of the humanist—albeit a Christian humanist—who failed to see that the enormity of man's sin needed more than instruction in righteousness. Erasmus could provide the basic tools of reform, and he did, but he lacked the very qualities that Luther possessed, which to a considerable extent made Luther the reformer that Erasmus could never be.

In a sense Luther embodied many of the distinguishing marks of earlier reformers. He possessed the soul of a mystic and the earnestness characteristic of devotees of the *devotio moderna.* He was trained in Scholastic theology of the late medieval type. Thus he was no stranger to the teachings of William Ockham or Gabriel Biel. Strains of humanist thought are reflected in his writings, including an appreciation for the early Erasmus, whose antipathy for Scholasticism he shared. His vigorous and creative mind discovered a vital theology in a fresh appropriation of Pauline thought that he found echoed by Augustine. But Luther was more than the apparent compilation of all that he had encountered. Above all else the inescapable impression is that here was an honest monk seeking God in a medieval maze of misrepresentation with an intensity of purpose born out of the depths of human despair. His was an earnest soul that would not—could not—accept a substitute for God. Once he was convinced that God's forgiveness was his, he attempted to understand and with rare courage to implement his newfound faith.

As Thomas Lindsay, Gerhard Ritter, Roland Bainton, and others have shown, there is no understanding of the Reformation or of Luther's role in it without first recognizing that whatever else it may have been—or has been made out to have been—it was initially a theological revolution within the religious experience of a once-obscure Augustinian monk.[1]

Few have put the matter as well as Lindsay when he writes,

> Humanism had supplied a superfluity of teachers; the times needed a prophet. They received one; a man of the people; bone of their bone, and flesh of their flesh; one who had himself lived that popular religious life with all the thoroughness of a strong, earnest nature, who had sounded all its depths and tested its capacities, and gained in the end no relief for his burdened conscience; who had at last found his way into the presence of God, and who knew, by his own personal experience, that the living God was accessible to every Christian. He had won the freedom of a Christian man, and had reached through faith a joy in living far deeper than that which Humanism boasted.[2]

Since the fortunes of the Reformation were so much a part of Luther's pilgrimage, it is wise to carefully follow his life and examine those forces and experiences that helped to make him the Reformer he became.

MARTINUS LUDHER EX MANSFELD

Martin Luther was born in Eisleben on November 10, 1483. His father was Gross-Hans Luder, or Lutter, a man from a staunch peasant family of Möhra in the vicinity of Eisenach. His mother was Margaretta Ziegler from Eisenach. Shortly after marrying, the young couple had moved to Eisleben, where Hans had hoped to find work in the mines. In 1484 Hans had moved his family to Mansfeld in hopes of improving his fortunes. He finally did achieve a degree of success in the mining industry and a place on the city council, but only after years of struggle and hard work.

Life in Mansfeld for young Martin and his family was harsh by any standard. Poverty and hard work were their inescapable companions—almost as unshakable as the discipline and superstition characteristic of German home-life at the time. Life was also hard at school, which young Martin began to attend at an early age. (It is difficult to determine the exact age from the sources; he may have been only five.) In 1497 his father sent him to Magdeburg to attend a school conducted by the Brethren of the Common Life. This was apparently the *Domschule* (cathedral school) where Luther saw a complete Bible for the first time in his life—an experience that left an indelible impression upon him. Three more years of schooling followed at Eisenach before he was ready for the university. The *Georgenschule* compared favorably with the *Domschule* of Magdeburg. Apparently Luther did well in his studies here, developing into an excellent Latinist. During his Eisenach years he was befriended by two prominent families, the Cottas and the Schalbes. All in all the Eisenach years were among the most satisfying of Luther's youth. In later life he frequently referred to his "beloved Eisenach."

His father, who had already invested a considerable amount in his son's education, sent him to the University of Erfurt, one of Germany's oldest and most respected universities. Thus, using the name Martinus Ludher from Mansfeld, Luther entered the university in April 1501. His progress was rapid. In less than two years he had earned his bachelor's degree, and by 1505, his master's. The fact that Luther finished the *trivium* and the *quadrivium* in such short order is indicative of both his intelligence and the excellence of his Latin-school education.[3] Lu-

---

1. There are currently several differing interpretations of the Reformation, all of which cite supporting evidence. The position assumed here is that which considers the Reformation to have begun as a religious phenomenon but does not ignore the factors that primed the age for reform. Nor does this position assume that what began as a religious protest against certain abuses and practices of the medieval church remained primarily a religious movement in its every manifestation. This was obviously not the case. For other positions, see Peter J. Klassen, *The Reformation: Change and Stability*, Problems in Civilization Series (St. Louis: Forum Press, 1980).

2. Lindsay, *A History of the Reformation*, 2 vols. Edinburgh: T. & T. Clark, 1907), 1: 190–91.

---

3. As we have seen, this was the standard curriculum leading to the bachelor's degree. The *trivium* consisted of grammar, rhetoric, and logic; the *quadrivium* consisted of arithmetic, astronomy, music, and geometry.

ther's studies leading to a master's degree involved a thorough knowledge of Scholasticism. At Erfurt it was the *via moderna* of Ockham and Biel that commanded the field. Two professors at Erfurt, Jodocus Trutvetter and Bartholomeus von Usingen, were particularly effective in attacking the *via antiqua* of Thomas Aquinas and, by the same token, the philosophy of Aristotle. They reinforced their attack by citing ancient authors, both Christian and pagan. There is little doubt that Luther's disenchantment with Scholasticism began during his Erfurt years. Through a number of professors and visiting humanist scholars he also developed a love for the ancient Latin classics—a love so strong that when he entered the monastery, though he discarded all his other books, he took his copies of Virgil and Plautus with him.

BROTHER MARTIN

On July 17, 1505, Luther entered the Augustinian monastery. This marked an abrupt change in his career. Only a few weeks before he had begun the study of law in the university's law school. To celebrate the event his father had bought him a copy of the *Corpus juris*. Hans entertained great ambitions for his gifted son. There is no indication that he ever considered an ecclesiastical career for Martin. But the master-of-arts graduate of Erfurt, second in his class of seventeen (as Hans proudly related to his friends on the city council), had only recently returned to the university after spending a few days at home when the shocking news reached Mansfeld that the promising law student had become a monk. Martin had already made the decision before he told his parents about it. It appeared very final, and that is exactly how the twenty-two-year-old novitiate viewed it.

The year 1505 was the year of crisis for Martin. If he was going to make a change, the sooner he did so the better. While it was increasingly apparent to him that his interests lay elsewhere than in law, it was difficult for him to deviate from the plans his father had made for him. It took a conviction greater than the fear of disappointing his father to drive him into the

monastery. During the previous year Martin had faced death a number of times (though sources are not entirely clear on this matter). Two close friends of his had died, and he had almost died when his dagger ran through its worn scabbard and severed an artery in his leg. But the occasion that triggered his final decision was the thunderstorm that overtook him on the road from Stotternheim to Erfurt. A nearby stroke of lightning sent him sprawling, and in the moment of terror he made a vow: "Save me, Saint Ann, and I will become a monk!" A bolt of lightning was the sure sign of the judgment of God—every German knew this. However, one suspects, as Roland Bainton indicates, that the thunderstorm simply brought to a head what had been more than a fleeting thought for some time. Thus, as Bainton suggests, Luther entered the monastery for the same reason that countless others had before him: "to save his soul."[4]

Of the twenty-two cloisters in Erfurt, Luther chose that of the Augustinians, which was a short distance from the *Georgenburse,* where he had lived as a student. The Observantine branch of the Augustinian order was known for the sincerity with which the brothers pursued the monastic life. The Erfurt chapter placed a premium on scholarship. Some members of the order were also on the university's faculty of theology. Once Luther was formally admitted to the order, he was given his own copy of the Vulgate and began the study of Biel's *Canon of the Mass.* The novitiate year was spent getting accustomed to the endless round of prayers and the menial tasks, a regimen designed to induce a life of piety and humility. By the end of his first year Luther had satisfied the requirements of the novitiate and had taken his final vows. Another year passed, and he was ordained to the priesthood amid much fanfare in the presence of his father and twenty of his fellow townsmen from Mansfeld. It was a gala occasion despite his father's informal remark about disobedient sons, for which he cited Scripture. From

---

4. Bainton, *Here I Stand: A Life of Martin Luther* (Nashville: Abingdon Press, 1959), p. 34.

1507 to the spring of 1509, Luther was hard at work on the basic theological degree, *Baccalaureus Biblicus,* which he received on March 9, 1509. Little more than three years later, on October 18, 1512, Luther was awarded the doctor of theology degree from the University of Wittenberg, where he had also been lecturing on moral philosophy.

Luther's academic progress in one of the most exacting of disciplines was truly remarkable, especially in the light of the inner conflict that seemed always just beneath the surface. Luther himself indicated the source of his frustration: "I was myself a monk for twenty years and so plagued myself with prayers, fastings, wakings, and freezings that I almost died of the cold. . . . What else did I seek through this but God? Who else was to see how I observed the rules and lived such a rigid life?"[5]

Luther had entered the monastery to find God and salvation through the surest means known to medieval man—the cowl. But despite his most strenuous efforts, he had found neither. He exhausted all the means the Roman Church had to offer to relieve a burdened conscience, but all to no avail. He spent hour upon hour in the confessional confessing all the sins he could remember, but he was never sure he had confessed them all. Finally he declared that he did not love God but rather hated him. Little did he realize at the time that the God he could not love was but a caricature of the God revealed in Jesus Christ. Finally he was sent to Rome on business for the Reformed Order of the Augustinian Eremites. Perhaps his superior, Johann von Staupitz, thought the glories of the Holy City would cure the melancholy of his brilliant young friar. If so, his hopes were doomed to disappointment.

Luther did indeed go to Rome, and he turned his opportunity into a religious pilgrimage. Like hundreds of thousands before him, he visited the holy places, heard the remarkable stories of miracles and angelic dedications, and worked

hard to claim the promised indulgences. He said mass at some of the most sacred altars in Christendom. As a faithful son of the church, he dutifully crawled up the *Scala sancta* (Pilate's Staircase) at Saint John's in the Lateran, repeating the Lord's Prayer on each step and kissing each in turn. However, his diligent efforts to take advantage of all the spiritual benefits the Eternal City had to offer the believing soul brought no ringing affirmation of faith—as d' Aubigné claimed—but doubt. His own sense of sin was not alleviated. Instead, Luther, like Isaiah, discovered himself to be a sinner in the midst of sinners. In the light of reality Rome had lost its halo. He entered the city with reverent words on his lips: "O Holy Rome, thrice holy from the blood of the martyrs, I greet thee." In retrospect he said, "I went with onions and left with garlic."

By the time Luther received his doctorate from Dr. Andreas von Karlstadt, he had wellnigh exhausted every means the Roman Church had to offer to bring peace to a troubled soul. Try as he might, he could not shake the specter of an angry God or his own guilt when confronted with God's righteousness. The God of his childhood he could fear or even hate, but love—never. Luther was not exhibiting the malaise of the sick soul who takes masochistic delight in a morbid preoccupation with his own sins. Here was a young monk whose honest search for the living God would not be satisfied until he had found Him or convinced himself that God did not exist.

THE *TURMERLEBNIS*

The fall of 1515 found Luther at the University of Wittenberg, beginning to lecture on Paul's Epistle to the Romans after two years of lecturing on the Psalms. He had begun to read the Bible as a monk, but now he had to learn it in order to teach. Forced to grapple with the biblical text as best he could, he ran into difficulty in the very first chapter of Romans. His problem was that he persisted in superimposing upon Paul his own medieval concept of God. The vision of an angry God so blocked his under-

---

5. Luther, cited by E. G. Schwiebert in *Luther and His Times: The Reformation from a New Perspective* (St. Louis: Concordia, 1950), p. 150.

standing that he could not perceive what the apostle was really saying. Writing some time after the event, he gave his own account of what has been called the *Turmerlebnis* (tower experience), or "evangelical breakthrough":

> All the while I was absorbed with the passionate desire to get better acquainted with the author of Romans. Not that I did not succeed, as I had resolved, in penetrating more deeply into the subject in my investigation, but I stumbled over the words (chapter 1:17) concerning "the righteousness of God revealed in the Gospel." For the concept "God's righteousness" was repulsive to me, as I was accustomed to interpret it according to scholastic philosophy, namely, as the "formal or active" righteousness, in which God proves Himself righteous in that He punishes the sinner as an unrighteous person . . . until, after days and nights of wrestling with the problem, God finally took pity on me, so that I was able to comprehend the inner connection between the two expressions, "The righteousness of God is revealed in the Gospel" and "The just shall live by faith."
>
> Then I began to comprehend the "righteousness of God" through which the righteous are saved by God's grace, namely, through faith; that the "righteousness of God" which is revealed through the Gospel was to be understood in a passive sense in which God through mercy justifies man by faith, as it is written, "The just shall live by faith." Now I felt exactly as though I had been born again, and I believed that I had entered Paradise through widely opened doors. I then went through the Holy Scriptures as far as I could recall them from memory, and I found in other parts the same sense: the "work of God" is that which He works in us, the "strength of God" is that through which He makes us strong, the "wisdom of God," that through which He makes us wise, and so the "power of God," are likewise to be interpreted.
>
> As violently as I had formerly hated the expression "righteousness of God," so I was now as violently compelled to embrace the new conception of grace and, thus, for me, the expression of the Apostle really opened the Gates of Paradise.[6]

What the church and its sacramental system had failed to do for Luther, the Scriptures did. Luther now read Romans 1:17 in context with Romans 1:16. In the process his concepts of Christ, God, the sinner, and salvation were permanently altered. Luther discovered that Christ died for the sinner, not for sins in the abstract; and whether or not the sinner could remember all his sins was not important—for once the commitment to Christ has been made, continued forgiveness is a reality for the truly repentant. God became the heavenly Father who knows and who cares, and the sinful man who commits himself to Christ in faith is completely forgiven. At last Luther had found God—and, through the experience, forgiveness. Within Luther's mind and heart a most profound change had taken place, the implications of which he could not possibly have known in 1515. He first alluded to the *Turmerlebnis* as a wonderful experience when lecturing on Galatians as early as 1516-17.[7] Although the precise date of Luther's evangelical breakthrough is a matter in dispute, there is no doubt that it occurred.[8]

CONFLICT—1517

After Luther completed his lectures on Romans, he turned to Galatians, which served to strengthen his new evangelical theology. In the unforgettable year 1517, he delivered his lectures on Hebrews and published *The Seven Penitential Psalms with a German Exposition. The German Exposition of the Lord's Prayer for the Laity* and an exposition on the Ten Commandments followed. In September 1517 he prepared his *Disputation Against Scholastic Theology,* consisting of ninety-seven theses in which he attacked Aquinas, Aristotle, Duns Scotus, Ockham, and Biel. It is clear that in the light of his own maturing thought, his disenchantment with Scholasticism had become complete. Based upon his own careful exegesis of Scripture and

---

6. Luther, cited by Schwiebert in *Luther and His Times,* pp. 285-86.

7. Schwiebert, *Luther and His Times,* p. 286.

8. While most biographers of Luther highlight the *Turmerlebnis,* some, such as Richard Friedenthal (*Luther: His Life and Times,* trans. John Nowell [New York: Harcourt Brace Jovanovich, 1967]), completely ignore it or fail to understand its importance.

Martin Luther, whose Ninety-five Theses launched the Protestant Reformation RELIGIOUS NEWS SERVICE

From the pulpit of the Castle Church in 1516, Luther began to point out the dangers of indulgences. On February 24, 1517, he condemned them because, he charged, they encouraged sinning and furthermore they kept people from knowing God. This was like biting the hand that fed him, because the university was supported in part by indulgences dispensed by the Castle Church. Its collection of relics was one of the largest and most auspicious outside of Rome. Frederick worked unceasingly at acquiring more and more for his church and university. In fact, the church by a special papal dispensation was given the right to grant complete remission of all sins to those who would view the relics and pay the stipulated fee. November 1, All Saints' Day, was the occasion of its proclamation. The collection of relics in 1509 included 5,005 fragments, the viewing of which reduced one's time in purgatory by 1,443 years. By 1518 it is estimated that there were 17,443 pieces on display in twelve aisles. Included among them were such remarkable relics as a veil sprinkled with the blood of Christ, a twig of Moses' burning bush, and a piece of bread from the Last Supper. By 1520 the collection had grown—despite Luther's opposition—to 19,013 holy pieces. Those who viewed the relics on All Saints' Day and made the required contribution would receive from the pope an indulgence that would reduce time spent in purgatory—either by themselves or others—by up to 1,902,202 years and 270 days.

reinforced by the teachings of Augustine, his new theology was rooted and grounded in grace, for as he insisted in thesis 67, "It is by the grace of God that one does not lust or become enraged."[9] In his confrontation with Scholastic theology, Luther inserted a word of caution that indicated his suspicion that his theses could be interpreted as an attack upon the Catholic Church: "Nor do we believe we have said anything that is not in agreement with the Catholic church and the ancient doctors of the church."[10] Despite his broadside against the *via moderna*, Luther's theses went virtually unnoticed. Of course Frederick the Elector's university was new and, as universities go, insignificant. Therefore, it is doubtful that anyone outside of Wittenberg and a few Augustinian monks at Erfurt had ever heard of this professor of the Bible, now dean of the faculty of theology. But Luther's attack on the indulgence traffic was to change all that.

The indulgence system was based upon the concept of works of supererogation. In other words, according to medieval Roman Catholic teachings, Christ, Mary, and the saints had lived without sin. They had also performed a great number of good works, which were stored up in heaven. Because the ordinary Christian ends this life with more sins than merits, a penalty must be paid, the church insisted: the sinner must endure untold suffering in purgatory before being admitted to heaven. Thus it was necessary for relatives and friends of the dead to have mass said and to purchase indulgences in order to reduce the time spent in purgatory. The pope alone could authorize the sale of indul-

9. *Weimarer Ausgabe*, 1: 221 (my translation). In subsequent notes this work will be referred to as *WA*.

10. *WA*, 1: 228.

gences that transferred the merits of Christ and the saints to the credit of the living and the dead. The concept of the exchange of merits for money had apparently first arisen during the Crusades. It proved so effective that the church soon saw its possibilities for raising enormous amounts of money for various projects, and the sale of indulgences became very popular.

Even though Frederick the Wise took exception to Luther's sermons on indulgences, he did not attempt to silence him. However, Luther was on safer ground when he published his Ninety-five Theses, for they were against Johann Tetzel and his claims, which Frederick also opposed. On the surface Luther appeared to be writing against the abuses of the indulgence traffic, yet his charges constituted an assault upon the very foundations of the system itself. Tradition has it that he nailed the Theses on the doors of the Castle Church on the eve of All Saints' Day, October 31, 1517. This was prompted by two things: the sale of indulgences across the river from Wittenberg and his growing hostility toward the practice because of a genuine pastoral concern. For the awakened Luther, the use of indulgences could no longer be tolerated in silence.

It was a most strategic confrontation on Luther's part. He had chosen to speak out when the sale of indulgences in Germany was at its peak. Tetzel, a Dominican monk, had come to the vicinity of Wittenberg to promote their sale with all the trappings of an ecclesiastical circus. He had been forbidden entrance to Wittenberg by Frederick the Elector. But the prohibition did not prevent him from coming as close as possible to the town in order to entice the people of Wittenberg to purchase his wares. When he visited a town, Tetzel would usually begin his sales pitch by building a huge bonfire in the town square. Business was usually brisk. Most thought the proceeds were going to the announced object of the sales: the construction of the new St. Peter's Basilica. The fact that Tetzel was a known heresy hunter didn't hurt business either.

Behind the sale of indulgences for St. Peter's was the need of Albert of Brandenburg, a noble-

man of the Hohenzollern line, to raise enough money to pay back the Fuggers of Augsburg, who had loaned him the cash necessary for the down payment toward the purchase of the archbishopric of Mainz. The papacy had struck a hard bargain. Since Albert held two sees when technically, at the age of twenty-three, he was not old enough to occupy even one, Pope Leo demanded ten thousand ducats above the regular fee of twelve thousand. The Hohenzollerns were ambitious. They longed to possess the archbishopric because it was both the most prestigious and the most lucrative in Germany. But even they did not have the ready cash to pay for it—hence the request for the sale of a plenary indulgence in Germany. It was agreed that, after expenses, half of the money was to go to Rome for the construction of St. Peter's Basilica, and half to Albert. Tetzel, the most successful of all indulgence salesmen, was secured for this occasion. The fact that Albert was to receive a certain share of the funds raised was not general knowledge. Albert certainly never breathed a word of it to the public; on the contrary, he emphasized the deplorable condition of the bones of Peter, Paul, and the saints in Rome, and the dire necessity of protecting them with an appropriate building. This was the announced object of the sale—to finish what Julius II had started. Furthermore, those who purchased an indulgence for themselves would receive a plenary (complete) pardon of all sins, which meant that they would be restored to a state of innocence like that enjoyed immediately after baptism and would be relieved of all the penalties of purgatory. Those buying indulgences for relatives already in purgatory needed only money, since neither contrition nor confession was necessary. The actual price of the indulgences varied according to the ability of the customer to pay.

Tetzel and his colleagues were very successful. He usually preached a brief but emotional sermon in which he called upon his hearers to be "contrite, to confess, and contribute" for the sake of their dear dead relatives for, as he promised, "As soon as the coin in the coffer rings, the soul from purgatory springs."[11]

For more than a year Luther had become increasingly critical of indulgences, refining his criticism and strengthening his arguments. The Ninety-five Theses represent a final stage in this development. In the Theses Luther attacked the object of expenditures—the building of St. Peter's—as an unnecessary task, a waste of money, and robbery of the German people. He further suggested that if the pope were so concerned he could build the basilica out of his own money, since he was richer than Croesus.[12] He was hardly in a position to know that fifty percent of the proceeds were going to Albert of Brandenburg. He questioned the pope's power over purgatory: "The pope can remove only those penalties which he himself has imposed on earth. . . ."[13] However, his most serious assault was against the concept of a storehouse of merits provided by the saints upon which the sinner could draw. Luther's scorn for the concept that his holiness possessed a treasure out of which he could grant indulgences can be seen in the following quotations:

62. The true treasure of the church is the most holy gospel of the glory and grace of God.

66. The treasures of indulgences are nets which now fish for the wealth of men.[14]

His attack upon papal claims over purgatory could not help but sting when he put into the mouths of anonymous laymen this question in thesis 82: "Why doesn't the pope evacuate purgatory for the sake of holy love if he redeems an infinite number for the sake of mere money to build a basilica or for such trivial reasons?"[15] Luther's indignation reached the boiling point when he became convinced that the sinner who

trusted in an indulgence for forgiveness was utterly deceived and therefore damned.

In addition to nailing the inflammatory document on the door of the Castle Church, as tradition has it, Luther mailed a copy to Albert, the archbishop of Mainz. In his letter the Augustinian friar asked that the archbishop examine his theses and do something about the sale of indulgences before the disgraceful situation got out of hand. (In recent years the traditional story has been questioned, but whether the Ninety-five Theses were nailed up, or mailed, or both is not terribly important.)

Luther wrote his Ninety-five Theses in Latin. Several copies were printed in folio by Johann Grünenberg of Wittenberg and were translated almost immediately into German. Within two weeks they were known and read all over Europe, and within a month they had reached England. Worried about the possible damage to the sale of indulgences in Germany, Albert sent a copy to Pope Leo X. The pope was preoccupied with other interests, however, and did not take the matter seriously. At worst he viewed it as a quarrel between the Augustinians and the Dominicans. In retrospect this was a costly blunder, but few in Luther's day would have realized the significance of Luther's assault, for indulgences had come under increasing attack ever since the time of Wycliffe. But this time there was a difference: the attack was sparked by a new dynamic, Luther's "theology of the cross."[16]

CONFRONTATION—1518-1521

Once thoroughly aware of the damage Luther could do, Leo began to take steps to silence him. Apparently his primary concern was money. The Ninety-five Theses had a sobering effect on the indulgence market. As sales fell off, alarm in Augsburg, Mainz, and Rome

---

11. Another version of this popular jingle is found on a woodcut in the Lutherhalle in Wittenberg: "As soon as the money in the coffer rings/ Immediately the soul to heaven springs."

12. This was a reference to Marcus Licinius Croesus, 115-153 B.C. a name synonymous with wealth and luxury.

13. *WA*, 1: 233.

14. *WA*, 1: 236.

15. *WA*, 1: 237.

16. The *Weimarer Ausgabe* (1:233-38) contains a critical edition of the original Latin version. English translations abound. Most readily available is that by C. M. Jacobs in *Career of the Reformer*, 3 vols. (vols. 31, 32, and 34 of *Luther's Works*), ed. Helmut T. Lehmann et al. (Philadelphia: Muhlenberg Press, 1957-69), 1: 25- 33.

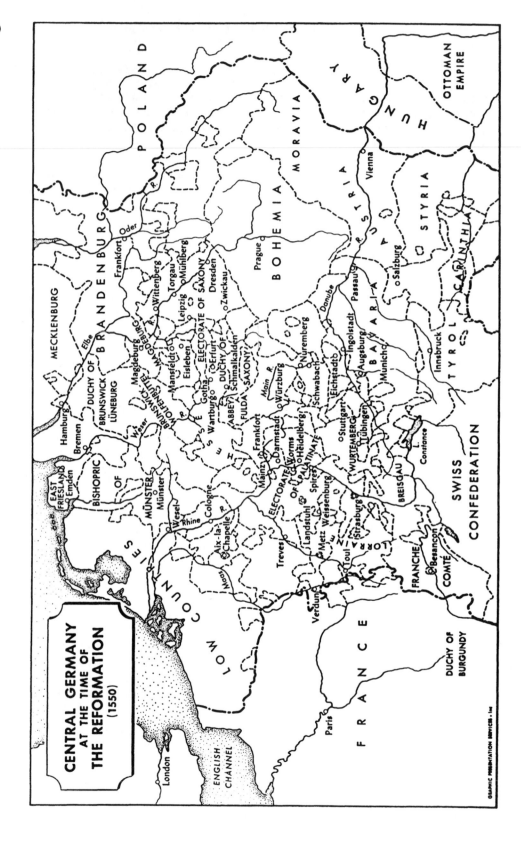

CENTRAL GERMANY
AT THE TIME OF
THE REFORMATION
(1550)

mounted. Seldom if ever had an academic matter had such repercussions in the financial centers of Europe. Although Luther proposed that the Ninety-five Theses be debated by competent theologians, it involved much more than academics or papal revenues. The whole medieval scheme of salvation as worked out by the Scholastics and taught by the church was implicated. The immense popularity of the Theses may have been due initially to the document's attack upon the money-raising scheme of a luxury-loving pontiff, but its lasting significance was due to the fundamental issues it raised concerning the nature of repentance, forgiveness, and salvation, to say nothing of the questions it raised regarding purgatory and the pope's power over the dead. All of this became increasingly clear even to Albert and Leo in the confrontations that followed.

Heidelberg, April 26, 1518

When Leo finally acted, it was with a gloved fist. He asked the newly elected general of the Augustinians, Gabriel della Volta (Venetus), to silence Luther. Volta turned the matter over to Luther's superior, Johann von Staupitz, vicar of the German congregation of the order. Luther was thus dutifully summoned to appear before the annual meeting of the German Augustinians at Heidelberg, scheduled for May. The moment of decision had arrived. Luther's closest friends advised him not to go. Tetzel had boasted that Luther would be burned at the stake—it was only a matter of time. Others were also convinced that the Dominicans could stop Luther, even in Heidelberg. Despite these ominous warnings, Luther was determined to go even if it meant "the cross."

Luther and a fellow Augustinian, Leonard Beier, set out on foot from Wittenberg on April 11. They were in Würzburg by Sunday evening, April 18. They rode the remaining few miles with friends who had also stopped at Würzburg en route to Heidelberg, arriving three or four days before the meeting, which was to begin on the twenty-fifth. On April 26, the day after the meeting convened, Luther presented forty

theses attacking Scholastic theology, which he called "the theology of glory." In contrast he set forth his "theology of the cross." In the process he made Aquinas and Aristotle responsible for misconceptions associated with a false theology and Augustine and Paul the main architects of biblical theology. These theses represented a refinement of the ninety-seven theses he had drawn up the year before at Wittenberg, published under the title *Disputation Against Scholastic Theology.* The occasion provided Luther with a perfect opportunity to reveal his rediscovery of Augustine. It was also clear that he was using the early church father to dethrone Aquinas. Even more evident was that he saw in Augustine an essentially Pauline and thus biblical faith, but in Aquinas he beheld the ghost of Aristotle, whom he had come to loathe.

The theses that Luther presented at Heidelberg were divided into two unequal parts. The first twenty-eight were theological, followed by twelve that were labeled philosophical. The latter theses constitute an attack upon Aristotle and Aristotelian philosophy. In the theological theses Luther set forth the major themes of his new evangelical theology. The law does not save, he claimed, but condemns. Man's will is not free but enslaved to sin. "Good works" are futile, because man can do nothing good in himself. He has no *potentia activa* but only *potentia subjectiva* (theses 14, 15).[17] "The theology of the cross" contradicts "the theology of glory." In commenting on thesis 21, Luther wrote,

> This is clear: He who does not know Christ does not know God hidden in suffering. Therefore he prefers works to suffering, glory to the cross, strength to weakness, wisdom to folly, and, in general, good to evil. These are the people whom the apostle calls "enemies of the cross of Christ" [Phil. 3:18], for they hate the cross and suffering and love works and the glory of works.[18]

---

17. *Luther: Early Theological Works,* trans. and ed. James Atkinson (Philadelphia: Westminster Press, 1962), p. 277. The Latin text of the *Heidelberg Theses* is found in *WA,* 1: 360.

18. Luther, *Career of the Reformer,* 1: 53.

Luther plumbed the depth of his own experience when he wrote about the personal implications of his "theology of the cross" in thesis
24:

> The truth of the matter is that whosoever has been
> brought to nought by suffering does not thereby
> do good works. On the contrary he simply knows
> that God is working in him and effecting every-
> thing. Therefore whether he is doing good works
> or whether he is not doing good works is all the
> same to him: he neither boasts if he does a good
> work nor is he ashamed when God is not working
> anything in him. Thus he knows that it is enough
> if he suffers and is broken through the cross, nay
> rather is utterly brought to nought. But this is
> exactly what Christ says in John 3:7: "Ye must be
> born again." If we are to be born again we must
> first die and be exalted with the Son of Man. I
> said, "Die," and that means to find death ever
> present in all experiences.[19]

With increasing feeling, which is evident
when one reads these theses today, Luther
echoed his tower experience as he placed good
works within the context of justification by faith:

> For the righteousness of God is not acquired by
> means of acts frequently repeated, as Aristotle
> taught, but it is imparted by faith, for "He who
> through faith is righteous shall live" (Rom. 1
> [:17]), and "Man believes with his heart and so is
> justified" (Rom. 10[:10]). Therefore I wish to
> have the words "without work" understood in the
> following manner: Not that the righteous person
> does nothing, but that his works do not make him
> righteous, rather that his righteousness creates
> works.[20]

Luther's presentation of his theses and Beier's
defense of them must have been electrifying. A
letter from Martin Bucer, who later became the
Reformer of Strasbourg, reveals something of
the feeling of those who were there and heard
Luther's enunciation of "the theology of the
cross" for the first time. His reliance upon Scripture, his courtesy in fielding questions, and the
courage with which he presented his position
appeared both admirable and convincing to
those who, like Bucer, became his disciples.

---

19. Luther, *Luther: Early Theological Works,* p. 293.
20. Luther, *Career of the Reformer,* 1: 55–56.

Of course, not everyone was so impressed.
For the first time those who were disposed to
accept or reject Luther's presentation caught a
glimpse of the enormous depth and power of
the new theology that underlay the Ninety-five
Theses. Before his fellow monks Luther had laid
bare his soul, disregarding the consequences. It
was now clear that Luther's quarrel was concerned not only with the "Holy Trade" but with
the Thomistic theology that undergirded the
entire sacramental system. The theological revolution that would spark the Reformation was
becoming increasingly evident.

Luther before Cajetan, October 1518

Since the Augustinians failed to silence Luther
or even to censure him, the Dominicans—led
by Tetzel, who had only recently been granted
a doctor's degree so that he could debate Luther—pressured Leo into initiating formal procedures against the unrepentant friar. Thus he
was summoned to Rome to answer charges of
heresy. Through the political maneuvering of
Frederick the Wise, Luther's prince, the city chosen for the hearing was changed from Rome to
Augsburg. Cardinal Cajetan, a Dominican and
the designated papal legate to the diet of the
German nation at Augsburg, was charged with
the responsibility of dealing with Luther. This
method of handling the problem more or less
satisfied all parties concerned—the pope, the
Dominicans, and Frederick; Luther was the one
least pleased. Frederick made a personal plea to
Cajetan to treat the Wittenberg professor fairly
and in a fatherly manner. He also instructed his
lawyers to assist Luther in his defense to insure
that the Augustinian monk would receive a fair
hearing before the Dominican cardinal.

The political situation facing Rome and the
diet was to Luther's advantage. Among his other
responsibilities, the cardinal was to enlist the
aid of the electors in mounting another war
effort against the Turks, who were still threatening Europe. However, the German princes and
electors were in no mood to launch a crusade
or even a campaign to raise the necessary revenues. It was evident that they were fed up with

Rome's financial exactions. To what extent this feeling was due to Luther's attack upon indulgences no one can say, but it was clear that the mood of the diet was favorable to Luther and his protest. Although Emperor Maximilian was opposed to Luther, Leo did not feel obligated to follow his desires in the matter because Maximilian was openly lobbying for his grandson, Charles I of Spain, to succeed him. The papacy stoutly opposed this strategy because of its designs on Naples, which Charles now ruled. Thus Frederick found himself in a good bargaining position. The papacy acceded to his request to move the hearing from Rome to Augsburg but rejected his wishes that Luther be heard by competent authorities before judgment was passed. However, no one really believed that papal policy ruled out the swift condemnation of Luther to the stake. For this reason Frederick refused to allow Luther out of the sight of his escorts until the emperor finally granted Luther a safe conduct on October 11.

Luther had just finished his *Explanations of the Ninety-five Theses* when he was summoned to Rome. He had been in the process of preparing it since 1517, and it had undergone numerous additions and revisions as his own insights and convictions had developed in the midst of intense study and haunting doubts. Once again he was called upon to put his life on the line and risk everything as an obedient son of the church. The danger Luther faced was no imaginary one: he would never be so close to the stake again. Once Luther was in Augsburg, Staupitz, his vicar and friend, arranged a series of interviews with Cardinal Cajetan.

The interviews took place over three days, from Tuesday, the twelfth, through Thursday, the fourteenth. Cajetan did treat Luther with the utmost kindness and courtesy, but he had no intention of giving the Augustinian monk a fair and impartial hearing. His instructions had been to obtain a recantation and, if this were forthcoming, to reconcile Luther to the church. However, Luther was not intimidated by the cardinal, nor was the cardinal impressed with Luther. Cajetan, a scholar in his own right, had prepared for the occasion. When Luther asked to be

shown his error, Cajetan answered that among Luther's errors was his denial of the treasury of merit as set forth in *Unigenitus,* the papal bull of Clement VI issued in 1343. At first Luther tried to interpret the concept in the light of his own position, but he found this a difficult task. Once again Luther asked that he be given a public hearing before competent judges or that his writings be submitted to the University of Basel, Freiburg, Louvain, or Paris for examination and evaluation. As Roland Bainton points out, this latter plea was a very undiplomatic one because it implied that Cajetan was incompetent to sit in judgment upon Luther. Doubtless this was the true feeling of the accused monk. Apparently no one in the Curia, least of all Leo, understood the depth of conviction out of which Luther had written his Ninety-five Theses or the profound difference between—to use Luther's terms—"the theology of glory" and "the theology of the cross." Luther wrote friends in Wittenberg that the cardinal was "no more fitted to handle the case than an ass to play on a harp."[21] But the cardinal was handling the case, albeit within certain limitations.

On the third day, in the presence of two lawyers provided by his prince, Luther presented a written document that left no doubt about his position. He stated quite flatly that the pope could and did make mistakes, that a general council constituted an authority superior to that of the papacy, that a sacrament without faith on the part of the one receiving it conveyed no grace, and that justification by faith had solid scriptural support. Luther's appeal was to the Bible as the Christians' supreme authority. The cardinal reminded Luther that Scripture had to be interpreted, and that only the pope was capable of this task. He went on to assert that the pope was above Scripture, above a council, and above everything in the church. But Luther would not be intimidated. He replied, "I deny that the pope is above Scripture. His holiness abuses Scripture." With this exchange the cardinal lost his temper and shouted that Luther

---

21. Luther, cited by Bainton in *Here I Stand,* p. 91

should leave and never darken his door again unless he were willing to say "*Revoco*"—"I recant."[22]

Once the stormy session was over, Staupitz had dinner with the cardinal and tried to patch things up, but the cardinal, whose patience was exhausted, was adamant. Staupitz next persuaded Luther to write a letter of apology for failing to give due respect to a prince of the church. However, neither Luther's letter nor the one that Staupitz wrote elicited a response. The signs were ominous. In a few days Staupitz released Luther from his vows to the Augustinian order and left town. Luther addressed an appeal to "Leo badly informed to Leo better informed" in which he claimed that his teachings were not heretical because they were based upon Holy Scripture: "I feel that I have not had justice because I teach nothing save what is in Scripture."[23]

It soon became obvious that Luther had nothing to gain by remaining in Augsburg. Rumors were rife. One had it that Cajetan's next move would be to arrest Luther and send him to Rome for trial. In the light of this rumor, Maximilian's safe conduct appeared to be no more valid than the one that Emperor Sigismund had given to John Huss a hundred years before. Luther was fortunate that Langenmantel, a canon of the cathedral, apparently had received some inside information. He sent a faithful servant to awaken Luther in the middle of the night on October 20 and rush him out a back gate of the walled city. Once outside the city, Luther was forced to ride a waiting horse, though he was wearing only his monk's habit, without pants or boots, and had no stirrups. The party did not stop until they reached Monheim some forty miles away. After a day's rest Luther was on the road again, and he reached Wittenberg by the thirty-first, a tired but grateful man. En route home he had seen at Nuremberg a copy of the orders to Cajetan authorizing his arrest at Augsburg.

---

22. Cited by Bainton in *Here I Stand,* p. 96.
23. Luther, cited by Bainton in *Here I Stand,* p. 97.

Once back in his study, Luther hurriedly wrote up an account of his experiences known as *Acta Augustana* (*Proceedings at Augsburg*) while the details were fresh in his mind. Frederick was in serious conversation with Cajetan on November 25, 1518, the day of its publication—hence its appearance was highly embarrassing to the elector. In spite of it all, Frederick was convinced that Luther had not been given an open and fair hearing. Therefore he still stood by the side of his professor whose theology was beyond him but in whose brilliance and utter sincerity he continued to believe.

The Leipzig Disputation, July 1519

The emperor of the Holy Roman Empire died on January 12, 1519, and papal politics immediately crowded into the foreground. This meant that Leo was to take a much more conciliatory attitude toward Luther than he had previously. In his determination to crush Luther, he was forced to reckon with Frederick, since he preferred as emperor the elector of Saxony to either Francis I of France or Charles I of Spain. It was a well-known fact that the electors preferred a German to a foreigner. Although a long shot, it was not altogether out of the question that Leo might have his way. Already by November 9 he had issued *Cum postquam,* a papal bull clarifying many of the issues that Luther had raised regarding the efficacy of indulgences. Karl von Miltitz, a German and a relative of Frederick, was appointed as a special assistant to Cajetan and given the delicate task of dealing specifically with Luther and bringing about a reconciliation.

Miltitz first met with Tetzel, whom he soon put out of business and allowed to retire in a monastery. Next he attempted to bribe Frederick with a golden rose, the traditional sign of papal favor, and a veiled hint that Luther might be in line for a cardinal's hat if he would only cooperate. Much to his dismay, however, Miltitz underestimated both Luther and his prince: neither would be bought or intimidated. He did get Luther to promise to discontinue the running battle with his critics if they would cease and desist—but therein lay the catch. At the time a paper debate was in progress between Johann Eck and Luther to which Karlstadt had become a party, championing the cause of Luther. The climax of this particular exchange of theses was the challenge Eck sent to Karlstadt to debate the issues raised by the whole controversy over indulgences, even though Eck's quarrel with Karlstadt had been over grace and the freedom of the will. In fact, it was not Karlstadt who had initiated the controversy, as everyone knew, nor were Eck's Twelve Theses of December 1518 confined to this subject. Rather, they involved the points at issue between Eck and Luther, particularly that on the origin and power of the papacy. Thus Eck's challenge to Karlstadt appeared to be a ploy whereby the proud and capable but unscrupulous Eck would have an opportunity to vanquish Luther in safe territory.

Leipzig, however, was something other than neutral ground. It was the heart of Ducal Saxony and a fierce rival of Electoral Saxony. The two Saxonies date from the time of the two sons of Albert I and Helena (the Hapsburgs). John, the older son, headed the Lauenburg line, while Albert II, the younger son, founded the Sachsen-Wittenberg line. Albert's Saxony became Electoral Saxony through a series of fortuitous developments. The rivalry between the two Saxonies had increased since Frederick the Wise had established his university at Wittenberg and Luther had brought both fame and students to the city. Leipzig, on the other hand, was historically conditioned to reject Luther and the Reformation. The Germans forced out of Prague by the Czechs had founded the University of Leipzig in 1409. Thus Leipzig was perfect for Eck's strategy. Its reputation for orthodoxy assured Eck of a sympathetic audience, and the fear of the Hussites gave Eck a decisive advantage. Eck really wanted to debate Luther, but that did not at first appear possible. Although the bishop opposed Luther's presence, Duke George insisted that theologians were of little use if they could not debate. Besides, he really wanted to know if Tetzel's jingle ("As soon as the coin in the coffer rings, the soul from purgatory springs") was true. It was Duke George who overruled the bishop and pressured the university faculty to host the disputation between Eck and Karlstadt.

Even though Eck's reputation as a debater had preceded him and Luther was well aware of the Ingolstadt professor's ability to clothe falsehood in attractive dress, Luther was determined to be heard. After all, had he not been seeking just such a hearing? For his expected role he had prepared diligently. The more he studied, the more apparent it became to him that the claims of papal supremacy based on the Pseudo-Isidorian Decretals rested on a false foundation. Through intensive critical-historical investigation, using the tools of textual criticism in the examination of the Greek text of the New Testament, he reached the conclusion that the church was founded upon Christ alone. Therefore the pope was not vicar of Christ but an imposter, possibly even the Antichrist or his apostle. In this frame of mind Luther went to Leipzig, making the trip in a wagon along with Karlstadt, his senior colleague, and Melanchthon, a recent addition to the faculty. Also in the company traveling under the safe conduct given Karlstadt and his party were Nicholas Amsdorf and Justus Jonas, accompanied by two hundred Wittenberg students, armed with spears and halberts, who walked beside the wagons. This seemed a necessary precaution because the safe conduct for Luther had not yet been issued. Even though Eck had not assured Luther that he would be allowed to participate in the oral battle, there is no question about Luther's readiness to confront Eck with the results of his studies. The Wittenberg professors arrived in Leipzig on June 24, 1519, a few days after Eck.

The disputation opened three days later with much fanfare. The opening address was followed by mass in St. Thomas Church and choir music prepared especially for the occasion, and still another address on theological disputations. The preliminaries ended with the choir of St. Thomas singing and the city band playing *Veni, sancte Spiritus* while everyone knelt. It was quite an auspicious beginning for what turned out to be a most pivotal event in Reformation history.

On the afternoon of the twenty-seventh,

Karlstadt and Eck faced each other. Eck had a rapier-like intellect and an extremely good memory. His ability as a debater was well known. He preferred the Italian method that allowed the debaters to interrupt, and charge and countercharge at will. The method initially adopted, however, was the German method, which allowed each debater thirty minutes for an uninterrupted presentation of his position, followed by a rebuttal from his opponent. But after two days in which Karlstadt relied greatly upon his sources for direct quotations from Scripture and the early church fathers, Eck, realizing how damaging the record would be, appealed to the audience, which sided with him in urging a change in procedure. When the debate resumed, all use of books and even notes was ruled out. This was all to Eck's advantage, and he made the most of it. With sarcasm, innuendo, and the usual misrepresentation of his opponent's position, he outperformed the careful and methodical professor from Wittenberg. To the immense satisfaction of most of the audience, Eck appeared invincible. This was exactly the scenario he had envisioned. Once he, the gifted controversialist, had demonstrated his superiority over Karlstadt, he was confident he could slay the "dragon" from Wittenberg. But the more astute members of the audience were not impressed. While Eck was admitted the master of extemporaneous speech and ready repartee, Karlstadt had gotten him to admit that in relation to divine grace and the will of God, man's will is no more than "a slave and a servant."[24] Apparently the debate on free will and grace had not been as one-sided as it had at first appeared.

On July 4, Eck faced an entirely different opponent in debate on a far more sensitive subject. Some time before, Eck had prepared Thirteen Theses, a revision of his Twelve Theses, for the occasion. He had spent the better part of the week debating thesis number seven on free will and grace with Karlstadt. With Luther he immediately raised the primacy issue as set forth in the thirteenth thesis (formerly the twelfth thesis), which reads, "We deny that the Roman Church was not over other churches before the time of Sylvester, but, on the contrary, we assert that he who possessed the seat and faith of St. Peter was always regarded as the successor of Peter and the general Vicar of Christ."[25]

In reply Luther went out of his way to be cordial and courteous, but he had no intention of accepting Eck's argument. Instead Luther began to present his evidence from Scripture, the early church fathers, and church history to support his contention that the church was founded upon Christ, not Peter, and that Christ, not the pope, was the head of the church militant. When Eck quoted the Pseudo-Isidorian Decretals to bolster his argument, Luther impugned them. In the course of his studies he had discovered by critical-historical analysis that the Decretals were forgeries and Rome's claims were likewise false. (Both Lorenzo Valla and Cusanus had, upon the basis of their independent research, questioned the genuineness of these documents, but their work was not available to Luther.) It became readily apparent to the alert that the Reformer was more than a match for Eck. Luther was Eck's equal in ability to recall from memory vast amounts of material, but his knowledge of Scripture was far superior to Eck's, and his commitment to truth was transparent. In the course of the debate on this one issue, which consumed five days, Eck said as much and even apologized for not being as well-prepared as Luther, but then, he pointed out, Luther was writing a book on the subject, and that explained why Luther's materials were better organized than his.

When Eck realized that he could not triumph in a fair skirmish, he decided to fight underhandedly. In a desperate move to label Luther a heretic, he accused him of being a Bohemian or at least one who could conceivably be called "a Saxon Huss." In fact, he charged, Luther's

---

24. Eck, cited by Schwiebert in *Luther and His Times*, p. 397. For a detailed account of the Leipzig debate, see pp. 391–417.

25. Eck, cited in *Career of the Reformer*, 1: 386.

position was that held by Marsiglio of Padua, John Wycliffe, and John Huss—all of whom had been condemned by the church. The implications were clear: Luther's call to be heard by a general council of the church could not but lead to condemnation also. In Leipzig this was a serious charge, and Luther at first denied it. However, he availed himself of the opportunity that the university library afforded to acquaint himself more thoroughly with the articles of Huss that had been condemned at the Council of Constance. Returning to the Pleissenburg when the issue of Huss's heresy was raised again, Luther suggested that not all of Huss's doctrines were wrong because some were undeniably Christian and evangelical. Eck had struck a telling blow in eliciting this most damaging admission from Luther. An eyewitness records the shock triggered by those words:

> One thing I must tell which I myself heard in the Disputation, and which took place in the presence of Duke George, who came often to the Disputation and listened most attentively; once Dr. Martin spoke those words to Dr. Eck when hard pressed about John Huss: "Dear Doctor, the Hussite opinions are not all wrong." Thereupon said Duke George, so loudly that the whole audience heard, "God help us, the pestilence!" (*Das walt, die sucht*), and he wagged his head and placed his arms akimbo. That I myself heard and saw, for I sat almost between his feet and those of Duke Barnim of Pomerania, who was then the Rector of Wittenberg.[26]

As Roland Bainton suggests, Duke George had not learned much about the release of souls from purgatory, but he had learned more than he bargained for about Luther's heresy. He decided that he had heard enough, and since the disputation had gone on for more than two weeks, perhaps he had. Before the debate was brought to a close, however, Luther and Eck continued the discussion on purgatory, indulgences, and penance. Finally, weary of Eck's habit of quoting Scripture out of context and numerous irrelevant sources in support of the

medieval church's teachings, Luther closed his remarks with this observation: "I grieve that the Holy Doctor penetrates the Scriptures as profoundly as a water spider the water; in fact, he flees from them as the devil from the Cross. Therefore, with all reverence for the Fathers, I prefer the authority of the Scriptures, which I commend to the future judges."[27] In a not-so-grand finale, Eck and Karlstadt resumed their interrupted debate on free will and grace. At the close of the debate, according to mutual agreement, the minutes were sent to the Universities of Erfurt and Paris for judgment. But the partisans of both sides had already decided who had won the debate.

It is difficult to overstate the significance of the Leipzig Disputation. In rejecting the Roman Church's teachings and claims, Luther took the boldest stand he had ever taken in public. His integrity had forced him to affirm the martyred Huss. His scholarship demonstrated that he had learned the lessons of Christian humanism well. At least he had been heard, and the younger humanists to a man rallied around him. While they sensed in Luther a spirit akin to their own, there was something more. They recognized and applauded his courage, and they recognized his commitment to the principles of grammatico-historical interpretation of Scripture fortified and clarified by the tools of the textual critic. But it was his God-consciousness, his utter devotion to the gospel of redemption as revealed in Christ and recorded in the New Testament, that most impressed them—and that provided the driving power of the new movement and filled the vacuum in Renaissance humanism. That which Erasmus had attempted with his facile pen, Luther was to do with his life.

THE FATEFUL YEAR: 1520

By 1520 Luther had left Wittenberg three times to stand his ground before his critics, and each time he had gone with fear and trembling and haunt-

---

26. Cited by Lindsay in *A History of the Reformation*, 1: 238.

27. Luther, cited by Schwiebert in *Luther and His Times*, p. 238.

ing doubts that Cajetan, Prierias, and Eck were not averse to reinforcing. The dangers lurking in the shadows were very real, but when the year 1520 arrived and he was still alive, he took heart. Apparently God was not done with him yet, he reasoned. Even though it was the year of his excommunication and of Erasmus's growing estrangement, it was also a year of unprecedented productivity for him. In the first six months after Leipzig, Luther wrote no fewer than sixteen treatises, amounting to about four hundred printed pages. And he did this in addition to attending to his preaching responsibilities, to his lectures at the university, and to the publication of his *Commentary on Galatians*. Thus his thought matured and his concepts were refined in the midst of conflict. His three Reformation treatises constitute the high-water mark of this development.

Exsurge Domine, June 15, 1520

"Arise, O Lord, and judge thy cause. A wild boar has invaded thy vineyard."[28] Thus began the introduction to *Exsurge Domine*, the papal bull published by Leo X against Luther. As Bainton suggests, Leo probably wrote only the preface and the conclusion—and that from his hunting lodge. He left it up to Cajetan, Prierias, and Eck to delineate which of Luther's errors were condemned. Of these there were forty-one. They make curious reading and indicate that even Luther's enemies were not agreed about what constituted error or the exact nature of the heresies involved. The list was marked by some glaring omissions. The indecision and the haste of Rome are both reflected in the document. The door was left slightly ajar, giving "the son of iniquity" sixty days in which to submit to the supreme pontiff or face excommunication, but it took the document three months to reach Germany.

Once a copy of the bull arrived in Wittenberg, the students and professors led by Luther made a

Opening paragraph of *Exsurge Domine*

festival occasion out of it. They built a huge bonfire into which they threw copies of the false decretals that Luther had exposed at Leipzig and the bull of excommunication. They also burned some of Eck's works for good measure, in retaliation for the burning of Luther's books in Cologne. Luther justified the action in this way: "Since they have burned my books, I burn theirs. The canon law was included because it makes the pope a god on earth. So far I have merely fooled with this business of the pope. All my articles condemned by Antichrist are Christian. Seldom has the pope overcome anyone with Scripture and with reason."[29] This action closed the door. On 3 January 1521, the bull of excommunication was published.

The Three Treatises

If the bull of excommunication did not mark the point of no return, the three little books that

---

28. See William Luck, *Reformation Documents* (Wittenberg: n.d.), p. xii for a reproduction of the title page and first page of the text. For the Latin text, see B. J. Kidd, ed., *Documents Illustrative of the Continental Reformation* (Oxford: Clarendon Press, 1911), pp. 75–79.

29. Luther, cited by Bainton in *Here I Stand*, p. 166.

Luther wrote in the autumn of 1520 did. The first, *An Open Letter to the Christian Nobility of the German Nation* (published in August), was politically oriented and designed to appeal to those caught up in the rising tide of German nationalism; the second, *The Babylonian Captivity of the Church* (published in October), was basically a theological treatise that attacked the church's sacramental system; and the third, *The Freedom of a Christian* (published in November), was a devotional treatise spelling out the practical implications of Luther's soteriology. The first two of the three tracts could be considered manifestoes of the German Reformation. The third arose out of somewhat different circumstances.

Luther wrote *The Freedom of a Christian* at the request of Karl von Miltitz. Miltitz was a German, the assistant to Cardinal Cajetan who had been assigned the task of reconciling Luther to the church. As a last-ditch effort, even after the bull of excommunication had been published in Germany, he persuaded Luther to write a devotional booklet to send, along with a conciliatory letter, to the pope. Luther complied and even agreed to date the letter September 6, which antedated the publication of the bull of excommunication in Germany. The booklet was written in Latin and breathed the spirit of medieval mysticism of *The German Theology*. Even here, however, Luther clearly enunciated his concept of justification by faith. It is particularly apparent in the discussion of the relationship between faith and works that concludes the book:

> Our faith in Christ does not free us from works but from false opinions concerning works, that is, from the foolish presumption that justification is acquired by works. Faith redeems, corrects, and preserves our consciences so that we know that righteousness does not consist in works, although works neither can nor ought to be wanting; just as we cannot be without food and drink and all the works of this mortal body, yet our righteousness is not in them, but in faith; and yet those works of the body are not to be despised or neglected on that account. In this world we are bound by the needs of our bodily life, but we are not righteous because of them. "My kingship is not of this world" [John 18:36], says Christ. He does not, however, say, "My kingship is not here, that is, in this world." And Paul says, "Though we live in the world we are not carrying on a worldly war" [II Cor. 10:3], and in Gal. 2[:20], "The life I now live in the flesh I live by the faith in the Son of God." Thus what we do, live, and are in works and ceremonies, we do because of the necessities of this life and of the effort to rule our body. Nevertheless we are righteous, not in these, but in the faith of the Son of God.[30]

It is difficult to summarize these booklets without doing Luther an injustice. Nothing else he wrote was more eloquent or constituted a more forceful presentation of his position than these forthright pamphlets. Even today, in translation, they convey Luther's emerging Reformation theology with remarkable potency. In *An Open Letter to the Christian Nobility*, Luther attacked the three walls that the "Romanists" erected around Scripture:

> First, when pressed by the temporal power, they have made decrees and said that the temporal power has no jurisdiction over them, but, on the other hand, that the spiritual is above the temporal power. Second, when the attempt is made to reprove them out of the Scriptures, they raise the objection that the interpretation of the Scriptures belongs to no one except the pope. Third, if threatened with a council, they answer with the fable that no one can call a council but the pope.

Luther demolished all three walls with his doctrine of the priesthood of believers, the basic concept of which is expressed in the following statement:

> Against the *first wall* we will direct our first attack. It is pure invention that pope, bishops, priests and monks are to be called the "spiritual estate"; princes, lords, artisans, and farmers the "temporal estate." That is indeed a fine bit of lying and hypocrisy. Yet no one should be frightened by it and for this reason—viz., that all Christians are truly of the "spiritual estate," and there is among

---

30. Luther, *The Freedom of a Christian*, trans. W. A. Lambert, in *Three Treatises* (Philadelphia: Muhlenberg Press, 1960), p. 311.

them no difference at all but that of office, as Paul says in I Corinthians 12. We are all one body, yet every member has its own work, whereby it serves every other, all because we have one baptism, one Gospel, one faith, and are all alike Christians; for baptism, Gospel, and faith alone make us "spiritual" and a Christian people.[31]

In *The Babylonian Captivity of the Church,* Luther launched an attack on the seven sacraments and the entire Roman sacramental system, which he held was based upon Thomas Aquinas and his misuse of Aristotle. In the place of the seven sacraments he supported at this point in his development only three: baptism, the Lord's Supper, and penance. He was most concerned to set forth his theology of the mass against the prevailing Roman Catholic teaching.

A sixteenth-century woodcut depicting a communion service in which Luther (left) and Huss serve both bread and wine to the House of Saxony. In this way the artist links Luther with the discredited Huss.
RELIGIOUS NEWS SERVICE

<hr>

31. Luther, *An Open Letter to the Christian Nobility,* trans. Charles M. Jacobs, in *Three Treatises,* pp. 13–14.

While he denied the miracle of transubstantiation and the distinction between substance and accidents, he affirmed the "real presence" of Christ in the bread and the wine. He also denied that the mass was in any sense a sacrifice but rather declared the Lord's Supper a "Testament." Faith, he said, was the indispensable element in the efficacious reception of this sacrament. Conscious of the similarity of his position to that of Wycliffe and Huss, he argued for its validity as the only biblical understanding, regardless of others who may have held similar views.

In 1520 Luther apparently believed that the primitive mode of baptism involved immersion, for this is the term he repeatedly uses. Even though he immersed his first son, Hans, he evidently abandoned the practice shortly after that baptism. He also reduced the sacraments to two and thus defined the empirical church as present "where the Word is preached and the sacraments are properly observed."[32]

In *The Freedom of a Christian* Luther took the paradoxical assertions that "A Christian is a perfectly free lord of all, subject to none" and "A Christian is a perfectly dutiful servant of all, subject to all," and worked out an exposition of the relationship of faith and works. In regard to faith he wrote,

Faith alone is the saving and efficacious use of the Word of God, according to Rom. 10[:9]: "If you confess with your lips that Jesus is Lord and believe in your heart that God raised him from the dead, you will be saved." Furthermore, "Christ is the end of the law, that everyone who has faith may be justified" [Rom. 10:4]. Again, in Rom. 1[:17], "He who through faith is righteous shall live." The Word of God cannot be received and

<hr>

32. William Mueller, *Church and State in Luther and Calvin* (Nashville: Broadman, 1954), p. 16. Also see article eight of the Augsburg Confession. In Luther the universal church is hidden but becomes visible under the proclamation of the Word and the proper observance of the sacraments. This is clearly enunciated in "Concerning the Ministry," in *Church and Ministry,* 2 vols. (vols. 40 and 41 of *Luther's Works*), trans. Conrod Bergendoff, ed. Helmut T. Lehmann (Philadelphia: Muhlenberg Press, 1958–66), 2: 21–28). One of the most incisive studies of Luther's ecclesiology is found in William Mueller's *Church and State in Luther and Calvin,* pp. 5–35.

cherished by any works whatever but only by faith. Therefore it is clear that, as the soul needs only the Word of God for its life and righteousness, so it is justified by faith alone and not any works; for if it could be justified by anything else, it would not need the Word, and consequently it would not need faith.[33]

In this devotional work Luther did not mean to imply that a Christian is free to live a life of wanton sinfulness because he is justified but rather that the new man in Christ lives no longer to himself or for himself but in Christ and for his neighbor:

We conclude, therefore, that a Christian lives not in himself, but in Christ and in his neighbor. Otherwise he is not a Christian. He lives in Christ through faith, in his neighbor through love. By faith he is caught up beyond himself into God. By love he descends beneath himself into his neighbor. Yet he always remains in God and in his love. . . . [34]

While it was evident even to Luther's contemporaries that the foundation of a new church was being laid, there was still one last appeal—to Emperor Charles V. Since his election in June 1519 as emperor of the Holy Roman Empire Charles had been too busy to deal with Luther, but that time would soon end, and Frederick the Elector, who seems never to have ceased in his efforts to secure a fair hearing for his professor, was determined to make the most of it.

THE DIET OF WORMS—1521

As great as the gap now appeared to be between Luther and Rome, there was still a chance for a reprieve, thanks to the tireless efforts of Frederick the Wise. The elector made it possible for Luther to appear before the diet of the German nation to be held at Worms in 1521. Frederick used the plea that Luther had not yet been heard by competent theologians and stood condemned without a fair hearing as a lever to secure a hearing before the diet for his contro-

versial professor. The fact that Frederick was the uncle of Charles V probably clinched the matter. Yet one wonders if the young emperor were not curious enough to want to hear Luther for himself.

Once again Luther set out for an appointment from which he did not expect to return. On April 16, after a long, hard journey from Wittenberg, he arrived in Worms with a few companions. Although he arrived at the dinner hour, about two thousand people ran out to greet him and escort him into the town. On the following day Luther was led into the presence of the emperor, the electors, and the representatives of ecclesiastical and civil authorities. J. A. Froude has called Luther's stand at Worms "one of the finest—perhaps the finest[—]scene in human history."[35] This may be an exaggeration, but Luther's appearance at Worms was doubtless one of the most significant moments in the entire sixteenth century. Here an excommunicated monk stood his ground before the most impressive symbols of power ever assembled for such an occasion and refused to compromise his convictions.

The first hearing was brief and inconclusive. A stack of Luther's books had been placed on a bench, and he was asked if they were all his. Before he could answer, Jerome Schurff, professor of canon law from Wittenberg, shouted, "Let the titles be read!" This done, Luther replied, in a voice subdued and hardly above a whisper, "The books are all mine, and I have written more." Luther's admission was sufficient to seal his doom, but the representative of the archbishop of Trier, who was doing the questioning, probed further. "Do you defend them all, or do you care to reject a part?" he asked. "To say too little or too much would be dangerous," Luther answered. "I beg you, give me time to think it over." To the amazement of the assembled dignitaries, the emperor granted Luther's request, giving him until the next day.[36]

On the following day (April 18) the diet met

33. Luther, *The Freedom of a Christian*, p. 280.
34. Luther, *The Freedom of a Christian*, p. 309.

35. Froude, cited in Gordon Rupp, *Luther's Progress to the Diet of Worms* (New York: Harper & Row, 1964), p. 97.
36. Luther, cited by Bainton in *Here I Stand*, p. 183.

in a larger assembly hall because so many wanted to hear Luther for themselves. The interrogator—Eck by name (not Dr. Johann Eck of Ingolstadt)—repeated the question of the previous day. Luther, who had apparently spent a restless night going over and over his answer, now responded without faltering.

He began his defense by addressing the audience in all humility: "Most illustrious and most mighty emperor, very illustrious princes, most gracious lords. . . ."[37] Next he asked their forbearance, noting that he was not accustomed to addressing men of such exalted ranks since he was only a monk. Then he turned to address his interrogator, first repeating the affirmation of the day before, and proceeded to enlarge upon the answer. "As to the second point," he declared, " . . . please to note that my books are not all of the same kind."[38] This was a thoughtful strategy. With this tactic Luther heightened the audience's curiosity and gained the right to speak. He then proceeded, for the sake of analysis, to place his books into three categories. The first included books that addressed themselves to the practical needs of the Christian life. They were devotional in nature and universally appreciated. To condemn these books, he claimed, would be to condemn those for which both friend and foe had expressed appreciation.

The second category, Luther insisted, included books that condemned the papacy in its abominable errors, along with a corrupt Curia and the unjust canon law—all of these had placed an intolerable burden upon the German people. Although the appeal to the rising tide of German nationalism was transparent, the thrust of Luther's argument here was that he had spoken out against the Roman Church in its attempt to enforce its very human laws upon the German people in violation of their consciences. How could he retract the charges

when to do so would surely increase the Roman tyranny in a wretched land?

In the third category were books he had written against certain individuals whom he perceived were enemies of the gospel. He admitted that he had at times been too caustic and sharp in his attacks, but that it was jealousy for the cause of Christ that compelled him to react in such a fashion. Therefore, he could not find it in his heart to retract those works any more than the others.

Luther then appealed to his subdued audience to point out his errors on the basis of Scripture. He expressed his willingness to recant if shown his error: "I shall be only too willing and ready to renounce all my errors; and I shall be the first to want to consign my little books to the flames."[39]

Since Eck had been waiting for just such an opportunity to make a speech, he countered with gusto, claiming that Luther's books contained the errors of the Beghards, the Waldenses, the Poor Men of Lyons, Wycliffe, and Huss, among others. Since all these errors had already been condemned by various councils, he claimed there was no point in reopening questions pertaining to these points. He asked if Luther thought that he alone understood Scripture, then hastened to add that he was not there to dispute with him. "I must again and again insist and demand that you give your answer sincerely, frankly, unambiguously, and without horns," said Eck. "Do you choose, or do you not choose, to revoke and retract your books and the errors which they contain . . . ?"[40]

Luther's reply was forthright and incredibly courageous:

Since then your serene Majesty and your lordships request a simple reply, I will give it without horns and hoofs, and say: Unless I am convinced by the testimony of Scripture or by plain reason (for I believe in neither the pope nor in councils alone, for it is well-known, not only that they have erred,

37. Luther, cited in *Reformation Writings of Martin Luther,* 2 vols., ed. Bertram Lee Woolf (London: Lutterworth Press, 1956), 2: 144.

38. Luther, cited in *Reformation Writings of Martin Luther,* 2: 145.

39. Luther, cited in *Reformation Writings of Martin Luther,* 2: 149.

40. Eck, cited in *Reformation Writings of Martin Luther,* 2: 155.

but also have contradicted themselves), I am mastered by the passages of Scripture which I have quoted, and my conscience is captive to the Word of God. I cannot and will not recant, for it is neither safe nor honest to violate one's conscience. I can do no other. Here I take my stand, God being my helper. Amen.[41]

A few days later, on April 24, a committee began the futile attempt to break Luther down. This was a more difficult situation. The atmosphere was cordial, even friendly, but the discussions accomplished nothing because Luther's antagonists failed to deal with the issues. Even though he had come to Worms under an assurance of safe conduct by the emperor, the German peasants were not taking any chances. They let their presence be known by posting placards all over the city displaying the symbol of the *Bundschuh*.[42] The message was ominous: if Luther were harmed, the emperor would be held accountable. After Luther left the city, Jerome Aleander, a papal agent, prepared the Edict of Worms, which the emperor called upon the electors to sign. The edict condemned Luther for his alleged errors and gave him twenty-one days (from April 15) of safe conduct, after which he was to be regarded as a convicted heretic: "When the time is up, no one is to harbor him. His followers also are to be condemned. His

books are to be eradicated from the memory of man."[43]

The edict was dated May 6, but it was not signed until May 26. Two of the electors, Frederick the Wise of Saxony and Ludwig of the Palatinate, refused to sign it. Aleander and his party were elated, however, because at last the emperor had declared Luther a *Vogelfreis* (outlaw), which meant that he could be murdered on sight.

Luther left Worms on April 26, a month before the edict was signed. At Eisenach his traveling party divided into two different groups because Luther had decided to visit his grandmother and the family of his Uncle Heinz in Moehra. As they were returning from Moehra through the Thuringian Forest on the road to Gotha, the travelers were attacked by four or five unknown assailants. Luther was wrestled to the ground, blindfolded, put on a horse, and led away in the darkness of the night to the Wartburg, a castle owned by Frederick high on a hill overlooking Eisenach. When word leaked out that Luther had been kidnapped, his friends were sure the Catholics had done the deed; the Catholics thought the same. From the beginning Luther resented the protective custody provided by his sagacious prince. Nevertheless, it provided a needed interlude. The strategy of confrontation had ended in exile for Luther. Indignant, he protested that he had been thrice excommunicated—first by Staupitz, then by the pope, and finally by the emperor—but he had not been refuted, if he had even been heard—and he would be heard.

---

41. Luther, cited in *Reformation Writings of Martin Luther*, 2: 155.

42. The banner of the *Bundschuh* carried the religious symbols of the Virgin Mary, the cross, and the kneeling peasant. A peasant's shoe also adorned the banner.

---

43. Cited by Bainton in *Here I Stand*, p. 189.

Die Epistel sanct Pauli zu den Romern.

Das Erst Capitel.

I

Unter-
schrifft

Aulus eyn knecht Jhe-
su Christi : beruffen zum
Apostel / ausgesondert zu predigen
das Euangelion gottis (wilchs er
zuuor verheyssen hat / durch seyne
propheten / yn der heyligen schrifft /
von seynem son / der yhm geporn ist
von dem samen Dauid / nach dem
fleysch / vñ krefftiglich erweyset eyn
son gottis / nach dem geyst der do
heyliget / sint der zeyt er aufferstan-
den ist von den todtenn / nemlich /
Jhesus Christ vnser her / durch wil-
chen wyr haben empfangenn gnad
vñ Apostel ampt vnter alle heyden /
den gehorsam des glawbens auffzurichten / vnter seynê namen / wil-
cher yhr zum teyl auch seyt / die da beruffen sind von Jhesu Christo)

(Nach dê geyst ic.)
Der geyst gottis ist
geben nach Chri-
stus auffart / von da
an / heyliget er die
Christen vnd ver-
kleret Christum in
aller welt / das er
gottis son sey / mit
aller macht / ynn
worte / wunder vñ
zeychen.

Uberschri-
fft.

Allen die zu Rom sind / den liebsten gottis / vñ beruffnen heyligê.

Grus.

Gnad sey mit euch vnd fride von got vnserem vater vnd dem herrn
Jhesu Christo.

Erbietüg.

Auffs erst / danck ich meynem got / durch Jhesu Christ / ewr aller
halben / das man von ewrem glawben ynn aller welt sagt. Deñ got
ist meyn zeuge / wilchem ich diene ynn meynem geyst / am Euange-
lio von seynem son / das ich on vnterlaß ewr gedenck / vnnd alletzeyt
ynn meynem gepet flehe / ob ich yhe der mal eyns eynen fertigen weg
haben mocht durch gottis willen zu euch zukomen. Denn mich ver-
langet euch zusehen / auff das ich euch mitteyle etwas geystlicher ga-
be euch zustercken (das ist) das ich sampt euch trostet wurde durch
ewren vnd meynen glawben / den wyr vnternander haben.

Ich wil euch aber nicht verhalten / lieben bruder / das ich myr offt
hab furgesetzt zu euch zukomê / byn aber verhyndert bißher / das ich
etwas guttis schaffete auch vnter euch / gleych wie vnter andern heyden. Ich byn eyn schuldner beyde der kriechen vnnd der vnkriechen /
beyde der weysen vñ der vnweysen / darumb / so viel an myr ist / byn
ich geneygt / auch euch zu Rom das Euangelion zupredigen.

Denn ich scheme mich des Euangelion von Christo nicht / denn
es ist eyn krafft gottis / die da selig macht / alle / die dran glewbenn /
die Juden furnemlich / vñ auch die Kriechê / syntemal dryñe offin-
bart wirt die gerechtickeyt die fur got gilt / wilche kompt auß glawben ynn   a

First page of Paul's Letter to the Romans in Luther's *September Bibel*

Chapter IX

NEW WINESKINS
FOR NEW WINE

lthough Luther found himself in exile and his activities severely curtailed against his wishes, he made the best of a bad situation. Chafing under Frederick's restraints, at first he complained that he would rather "burn on live coals than rot here."[1] He found unbearable the prospect of wasting away in the elector's abandoned castle, ignored by his colleagues and forgotten by his enemies. But after some reflection he began to see, ever so faintly, the hand of God in his misfortunes. At least he was alive—although plagued by the infirmities of the flesh (constipation and insomnia)—and safe from his enemies. At least he had time to study, think, and write. Since he was relieved of his preaching and lecturing responsibilities, his pen became the means by which he continued to spark the Reformation from his "Patmos." A glimpse into this aspect of his Wartburg exile is caught in a letter he wrote to a friend in Strasbourg:

> It would not be safe to send you my books, but I have asked Spalatin to see to it. I have brought

out a reply to Catharinus and another to Latomus, and in German a work on confession, expositions of Psalms 67 and 36, a commentary on the Magnificat, and a translation of Melanchthon's reply to the University of Paris. I have under way a volume of sermons on the lessons from the epistles and Gospels. I am attacking the Cardinal of Mainz and expounding the ten lepers.[2]

After the rather decisive events of Worms, Luther could not beguile himself into thinking that he was still a Roman Catholic. His mind invariably turned to the needs of the church in Saxony, and it was inconceivable to him that a German church could prosper or long exist without a fresh translation of the Scriptures into the German language. It was also apparent to him that the new German Bible would have to be something other than a translation of the Latin Vulgate. There were already fourteen editions in High German and three in Low German—and still another in Low German had appeared just before Luther's New Testament. But these editions were quite inadequate, and Luther found them unacceptable. They frequently contained errors of all kinds and unforgivably poor sentence structure. They were also quite elaborate publications, and consequently

---

1. Luther, cited by Roland H. Bainton in *Here I Stand: A Life of Martin Luther* (Nashville: Abingdon Press, 1959), p. 195.

2. Luther, cited by Bainton in *Here I Stand,* p. 197.

Luther working at Wartburg Castle RELIGIOUS NEWS SERVICE

were expensive.³ Luther felt that no new German edition of the New Testament could ignore the appearance of Erasmus's second edition of the Greek New Testament and his Latin translation of 1519.

THE *SEPTEMBER BIBEL*

By September 1522 Luther, with the help of Melanchthon and Spalatin, had succeeded in

seeing through the press his translation of the New Testament. He had completed the initial translation in less than three months while he was still at the Wartburg. Doubtless he had felt the need for a new German translation long before this time. In fact, earlier he had translated certain sections from the Vulgate into the German, and in 1514 he had begun to give serious attention to improving his knowledge of the Greek language. After the appearance of Erasmus's New Testament in 1516, he had become increasingly conversant with the Greek text. Luther revealed his intention to translate the New Testament into German in a December letter to Johann Lang of Erfurt, in which he told Lang, "I plan to write the Postil [Matt. 2:1-2] and to translate the New Testament into the vernacular, which our friends desire."⁴ By March he had

3. For a detailed discussion of these Bibles, see Kenneth A. Strand, *German Bibles Before Luther* (Grand Rapids: Eerdmans, 1966). In his *Luther's German Bible*, Johann Reu writes, "We have to read chapter after chapter in the German Bible of the middle ages with its terrible poverty of expression, its unbearable monotony and its pathetic helplessness, and then turn to Luther's version in order to appreciate the richness and delicacy of the language of his German Bible" (cited in Kenneth A. Strand, *Luther's "September Bible" in Facsimile* [Ann Arbor, Mich.: Ann Arbor Publishers, 1972], p. 11 of the appendix).

4. Luther, cited by Strand in *Luther's "September Bible,"* Part II, p. 2.

completed the first draft, but much hard work remained before the manuscript was ready for the printer.

Once back in Wittenberg and free of the problems that had demanded his immediate attention, Luther turned once again to the revision of his first draft. This time his efforts were reinforced by those of his colleagues. The final product, however, was the result of Luther's genius. Luther was a master of his native tongue—in fact, it is now recognized that through his work as translator he created the modern German language, which, as Albert Hyma writes, "is a tremendous feat, worthy of untold eulogy."[5] Once the New Testament appeared in print, it was subjected to severe criticism by Luther's antagonists, who claimed that his was not a literal translation. Rather, they pointed out, Luther had inserted words that were not in the Greek or the Latin texts. They cited Romans 3:28 as a case in point. Here the text reads that "a man is justified by faith apart from the works of the Law," but Luther had added to the phrase "justified by faith" the word "alone" (*allein*). Luther responded by pointing out that while the word *allein* was not in the Greek, the meaning was, and "the word belongs there if the translation is to be clear and strong. I wanted to speak German, not Latin or Greek, since I had undertaken to speak German in the translation."[6] While Luther was intent on translating meaning, not words, so that the most ordinary of Germans—i.e., the "mother in the home, the children on the street, the common man in the market-place"—might hear or read and understand, he was not unaware of the translator's responsibility to be true to the biblical text, and for this reason he explained, "I have not disregarded literal meanings too freely, but with my helpers, I have been very careful to see that when a passage is important, I have kept the literal meaning, and not departed freely from it."[7]

It has long been a matter of controversy whether Luther's work was really an original translation of the Greek text or simply a compilation of earlier German versions informed by the Latin Vulgate. Albert Hyma, Heinz Bluhm, Johann Reu, A. Freitag, and Kenneth Strand, to name only a few, have made these questions the object of careful investigation. They have found indications that Luther relied on Erasmus's Greek text both for his organization and for the disputed and controversial passages. But they have also uncovered evidence that he used the Vulgate and possibly the Zener German Bible (ca. 1475) as well as the Loberger Bible of 1483. Bluhm detects a fundamental difference between Luther's Postil on Matthew 2:1–12 and his translation of the New Testament. The Postil is a translation of the Vulgate, whereas his New Testament, especially the earliest edition, shows a basic dependence in its word order upon the Greek text. How carefully Luther selected his words and refined his style may be seen in a comparison of the 1522 edition with the 1546 edition. As Reu has pointed out, Luther deliberately moved the verb closer to the subject in many sentences so that those who were unable to read the text and so could only listen to a reading of it could get a better grasp of the meaning than would have been possible if he had retained the older, more traditional German style. He also added verve and force to the German text by utilizing verbs as much as possible rather than nouns and adjectives. Finally, with the help of Melanchthon, who was his superior in knowledge of the Hebrew language, Luther turned to the translation of the Old Testament. It came out in bits and pieces, and eventually, by 1534, Luther had translated the entire Bible.

Roland Bainton calls the translation of the Bible into German "Luther's noblest achievement."[8] And Albert Hyma, often a severe critic

---

5. Hyma, cited by Strand in *Luther's "September Bible,"* Part II, p. 8.

6. Luther, cited by Strand in *Luther's "September Bible,"* Part II, p. 3.

7. Luther, cited by Strand in *Luther's "September Bible,"* Part II, pp. 4–5.

8. Bainton, *Here I Stand,* p. 326.

EUROPE
AT THE TIME OF
THE REFORMATION

||||| Hapsburg possessions

GRAPHIC PRESENTATION SERVICES · Inc

of the Reformer, writes, "Even his debate with Eck at Leipzig is not a matter of world-shaking importance, as compared with his translation of the New Testament."[9] Indeed, Luther's German Bible was basic to all else he did as a Reformer. It was the indispensable source of his theology and the authority above all others to which he constantly appealed.

Despite its critics, Luther's New Testament was an instant success. Melchior Lotther, a Wittenberg printer, ran it off on three different presses. Three to five thousand copies are thought to have been printed in the first edition, and they were sold out in less than three months. A new edition came out in December, which was actually a revision with no less than 574 corrections and improvements in style. Before the complete Bible was printed in 1534, eighty-seven editions had appeared in High German and nineteen in Low German. It is estimated that in the intervening twelve years, at least 200,000 copies of the New Testament were printed. This represents something of a publishing phenomenon, since an estimated total of only thirty thousand copies of Bibles were printed in German before 1522.

Luther's Bible marked the beginning of a significant increase in the production of Bibles in Europe. A similar development was taking place in Zürich. Vernacular versions in English and Spanish would soon follow the familiar pattern: first the New Testament would appear; then shortly thereafter a new edition, with corresponding changes, corrections, and improvements; and finally the complete Bible. The Bibles were then subject to immediate revisions. New editions continued to pour from the presses in an ever-increasing stream throughout the sixteenth century. Everywhere the Reformation was spurred on by the study of the new Bibles, study that fed the rising tide of literacy across Europe.

---

9. Hyma, cited by Strand in *Luther's "September Bible,"* Part II, p. 8.

WITTENBERG IN TURMOIL

The city council of Wittenberg sent out an urgent call for Luther to return, a call prompted by the outbreak of iconoclasm and conflicting opinions over the Zwickau Prophets, which threatened to destroy the Reformation in its cradle. Frederick the Elector, while deploring the chaos that had enveloped the little town, forbade Luther to return, or at least not to do so without his permission and protection. In the meantime the situation steadily worsened despite all that Melanchthon and Spalatin (among those with cooler heads) could do. The pressure mounted. Melanchthon was confused because he could not discern the spirits; Spalatin described the situation as a "mess." But the elector hesitated to call Luther back, fearing for his safety. So without the elector's protection Luther set out for Wittenberg disguised as Junker Jörg, a German knight with a full beard and a sword at his side. Upon his arrival in Wittenberg he found things basically as they had been described: everything was coming unglued.

Karlstadt et al.

With Luther hidden away in the Wartburg, the fortunes of the church in Wittenberg were entrusted to Karlstadt and his colleagues. Andreas Bodenstein von Karlstadt (1480–1541) was Luther's senior by a few years. Before his younger colleague's meteoric rise to fame, he had been the brightest star in the fledgling university's galaxy. it was he who had bestowed on Luther the doctorate in theology. But he had early become one of Luther's most ardent disciples, forsaking his Thomism for the "new theology." Now that Luther was out of the picture, Karlstadt, already archdeacon of the Castle Church and provost of the university, became the leading Reformer of Wittenberg. He was supported by Melanchthon, Nikolaus von Amsdorf, and other members of the faculty who had supported Luther.

After much thought and considerable caution, Karlstadt reversed an earlier decision and announced that the mass would be celebrated in a new evangelical manner on Christmas Day, 1521. On that day the church was packed. Here two thousand communicants witnessed a priest, without the usual vestments, using for the first time an abbreviated Latin form of the mass from which all references to sacrifice had been removed. The elevation of the host was also eliminated, and when the bread and wine were both offered to the laity, the priest began speaking in German. Even though there had been a growing demand for just such a change, a change that Karlstadt had for a time resisted, its actual implementation was a nerve-shattering experience for the average parishioner.

This departure from the traditional practice was soon followed by a reordering of church life in Wittenberg. The city council adopted the Ordinance of the Town of Wittenberg, which was published on January 24, 1522. In addition to enjoining Luther's program of social reform, the ordinance called for the removal of images from the churches. Three days after the publication of the ordinance, Karlstadt issued his *Von abtuhung der Bylder,* in which he argued from the Old Testament that the worship of images was idolatrous. This new thrust triggered an iconoclastic riot in which Gabriel Zwilling and those whom Luther dubbed the "Zwickau Prophets" were involved. Even though Karlstadt did not personally take part in the outburst, the council asked him to give up preaching and stick to teaching so that they might get Frederick to approve the ordinance.

When Luther returned to Wittenberg he confronted Karlstadt about his "radicalism." Karlstadt could have justifiably defended himself upon the grounds that he was simply implementing what Luther had been teaching since 1520. Luther, however, speedily restored the Roman mass with the exception of the references to sacrifice. Karlstadt was allowed to retire to the parish church of Orlamünde. There he dressed like a peasant and tilled the fields to support himself. Up until this time Karlstadt, like Luther, had continued to hold and teach the concept of the "real presence" of Christ in the Eucharist. But once Karlstadt was free to develop his own theology of the mass, he rejected the idea that the sacrament became Christ's flesh and blood, holding that when Christ said "This is my body," he pointed to himself. Luther, on the other hand, defended the concept of the "real presence," resorting to a philosophical argument based upon the concept of the ubiquity of Christ. Eventually Luther's alienation from and rejection of Karlstadt's radicalism led the elector to banish him from Saxony.

The Zwickau Prophets

Just two days after Karlstadt's Christmas mass in the Castle Church, the Zwickau Prophets—Nicholas Storch, Thomas Drechsel, and Marcus Thomas Stübner—arrived in Wittenberg. Storch, a weaver, was a charismatic leader well-versed in the Bible. Stübner, however, was the only one of the trio with a university degree. But what the prophets lacked in formal theological education they made up for in zeal. The movement of which they apparently became the first representatives grew out of a group of earnest laymen intent on studying the Scriptures and following its mandates. Informed by the writings of Luther and encouraged by the recent events in Wittenberg, they descended upon the town to make Luther's disciples their own, converts to what they considered a more enlightened and Spirit-led fellowship. Before long they had the town in an uproar. Karlstadt looked upon them with favor; Zwilling became their constant companion and staunch supporter. Melanchthon and Amsdorf were fascinated by them but not sure whether they were of God or the devil. Spalatin viewed the whole scene with despair.

What appeared most disturbing about these self-assured would-be prophets of the new order was not their questioning of the biblical support for infant baptism (which Melanchthon had also questioned) but their spiritualism. They apparently held that the authority of immediate revelation to the individual believer through the Holy Spirit was superior to that of the Bible. They claimed that God spoke through visions and dreams and had given them the ability to read minds. They seemed to have been influenced by Taborite ideas, ideas that led them to embrace a revolutionary eschatology that became more clearly pronounced in the teachings of Thomas Müntzer. It did not take Luther long to "discern the spirits." He quickly recognized that to acknowledge the claims of the *Schwärmer* (fanatics), as he would call them, would be tantamount to surrendering the reins of the Reformation to those for whom the Bible was no longer the supreme authority. Thus he rejected their claims and attributed their works to the devil. His preaching and his personal denunciation of the prophets soon created a climate in Wittenberg that was inhospitable to these earnest apostles of the free spirit. Eventually they left, but by that time they had won two notable converts, Martin Cellarius and Dr. Gerhard Westerburg.

Thomas Müntzer (1490-1525)

Thomas Müntzer, a follower of Luther and a friend of Nicholas Storch, was not with the Zwickau Prophets when they descended upon Wittenberg. However, when he did arrive, he found it expedient to leave very shortly thereafter.

Müntzer first made contact with the prophets when he went to Zwickau to supply the pulpit of Johann Wildenhauer (called Ergranus) upon Luther's recommendation. During the interim he had fallen under the spell of Nicholas Storch and the "Storchites." From the very beginning of his Zwickau sojourn, he was involved in controversy. Finally he was summoned to appear before the city council to answer the charges that at an infant's baptism he had denied the efficacy of the godparents' faith and had exalted the Spirit over the Word. On the evening of his trial he left Zwickau for Prague. Here he identified with the eschatological and revolutionary tenets of the Taborites. On November 1 he posted his Prague Manifesto, in which he blamed the ills of Christendom on scholars and priests who had obscured or completely distorted the gospel. He held that the task of restoration belonged to the common people, who have the right to elect their own pastors.

Müntzer also asserted that the bestowal of the sevenfold gift of the Spirit was the goal of redemption. An aspect of this gift, he claimed, was the ability to receive direct instruction from the Holy Spirit in the form of visions, dreams, ecstatic utterances, or inspired exegesis. Despite a certain affinity for teachings of the more radical Hussites, it does not appear that Müntzer sparked the mass response that he apparently had anticipated. Perhaps part of the problem was that he was a German, not a Bohemian. Also, the plan of reform that Müntzer offered was somewhat confused; his was an uncertain trumpet. At any rate, he apparently returned to Germany and visited Luther in Wittenberg in the spring of 1523 before becoming pastor at Allstedt, some twenty miles south of Eisleben.

In Allstedt Müntzer married a former nun and settled into the life of a pastor. Apparently content to serve in this capacity, he turned his attention to the practical aspects of his new responsibilities. The result was his *German Church Order*, the first such order sparked by the Reformation. The next year (1524) he brought out the *German Evangelical Mass* and the *Order* and *Structure of the German Office*. In these efforts Müntzer anticipated Luther, who at the time did not feel it necessary to eliminate Latin from the liturgy of the new evangelical worship service. Although the *German Evangelical Mass* was little more than a German translation of the *Roman Catholic Mass,* there were some changes: the words of institution were spoken by the entire congregation, and the Scripture lessons became much longer.

In 1524 Müntzer published two tracts, *On Phony Faith* and *Protestation.* They indicate that he was becoming increasingly critical of Luther. He claimed that there was no genuine understanding of the true Christian faith in either the old church or the new. He insisted that to be Christian means to be crucified with Christ. The evidence of this commitment is seen in a new Christian life-style of self-denial and obedience to Christ. He also claimed that baptism had not been correctly understood, noting that infant baptism is not found in the Scriptures. He went on to assert that "in the days of the apostles only adults were accepted after a lengthy period of instruction and were called *Catechumenos*."[10]

Apparently Müntzer's baptismal theology was in a state of flux. In the same year of the *Protestation*, in which he raised questions about the New Testament teachings on baptism, Müntzer brought out a new baptismal liturgy, *Von der Tauff wie man die heldt*, in which he provided for infant baptism. It appears that he, unlike the Anabaptists, never baptized adults when they made professions of faith, but that he continued to baptize infants or young children. He apparently made less and less of baptism, insisting that "neither Mary, the mother of God, nor the disciples of Christ had been baptized with water."[11] The direction of his ministry was rapidly moving toward violence in the interest of social justice. When rumors of the revolutionary nature of his sermons—which drew huge crowds from the countryside—reached Count Ernst of Mansfeld, he promptly prohibited their attendance. This led to a fateful encounter.

Sermon before the Princes—July 13, 1524

Sometime in March 1523 a small chapel near Allstedt that housed an image of the Virgin Mary was burned to the ground. Even though Müntzer was not a party to the action, he had previously preached against idol worship in the chapel with his usual vehemence. This event—coupled with his vigorous attack on "Brother Fattened Swine and Brother Soft life" (Luther) and those who preached a "sweet sinful Jesus" (Luther and his colleagues) instead of the cross and a "bitter Christ"—brought him to the attention of Frederick the Wise and his brother, Duke John. The duke decided that it was time to hear for himself what Müntzer was preaching. Thus in July he and his son John Frederick made the trip to Allstedt and invited Müntzer to preach before them in Duke John's castle there.

Müntzer felt that this occasion offered him a superb opportunity to enlist the support of the princes for his vision of "a complete reformation." Duke John did in fact seem to favor a more radical version of reformatory efforts than Luther advocated; however, his son was an ardent admirer of Luther. Regardless of what one may say about Müntzer's tactlessness, he was not guilty of duplicity. He frankly set forth his bold theology of history and in the process revealed his contempt for Luther while affirming his own faith in dreams and visions as means by which God speaks to "the elect." Following the example of the Old Testament prophets, he preached that "the Stone [made] without hands" would crush in judgment the fifth kingdom (Dan. 2:34), a kingdom of iron and clay. He explained that God would do this by using the godly to slay the godless: "The sword was the means, as eating and drinking is for us the means of living. In just this way the sword is necessary to wipe out the godless (Rom. 13:4)." He then appealed to the princes to join the battle against the godless. But if they refused, he preached, "they may be slain without mercy as Hezekiah . . . destroyed the priests of Baal, otherwise the Christian church (*Kirche*) cannot come back again to its origin."[12]

There was no immediate reaction to Müntzer's sermon. If the princes understood it, they probably took it to mean that God would vindicate his own at the end of the age. But this is not how Luther understood it, and he became increasingly wary of the developments in Allstedt. Müntzer formed a *Bund* (union) of the elect for, he claimed, the defense of the gospel. Since the gospel was not under attack in Saxony, questions were raised about the true nature of this new group. On August 1 Müntzer and four members of the city council answered a summons to appear before Duke John at Weimar. When he returned, Müntzer discovered that his printer had disappeared, the print shop had

---

10. Müntzer, cited by Hans J. Hillerbrand in *A Fellowship of Discontent* (New York: Harper & Row, 1967), p. 10.

11. Robert Friedmann, "Thomas Muentzer," in *The Mennonite Encyclopedia*, 4 vols., ed. Harold S. Bender and C. Henry Smith (Scottdale, Pa.: Herald Press, 1956–1969), 3: 786.

12. Müntzer, "Sermon before the Princes," in *Spiritual and Anabaptist Writers*, ed. G. H. Williams and Angel M. Mergal, vol. 25 of the Library of Christian Classics (Philadelphia: Westminster Press, 1957), pp. 63–68.

been closed, and the *Bund* had been dissolved by the city council. The tide had turned against him. On the night of August 7 he abruptly left the city by scaling a wall in the company of a goldsmith. His destination, as it turned out, was Mühlhausen, a free city of about five thousand people approximately forty-five miles southwest of Allstedt. Here he joined forces with Heinrich Pfeiffer, a former monk who had embraced "the new church teaching." At the time, Pfeiffer, a native of the city, was a popular but controversial preacher. However, despite widespread support for their proposed reforms, both he and Müntzer were expelled from the city by the city council before the end of September.

THE PEASANTS' REVOLT

The Peasants' Revolt is the term given to the widely scattered outbursts of peasant rebellion that occurred from June 1524 to July 1525. These uprisings were not a response to Müntzer's incendiary preaching; rather, they were the flaming up of long-smoldering discontent that had become increasingly apparent as the nobility, hard-pressed for ready cash, began to take away the traditional privileges and rights of a downtrodden people. A difficult situation rapidly became an intolerable one. Some peasant leaders may have remembered Joss Fritz and Hans Böhm and their ill-fated movements, but they were encouraged to think that their own protests would not suffer a similar fate. Perhaps such encouragement originally came from Luther and the Bible more than from the preaching of men like Müntzer, Pfeiffer, and Karlstadt. In his *Freedom of a Christian,* Luther had laid the theological groundwork for an egalitarian society where every person, regardless of status, is a priest and is accountable to God for being a Christ to his neighbor. And certainly the Bible championed the cause of the disadvantaged. Once the level of literacy began to rise and peasants began to read for themselves the gospel accounts of the life and teachings of Christ, they realized that Christ was on the side of the poor, not necessarily on the side of the rich or the high and mighty. But the peasant *Bunds* of

1524–1525 did not always reflect the new evangel; in fact, their interests for the most part turned out to be quite worldly and self-centered. Even Müntzer was finally forced to admit that social class alone did not determine virtue—that a peasant was not necessarily godly and a prince necessarily ungodly.

The Beginning of Conflict

A relatively trivial matter triggered the first peasant uprising. On June 23, 1524, the countess of Lupfen-Stühlingen interrupted some of her peasants while they were in the middle of haying and sent them to collect snails. The resentment they felt soon expressed itself in the organization of peasants to prevent future episodes of similar exploitation. A man named Hans Müller arose to lead the Stühlingen peasants to seek support in Klettgau and Waldshut. Waldshut was already in trouble with the Austrian authorities because it had embraced the Reformation and had sought to align itself with the Swiss Confederation. In fact, Zürich sent a contingent of 170 volunteers to help protect the town from the Austrian menace in October 1524. When Swiss troops were withdrawn (in December), Müller's band of 550 peasants, camped on the hillside overlooking Waldshut, constituted the town's only tangible defense against Archduke Ferdinand.

During this time of peasant unrest—November and December 1524—Thomas Müntzer was in Klettgau and Hegau. Little is known of his activities in these cities. Regardless of what Heinrich Bullinger and others since him have written, there is really no evidence to suggest that Müntzer influenced the Upper Swabian peasant movement in the slightest degree. He does seem to have become captive to the social program of the peasants and to have championed their cause from this time on. But Müntzer's spirit was far more militant than that of the South German peasants.

The Twelve Articles

The Twelve Articles reflect in a remarkable way the mixture of peasant grievances and what the peasants perceived to be the social implications of the gospel. The articles were published by Sebastian Lotzer of Memmingen on March 1, 1525. These articles called for the end of serfdom because

> Christ has delivered and redeemed us all, without exception, by the shedding of his precious blood, the lowly as well as the great. Accordingly it is consistent with Scripture that we should be free and wish to be so. Not that we would wish to be absolutely free and under no authority. God does not teach us that we should lead a disorderly life in the lusts of the flesh, but that we should love the Lord our God and our neighbor.[13]

In addition, these peasants asked for the right to select their own pastors[14] and for an end to the hated death tax. They appealed to the teachings of Scripture for the justification of their requests. Even though the concluding statement was firm and open-ended, nowhere was there a call to arms.[15] Dr. Balthasar Hubmaier, the parish priest of Waldshut who became a Reformer, confessed under torture that he wrote these articles. This confession probably meant no more than that he edited them for the peasants, although the articles' evangelical spirit and lack of violent overtones may indeed be due to his influence. Whatever the case may be, there is little doubt that they contain a true list of the peasants' complaints.

Violence did flare up among some peasant bands that besieged cities and castles in the area. Despite these forays, which were sometimes cruelly suppressed, the Swabian peasants continued to pursue a course of nonviolent protest while preparing themselves for armed conflict. By April 17, 1525, the peasants were confronted by twelve thousand troops led by Seneschal George of Waldburg. Bloodshed was avoided when Seneschal George granted some of the peasants' demands, and the Weingarten Treaty was signed. As if to emphasize both the peasants' peaceful intent and their relentless pursuit of what they considered justice, Sebastian Lotzer led in the formation of a Christian union made up of peasant bands from around Lake Constance, Allgau, and Baltringen. With the formation of similar bands in and around Rottenburg, the patience of the peasants finally ran out. Violence erupted, and the peasants suffered a bitter defeat at the hands of Seneschal George and his well-equipped army. Peasant villages, orchards, fields, and houses were left in flames. On July 9 one of the most sincere and competent leaders of the peasants, the moderately wealthy Florian Geyer, died at the head of a peasant band at Schwäbisch Hall.

As the Peasants' Revolt moved north, preachers like Hubmaier and Karlstadt attempted to direct the movement into constructive evangelical channels. One of these preachers was Karlstadt's brother-in-law, Dr. Gerhard Westerburg, who introduced the Reformation to Frankfurt. For this purpose Westerburg drew up the Forty-two Articles, similar in tone and content to the better-known Twelve Articles. Westerburg and his colleagues met with unusual success. The Frankfurt city council adopted the articles, and the pulse of reform quickened. But the city was unable to resist the pressures of feudal lords. The Swabian League, now able to turn its attention to the peasants since Francis I had been taken prisoner at Pavia, joined the efforts of George of Waldburg to suppress the uprising and reverse whatever small concessions the peasants had won.

Thomas Müntzer and the Sword of Gideon

The peasant bands were often accompanied by chaplains such as Karlstadt. Thomas Müntzer also accompanied these bands, but he was more than a chaplain—or so he thought. It is clear that Müntzer considered himself a warrior-priest

---

13. "The Twelve Articles of the Peasants, March 1525," cited in *Documents Illustrative of the Continental Reformation*, ed. B. J. Kidd (Oxford: Clarendon Press, 1911), p. 176.

14. Hubmaier had set forth this concept as early as April 1524 in his Eighteen Articles, and he had implemented the idea of congregational rule and support of pastors when he led the Waldshut church to embrace Anabaptism a year later. This was simply carrying a step further the ideas that Luther had expressed in his *Open Letter to the Christian Nobility.*

15. See "The Twelve Articles of the Peasants, March 1525," pp. 174–79.

Thomas Müntzer, who patterned himself after the Old Testament model of Gideon RELIGIOUS NEWS SERVICE

and patterned himself after an Old Testament model: he signed his letters "Thomas Müntzer with the Sword of Gideon" or "Thomas Müntzer with the hammer." He has frequently been portrayed as the main instigator and greatest leader of the Peasants' Revolt as well as the founder of the Anabaptist movement. However, it is now apparent that this description is not true. The Peasants' Revolt began with the uprising of Stühlingen peasants led by Hans Müller. It was Heinrich Pfeiffer of Mühlhausen who formulated a program of social reform that led to that tragic confrontation at Frankenhausen (in which Müntzer took part). The origins of Anabaptism are Swiss, not German, because it was Zürich,

not Wittenberg or Allstedt, that witnessed the first baptism of adult believers.

If Müntzer was neither strategic peasant leader nor Anabaptism's founder, then what was he? He can best be seen as a pamphleteer who with a bitter and vindictive pen hurled scathing words of denunciation against those whom he perceived to be the enemies of God; chief among them he counted Luther and Count Ernst of Mansfeld. He was primarily a religious reformer with a deep sympathy for the oppressed and an absolute confidence in his ability to decipher the signs of the times and to discern the voice of God in the mounting conflict. He returned to Mühlhausen to prepare for the great eschatological event that he was convinced was near at hand. By this time he had written off the princes as the godless whom the godly—the peasants—were called upon to slay. Together with Pfeiffer, who had returned to the city even earlier than Müntzer to promote his program of social reform, he led the citizens of Mühlhausen to replace their city council with men of their choosing who were called "the Eternal Council." Thus the city that had unceremoniously expelled the two men less than a year before was now captive to their program of reform.

A large throng of peasants, convinced that the time had come to inherit the earth, began to assemble near Frankenhausen around the first of May for the victorious march on the bastions of power. They sent a request to Mühlhausen for two hundred additional reinforcements. Müntzer thought the request much too modest and volunteered that "all would come." In response he rode forth on the twelfth of May to do battle along with the Mühlhausen contingent, encouraging them and exhorting them to valor. On the same day, the "warrior-prophet" wrote to Count Ernst of Mansfeld, obviously sensing that victory was within the peasants' grasp, asking

that for the sake of the name of the living God you desist from your tyrannical raging lest you continue to incite God's wrath over you. You have begun to torture the poor Christians. You have labeled the holy Christian faith a roguery. You have dared to suppress the Christians. Tell me you miserable bag of worms, who made you a ruler of the people whom God has purchased with his precious blood?

He signed the letter "Thomas Müntzer with the Sword of Gideon."[16]

Rumors that the princes were assembling a strong force of crack troops to meet the peasant challenge had doubtless reached the Frankenhausen peasants by the time Müntzer and his Mühlhausen company arrived, because on the following day Müntzer got off a hurried letter to Wittenberg asking for help. In support of his frantic pleas he cited an Old Testament passage, Ezekiel 39:25: "I will redeem you from them who command you in tyranny." He went on to express again his faith in the cause of the peasants, saying, "God's elect are called upon to aid God in the fulfillment of his eternal purpose."[17]

Luther and his Wittenberg disciples turned a deaf ear to Müntzer's plea for help. The die was already cast. Duke George of Saxony and Philip of Hesse commanded an imposing army of well-equipped cavalry and infantry. The prince gave the peasants one last chance at a reprieve provided they turned over "the false prophet Thomas Müntzer." The peasants refused, and in the subsequent battle they were virtually annihilated. Müntzer and a few others managed to escape, but five thousand were killed outright. Müntzer was discovered hiding in the attic of a farmhouse, pretending to be a "poor sick man." On May 27, 1525, Müntzer and Pfeiffer were beheaded outside Mühlhausen.

Luther and the Peasants

The Catholics were not slow to blame Luther for the Peasants' Revolt. This allegation touched a sensitive spot; Luther realized that if the charge were allowed to stand, the results could be devastating. It was all the more damaging because Luther's initial response to the Twelve

Articles had been an expression of sympathetic concern in which he encouraged the princes to deal justly with their subjects. However, three weeks after publishing *An Admonition to Peace: A Reply to the Twelve Articles of the Peasants in Swabia* (April 19, 1525), Luther wrote an angry tract, "Against the Robbing and Murdering Hordes of Peasants," in which he declared that anyone who killed a peasant did God a service.[18] The Luther who had returned from the Wartburg against the advice of his prince, Frederick the Wise, denying his need of the elector's protection, realized that the peasants could not possibly win out against the superior forces of the rulers of Europe, and in their inevitable fall they were likely to pull down the whole Reformation if he did not divorce his movement from theirs. However, to hold that this was the only reason that moved Luther to oppose the peasants would be a serious misrepresentation of the Reformer. Doubtless the fact that Thomas Müntzer had so identified himself with the peasants' cause did not help them in Luther's sight. He was primarily a man of peace to whom war was abhorrent, but if war were necessary he would side with the rulers rather than the rebels. His medieval mentality could not fathom how peasants could rule themselves or bring order out of chaos. Then too, he, unlike Müntzer, was never deceived regarding the very earthy and selfish motives of "the hordes." For Luther the tragedy of this turmoil was twofold: he lost his faith in the common man, and his cause was weakened by the peasants' subsequent alienation from him and "the Magisterial Reform."[19] Perhaps the peasants had forgotten that the Roman Catholic rulers were just as determined as Luther to stamp out their movement for human rights. But even if they had not, their reaction was a matter of differing expecta-

---

16. Müntzer, cited by Hillerbrand in *A Fellowship of Discontent,* p. 24.

17. Müntzer, cited by Hillerbrand in *A Fellowship of Discontent,* p. 24.

18. See Luther, "Against the Robbing and Murdering Hordes of Peasants, May 1525," in *Martin Luther,* ed. E. G. Rupp and Benjamin Drewery (New York: St. Martin's Press, 1970), pp. 125–26.

19. The Magisterial Reform is the term used to identify the reformation that relied upon the government for its defense and support. It was in effect a reformation carried forward by the state.

tions: they had anticipated resistance from the rulers but not from Luther.

The truth of the matter is that the peasants themselves often had no deep religious convictions. There is no doubt that preachers like Karlstadt, Westerburg, Müntzer, and Pfeiffer held such convictions, but the peasants for the most part were fighting not out of a religious idealism but for a restoration of ancient privileges that had been usurped by the lords. In the emerging Protestant Reformation they saw the chance for a redress of grievances and possibly for a new day when they would be treated as persons and not simply as objects to be exploited. In these expectations they were doomed to be disappointed. But some of the peasants survived to become a part of the Anabaptist movement, which had a strong appeal for those who had lost faith in Luther and the princely advocates of the new faith.

ASSAULT ON CELIBACY

For the brief time during which Frankfurt was captivated by the reforming zeal of Dr. Gerhard Westerburg, the Reformers addressed the problem of clerical libertinism. The Forty-two Articles demanded that parish priests either observe their vows of chastity or marry. At the time, violation of the vows of celibacy had been creating such scandal that many of the more sensitive were convinced that something had to be done. Insisting that the clergy marry, legally and publicly, was one answer.

While Luther was still at the Wartburg, Karlstadt married. When Luther heard the news, he is reported to have said, "Good heavens! Will our Wittenbergers give wives to monks? They won't give one to me!"[20] Luther was not condemning marriage of clergy, secular or religious; he was simply expressing his commitment to the celibate life. However, in 1523 a group of nuns who had deserted the convent because of the impact of the Reformation arrived in Wittenberg, and by 1525 one of the

nuns, Katherine von Bora, had changed Luther's mind. After Luther failed to find her a suitable husband or one whom she would accept, Katie sent word that she really was not impossible to please; for she was willing to marry Dr. Amsdorf or even Dr. Martin himself. At first Luther treated the suggestion as a huge joke, but as he thought about it and shared it with his father and friends, it began to take root. By May he had decided to marry Katie even if he should be martyred shortly thereafter.

By June 13, 1525, Luther and Katie were publicly married. Luther gave three reasons for his change of heart: he wished to please his father, spite the pope, and give Katie a name before he died. In the last of the three reasons we catch a glimpse of genuine concern, if not love. Luther was not the first former priest or monk to marry, but because of his role in the Reformation his marriage became something of a symbol for the new attitude of the reforming clergy toward marriage, and as such did more for the establishment of the "Protestant parsonage" than the earlier marriages of Karlstadt, Zwingli, and others. The former Augustinian monastery became home for Luther and Katie. A year after their marriage, on June 7, 1526, Hans was born, and after Hans five other children came along in due time. Upon occasion the Luther household would number as many as twenty-five because the Luthers took in four orphaned children of relatives and were also forced to take in student boarders to augment the family income. Katie was an exceptional person who possessed almost infinite patience, an invaluable asset in living with her gifted but irascible husband. She was also intelligent and effective as an administrator. She as much as Luther was responsible for providing an attractive model for Protestant family life. Gradually a viable alternative to priestly celibacy in the medieval church was taking shape.

CUJUS REGIO, EJUS RELIGIO

The Catholic princes viewed with growing alarm the rapid spread of the Lutheran heresy. Thus, led by Duke George of Ducal Saxony and

---

20. Luther, cited by Bainton in *Here I Stand,* p. 200.

Archbishop Albert of Mainz, they organized a league of defense against the supposed menace in July 1525. By February of the following year Elector John of Electoral Saxony and Philip of Hesse had responded by forming an alliance with a number of other princes and free imperial cities for their mutual protection. It was in this atmosphere of tension and suspicion that the First Diet of Speyer was held in 1526.

The First Diet of Speyer, 1526

Even though Charles V was victorious over Francis I, his struggle with Leo and papal intrigue contrived against his attendance at the diet. Consequently, his brother, Archduke Ferdinand of Austria, took his place with instructions to enforce the Edict of Worms and bring the German princes into line.

Once the diet had convened, it became obvious that the supporters of the Reformation were in no mood to do the bidding of Rome or of Charles V as far as Luther was concerned. They countered the Catholic charge that the Reformation had fomented the Peasants' Revolt with an allegation of their own. The real culprit, they claimed, was Rome: it was common knowledge that the clerical lords, bishops, and abbots were merciless in exacting the last farthing from the impoverished peasants, and once the revolt had been put down their cruelty had been untempered by mercy. In every respect, the princes pointed out, the peasants fared better under secular rulers than under clerical landlords. Ferdinand and the Catholic party were also rebuffed in their attempt to secure a reaffirmation of the Edict of Worms. A committee of princes brought back a report to the full meeting of the diet that supported virtually all of the changes in the worship and the practice of the church proposed by Luther, even insisting that Scripture be interpreted by Scripture. The committee proposed that "until the meeting of a General Council to be held in a German city each State should so live as it hoped to answer for its conduct to God and to the Emperor."[21] Since

Ferdinand was both outmaneuvered and outnumbered, and the emperor was at the moment at war with the pope, the proposals were allowed to stand.

The Protestant princes interpreted the actions of the diet as giving them a certain legal sanction that advocates of the Reformation had never enjoyed before. This quasi-legal recognition brought many a closet Protestant out into the open. Practically all of North Germany—with the exception of Brandenburg, Ducal Saxony, and Brunswick-Wolfenbüttel—became Lutheran within three years. This did not necessarily mean that there were no holdouts, but it did mean that the formula associated with the First Diet of Speyer— *cujus regio, ejus religio*—was respected. This meant that the prince's personal religious affiliation would determine the legal religion of his territory. It had the effect of making the princes in Lutheran lands acting bishops and establishing the Lutheran Church as the *Landeskirche* (state church). While Luther indicated that the church "is where the gospel is preached and the sacraments are rightly observed,"[22] in reality there could be no such recognized church without the approval of the prince. Even though Luther had very little interest in providing a new structure for the church, he was forced to give his movement some viable structure and in so doing became a party to an Erastian concept, in which the state is the dominant partner and the church is subservient to its needs and demands.

For the moment at least, the Reformation was assured a future in the eyes of Luther's followers. As far as Ferdinand and Charles were concerned, the First Diet of Speyer represented the politics of the possible. The two men had made concessions, determined that these would not become permanent imperial policy. This became all the more apparent with the convening of the Second Diet of Speyer three years later.

---

21. Thomas M. Lindsay, *A History of the Reformation*, 2 vols. (New York: Scribner's, 1907, 1928), 1: 343.

22. Luther, cited in *Documents Illustrative of the Continental Reformation*, p. 264.

The Second Diet of Speyer, 1529

Charles V was absent from the Second Diet of Speyer, but members of the Roman Catholic party were in the majority and determined to carry out the mandates of their emperor. The commissioners stated at the beginning of the proceedings that the emperor "by his imperial and absolute authority (*Machtvollkommenheit*)"[23] had abolished the clause of the First Diet of Speyer, which the Lutheran princes had interpreted as giving them the legal right to establish the Reformation in their territories. The majority of those present voted to implement the emperor's wishes. The diet went on to insist that those territories that had begun to enforce the Edict of Worms must continue to do so and those that had departed from its provisions must cease from any further innovations. This meant that Catholics were to be tolerated in Lutheran lands but that Lutherans were not to be given the same treatment in Catholic territories. The diet also ruled that Zwinglians were not to be tolerated any more than Anabaptists were. As for the Anabaptists, they were to be put to death. For this severe treatment the diet cited the Justinian code against the Donatists, which called for the death penalty for those who practiced rebaptism. It further declared that "no ecclesiastical body should be deprived of its authority or revenues."[24] This last ruling was designed to deal a mortal blow to the new territorial churches.

Outnumbered as they were, the Lutherans had no other choice than to protest these actions. On April 19, 1529, they read their protestation before the diet. They began by questioning the legality of the proceedings of the second diet, which attempted to reverse the decisions of the first; they insisted that what one diet had done, another could not undo. They further stated that if their plea was not heard, then

we herewith protest and testify publicly before God . . . that we for ourselves, our subjects and in behalf of all, each and every one, consider [the entire transaction] null and not binding; and we desire, in matters of religion . . . so to live, govern, and carry ourselves in our governments, . . . as we trust to answer it before God almighty and his Roman Imperial Majesty, our most gracious Lord.[25]

The word "protest" struck a resounding note, and Lutherans became known as Protestants. Eventually the term was applied to all non-Catholic Christians.

Since Ferdinand and the commissioners of the emperor would not allow the protestation to be included in the minutes, it was published along with supporting documents and the signatures of Elector John of Saxony, Margrave George of Brandenburg, Dukes Ernest and Francis of Brunswick-Lüneburg, Landgrave Philip of Hesse, and Prince Wolfgang of Anhalt. Representatives of fourteen free imperial cities, some of whom adhered to the Zwinglian form of the Reformation, also signed. That Charles V got the message was evident that next year when the diet of the German nation met at Augsburg.

THE AUGSBURG CONFESSION

Unknown to Luther, the protesting princes and their co-religionists entered into a secret agreement after the Second Diet of Speyer for the defense of the faith. Philip of Hesse perhaps saw more clearly than others the necessity of a political and military alliance between the Protestant territories and the free imperial cities. Luther disagreed. He was dead set against the use of the sword in defense of the faith, and he also opposed the doctrinal position of the Zwinglians. As a result, a more formal union was scrapped. But Philip would not give up. He felt the future of the evangelical cause hung in the balance. His strenuous efforts and astute diplomacy led to the Marburg Colloquy, which took place from September 30 to October 5, 1529.

---

23. Cited by Lindsay in *A History of the Reformation*, 1: 345.

24. "The Resolution of the Majority, 7 April 1529," in *Documents Illustrative of the Continental Reformation*, p. 242.

25. "The Resolution of the Majority, 7 April 1529," in *Documents Illustrative of the Continental Reformation*, p. 242.

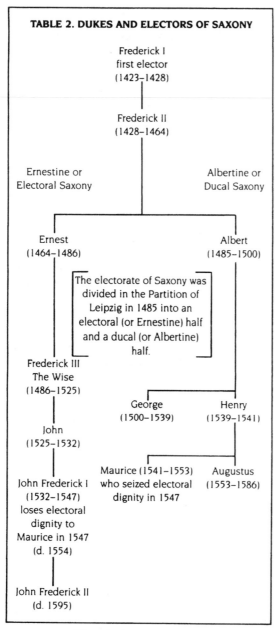

TABLE 2. DUKES AND ELECTORS OF SAXONY

Frederick I
first elector
(1423–1428)

Frederick II
(1428–1464)

Ernestine or
Electoral Saxony

Albertine or
Ducal Saxony

Ernest
(1464–1486)

Albert
(1485–1500)

The electorate of Saxony was
divided in the Partition of
Leipzig in 1485 into an
electoral (or Ernestine) half
and a ducal (or Albertine)
half.

Frederick III
The Wise
(1486–1525)

George
(1500–1539)

Henry
(1539–1541)

John
(1525–1532)

John Frederick I
(1532–1547)
loses electoral
dignity to
Maurice in 1547
(d. 1554)

Maurice (1541–1553)
who seized electoral
dignity in 1547

Augustus
(1553–1586)

John Frederick II
(d. 1595)

The Marburg Colloquy

While Philip himself probably did not understand the theological distinctions that appeared
to separate the Lutheran and the Zwinglian positions, he did recognize the delicacy of the task
facing him. Thus he arranged for Zwingli to be
absent from the opening banquet. When discus-

sions actually got under way, Luther faced Oecolampadius, and Zwingli faced Melanchthon.
On October 2 at six in the morning Luther and
Zwingli faced each other for the first time. Each
was a Reformer in his own right, but each had
arrived at his convictions by a different route.
Zwingli claimed that his position was the result
of independent study. Luther had long considered Zwingli's part in the execution of Anabaptists barbarian and his views of the Eucharist
heretical. Although they both rejected the miracle of transubstantiation and the mass as a sacrifice, they disagreed on the doctrine of the real
presence. Before the discussion began, Luther
wrote in chalk on the table in the great banquet
room *Hoc est corpus meum* ("This is my
body"), which he interpreted literally. For his
part Zwingli set forth his memorial view of these
words, indicating that the word *est* (is) could
best be understood as *significat* (signifies).
Therefore, Zwingli emphasized, the Lord's Supper should be observed in remembrance of the
one sacrifice of Christ on the cross for us. Luther
saw Zwingli as a proponent of Karlstadt's view,
and Zwingli saw Luther as an insufferable obscurantist. Neither Reformer was at his best.
Both were adamant. Melanchthon, who had
never favored the idea of a colloquy with the
Zwinglians in the first place, was just as inflexible. Oecolampadius and Martin Bucer sought
and found mediating positions.

Philip had obviously underestimated the
depth of the theological gulf separating Luther
and Zwingli. In a last-ditch effort to salvage
something from the meeting, the participants
drew up fifteen articles consisting of doctrinal
statements upon which they could agree. The
fifteenth, which concerned the nature of the
Lord's Supper, was an ambiguous article that
could be interpreted in different ways. It was
followed by a frank admission that a difference
of opinion still existed regarding the Eucharist.
Philip's plans, it would appear, had come to
nought.

Despite his abortive efforts at Marburg, Philip
persisted in his attempt to form a Protestant
defensive league upon the basis of common
theological commitment. For that purpose, Lu-

ther—although he still resisted the idea of a political alliance—formulated a confession of seventeen points that were based upon the Marburg articles but were strictly Lutheran in the interpretation of the Lord's Supper. But Philip's hopes of forming a Protestant union were frustrated once again when the representatives of Ulm and Strasbourg refused to sign the confession. Hence the Schwabach articles (of November 1529) met the fate of the Marburg articles, and the Protestants, divided, awaited an aggressive and confident Roman Catholic emperor.

The Diet of Augsburg, 1530

Charles V had emerged from a series of conflicts completely triumphant. He had defeated Francis I at Pavia, and in the papal test of his power he had once again been victorious. In addition, the Austrian army had turned back the Ottoman Turks in their siege of Vienna. But the Turkish threat was a real one that Charles felt only a united empire could successfully withstand. The reconciliation of the Protestants was urgent, but for Charles, as for Ferdinand, it was more than a political necessity. Both brothers were men of conviction and devout Catholics. In order that his brother might succeed him (Ferdinand had inherited the crown of Hungary and Bohemia), Charles planned to have him crowned king of the Romans. But before this could be smoothly accomplished, the religious questions that had threatened the unity of the Holy Roman Empire had to be faced. Since Charles recognized the theological nature of the issues, he hoped to attempt a reconciliation by bringing the Roman Catholic and Protestant theologians together at Augsburg for a face-to-face dialogue. If this failed to effect a union, he was prepared to bring about submission by force. But first he would offer the olive branch.

Melanchthon, who had entertained serious misgivings about including the Zwinglians in the protestation at the Second Diet of Speyer, was in a very conciliatory mood. He and the other Lutheran theologians agreed to attend the conference at Augsburg. Since the Edict of Worms was still in effect, Luther was not present

at Augsburg but remained nearby at Coburg, where Melanchthon could keep him well-informed of developments. Thus the stage was set for the possible reunion of the Protestants with Rome.

Charles arrived in the city on June 15 with all the pomp and circumstance due the emperor of the Holy Roman Empire. Later he took part in the Corpus Christi procession, from which the Protestants abstained. On June 20 the diet was opened with appropriate ceremonies, and by June 25 an imperial diet of the German nation heard for the first time a Protestant confession of faith. Presented in both Latin and German, it consisted of two parts. The first part contained twenty-two articles, the last of which was a summary that attempted to establish the claim that the Lutherans held to the true Catholic faith of the unfallen church, a part of which reads as follows:

> This is about the sum of doctrine among us, in which can be seen that there is nothing which is discrepant with the Scriptures, or with the Church Catholic, or even with the Roman Church, so far as that Church is known from writers [the writings of the Fathers]. This being the case, they judge us harshly who insist that we shall be regarded as heretics. But the dissension is concerning certain [traditions and] abuses, which without any certain authority have crept into the churches; in which things, even if there were some difference, yet would it be a becoming lenity on the part of the bishops that, on account of the Confession which we have now presented, they should bear with us, since not even the Canons are so severe as to demand the same rites everywhere, nor were the rites of all churches at any time the same. Although among us in large part the ancient rites are diligently observed. For it is a calumnious falsehood, that all the ceremonies, all the things instituted of old, are abolished in our churches.[26]

The second part of that confession consisted of a discussion of seven abuses alleged to have crept into the Catholic Church, abuses that the

---

. 26. The Augsburg Confession, in *The Evangelical Protestant Creeds, with Translations*, vol. 3 of Philip Schaff's *Creeds of Christendom* (Grand Rapids: Baker Book House, 1966), pp. 26–27.

Lutherans claimed to have corrected. This section began on the same note with which the first part ended:

> Inasmuch as the churches among us dissent in no article of faith from [the holy Scriptures, or] the Church Catholic [the Universal Christian Church], and only omit a few of certain abuses, which are novel [in part have crept in with time, in part have been introduced by violence], and, contrary to the purport of the Canons, have been received by the fault of the times, we beg that Your Imperial Majesty would clemently hear both what ought to be changed and what are the reasons that the people ought not to be forced against their consciences to observe those abuses.[27]

Melanchthon was the chief architect of the confession. He took the Schwabach articles that Luther had formulated and reworked them to make them sound as inoffensive as possible to Roman Catholic ears. He made it clear that the Augsburg Confession was not intended to replace the historic creeds but was in perfect accord with them and in agreement with Scripture and the early church fathers. The previous March Johann Eck had presented the emperor with a list of 404 errors in which he attributed to the evangelicals the heresies (in their most offensive form) supposedly held by Lutherans, Zwinglians, and Anabaptists. Thus Melanchthon took special pains to condemn both the Zwinglians and the Anabaptists and to distinguish the Lutherans from those whom both Catholics and Lutherans considered heretics. He also emphasized that they held with the Catholics "one faith, one Lord, and one baptism."

Despite Melanchthon's skillful and irenic attempt to placate the emperor and the Roman Catholic theologians, the discussions reached an impasse. In the course of the diet Melanchthon indicated a willingness to compromise even further and made a number of potentially damaging concessions—at least they appeared so to the Protestant princes. His conduct caused Philip of Hesse to remark, "Master Philip goes backward like a crab." However, the final printed version of the confession embraced the heart of the Reformation faith. Even though the article on justification by faith (Article 4) was briefly and simply stated, the concept appeared repeatedly and was more forcefully expressed and explained in Article 20, "Of Good Works." Here faith was defined as *fiducia* (trust) and not in the traditional sense of *assensus* (mental assent to certain propositions the Roman Church held to be true). It was further explained that the new life in Christ produced good works—not good deeds that the believer performed to achieve merit in God's sight and thus win salvation, but, as both Augustine and Paul taught, the natural fruit of a life changed by divine grace. "He, therefore, that trusteth by his works to merit grace, doth despise the merit and grace of Christ, and seeketh by his own power, without Christ, to come unto the Father; whereas Christ hath said expressly of himself, 'I am the way, the truth, and the life' (John xiv.6)."[28]

The Catholic theologians—led by Johann Eck, Johann Fabri (von Leutkirch), and Johann Cochlaeus—prepared for the "Confutation," which was promptly rejected by Charles because of its bitter tone. Five revisions later the refutation was allowed to stand, although it was still not what the emperor had desired. By this time (August 3) Charles had begun to get a glimpse of what he was up against. In the face of Melanchthon's apparent weakness in a toe-to-toe encounter with the Catholic theologians and the nuncio, the resistance of the Lutheran princes increased. Charles did not press the issue but agreed in a public statement of policy on November 19, 1530, to give the Lutherans until April 15, 1531, to submit. The fifteenth of April came and went, and nothing happened. The emperor was beset with difficulties and found the German Catholic princes unwilling to use force to stamp out the Lutheran heresy. In addition, the Lutheran princes proved more willing than their Catholic counterparts to send

27. The Augsburg Confession, in Schaff's *Evangelical Protestant Creeds*, p. 28.

28. The Augsburg Confession, in Schaff's *Evangelical Protestant Creeds*, pp. 20–21.

troops to defend Vienna against the Turks. Thus, after the Diet of Nuremberg in July 1532, the emperor once again granted a degree of toleration and left his Protestant subjects in Germany unmolested another nine years.

However, the Diet of Augsburg precipitated some unexpected results. During the diet Martin Bucer and Wolfgang Capito, Reformers of Strasbourg, presented their own confession of faith on behalf of the cities of Strasbourg, Constance, Memmingen, and Lindau—hence it was called the Tetrapolitana Confession, or the Confession of the Four Cities. Even though these cities were Zwinglian, Zwingli presented his own confession on behalf of the Swiss. At the same time, the Lutheran princes and representatives of the cities were genuinely alarmed over the attitude of the emperor and his supporters. Immediately after Charles's proclamation of November 19, they laid plans to meet at Schmalkald to discuss measures to defend themselves against his designs. Certain questions arose regarding the legality of their actions, but by December 31 they had formed the Schmalkald League. Although its beginnings were shaky, this new alliance became a formidable force in the life of Europe; eventually it had disastrous consequences for Catholics and Protestants alike. However, war did not break out until 1546, the year of Luther's death.

LAYING THE FOUNDATIONS

What had begun as a protest against the indulgence traffic and its abuses was rapidly developing into a new church structure. While the Augsburg Confession stressed the unity of Luther's followers with the Roman Catholic Church, the same confession revealed the profound theological differences that underlay the theologians' failure to achieve a reconciliation. Luther must have recognized by the end of the diet—if not before—the permanence of the divisions his teachings had precipitated. It is evident that he had begun some time earlier to lay the foundations for an evangelical church in Germany, the leadership for which he continued to provide until his death.

The German Bible

Basic to all else Luther did was the German Bible. Long before 1522 he had started studying biblical languages, preparing for the day when he would translate the Bible into the language of the people. The Wartburg exile provided him the opportunity to undertake the task, and by 1534 the complete German Bible was in the hands of the people. Even though Luther never completely freed himself from the Vulgate, for the evangelical world it was the Bible in the vernacular languages that was to take precedence over the Latin version. Beginning with the German editions, new Protestant Bibles became the most significant influence in shaping the spoken language in half a dozen European countries. Without new vernacular versions of the Bible, it would have been difficult if not impossible for the Reformation to gain enough momentum to have been of any lasting significance. In his work of translation Luther set a pattern that was soon followed by Zwingli, Tyndale, Calvin, Encinas, and numerous others who devoted themselves to the demanding work of translating the Bible into their native tongues. In certain cases the results were remarkable.

Music for the Church

Luther wrote to the Bavarian composer Ludwig Senfl that he had always loved music. In fact, he ranked it second only to theology as an incomparable art:

> I am not ashamed to confess publicly that next to theology, there is no art which is the equal of music, for she alone, after theology, can do what otherwise only theology can accomplish, namely, quiet and cheer-up the soul of man, which is clear evidence that the devil, the originator of depressing worries and troubled thoughts, flees from the voice of music just as he flees from the words of theology.[29]

---

29. Luther, cited by Walter Buzzin in "Luther on Music," *The Musical Quarterly* 32 (Jan. 1946): 84.

Luther was also a noted musician: he played the flute and sang. Hans Sachs, the famous Meistersinger of Nuremberg, called him *"Die Wittenbergisch Nachtigall"* ("the Wittenberg Nightingale"). Zwingli surpassed Luther as an instrumentalist; whereas he gave up entirely on using music in worship, Luther saw the immense potential music held for evangelical worship, and for this reason he studied music and the principles of composition. As early as 1523 he began to collect hymns and psalms for a hymnbook that was published in 1524. In the same year he translated the mass into German, a work for which he composed new chants. Thus, as with Thomas Müntzer's German Mass, the congregation sang certain parts of the service.

Luther actually composed the music and wrote the lyrics for a number of hymns himself. The most famous of these is *A Mighty Fortress Is Our God.* Written in 1528, it reflects Luther's position against the proposed political alliance of evangelicals. His "fortress" was God, not man's puny sword. Filled with imagery with which every sixteenth-century European was familiar, the song became the battle hymn of the Reformation.

The sources for Luther's hymns varied. Luther translated some of the great Latin hymns of the Roman Church into German. Thus *Veni, Creator Spiritus* (*Come, O Creator Spirit, Come*) became *Komm, Gott Schöpfer, Heiliger Geist.* (Other composers followed suit, and thus Latin church music was adapted for Protestant worship.) Luther also pressed into service secular folk tunes, providing them with new lyrics. Luther did not invent this "contractual technique," but no one before him used it so widely or so well. In addition to borrowing the "Barform Chorale" made popular by the German Meistersingers in the previous century, Luther and Johann Walther, the court musician of Frederick the

Komm, Gott Schöpfer, Heiliger Geist, Luther's translation of the Latin hymn *Veni, Creator Spiritus*

Wise, used rhythmic chorales and composed original chorale melodies. These chorales composed for *novias* brought a new vitality to choral music in church worship, because the whole congregation began to sing.

Luther did more than borrow from others and imitate what was traditional. Johannes Riedel attributes the introduction of the Ionian mode to Luther. "He extended the eight church modes to twelve," Riedel points out, "clearing the way for the major and minor scales of today."[30] As much as Luther enjoyed hearing a complex composition sung by the choir, he longed to hear the members of the congregation blend their voices in song. Therefore he was the guiding spirit in the production of the *Geystliche Gesang Büchleyn* (*The Sacred Hymn Book*), which he and Johann Walther brought out in 1524. Another German hymnal was published in Erfurt in the same year. It contained twenty-five hymns, eighteen of which were attributed to Luther. Luther brought out a second hymnbook in 1529, and two more followed: the third was published in 1542, and the last in 1545, a year before his death. As many as thirty-six hymns have been ascribed to Luther; he composed the music for at least ten of these.

Luther's contribution to Protestant church music has been variously assessed. Some have called him the father of Protestant hymnody; others ascribe this title to Johann Walther. While he cannot be compared with the master musicians such as Johann Sebastian Bach who would follow in his train, their work, as Albert Schweitzer has suggested, would have been impossible without Luther's. Whatever else one may say about Luther, it must be said that he

---

30. Riedel, *The Lutheran Chorale: Its Basic Tradition* (Minneapolis: Augsburg, 1967), p. 49. Heinrich Glareanus first recognized the change of modes from eight to twelve in his *Dodecachordon*, published in 1547, a fact that has led some students such as Michael Linder to question Luther's originality. But there is no question that Luther's greatest contribution to music was the introduction of congregational singing into Protestant worship. Even though Thomas Müntzer may have anticipated him in this, Luther was the one who was instrumental in making this a lasting element in evangelical worship.

taught the church—not just the clergy—to sing. It is because of him that music became an effective means of advancing the cause of reform across Europe.

Preaching the Word

As much as Luther loved music, it was preaching, not music, that became the central act of Protestant worship. With Luther the sermon came into its own. The worship of the medieval church had previously centered on the sacrament of the altar, the mass; preaching was an occasional exercise and by no means central. Through the centuries there had been great preachers, but they had become increasingly rare, and frequently the greatest of them had become the objects of suspicion and persecution. But from the time of Luther onward the sacrament of the altar became secondary and the "sacrament" of preaching became primary. Thus the Reformation made preaching the heart of evangelical worship and life, and so it has remained.

In this transition of emphasis from altar to pulpit, Luther set the pattern and became the model. Through the challenge of his responsibilities as pastor and preacher, Luther's concept of the ministry took shape and found expression. For him the preaching of the Word was not just biblical exposition; it was the proclamation of the gospel. Indeed, for Luther any preaching that did not enunciate the gospel of redemption was not preaching. Although he was not averse to devoting whole sermons to the denunciation of the indulgence traffic or the condemnation of drunkenness, he usually chose a text from the Bible and treated it with respect and integrity. His language was forthright, at times even crude and pungent. However coarse and earthy his language, his listeners were never in doubt about his meaning. Luther explained that his lack of eloquence and polish was intentional, because he was directing his words to the ordinary parishioner: "When I preach I sink myself deeply down; I regard neither doctors nor masters, of which there are in the church above forty. But I have an eye to the multitude of young people, children, and servants, of which there are more than two thousand."[31] As Heinrich Heine has pointed out, "The fine discernment of Erasmus, and the gentleness of Melanchthon has never done so much for us as the divine brutality of Brother Martin."[32]

This robust German, in mortal combat with the papacy and other enemies both real and imaginary, possessed the soul of a poet and a sensitivity to the world around him that enabled him to find the inspiration for sermons in everything, including animals—birds, dogs, rabbits, cows, even pigs. His mastery of the German vernacular was never more evident than when he was preaching, yet he never contrived to produce an effect. His words flowed from a soul deeply moved by a conviction refined in the fires of doubt and suffering. Luther gives a glimpse into his concept of a balanced sermon in a few direct sentences:

> A preacher should be a logician and a rhetorician—that is, he must be able to teach and admonish. When he preaches on any article, he must first distinguish it, then define, describe, and show what it is; thirdly, he must produce sentences from the Scripture to prove and to strengthen it; fourthly, he must explain it by examples; fifthly, he must adorn it with similitudes; and, lastly, he must admonish and arouse the indolent, correct the disobedient, and reprove the authors of false doctrine.[33]

It is no accident that from the time of Luther onward, Protestant ministers were referred to not as priests but as preachers, and the unwritten law of the Protestant ministry became "He must be married."

The Teaching Church

It was Luther's family life and that of his friends like Melanchthon that brought out the best in

him and elicited his most tender moments of feeling and reflection. The death of his daughter Magdalena at fourteen caused him untold anguish and unspeakable sorrow, but it did not diminish his devotion to children. The responsibility of teaching his own children as well as those in the churches of the Reformation resulted in his *Small Catechism*.

For Luther the pulpit was also the means of teaching God's people, but he soon realized there must be more. The Reformation had swept many a priest and church into its orbit, but often both priest and people had only the faintest notion of the nature and demands of the new faith. The people rejoiced in their newfound freedom from church tithes (taxes), but the result was that the priests were further impoverished. Often the priests as well as the people were abysmally ignorant. They could repeat the Lord's Prayer, the Apostles' Creed, and perhaps the Ten Commandments, but often little more. The new abandonment of morals went hand in hand with such ignorance. The common people generally understood little about "the new church teachings": to them it meant simply that the mass was now in both kinds (the congregation received both bread and wine) and that, according to Luther, a man was justified before God by faith in Christ alone. In fact, Luther's doctrine of justification by faith had in some cases produced a new antinomianism.

In light of the deplorable conditions of the church in Saxony, teaching was not optional; it was imperative. The first visitation in Saxony had underlined this fact. A program of teaching was inaugurated in every parish, and Luther's *Small Catechism* became the first textbook to be used. Luther wrote it in 1529, shortly after he (along with Justus Jonas and the lawyers) had returned from the visitation. In the introduction he explains the need for the book:

> The deplorable conditions which I recently encountered when I was a visitor constrained me to prepare this brief and simple catechism or statement of Christian teaching. Good God, what wretchedness I beheld! The common people, especially those who live in the country, have no knowledge whatever of Christian teaching, and un-

31. Luther, cited by T. Harwood Pattison in *The History of Christian Preaching* (Philadelphia: American Baptist Publication Society, 1903), pp. 136–37.

32. Heine, cited by Pattison in *The History of Christian Preaching*, p. 137.

33. Luther, cited by Pattison in *The History of Christian Preaching*, p. 137.

fortunately many pastors are quite incompetent and unfitted for teaching. Although the people are supposed to be Christian, are baptized, and receive the holy sacrament, they do not know the Lord's Prayer, the Creed, or the Ten Commandments, they live as if they were pigs and irrational beasts, and now that the Gospel has been restored they have mastered the fine art of abusing liberty.

How will you bishops answer for it before Christ that you have so shamefully neglected the people and paid no attention at all to the duties of your office? May you escape punishment for this! You withhold the cup in the Lord's Supper and insist on the observance of human laws, yet you do not take the slightest interest in teaching the people the Lord's Prayer, the Creed, the Ten Commandments, or a single part of the Word of God. Woe to you forever! I therefore beg of you for God's sake, my beloved brethren who are pastors and preachers, that you take the duties of your office seriously, that you have pity on the people who are entrusted to your care and that you help me to teach the catechism to the people, especially those who are young.[34]

Another result of the first visitation was the publication of *Instruction,* a book of advice and direction for the evangelical churches in Electoral Saxony. As Thomas Lindsay has pointed out, this was the first attempt to give the Lutherans a model for church organization. Because there were no bishops, the "visitors" became in effect a consistory to "ride herd" on the churches. The responsible authority for redirecting ecclesiastical revenues was the elector of Saxony, who in reality was, to use Karl Holl's term, an "emergency bishop" of the *Landeskirche* (territorial church).[35] Luther always viewed this as a temporary arrangement to be observed only until the rule of true bishops could be restored. But what was a temporary expedient became rather permanent in German

Lutheranism, and in the process was born the state church, in which religious concerns became subservient to the concerns of the state.

The Church Is . . .

Luther hammered out much of his ecclesiology in controversy with Rome and his evangelical adversaries. At times he seems to have viewed wistfully the possibility of implementing the concept of the *Freiwilligkeitskirche* (free church), according to which churches would be comprised of committed Christians who voluntarily formed fellowships for the purpose of mutual edification and service. "But," he wrote in the German Mass, "as yet I neither can nor desire to begin, or to make rules for such a congregation or assembly. I have not yet the people necessary to accomplish it; nor do I observe many who strongly urge it." He went on to say, "For every Christian peasant you will find a thousand non Christian peasants."[36] The whole idea of the free church was dismissed because, however attractive it might appear, it was clearly impossible.

With the rejection of churches made up of only believers went the rejection of believer's baptism. Luther may even have entertained the possibility of implementing it, but he was restrained by his pessimistic appraisal of the common man's response: "If from now on only adults and older people were to be baptized, I venture to assert that not more than a tenth of our people would allow themselves to be baptized."[37] Even though Luther referred to the evangelical congregations composed of pagans as being "under a Christian guise,"[38] he admitted that the church was present in their midst. While it was apparently hidden from the eyes of

34. Luther, *Small Catechism,* in *The Book of Concord,* trans. and ed. Theodore G. Tappert (Philadelphia: Muhlenberg Press, 1959); cited in *Creeds of the Churches: A Reader in Christian Doctrine from the Bible to the Present,* ed. John H. Leith (Garden City, N.Y.: Doubleday, 1963), p. 108.

35. Holl, cited by Mueller in *Church and State in Luther and Calvin: A Comparative Study* (Nashville: Broadman Press, 1954), p. 33.

36. Luther, cited by Mueller in *Church and State in Luther and Calvin,* p. 27.

37. Luther, cited by Mueller in *Church and State in Luther and Calvin,* pp. 26–27.

38. Luther, cited by Mueller in *Church and State in Luther and Calvin,* p. 27.

man, there were certain signs by which one could determine its presence. In a tract he wrote in 1539 entitled "On the Councils and the Churches," Luther gives seven marks that distinguish "the holy Christian Church of Christ" on earth: the Word of God, the sacrament of baptism, the sacrament of the altar, the keys of Matthew 18, ministers called by the church, the offering of prayer and praise, and suffering for the sake of Christ (the Holy Cross).

When Luther summarizes the indispensable features of the functioning church, he reduces them to two: "the church may be known where the Word is preached and the sacraments are properly observed."[39] "The Word" in this case means the gospel, but it is closely related to Scripture. (Contrary to what many have asserted, Luther's use of the term "the Word of God" varies. Often he uses it to mean the Word preached or the proclamation of the gospel; he also uses it to mean Christ or the Bible.)

By the proper observance of the sacraments Luther meant infant baptism as practiced in the Catholic Church. The sacrament of the altar was revamped according to his teachings, which means that it was offered in both kinds (bread and wine) and with his understanding of the "real presence" (corporal presence) of Christ. Luther believed that participants needed to have faith if the sacrament was to convey the grace of God. Thus infant faith was necessary for infant baptism:

> If we then cannot prove that young children do themselves believe and have faith of their own, I should forthwith counsel that at once we let off this practice, the sooner the better and never again baptize another infant in order that we may not mock and blaspheme the adorable majesty of God by such nonsensical and magical work.[40]

In his early writings Luther insisted that the New Testament taught baptism by immersion and included penance as a sacrament. The ma-

ture Luther, however, abandoned both of these positions. In his later years he placed less emphasis on faith and more on the necessity of baptism for salvation. Perhaps those whom he labeled *Schwärmer* (fanatics) caused him to put increased emphasis on the importance of the sacraments.

Theology

There have been many attempts to reduce Luther's theological concepts to one proposition. This is, of course, impossible; it is even difficult to summarize Luther's often contradictory writings. Still, although Luther was not a systematic theologian, all of his work was rooted in theology, and his theological insights stimulated numerous attempts at structuring a Protestant theology. To ignore Luther as a theologian, therefore, is to ignore Luther.

Early on it became quite apparent that Luther was attempting to reformulate Augustine's thought within his growing commitment to biblical truth. Like Wycliffe and Huss before him, he considered himself an Augustinian, because in Augustine he found the support from an ancient and respected father with which he could reject Aquinas and Aristotle. But his reconstruction of Augustine was far more dynamic than that of Wycliffe or Huss. It had been tested in the crucible of his own experience and reshaped according to his understanding of Scripture, Scripture that had come alive in his quest for a gracious God. It was through this struggle that he had made his discovery that "the just shall live by faith."

Although the principle of justification by faith is pervasive and fundamental to all else in Luther's thought, it can never stand alone. It is also an inadequate reduction that sums up Luther's theology in the three *solas—sola scriptura, sola fides, sola gratia—*and the priesthood of believers. But it would be difficult to come up with a more basic summary of Luther's theology. For there is a strong relationship between Luther's discovery of the scriptural truth that man is justified by faith alone in God's sight, and his realization that this is the expression of God's

---

39. See Mueller, *Church and State in Luther and Calvin,* p. 12.

40. Luther, cited by Mueller in *Church and State in Luther and Calvin,* p. 23.

grace of which Augustine made so much. In Luther's thought the priesthood of believers is the result of justification. At the same time, it enhances the believer's status before God, sanctifies his vocation, and provides the motivation for a life of Christian service.

However, there is little that one can say about Luther without fear of contradiction. The reasons for this are fairly obvious. Perhaps no other single figure of the Reformation era has been the subject of such intense investigation. In addition, confessional bias either deliberately or subconsciously affects one's interpretation. And then there is the challenge of Luther himself. His was a complex personality, and he was fond of stating his thoughts in paradoxical equations that often seem contradictory. Things are further skewed by the changes he underwent. From 1515 to the end of his life his inquisitive and creative mind was constantly working out the implications of his own experience of grace. There is no doubt that "the young Luther" was more creative and evangelical than "the old Luther." With age came more responsibility and more enemies. Luther reacted in different ways to his enemies and to other expressions of the Reformation, but he seldom responded with restraint. Thus various historians of the Reformation perceive Luther in different ways. Erich Hassinger believes that Luther's unique contribution lay in his "rediscovery of the historical core" of the Christian religion:

As for the claim that Luther was in no sense original, there is no better reply than that to be found in the recent work of Erich Hassinger, who finds Luther's contribution to have been his rediscovery of the historical core of Christianity. The claim of the Christian religion is that God did something unique in history. In the year that Caesar Augustus ordered all the world to be taxed, the Word became flesh. The Incarnation, the Crucifixion and the Resurrection constituted a unique self-disclosure of God in Christ. To Him the ages lead up, and from Him the centuries lead out. By faith in His redeeming work man is forgiven and remade. The assertion of the unique historical role of Christ is an offense because it assumes unevenness in the work of God, who, if this be true, declared Himself more manifestly to the men of

the first century than to those in any other. There are various ways of escaping from the historical singularity of Christ. One is mysticism: God is accessible at all times equally to the waiting heart. Another is moralism: man is saved by his own good deeds done here and now. And still another is institutionalism: the Church is the custodian and continuator of the revelation once and for all given. Luther asserted unequivocally the historical uniqueness of the work of God in Christ. Its continuance in the present is mediated through Scripture, which is the record of the event. And though it must be interpreted by the Spirit, yet the Spirit can never be disassociated from the outward Word. This position divided Luther from Catholics on the one side and from Protestant sectaries on the other.[41]

It was the Renaissance that set the pattern that Luther followed when he sought to determine the essence of the Christian faith in the light of Scripture. His search was in part a personal pilgrimage that did not stop until he had encountered God and received the assurance of forgiveness. The Renaissance (as mediated by Erasmus) also gave him the tools with which he pursued his quest and the critical criteria he utilized to sift the biblical wheat from the medieval chaff. But it was personal experience that convinced Luther, as it had others before him, that the revelation of God in Christ was historically mediated, and that a faith commitment, *fiducia* (trust), to Christ alone was the way of salvation. In all of this the medieval church contributed little. It had, however, preserved the sources—the Bible and the early church fathers—with which the earnest searcher could explore the terrain if he possessed the linguistic tools necessary for the task.

When Luther died in 1546, all of Europe—Luther's enemies as well as his friends—recognized that one of history's greatest figures had exited from the drama of human affairs. But by this time there were numerous Reformers, and

---

41. Hassinger, cited by Roland Bainton in *Studies on the Reformation* (Boston: Beacon Press, 1963), pp. 107-8.

the Reformation was spawning new forms in almost every city in Northern Europe. Perhaps the greatest challenge to Luther's leadership was coming from Geneva. All of this indicated that the churches of the Reformation were here to stay. The new wine demanded new wineskins; the old simply could no longer contain the ferment of the rediscovered gospel.

Chapter X

ZWINGLI: HUMANIST TURNED REFORMER

Zwingli, the Reformer of Switzerland, and Luther met face to face only once—at Marburg in 1529. Instead of providing an occasion for a meeting of the minds, the colloquy turned out to be a confrontation in which each Reformer sharply rejected the theology of the other. Perhaps a clash between these two strong-willed champions of Reformation truth was inevitable. Their theological differences were too profound to be resolved in a few days, and their divergent viewpoints had been forged in quite different cultural and religious milieus. Luther was a German of the Germans surely as much as the Apostle Paul was a Hebrew of the Hebrews. And the Germans viewed the Swiss as uncouth people just one step from barbarism whose mercenaries were the terror of Europe.

But the meeting at Marburg failed because of more than cultural and national differences. Luther had become a Reformer out of a deep travail of the soul, after a long spiritual struggle that had driven him into the monastery. Zwingli, on the other hand, trod the humanist path to reform; his upbringing and education reflected a more rationalistic—and hence a more humanistic—approach to religion. In the early stages of his ecclesiastical career Zwingli was a disciple of Erasmus, just as Luther was a disciple of Augustine.

To the dismay of Philip of Hesse, the verbal battle at Marburg became explosive when Zwingli, who was a superb linguist, confronted Luther with the meaning of John 6:63 in the Greek text. Luther responded that Zwingli's text had nothing to do with the discussion in progress. "No!" retorted Zwingli. "This will break your spine!" Luther shot back, "Do not brag too much. Here, necks are not broken. You are in Hesse now, not in Switzerland!" Zwingli apologized, but the damage had been done.[1] Later, in writing about Zwingli and his compatriots, Luther ridiculed them in a parody of Psalm 1:1: "Blessed is the man who walketh not in the counsel of the sacramentarians nor standeth in the way of the Zwinglians nor sitteth where the Zürichers are sitting."[2] It is quite evident that Zwingli, despite his willingness to seek some common ground with Luther, was not a "Lu-

---

1. Cited by Jean Rilliet in *Zwingli: Third Man of the Reformation,* trans. Harold Knight (Philadelphia: Westminster Press, 1964), p. 260.

2. Luther, cited by William A. Mueller in *Church and State in Luther and Calvin: A Comparative Study* (Nashville: Broadman Press, 1954), p. 18.

theran." Neither was the Reformation in Switzerland a carbon copy of that in Saxony; rather, it was a relatively independent and indigenous development. Zwingli's life and reformatory efforts are an indispensable part of the history of this movement.

THE EARLY YEARS: 1484-1505

Ulrich Zwingli was born on January 1, 1484, approximately seven weeks after the birth of Luther. He was named after his father, Huldrych (Uly), who served as magistrate of the village of Wildhaus as his father had done before him. His mother was the former Margaretha Bruggmann Meili, a cousin of the abbot of Fischingen. To Margaretha and Uly were born eight children, two girls and six boys. Ulrich was the third child born to the most prominent family in Wildhaus.

Wildhaus was hardly a village. It was actually a scattering of homes—a patchwork of houses, barns, gardens, and orchards—among green alpine pastures. It was located high in the Toggenburg Valley—so high, in fact, that the fruit was not yet ripe before the winter chill began to drive man and beast indoors. The location of Wildhaus was symbolic of its dual Latin and Germanic heritage. It was said that the rain falling on one side of the roof of the parish church eventually found its way into the Rhône, but the rain falling on the other side fed the rivulets that flowed into the Rhine. Similarly divided was the political and religious jurisdiction of the village. The magistrate was appointed by the abbot of the Benedictine Abbey of St. Gall, but the parish priest was answerable to the bishop of Chur, and Chur was the capital of the Grissons. Thus Zwingli's father was answerable to one authority, and his Uncle Bartholomew, who was the parish priest, was answerable to the other. Although Wildhaus was technically outside the thirteen cantons that made up the Confederation, no village was more Swiss. The Toggenburgers were Alamanni and heirs of the proud Swiss traditions of independence and self reliance.

Latin School

In 1487 Zwingli's uncle became dean of Wesen on Lake Wallenstadt, and in 1489 Zwingli, then five, left the crowded household of his childhood to live with his uncle. For the next five years he attended a Latin school in Wesen. When he was ten he was sent to Basel, where he lived with a distant relative while attending an advanced Latin school. But two years later he was transferred, probably upon the advice of an outstanding schoolmaster and follower of Erasmus (Gregory Bünzli), to a school conducted by Heinrich Wölflin in Bern. Bern, a free imperial city, was rapidly becoming a most promising political center of Switzerland. At the time, religious life was flourishing, and monasteries vied for young recruits. Zwingli, who was developing into an excellent Latin scholar and possessed remarkable musical talent as well, was an attractive prospect, and the Dominicans persuaded him to become one of them. He may even have begun his novitiate at the age his uncle had expected him to enter the university. The news of Ulrich's change in career was quite as unwelcome to his parents and uncle as Martin Luther's news had been to his father. The Zwinglis reacted by immediately removing their son from the monastery. They had no intention of allowing his decision to stand or at least to remain unchallenged. A few months later, Zwingli had arrived safely in Vienna to begin his university studies, but his father was still playing watchdog. In reply to a letter from his son describing his accomplishments as a musician, he wrote, "I would rather have a philosopher [for a son] than a play-actor."[3]

University Days

Zwingli's first attempt—in 1498—to pursue university studies was brief. Soon after he entered the famous University of Vienna, founded in 1368, he was expelled. At that time feelings were running high between Austrian students

---

3. Huldrych Zwingli, cited by Rilliet in *Zwingli*, p. 23.

and the Swiss, and this, coupled with Zwingli's expulsion, may account for the fact that he stayed in Vienna less than a year. However, he returned for another stint, which lasted somewhat longer. Vienna offered Zwingli opportunities he had only dreamed of before. The university counted five thousand students or more within the three traditional faculties of theology, law, and medicine. In the early years of the Renaissance the university had embraced Italian humanism and the conciliar movement. Heinrich von Langenstein's move from the University of Paris to the University of Vienna had strengthened the advocates of the *via moderna* in Vienna. Conrad Celtis spent his last years in Vienna organizing his humanist literary societies, which were strongly tinged with German nationalist feeling. New disciplines like geography had been added to the traditional *trivium* and *quadrivium*. Besides having a well-known academic reputation, the university, like those of Oxford and Paris, was infamous for student brawls, drunkenness, and immorality. Thus Zwingli's Vienna experience must have been both enlightening and shocking. In any case—perhaps because his funds ran out, perhaps because he was much too Swiss to ever feel at home in Vienna—Zwingli left Vienna for Basel sometime before October 1502.

Basel was certainly no Vienna, and its university was a proud but small institution with only about a hundred students—but it was Swiss. It was not lacking in able scholars, among whom were Sebastian Brant and Johann Reuchlin. And it could boast that it was one of the first universities north of the Alps to embrace the Renaissance. At the time of Zwingli's appearance there the faculty was composed of equal numbers of advocates of the *via moderna* and the *via antiqua*, with a sprinkling of humanist followers of Erasmus. On September 18, 1504, Zwingli received his bachelor of arts degree, and in 1506 he received his master's.

Before Zwingli had completed his studies at Basel, Thomas Wyttenbach arrived from Tübingen to lecture on Peter Lombard's *Sentences* and Paul's Epistle to the Romans. It would have been strange indeed if Zwingli had not availed himself of the opportunity to attend the lectures of the new professor. In retrospect Zwingli attributed to Wyttenbach his first awakening "to several abuses of the Church, especially the indulgences," and claimed that Wyttenbach "taught him not to rely on the keys of the Church, but to seek the remission of sins alone in the death of Christ. . . ."[4] Leo Jud, a fellow student of Zwingli's and later a priest in Zürich, related that it was Wyttenbach who taught his students to study the Scriptures and forsake the "sophists." Whether or not Zwingli and Jud heeded this advice (and they may have invested Wyttenbach's lectures with more than was there) is not known. But there is no doubt that during his Basel years Zwingli was introduced to Aquinas and consequently to Aristotle.

Little is known of Zwingli's personal life during his university career. That he had the capacity to form lasting friendships is evident from his close ties with Joachim von Watt (Vadianus), a friend from his Vienna days, and Leo Jud. The source of his financial support has remained largely a mystery. Doubtless he went to Vienna with some assistance from his Uncle Bartholomew. There are some indications that he was forced to resort to begging, not an uncommon experience of university students in those days. But once he was back in Basel his fortunes improved considerably. He received a small stipend from St. Peter's Cathedral and some pay for his tutorial work in Latin. He might have remained in Basel or considered undertaking more formal theological studies if his uncle had not stepped in to change the course of his career.

GLARUS, 1506-1516

Zwingli's enterprising uncle learned that the priest at Glarus had recently died, and even though Zwingli had not yet been ordained to the priesthood, his uncle recommended him to

---

4. Zwingli, cited by Samuel Macauley Jackson in *Huldreich Zwingli: The Reformer of German Switzerland, 1484-1531* (New York: Putnam, 1901), p. 59.

the parish. (Glarus was a town in the Swiss Alps near the headwaters of the Rhine, about forty-three miles southeast of Zürich.) But according to custom another priest, Heinrich Göldi of Zürich, who was already receiving benefices from two other churches, was given Glarus. It was widely known that Göldi, who had no intention of serving Glarus himself but planned to send a substitute to fulfill the minimum obligations, demanded a hundred florins in payment before he would relinquish his claim to the position. Thus Zwingli was forced to purchase the "franchise" to serve as parish priest at Glarus. He agreed to pay in installments after the men of Glarus let it be known that they preferred the young Ulrich to an absentee vicar. He was hurriedly ordained a priest and celebrated his first mass on September 29 in his native village of Wildhaus. The coming of a young new parish priest to Glarus was a major event in the town of thirteen hundred inhabitants, especially since the men of Glarus felt they had had a hand in Zwingli's selection.

Weaving was the town's major industry, but, like most of Switzerland, Glarus was also agrarian. It produced an abundance of milk and cheese and some wine. The townspeople also produced many children, and the "cash crop" came from the ready supply of sturdy young men who, according to custom, hired themselves out as mercenaries.

The tradition of Swiss valor in battle was an honored one. The three cantons of Uri, Schwyz, and Unterwalden, the nucleus of the Confederation, were soon joined by Lucerne, Glarus, Zug, Zürich, and Bern. Together they proved their mettle on the battlefield, and by the end of the fourteenth century they had thrown off the yoke of the Hapsburgs and made good the independence that they had claimed as early as 1291. Largely independent and self-governing with differing ethnic and linguistic characteristics, the cantons were bound together by a mutual need for defense and a common love of freedom and independence. Even though the country that the Swiss inhabited was strikingly beautiful, it was barren. With much toil and ingenuity (and some cows), they managed to

survive, but money and luxuries were in short supply—hence the mercenary traffic. By Zwingli's time the Confederation could field an army of ten thousand or more for purposes of defense or attack. After a series of stunning victories in 1476 and 1477, Swiss soldiers became the most sought-after mercenaries in Europe. They appeared invincible.

Since Glarus was a major supplier of hardy young recruits, Zwingli became involved in foreign excursions, serving as a chaplain with a Swiss contingent from Glarus. Pope Julius II, the "warrior pope" detested and ridiculed by Erasmus, was in constant need of mercenaries to "liberate" Italian cities from foreign domination. Zwingli may have been with the estimated eighteen thousand Swiss troops who defeated the French at the battle of Pavia in 1512. It is certain that he was with the four thousand Swiss soldiers at Novara (in 1513), where once again the French were defeated. The Swiss profited greatly from these two successful expeditions, and the pope was not ungrateful. For his services on behalf of pope and church, Zwingli was granted a yearly pension of fifty florins. Thus in 1515 he was again with the Swiss troops, exhorting them to fight manfully in the cause of his holiness against the French at Monza. But this time the French succeeded in buying off the soldiers from a number of Swiss cantons. Reinforced by Venetians and supported by heavy artillery, the French dealt a mortal blow to the remaining Swiss forces during twenty hours of hand-to-hand combat. For the first time in history a Swiss army was utterly beaten. The carnage was indescribable. Ten thousand of the flower of Swiss manhood lay dead. Zwingli never succeeded in escaping the memories of that experience. His subsequent opposition to Swiss mercenary traffic can be dated from this time. Erasmus and his vigorous tracts against war reinforced the young chaplain's misgivings about Swiss military exploits. During his years in Glarus, however, Zwingli tended to lay all the blame for the massacre on Francis I and the French.

At Glarus, Zwingli began to acquire a library. In addition to the ancient classics, such as the works of Aristotle, Origen, Jerome, and Augustine, he purchased every available work of Erasmus, and he actually began to teach himself Greek in order to be able to read the Greek New Testament when it appeared. In fact, Zwingli purchased one of the first copies of the 1516 edition published by Froben in Basel. This edition carried the Latin text on one side and the Greek text on the other, an invaluable aid for one who knew the Latin well and was attempting to learn Greek. Zwingli was so inspired by the work that before the end of the year he made the long and difficult journey to Basel just to talk with Erasmus personally.

While in Glarus, Zwingli founded a Latin school for the promising boys of the parish. He also proved a faithful pastor to his troubled congregation. But despite his unquestionable devotion to his people, his opposition to the mercenary traffic, which he denounced with increasing conviction, forced him to leave. The traffic was too profitable for those for whom the fear of poverty was more threatening than the risk of battle. That Zwingli's departure from Glarus was not of his own choosing is evident from a letter he wrote to Vadianus, his friend from his Vienna days:

> I have changed my residence, not at the stimulus of desire or of avarice, but because of the evils of the French and now I am at Einsiedeln. . . . What disaster that French faction has at last brought me the wind of rumor has doubtless wafted to you. In the things done I too have had a part, but I have borne or have learned to bear my misfortune.[5]

EINSIEDELN, 1516-1518

Although Zwingli left Glarus, he did not give up his benefice. He moved to Einsiedeln, about thirty miles from Glarus, to serve as chaplain of the Shrine of the Virgin of Meinrod (the Black Virgin), which was (and is) the center of the cult-of-Mary worship in Switzerland. Today the Chapel of the Black Virgin is located in the basilica of the Benedictine monastery. Twice ravaged by fire, the ornate baroque edifice bears

little resemblance to the building that housed the shrine in Zwingli's day, but the worship remains virtually the same.

Tradition holds that the chapel was dedicated by an angelic host in 948 A.D. In Zwingli's time a celebration of the angelic dedication was held every seven years. A number of pilgrims among the thousands that visited the shrine every year testified that miracles occurred there regularly. This Lourdes of Switzerland attracted the credulous and devout from Germany and Italy as well as from the cantons of Switzerland. Thus Zwingli enjoyed frequent opportunities to preach to people from near and far, and the news of his eloquence began to create a stir in Zürich some twenty miles distant. In addition to fulfilling his duties as chaplain, Zwingli served as parish priest to the citizens of Einsiedeln. Neither his preaching responsibilities nor his pastoral duties were extremely demanding, so he had time to continue his theological studies, which commanded his attention more and more.

The situation was made to order for a person with Zwingli's interests. The Benedictine monastery, of which the shrine was a part, had almost ceased to exist. Only two or three monks were left to rattle around its empty corridors, and only one of them—Diebold von Hohengeraldseck, the administrator—was active. He became Zwingli's close friend and supporter, opening to him the treasures of the ancient library with its priceless manuscripts. Diebold was also a patron of the new learning and supported Zwingli's Christian humanism.

The Einsiedeln years can be called the Erasmian years. Zwingli had become increasingly enamored with Erasmus. He tried to read everything Erasmus wrote and began to refer to his own understanding of the Christian faith as "the philosophy of Christ." During these years he also became an accomplished Greek scholar. G. R. Potter, his latest biographer, writes,

> He had by now mastered the Greek language as well as any man north of the Alps—More, Vadian, Budaeus, even Erasmus. From the Greek New Testament, and from Tertullian, Jerome and Lactantius, he was drawn to the study of the Greek

---

5. Zwingli, cited by Jackson in *Huldreich Zwingli*, p. 94.

Fathers, Origen, Cyril of Alexandria and Chrysostom in particular, and he noticed that the earlier they wrote the less their teaching seemed to support current doctrine, especially about purgatory.[6]

It was while he was chaplain in Einsiedeln that Zwingli had his first skirmish with Berhardin Samson, a peddler of indulgences like Tetzel, his German counterpart. Because of Zwingli's sharp attack upon the traffic as well as strong local opposition to it, Samson beat a hasty retreat. Zwingli's opposition may have been no more than the outrage of an enlightened humanist who deplored the fleecing of the sheep, or it may have been a righteous indignation that ran much deeper than that. Erasmus had raised questions about indulgences in *The Praise of Folly,* the force of which could hardly have escaped Zwingli's notice. And, of course, both Thomas Wyttenbach and Luther had questioned indulgences. Only eight months before, Luther had attacked the issue again and with far more urgency than either Wyttenbach or Erasmus had expressed.

In retrospect Zwingli claimed to have begun to preach the gospel as early as 1516. He wrote, "I began to preach the gospel before anyone in my locality had so much as heard the name of Luther: for I never left the pulpit without taking the words of the gospel as used in the mass service of the day and expounding them by means of the Scriptures; although at first I relied much upon the Fathers [Origen, Ambrose, Jerome, and Augustine] as expositors and explainers."[7]

Two comments by his contemporaries help put Zwingli's self-understanding in proper perspective. Beatus Rhenanus, one of Zwingli's friends, wrote on December 6, 1518, "For it does not escape me that you and those like you bring forth to the people the pure philosophy of Christ, straight from the fountain, uncorrupted by interpretation of Scotists or Gabrielists, but expounded by Augustine, Ambrose,

Cyprian, Jerome, faithfully and correctly."[8] In the same vein Casper Hedio wrote on November 6, 1519, after Zwingli had gone to Zürich, "I was greatly charmed by an address of yours, so elegant, learned, and weighty, fluent, discerning, and evangelical such a one as plainly recalled the energy of the old theologians. . . . "[9]

But even after Zwingli claimed to have arrived at evangelical truth, he was still accepting the papal pension. In fact, on September 1, 1518, he was appointed an acolyte chaplain by Leo X. However, he did refuse the pope's offer to double his grant. That he was a priest on the move and possibly in theological transition may have become known in Rome—hence the Curia's attempt to tie him more securely to the papal see.

Zwingli's preaching had become a topic of conversation in certain circles in Zürich. Two weeks after Easter Sunday, fifteen hundred men from Zürich walked on foot to the Shrine of the Black Virgin to pray. Zwingli's sermon upon this occasion made quite an impression on them, so when the office of people's priest became open at the *Grossmünster* (Great Minster) in Zürich, Oswald Myconius's recommendation of Zwingli did not fall on unheeding ears. Zwingli had friends in high places, one of whom was Cardinal Schinner, which was also in his favor. The twenty-four canons (priests attached to the church living under a semimonastic rule) who had the responsibility of selecting the next people's priest did not find the choice a difficult one.

But Zwingli's election to the new post did not come without some opposition. Some canons raised questions about Zwingli's morals. It was rumored that a woman in Zürich, a nobleman's daughter, claimed that Zwingli was the father of her baby. Zwingli's response revealed much, about both his life-style and the problems that clerical celibacy had created. Zwingli

---

6. Potter, *Zwingli* (London: Cambridge University Press, 1976), pp. 42–43.

7. Zwingli, cited by Jackson in *Huldreich Zwingli,* p. 108.

8. Rhenanus, cited by Jackson in *Huldreich Zwingli,* p. 107. Rhenanus is referring to Duns Scotus and Gabriel Biel. Scotus was a Realist, and Biel was a Nominalist. Both were sharp logicians of late medieval Scholasticism.

9. Hedio, cited by Jackson in *Huldreich Zwingli,* p. 108.

replied that the woman was not a nobleman's daughter but a barber's daughter from Glarus whose loose morals had caused her to be thrown out of her father's home. Thus it was impossible to say who the baby's father was. He frankly admitted that he was unable to remain chaste, regardless of how hard he tried. It was his rule, however, never to violate a nun, a virgin, or the marriage bed.

Since his only serious competitor for the post was a German priest who reportedly kept three concubines by whom he had fathered eight children, Zwingli was elected despite his painful admission. Perhaps the canons felt that his honesty and his attempts to live morally reflected a more ethical life-style than they could expect most priests of the day to follow. In that supposition they were correct. The bishop of Constance fined any priest in his diocese four florins if it was discovered that he had fathered a child, and at that time the average annual income from this source amounted to four hundred florins.

THE BEGINNING OF THE REFORMATION IN ZÜRICH, 1519

Zwingli moved to Zürich on December 27 in order to assume his new responsibilities on the first day of January 1519. Only then did he formally take leave of his church in Glarus. Since he still owed twenty florins on the purchase price of the office, the citizens of Glarus raised the money and paid off his debt. It was truly a new beginning for the new people's priest, who began his ministry on his thirty-fifth birthday.

Zürich was the chief city in the canton and one of the more important cities of the thirteen cantons in the Confederation. The city with its surrounding villages had seven thousand inhabitants. Several churches dominated the skyline of this old city, which was located on the shores of Lake Zürich and the banks of the Limmat River. The most impressive was the *Grossmünster,* with its twin steeples rising high over the Limmat. There were fifty-seven secular priests of one kind or another attached to the churches of the city in addition to the two

hundred monks, nuns, and priests who belonged to the four orders with their monasteries and priories. It was truly an impressive and important religious center of German-speaking Switzerland to which the priest from Wildhaus had come.

The role of the people's priest of the *Grossmünster* was pastoral. It was his responsibility to say mass, visit the sick and dying, and preach. From the beginning it was evident that Zwingli intended to give preaching a prominent role in the worship experience of the people. After his formal induction on Saturday, January 1, he thanked the canons for electing him and asked for their prayers. He then announced that on the following day he would begin a series of sermons based on the Gospel of Matthew.

Apparently Zwingli did not intend to start a religious revolution with this deviation from tradition, but he did. He was still working within the context of Erasmus's concept of reform, which called for a cleansing of the church through a return to Scripture and canon law. He also continued to count among his friends Cardinal Schinner and Johann Fabri (Heigerlin von Leutkirch), vicar-general of Constance. Apparently at this time Zwingli saw no basic difference between Erasmus and Luther, nor had he faced the possibility of separation from Rome.

But before Zwingli had a chance to finish his exposition of Matthew's Gospel, the plague descended upon Zürich with a vengeance. More than a fourth of Zürich's seven thousand residents were buried as a result. The bodies were stacked in the streets like cords of wood because graves could not be dug fast enough.[10] Through it all Zwingli proved himself a faithful priest who put the welfare of his people before his own. But the strain and exposure were too much, and he too became deathly ill. The worst blow came when his younger brother, Andrew, for whom he held a special affection, contracted the disease and died. These tragic events precipitated the most serious spiritual crisis that Zwingli had yet experienced.

---

10. Chroniclers differ on the exact numbers. One records that 2,000 died; another says that 3,500 died.

Ulrich Zwingli, Reformer of German-speaking Switzerland RELIGIOUS NEWS SERVICE

THE CRISIS OF 1519

Zwingli had faced his first spiritual crisis at Monza, and it had left its mark. But this second crisis was far more personal and threatening. If the carnage on the plains of Milan had made Zwingli think seriously for the first time about the fleeting nature of life, the plague that enveloped the city on the Limmat became an even more potent reminder of that fact.

When Zwingli himself was stricken by the plague, he feared he would die, and he expressed his feelings in three poems written at various stages of his illness. They reveal a man, now sobered by thoughts of his impending death, who had become acutely aware of his sins. When he was safely out of danger, tragedy struck: his younger brother contracted the disease and died. Zwingli was crushed, but he refused to blame God. Instead he wrote, "I have learned to submit myself completely to his divine will." The passage in which this admission appears reads like a psalm.

> Do as Thou will
> Nothing is too severe for me
> I am Thine to
> Make whole or to break
> So I will still
> Defy the Lordships of this world
> And bear joyfully its blows
> With Thy help
> For without Thee, nothing is
>   possible.[11]

One cannot know for sure whether or not Zwingli was converted in the usual sense of the word, but certainly there was a new seriousness about him. It could be that his brush with death and his anguish over the loss of his brother marked his transformation from enlightened humanist to earnest Reformer. At the time he had not yet broken with Rome. In fact, the papal legate's personal physician had been sent to Zürich to treat Zwingli during his illness. However, a year later (in 1520) he publicly rejected the papal pension and asked forgiveness for

having accepted it for so long. One thing is certain: Zwingli's faithfulness in discharging his pastoral functions had endeared him to the people of Zürich and the canons of the *Grossmünster*. He wrote enthusiastically to Myconius in December 1519 that there were more than two thousand somewhat enlightened people in Zürich.

On April 29, 1521, he became a canon of the *Grossmünster*, taking the place vacated by Dr. Heinrich Engelhard, who had become a canon and people's priest at the *Fraumünster* across the river. With this new position Zwingli became a full citizen of the city. He was allowed a house, a horse, and an income of seventy gulden. He welcomed the promotion. "I am in this city of Zürich bishop and pastor," he wrote. "The cure of souls has been laid upon me. I have taken an oath to this effect which the monks have not done."[12]

Zwingli could not have been unaware of what was happening in Germany at the time. By 1521 Luther's books were circulating freely in Switzerland, and all of Europe waited anxiously for news from the Diet of Worms, fearing the worst. For the supporters of Luther "the worst" meant one thing, and for those who clung to Rome it meant quite another. At the same time Zwingli was conditioning his people for the coming Reformation and consolidating his support. The people's priests in each of the other major churches, Heinrich Engelhard of the *Fraumünster* and Leo Jud of St. Peter's Church, were of one mind and heart with Zwingli. If Zwingli were indeed determined to follow a reformatory course in Zürich, he had been both shrewd and cautious up to this point.

ZWINGLI'S REFORMATORY METHOD

Whether or not Zwingli had so intended, he had launched the Reformation in Zürich from his pulpit. After recovering from his near-fatal bout with the plague, he resumed his exposition of Matthew's Gospel. Such a departure from the

---

11. Zwingli, cited by Potter in *Zwingli,* p. 70.

12. Zwingli, cited by Potter in *Zwingli,* p. 73.

traditional worship of the medieval church must have evoked considerable comment among the parishioners. The church calendar was ignored, and mass ceased to be the only act of worship.

Preaching the Evangel

In 1520 Zwingli concluded his sermons from Matthew and promptly moved on to a consideration of Acts; in 1521 he preached from First Timothy and Galatians. Since some criticized him for being too Pauline, he turned to First and Second Peter, followed by Hebrews. In 1523 he returned to the Gospels, preaching first from Luke and then John. He did not turn to the Old Testament for his regular Sunday sermons until the middle of 1525. Then the shift was significant.

These choices were very probably part of Zwingli's strategy. If Conrad Hofmann, one of the canons who had opposed Zwingli's election, recognized the revolutionary implications of such preaching, Zwingli must have, too. In fact, Hofmann was so distressed that during Zwingli's illness he visited him in the hope of helping the people's priest see the error of his ways before it was too late. He even went so far as to register a formal complaint with the provost of the *Grossmünster,* claiming that Zwingli was flouting long-standing tradition by refusing to follow the designated Scripture selections for each Sunday. Zwingli defended himself by citing the practice of Chrysostom and Augustine, who had followed no such list. He also pointed out that the list did not exist before Charlemagne's time.

Zwingli's preaching became his most effective means of advancing the cause of reform. His progress toward Reformation truth is difficult to follow because rarely were his sermons written out or recorded by a stenographer. His style was more informal and extemporaneous than that of Luther. Even though his voice was not strong and his delivery was rapid, he enlivened his sermons with humor and frequent anecdotes. He evidently kept his congregation awake and alert, and in the process he introduced them to Reformation concepts.

Although Rome became increasingly restive concerning the rumors of Zwingli's provocative sermons, his friendship with Cardinal Schinner and his hopes for a genuine reform within the church forestalled an open break with the Reformer. Rome's tolerance for heresy in Zürich doubtless went well beyond previous limits because the papacy was so dependent upon Swiss troops in its ongoing power struggle with the princes of Europe. There was also a growing conviction among some highly placed and respected members of the hierarchy that internal reform was the only adequate answer to the church's plight. Hints from Rome late in 1523 relayed the message that if Zwingli would only be patient and conform, he would be rewarded—both with a reform of the church and a cardinal's hat.

The Affair of the Sausages

Two events in 1522 indicated the direction in which Zwingli and the Swiss Reformation were moving. The first of these was "the affair of the sausages." For some time Zwingli had been preaching that many traditions and practices of the Roman Catholic Church lacked biblical support. Among those failing the test was the traditional Lenten fast. It was during Lent that some members of Zwingli's congregation decided to take matters into their own hands. Christopher Froschauer, a Zürich printer, was in the process of running off a new edition of Paul's Epistles for the Frankfurt fair to be held immediately after Easter. His presses had been running overtime, and his workers were exhausted. He wished to express his appreciation for their efforts by treating them to a substantial dinner, so he instructed his wife to serve them *Wurst* (sausage) instead of fish. After all, he reasoned, it was unthinkable to offer these tired and hungry people a few morsels of fish—and besides, if abstaining from eating meat during Lent had no biblical support, as Zwingli had been preaching, why bother? The sausage was served, and with the exception of Zwingli, everyone—including two other priests who were present—partook.

The fat was in the fire, literally and figuratively. News of the precipitous action was carried to the city council, and the sausage-eaters were jailed. But Zwingli rose to their defense and preached a sermon on March 30, the third Sunday in Lent, about the freedom to choose what one ate. This sermon received special treatment. It was written out, revised, and printed on April 16 under the title *Von Erkiesen und Freiheit der Speisen* (*Of Choice and Freedom Regarding Foods*). In this tract Zwingli cautiously rejected obligatory fasting on Fridays and certain other holy days, including those of Lent. While he respected the rights of anyone who so wished to abstain from eating meat, he claimed that it was a matter of indifference. However, he was careful to point out that in Christ there is freedom and not law, that the principle Christ taught regarding the Sabbath holds true for fasting as well because eating and drinking are necessary to sustain life. To support his position he cited the example of Peter in Acts 10:10-16 and the teachings of Paul in First Corinthians 6:12-14.[13] The council compromised. In the face of such stout defense, it was freely admitted that while there was no clear scriptural support for fasting, it was good to observe the traditional rules for the sake of peace.

Upon hearing of the sausage episode and Zwingli's sermon, Bishop Hugo von Hohenlandenberg of the diocese of Constance sounded the alarm. He first sent a letter to the Zürich city council and another to the chapter of the *Grossmünster* urging both to adhere to the age-old practices of the church. On April 7 a commission was deployed to investigate the situation, a commission that also took upon itself the responsibility of warning council and church about heretical teachings in their midst. Even though Zwingli was not mentioned, he was present on the second day of the commission's appearance before the city council. He vigorously rebutted the charges against him but stopped short of calling for an end to fasts. The council took the matter farther than the delegation had cared to go when it petitioned the

bishop to carry the question before the hierarchy, "that there should be no conduct contrary to the precepts of Christ."[14] But Bishop Hugo had other ideas. He persuaded the Swiss diet, which met annually at Baden, a few miles from Zürich, to pass a mandate prohibiting the preaching of Reformation doctrines.

While the diet was still in session, Zwingli was drawing up a petition that would give the bishop an even greater headache. The rather long title of the document reads, "Petition of Certain Preachers of Switzerland to the Most Reverend Lord Hugo, Bishop of Constance, That He Will Not Suffer Himself to Be Persuaded to Make Any Proclamation to the Injury of the Gospel, Nor Longer Endure the Scandal of Harlotry, but Allow the Priests to Marry Wives, or at Least to Wink at Their Marriages." This was tantamount to announcing that those who signed the petition either were planning to make their clandestine relationships official or intended to be married with the sanction of their fellow priests and local congregations. This petition carried eleven signatures, including Zwingli's. A few days later a similar document, this time in German, was addressed to the Swiss Confederation. The document's title took the form of an announcement, asking that "the preaching of the Gospel not be prohibited and that no one take offense when priests married in order to avoid scandal."[15]

As S. M. Jackson has suggested, Zwingli was probably the author of both documents. They were printed by Froschauer and distributed by Zwingli and his friends. Each petition pointed out that God had not given the priests who were a party to the petition the gift of continence, and went on to confess with shame their lack of chastity. At the time Zwingli was living with Anna Rhinehart, whose first husband, Hans Meyer von Knonau, had been killed in battle. It was a so-called clerical marriage, commonly recognized by the people but forbidden by canon law. The proscription apparently made little dif-

---

13. See Emil Egli and Georg Finsler, eds., *Huldreich Zwinglis Sämtliche Werke,* 12 vols. (Munich: Kraus-Thomson, 1981), 1: 109-10.

14. Cited by Rilliet in *Zwingli,* p. 70.
15. Jackson, *Huldreich Zwingli,* p. 166.

ference: it is estimated that at that time in the diocese of Constance there were as many as fifteen hundred children who had been fathered by priests.

The Printed Page

At this time Zwingli was quietly acquiring another weapon besides preaching with which to carry on his warfare: the printed page. On August 22, 1522, he finished the preface to his studied answer to the bishop's charges entitled *Apologeticus archeteles* (*An Apology: The Beginning and the End*), and on the twenty-third it was printed. Even though it was neither the beginning nor the end of Zwingli's theological development, it was a forthright answer to the letter the bishop had sent to the chapter of the *Grossmünster* three months before. The title of the treatise is Greek, the second of the two words being one that Zwingli fashioned from two Greek words. The treatise itself was written in Latin.

The *Archeteles* was followed on September 6 by a tract, "On the Clarity and Certainty of the Word of God." This treatise, like that on fasting and the *Archeteles,* grew out of a local episode. One of the bastions of Roman Catholicism in Zürich was Oetenbach, the wealthy and prestigious convent of Dominican nuns. The direction of their spiritual life was in the hands of the *Predigerkloster* (the Dominican monastery), as it had been for two hundred years. The convent had become a center of the opposition to Zwingli and his reforms. Zwingli determined to put an end to this private preserve of orthodoxy and opposition. With council backing the Reformer succeeded in gaining a hearing before the nuns. He prepared a sermon for the occasion, the revised edition of which became the printed tract. It was undoubtedly a factor in eliciting council support for his program of reform. By March 7, 1523, the council had replaced the Dominican monks with Leo Jud as chaplain of the nuns, and thus the struggle with the friars of the city shifted in Zwingli's favor.

In "On the Clarity and Certainty of the Word of God," Zwingli set forth the claims of Scripture over the authority of the Roman Church, which claimed the exclusive right of interpreting Scripture. According to Zwingli the Word of God is inseparable from Scripture, but it is not identical with Scripture. In the introduction of the tract Zwingli pointed out that man was made in the image of God and thus there is in him an insatiable thirst for the Word of God. This longing can be satisfied only when man receives the Word by faith, listens to it as the Holy Spirit illuminates his mind and heart, and believes it. The image of God is then renewed within him. "And on the basis of the fact that he is the image of God this new man studies more and more to come to knowledge—the knowledge of him that created him and impressed this image upon him—in order that he may be made new."[16]

Zwingli went on to cite numerous passages of Scripture, first from the Old Testament and then from the New, to support his argument that when the Word of God comes to man, it is both powerful and self-evident in its meaning and truth. Then, using the format of a debate, he raised objections that the Romanists either had presented or were likely to bring against his position. The sermon reached its climax when Zwingli related his own personal experience as a conclusive argument that the Scriptures apart from philosophy or theology bring the Word of God to the receptive heart. An excerpt as translated by G. W. Bromiley gives a glimpse into Zwingli's style of argument:

> No matter who a man may be, if he teaches you in accordance with his own thought and mind his teaching is false. But if he teaches you in accordance with the word of God, it is not he that teaches you, but God, who teaches him. For as Paul says, who are we but ministers of Christ and dispensers or stewards of the mysteries of God? Again, I know for certain that God teaches me, because I have experienced the fact of it. . . . When I was younger, I gave myself overmuch to human teaching, like others of my day, and when

---

16. Zwingli, "On the Clarity and Certainty of the Word of God," in *Zwingli and Bullinger,* trans. and ed. G. W. Bromiley, vol. 24 of the Library of Christian Classics (Philadelphia: Westminster Press, 1953), p. 65.

about seven or eight years ago I undertook to devote myself entirely to the Scriptures I was always prevented by philosophy and theology. But eventually I came to the point where led by the Word and Spirit of God I saw the need to set aside all these things and to learn the doctrine of God direct from his own Word. (48) Then I began to ask God for light and the Scriptures became far clearer to me—even though I read nothing else—than if I had studied many commentators and expositors. Note that that is always a sure sign of God's leading, for I could never have reached that point by my own feeble understanding. . . . (49) Hear the words of Paul (I Cor. 2): "But the natural man receiveth not the things of the Spirit of God: for they are foolishness unto him: neither can he know them, because, they are spiritually discerned. But he that is spiritual judgeth all things, yet he himself is judged of none. For who hath known the mind of the Lord, that he may instruct him." These words of Paul are more precious than all the gold upon earth. The natural man is he who brings his own mind: the spiritual man he who does not trust any mind but that which is given by God: he is pure and simple, and quite free from worldly ambition or covetousness or carnal lust. The spiritual man judges all things, that is, he sees at once whether the doctrine is of God or not. But he is judged of none, that is, even if he is judged, which for this reason he cannot be, he will not let himself be torn or turned aside.[17]

In bringing his sermon to a close Zwingli summarized his message in twelve points. Points nine and ten give the thrust of what he wished to convey:

Ninth, when you find that the Word of God renews you, and begins to be more precious to you than formerly when you heard the doctrines of men, then you may be sure that this is the work of God within you.

Tenth, when you find that it gives you assurance of the grace of God and eternal salvation, it is of God.[18]

17. Zwingli, "On the Clarity and Certainty . . . , " pp. 90-91.
18. Zwingli, "On the Clarity and Certainty . . . , " p. 94.

The Prophecy Meetings

Even though Zwingli emphasized with the nuns of Oetenbach the self-evident nature of the biblical record, he did not mean to disparage scholarship, particularly that of the Bible. In fact, his own diligence in studying both Greek and Hebrew is indicative of the importance he placed upon philology and the necessity of examining the Scriptures in their original languages. As early as 1519 he had begun to attract to himself several young university students who wished to learn Greek in order to read Plato and other Greek classical authors. However, it was not long until these would-be scholars with humanist leanings forgot Plato and became engrossed in the study of the Greek New Testament. This was the beginning of what later became known as the Prophecy Meetings.

Among those who attended the Prophecy Meetings were Conrad Grebel, the son of Jacob Grebel, a member of the city council; Felix Manz, son of the former provost of the *Grossmünster;* and Simon Stumpf, the parish priest at Hönng. It was a select group of young men that began to reflect Zwingli's own interests and convictions regarding the nature of the Christian faith. One by one they became his ardent disciples and earnest students of the Bible. Naturally the Bible became the major textbook of the group. They read it in Latin and then examined it in Greek and, beginning in 1522, in Hebrew as well. After carefully scrutinizing the glosses (definitions of words) and *scholia* (interpretative notes), they arrived at the correct exegesis, apparently by group consensus. Then one of the group would be asked to prepare a sermon in the local Swiss dialect. Very soon Conrad Grebel began to excel in the knowledge and use of Greek, and Felix Manz became the outstanding Hebraist of the group. From these first attempts at putting the Scriptures into Swiss German we may detect the beginning of the Züricher or Froschauer Bible, the first edition of which came out in 1529.

The Prophecy Meetings became a means by which Zwingli consolidated his support among the most influential families of the canton. In this way he added the undergirding strength of the classroom to his pulpit and pen. His own dedication to biblical studies was enhanced by the congenial companionship of gifted students.

The Disputation

By the end of 1522 Zwingli's carefully thought-out reformatory methodology was beginning to take shape. To preaching, covert agitation, writing, and teaching he was ready to add an adaptation of the academic disputation. In the time-honored tradition of the medieval university, where students and professors debated the most questionable subjects with episcopal permission, Zwingli saw the perfect vehicle for educating the common people and promoting reform. Doubtless the publicity given Luther's Leipzig Disputation with Johann Eck as well as the successful defense of his "theology of the cross" at Heidelberg suggested the possibilities of the technique to Zwingli.

Before the First Disputation became a reality, however, Zwingli sent up a couple of trial balloons, the first on July 16 and the second on July 21. In these two lesser-known disputations Zwingli debated with representatives of the monastic orders. The first involved a Franciscan, Francis Lambert from Avignon, and focused on the worship of Mary and the saints. In the second the Dominicans and the Augustinians debated with Zwingli on the authority of Scripture. Echoes of the second debate are readily apparent in the printed version of the sermon entitled "On the Clarity and Certainty of the Word of God." After these preliminary bouts, the Reformer was ready for the main event. It wasn't long in coming.

THE FIRST DISPUTATION: JANUARY 29, 1523

Since the previous September, Zwingli had been acting more and more like a Reformer. He had actively promoted the distribution of Luther's tracts and German New Testament. He had even carried the battle into the convents. One significant action after another supporting

him and his teaching had issued from the city hall. Rumors of what was afoot had reached Rome. Pope Adrian VI, who genuinely longed for reform within the church, had hastened to write Zwingli a letter of reconciliation on January 23. But it was too late: the disputation had already been announced on January 3, and Zwingli would not be turned aside. Zürich was alive with rumors and anticipation.

The bishop of Constance was invited to Zürich for the First Disputation, for which Zwingli had prepared Sixty-seven Articles (*Schlussreden*). The bishop declined the invitation but sent his very able vicar general, Johann Fabri (Faber), along with lesser-known and less able colleagues. On January 29 six hundred men turned out for the occasion. The meeting was held in the city hall (*Rathaus*) in the presence of the city council. The setting was exactly as Zwingli had planned it, although the Swiss diet sent no representative, and some prominent scholars failed to attend. Indeed, certain of Zwingli's learned friends—such as Oecolampadius and Glareanus from Basel and Hubmaier from Waldshut—were not there.

In fact, the assembled body was not a particularly auspicious one. Bishop Hohenlandenberg called it a *Kesslertag*, a tinker's assembly. It did resemble an annual meeting of the canton of Zürich, but it was sufficient for the purpose. All the clergy from the canton and representatives of every stratum of the canton's society were there, as well as the all-important city council. Other absences did not matter as long as the *Bürgermeister* Marx Röist and the Council of the Two Hundred were in attendance and were sympathetic. Zwingli, the renowned Swiss patriot, stood in their midst with the Hebrew, Greek, and Latin texts of Scripture open on a table before him. The German Fabri, representing the bishop of Constance and, in effect, the papacy, was at a distinct disadvantage. He was a foreigner in a strange land, representing the Roman Church whose pontiff had not paid the long-standing debt to Zürich for the services of its mercenaries. He had few supporters in the audience.

Röist, who presided over the disputation, delivered a speech that could have been written by Zwingli himself, it so frankly set forth the purpose of the disputation:

> Very learned, venerable, noble, steadfast, honourable, wise, ecclesiastical lords and friends: In my lords' city of Zurich and in its territories there has risen for some time discord and strife on account of the sermons and doctrine given to the people from the pulpit by our preacher here in Zurich, Master Ulrich Zwingli. Wherefore he has been reproached and spoken against by some as a false guide, by others as a heretic. So it has come about that not alone in our city of Zurich but in the country under the authority of my lords such discord among the priests, also among the laity, increases, and daily come complaints to my lords about it, until it seems that there is no end to such angry words and quarrelling. On this account Master Ulrich Zwingli has offered often from the public pulpit to give before everybody the rationale and ground of his preaching and doctrine delivered here in Zurich in an open disputation before numerous clergy and laity. The honourable Council has granted this request of Master Ulrich with a view to stop the great unrest and disputing, has allowed him to hold a public disputation in the German language before the Great Council of Zurich, as the Two Hundred are called, to which the honourable wise Council has invited all the people's priests and curates of the canton; also solicited the venerable lord and prince, etc., Bishop of Constance; on which his grace has kindly sent the deputation here present, for which the honourable council of Zurich expresses especial great thanks. Therefore, if anyone now present has any displeasure or doubts over the preaching and doctrines [that] Master Ulrich here has given from the pulpit, or knows to speak about the matter, as that such preaching and doctrine were and must be not correct but seditious or heretical, let him here before my lords convict the oft-mentioned Master Ulrich of untruthfulness, and in this presence here confute his error by Holy Scripture freely, boldly, and without fear of punishment, so that my lords may be spared hereafter daily complaints, whence originate discord and disunity. For my lords are tired of such complaints, which tend to increase constantly from the clergy and laity alike.[19]

The *Bürgermeister* then opened the floor for discussion. Fabri declared that he had not come to debate but to investigate and to reconcile. He claimed that he had not seen a copy of Zwingli's articles until he had reached Winterthur on his way to Zürich. He also contended that this was no proper forum for such a discussion. They should wait for a general council of the church, which the Diet of Nuremberg had called to be held a year hence. Besides, he insisted, the Universities of Paris, Cologne, and Louvain were the only competent judges of such matters. At this point Zwingli broke in. "Why not Erfurt or Wittenberg?" he asked. This comment brought a roar of laughter. "No," replied the dour-faced Fabri. "Luther is too near there, and then all evils come out of the North."[20]

The debate was about to degenerate into a wrangle almost before it began. Zwingli then went to the heart of the matter. He asserted that the question before them regarding the legitimacy of certain practices of the Roman Church was not about how old certain practices were but whether or not they had been established by God. Therefore it was not necessary to appeal to a general council or the universities to decide the issue. The Word of God alone was competent to judge.

Finally, when a priest of the canton pointed out that the bishop of Constance had arrested a priest, Urban Wyss of Fislisbach (a village on the border of Switzerland near Constance), for preaching Reformation doctrines, the debate began in earnest. Fabri claimed that he had used Scripture to convince the erring pastor to renounce his heretical teachings. Thereupon Zwingli asked Fabri to cite those same passages against his teachings if they were in error. This Fabri failed to do. It was obvious that he was no match for Zwingli.

When at last the long day came to an end, Zwingli had not been vanquished. According to S. M. Jackson, the *Bürgermeister* was heard to say, "That sword which pierced the pastor of Fislisbach, now a prisoner at Constance, has got

---

19. Röist, cited by Jackson in *Huldreich Zwingli,* pp. 186–87. For a more recent translation (which differs in no essential detail), see pp. 45–46 of the 1972 edition (New York: AMS Press).

20. Fabri, cited by Jackson in *Huldreich Zwingli,* p. 188.

stuck in its scabbard."[21] The members of the city council apparently agreed with Röist. They issued a mandate approving Zwingli's teachings and demanding that all clergy follow his lead: "Furthermore, all your people's priests, curates, and preachers in your cities and canton and dependencies, shall undertake and preach nothing but what can be proved by the Holy Gospel and the pure Holy Scriptures: furthermore, they shall in no wise for the future slander, call each other heretic, or insult in such manner."[22]

The right to freely preach the gospel as Zwingli understood it could hardly have been stated more forcibly. The Reformation had won a significant battle in Zürich. What this meant was spelled out in the Sixty-seven Articles.

THE SIXTY-SEVEN ARTICLES

Zwingli's Sixty-seven Articles are divided into two unequal parts: the first fifteen articles are positive affirmations of evangelical truth, and the other fifty-two condemn ancient rules, regulations, and practices of the Roman Church. The first fifteen articles are Christocentric. In them Christ is set forth as the "true Son of God" who has revealed the Father's will and has "released us from death and reconciled God" (Art. 2). He is further presented as the only all-sufficient Savior (Art. 3), the promised guide and leader of all men (Art. 6), the eternal Savior and head of all believers who are his body (Art. 7). "From this it follows that all who live in the head are [his] members, children of God that is the church," the communion of saints, the bride of Christ: "*Ecclesia catholica*" (Art. 8).[23]

It is clear that for Zwingli the "gospel" revealed in Jesus Christ is superior to all human instruction (Arts. 5 and 15).[24] In the fifty-two articles beginning with Article 16, Zwingli proceeds to demolish long-held teachings of the church in the light of his new understanding.[25] These articles reveal Zwingli's true radicalism. He denounces the papal office, purgatory, priestly garments, the priesthood itself, clerical celibacy, and the mass as completely unsupported by the gospel. In Article 18 on the mass Zwingli sets forth his concept of the Lord's Supper, from which he never retreated: "That Christ himself, having sacrificed himself once, is for eternity a certain and valid sacrifice for the sins of all believers; therefore, the mass is not a sacrifice, but is a memorial (*Widergedächtnus = Wiedergedächtnis*) of the sacrifice and assurance of the forgiveness which Christ has already provided us."[26]

This concept of the mass was not entirely original with Zwingli, but his more biblical approach to the age-old practices of the church made it a central issue in his program of reform. But the attempt to put the new teaching into practice became a problem for Zwingli and his zealous young disciples, and its implementation subsequently became a stumbling block that prevented any genuine understanding between Zwingli and Luther.

Zwingli explained his teaching on the Lord's Supper in greater detail in his "Essay on the Canon of the Mass." Using John 6:60–65, he explained that the Lord's Supper did not involve a physical eating of the body or a literal drinking of the blood but a spiritual feeding upon Christ. However, he was not yet ready to put his new teaching on the mass into practice; according to his cautious plan, the time was not ripe. In spite of this, the Reformation in Zürich did proceed—but not according to plan.[27]

21. Cited by Jackson in *Huldreich Zwingli,* p. 192.
22. Cited by Jackson in *Huldreich Zwingli,* p. 191.
23. *Zwingli Hauptschriften,* ed. Fritz Blanke, Oskar Farner, and Rudolf Pfister, 9 vols. (Zürich: Zwingli-Verlag, 1947), vol. 4, *Zwingli der Verteidiger des Glaubens,* ed. Oskar Frei, Part 1, p. 4.

24. *Hauptschriften,* 4/1: 3–5.
25. *Hauptschriften,* 4/1: 5–11.
26. *Hauptschriften,* 4/1: 5.
27. See *Hauptschriften,* 4/1: 143, for Zwingli's commentary on this essay.

Chapter XI

THE PARTING OF THE WAYS

isputation was both an interesting and important feature of academic life in the medieval university. Luther's early theses against Scholastic theology and the indulgence traffic were first meant for such an audience; it was Zwingli who first moved such disputations from the confines of the university to the city hall. Thus the Zürich experience set a new pattern for advancing the Reformation. The concept of an academic disputation gradually broadened to include not only a university forum but also the semi-annual meeting of a Swiss canton. Thus the Council of Two Hundred became an integral part of the process. By 1522 the city council had become involved in making a series of decisions regarding the internal life of the church and the monastic orders of Zürich. While Zwingli considered the members of the Small and Large Councils his allies in the cause of reform, he had no intention of surrendering his role of leadership to them. However, he was careful not to run too far ahead. Thus the disputation became an important instrument in the education of these laymen as well as that of the priests and friars of the canton. They in turn were becoming more and more involved in the decision-making process that was helping to make Christianity in Zürich a state church

(*Volkskirche*) similar to that in Saxony (*Landeskirche*). Until the Second Disputation in October 1523, Zwingli was able to guide the Reformation with a considerable degree of harmony and unanimity. But with this historic event a crack began to appear in the new Swiss evangelical edifice.

THE SECOND DISPUTATION: OCTOBER 26-28, 1523

The Second Disputation, like the First, was called to debate certain theses or issues raised by the action of some of Zwingli's more enthusiastic followers. In this case one of the issues involved the use of images in Christian worship. Zwingli also used the occasion to introduce his unique teachings on the nature and theology of the mass. The three-day agenda originally called for a discussion of images on the first day, of the mass on the second, and of purgatory on the third. But the participants became bogged down in the debate over the mass and never got to the discussion of purgatory. The episode that had triggered the calling of the disputation was an outbreak of iconoclasm that eventually involved all three of the leading priests and the city council.

Iconoclasm in Zürich

The preaching and teaching of the reform-minded priests of Zürich precipitated a somewhat unruly if not unexpected response. Lorenz Hochrütiner and Wolfgang Ininger smashed some glass candelabra and deliberately sprinkled holy water on the floor of the *Frau-münster*. Lorenz Meyer led a group of men in pulling down some pictures in St. Peter's, leaving the debris on the floor. At Hönng, Thomas Platter burned a wooden image of Saint John to the accompaniment of church bells. Just prior to the action, Leo Jud (1482-1542)—the people's priest since June 7, 1522, at St. Peter's—had vigorously denounced the use of images and pictures as idolatrous.[1] But the most notorious of these episodes was the destruction of the crucifix at Stadelhofen. Klaus Hottinger, one of the original "sausage eaters," and Hans Ockenfuss were the alleged culprits. This act, which was most offensive to good Catholics, was most courageous in their eyes. For what could be more idolatrous than a sculptured image of deity in wood or stone?

However justified the acts were in the eyes of these advocates of reform, they were too much for the Small Council. The offenders were taken into custody and placed in the Wellenberg prison tower. However, the grass-roots support for what had occurred was widespread and vocal. On September 29 the whole matter was turned over to a commission consisting of *Bürgermeister* Röist, eight prominent councilors, and the three people's priests: Englehard of the *Frau-münster*, Jud of St. Peter's, and Zwingli of the *Grossmünster*. By October 15 the commission had reached a decision. They recommended that those arrested be released on bail until a disputation could be held to debate the place of images in Christian worship. The city council accepted the recommendation and set October

---

1. Leo Jud was a close friend and confidant of Zwingli. He had come to the Confederation from Alsace and had followed Zwingli as chaplain at Einsiedeln. He had arrived in Zürich in 1519, and became people's priest three years later.

26-28 as the dates for the forthcoming disputation.

The Agenda

Zwingli's membership on the commission appointed to deal with the problem gave him an excellent opportunity to lay the groundwork for the Second Disputation. It appears that almost immediately both the projected size and the agenda of the debate were expanded. For one thing, Zwingli and his elite band of students, who had been engrossed almost daily in the Prophecy Meetings, were far more concerned about implementing Zwingli's concept of the Lord's Supper than about images. Their studies in both the Old and the New Testament had long ago convinced them that Scripture did not justify using images as aids in worship. For them the burning issue was the implementation of the Lord's Supper in a form that they were convinced was the simple apostolic pattern established by Christ and enunciated by the Apostle Paul. Zwingli had taught them well. They were now ready for action. Doubtless the rumors of what had transpired in Wittenberg and Allstedt had raised their hopes that soon they too could take the mass in both kinds and hear the words of celebration in their own tongue. Zwingli was neither insensitive to nor unsympathetic with their desires—in fact, he had encouraged them. Thus the expanded agenda included three subjects for discussion: images, the mass, and purgatory.

The invitation list went beyond the borders of the canton to include the bishops of Constance, Chur, and Basel as well as prominent university-educated priests and scholars. The bishops declined to attend, but a number of the priests and scholars showed up, ten of whom had doctorates. The assembly was by far the most impressive gathered for such an occasion. Altogether there were more than 800 men present, including 350 to 500 priests and monks. Among the more prominent foreign visitors were Dr. Joachim von Watt (Vadianus) from St. Gall, Dr. Balthasar Hubmaier from Waldshut, Dr. Sebastian Hofmeister from Schaffhausen, and Christopher Schappelar (Sertorius) from Memmingen.

October 26

When October 26 dawned, hundreds of men made their way to the *Rathaus*. After the *Bürgermeister* had set the stage and turned the disputation over to the speakers, it soon became evident that there would be no debate on the propriety of the use of images in worship. Their use was declared an abomination in the sight of God and repeatedly condemned by one speaker after the other. Dr. Hubmaier spoke out eloquently against images, emphasizing that the Scriptures alone provided the standard of judgment. As Torsten Bergsten points out, "With reference to the Second and Fifth Book of Moses, he declared that God had forbidden the making of idols and their worship and had therefore commanded that they should be burned."[2]

October 27

By the end of the first day, no one had risen to defend the continued use of images. Thus the second day the disputation moved on to a consideration of the mass. Like the use of images, the mass was described as an abomination in the sight of God, and its idolatrous aspects were roundly denounced by various speakers. At the close of the day the *Bürgermeister* declared that since the mass had been thoroughly discussed, he was prepared to adjourn if "my lords" agreed. He then announced that they would assemble again the next day at noon for a discussion of purgatory.

Clearly disappointed that no instructions had been given for the abolition of what was such an abomination, Conrad Grebel "stood up and expressed the opinion that since the priests were all present that they should be instructed

regarding the mass so that from this time on the mass would be dispensed with. If this were not done the disputation would be in vain. While it was true that much had been said about the mass up to that point, no one was willing to forsake this great abomination before God. Also, there were still many more serious abuses in the mass about which one must speak."

Zwingli replied, "My Lords [the Large Council] will decide what measures are to be taken from this point on regarding changes in the mass." Then Simon Stumpf (priest at Hönng) arose and said, "Master Ulrich, this power is not in your hand to turn over to my Lords . . . for that decision has already been made: the Spirit of God judges. So, if my Lords arrive at some other decision and judgment that is against the judgment of God, I will ask Christ for His Spirit and will teach and act against it."[3]

Zwingli immediately answered, "That is right. I will also preach and act against it, if they render another decision. I do not deliver that judgment into their hand. They are not to sit in judgment over God's Word and that goes not only for them but also for the whole world. Also, this assembly is not called to decide what they should do but to determine in the light of Scripture whether the mass is a sacrifice for sins or not. So, later on the members of the council will determine what measures will be taken concerning these matters."[4]

October 28

After this rather sharp exchange, the *Bürgermeister* got to his feet once again to announce that the disputation would proceed the next

---

2. Bergsten, *Balthasar Hubmaier: Anabaptist Theologian and Martyr*, ed. W. R. Estep, Jr. (Valley Forge, Pa.: Judson Press, 1978), p. 83.

3. Cited in *Anabaptist Beginnings (1523–1533): A Source Book*, ed. W. R. Estep, Jr. (Nieuwkoop: B. de Graaf, 1976), p. 17. This work contains the author's translation of Ludwig Haetzer's minutes from *Huldreich Zwinglis Werke*, ed. Melchior Schuler and Johann Schulthess (Zürich: ben Friedrich Schulthess, 1828), 1: 459–540. The minutes are also available in vol. 2 of a modern edition entitled *Huldreich Zwinglis Sämtliche Werke*, ed. Emil Egli and Georg Finsler (Munich: Kraus-Thomson, 1981), 671–813.

4. Zwingli, cited by Estep in *Anabaptist Beginnings*, pp. 17–18.

day. But the following day the session opened with a continuation of the discussion of the mass. Apparently on the previous evening Zwingli, Vadianus (who was presiding), and Grebel had agreed to continue the previous day's discussion before going on to a consideration of purgatory. It appears, in fact, that the assembly never got around to discussing purgatory. It was probably quite a dead issue, since both Erasmus and Luther had raised serious questions about its very existence. But the mass was still a live issue.

According to the minutes taken by Ludwig Haetzer, Grebel was the first to speak. He pointed out that there were many more abuses in the mass than had been brought out in the discussion the day before. He was followed by Hubmaier, who delivered a carefully thought-out five-point attack on the mass, revealing in the process his basic agreement with Zwingli. Among these points was a call for the celebration of the mass in the language of the people, not in Latin: "Without a doubt Christ did not speak gibberish [*calecutisch,* a term referring to the language of Calcutta, which was nothing but gibberish to Europeans] with his disciples when He instituted the Lord's Supper but used language which was clear and understandable." He insisted that when mass is observed, the Gospel must be preached, for "he who does something other than this does not celebrate the true mass."[5] He also suggested that the Scriptures know nothing of private masses but teach that the observance of the mass is an act of fellowship among believers. He implied that both bread and wine are to be taken by all the brethren. He claimed to have had misgivings about other abuses of the mass such as those that Grebel had suggested. Characteristically, Hubmaier qualified his statements by saying, "I may err, I am a man; but a heretic I cannot be. I (desire from the heart) and will receive correction and give many thanks to those who make

known my error for I will follow God's Word willingly. . . . "[6]

The next speaker was Zwingli, who joined in the condemnation of other abuses connected with the mass. He closed his remarks by making a strong appeal for a careful study of the Scriptures. But Grebel had not finished. For a short time the disputation became little more than a dialogue between Grebel and Zwingli. The minutes suggest that Grebel took the offensive and consequently put Zwingli on the defensive. At times Zwingli agreed with Grebel, but more often than not he claimed that one could not be absolutely sure about the details of the Last Supper instituted by Christ. On those points on which the Bible is not clear, Zwingli said, the parish church (*kilchböre*) must determine how and under what circumstances the Lord's Supper should be observed. Finally, Zwingli expressed the desire "that my Lords will permit the scandal of the mass to come to an end in an orderly manner, maintaining peace."[7]

Zwingli doubtless knew that in such company he must move cautiously. There were present, in addition to the convinced and the confused, defenders of Rome ready to spring to the attack. The half-convinced were reluctant to give up such an awe-inspiring ceremony so abruptly. It is clear that Grebel and Stumpf represented those of a vigorous and aggressive spirit who desired action on those points on which the teachings of the New Testament were so "self-evident." The tension was growing. No one could know for sure how many held views either more traditional or more radical than those expressed. Toward the end of the day Zwingli spoke again, this time clearly agitated. With deep earnestness he pled with the assembly not to hesitate to learn from God's Word. In the minutes Haetzer noted that Zwingli spoke with such strong feelings for Christian unity that he began to weep, and many others with him.

5. Hubmaier, cited by Estep in *Anabaptist Beginnings,* p. 19.

6. Hubmaier, cited by Estep in *Anabaptist Beginnings,* p. 19.

7. Zwingli, cited by Estep in *Anabaptist Beginnings,* p. 21.

After the leaders had regained their composure, the disputation was brought to a close.

The disappointment that Grebel expressed at the end of the second day increased during the weeks that followed. On December 8 the minutes of the disputation were published, provoking new protests against the mass and the use of images in worship. But the new demonstrations produced no change of mind or heart on the part of the city council, and by December 19 Zwingli bowed to the authority if not the judgment of the council. Thus, to the great consternation of some of his followers, he abandoned his earlier plans to observe the Lord's Supper in a simple apostolic manner on Christmas Day. In the eyes of Grebel and his friends, the authority of the Word of God had been sacrificed upon the altar of human expediency. The youthful disciples felt that they had been betrayed.

In the break between Zwingli and his critics Harold Bender detects the beginning of the free-church movement, which he views as the first attempt within the Reformation to establish a church without state cooperation or support: "The decision of Conrad Grebel to refuse to accept the jurisdiction of the Zürich Council over the Zürich church is one of the high moments of history, for however obscure it was, it marked the beginning of the modern 'free church' movement."[8]

DIALOGUE AND ESTRANGEMENT, 1524

Whether the disagreement that surfaced during the Second Disputation reflected a break between Zwingli and his students remains a matter of debate. But there is no question that by the end of December 1523, they were estranged. The group of dissidents was small, numbering no more than seven. Before alienation appeared permanent, Felix Manz and Conrad Grebel attempted to persuade Zwingli and Leo Jud to adopt a more biblical program of reform, but

their attempt failed. Positions hardened on both sides, and hopes of reconciliation faded. Grebel and Manz emerged as leaders of a new conventicle that began to meet regularly for worship and serious Bible study. Frequently the group met in Manz's home on *Neustadt Gasse,* directly in back of the *Grossmünster.*

The group found themselves isolated and ostracized by Zwingli and his close associates, and Grebel began to cast around for outside support, writing Luther, Karlstadt, and Thomas Müntzer. Only the letter to Müntzer is extant. It is quite revealing of the state of mind and the convictions of the dissenting faction, which was in the process of becoming Anabaptist.

Grebel had apparently read some of Müntzer's earlier tracts and had received encouraging reports about his earnest preaching. He wrote his letter of inquiry hoping that once he had revealed the group's dissenting opinion, he would gain an ally. The letter, however, is not one of humble submission; the information it transmits shows Grebel and his colleagues doing a lot more telling than asking. This letter and its postscript clearly demonstrate the independent nature of the origin of the Grebel-led Swiss Brethren and give only a hint of the possible influence of Thomas Müntzer and his *Bund.*

After giving a brief account of their separation from Zwingli, Grebel expressed joy at the reports reaching Zürich of Müntzer's preaching and the recent tracts that the group had seen:

> While we were taking note of and lamenting these things your writing against spurious faith and baptism was brought to us, and we were more fully informed and confirmed. It made us wonderfully happy to have found one who was one with us in a common Christian understanding, and who ventured to point out to the evangelical preachers their deficiency.[9]

Just to be sure Müntzer understood the group's position, Grebel offered him their advice:

8. Bender, *Conrad Grebel, c. 1498-1526* (Goshen, Ind.: Mennonite Historical Society, 1950), pp. 99-100.

9. Grebel, cited by J. C. Wenger in *Conrad Grebel's Programmatic Letters: 1524* (Scottdale, Pa.: Herald Press, 1970), p. 17.

We therefore entreat and admonish you as a brother, by the name, power, Word, Spirit, and salvation which all Christians receive through Jesus Christ our Master and Savior, to seek earnestly to preach only the divine Word, and unafraid, to set up and defend only divine rites, to esteem as right and good only what is found in crystal-clear Scripture, to reject, hate, and curse all proposals, words, rites, and opinions of all men, even your own.[10]

Applying the principle just enunciated, Grebel attacked singing in worship, something that he and his colleagues ruled out at this stage as unscriptural, even in German. But the mass received the severest criticism. Grebel's delineation of the necessary steps in the restoration of the Lord's Supper has a familiar ring to it, echoing as it does the points that he and others attempted to score in the Second Disputation. Following Zwingli's understanding of the symbolism of the observance, he wrote, "Although it is simply bread, where faith and brotherly love prevail it shall be partaken of with joy. When observed in that way in the congregation it shall signify to us that we are truly one loaf and one body, and that we are one and intend to be true brothers one with another." He continued, "The Supper . . . is to be a sign of unity. It is not a mass or a sacrament. Therefore no one shall receive it alone, neither on a deathbed nor otherwise."[11] Grebel went on to spell out in minute detail the proper observation of the mass.

From a discussion of the mass the letter shifted once again, raising the possibility that Müntzer was not as "simon pure" as his well-wishers might desire. The Swiss suggested that if Müntzer was still receiving benefices, he should stop doing so. They also expressed their sorrow and disappointment over the recent rumor that he had made tablets of stone to call his congregation back to the law of God. They feared that such action would result in a return to idolatrous worship.

The Swiss had been misinformed regarding Müntzer's teachings on the sword. In the first letter they assumed that he subscribed to a thoroughgoing pacifism that rejected any use of the sword even in matters of defense. In the postscript, which was actually a second letter, they denounced unequivocally Müntzer's call to arms against the nobility. The apparent arrogance of such youthful zealots would have been difficult to explain and even more difficult to accept if it had not been for their utter sincerity in rejecting any practice in the life of the church not rooted and grounded in the Bible.

Although they had obvious misgivings regarding what they had read and heard about Müntzer's program of reform, they offered to befriend him because of his teaching on baptism. Here they felt they shared common ground. In this regard the letter took on the ring of absolute certainty. On the basis of Scripture the group rejected infant baptism: "From the above Scriptures which alone apply to the whole subject of children, and all other Scriptures (demanding faith) do not apply to children, we conclude that infant baptism is a senseless, blasphemous abomination, contrary to all Scripture."[12]

By September 5, 1524, the estrangement between Zwingli and his former disciples—which had begun in a disagreement over whether the secular authority had the right to retain the Roman mass—had developed into a full-fledged separatist movement that raised basic questions regarding the nature of the church, the church's relation to the state, Christian discipleship, baptism, and the Lord's Supper. At this point the group had not yet reached the point of no return; others before them had gone almost as far as they had. But with the inauguration of believer's baptism and the formation of a church upon the principle of individual voluntary commitment, they went much further

10. Grebel, cited by J. C. Wenger in *Conrad Grebel's Programmatic Letters*, p. 19.

11. Grebel, cited by J. C. Wenger in *Conrad Grebel's Programmatic Letters*, p. 23.

12. Grebel, cited by J. C. Wenger in *Conrad Grebel's Programmatic Letters*, p. 31.

than their medieval predecessors. The Bohemian Brethren, under the tutelage of Peter Chelčický (ca. 1380–1460) and the leadership of Gregory of Prague (d. 1474), founded a new church at Kunvald in 1457–58. They apparently came the closest to anticipating the Anabaptist movement of any group of the Middle Ages.[13]

THE ANABAPTIST WAY

With the inauguration of believer's baptism came the parting of the ways between Zwingli and his former disciples. Since September, Zwingli and Leo Jud had attempted to refute the arguments advanced by Grebel, Manz, and others, but they were unsuccessful. Fearing schism, Zwingli prodded the city council into calling the Third Disputation. This debate, like the others, was held in the *Rathaus* (city hall). Unlike the others, however, it was designed to put down what Zwingli had come to view as an insidious rebellion.

The Third Disputation convened on January 17 to consider one question: believer's baptism. The issue of baptism had forged to the front as the most divisive and explosive of the lot. Grebel, Manz, and George Blaurock argued for their cause with frequent reference to the New Testament, but they made no headway with Zwingli or the city council. Zwingli's "torrent of words" and arguments of dubious merit overwhelmed his opponents and persuaded the council. It was clear that Zwingli was greatly agitated. Among the leaders of the group were his brightest students. They claimed to be following the principles he had taught them and to hold positions he had once held but had abandoned. Possible damage to the fledgling reformation that Zwingli was leading in Zürich loomed large on the horizon—hence the outcome was a foregone conclusion. Zwingli was declared the victor, and those whom Zwingli first dubbed "Anabaptists" (*Wiedertäufer*) lost. The next day, January 18, the first of two mandates de-

signed to suppress the movement was handed down by the city council. The second followed on January 21.

The dissidents were ordered to cease meeting together and to have their unbaptized children baptized; if they refused to comply, they were to leave the canton within eight days. The mandate of the twenty-first also listed those who were not citizens of the canton; they were to be banished in eight days. Among these were Wilhelm Reublin, pastor at Wytikon, the first of the Zürich clergy to take a wife; Johannes Brötli, an elderly "retired" priest at Zollikon; Ludwig Haetzer, a brilliant Hebraist; and Andreas Castleberger, a bookseller from Graubunden.

The First Baptisms

Even though Reublin was the first among the Swiss Brethren to raise the question concerning baptism, he was not the first to be baptized or to baptize. Grebel was the first baptizer, and George Blaurock, a former priest from Chur, was the first to be baptized. It was the night of the twenty-first. The place was the home of Felix Manz and his mother. *The Large Chronicle of the Hutterian Brethren* records the stirring events of that unforgettable night:

And it came to pass that they were together until anxiety (*Angst*) came upon them, yes, they were so pressed within their hearts. Thereupon they began to bow their knees to the Most High (*hochstenn*) God in heaven and called upon him as the Informer of Hearts (*Hertzenkundiger*), and they prayed that he would give to them his divine (*gotlichen*) will and that he would show his mercy unto them. For flesh and blood and human forwardness did not drive them, since they well knew what they would have to suffer on account of it.

After the prayer, George of the House of Jacob stood up and besought (*gebeeten*) Conrad Grebel for God's sake to baptize him with the true (*recht*) Christian baptism upon his faith and knowledge (*erkanndtnus*). And when he knelt down with such a request and desire, Conrad baptized him,

13. See the works on the Bohemian Brethren by Jarold Knox Zeman cited in the bibliography.

since at that time there was no ordained minister (*dienner*) to perform such a work.[14]

After his baptism, Blaurock proceeded to baptize others who requested it. The baptized then covenanted together as faithful disciples of Christ to live lives separate from the world, to faithfully teach the gospel, and to hold steadfastly to the faith.

With this first baptism, the earliest church of the Swiss Brethren was formed, and Anabaptism was born. Although it may not have been evident at the time, this was the most revolutionary act of the Reformation. No other event so completely symbolized the break with Rome and the medieval sacral society. For the first time in the course of the Reformation a group of Christians dared, without the support or approval of the magistrates, to form a church modeled after what they believed was the New Testament prototype. By so doing, they affirmed the absolute Lordship of Christ and the voluntary nature of the personal commitment to him. This act was an obvious refutation of the church's concept of baptism and at the same time a rejection of the authority of the state in religious matters.

In the Byways and Hedges

On January 21 the little band, possibly numbering no more than twelve, dispersed to carry their witness to nearby communities, the first of which was Zollikon. The next day Brötli baptized a number of converts at the village well.

Within the week more baptisms followed. For a brief period Brötli, Manz, Blaurock, and Klaus Hottinger worked together in forming the first Anabaptist congregation at Zollikon. Their efforts were interrupted when a number of the baptized were arrested and subsequently confined in the Wellenberg prison tower and the former Augustinian monastery. Thus a pattern in Anabaptist evangelism emerged: proclamation of the gospel, response, baptism, observance of the Lord's Supper, witnessing of the new converts, arrest, imprisonment, and final suppression.

The Swiss Brethren performed the first baptism by pouring water over the believer's head. Even though the early leaders doubtless knew that the Greek word *baptizein* meant "to immerse," they probably did not consider immersion a true option. For one thing, they had gone to Manz's home—having suffered the harsh mandate of the Zürich city council—primarily to pray and seek divine guidance in the crisis facing them. The possibility of baptism may have been in the back of their minds. But it is one thing to embrace a concept and quite another to practice it. When the impetuous Blaurock asked Grebel to baptize him, apparently no one thought of "gathering at the river" a few hundred feet from where they were meeting. It was January, and Januaries in Zürich are cold. Perhaps the Limmat was even frozen over. At any rate, the major concerns of the small band of bold pioneers that night were the formation of a church made up of committed disciples baptized upon the basis of their confession of faith, and the voluntary decision to act out that commitment.

Less than a month later one of the Swiss Brethren, Grebel, did perform baptism by immersion for the first time. On the way to Schaffhausen, he met and baptized Wolfgang Ulimann, a former monk.[15] Luther had earlier attempted to reinstate the New Testament form of baptism by immersing his firstborn son,

---

14. From *Die älteste Chronik der Hutterischen Brüder,* ed. A. J. F. Zieglschmid (New York: Carl Schurz Memorial Foundation, 1943), p. 47. The full account is also given in *Das Klein-Geschichtsbuch der Hutterischen Brüder,* also edited by Zieglschmid (Philadelphia: Carl Schurz Memorial Foundation, 1947). Joseph Beck gives essentially the same account on pp. 19–20 of his *Die Geschichte-Bücher der Wiedertäufer in Oesterrich-Ungarn* (Vienna: Carl Gerald, 1883). English translations of the record of this first baptism are given in *Glimpses of Mennonite History and Doctrine* by John C. Wenger (Scottdale, Pa.: Herald Press, 1947), pp. 24–25, 137; and in *Spiritual and Anabaptist Writers,* ed. G. H. Williams and A. M. Mergal, vol. 25 of the Library of Christian Classics (Philadelphia: Westminster Press, 1957), pp. 41–46.

15. *Quellen zur Geschichte der Täufer in der Schweiz,* vol. 2, *Ostschweiz,* ed. Heinold Fast (Zürich: Theologischer Verlag, 1973), p. 604.

Hans, but he did not continue the practice. As early as 1520 Luther had arrived at the conviction that believers should be baptized by immersion,[16] but apparently he refused to take the decisive step of affirming the baptism of adult believers.

Ulimann is an example of a convert clearly convinced that only the immersion of a believer in water conformed to·apostolic baptism. Grebel must have agreed with him, because he accompanied Ulimann down to the Rhine, where, according to Johannes Kessler, a contemporary chronicler from St. Gall, Grebel "put him under [*undergetruckt*] and covered him over [*und bedeckt werden*] in the waters of the Rhine."[17]

It was Ulimann who returned to his native St. Gall and, along with Gabriel Giger and Lorenz Hochrütiner, began to sow the seeds of Anabaptism. When a revival took root, he called for help, and Manz and Grebel soon joined in the mission effort. Within a few weeks hundreds responded and were baptized, not in the small stream that flowed through the city but in the Sitter (Sytern) River about three kilometers away. Due to the energetic efforts of the Zürich Anabaptists, Anabaptism was beginning to take root in St. Gall and the surrounding area.

Arrest and Imprisonment

Grebel chose his boyhood home of Grüningen, northeast of Zürich, for the scene of his labors. Here he worked with extraordinary success from the end of June until the beginning of October 1525. For the better part of these three months Grebel went from house to house, witnessing to one or two people or to small groups. His messages emphasized the necessity of repentance and faith in the authority of the Scriptures. The point of departure from the standing order always seems to have been the issue of baptism. The Brethren from Zollikon, Chur, and Waldshut often worked together in an intensive effort to spread the gospel of Anabaptism. One of their meetings was to take place on October 8—but a mass arrest brought activity to a halt. As Grebel, Manz, and Blaurock were preparing for the meeting in a woods near Grüningen, Grebel and Blaurock were arrested by Magistrate Berger and imprisoned in the castle at Grüningen. Three weeks later Manz, who had escaped the clutches of the magistrate on the eighth, was seized and incarcerated in the same prison.

After more than a month in confinement, the three ring-leaders were finally brought to trial and sentenced to indefinite prison terms on November 18, 1525. They were condemned "because of their Anabaptism and their unbecoming conduct to lie in the tower on a diet of bread and water, and no one was permitted to visit them except the guards."[18]

Despite this stern judgment, the case against the Anabaptists was weak. Upon rather dubious evidence, Zwingli accused them of sedition. Actually the charges were based in part upon a misunderstanding—if not a distortion—of Anabaptist teachings. They did not deny the magistracy, as Dr. Hofmeister, formerly of Schaffhausen, had charged; they believed, as Manz put it, that "no Christian could be a magistrate, nor could he use the sword to punish or to kill anyone, for he had no Scripture for such a thing."[19]

The accused also denied that they taught that Christians should own all material possessions

---

16. See Luther, *The Babylonian Captivity of the Church*, trans. A. T. W. Steinhäuser, rev. Frederick C. Ahrens and Abdel Ross Wentz, in *Three Treatises* (Philadelphia: Muhlenberg Press, 1960), pp. 178-206. Luther also taught that faith was necessary for valid baptism. When he realized that this position would normally exclude infant baptism, he posited the unlikely concept that infants were capable of such faith. Thus he sought to justify the continuation of infant baptism. He was also convinced that relatively few adults would seek baptism on their own initiative.

17. Kessler, *Sabbata mit Kleineren Schriften und Briefen*, ed. Emil Egli and Rudolf Schoch (St. Gallen: Huber, 1902), p. 144.

18. Cited by Bender in *Conrad Grebel*, p. 155. For the text of the order, see *Quellen zur Geschichte der Täufer in der Schweiz*, vol. 1, *Zürich*, ed. Leonhart von Muralt and Walter Schmid (Zürich: S. Hirzel Verlag, 1952), pp. 141-42.

19. Manz, cited by Bender in *Conrad Grebel*, p. 159.

in common. Rather they insisted that a Christian must share his material goods with those in need. Manz and Grebel also asserted that infant baptism lacked biblical support and affirmed their conviction that believer's baptism was the sign of the true church.

Others were imprisoned and the Brethren who at one time (along with Zwingli) had even questioned the scriptural basis for singing in worship began to sing. It is not known whether their actions were based on a more complete understanding of the Scriptures or simply reflected the irrepressible desire of the Brethren to worship in song in the midst of adversity. In any case, the harshness of their imprisonment apparently was relieved by the joy of Christian fellowship. Their days were full of praise and prayer even though the provision for their physical needs was meager.

It was ironic that Grebel now found himself imprisoned in the tower of the castle in which he had roamed at will as a small boy. (Upon two different occasions Jacob Grebel, a Hapsburg, and his family had lived there.) But Grebel did not waste his time reminiscing or feeling sorry for himself. Instead he produced a manuscript on baptism and even asked for permission to have it published. Such exasperating audacity provoked an irritated response. The rejection of his request could not have been unexpected, since it came just after a second trial held on March 5 and 6, 1526. On March 7, Grebel, Manz, Blaurock, and a number of others were sentenced to life in prison. On the same day the city council handed down a new mandate making the act of "rebaptism" a crime punishable by death. But fourteen days later some unknown benefactor left the prison doors unlocked, and the prisoners escaped.

The First Martyr at the Hands of Protestants

After spending five months in prison followed by another five months as a fugitive, Grebel died. The numerous imprisonments and the hardships of a hunted heretic weakened his already frail body, and when he was stricken with the plague he could not withstand it. In a

sense his death in exile at Maienfeld in the Oberland was a martyr's death. But Felix Manz became the first Anabaptist executed at the hands of Zürich authorities. Even before Grebel's death, Manz and Blaurock had begun to take over the leadership of the movement. On October 12, almost a year to the day since his arrest in Grüningen, Manz was imprisoned in St. Gall but was soon released. However, he was arrested again in a Grüningen forest, this time with Blaurock. Two months later he was transferred to the Wellenberg prison in Zürich. From there he was taken to the site of his execution. On January 5, 1527, Felix Manz was sentenced to die,

> because contrary to Christian order and custom he had become involved in Anabaptism, . . . because he confessed having said that he wanted to gather those who wanted to accept Christ and follow Him, and united himself with them through baptism, . . . so that he and his followers separated themselves from the Christian Church and were about to raise up and prepare a sect of their own . . . because he had condemned capital punishment . . . since such doctrine is harmful to the unified usage of all Christendom, and leads to offense, insurrection, and sedition against the government, . . . Manz shall be delivered to the executioner, who shall tie his hands, put him into a boat, take him to the lower hut, there strip his bound hands down over his knees, place a stick between his knees and arms, and thus push him into the water; thereby he shall have atoned to the law and justice. . . . His property shall also be confiscated by my lords.[20]

According to the sentence, Manz was taken bound from the Wellenberg prison past the fish market to the boat. All along the way he witnessed to the members of the dismal procession and to those standing on the banks of the Limmat River, praising God that even though he was a sinner, he would die for the truth. He also declared that believer's baptism was the true

---

20. See the original indictment and sentence in *Zürich*, pp. 224-25. This translation is from Harold Bender's "Felix Manz," in The Mennonite Encyclopedia, 4 vols., ed. Harold S. Bender and C. Henry Smith (Scottdale, Pa.: Mennonite Publishing House, 1956-69), 3: 473.

baptism according to the Word of God and the teachings of Christ. His mother's voice could be heard above the sounds of the subdued throng and the ripple of the swift-flowing stream, entreating him to remain true to Christ in the hour of temptation. After the sentence was pronounced, he was placed into a boat just below the *Rathaus* (council hall); the boat moved downstream to a fish hut that was anchored in the middle of the Limmat. As his arms and legs were being bound, Manz sang out in a loud voice, *"In manus tuas, Domine, commendo spiritum meum"* ("Into thy hands, O Lord, I commend my spirit"). A few moments later the cold water of the river closed over his head. According to the Zürich chronicler Bernhard Wyss, Manz's execution took place on January 5, 1527, at three o'clock on Saturday afternoon.[21]

Manz thus became the first victim of Protestant intolerance; unfortunately, he was not the last. Before Zwingli himself met death on the battlefield of Kappel, other Anabaptists were drowned in the Limmat at the same place where Manz died. Thus progress of Anabaptism was accompanied by persecution, and martyrdom became the hallmark of "the church under the cross." Once again the blood of the martyrs became the seed of the church.[22] As the movement spread from its cradle in Zürich and Zollikon throughout German-speaking Europe, death stalked its way. Imprisonment and execution by drowning or by sword and fire—these were the means used to suppress the movement. In Roman Catholic territories Anabaptists were most severely persecuted; in areas under Protestant influence they faced suppression with various degrees of severity. As a result, a mounting stream of refugees began to carry the message to new centers of activity. Claus-Peter Clasen holds that with the death of the more

biblical and responsible leaders, leadership of the movement fell into the hands of the unstable and the untutored. Consequently, Anabaptism in some areas lost its original vision and became captive to the fantasies of some unscrupulous men. This seems to have been the case at Münster under Jan of Leiden.[23] This development in turn led to further suppression and fragmentation. Thus a small remnant of what had never been a large movement struggled to survive into the seventeenth century and the centuries thereafter. Among the remnant were a few Swiss and South German Anabaptist churches, the Hutterites in Moravia, and the Mennonites of the Netherlands, none of whom had been a part of the "New Jerusalem" at Münster or succumbed to the distortions of the Münsterites.

THE ZWINGLIAN WAY

Before Zwingli met death in battle on October 11, 1531, he had become an embittered enemy of the Anabaptists, who had formerly been either his colleagues or students. G. R. Potter attempts to justify Zwingli's and the council's harsh treatment of the Anabaptists on the grounds that the movement was seditious, that the followers had actually planned to set up a state within the state as the early Mormons did.[24] But this interpretation seems farfetched. Potter may be using the Münster episode to read into the Zürich situation something that was never a part of the Swiss Anabaptist vision. Admittedly, factors other than the purely religious merged to produce the Anabaptist movement: the impetuosity of youth, the insensitivity of those without leadership responsibilities to the possible implications of their actions, and the obvious disappointment with the slow pace of the Reformation in Zürich. (This disappointment was somewhat understandable: by the time of the first baptisms among the Swiss Brethren, the

---

21. Ekkehard Krajewski, *Leben und Sterben des Zürcher Täuferführers, Feliz Mantz* (Kassel: J. G. Oncken Verlag, 1957), pp. 22-23. Krajewski's work is the definitive biography of Felix Manz. It is a careful and detailed account of one of the more important leaders in early Anabaptism.

22. In his *Apologeticus* Tertullian wrote, "We multiply whenever we are mown down by you, the blood of Christians is seed."

23. See Clasen, *Anabaptism: A Social History, 1525-1618* (Ithaca: Cornell University Press, 1972).

24. See Potter, *Zwingli* (London: Cambridge University Press, 1976).

mass was still being said by Zwingli and the priests of Zürich, and despite the two disputations of 1523, most Roman Catholic practices remained intact.) All in all, however, it is impossible to escape the impression that these first Anabaptists were earnest and dedicated men whose supreme allegiance to Jesus Christ became the guiding star of their pilgrimage. The refusal to swear, the refusal to bear arms, the insistence upon a personal discipleship and a church made up of only committed disciples baptized upon their own volition in obedience to the command of Christ—these practices did not indicate that they wanted to set up a state of their own. They were, as James M. Stayer has shown, essentially apolitical.[25] It did mean, however, that they intended to form churches patterned after the New Testament model as they understood it.

Zwingli's Reaction

The ecclesiology of the Anabaptists did have certain implications for the state that were unacceptable to Zwingli and to Luther as well. The Anabaptists saw more clearly than either Reformer that the proclamation of the gospel was predicated upon an uncoerced response. As Hubmaier wrote in 1524 in his *Concerning Heretics and Those Who Burn Them* (*Von Ketzern und ihren Verbrennern*), even the atheist (*Gotssfind*) had a right to his unbelief as long as he obeyed civil law. Hubmaier made the distinction that all Anabaptists made between "heretics" and "criminals." The state, he insisted, had the right to punish criminals but had absolutely no right to prescribe or proscribe a man's religious confession or lack of it.[26]

Zwingli was well aware of Hubmaier's views

25. Stayer, *Anabaptists and the Sword* (Lawrence, Kans.: Coronado Press, 1972).

26. Potter only confuses matters when he implies that Hubmaier was a Baptist (*Zwingli*, p. 178). While the Baptist movement owed certain of its insights and practices to Anabaptism, it was a development of the seventeenth century that came out of English Separatism. To confuse the two indicates a failure to understand the difference between them.

and apparently took no exception to them until Hubmaier was baptized by Wilhelm Reublin during Lent in 1525. By this time Zwingli's state church had become firmly established, and dissent was not tolerated. As a result, Zwingli's theological stance underwent a number of changes. He pushed Anabaptism aside, preferring to consider it a mindless interruption in the progress of reform in Zürich, but it would not go away. It still presented a threat to the unified front that Zwingli wished to present to his Catholic foes.

Zwingli may have decided to go along with the city council primarily for political reasons, but his appropriation of Augustine's teaching on predestination gave his decision theological support. For his new views he turned to the Old Testament, in which he now discovered that circumcision was the Old Covenant's counterpart to the New Covenant's baptism of infants. Once fortified with this idea, which appeared both biblical and plausible, he was intellectually prepared to do battle with his opponents. He subjected his entire theological system to intense scrutiny and revision.

Ever since Zwingli had established a refuge on an island in Lake Zürich for the errant knight Ulrich von Hutten, Erasmus and Zwingli had been drifting apart. Increasingly, Zwingli found himself disagreeing with Erasmus as he continued to press for the reform of the church in the canton of Zürich. When violence erupted in dealing with the Anabaptists and later with the Roman Catholic cantons, Erasmus's denunciation of Zwingli and his colleagues became widely known. This was evidence enough that Zwingli had forsaken his earlier leanings toward pacifism, which had been inspired in part by Erasmus. By 1529 Zwingli had identified completely with Luther's Augustinian predestinarian theology. Augustine's view of election and grace fitted his new defense of infant baptism far better than Erasmus's teachings on the nature of man and the freedom of the will. Since Zwingli's theology underwent such a drastic revision in midstream, it was somewhat disjointed and incomplete in its final form, as G. W. Bromiley has pointed out.[27]

In 1525, for the first time in his preaching at the *Grossmünster*, Zwingli turned to the Old Testament for his texts, where he found justification for infant baptism. Since the sign of the Old Covenant was circumcision, Zwingli reasoned, the sign of the New Covenant was infant baptism. Thus he did not seek the justification of infant baptism as necessary for the removal of Adamic guilt, because he held that infants, although heirs of Adamic sin, were not guilty in the sight of God. Nor was baptism necessary to salvation. Unlike Luther, Zwingli refused to posit faith in the infant. For him faith was expressed by the congregation on behalf of the baptized, who were surely among the elect.

The Christian Civic Union

Zwingli's Old Testament studies and preaching also provided him with the biblical support he sought for his theocracy and for his argument for the necessity—even the divine sanction—of defending it from all opponents, internal and external, by the sword. All of this apparently led Zwingli to launch a campaign of military conquest of the Catholic cantons in hopes of uniting the whole Confederation in the cause of reform. In 1528 Bern officially supported the Reformation, and by 1529 Bern, Zürich, and Constance formed an alliance called the Christian Civic Union (*das Christliche Burgrecht*), which was soon joined by other Protestant cities, including Basel. The Catholics responded with the formation of the Christian Alliance (*die Christliche Vereinigung*) with the proffered support of Archduke Ferdinand. The new alignments prepared the way for the disastrous Kappel wars.

Zwingli perceived that he had two different kinds of enemies: the Anabaptists, who existed largely because of his earlier teachings and in-

fluence; and the Roman Catholics, whom he suspected of sinister designs on the Protestant cantons. He was also convinced that a plot existed to overthrow the Reformation by force, a plot in which Charles V and his brother, Archduke Ferdinand, were the chief conspirators. Once he had effectively suppressed the Anabaptist movement by means of imprisonment, banishment, and execution, Zwingli turned his attention to the remaining threat: the resurgent Catholic cantons.

In the midst of the political maneuvering, undergirded by his new theological insights, Zwingli kept his position on the Lord's Supper virtually unchanged. This remained the one point on which he and his former disciples found themselves theologically very close. By the same token it was the one issue that drove the final wedge between Zwingli and Luther at Marburg.

Zwingli and Marburg

Why did Zwingli hasten to Marburg at the behest of Philip of Hesse when he knew that he and Luther were worlds apart in their understandings of the Eucharist? The answer is multifaceted. He and Philip thought alike in regard to the necessity of a military alliance of Protestants against the growing Catholic menace. Scarcely two months before, the First Kappel War had ended with an uneasy truce on July 23 (*"Erste Kappeler Land Frieden"*). Zwingli was seeking additional allies. He also felt so confident in his knowledge of the biblical languages and his ability as a debater that he probably thought that he could convince Luther to adopt the "correct" biblical understanding of the Lord's Supper or at least that he could clear the air of misunderstanding and suspicion to the extent that a strong alliance between the German and Swiss Protestant states could become a real possibility. At any rate, Zwingli set out for Marburg with the utmost secrecy. His wife was told only that her husband had urgent business in Basel. At Basel he and Rudolf Collin were joined by Oecolampadius and his party. By the end of September, Philip of Hesse had managed to assemble in

27. See Bromiley, trans. and ed., *Zwingli and Bullinger*, vol. 24 of the Library of Christian Classics (Philadelphia: Westminster Press, 1953), p. 127.

Marburg the most auspicious group of Protestant theologians, Lutheran and Zwinglian, ever gathered together. Because of Zwingli's theological works and his energetic efforts to advance the Reformation in Switzerland, the Swiss and the South Germans considered him to be equal if not superior to Dr. Martin. Each man, a Reformer in his own right with an admiring circle of friends and supporters, felt enormous pressure to defend his own position at all costs.

To a layman like Philip of Hesse the differences between them were not all that great. He fondly imagined that Luther and Zwingli and their compatriots, once face to face, could work through their difficulties in a matter of days. As imperceptible as the gulf may have been to Philip and other laymen, however, it was formidable enough to the participants.

Luther's doctrine, generally referred to as the doctrine of *consubstantiation,* was based upon a literal interpretation of the scriptural accounts of the Last Supper undergirded by a philosophical concept of the ubiquity of Christ. Since Christ is everywhere and in all things, Luther claimed, to deny his presence in the elements is to deny the plain meaning of the words of Christ as well as his ubiquity. The miracle of *transubstantiation* was thus taken out of the hands of the priests; the "real presence" of Christ was for those who possessed the faith to realize it. Although Luther denied that the mass was a sacrifice for sin (as the Roman Church taught), he still maintained that in some sense it was a means of grace.

Zwingli—stimulated by the work of Cornelius Hoen, a Dutch theologian who first called his attention to a different interpretation of the Eucharist—became the best-known exponent of "the memorial view." Hoen had suggested that the "is" in "This is my body" meant "signifies." Zwingli concurred. After checking with Erasmus as well as reviewing Luther's writings on the subject and the works of Karlstadt, Zwingli was convinced that his understanding was supported by the clear meaning of Scripture. Thus Zwingli developed his memorial view of the Lord's Supper quite independently of Luther.

According to Zwingli, the purpose of the Lord's Supper was to help the participant call to mind Christ's sacrifice for our sins—hence it was not a repetition of the sacrifice. Christ was thus present only in a spiritual sense; his body had ascended into heaven. To Zwingli it was not biblical to speak of the "real presence." The Lord's Supper was truly a *eucharist* in which the believer gave thanks to God for the one sacrifice of the cross. Thus Zwingli denied the literal meaning of the words that implied the bodily presence of Christ. Against Luther's interpretation, Zwingli argued on the basis of John 6:63 that these words were not to be interpreted literally but only spiritually. Luther contended that Zwingli's text had nothing to do with the discussion in progress. When Zwingli retorted that his argument would break Luther's neck, Luther replied acidly, "Here, necks are not broken. You are in Hesse now, not in Switzerland."[28] Zwingli apologized, but the damage had been done. Luther refused to shake Zwingli's outstretched hand, and the conference had reached a stalemate.

After some pleading by Philip, their host, who insisted that they should at least be able to arrive at some consensus regarding what constituted the Protestant faith, fifteen articles were drawn up and signed. The last article reflected a compromise that left each side free to disagree. It reads,

> Although we have been unable to agree on the issue as to whether the true vine and blood of Christ are corporally present in the bread and wine of the eucharist, nevertheless each party will prove towards the other its spirit of Christian love, in so far as his conscience will permit. Both will fervently pray to God Almighty that He may grant us and confirm us in true understanding of the matter.[29]

IN THE MIDST OF BATTLE

The Marburg interlude occurred between outbreaks of hostility. The First Kappel War had begun with the refusal of Schwyz and Lucerne

---

28. Luther, cited by Jean Rilliet in *Zwingli: Third Man of the Reformation,* trans. Harold Knight (Philadelphia: Westminster Press, 1964), p. 260.

29. Cited by Rilliet in *Zwingli,* p. 265.

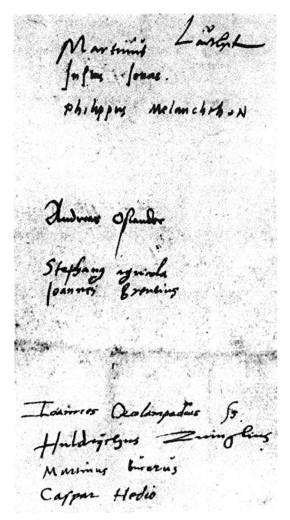

Signatures of the Marburg Confession

and, although a native of Uznach, he represented an attempt on the part of Zürich to export the Reformation into Catholic territories.

The emissaries of the Swiss reform had already won a number of cities and cantons for the cause: Ulm, Memmingen, Constance, and Augsburg in South Germany, and St. Gall, Basel, and Bern in Switzerland. The battle for Bern is illustrative of Zwinglian tactics. Under the leadership of Berchtold Haller of the cathedral and another Bernese priest, Franz Kolb, steps were taken—with the support of the city council—to educate the citizens of the city regarding the differences between "the new church teaching" and "the old church teaching." For this purpose the two priests compiled ten articles, drawing heavily upon the Sixty-seven Articles of Zwingli and those that the Reformer Johannes Comander had used in the Ilanz Disputation. As Oskar Farner suggests, the articles breathed the spirit of Zwingli (*Zwingligeist*) as much as if Zwingli himself had written them.[30] They were ready by November 19 and published shortly thereafter. Haller left nothing to chance. Sermons on and discussions of the articles were spread over a five-day period, from January 14 to 19; Zwingli, Martin Bucer, Oecolampadius, and Haller himself took part in them, as did a number of lesser-known Reformers. On February 7, 1528, Bern officially joined the Reformation by vote of the city council.

With Bern's approval of the Reformation, it appeared to Zwingli that everything was going his way. He envisioned that, with the support of St. Gall, Basel, Bern, Constance, and numerous outlying villages and hamlets, the Reformation would capture the loyalties of the solidly Catholic cantons; arms would be used if necessary. The success of the First Kappel War appeared to confirm this projected scenario. However, Zwingli was restless and quite dissatisfied with what he considered the failure of the victors to press on against the five districts for a total surrender and consequently gain a hearing for

to permit within their borders the preaching of the gospel according to the Zwinglians. The immediate occasion was the execution of an evangelical preacher, Jakob Kaiser, who was burned at the stake. The magistrates of Schwyz may not have anticipated such a severe reaction; in Schwyz on May 29, 1525, Eberli Bolt, an Anabaptist preacher from St. Gall, had been burned together with a friend, a priest who had shared his faith but had not yet been baptized, and the incident had not elicited so much as a flicker of protest from Zürich. But the case of Kaiser was different. He was not an Anabaptist,

---

30. See Farner, *Huldrych Zwingli: Reformatorische Erneuerung von Kirche und Volk in Zürich und in der Eidgenossenschaft, 1525-1531*, 4 vols. (Zürich: Zwingli-Verlag, 1943-60), 4: 277-80, for a list of the articles and an account of the disputation.

the Protestant cause. In the meantime he tightened the reins on the citizens of Zürich.

Reform Measures in Zürich

Hans Salat, chronicler of Lucerne, critically observed, "In Zürich Zwingli is already *Bürgermeister,* chronicler (*schryber*) council, etc. all in all with total power."[31] Although this was not entirely true, it certainly appeared to be. Early in his career of reformatory efforts, Zwingli attempted to bring the monastic orders within the orbit of the Reformation. Under his direction the city council ordered convent life, including instruction in Bible and Latin, to guarantee that the gospel be taught and that those remaining in the cloisters understand what was being taught. The monasteries and convents subjected to such strictures were quite rapidly abandoned. The vacated buildings were at the disposal of the city council, which, again under Zwingli's direction, turned them into centers to care for the poor.

The worship of the churches was also revamped. The organ was removed from the *Grossmünster,* and for some time music found no place in the Reformed worship service. All images were also removed from the church, although stained-glass windows were allowed to remain intact, since the idolatrous worship of glass saints was an unlikely development. The preaching of the gospel and the reading of the Old and New Testament lessons, along with appropriate prayers, became the central acts of the new Protestant worship. Attendance of the services was obligatory.

The whole of life came under the close scrutiny and direct supervision of the authorities in both city and canton. Adultery and prostitution were prohibited. Even the wearing of gold jewelry, silk and velvet apparel, and low-cut shoes was outlawed. All disorder was dealt with rigorously. On May 26, 1530, a curfew was introduced that made it illegal for a citizen to frequent public houses or "clubs" after nine o'clock in the evening.

---

31. Potter cites this observation (*Zwingli,* p. 390), but he questions its accuracy.

Religious conformity was imposed not only upon unrepentant Anabaptists—who were often imprisoned and, if they were among the more serious offenders, executed—but also upon the few Roman Catholics remaining in the city. To Zwingli and the city council, deviation from the Reformed Church order was tantamount to treason. In the eyes of the church, sin became a crime against the state. The sacral society that the Reformer had created would tolerate no dissent. Apparently Zwingli felt the success of the Reformation in Zürich depended upon the power of the state. Indeed, it was a short step from this conviction to the promotion of the cause outside Zürich at the point of the sword.

The Second Kappel War, 1531

Zwingli's dissatisfaction with the provisions of the truce following the First Kappel War became something of an obsession. He urged Bern to unite with Zürich and the other Protestant cantons to raise an army and strike while the iron was hot, to win a victory for the evangelical cause. Bern hesitated. The recently won canton still had some Catholic sympathizers and others who were none too happy about the prospect of a bloody conflict that would pit Swiss against Swiss. While the two powerful Protestant cantons were divided about the next step, the Catholic cantons were feeling the pinch because the Protestants had imposed a food blockade, and they were thus shut off from both supplies and markets for their products. Secretly they prepared for war.

Zürich maintained a small garrison beyond a range of mountains on the plain of Kappel between Zürich and Lucerne. As the Catholic army approached, it was clear that the small garrison, numbering no more than three hundred, was hopelessly outnumbered. The city council sent out the call for reinforcements too late. After the battle had begun and the Zürichers had made a number of costly blunders, a contingent of seven hundred reinforcements, hastily assembled and poorly organized, rushed out, at Zwingli's urging, to try to save the beleaguered outpost, but they were overwhelmed on the marshy land and put to flight. The victors were merciless. Zwingli was knocked from his horse and run through with a sword. Once his identity was discovered, he was decapitated and his head was placed on a pole. His body was quartered and burned, and the ashes were mixed with manure and scattered across the countryside. Five hundred Zürichers died with Zwingli on that disastrous day in October. Some families suffered multiple losses. Zwingli's wife, Anna, lost not only her husband but also her oldest son, a son-in-law, a brother, and a brother-in-law.

As the war continued, more from other cantons died in what was in the end an unnecessary conflict: when the war ended, the Protestants lost virtually all the concessions they had wrested from the Catholic cantons in the first bloodless conflict. The result was that the Protestants were stymied, and the Catholic cantons hardened their positions; in fact, they have remained almost totally Roman Catholic through the subsequent four-and-a-half centuries.

REFORM AFTER KAPPEL

Sometime in August, according to Myconius, a comet was observed in the heavens above Zürich. In an age when astrology still held some credibility even for the most liberated humanist, Zwingli took it to be an ill omen for himself and another. But the war to which the battle at Kappel gave its name proved an unmitigated disaster for the hundreds who died, and dealt a serious blow to the Reformation in the cities of Zürich and St. Gall.

The reaction in Zürich was severe. Myconius reports that he was forced to go into hiding for a number of days. Once he dared to show his face, he discovered that he stood almost alone in defending Zwingli's actions during those last fateful years. The city council regrouped to pass several resolutions designed to remove preachers from the political arena. They were not to meddle in politics, and war could not be promoted without the council's consent. The council assumed the right to appoint all preachers in the canton to their respective parishes. But the Protestant faith still remained the established

religion of the city and canton, as it did in St. Gall.

The recovery of the Swiss Reformed Church from the war's devastating effects was due to a large extent to the superb leadership of Zwingli's successor, Heinrich Bullinger (1504-1575). Bullinger was the son of the parish priest at Bremgarten. After studying at Emmerich in a school conducted by the Brethren of the Common Life, he attended the University of Cologne, where he was educated in the *via antiqua* but at the same time became acquainted with the writings of Erasmus and Luther. He returned to Bremgarten to succeed his father, but the war compelled him to take refuge in Zürich. Although a fervent admirer of Zwingli, he had opposed the military adventurism of the Reformer. On December 9, when he was only twenty-seven, he was appointed by the city council to serve the *Grossmünster* after a mutual understanding had been reached regarding the freedom of the pulpit. The youthful minister soon justified the confidence of Zürich councillors. His doctrinal sermons reinforced the Zwinglian foundation of the church. He organized both the academic and the ecclesiastical institutions of the city. Even though basically Augustinian in his theology, Bullinger was not as rigorous in his predestinarian views as Calvin. His irenic approach to the brilliant Reformer of Geneva made possible a common confessional understanding of 1566, *The Second Helvetic Confession,* which united the Reformed Church of Switzerland.[32] However, in his attempts to find some common ground with the Lutherans

---

32. *The First Helvetic Confession* was drawn up by Bullinger, Myconius, and others assembled for the purpose at Basel in 1536. Other confessions followed: the Consensus of Zürich in 1549 (*Consensus Tigurinus*) and the Consensus of Geneva in 1552. Elements of both are found in *The Second Helvetic Confession,* which Bullinger wrote in 1562, two years before Calvin's death. It was first published in 1566 in three languages: Latin, German, and French. It became the basic confession of almost all of the Reformed churches on the Continent and in England and Scotland as well. See the Latin text in *The Evangelical Protestant Creeds, with Translations,* vol. 3 of Philip Schaff's *The Creeds of Christendom* (Grand Rapids: Baker Book House, 1966), 233-306.

he was no more successful than Calvin had been.

As for the Anabaptists, Bullinger, like Zwingli, saw them as a threat to both church and state. In fact, his polemics led him to distort the history of the movement. In order to remove from the Swiss Reformation the odium that had been associated with the name "Anabaptists" after the Münster fiasco, Bullinger wrote in his *Rise of the Anabaptists* (*Der Widertöufferen Ursprung*), published in 1560, that Thomas Müntzer was the founder of the movement. Johann Eck, on the other hand, attributed the movement to Zwingli's teachings. In this, Eck, the Catholic antagonist of Luther, was more nearly correct than Bullinger. However, Bullinger deserves credit equal to or greater than that given Calvin for salvaging the work of Zwingli and thus helping to shape the Reformed Church into possibly the most influential and international form of Protestantism to emerge out of the sixteenth-century Reformation.

Chapter XII

THE ANABAPTISTS

t was Zwingli who first gave his former disciples, the Swiss Brethren, the name *Wiedertäufer* (Anabaptists). It caught on and remained a convenient tag by which their enemies could identify those who preferred to call themselves Brethren in Christ. However, it remained for Zwingli's successor, Heinrich Bullinger, to link Thomas Müntzer of Allstedt with the Swiss Anabaptists.

Bullinger's theory was rather tardy in appearing. In his first published statements on the subject, he asserted that Anabaptism had originated in Zürich, but by 1570 he had succeeded in tracing the beginnings of the movement to Thomas Müntzer. Bullinger's revisionist history proved attractive, and for the better part of three centuries it remained virtually unchallenged by many historians of the Reformation. C. A. Cornelius (1819–1903), a Catholic historian, was the first to raise serious questions about Bullinger's version of the historical development of Anabaptism. He was followed in his rejection of Bullinger's thesis by Ernst Troeltsch, Fritz Blanke, and the American Mennonite historian Harold Bender. Troeltsch went on to assert that in Anabaptism lies the beginning of the modern free-church movement. Both Roland Bainton and George Huntston Williams are in substantial agreement with this position.

However, these two American church historians have suggested umbrella terms that include Anabaptists as well as Spiritualists (like Müntzer) and Rationalists (Socinians) without erasing finer distinctions. Bainton coined the phrase "the left wing of the Reformation," and George Huntston Williams suggested "the Radical Reformation." Williams also introduced the term "Magisterial Reformation" to refer to the movements of Reformers like Luther, Zwingli, and Calvin. The major groupings included in this term are essentially the same as those of Bainton. However, Williams further divides the Radical Reformers into three groups: Revolutionaries, Contemplatives, and Evangelical Anabaptists. While questions may be raised about Williams' labels, apparently his distinction between the "Magisterial" and the "Radical" Reformations has been widely accepted by historians of the Reformation era.[1]

---

1. In *Spiritual and Anabaptist Writers,* Williams and Angel M. Mergal note, "All three groupings within this Radical Reformation agree in cutting back to that root and in

Williams further subdivides his three major categories. Consequently, the Anabaptists fall into three groups—Revolutionary, Contemplative, and Evangelical—and the Spiritualists fall into three groups—Revolutionary, Evangelical, and Rational. The Rationalists, known as both Socinians and Antitrinitarians, could be differentiated by further division but are not. However, it is not necessary to accept Williams' subgroupings to recognize that his basic categories are substantially correct. His work emphasizes that the historical development of Anabaptism demands a more careful delineation of relationships with kindred movements not always sufficiently distinguished. Admittedly, this is a difficult task but not an impossible one. As early as 1531 an English bishop who had lived in Switzerland wrote in his *Dyaloge* that Luther was the "chief captain of new heretics," of which there were three main parties. "And whereas there was only one faction before, that of the Lutherans, there arose another, which he called Oecolampadians or Zwinglians, out of whom came a third faction named Anabaptists, consisting of more than eleven sects of different heresies and opinions."[2]

While there are still unresolved questions about the origins of Anabaptism and its relationship to the Spiritualists and the Rationalists, the available evidence indicates that Anabaptism was primarily a reform movement that developed within the context of the Swiss Reformation. Only by correctly placing the rise of the Anabaptist movement within its Swiss context can one restructure the nature of the movement and recapture its original vision.[3] But it is also important to remember that it soon demonstrated the distinctive features that characterized its unique contribution, which became cause first for concern, then for alarm, and finally for suppression.

Certain other historians such as Albrecht Ritschl, Ludwig Keller, and Thomas M. Lindsay have held that the roots of the Anabaptist movement lay deep within one or more of the dissenting groups of the medieval period. While there are undoubtedly certain similarities between the Anabaptists and—to name only two such groups—the Czech Brethren and the Waldenses, these similarities do not appear to have been due to any direct historical connections. The entire leadership of the early Anabaptists of Switzerland and South Germany came out of the Roman Catholic Church with intermediate stops within the Zwingli-led Reformation. In fact, George Blaurock, Johannes Brötli, Eberli Bolt, Wilhelm Reublin, Michael Sattler, and Balthasar Hubmaier were all priests. This is not to deny that communities in Switzerland where Waldenses once flourished eventually became havens for Anabaptist house churches, or that certain areas in England that once saw Lollards in abundance became (early in the sixteenth century) fertile fields for Anabaptist cultivation. However, in cases where such kindred groups did coexist—for example, the Czech Brethren and the Anabaptists—they moved, as Jarold Zeman has demonstrated, like two ships passing in the night.[4]

Even though the Anabaptist movement may have been nothing "more than a minor episode in the history of sixteenth-century German society," as Claus-Peter Clasen contends,[5] no other

---

freeing church and creed of what they regarded as the suffocating growth of ecclesiastical tradition and magisterial prerogative. Precisely this makes theirs a 'Radical Reformation'" ([Philadelphia: Westminster Press, 1957], p. 22). Those who wish to study these movements in more detail can consult two of Williams' other works: *The Radical Reformation* (Philadelphia: Westminster Press, 1962), and *The Polish Brethren*, 2 vols., Harvard Theological Studies, no. 30 (Chico, Calif.: Scholars Press). The finest work on the history of Anabaptism (among other things, it gives a balanced account of Münster), is Cornelius Krahn's *Dutch Anabaptism: Origin, Spread, Life, and Thought (1450–1600)* (The Hague: Martinus Nijhoff, 1968).

2. Cited by Irvin Buckwalter Horst in *The Radical Brethren: Anabaptism and the English Reformation to 1558* (Nieuwkoop: B. de Graaf, 1972), pp. 44–45.

3. For a fuller discussion of Thomas Müntzer's relationship with the Swiss Brethren, see Harold S. Bender, *Conrad Grebel, c.1498–1526* (Goshen, Ind.: Mennonite Historical Society, 1950), pp. 108–16.

4. Zeman, *The Anabaptists and the Czech Brethren in Moravia, 1526–1628: A Study of Origins and Contacts* (Paris: Mouton, 1969), pp. 26–38.

5. Clasen, *Anabaptism: A Social History, 1525–1618* (Ithaca: Cornell University Press, 1972), p. 428.

Reformation movement so symbolized the break between the medieval and the modern worlds. Further, the influence of Anabaptism far outweighed the number of its adherents, not only in German-speaking Europe but in France, the Netherlands, and England as well. And while its ongoing influence may be difficult to assess, it is far too early to close the books on this point.

A PEOPLE'S MOVEMENT

The beginnings of the Anabaptist movement were hardly indicative of the popular appeal it was to have. It was born in the minds and hearts of a handful of priests and intellectuals (there were no more than fifteen of them).[6] But when these zealous advocates began preaching about their new faith, it soon demonstrated its popular appeal.

Zollikon

The first baptisms among the Swiss Brethren took place in Zürich on January 21, 1525, a Saturday. The next day, Johannes Brötli, a former Roman Catholic priest and apparently one of the early converts, baptized his landlord, Fridli Schumacher, at the well of Hirslanden in Zollikon, a small farming village near Zürich. Fritz Blanke relates this stirring event in a matter-of-fact way, using almost the identical wording of the court record:

> Arriving at the well of Hirslanden they both stopped, and Schumacher said to Brötli: "Now then, Hans, you have taught me the truth. For this I thank you and now please give me the sign." Schumacher had been instructed about baptism by his tenant, Brötli, and had accepted these teachings. Now he wished to take a further step, the step from theory to practice. And although he had been baptized as a small child, once more he asked for the sign of baptism. Without hesitation

Brötli proceeded to baptize Schumacher sprinkling him with well water.[7]

Hans Oggenfuss (Oakenfüss), a tailor, on his way to deliver a coat to Wilhelm Reublin, saw and reported this baptism of the shoemaker by the former Roman Catholic priest. This was but a foretaste of things to come. During the next few days many others—farmers and artisans from Zollikon—committed their lives to Christ, a commitment signified by believer's baptism. The simple baptisms were followed by an equally simple observance of the Lord's Supper. Brötli, Blaurock, and Felix Manz were the leaders in introducing the Anabaptist message to Zollikon.

In the churches of Switzerland, many of which no longer held to transubstantiation, priests were still saying the mass in Latin. In Zürich churches only the words referring to the mass as a sacrifice had been omitted. Two years after the First Disputation, Conrad Grebel led in the first known evangelical observance of the Lord's Supper. Grebel read a passage of Scripture, and those sitting at the table who had been baptized took the wine and the *Hausbrot* (leavened bread) in their own hands in remembrance of the sacrifice of Christ. These early observances were memorable experiences. Jörg Schad, a Zollikon farmer and new convert, testified in court that "they had broken the bread and eaten it in order that they might always have God in their hearts and think of Him and show brotherly love to every man."[8] Implicit in the early observances of the Lord's Supper among the Swiss Brethren were those concepts that became more clearly defined as the Anabaptist movement progressed. The Lord's Supper was primarily a *eucharist*—that is, a thanksgiving memorial of the sacrifice of Christ. It was also conceived of as a sign of fellowship in which one pledged peace and love to his brethren,

---

6. Fritz Blanke, *Brüder in Christo* (Zürich: Zwingli-Verlag, 1955), p. 16.

7. Cited by Blanke in *Brüder in Christo*, p. 23. See also *Quellen zur Geschichte der Täufer in der Schweiz*, vol. 1, *Zürich*, ed. Leonhard von Muralt and Walter Schmid (Zürich: S. Hirzel Verlag, 1952), pp. 41–42.

8. Cited in *Quellen zur Geschichte der Täufer in der Schweiz*, 1: 41.

and a reminder of the ethical demands of Christian discipleship. Therefore the transformed
mass had become both personal and communal, incorporating in its observance the ethical dimensions of the Christian life for both the
individual and the congregation (*Gemeinde*.)[9]

With the emergence of the Swiss Brethren, a
new kind of Reformation Christianity was clearly
taking shape. Even though the group stressed
the importance of personal belief, it also incorporated the baptized into a community of believers. Although there were cases of individual
baptisms, such as those of Fridli Schumacher
and Wolfgang Ulimann, from its very beginning
the theology of baptism among the Anabaptists
implied incorporation into a witnessing community of believers. In Switzerland and most
other European states, this meant that Anabaptism was to remain a small minority composed
of recruits from the ranks of the humbler sort;
few people of wealth and position cared to
break with the state churches and risk losing
everything, including their lives.[10]

By their new faith these poor and powerless
were lifted out of the wretchedness of poverty
and ignorance and became bold witnesses of a
dynamic movement that commanded their
steadfast loyalty until death. Two exceptions to
this pattern were the churches led by Hubmaier

---

9. An example of the implication of baptism and the
Lord's Supper for the first Anabaptists of Zollikon is found
in the testimony of Cünrat Hottinger. Hottinger was one of
those baptized (at his own request) in Zollikon by Johannes
Brötli. Afterwards, Hottinger related, he and the others sat
down at a table and celebrated the Lord's Supper after the
example of Christ and his disciples, who "at the Last Supper
broke bread together as a sign of brotherly love and peace"
("*das es ein zeichen sölte sin brüderlicher lieby und dess
fridens*"). "So had *der helffer* [Johannes Brötli] broken it
and gave it to them. In the same way he followed this with
presenting the cup" (*Quellen zur Geschichte der Täufer in
der Schweiz*, 1: 41).

10. In a statistical summary Clasen gives numerical esti-
mates of the classes of adherents of Anabaptism in the
sixteenth century with the exception of North Germany, the
Netherlands, England, and France: there were 154 intellectuals, 4,552 craftsmen, and 7,647 farmers. If these figures are
representative, it would be safe to conclude that the movement was indeed a "people's movement." For a breakdown
of the figures, see Clasen's *Anabaptism*, p. 432.

in Waldshut and Nikolsburg, Moravia, where the
Anabaptist's gospel captured the majority of the
inhabitants (not only the poor) and took over
former Roman Catholic edifices. In Switzerland
Anabaptism conformed to the general pattern;
it was most popular in St. Gall.

St. Gall

Wolfgang Ulimann was a native of St. Gall.
Shortly after Conrad Grebel baptized him in the
Rhine River, he returned to his native environs
and discovered the people to be quite receptive
to his message. He sent for Grebel, and together
they became involved in a door-to-door campaign that proved quite fruitful. Two hundred
were baptized on Palm Sunday 1525 in the Sitter
River, which was about three kilometers from
the city. Within the next six weeks possibly as
many as four hundred were baptized.

At first the authorities were reluctant to act,
perhaps out of deference to Grebel's brother-in-
law, Dr. Joachim von Watt (Vadianus). However,
after receiving a letter from Zwingli, Vadianus
himself opposed the Anabaptists before the city
council. By this time Grebel had already left
town, but he wrote a letter on behalf of the
beleaguered converts that was read before the
city council. The authorities sought to control
the growing movement by imprisoning or ban-
ishing its leaders, a strategy that proved quite
effective. After Eberli Bolt and Ulimann had
been expelled from the city, the movement
failed to prosper, although it lingered on for
some time in the canton. Bolt, Ulimann, and
Manz, all of whom labored for a time in St. Gall,
were executed elsewhere for heresy, and Grebel
died in the summer of 1526. This doubtless left
the St. Gall Anabaptists without effective leaders
and with little heart to pursue a course that led
to such reprisals.

THE CHURCH UNDER THE CROSS

The fate of the Anabaptists of St. Gall became to
some extent the Anabaptist story. It is a history
of martyrdom. Although Grebel and the small
courageous band who had gathered in the

home of Felix Manz had anticipated persecution for their defiance of the mandates of the Zürich authorities, they had no way of knowing how severe the attempt to suppress the movement would eventually become. According to Claus-Peter Clasen, "Anabaptism in our area (Switzerland, south and central Germany, Austria, Bohemia) was already largely destroyed in 1528 and 1529, several years before the Kingdom of Münster."[11] But this did not mean that the persecution of Anabaptists ceased. In fact, Clasen indicates that there were 370 known executions from 1530 to 1539. In Switzerland executions took place as late as 1618, the last year covered in the study. And Anabaptists continued to be the objects of persecution and imprisonment in the canton of Bern until Napoleon's armies brought religious liberty to Switzerland in the nineteenth century.

As for the rest of Europe, the record is a checkered one. The siege of Münster itself was not a particularly noble episode. However, Philip of Hesse was one Protestant prince who refused to put Anabaptists to death within his domains. Although he still had arrested and imprisoned those who passed through his territory, he found that persecution tended to scatter the sheep. They fled from Moravia to Hungary and back again, and eventually the Hutterites and the Mennonites from various European countries immigrated to the United States after a sojourn in Russia. In the sixteenth century they traveled from the Netherlands and Flanders to the east coast of England, and when persecution became their lot there, they retraced their steps. At times the execution of the Anabaptists defeated the ill-conceived purpose of the authorities: it tended to magnify the influence of this relatively small group of believers. The martyrdom of Michael Sattler is a case in point.

Michael Sattler (ca. 1490-1527)

The execution of Michael Sattler became the best known of that of any sixteenth-century Ana-

baptist. Several factors explain this phenomenon. Sattler himself was a pivotal figure. He had been a prior in a monastery at Freiburg in Breisgau and was the probable author of the Schleitheim Confession, the first group confession of the Anabaptists, which had been drawn up shortly after the execution of Felix Manz. The fact that the authorities wanted to make Sattler an example compelled them to make something of a production of his trial, which lasted for two days. Afterward Sattler was subjected to prolonged torture, then burned alive. Four accounts of the death of Sattler and his faithful wife are extant. His courageous defense and valiant death created a boomerang effect that Rottenburg had not anticipated. Perhaps no other martyrdom of an Anabaptist so publicized the faith and faithfulness of Anabaptists to a German-speaking audience. For this reason a closer look at Sattler and his execution is particularly important.

After the death of Manz, Sattler emerged as the most able leader among South German Anabaptists. Prior to the Schleitheim conference on the outskirts of Schaffhausen in February 1527, Sattler had served as an evangelist in both Zürich and the Strasbourg area. It was in Zürich that he had become an Anabaptist under the influence of Wilhelm Reublin. No other Anabaptist leader remained active in the area: Hubmaier was in Moravia, Blaurock was in the Tyrol, and Hans Denck was attempting to witness in the Jewish communities along the Rhine. Grebel and Manz were dead. Reublin was apparently not the leader that Sattler was—hence it was Sattler rather than Reublin who stood in the breach at Schleitheim. Some of the Brethren, perhaps at St. Gall, had begun to express attitudes not at all in keeping with the basic tenets of the faith. Schleitheim was designed to counteract these tendencies and to provide an opportunity for reaffirmation of and rededication to the original vision.

The Schleitheim Confession, 1527

For the meeting Sattler had probably drawn up the articles, at least in a preliminary draft, sub-

---

11. Clasen, *Anabaptism*, p. 371.

sequently known as the Schleitheim Confession. The term "confession" is somewhat misleading, because the articles contain no strictly doctrinal statements other than a general affirmation of commonly held Christian concepts about God. The confession is concerned with order and discipline within the small, widely scattered congregations; therefore baptism, excommunication, the Lord's Supper, separation from the world, pastors, the sword, and the oath comprise the subjects addressed. Although the work resembles a church manual on the order of the primitive *Didache* (*The Teaching of the Twelve Apostles*) rather than a confession of faith, throughout it there are implications that reflect the theology of Anabaptism. This is particularly true of the statements made about baptism and the Lord's Supper. On baptism, for example, the Brethren agreed,

> Baptism shall be given to all who have learned repentance and amendment of life, and who believe truly that their sins are taken away by Christ, and to all those who walk in the resurrection of Jesus Christ, and wish to be buried with Him in death, so that they may be resurrected with him, and to all those who with this significance request it [baptism] of us and demand it for themselves. This excludes all infant baptism, the highest and chief abomination of the pope. In this you have the foundation and testimony of the apostles. Mt. 28, Mk. 16, Acts 2, 8, 16, 19. This we wish to hold simply, yet firmly and with assurance.[12]

This initiatory rite was to be administered only to those "who have learned repentance and amendment of life . . . and all those who walk in the resurrection of Jesus Christ."[13] Here are reflected the moral implications of the Anabaptist theology of baptism. The Anabaptists rejected infant baptism because it failed the biblical tests they applied to it. Instead they insisted upon baptism for those who had been truly converted and who had so demonstrated the change in their life-styles. Of course it was

meaningless if it was not a voluntary act. Baptism by immersion seems to be suggested by the phrasing " . . . buried with Him in death, so that they may be resurrected with Him, and to all those who with this significance request it." However, the imagery here is figurative, as it is in Romans 6:4, and was apparently never intended to prescribe immersion as the correct form of baptism.

The Lord's Supper is referred to as "the breaking of bread" and is simply and briefly elaborated:

> All those who wish to break one bread in remembrance of the broken body of Christ, and all who wish to drink of one drink as a remembrance of the shed blood of Christ, shall be united beforehand by baptism in one body of Christ which is the Church of God [*in die gmein gottes*] and whose Head is Christ. For as Paul points out we cannot at the same time be partakers of the Lord's table and the table of devils; we cannot at the same time drink the cup of the Lord and the cup of the devil. That is, all those who have fellowship with the dead works of darkness have no part in the light. Therefore all who follow the devil and the world have no part with those who are called unto God out of the world. All who lie in the evil [*in dem argen ligen*] have no part in the good.
>
> Therefore it is and must be [thus]: Whoever has not been called by one God to one faith, to one baptism, to one Spirit, to one body, with all the children of God's church, cannot be made [into] one bread with them, as indeed must be done if one is truly to break bread according to the command of Christ.[14]

The memorial nature of the Lord's Supper is paramount in this article, but it is clear that the prerequisites for participation are baptism and a blameless life. The article also emphasizes communion as a sign of unity among the Brethren.

Two of the most important articles in the confession were those on separation and the sword. Besides calling for separation from Roman Catholic churches, those assembled at Schleitheim agreed to abstain from all civic af-

---

12. Cited by William L. Lumpkin in *Baptist Confessions of Faith* (Philadelphia: Judson Press, 1959), p. 25.

13. Cited by Lumpkin in *Baptist Confessions of Faith*, p. 25.

14. Cited by Lumpkin in *Baptist Confessions of Faith*, pp. 25–26.

fairs as well as the "sword, armor and the like."[15] In the article on the sword, the Brethren recognized that God had given the sword to the state for the maintenance of law and order, but they held that the Christian was to have nothing to do with this. In a summary of their position, the dichotomy between those of the world who use the sword and the Christian who follows Christ is sharply drawn:

Finally, it will be observed that it is not appropriate for a Christian to serve as a magistrate because of these points: The government's magistracy is according to the flesh, but the Christians' is according to the Spirit; their houses and dwelling remain in this world, but the Christians' citizenship is in heaven; the weapons of their conflict and war are carnal and against the flesh only, but the Christians' weapons are spiritual, against the fornication of the devil. The worldlings are armed with steel and iron, but the Christians are armed with the armor of God, with truth, righteousness, peace, faith, salvation and the Word of God. In brief, as is the mind of Christ toward us, so shall the mind of the members of the body of Christ be through Him in all things, that there may be no schism in the body through which it would be destroyed.[16]

Historians working in these materials have rarely agreed about the identity of those Anabaptists considered in error. Beatrice Jenny thought certain wayward souls at St. Gall were intended. If this were so, then some may have been present at Schleitheim and joined in the consensus that resulted in the acceptance of the articles. It appears that in the wake of Manz's martyrdom some of the Brethren had taken the position that Anabaptists should participate in government and bear arms under certain circumstances. This was Hubmaier's position, and Waldshut, where Hubmaier had reorganized his church into an Anabaptist congregation, was only a few kilometers away. Hubmaier was also well-known in Schaffhausen, where many

friends held his name and teachings in high regard, and he was still not without influence among the Anabaptists of Moravia. It seems that those who held to his teachings on the sword and civic responsibility were the most likely targets of the articles on the ban, separation, and the sword. That this is a safe conjecture is supported by the appearance of Hubmaier's work *On the Sword* on June 27, 1527, in which he attempts to give biblical justification for his more positive position on the state and even the desirability of a Christian magistrate.

The article dealing with an Anabaptist pastor's relationship to his church reveals the precarious existence of small Anabaptist congregations within a hostile environment. However small a local congregation may have been, the Brethren agreed that it was responsible for supplying its pastor's material needs. The congregation also had the authority to discipline an erring pastor as well as the right to replace him with another. This is spelled out very briefly: "But should it happen that through the cross this pastor should be banished or led to the Lord [through martyrdom] another shall be ordained in his place in the same hour so that God's little flock and people may not be destroyed."[17]

Sattler's Trial and Execution

Upon his return to Horb from Schleitheim in the company of a few of the Brethren, Sattler was arrested and placed in the prison tower at Binsdorf. Certain incriminating documents were found on him. As a result, the authorities decided to make an example of him in an attempt to intimidate other Anabaptists or would-be

15. Cited by Lumpkin in *Baptist Confessions of Faith*, p. 27.

16. Cited by Lumpkin in *Baptist Confessions of Faith*, p. 28.

17. Cited by Lumpkin in *Baptist Confessions of Faith*, p. 27. The Schleitheim Confession is translated by John C. Wenger. Those interested in a history of the earliest known texts should consult *The Legacy of Michael Sattler*, trans. and ed. John Howard Yoder (Scottdale, Pa.: Herald Press, 1973), pp. 13-15. The most recent critical version of the Schleitheim Confession can be found on pp. 26-35 of *Quellen zur Geschichte der Täufer in der Schweiz*, vol. 2, *Ostschweiz*, ed. Heinold Fast (Zürich: Theologischer Verlag, 1973).

Anabaptists along the Neckar. A jury was convened, some jurors coming from as far away as Ensisheim. The trial began on May 17. There were fourteen defendants on the bench of the accused, and seven charges were brought against all fourteen. Two additional charges were brought against Sattler alone. Count Joachim began the proceedings by asking for a reading of the charges:

1. That he and his adherents acted contrary to the decree of the emperor. 2. He taught, maintained, and believed, that the body and blood of Christ were not present in his sacrament. 3. He taught and believed, that infant-baptism was not promotive of salvation. 4. They rejected the sacrament of extreme unction. 5. They despised and reviled the Mother of God, and condemned the saints. 6. He declared, that men should not swear before a magistrate. 7. He has commenced a new and unheard of custom in regard to the Lord's Supper, placing the bread and wine on a plate, eating and drinking the same. 8. Contrary to the rule, he has married a wife. 9. He said if the Turks invaded the country, we ought not to resist them, and if he approved of war, he would rather take the field against the Christians than against the Turks, notwithstanding, it is an important matter to set the greatest enemies of our faith against us.[18]

After the charges were read, Sattler asked that the articles be reread. In response to this request the secretary, who was from Ensisheim, sneered, "He has boasted of the Holy Ghost. Now if this boast is true, it seems to me, it is unnecessary to grant him this; for, if he has the Holy Ghost, as he boasts, the same will tell him what has been done here." Unperturbed, Sattler repeated his request, which was begrudgingly granted.[19]

Sattler's defense was both skillful and courageous. In answer to the first charge, he pointed out that the imperial mandates were against the Lutherans. The mandates directed that the gos-

pel and the Word of God be followed, not Lutheran doctrine and error. "This we have observed," he stated, "for I am not aware, that we have acted contrary to the gospel and word of God; I appeal to the word of Christ."[20] He accepted the second charge as valid, defending the Anabaptist position with numerous Scripture references. The third charge he did not deny, but used the opportunity to affirm believer's baptism. In speaking to the fourth article, he refused to distinguish between oil as a creation of God, which is good, and the oil of extreme unction. Concerning the Virgin Mary, he said,

We never reviled the mother of God, and the saints; but the mother of Christ should be esteemed above all women; for she had the favor of giving birth to the Savior of the world; but that she shall be an intercessor, is not known in Scripture. . . . As to the saints, we say, that we who live and believe are the saints; in evidence of this I appeal to the epistle of Paul to the Romans, Corinthians, Ephesians, etc. He always writes: To the beloved saints. We, therefore, who believe, are the saints: those who die in the faith, we consider the "blessed."

Sattler accepted the sixth charge as valid and defended his position by citing Matthew 5:34, 37. He ignored the seventh charge.[21]

Sattler then turned his attention to the last two charges brought against him personally. Regarding his teaching about the Turks, Sattler asserted the principle of nonresistance:

If the Turks should make an invasion, they should not be resisted; for it is written: Thou shalt not kill. We ought not to defend ourselves against the

---

18. Cited by Gustav Bossert, Jr., in "Michael Sattler's Trial and Martyrdom in 1527," trans. Elizabeth Bender, *Mennonite Quarterly Review* 25 (July 1951): 209–10.

19. Cited by Williams and Mergal in *Spiritual and Anabaptist Writers,* p. 139. Bossert asserts that the articles were not reread even then but that only their substance was given ("Michael Sattler's Trial," p. 209).

20. Sattler, cited by Williams and Mergal in *Spiritual and Anabaptist Writers,* p. 140.

21. Sattler, cited by Thieleman J. Van Braght in *Martyrs' Mirror* (Scottdale, Pa.: Herald Press, 1938), p. 345. There are four extant accounts of Sattler's trial and death. Wilhelm Reublin's account is found on pp. 250–53 of vol. 1 of *Quellen zur Geschichte der Täufer in der Schweiz.* Klaus von Graveneck's account is in the Wolfenbüttel Library. An original German account edited by W. J. Köhler is found in *Flugschriften aus den ersten Jahren der Reformation II* (Leipzig, 1908). It differs from the others in some slight details. It is this last account from which the version in *Martyrs' Mirror* is taken.

Turks and our persecutors; but earnestly entreat God in our prayers, that he would repel and withstand them. For my saying, that if I approved of war, I would rather march forth against the so named Christians who persecute, imprison, and put to death, the pious Christians, I assign this reason: The Turk is a true Turk, knows nothing of the Christian faith, and is a Turk according to the flesh; but you, wishing to be Christian, and making your boast of Christ, persecute the pious witnesses of Christ, and are Turks according to the Spirit. Exodus XX.30. Matthew VII.7. Titus I.16.

In his closing argument Sattler established the legitimacy of the office of magistrate, defining its jurisdiction, limitations, and responsibilities. His final plea was for an opportunity to discuss the Scriptures with the judges in the language of their choice. He expressed a desire that the judges would "repent and receive instruction."[22]

The response, according to the account, was reminiscent of apostolic days, and indicative of the spirit of the court: "The judges laughed at the discourse, and after consultation, the town clerk of Ensisheim said: 'Oh, you infamous, desperate villain and monk, you would have us engage with you in a discussion! The executioner will dispute with you, we think for a certainty.' Sattler exclaimed: 'Let the will of God be done.'"[23] More of the same followed. The town clerk of Ensisheim even became violent. Caught up in an emotional frenzy, he threatened to take Sattler's life then and there. The prisoner's patience and composure were obviously exasperating to his would-be judges.

During the hour and a half that the judges deliberated, Sattler was alternately threatened and ridiculed. Some cried out, "When I see you get away, I will believe in you." Another seized his sword and said, "See, with this we will dispute with you."[24] A voice from the crowd asked why he had not remained a lord in the monastery. Sattler replied, "I was a lord according to

the flesh, but it is better thus."[25] Klaus von Graveneck, an eyewitness, wrote of Sattler's conduct, "All this I saw myself. May God grant us also to testify of Him so bravely and patiently."[26]

These events took place over a two-day period. Sattler was sentenced on May 18 and executed two days later.[27] The torture, a prelude to the execution, began at the marketplace, where a piece was cut from Sattler's tongue. Pieces of flesh were torn from his body twice with red-hot tongs. He was then tied to a cart. On the way to the scene of the execution he was torn with the tongs five more times. In the marketplace and at the site of the execution, still able to speak, the unshakable Sattler prayed for his persecutors. After being bound to a ladder with ropes and pushed into the fire, he admonished the people, the judges, and the mayor to repent and be converted. Then he prayed, "Almighty, eternal God, Thou art the way and the truth: because I have not been shown to be in error, I will with thy help to this day testify to the truth and seal it with my blood." When the ropes on his wrists had burned, Sattler raised both forefingers, giving the promised signal to his fellow Anabaptists that a martyr's death was bearable. Then the assembled crowd heard coming from his seared lips, "Father, I commend my spirit into Thy hands."[28]

Three others were then executed. And Sattler's faithful wife was drowned eight days later in the Neckar; she had refused to recant, turning down an attractive offer of amnesty and a comfortable home in a congenial environment.

Perhaps no other execution of an Anabaptist had such far-reaching influence. Lutheran, Reformed, and even Catholic witnesses were never

22. Sattler, cited by Van Braght in *Martyrs' Mirror*, pp. 345–46.

23. Sattler, cited by Van Braght in *Martyrs' Mirror*, p. 346.

24. Cited by Bossert in "Michael Sattler's Trial," p. 214.

25. Sattler, cited by Van Braght in *Martyrs' Mirror*, p. 346.

26. Von Graveneck, cited by Bossert in "Michael Sattler's Trial," p. 215.

27. There is a difference of opinion about the date of Sattler's execution. Some accounts report that he was put to death on Monday, May 20, 1527; others say he was killed the following day. See Bossert, "Michael Sattler's Trial," p. 215, for a rather detailed discussion of this matter.

28. Sattler, cited by Bossert in "Michael Sattler's Trial," p. 214.

quite able to forget the scene of that infamous day in Rottenburg. Martin Bucer and Wolfgang Capito were grieved at the news of the execution. And Wilhelm Reublin's booklet containing an account of Sattler's execution found its way throughout Germany, Austria, and Switzerland. Indeed, the impact of Sattler's superlative witness is felt to this day. Testifying to this fact is Gustav Bossert, Jr., a contemporary Lutheran pastor and Anabaptist scholar of Wurttemberg. He writes, "Sattler's character lies clearly before us. He was not a highly educated divine and not an intellectual; but his entire life was noble and pure, true and unadulterated."[29]

In his final defense Sattler set forth the Anabaptist theology of martyrdom even as he denied the authority of the state to rule in matters of faith:

> You servants of God, I have not been sent to defend the Word of God in court. We are sent to testify thereto. Therefore we cannot consent to any legal process, for we have no such command from God. If, however, we have not been able to be justly convinced, we are ready to suffer, for the Word of God, whatever will and may be laid upon us to suffer, all for our faith in Christ Jesus our Savior, as long as we have in us a breath of life, unless we should be convinced otherwise with Scripture.[30]

Even if it were possible to arrive at an accurate estimate of the number of Anabaptist martyrs, statistics alone can never tell the whole story. These were individuals who, like all people, were driven by hopes and fears, fortified by convictions. They were young and old, male and female. Children in their teens, even though not yet baptized, testified to their faith before being put to death. *Martyrs' Mirror,* which gives an account of hundreds of martyrdoms, is aptly named, for it not only gives the personal accounts of multitudes of the persecuted but also paints a less than spotless picture of state churches, both Protestant and Catholic. As Claus-Peter Clasen has shown, the most se-

vere and extended persecutions in Germany, Switzerland, and Moravia took place long before the Münster tragedy (in which a miscellaneous collection of Spiritualists and Anabaptists led by self-appointed opportunists led in the rise and fall of the New Jerusalem at Münster, Germany, in 1534-35), and may have constituted one of the most significant factors contributing to that grand fiasco.

ANABAPTIST THEOLOGIANS

The Anabaptists took seriously the Reformation concept of the priesthood of believers. This meant in many instances that individual Anabaptists considered themselves theologians whether or not they had been educated as such. This vocational commitment had both strengths and weaknesses. On the positive side, few religious movements in history have involved laymen so extensively. On the negative side, a theological consensus became increasingly difficult to achieve. The result was the fragmentation of a movement that could ill afford division. Despite great diversity, however, some major points of agreement emerged and remained characteristic of sixteenth-century Anabaptism.

Among sixteenth-century Anabaptists there were relatively few theologians who were writers. Among these, three stand out: Balthasar Hubmaier, Pilgram Marpeck, and Menno Simons. None, however, were systematic theologians; they all had much in common with the major Continental Reformers. Thus there was no quarrel between the Anabaptists and the Magisterial Reformers on the nature of God, the reality of the Trinity, the deity of Christ, and the authority of Scripture. Nevertheless, though they shared many of the presuppositions of both Luther and Zwingli, there were Anabaptist variations and differing emphases within the context of Reformation theology.

Anabaptist theology, therefore, can be described as biblical but also as existential because it developed in dialogue—in dialogue with the Reformers of the Magisterial Reformation and in dialogue with the various factions within the Radical Reformation. Thus it is that

---

29. Bossert, "Michael Sattler's Trial," p. 217.
30. Sattler, cited in *The Legacy of Michael Sattler*, p. 74.

Maria and Ursula van Beckum were burned at the stake on November 13, 1544, at Deventer for their Anabaptist faith.

Hubmaier found himself in dialogue first with the Roman Catholics over the nature of the Christian faith and the freedom of dissent, and then with Zwingli over the nature of baptism and the freedom to engage in dialogue itself without fear of reprisals. Some of his most creative insights came out of dialogue with Luther's followers over the possibility and the necessity of a free and uncoerced response to the gospel. And in dialogue with Jacob Wiedemann and the *Stäbler* and perhaps in response to Schleitheim, Hubmaier set forth his own understanding of the biblical teachings on the sword.

Although the theological writings of Pilgram Marpeck and Menno Simons are more systematic than those of Hubmaier, neither of these men was unmindful of opposing positions. As William Klassen and Walter Klaassen indicate, Marpeck very clearly had in mind Caspar Schwenckfeld even in his *Testamentserleutterung* (*Explanation of the Testaments*), as well as in the more polemical *Verantwortung*, which was specifically directed against Schwenckfeld and his teachings. Although Klassen and Klaassen claim that Marpeck never developed a comprehensive theological system,

It is generally agreed that Christology formed the center of his concern. In respect to his doctrine of Christ he laid emphasis on the humanity of Christ and its implications for church order. For him Christ was true God and true man and the implications of the latter for the Christian life and for the corporate body of Christ attracted him like a magnetic field.[31]

Perhaps Menno Simons was even more systematic in the presentation of his version of the Anabaptist faith than Marpeck, but he was also in constant dialogue with representatives of the Reformed Church. Gellius Faber and John à Lasco figure prominently in his writings.

Other Anabaptists could also be cited in support of the dialogic characteristics of Anabaptist theology; when this is done, the impression grows that Anabaptist theology was a people's theology in which neither creed nor any single Reformer had the last word. Thus I have chosen to focus on Hubmaier not because his theological position became normative, without alteration or addition, for sixteenth-century Anabaptism, but because he best illustrates in his brief career the nature of the development of Anabaptist theology. Other Anabaptist theologians such as Pilgram Marpeck and Menno Simons formulated their own theologies without either duplicating or ignoring Hubmaier's work.

Balthasar Hubmaier (1480-1528)

Among the Anabaptist theologians, only Hubmaier completed formal theological studies leading to a doctor's degree. Hubmaier was a native of Friedberg, a city five miles from Augsburg. He apparently studied for the priesthood at the cathedral school in Augsburg but transferred to the University of Freiburg on May 1, 1503. He interrupted his university studies for a brief stint as a teacher in the nearby city of Schaffhausen, then returned to the university to take his bachelor of divinity degree in August 1511. For a while he headed the *Pfauenburse* (a Nominalist student house called Peacock Hall), a post that had been vacated by his teacher, Dr. Johann Eck, when he left Freiburg for the University of Ingolstadt. Not long after-

ward Eck was joined by Hubmaier, who was awarded the doctor of theology degree by the university on September 29, 1512.

Of Ingolstadt, Regensburg, and Waldshut

At Ingolstadt Hubmaier served in a dual capacity. He was the chaplain of the Church of the Virgin, the university church, and lecturer in theology at the university. Three years later he became vice-rector of the university, but his tenure was short-lived. He left for the nearby city of Regensburg less than a year later, when the post of cathedral preacher became vacant there; apparently the pulpit appealed to him more than the classroom.

At Regensburg he became involved in an unholy campaign to rid the city of its Jewish population.[32] This was a testimony both to his effectiveness in the role of cathedral preacher and to his lack of conscience in the matter. Once the Jews had left the city, he had an empty synagogue on his hands. But the enterprising priest was equal to the task: the deserted synagogue became a Catholic chapel dedicated "to the beauteous Mary" (*zur Schönen Maria*).

The new chapel was an immediate success. According to Hubmaier, miracles occurred there daily. This news traveled rapidly over the countryside, and the city was soon filled with credulous pilgrims. Hubmaier listed fifty-four miracles that he testified had taken place since the chapel's inauguration. But there was a fly in the ointment. Pilgrims' offerings to the shrine aroused the hostility of local monks, who suffered from the loss of income and prestige. In addition, a quarrel arose between the city council and church authorities regarding chapel revenues. And more questions about the pil-

---

31. *The Writings of Pilgram Marpeck*, trans. and ed. Klassen and Klaassen (Scottdale, Pa.: Herald Press, 1978), pp. 555, 507.

32. One of the responsibilities of the cathedral preacher in Regensburg was to see that the Jews were under "proper restraint." Most German cities had already expelled the Jews. Hubmaier apparently resented the high interest rates the Jews were charging on loans. But he does not seem to have been personally anti-Semitic; in fact, he helped an elderly Jew by translating an important Hebrew document for him, a document that was strategic in a lawsuit that his Jewish friend was bringing against some members of his family who were attempting to defraud him.

grimage movement were raised after an unfortunate incident occurred at the shrine: pilgrims engaged in "wild" dancing in front of the chapel. Hubmaier, who witnessed the orgy himself, was sick at heart. He immediately set himself against such scandalous conduct, which doubtless became a factor in his leaving Regensburg.

About the time that Hubmaier left Regensburg for Waldshut, a small town on the Rhine, the plague was threatening the city. This became an added incentive for him to consider a change in residence and responsibility. Perhaps he was even now beginning to question the traditional beliefs of Catholicism. The city fathers, whose gratitude he so well deserved, presented him with forty gulden in appreciation of his efforts on behalf of city and cathedral.

By the beginning of the year 1521, Hubmaier was in Waldshut. During his first year in his new parish, he conscientiously performed the duties of a typical medieval parish priest. Waldshut had never before witnessed such elaborate processions or such impressive ritual. The reverend doctor reverenced Mary and all the saints and was in turn revered by the citizens of Waldshut.

All of this was destined to change, but it may not have been apparent to anyone but Hubmaier in 1522. This was the year of decision for him. Sometime before, perhaps more than a year earlier, he had begun to study the Scriptures, paying special attention to the Pauline epistles. In June 1522 he journeyed to Basel, where he made the acquaintance of Erasmus and Glarean, Conrad Grebel's old teacher. After visiting other Swiss cities and noting the progress of the Reformation, he returned to Waldshut, becoming more intent than ever on a study of the New Testament, which was increasingly the source book of his theology.

Hubmaier Becomes an Evangelical

Later in 1522 a new call came from Regensburg. Without actually giving up his church at Waldshut, Hubmaier decided to give the Bavarian city another try. He returned to take up his responsibilities as chaplain of the Chapel of the Beautiful Mary and signed a contract to this effect on December 22. However, instead of preaching on the Regensburg Madonna, he resumed his ministry with a message from the Gospel of Luke. He also began to attend a Bible study group led by a tanner, Hans Blabhans. It was perhaps during these days that Hubmaier became a firmly committed disciple of Jesus Christ. There is no record of the event, but in a letter to the Regensburg city council of 1524, he wrote,

> Therefore I openly confess before God and all men, that I then became a Doctor and preached some years among you and elsewhere, and yet had not known the way unto eternal life. Within two years has Christ for the first time come into my heart to thrive. I have never dared to preach him so boldly as now, by the grace of God. I lament before God that I so long lay ill of this sickness. I pray him truly for pardon; I did this unwittingly, wherefore I write this.[33]

Hubmaier's second tenure in Regensburg didn't last long because he found himself in an impossible position. Previously he had been the prime mover in the cult of the Beautiful Mary; images of silver and lead had been sold by the thousands. Now he could no longer promote the pilgrimages, the sales, or the cult of the Regensburg Madonna even though he, like Luther and Zwingli, still held to the perpetual virginity of the Virgin Mary and esteemed her above all womankind. By March 1, 1523, he was back in Waldshut.

In October of the same year, Hubmaier took part in the Second Disputation in Zürich. While in Switzerland he preached in St. Gall, compared notes with Zwingli, and made the acquaintance of Grebel, Reublin, Felix Manz, and others who eventually became Anabaptists. His friendship with both Zwingli and his more rad-

---

33. Hubmaier, cited by Henry C. Vedder in *Balthasar Hubmaier: The Leader of the Anabaptists* (New York: Putnam, 1905), p. 78. Torsten Bergsten points out that Hubmaier's inner struggle finally ended during his second stay in Regensburg, something he deduces from Hubmaier's interview with Fabri in 1527. See his *Balthasar Hubmaier: Seine Stellung zu Reformation und Täufertum, 1521–1528* (Kassel: J. G. Oncken Verlag, 1961), p. 106.

ical followers indicates that up to this time no rift had developed between Zwingli and his disciples.

The Eighteen Articles

Once back in Waldshut, Hubmaier began the work of reform in earnest. Zwingli's influence on him was apparent. However, it soon became clear that the Reformation in Waldshut was a phenomenon neither Lutheran nor Zwinglian; it was an indigenous development. The Eighteen Articles of April 1524 constitute Hubmaier's first reformatory writing.

Hubmaier drew up these articles to serve as a basis for discussion in the chapter meeting of the Waldshut clergy. They reflect both Lutheran and Zwinglian influences but with some interesting differences. The first three articles define the nature of true Christian faith. In them it is immediately apparent that Hubmaier's concept of faith was more dynamic than that of the medieval church. To him it was much more than an intellectual response (*assensus*). This faith, Hubmaier wrote, "can not remain passive but must break out [*aussbrechen*] to God in thanksgiving and to mankind in all kinds of works of

Balthasar Hubmaier, the first major theologian among the Anabaptists

brotherly love."[34] It is possible that Hubmaier was even suggesting believer's baptism in article eight, which reads, "As every Christian believes for himself and is baptized [*Wie ein yeder für sich selbs glauwbt unnd getaufft wirt*], so each individual should see and judge by the Scriptures if he is rightly provided food and drink by his pastor."[35] Hubmaier even suggested a new financial basis for the support of pastors. It was his opinion that they should be supported by the members of the church without having to resort to the traditional means of support. He denounced the reliance upon Scholastic theologians such as Scotus, Bonaventure, and Ockham. Like Zwingli, he advocated the marriage of priests. The two articles devoted to the Lord's Supper reflected the position he articulated at Zürich and were in substantial agreement with the views of Zwingli.

The progress that the Reformation was making under Hubmaier's leadership in Waldshut during the spring of 1524 became a matter of grave concern to Archduke Ferdinand. Since Waldshut was under Austrian jurisdiction, its moves were closely monitored by Ensisheim, a fanatical Catholic city that was only too happy to be charged with such a responsibility. In fact, Austria sent a delegation to Waldshut to warn the city of the grave consequences of its departure from the faith and demanded the surrender of Hubmaier to Austrian justice. The city council of Waldshut steadfastly refused to meet the delegation's demands, defending its freedom to follow the teachings of its chief preacher and to embrace the evangelical faith. Of course, Archduke Ferdinand and the Austrian government had no intention of allowing a town under Austrian rule to become evangelical, and preparations were made for military intervention. To prevent an invasion and its inevitable conse-

---

34. *Balthasar Hubmaier: Schriften*, ed. Gunnar Westin and Torsten Bergsten, vol. 9 of *Quellen zur Geschichte der Täufer* (Gütersloh: Verlagshaus Gerd Mohn, 1962), p. 72.

35. Hubmaier, cited in *Anabaptist Beginnings (1523–1533): A Source Book*, ed. William R. Estep, Jr. (Nieuwkoop: B. de Graaf, 1976), p. 25. The German phrase is from Hubmaier's *Achtzehn Schlussreden*.

quences, Hubmaier left Waldshut for Schaffhausen on August 29, 1524.

At Schaffhausen Hubmaier found refuge in the Benedictine monastery that was in the process of dissolution. It was during this period of exile that Hubmaier wrote one of the most important treatises of the entire Reformation. He addressed three letters (which were later published) to the Schaffhausen city council, asking for the privilege of remaining in the monastery. In addition, he wrote *Concerning Heretics and Those Who Burn Them* (*Von Ketzern und ihren Verbrennern*), and a polemical tract against his former teacher, Dr. Johann Eck, entitled *Axiomata.*

Concerning Heretics

In *Concerning Heretics* Hubmaier set forth in the form of an abstract of principles a plea for religious liberty. It was the first treatise on behalf of complete freedom of religion that the sixteenth century produced, one that went beyond both Erasmus and Luther. In it Hubmaier argued that the nature of the gospel precludes coercion. To persecute a man for his religious opinions or affiliation is to deny the incarnation (art. 28)—hence the preaching of the gospel is predicated upon an uncoerced response (art. 14). The nature of the church precludes persecution (arts. 14, 21). Hubmaier's position is most dramatically stated in the twenty-second article, which reads, "Therefore, it is well and good that the secular authority puts to death the criminals who do physical harm to the defenseless, Romans 13. But no one may injure the atheist [*Gottsfind*] who wishes nothing for himself other than to forsake the gospel."[36] In this article Hubmaier's radicalism is most evident. By no stretch of the imagination could Hubmaier be accused of atheism or sympathy for the atheistic cause. He was a fervent believer in the gospel and in the necessity of a faith commitment to Christ for salvation. Yet his plea for freedom includes even those who refuse to acknowledge

the existence of God yet continue to obey the civil law. This lifts the treatise out of the category of a personal plea. It is an abstract of universal principles on religious liberty. The separation of church and state is also implied in this article. Hubmaier recognizes the legitimacy of the state and even its right to punish criminals but insists that it has no jurisdiction in religious matters.

His final argument against persecution is found in his motto *Die Warheit ist Untödlich* (Truth Is Undying). With this statement, which appears on everything that he ever published, Hubmaier is saying, "You may burn a man to death for heresy, but if he believes the truth, you have not destroyed it, and even if he believed a lie, you have not advanced the truth by burning a heretic, real or imaginary, for such a person needs to be instructed in love with Scripture and prayer." According to Hubmaier, to convince a man of his error and present the truth in this manner "is art" (art. 35).[37]

Return to Waldshut

By October Hubmaier had returned to his beloved parish and city. The little town now found itself under the scrutiny of both Austria and the canton of Bern. Like Schaffhausen, Bern had not yet decided for the Reformation, but unlike Schaffhausen, it seemed in the process of stiffening its traditional Roman Catholic stance. Its ties to Waldshut lay in its relationship to the convent in Königsfeld, which had the right of patronage over Waldshut. Bern protested that the town had misappropriated for its own use the wine and corn that was intended for the priests of the area. Bern also accused Waldshut of discontinuing the singing and reading of the mass. Waldshut rejected the allegations, claiming that the "holy gospel" was preached, the physical needs of its priests were being provided for by the city, and the priests themselves were more studious than ever before. There is

---

36. Hubmaier, cited by Estep in *Anabaptist Beginnings,* p. 51.

37. Sebastian Franck was later to echo these convictions in a more rationalistic vein in his *Chronica* of 1536. Sebastian Costellio drew generously on this volume in his *Concerning Heretics.*

little doubt that Hubmaier was mainly responsible for framing this reply.

The immediate threat of an invasion by Austrian forces had subsided. Armed peasants were encamped on the nearby hillside under the leadership of Hans Müller. There was also hope of additional help from Zürich. The little city took heart and prepared to bolster its defenses. Following Hubmaier's return, the pace of reform quickened. The remainder of the year saw the eradication, one by one, of the traditional Roman Catholic practices. On January 13, Hubmaier, convinced that marriage was God-ordained even for priests, married Elsbeth Hügline of Reichenau. By this time all the services, including the celebration of the mass, were in German. It also appeared that Hubmaier enjoyed the friendship and support of both Oecolampadius of Basel and Sebastian Hofmeister of Schaffhausen.

During this time Hubmaier's critique of infant baptism was becoming sharper, which in itself caused Zürich to question its alliance with Waldshut. An attempt of Waldshut to come under the protection of the Swiss Confederation failed. By April the town, left to fend for itself, became involved in the South German Peasants' War. During this time in which the political fortunes of the town were very much in doubt, both Conrad Grebel and Wilhelm Reublin visited Waldshut. Reublin was there as early as January, and Grebel was there by March. However, Hubmaier and his church did not become formally identified with the Anabaptists until April 15, 1525, the day before Easter Sunday. The Easter season provided the best possible time to dramatize this event.

Baptism According to Hubmaier

The baptism of Hubmaier was no impetuous action; the Reformer had contemplated it for some time. While the Swiss Brethren were in the process of crystalizing their convictions, Hubmaier was moving in the same direction. The principles he set forth in the Eighteen Articles and *Concerning Heretics and Those Who Burn Them* indicate that he was rapidly moving in the direction of Anabaptism. His progress is revealed in a letter to Oecolampadius on January 16, 1525:

> The meaning of this sign and symbol (baptism), the pledge of faith until death, in hope of the resurrection to the life to come, is to be considered more than a sign. This meaning has nothing to do with babes, therefore infant baptism is without validity. In baptism one pledges himself to God, in the Supper to his neighbor.[38]

Hubmaier confessed that he baptized infants when the parents insisted on it, but "As to the word, . . . I do not yield to them in the least point. I have written twenty-two theses with sixty-four remarks, which you will soon see."[39] By February 2 he had published a tract called *The Open Appeal of Balthazar of Friedberg to All Christian Believers*. In this he was even more definite about rejecting infant baptism. After issuing the challenge to anyone to prove on the basis of Scripture that infants ought to be baptized, he asserted, "Balthazar of Friedberg pledges himself, on the other hand, to prove that the baptism of infants is a work without any ground in the divine word, and that he will do this in German with plain, clear, simple Scriptures relating to baptism, without any addition."[40]

Two months later, in April 1525, Wilhelm Reublin, who had been driven out of Zürich, returned to Waldshut, probably by a prior arrangement made in January. While there he baptized Hubmaier and about sixty others. On Easter Sunday Hubmaier himself baptized over three hundred people. On the Monday after Easter the Lord's Supper was observed in a simple ceremony, with the participants receiving both the bread and the wine. In the following days many others were baptized, and foot-washing (soon discontinued) was engaged in by the newly baptized. In every way possible Hubmaier sought to reproduce the pattern of what

---

38. Hubmaier, cited by Vedder in *Balthasar Hubmaier*, p. 108.

39. Hubmaier, cited by Vedder in *Balthasar Hubmaier*, p. 109.

40. Hubmaier, cited by Vedder in *Balthasar Hubmaier*, pp. 109–10.

he then considered the New Testament faith and practice.

On May 28 Zwingli's pamphlet entitled *On Baptism, Anabaptism, and Infant Baptism* was published. It was an attack on the Anabaptist view of believer's baptism. Hubmaier's response was thorough and appeared the following July under the title *The Christian Baptism of Believers.* In this book Hubmaier was at his best. Loserth writes, " *Von Christlichen Tauf der Glaubigen* is correctly regarded as the classic presentation of his teaching on baptism and as one of the best defenses of adult baptism ever written."[41]

Excerpts from this work reveal something of the style, logic, and use of the Scriptures that characterized Hubmaier's presentation of the Anabaptist view of baptism:

Every devout Christian who permits himself to be baptized with water should beforehand have a good conscience toward God through a complete understanding of the Word of God, that is, that knows and is sure that he has a gracious, kindly God, through the resurrection [*Urstand*] of Christ. . . .

Then afterwards follows water baptism; not that through it the soul is cleansed, but the "yes" [of] a good conscience toward God, previously given inwardly by faith.

Therefore the baptism in water is called a baptism in *remissionem peccatorum* (Acts second chapter), that is, for the pardon of sins. Not that through it or by it sins are forgiven, but upon the strength of the inward "yes" of the heart, which a man outwardly testifies to on submitting to water baptism, saying that he believes and is sure in his heart that his sins are forgiven through Jesus Christ.[42]

As his numerous references to the matter affirm, Hubmaier denies that baptism is necessary for salvation. He insists, however, that it is essential to the life of the church and its discipline:

Where baptism in water does not exist, there is no Church, no brother, no sister, no brotherly discipline, exclusion or restoration. I speak here of the visible Church as Christ said (Matt. 18). For there must be some outward sign of testimony by which brothers and sisters can know one another, though faith be in the heart alone. By receiving baptism, the candidate testifies publicly that . . . he had submitted himself to his brothers and sisters . . . that is, to the Church.[43]

On the other hand, he denounces infant baptism as a sign without meaning. Those who practice infant baptism "rob us of the true baptism, and show us a sign before an inn in which is not wine." To the charge "that there is nowhere in the Scriptures a clear word to the effect that one must not baptize infants," Hubmaier answers in inimical style,

It is clear enough for him who has eyes to see it, but it is not stated in so many words, literally: "do not baptize young children." May one then baptize them? To that I answer "if so I may baptize my dog and my donkey, or I may circumcise girls . . . I may bring infants to the Lord's Supper, bless palm branches, vegetables, salt, land, and water, sell the Mass for an offering." For it is nowhere said in so many words that we must not do these things.[44]

In the chapter entitled "Order of Christian Godliness," Hubmaier suggests that the prerequisites of scriptural baptism are "hearing the word, repentance, faith, and confession." Then he (the convert) must be baptized in water by which means he publicly professes his faith and purpose. According to Hubmaier, baptism is not a part of the saving process but an act in which the new disciple confesses his allegiance to Jesus Christ:

Baptism in the name of the Father and of the Son and of the Holy Ghost is when a man first confesses his sins, and pleads guilty; then believes in the forgiveness of his sins through Jesus Christ and therefore proceeds to live according to the rule of Christ by the grace and strength given him by God the Father, the Son, and the Holy Ghost.

41. Loserth, "Balthasar Hubmaier," in *The Mennonite Encyclopedia,* 4 vols., ed. Harold S. Bender and C. Henry Smith (Scottdale, Pa.: Herald Press, 1956–69), 2: 287.

42. *Balthasar Hubmaier: Schriften,* pp. 136–37.

43. *Balthasar Hubmaier: Schriften,* p. 160

44. *Balthasar Hubmaier: Schriften,* p. 152.

Then he professes this publicly, in the eyes of men, by the outward baptism of water.[45]

Evidently Hubmaier's book on baptism was widely circulated among the Anabaptists. Its effect upon non-Anabaptists must have been quite disconcerting, because by November 5 Zwingli was ready with a reply entitled *A True, Thorough Reply to Dr. Balthasar's Little Book on Baptism.* Zwingli's style is caustic and bitter; he adds very little to his previous arguments. His main point is that Anabaptists were schismatics and would ultimately destroy the existing order in Switzerland if allowed to continue unchecked. The dialogue between Zwingli and Hubmaier was temporarily brought to a halt by Hubmaier's delayed response, *A Dialogue between Balthasar Hübmaier of Friedberg and Master Ulrich Zwingli, of Zürich, on Infant Baptism.* Even though Hubmaier had composed it immediately, it was not published until the following year, after Hubmaier had gone to Nikolsburg. This was the last work that he wrote at Waldshut.

The Nikolsburg Ministry

At last freed from other military engagements, having recently won a decisive victory over the peasants, Archduke Ferdinand was able to turn his attention to Waldshut. Hubmaier and his wife fled on the fifth of December, just a step ahead of the invading forces. Because of the advancing army Hubmaier and his wife were forced to seek refuge in Zürich, even though Hubmaier preferred Strasbourg. Shortly after arriving, he was arrested and imprisoned in the Wellenberg Prison Tower. He was released when he issued a recantation, but soon he publicly withdrew it, so he was tortured and imprisoned again; finally he was banished from Zürich. After a brief stop in Constance and Augsburg before the end of the year, he found a new refuge in the city of Nikolsburg (Mikulov) in Moravia. By 1526 the Reformation had already captured the area. Hubmaier soon won the leading clergy and the leading nobleman, Baron Leonhard Liechtenstein, for Anabaptism.

Anabaptists and would-be Anabaptists poured into Moravia from many German-speaking sections of Europe. Soon Hubmaier was joined by Simprecht Sorg, the nephew of Christoph Froschauer, the famous Zürich printer. Sorg enabled Hubmaier to publish the products of his facile pen, an opportunity few Anabaptists enjoyed. Despite Hubmaier's heavy pastoral responsibilities and the serious challenges to his leadership by Jacob Wiedemann, Hans Hut, and the *Stäbler* (the communitarian Anabaptists), Hubmaier's Nikolsburg ministry was remarkable. Hundreds were baptized—perhaps as many as six thousand, a figure given by Kessler, the chronicler of St. Gall. Numerous books and tracts were also printed to provide for the needs of the growing Anabaptist community.

Two of the most important publications were two works on the freedom of the will. Hubmaier also wrote a treatise entitled *On the Sword,* which not only set him apart from Wiedemann and his followers but can be considered an Anabaptist alternative to Schleitheim. Even though Hubmaier's views on the Christian's obligation to support the state—even to the extent of engaging in defensive warfare—were rejected by most Anabaptists in the sixteenth century, his soteriology became characteristic of the movement.

While most Anabaptists apparently accepted Hubmaier's teachings on baptism, free will, and salvation, they rejected his views on the sword and his more positive attitude toward the state. Basing his position upon a careful exegesis of relevant Scripture passages, Hubmaier established the legitimacy of the state. He even suggested that the position of magistrate could be better filled by a Christian than a pagan. But Hubmaier also believed that the Christian's faith imposed certain constraints on him as a citizen. For example, a Christian was obliged to suffer under the rule of a tyrant if he could not participate in a nonviolent move to replace the ruler or leave his territory for a hospitable land. Under no circumstances could a Christian take up arms to overthrow a tyrannical government, and he could bear arms in defense of his country only under certain conditions. While Hub-

---

45. *Balthasar Hubmaier: Schriften,* pp. 156-57.

maier was not an absolute pacifist, he opposed war and can be considered a modified pacifist in the Erasmian tradition.[46]

Salvation

It is possible to reconstruct Hubmaier's soteriology from the direct and indirect references to salvation in all his writings. However, two of his works—*On the Freedom of the Will* and *The Second Booklet on the Free Will of Men*, both published in 1527—deal specifically with his view of salvation. In the introduction to the first treatise, Hubmaier deplores the moral collapse of Europe, calling upon history as his witness. He claims that the world had not seen such moral degradation in a thousand years, and "all this had taken place (as painful as it is to say so) under the appearance of the gospel. As soon as one says to them: 'It is written (Ps. 37): Forsake the evil and do good,' they answer, 'We cannot do good. All things happen according to the plan of God and out of necessity.' By which they mean that they are already allowed to sin."[47] Hubmaier charges that some of the guilty claimed that since they had been saved by faith apart from works, they could do as their sinful hearts desired. The purpose of his book, he writes, is to offer a corrective to such "half-truths" and put an end to what he terms the greatest blasphemy on earth: man blaming God for his sins. He also proposes to show "what man in and outside of God's grace is and is able to do."[48]

According to Hubmaier, man has a tripartite nature consisting of body, soul, and spirit. Before the fall of Adam, all three parts were good: "So, God has pronounced all things that he created good, especially man who was made in his image."[49] Hubmaier understands this goodness to mean that man was free to choose be-

tween good and evil, but with the fall he lost this freedom, not only for himself but also for his descendants. Thus the result of the fall was death. With Paul, Augustine, and Luther, Hubmaier holds that in Adam all die. Man's only hope "is to be born again by the Spirit of God and his living Word."[50]

It is important to note that despite such a pessimistic appraisal of man's sinful condition, Hubmaier cannot abandon hope:

> The divine image (*imago Dei*) is like a little fire (*scintilla*) covered with ashes and yet still a burning cinder. The spirit may be variously seen as the scintilla of medieval mysticism, the breath of God, or the remaining *imago Dei*. [This is the only time Hubmaier uses the term *imago Dei*.] It is this spirit within man that has never lost its capacity to will the good, but it is powerless because of its enslavement to the flesh to do the good. Through the Word of God and the Holy Spirit, it is liberated from its bondage to sin through the new birth.[51]

The Word of God and the New Birth

The new birth lies at the heart of Hubmaier's teaching on the freedom of the will. According to him, the will to do good, which comes from the spirit of man, is completely impotent until man is born again (*Wiedergeburt*). Then the spirit is liberated from its bondage to sin, and the soul is restored to its original health. But since the flesh remains unaffected, an inner tension is created within man. The liberated spirit and the redeemed soul are in constant conflict with the unregenerate flesh. This means that the Christian life involves a struggle between good and evil. The difference between the newborn man and one who has not experienced the new birth is that the Christian is capable of making the right choices and doing good. However, although he is no longer a slave to the flesh, it does not necessarily follow that he cannot sin.

According to Hubmaier, this liberation is the work of God, which is effected by means of the Word of God. Hubmaier's use of the term "Word

46. For a more thorough discussion of the differences between Hubmaier and other Anabaptists, see James M. Stayer, *Anabaptists and the Sword* (Lawrence, Kans.: Coronado Press, 1972), pp. 137–39.

47. *Balthasar Hubmaier: Schriften*, p. 381.

48. *Balthasar Hubmaier: Schriften*, p. 382.

49. *Balthasar Hubmaier: Schriften*, p. 386.

50. *Balthasar Hubmaier: Schriften*, p. 386.

51. *Balthasar Hubmaier: Schriften*, p. 322.

of God" is essentially the same as Luther's. The Word of God is the preached Word by which men hear the gospel. By this Word fallen man becomes reborn and is made alive by the Holy Spirit. Often "the Word" as Hubmaier uses it refers to the Bible, which without the Spirit's work remains only a "deadening letter" (*töten-der Büchstabe*). At times "the Word" also refers to the incarnate Christ, "who is living and eternal." It is clear in Hubmaier that man's salvation depends upon both the Bible and the work of the Holy Spirit.[52]

Hubmaier's thought reveals an affinity with that of Luther in regard to the fallen nature of man. Both were indebted to Augustine but even more to the Apostle Paul. As Torsten Bergsten affirms, Hubmaier emphasizes that all men are children of wrath: "As an Anabaptist theologian, from the beginning he accepted the doctrine of original sin, and he did not depart from this during the whole of his life."[53] If Hubmaier's teachings on the nature of man and the Fall reflect both Lutheran and Erasmian influences, the resulting synthesis is one that he was certain the Scriptures taught. In this he was very close to Hans Denck, with whose writings he was familiar—indeed, there are some verbal parallels between Hubmaier's work and that of Denck.[54] (Hubmaier had baptized Denck in 1526 at Augsburg while en route to Nikolsburg.)

The truth of the matter is that Hubmaier was no slavish disciple of either Luther or Erasmus—in fact, many of the ideas he espoused were markedly different from theirs. He taught the threefold nature of man that Luther had condemned as "Origen's fable." In Luther's soteriology it was justification by faith that is central, while in Hubmaier's it was the new birth that comes to man through the Word and the Holy Spirit in response to man's faith. Luther's concern was for an imputed righteousness, whereas Hubmaier's emphasis was upon a change within man that is brought about by the preaching of the Word and the work of the Spirit. For Hubmaier the result of the new birth was a life of discipleship characterized by good works. It is abundantly clear that Luther stressed the necessity of faith and mentioned the new birth, but for Hubmaier the evidence of its reality was apparent in the fruits of the new life. Both Hubmaier and Denck drew upon Erasmus for certain concepts, but neither duplicated Erasmian thought. The two men parted company on the role of the Bible in bringing men to God. For Hubmaier it was an indispensable witness, a converting Word, but for Denck it was a confirming Word, since he held that salvation was wholly dependent upon the work of the Spirit.[55]

Apparently Hubmaier's adversaries had understood Luther and Zwingli to teach a doctrine of predestination that excluded any possibility of a personal decision on the part of the individual. In fact, they understood Luther to teach that human depravity was such that man was wholly incapable of even desiring salvation. It was against such "half-truths" that Hubmaier directed his most carefully thought-out teachings on salvation. For him predestination is clearly rooted in the sovereignty of God: "God indeed has full right and power to do with us whatever he will."[56] This aspect of God's will Hubmaier calls *voluntas absoluta* (absolute will), a Scholastic term. But he argues that no one can know God's absolute will, because it is hidden from the eyes of man. God's revealed will is something else, according to Hubmaier: the revelation of God in Christ clearly indicates that God wills that all men be saved. "Christ showed us this very plainly when he said (John 3:16): 'God so loved the world that he gave his only begotten Son, that whosoever believes on him should not perish, but have eternal life.'" He suffered for our sins, not for ours alone, but for the sins

52. See "*Ein christenliche Leertafel*," pp. 311–26 in *Balthasar Hubmaier: Schriften,* for Hubmaier's characteristic teachings on the role of the Bible in salvation. The role of the Word and the Spirit in bringing men to God is a familiar Reformation theme among both the Magisterial Reformers and the Anabaptists.

53. Bergsten, *Balthasar Hubmaier,* pp. 440–41.

54. Bergsten, *Balthasar Hubmaier,* pp. 444–45.

55. See *Anabaptist Beginnings,* p. 133.

56. *Balthasar Hubmaier: Schriften,* p. 415.

of the entire world (I John 2:2). He also quotes John 1:9, 12 and Mark 16:15, and says, "From these passages one can easily conclude that God, according to his preached and revealed Word, absolutely does not want to harden, blind, or damn anyone except those who out of their own evil desire and choice wish to be hardened, blinded, and damned."[57]

Even though all men will not be saved, Hubmaier insists that God cannot be held guilty, for he sent his "most beloved son to die for us all." It is Hubmaier's conviction that a careful study of Scripture will help one to know which passages refer to God's secret will and which refer to his revealed will:

> The revealed will is also called in scholastic parlance the ordained will because it is according to the preached Word of Holy Scripture in which he has revealed his will to us. Hence the distinction between the hidden and the revealed will of God. Not that there are two wills in God, but rather the Scripture speaks in a way for our human understanding. So we know that although God is all powerful, and can do all things, yet he will not act toward us poor human beings according to his omnipotence, but according to his mercy, as he amply proved to us by his most beloved son, and through all this as the whole Old and New Testaments have sufficiently shown.[58]

Thus Hubmaier holds that God must act toward man according to his revealed will; his very nature is at stake. Therefore his invitation to salvation is not a charade but an utterly sincere proffering. If it were not, its insincerity would reflect badly upon God, not man:

> Only a foolish king could place a goal before his subjects and then say, "Now run that you may get there," when he already knows before hand that they are bound in iron and that they cannot run. It were certainly a cunning God, who invites all men to the supper, and really offers his mercy to everyone, if he after all did not wish the invited to come. It were a false God who should say in words, "Come here," and yet in secret in his heart should think, "Sit yonder." It would be an unfaith-

ful God who should publicly offer grace to man, and should clothe him in new raiment, yet in secret take it away from him and prepare hell for him.[59]

Thus Hubmaier reinforces his argument that fallen man does indeed have a free will. While that will is certainly limited in its capacity to do good by man's inherited sinful nature, it nevertheless possesses the capacity—even though captive to the flesh—of desiring the good. Through the gospel God has taken the initiative—first, by providing a way of salvation through the atoning work of Christ, and second, by drawing men to him. This drawing is twofold, outward and inward. God calls men to himself outwardly by the proclamation of his "holy gospel, which Christ commanded to be preached to every creature." The inward drawing is the work of God, who enlightens the soul that is convicted by the Holy Spirit through the preached Word and led to confess Christ before men. While God takes the initiative, he cannot make the decision for man. "By his attracting, drawing will, he wills and draws all men to salvation," writes Hubmaier, but "choice is still left to man since God wants him without pressure, unconstrained, under no compulsion."[60]

Martyrdom

Upon the death of King Louis of Hungary, Moravia came under the authority of Ferdinand I, who was crowned king of Bohemia in February 1527. This ended the relative independence that Moravia had enjoyed for some time.[61] Under a

---

57. *Balthasar Hubmaier: Schriften*, pp. 414, 416.
58. *Balthasar Hubmaier: Schriften*, p. 417.
59. Hubmaier, cited by Vedder in *Balthasar Hubmaier*, p. 197.
60. Hubmaier, cited in *Spiritual and Anabaptist Writers*, p. 135.
61. Jarold Zeman says of this event, "Ferdinand was elected king by the Bohemian diet (acting without any agreement with the Moravian estates) in Prague on October 23, 1526. The Moravian estates received him, without election, as king and margrave on the basis of the hereditary rights of his wife Ann (sister of the deceased King Louis) at a diet in Olomouc, November 11–18, 1526, on condition that he would confirm their freedoms and rights, including the broad religious freedom" (*Anabaptists and the Czech Brethren*, p. 132).

general edict of August 20, 1527, which required the strict enforcement of the Edict of Worms, Hubmaier was arrested and imprisoned along with his wife in the Kreuzenstein Castle, which was a short distance north of Vienna. After several months' imprisonment, Hubmaier was taken to Vienna on March 3 and tortured. But the rack forced no last-minute recantation from the lips of the condemned man. When urged to confess to a priest and receive the last rites of the Roman Church before his execution, he refused. On March 10, 1528, he was burned at the stake in Vienna. His last words as they rubbed sulphur and gunpowder into his beard were "O dear brothers, pray God that he will give me patience in this my suffering. I will die in the Christian faith." As his head and hair caught fire, he cried out, "O Jesus, Jesus." Three days later his faithful wife was drowned in the Danube.[62]

Hubmaier was the first major theologian among the Anabaptists. His influence became pervasive: his teachings upon the role of faith and the necessity of the new birth that occurs with the hearing of the Word under the convicting power of the Holy Spirit became a major thrust of sixteenth-century Anabaptism. He undergirded with solid biblical exegesis the Anabaptist positions on the necessity of the new birth, believer's baptism, the nature of the church, and the limitations of the authority of the state. The churches he fostered at Waldshut and later at Nikolsburg, while true to the ecclesiological insights of Anabaptism, were more positively oriented toward the state than were Anabaptist churches elsewhere. However, his position on the sword never became widely accepted by sixteenth-century Anabaptists.

Regardless of Hubmaier's view of the Christian's obligation to support the magistracy, his final position was one that advocated personal nonresistance. According to Ethelbert Stauffer,

Hubmaier was the most vigorous and impassioned thinker of the Anabaptist movement. In him can be seen the Anabaptist conception of the cross both as an event that happened once and for all in the history of redemption and also as a principle of life for the people of God. Through his martyr's death, Hubmaier showed that he adhered to the "original Anabaptist" demand for individual nonresistance. Stauffer also says that Hubmaier was the only leading Anabaptist to show that he understood the "divinely-ordained office of the valiant martyr."[63]

Pilgram Marpeck (ca. 1490-1556)

After the death of Hubmaier, no theologian of outstanding ability or influence arose among the Anabaptists until Pilgram Marpeck became prominent. Marpeck was a native of Rattenberg on the Inn River in Austria's Tyrol. He was first a follower of Luther and then an Anabaptist. His decision to become an Anabaptist cost him dearly. On January 28, 1528, he lost his position as city mining engineer. In addition, the orphaned children he and his wife had adopted were taken from him, and his property was confiscated. Banished from Rattenberg, he became an itinerant, referring to himself as a wandering citizen of heaven.

Four years after leaving Austria, Marpeck was compelled to defend himself against the charges of heresy brought against him by Martin Bucer and the Reformers of Strasbourg. His "confession of faith" was rejected as heretical, and as a consequence he was banished. For the next twelve years he was unable to find a secure refuge. Finally his genius won him employment as city engineer in Augsburg, a position that he held until his death in 1556.

Relying heavily upon the work of Hubmaier and Bernard Rothmann, Marpeck added his own insights. Marpeck's most creative contribution to Anabaptist thought was his interpretation of the Scriptures. While holding the entire Bible to

---

62. Hubmaier, cited by Johann Loserth in *Doctor Balthasar Hubmaier und die Anfänge der Wiedertäufe in Mähren* (Brunn, 1893), p. 187. Loserth's account of Hubmaier's martyrdom is taken from Stephan Sprügel's eyewitness report.

63. Stauffer, cited by Bergsten in *Balthasar Hubmaier*, p. 43.

be the Word of God, he made a distinction between the purpose of the Old Testament and that of the New. As the foundation must be distinguished from the house, so the Old Testament must be distinguished from the New. The Old Testament was promise; the New, fulfillment. The New Testament comprised the apostolic witness to the revelation of God in Christ. Therefore, to hold that the Old Testament was equally authoritative for the Christian was to fail to recognize the difference between God's preliminary word to man and his final word to him. This failure to place the Old and New Testaments in proper sequence and relationship, Marpeck held, was disastrous. For to make the Old Testament normative for the Christian life was to seriously misinterpret the biblical message. In Marpeck's eyes the pope, Luther, Zwingli, and the "false Anabaptists" were all guilty of this fundamental error.

Marpeck's heremeneutical principle was not original with him: it was a common understanding that amounted to a consensus among the Anabaptists. Nevertheless, Marpeck enunciated it more clearly than most, and in so doing he distinguished the true Anabaptist witness from that of the deviate Münsterites.[64]

Menno Simons (1496-1561)

Menno Simons, the major Dutch Anabaptist theologian, constructed his theology over against the Münster tragedy. Menno became an Anabaptist in 1536, some twelve years after his ordination to the Roman Catholic priesthood. He immediately rose to prominence among the Dutch Anabaptists. Even before his death in 1561, the Anabaptists in the Netherlands were often referred to as Mennonites (Menists). His

---

64. Jan J. Kiwiet has carefully delineated Marpeck's views on this point in his *Pilgram Marbeck* (Kassel: J. G. Oncken Verlag, 1957), pp. 94-102. For a somewhat different approach, see William Klassen's *Covenant and Community* (Grand Rapids: Eerdmans, 1968). William Klassen and Walter Klaassen have translated and edited several of Marpeck's more important works for an English-speaking audience, collected in *The Writings of Pilgram Marpeck* (Scottdale, Pa.: Herald Press, 1978).

Menno Simons, the major Dutch Anabaptist theologian from whom the Mennonites take their name
RELIGIOUS NEWS SERVICE

conversion and call were such deeply moving experiences that they left an indelible stamp of utter sincerity upon his character and ministry.

The cross of persecution was an inescapable reality for Menno, and at times he chafed under its galling weight. In his *Reply to Gellius Faber,* he contrasted the life of the well-paid priest of the state church with that of the Anabaptist preacher:

I with my poor, weak wife and children have for eighteen years endured excessive anxiety, oppression, affliction, misery, and persecution. . . . Yes, when the preachers repose on easy beds and soft pillows, we generally have to hide ourselves in out-of-the-way corners. . . . We have to be on our guard when a dog barks for fear the arresting officer has arrived. . . . In short, while they are gloriously rewarded for their services with large incomes and good times, our recompense and portion be but fire, sword, and death.[65]

Many witnesses have abundantly testified that Menno's picture of the harrassed life of an Anabaptist preacher was not overdrawn.

An edict was published in the province of Groningen on January 21, 1539, commanding all Anabaptists to leave. Menno fled to the Dutch province of Friesland, where he resumed his ministry. During a previous visit there, he had stayed in the home of a "very pious and God-fearing man" by the name of Tjard Reynders. Shortly afterward, on January 8, 1539, his bene-factor was arrested, broken on the wheel, and executed. In 1541 the "counselors" of Leeuwarden made plans to seize Menno himself. His success was so great that the authorities despaired of ever eradicating Anabaptism as long as he was free. Pardon was offered to any Anabaptist then in confinement who would deliver Menno into their hands, but no Judas was forthcoming. Placards spread throughout the province of Friesland brought no results. Charles V, emperor of the Holy Roman Empire, published an edict against Menno and placed a price of a hundred guilders on his head. All persons were enjoined against giving Menno food or shelter. His followers were to be arrested immediately. Complete pardon for any crime committed continued to be promised to anyone delivering the renowned heretic into the hands of the authorities.

For the next two years Menno labored in and around Amsterdam with a measure of success. Those baptized were usually executed, but Menno somehow remained free. What is even more amazing is that he found time to write. Three books came from his pen during the initial period of his ministry in North Holland: *Christian Baptism* (1539), *Foundation of Chris-*

tian Doctrine (1540), and *True Christian Faith* (1541).

Menno's work in Amsterdam was a brief interlude between his ministry in North Holland and the final phase of his outreach. Late in 1543 he left Holland for the more tolerant climate of North Germany. Here he would spend eighteen years, the remainder of his life. He spent about two years in the Diocese of Cologne, then from 1546 to 1561 labored in Holstein and the Baltic seacoast region.

Menno's major task appears to have been that of a leader intent on calling the Anabaptists back to their original vision. In this effort he was eminently successful. His stress upon the necessity of the new birth could warrant one's calling him "the Theologian of the New Birth." Yet his intense desire to cleanse the fellowship of all Münsterites and others unwilling to hold to the Anabaptist faith and life-style led to a rather strict adherence to the ban—so strict, in fact, that the movement became fragmented as a result.

Menno himself brought a form of Christology into Dutch Anabaptism that was to prove troublesome and was never widely accepted outside of Dutch Anabaptist circles. It was called "Hofmannite" because Melchior Hofmann had introduced the concept into Dutch Anabaptist life.[66] In brief, Menno held that the Incarnation of Christ was a miraculous work wholly of God. Therefore Christ was said to possess "celestial flesh," or heavenly flesh. Menno did not intend to deny the humanity of Christ and did not do so, but he was hard put to explain how Christ could be human without partaking of Mary's flesh. Subsequently virtually all Mennonites as well as other evangelicals have felt that the tra-

---

65. Simons, Reply to Gallius Faber, in *The Complete Writings of Menno Simons, c. 1496-1561,* trans. Leonard Verduin, ed. John C. Wenger (Scottdale, Pa.: Herald Press, 1956), p. 674.

66. Hofmann was a Lutheran who became an Anabaptist without ever really grasping the distinctive Anabaptist hermeneutics. For him the Old Testament coupled with visions and dreams provided the clue to history and the second coming of Christ. He was led to believe that he was Elijah sent to prepare the way for the Lord's return. For this reason he went to Strasbourg, which he was convinced would be the New Jerusalem. Here, after ten years' imprisonment, he died. See the article "Melchior Hofmann" in *The Mennonite Encyclopedia,* 2: 778-85.

ditional view of the Incarnation comes closer to doing justice to both the human and the divine in Christ than the view made famous by Menno.

Menno's writings were voluminous. They were soon printed in half a dozen languages, including English. Doubtless Menno became the best-known Anabaptist theologian the sixteenth century produced. Hans de Ries and Lubbert Gerrits were to reflect Menno's influence in the Waterlander Confession, published in 1580-81. In 1609–1612 this had a great influence upon John Smyth and his followers, the group to whom the English Baptists trace their beginnings.[67]

THE ESSENCE OF ANABAPTISM

Jarold Knox Zeman suggests, "Sooner or later, every student of Anabaptism must answer the question: What constitutes Anabaptism and how can it be delineated from other radical groups of the sixteenth century?"[68] As Zeman indicates, this question has been given a variety of answers. The reason for such divergent answers, he insists, is the extremely complex nature of sixteenth-century Anabaptism. However, although it may not be possible to suggest a single concept by which "normative Anabaptism" can be identified, if the Anabaptist concept of the church with all of its ramifications is properly understood, it may provide a clue to the essence of Anabaptism.

If the matter of authority—the Bible versus the magisterium of the church—was the major line of demarcation between Protestantism and Roman Catholicism of the Reformation era, it appears that the implementation of the believer's church was that which separated the Anabaptists from the Magisterial Reformation. Historically this was the case. The concept of the church as embraced and established by the

Swiss Brethren did involve a number of ideas held in common with the Reformers, but distinctive Anabaptist ideas nevertheless stood out. For example, the Anabaptists held with the Reformers to the authority of Scripture, but they found the guidelines for the church and the Christian life in the New Testament alone; the Old Testament could never be used to justify state churches and the persecution of heretics, which they considered sub-Christian. For them the church was made up of committed disciples who bore witness to the new birth in believer's baptism, which also constituted a pledge of discipleship. Discipleship involved the ethical and moral dimensions of the Christian life. All Anabaptist concepts of church, baptism, and discipleship implied that the Christian's ultimate loyalty belonged to God rather than Caesar. Although with the Magisterial Reformers the Anabaptists acknowledged the legitimacy of the state as God-given, they denied its jurisdiction in matters of religion. For them the very nature of the gospel demanded an uncoerced response. But once commitment was freely made, the new disciple was expected to demonstrate the change wrought by the new birth by a new life-style. The Lord's Supper then became a sign of the fellowship of committed disciples as well as a memorial of the one sacrifice of Christ.

The concept of the church also had certain implications for the state: the state must recognize both its limitations and its responsibilities. For the Anabaptists the state was not the church and therefore had no ecclesial functions. But it was responsible to God for discharging justice and protecting the innocent. Some Anabaptists believed that the Christian could participate with certain reservations in the proper functioning of government, but all Anabaptists believed that the demand for religious liberty was nothing less than a biblical principle inherent in the gospel itself. Clearly, if one were forced to select among competing concepts the one that best explains the essence of sixteenth-century Anabaptism and that distinguishes Anabaptism from all other movements of the age, it would be

---

67. Menno Simons' works are available in English: see *The Complete Writings of Menno Simons, c. 1496-1561*. Biographies are also available. See Franklin H. Littell's *A Tribute to Menno Simons* (Scottdale, Pa.: Herald Press, 1961).

68. Zeman, *Anabaptists and the Czech Brethren*, p. 35.

difficult to find a concept more basic than that of the church.[69]

Even though at first glance the Hutterites might appear to contradict the concept of the church envisioned by the Swiss Anabaptists, this is not necessarily so. Virtually all Anabaptists held that the Christian was only a steward and not the owner of the property he possessed. He was compelled by brotherly love to share with anyone in need, particularly one of the same household of faith. But it remained for the Hutterites to make the community of goods the indispensable mark of both discipleship and the church.

The Hutterites trace their beginning as a distinct expression of sixteenth-century Anabaptism to Nikolsburg, Moravia, where under the leadership of Jacob Wiedemann they began to practice the community of goods in 1528. Their name was derived from Jacob Hutter, a courageous and able man who first put the *Brüderhof* (community of brothers) at Auspitz on firm economic footing. However, it was Peter Riedemann who gave literary expression to the concept in his second confession, which he wrote in 1545 while he was in prison at Hesse.

Riedemann held that unfallen man had no desire to own property—hence it follows that the desire to possess things is an expression of man's fallen nature. God did not intend for man to appropriate his creation for his own selfish purposes. This is the way of the world, and the true disciple cannot conform to the world. He who will not forsake private property cannot be a disciple of Christ. The example of the Jerusalem Church was cited to support this viewpoint. Thus Riedemann and the Hutterites reasoned that the nature of creation, of discipleship, and of the primitive church itself demanded the community of goods without which the true church cannot exist.[70]

While it can be argued, as scholars have frequently done, that the essence of Anabaptism can best be seen in a single concept—that of the authority of the New Testament, or baptism, or discipleship, or a two-world tension, or the church—it must be admitted that all of these ideas are indispensable for a complete understanding of the Anabaptist teachings; none of them can be left out. Yet in the final analysis, it appears that the concept of the church gave the movement its unique character and separated it from both the Magisterial Reformers and other groups within the Radical Reformation.

---

69. For a survey of various other viewpoints, see Zeman, *The Anabaptists and the Czech Brethren*, pp. 30–38.

70. See Peter Rideman, *Confession of Faith* (Rifton, N.Y.: Plough Publishing House, 1970). For additional information on the Hutterites, see Leonard Gross, *The Golden Years of the Hutterites* (Scottdale, Pa.: Herald Press, 1980); and John Horsch, *The Hutterite Brethren, 1528-1931* (Goshen, Ind.: Mennonite Historical Society, 1931).

Chapter XIII

CALVIN AND
THE CITY OF REFUGE

y the time Jean Cauvin (Calvin, the anglicized form of the French "Cauvin," is extracted from the Latin Calvinus) of Noyon transferred from the Collège de la Marche to that of Montaigu, Martin Luther had appeared before Charles V at Worms and had subsequently translated the Greek New Testament into German. Even before Calvin's conversion, the Reformed Church, founded by Zwingli, had arisen to challenge not only Rome but also the Lutheran Reformers. By this time (ca. 1530), the writings of both the German and the Swiss Reformers were finding an eager audience in France. The Christian humanists in particular welcomed the fresh air that had begun to blow in from German lands and to pervade even the University of Paris. Reform was on the way, and young Calvin could not fail to take notice of it, even though the Collège de Montaigu was known for its obscurantist position, championed by one of its most outspoken heresy hunters, Noël Bédier (Beda).

This defender of Catholic orthodoxy attacked Erasmus and the Bible translator Jacques Lefèvre d'Étaples, labeling them Arians, Sabellians, Donatists, Wycliffites, and Hussites. Bédier claimed to have discovered 143 Lutheran errors in Lefèvre's commentaries on Paul's epistles, and he condemned Erasmus's *Paraphrases of the New Testament* as well. Erasmus retaliated by claiming that he had found no fewer than 181 lies, 310 calumnies, and 47 blasphemies in Bédier's book, and that there were no doubt many more. To him Bédier was "more a block of wood than a man."[1]

It is not surprising that during his university studies in Paris Calvin was a staunch defender of the old ways and the traditional dogmas of the medieval church. It wasn't until he had left Paris for Orléans to study law that he came under the influence of the new Protestant movement.

Nowhere in Europe did the Renaissance provide greater preparation for the Reformation than in France. Lefèvre (Faber Stapulensis) and his prominent student, Guillaume Briçonnet, were the leading lights in this revival of Christian humanism. Perhaps it was Briconnet's experiences as a French envoy in the courts of Julius II and Leo X that fired him with the zeal of a Reformer. A man of wealth and prestige, he had been appointed bishop of Meaux in 1516.

---

1. T. H. L. Parker, *John Calvin: A Biography* (Philadelphia: Westminster Press, 1975), p. xiv.

FRANCE
IN THE RENAISSANCE
AND THE REFORMATION

From the beginning of his residence there in 1518 he moved to reform the diocese. He divided the territory into twenty-six districts and sent a reform-minded preacher to each during Advent and at Easter. In 1521 Briçonnet intensified his efforts: he brought in a number of preachers who shared his zeal for reform. Among them were his teacher, Lefèvre, as well as Gérard Roussel, Pierre Caroli, and Guillaume Farel. Biblical lecturers were established in four major towns of the diocese. Briçonnet's efforts soon began to bear fruit as laymen embraced the gospel and sought to act out its implications for more Protestant forms of worship. This triggered iconoclastic outbursts; *parlement* and the Sorbonne became thoroughly aroused. The repression urged by Pope Clement VII soon followed. Under the mounting pressure Briçonnet felt it expedient to condemn Luther and his teachings; Luther's books were now forbidden to the faithful. Some of the more ardent preachers were dismissed, and Farel was exiled, although he and Briçonnet remained friendly. In spite of growing suspicion and open opposition, by the mid-fifteen-twenties the incipient reformatory movement had spread to most of the large population centers of France, including Paris, Lyons, and Noyon.

These early advocates of reform, whether they were Erasmians or disciples of Luther, were all called Lutherans. Recognizing the enormous potential of a Protestant coup, Zwingli and the Swiss Reformers hastened to direct their attention to France. In March 1525 Zwingli dedicated his *Traité de la vrai et fause religion* (*Treatise on True and False Religion*) to the king of France. It set forth Zwingli's teaching on the mass, a viewpoint that the French monarch abhorred, though he may not have understood it. Not only did this work of Zwingli fail to make a favorable impression upon Francis, but it served to alert *parlement* to the evangelical threat against the traditional Catholic faith. On February 5, 1526, just before the king returned from prison in Spain, *parlement* prohibited "the preaching or teaching of any doctrines of Luther, or the contradiction, in any manner, of Catholic doctrines of the Sacrament, the Virgin,

saints, images, prayers for the dead, or fasting."[2] Due to his strained relationship with *parlement* and out of consideration for his sister, Marguerite, who was an ardent supporter of Briçonnet's early reform efforts at Meaux, Francis was not yet prepared to crush the emerging evangelical movement. But he was now deeply indebted to Clement VII and the church for his release from prison, and he eventually repaid his debt by suppressing "Lutheranism." He had, in short, been bought. As T. H. L. Parker observes, "Kings may be wooed, but they more effectively may be bought."[3] Nevertheless, at this point Francis seemed intent—more for political than religious reasons—on following a more lenient course than *parlement,* the Sorbonne, and Clement VII demanded. It is N. M. Sutherland's opinion that it was the concept of sacrament of the altar by which Francis discriminated between pernicious Protestantism and Christian humanism, which he considered relatively harmless:

> While Francis was certainly still anxious to protect and foster the remarkable intellectual activity of his world center of learning, he nevertheless ordered the new papal *juges délégués* to proceed diligently against the "quelque erreur touchant le sainct sacrement de l'autel." A determination to permit no interference with the Sacrament of the Eucharist was then, and continued to be, Francis's definitive attitude towards heresy.[4]

If Sutherland is correct, as the documents he cites seem to indicate, Francis's position was always one of expedience, based on an international situation that compelled him to seek allies among Lutheran princes and the Swiss alike. He seems to have followed a fairly moderate policy until "the affair of the placards." On the night of October 17, 1534, posters appeared in many of the cities of France, including Paris and Amboise, where the king was staying. They had been printed in Neuchâtel, where Farel and

2. N. M. Sutherland, *The Huguenot Struggle for Recognition* (New Haven: Yale University Press, 1980), p. 17.

3. Parker, *John Calvin*, p. xvii.

4. Sutherland, *The Huguenot Struggle for Recognition*, p. 17.

Antoine Mercourt were preaching. The posters denounced the mass as an abomination in the sight of the Lord and a ritual utterly against "the true Supper of our Lord, the sole Mediator, and only Saviour."[5]

Even though the first French evangelical martyr had been put to death as early as 1520, only a few scattered executions had followed until "the affair of the placards." This episode gave the king the occasion to launch a campaign of terror against the culprits: he levied the death penalty against heretics with a particular vengeance. Two hundred arrests were made by November, and within the next three months twenty Protestants were executed. This episode and the Nicholas Cop affair ushered in a new day of repression for the fledgling Protestant movement. In the wake of the reprisals, Etienne de la Forge, in whose home Calvin had often stayed, was burned to death. Fortunately, both Calvin and Cop had already fled the city for safer quarters.

At the time, Calvin had not yet published anything that would identify him with the advocates of reform. But he was implicated by association with both Cop, the rector of the University of Paris, and Étienne de la Forge. He emerges as a Reformer with the publication of the *Institutes of the Christian Religion* (*Christianae religionis institutio*). Thus Calvin made his debut in the world of the Reformation not in the pulpit or the classroom but via the printed page. By 1536 evangelicals and Catholics alike were asking, Who is this Jean Calvinus? For those who still ask this question, the next few pages may serve as an introduction.

THE EARLY YEARS

John Calvin was born in Noyon on July 10, 1509, the second of four sons born to Gérard Cauvin and his wife, Jeanne le Franc. Noyon was a cathedral town about fifty miles northeast of Paris. Calvin's father was notary apostolic and notary fiscal to the bishop. He was also notary

and *promoteur* of the cathedral chapter and registrar of the diocesan court. In addition to holding these positions, he did legal work for many of the powerful families of Noyon, and so was able to give his gifted son many of the advantages of the privileged class. In fact, the children of the nobility were Calvin's classmates and friends. He frequently visited their homes and evidently lived for a time after his mother's death in 1515 with the Montmors, a prominent Noyon family. It was this early association with the Montmors and with another prominent family, the Hangests, that gave Calvin his aristocratic bearing, which enabled him to associate with French nobility with ease and which set him apart from previous Reformers.

Calvin's education was underwritten by certain benefices provided by income derived from endowed altars and churches in the diocese. At twelve he was tonsured and granted the status of a cleric. Upon this occasion the bishop designated a part of the income from the Chapel of La Gesine as his benefice. From all appearances both Calvin and his older brother Charles were being groomed for ecclesiastical careers by their ambitious father.

Calvin was probably twelve when he was sent to Paris to study at the Collège de la Marche. His studies there consisted primarily in improving his knowledge and use of the Latin tongue. Since all classes on the university level were conducted in Latin and textbooks and lectures were in Latin, it was imperative that the would-be scholar have a good grasp of the language. After about a year Calvin transferred to the Collège de Montaigu, where he pursued the usual curriculum for the bachelor of arts degree, which consisted of the *trivium*—grammar, logic, and rhetoric—and the *quadrivium*—arithmetic, music, geometry, and astronomy. During his Paris years he was a diligent student, sleeping little and studying much. It was his habit to repeat everything new he had learned during the day before going to sleep at night, and to call to mind the previous day's lectures when he awoke the next morning. In this way his remarkable ability to retain an enormous amount of information was greatly enhanced.

----

5. Parker, *John Calvin*, p. 32.

Life at Montaigu was demanding. Rules were strict and strictly enforced. The spirit of the Brethren of the Common Life was still in evidence during Calvin's day—thus discipline was severe, and emphasis upon the devotional life was heavy. Like other colleges of the University of Paris, Montaigu was thoroughly medieval in its approach to education and theology. Scholasticism reigned supreme, and heresy, real or imagined, was suppressed. After completing his bachelor's degree, Calvin earned his master's in philosophy in 1526. Whatever plans he may have had for further studies in Paris were interrupted shortly thereafter by his father's change in fortunes. While his gifted son had been attending the university, Calvin's father had been coming into increasing conflict with the cathedral chapter in Noyon. Gérard's problems were not theological but financial: he was accused of mishandling funds from a will that he was pro bating. This he stoutly denied. The upshot of the squabble was that Gérard was excommunicated, and Calvin, at his father's insistence, changed his course of studies from philosophy to law. Therefore, in accordance with his father's wishes, he left Paris for the university at Orléans, which was famous for its law faculty.

Calvin seems to have undertaken his new studies with his usual dedication to academics. After a year or so at Orléans, he (along with a number of other students) was attracted to Bourges, where a famous Italian professor by the name of Andreas Alciati had recently begun to lecture. Even though Calvin soon registered his disappointment with his new mentor, the two years he spent at Bourges were among the most important in his life. For here he came under the influence of a German Protestant, Melchior Wolmar. Wolmar taught him Greek and introduced him to the Greek New Testament, something for which Calvin could never sufficiently thank him.

Even before his Bourges days, Calvin's kinsman from Noyon, Pierre Robert (Olivétan), had begun to exert considerable influence upon him. Olivétan was already a convinced Protestant and had taken refuge in Strasbourg, which had embraced the Reformation under the leadership of Martin Bucer, Wolfgang Capito, and Matthäus Zell. It is from this period (1529-1531) that T. H. L. Parker dates Calvin's conversion. Although Calvin himself does not say specifically where or when it happened, he describes the event as a sudden experience: he felt "overtaken and caught up short" like the apostle Paul. In Calvin's case, however, it was the Roman church he sought to defend—not Israel—before he was "caught up short."[6] In the preface to his *Commentary on the Psalms*, Calvin gives the longest autobiographical account found anywhere in his writings, which includes a brief glimpse of his conversion experience:

> God drew me from obscure and lowly beginnings and conferred on me that most honourable office of herald and minister of the Gospel. My father had intended me for theology from my early childhood. But when he reflected that the career of the law proved everywhere very lucrative for its practitioners, the prospect suddenly made him change his mind. And so it happened that I was called away from the study of philosophy and set to learning law: although, out of obedience to my father's wishes, I tried my best to work hard, yet God at last turned my course in another direction by the secret rein (or curb—*freno*) of his providence. What happened first was that by an unexpected conversion he tamed to teachableness a mind too stubborn for its years—for I was so strongly devoted to the superstitions of the Papacy that nothing less could draw me from such depths of mire. And so this mere taste of true godliness that I received set me on fire with such a desire to progress that I pursued the rest of my studies more coolly, although I did not give them up altogether. Before a year had slipped by anybody who longed for a purer doctrine kept on coming to learn from me, still a beginner, a raw recruit.[7]

---

6. For a discussion of Calvin's conversion, see John T. McNeill, *The History and Character of Calvinism* (New York: Oxford University Press, 1959), pp. 107-10.

7. Calvin, cited by Parker in *John Calvin*, p. 163. See also *John Calvin: Selections from His Writings*, ed. John Dillenberger (Garden City, N.Y.: Doubleday, 1971), pp. 26-27; and *Calvin: Commentaries*, trans. and ed. Joseph Haroutunian, vol. 23 of the Library of Christian Classics (Philadelphia: Westminster Press, 1958), p. 52.

This is a reference to Calvin's inner turning from Rome to Christ, which must have occurred while he was still a law student. However, Williston Walker, François Wendel, and others date Calvin's conversion in his twenty-fourth year. They find no evidence of an earlier evangelical experience. Whatever the case, it took a while for Calvin to make a clean break with his old allegiances. Apparently he and many other Christian humanists had hoped for a complete sweep for the evangelicals in France. By staying within the Roman Church, they thought they might be able to influence it in this direction. Apparently while still at Bourges Calvin began to preach, although he was not ordained. (Upon one occasion at least, he is reported to have preached in a barn.)

Before leaving Orléans Calvin received his licentiate in law, which was the last step before the bestowal of the doctorate. Perhaps because his mind and heart were now set upon another course, he never formally received the degree. By this time he had lost interest in pursuing law as a career, and his father's death on May 26, 1531, freed him from any obligation he may have felt to continue this pursuit. That he may have considered himself relieved of a burden could account for the fact that his correspondence reveals little remorse over his father's death. Then too, he had been away from Noyon for some ten years and had made only an occasional visit home, so it is possible that he no longer felt close to the one who had brought the family name into disrepute, a disrepute from which he and his brothers also suffered. He and his brother Charles, for example, were censured for not attending the chapter meetings, something that would not have happened under ordinary circumstances. Later, however, both John and Antoine, the younger brother, received benefices through the bishop's good graces and those of Claude de Hangest, who was abbot of Saint-Eloi,[8] a clear indication of the strong personal ties between Calvin and these families.

---

8. Parker, *John Calvin*, p. 19.

Within a year of his father's death Calvin brought out his first book. It was a commentary on Seneca's treatise entitled *De Clementia* (*On Clemency*). Erasmus had published the text in 1515 and a corrected version as late as January 1529. In the revised edition he had expressed the hope that someone might write a commentary on the treatise so that Seneca might be better understood. Calvin accepted the challenge, and by April 1532 he had completed and published the book at his own expense.

It was a remarkable achievement for one so young. In the work Calvin cites or quotes no fewer than seventy-four Latin authors and twenty-two Greek authors. Even though he does not quote from the original sources in every instance, as T. H. L. Parker points out, he demonstrates a remarkable knowledge of the ancient classics. At the time the book did not sell well, despite Calvin's strenuous efforts to promote it to his friends and various book dealers. But it did not go unnoticed in French humanist circles, although it got a cool reception. Apparently the humanists resented the arrogance of the young Frenchman who dared to correct Erasmus; they may also have been jealous of his learning.

While the work is not specifically a Christian apology, Calvin may have thought of it as exactly that. While Francis I was in Spain, where he had been taken captive after the French defeat at Pavia, the first Protestant martyrs were put to death in France. Although Francis was thought to be kindly disposed toward Christian humanist learning, it was increasingly apparent that the king had not yet decided on a firm course of action regarding the growing evangelical movement. Conceivably Calvin longed to tip the scales in favor of toleration of the evangelicals. The theme of his work, as its title makes apparent, is clemency. He stresses that it becomes a good ruler to promote toleration and to rule with justice, an emphasis that can be interpreted as a plea for mercy on behalf of the persecuted Protestants. "We should be fully persuaded that pity also is virtue," he writes; "that a man cannot be good if he is not merciful, whatever may be argued by these sages, idle in their ignorance."[9]

The work of Seneca also had a certain appeal for a person of Calvin's elitist feelings. Like many humanists, he distrusted the "ignorant rabble." This work gave him an opportunity to affirm the monarchy and to identify with the humanists who were the forerunners of the Reformation in France, as well as to score a point for religious toleration. It was certainly not a direct appeal for clemency on behalf of the persecuted, but given Calvin's shy and cautious disposition, it can be viewed as a veiled attempt on his part to influence the policies of the French crown toward the handful of evangelicals who had begun a fearful existence in the land of the Franks. Doubtless Calvin had other reasons for spending time and money on this theme, one of which was to correct Erasmus's text. This he claimed to have done in the preface, which he wrote in the form of an introductory letter to Claude de Hangest, his old friend from Noyon. However, as a Christian humanist who had not yet made his break with the Roman Church, he may also have hoped to influence his native country in exercising a more lenient policy toward Protestantism.

Calvin was forced to leave Paris in 1533 when his friend Nicholas Cop, the rector of the university, became the victim of Catholic reaction to his inaugural address on All Saints' Day. After he failed in his attempt to defend the university's independence and his immunity from prosecution, Cop fled. Calvin was suspected of having something to do with the address because it had strong evangelical overtones and was punctuated by quotations from Erasmus and Luther. With Cop gone, the frustrated ecclesiastics focused their wrath on Calvin. He was warned and left Paris in haste. It is difficult to follow his movements precisely from there. Noyon, Angoulême, Strasbourg, and Meaux all became his home for brief periods. He was back in Noyon by the fourth of May, when he resigned the chaplaincy of La Gesine.[10] And before the end of 1535 he had arrived in Basel to complete work on the first edition of the *Institutes of the Christian Religion.*[11]

CHRISTIANAE RELIGIONIS INSTITUTIO

Calvin may have gotten his idea for the *Institutes* during his years as a law student. All law students had to become thoroughly familiar with the *Corpus iuris civilis* (*Body of Civil Law*) based upon the Justinian codification of 529 and 534. Its major elements were set out in three basic textbooks: *Codex, Digesta,* and *Institutiones.* The *Codex,* or *Code,* contained the authoritative statement of Roman law. The *Digesta* contained the legal opinions of ancient lawyers and a historical commentary on the *Codex.* The *Institutiones* was the elementary but authoritative textbook of law students. Calvin apparently conceived the idea of using the pattern of this text to write an elementary textbook of the Christian faith that would be for Christianity what the *Institutiones* was for civil law.

<hr/>

9. Calvin, cited by François Wendel in *Calvin: The Origins and Development of His Religious Thought,* trans. Philip Mairet (New York: Harper & Row, 1963), p. 32.

10. Parker's explanation of the so-called imprisonment of Calvin sounds plausible:

The older writers and even, surprisingly enough, some modern, think that Calvin had an eventful month now. They accept Lefranc's misreading of the Register entry for 26 May, according to which "M. Iean Cauvin [then two words illegible] was put in prison at the gate Corbaut, for an uproar made in church on the eve of Trinity Sunday." He was released on 3 June but reincarcerated on 5 June. The correct reading, however (which Doumergue gave us as long ago as 1927), runs: "Un Iean Cauvin, dict Mudit, was put in prison . . . "—"A Jean Cauvin, called Mudit . . . " This namesake was presumably the same who in 1551-2 (when our Jean Cauvin had a water-tight alibi, being in Geneva at the time) was evicted from his canonry for having kept in his house "une femme de mauvaise gouvernement" (*John Calvin,* p. 31).

11. The complete title is a formidable one: *The Basic Teaching of the Christian Religion, Comprising Almost the Whole Sum of Godliness and Whatever It Is Necessary to Know on the Doctrine of Salvation. A Newly Published Work Very Well Worth Reading by All Who Are Studious of Godliness. A Preface to the Most Christian King of France, Offering to Him This Book as a Confession of Faith by the Author, Jean Calvin of Noyon.*

Dedicated to Francis I, Calvin's *Christianae religionis institutio* (*Institutes of the Christian Religion*) was also designed as an apology for evangelicals who were the objects of persecution in France. This much is evident in the "Prefatory Address" to Francis I:

> Sire,—When I first engaged in this work, nothing was farther from my thoughts than to write what should afterwards be presented to your Majesty. My intention was only to furnish a kind of rudiments, by which those who feel some interest in religion might be trained to true godliness. And I toiled at the task chiefly for the sake of my countrymen the French, multitudes of whom I perceived to be hungering and thirsting after Christ, while very few seemed to have been duly imbued with even a slender knowledge of him. That this was the object which I had in view is apparent from the work itself, which is written in a simple and elementary form adapted for instruction.
>
> But when I perceived that the fury of certain bad men had risen to such a height in your realm, that there was no place in it for sound doctrine, I thought it might be of service if I were in the same work both to give instruction to my countrymen, and also lay before your Majesty a Confession, from which you may learn what the doctrine is that so inflames the rage of those madmen who are this day, with fire and sword, troubling your kingdom. For I fear not to declare, that what I have here given may be regarded as a summary of the very doctrine which, they vociferate, ought to be punished with confiscation, exile, imprisonment, and flames, as well as exterminated by land and sea.[12]

The Apostles' Creed provided the outline for the *Institutes*, as it had for the confessional statements of Luther, Hubmaier, and others. Calvin was careful to distinguish the doctrines set forth in the *Institutes* from the taint of Anabaptism. The siege of Münster by Catholic and Protestant armies had destroyed the "New Jerusalem" with a merciless bloodbath, and Anabaptists everywhere suffered from the aftereffects of this tragedy. Thus, on February 1, 1535, Francis I had

excused the policies of persecution carried out by the crown and the Lutheran princes by claiming that the placards of 1533 denouncing the mass were the work of anarchists who were in reality Anabaptists.[13] The evidence, however, implicated Guillaume Farel. That Calvin knew the allegation against the Anabaptists was in error is revealed in the preface to his commentary on the Psalms, in which he also gives the underlying reasons for writing the *Institutes* in the first place:

> I left my own country and departed for Germany to enjoy there, unknown, in some corner, the quiet long denied me. But lo, while I was hidden unknown at Basel, a great fire of hatred [for France] had been kindled in Germany by the exile of many godly men from France. To quench this fire, wicked and lying rumors were spread, cruelly calling the exiles Anabaptists and seditious men, men who threatened to upset, not only religion, but the whole political order with their perverse madness. I saw that this was a trick of those in [the French] court, not only to cover up with false slanders the shedding of the innocent blood of holy martyrs, but also to enable the persecutors to continue with the pitiless slaughter. Therefore I felt that I must make a strong statement against such charges; for I could not be silent without treachery. This was why I published the *Institutes*—to defend against unjust slander my brothers whose death was precious in the Lord's sight. A second reason was my desire to rouse the sympathy and concern of people outside, since the same punishment threatened many other poor people. And this volume was not a thick and laborious work like the present edition; it appeared as a brief *Enchiridion*. It had no other purpose than to bear witness to the faith of those whom I saw criminally libeled by wicked and false courtiers.[14]

Little did Calvin realize when the Institutes were published in 1536 that this was only the first edition of a book that would demand his best efforts for the next twenty-three years. He wrote the original text in Latin. His French translation did not come out until 1541, two years

---

12. John Calvin, *Institutes of the Christian Religion*, 2 vols., trans. Henry Beveridge (Grand Rapids: Eerdmans, 1933), 1: 3–4.

13. Parker, *John Calvin*, p. 34.
14. *Calvin: Commentaries*, p. 52.

after the greatly enlarged edition of 1539. The final edition appeared in 1559, five years before his death. In all there were eight editions. The first edition had only six chapters; the last consisted of eighty chapters in four books. But the first edition was hardly a pocket-size handbook: in *Johannis Calvini Opera* it numbers 248 pages.[15]

The first edition admirably fulfilled the purpose that Calvin had in mind, even though he himself felt that it was an inferior product that could be greatly improved—and improve it he did. In the first edition he set out to present a compendium of the Christian religion in catechetical fashion based upon an exposition of the Ten Commandments, the Apostles' Creed, and the Lord's Prayer. In the second edition of 1539 he incorporated some significant changes. Only with the last edition was Calvin satisfied with his work: "Although I did not regret the labor spent, I was never satisfied until the work had been arranged in the order now set forth." After citing this quotation, Ford Lewis Battles goes on to suggest that Calvin is really saying, "Here in these successive editions of my *magnum opus* is the story of my own gradual growth in the Christian life."[16] Few books have mirrored an author's changing thought as the *Institutes* do.

Some of the changes that characterized the subsequent editions were due to Calvin's increased knowledge and appropriation of the church fathers, particularly Augustine and Chrysostom; the influence of Martin Bucer, who helped him to reach a "deeper understanding of predestination"; and Calvin's experience as pastor of a small congregation of French refugees during the Strasbourg interlude of 1538–1541. In regard to the last development, Battles writes, "Calvinism would be a poor, or at least inadequate, theological system for the church

indeed were it deprived of the significant insight into the life and discipline of the worshiping congregation set down in 1543."[17] Although there was a considerable amount of juggling of chapters in the final edition, the work began as it did in 1539 with a section on the knowledge of God—although this section, which was one chapter in the first edition, had grown to ten chapters in the 1559 edition. This edition ends as the first one did: with a chapter devoted to civil government. In the intervening chapters Calvin devotes himself to a systematic presentation of the Christian faith as he understood it. His retentive mind and breadth of knowledge enabled him to marshal enormous amounts of material from his vast array of sources. Thus concepts he borrowed—from Erasmus, Luther, Melanchthon, Zwingli, and Heinrich Bullinger as well as from the church fathers—and made his own may be readily discerned within the book's pages. In this fact lies something of the strength and genius of Calvin. Within the general framework of Augustinian theology, which was also the theological orientation of the older Reformers, he articulated more clearly than anyone had before him the basic theological truths of the Reformation while integrating within his synthesis the Christian humanism of Erasmus and the mysticism of Lefèvre. This is evident in his emphasis upon union with Christ that comes only through faith.

Like Luther and Zwingli, he held to only two sacraments: baptism and the Lord's Supper. Like Luther, he affirmed that infants have faith, and like Zwingli, he asserted that infant baptism under the New Covenant is analogous to circumcision in the Old. Therefore he rejected the Anabaptist insistence upon believer's baptism. He took a mediating position between Luther and Zwingli on the Lord's Supper, admitting that it had been very difficult for him to read Zwingli's works on the subject. However, with Zwingli he emphasized the Lord's Supper as a *Eucharistia*, a thanksgiving remembrance, and a confes-

15. *Johannis Calvini Opera quae supersunt omnia*, vol. 1, ed. Guilielmus Baum, Edwardus Cunitz, and Edwardus Reus (Braunschweig: C. A. Schwetschke & Son, 1863).

16. Battles and John Walchenbach, *An Analysis of "The Institutes of the Christian Religion" of John Calvin* (Grand Rapids: Baker Book House, 1980), p. 12.

17. Battles and Walchenbach, *Analysis of "The Institutes,"* p. 13.

sion of one's faith in the atoning work of Christ. He rejected Luther's concept of corporal presence, "real presence," preferring instead a concept of the spiritual presence that the participant "truly and effectually" (*vere et efficaciter*) receives in the Supper.[18]

Calvin's teaching on the nature of the church reveals perhaps the greatest change in various editions of the *Institutes*. In the first edition Calvin perceived the church as without "form or void."[19] It is composed of all the elect, including angels. However, on earth the church is the place where the Word is preached, the sacraments are properly observed, *and discipline is practiced.* Although Luther occasionally referred to discipline as one of the many marks of the church, for Calvin discipline became indispensable for *une église bien ordonée* (a well-ordered church). In the *Ordonnances écclesiastiques* that he drew up for the church in Geneva, Calvin spells out how discipline was to be administered. The fourfold ministry of the church—carried out by pastor, teacher, elder, and deacon—set forth in the *Ordonnances* is further refined in book 4, chapters 3-5 of the 1543 edition of the *Institutes*. Battles suggests that Calvin borrowed this concept of the ministry from Martin Bucer. In the final edition of the *Institutes*, according to J. S. Whale, Calvin perceived the church as far more institutionalized and considered it a means of grace.[20]

Another noticeable change between the first edition and subsequent editions involved that doctrine with which Calvin's name is most often associated: predestination. There is little doubt that Calvin's increasing appropriation of Augustine's teachings on the subject accounts for the heavier emphasis that predestination received beginning with the second edition. (Bucer's influence has also been credited as a factor in this development.) Of course, in reading the Bible with Augustinian glasses, Luther and (eventually) Zwingli quite readily found biblical support for the teaching. It is Calvin, however, who is most often associated with the concept. It is therefore easy to exaggerate the role of predestination in Calvin's theological development at the expense of his other doctrinal emphases both in the *Institutes* and in his commentaries. On the other hand, he made predestination such an integral part of his system that it cannot be overlooked.

Calvin gradually began to pay more and more attention to the concept of predestination in the *Institutes*. In the first edition predestination does not receive special attention. Instead, it is interwoven with other topics—the articles on the church, the communion of the saints, the remission of sins, resurrection from the dead, and eternal life—all of which are discussed in the fourth section of chapter 2, *"De Fide"*. The entire discussion takes less than ten pages.[21] In the 1539 edition predestination is discussed along with providence in a greatly enlarged section. In the 1559 edition of the *Institutes*, four chapters (3.21-24) are devoted to predestination alone. Surely a few lines lifted out of the volumes that Calvin wrote on the subject can never do complete justice to him or to the concept of predestination as he understood and taught it. But the following quotation, taken from chapter 21 of book 3, does provide his definition of predestination:

> By predestination we mean the eternal decree of God, by which he determined with himself whatever he wished to happen with regard to every man. All are not created on equal terms, but some are preordained to eternal life, others to eternal damnation; and, accordingly, as each has been created for one or other of these ends, we say that he has been predestinated to life or to death.[22]

18. Parker, *John Calvin*, p. 45. See chapter 17 of Beveridge's translation of the *Institutes*, "Of the Lord's Supper, and the Benefits Conferred by It."

19. For Calvin's view of the church at this early stage of his reformatory career, see the 1536 *Institutes* as reproduced in Dillenberger's *John Calvin*, pp. 295-307.

20. Whale, cited in *Calvin and the Reformed Tradition*, ed. James Leo Garrett, Jr. (Nashville: Broadman Press, 1980), p. 37. See also William Mueller, *Church and State in Luther and Calvin: A Comparative Study* (Nashville: Broadman Press, 1954), pp. 116 25.

21. *Johannis Calvini Opera*, pp. 72-81.

22. Calvin, *Institutes*, 3.21.5.

The form of the doctrine set forth here by Calvin is known as double predestination, which means that every person is destined to be either saved or lost. Calvin was careful to point out that God's choice of individuals in the matter did not rest upon foreknowledge—even though God possessed this knowledge—but upon his own sovereign and inscrutable will. Despite heavy criticism from a number of quarters, Calvin insisted that his understanding of election was taught by Scripture and that only arrogant, sinful men would question its justice. This became one of the running controversies he carried on with a number of his detractors. He remained convinced that Augustine as well as the Scriptures taught such a doctrine.

Few works on theology have had the influence that Calvin's *Institutes* have had. Luther, Zwingli, Melanchthon, Balthasar Hubmaier, Menno Simons, Pilgram Marpeck, and William Farel had all attempted something of the kind, but none was able to produce a work with the thoroughness, erudition, and force of the *Institutes*. Calvin's success lay in his ability to take Protestant theological insights and reshape them—in the light of Scripture and the teachings of the church fathers and with the help of humanist learning—into what was to become one of Protestantism's greatest attempts at erecting a systematic theology.

GENEVA BEFORE CALVIN

Calvin's magnum opus would never have become such without Geneva—or without Strasbourg, for that matter. It is amazing that this religious exile—a man who had been converted to the Protestant faith for less than five years and who had no formal theological education or even so much as experience in serving a church as pastor or vicar—produced that remarkable first edition of the *Institutes*. His lack of pastoral experience coupled with his inflexible idealism were to prove costly once he had settled in as "teacher to the Church of Geneva." But the Reformation had already been officially established in Geneva by the time Calvin arrived on the scene, though the acceptance of the Reformed

John Calvin, who formulated more systematically than anyone before him the basic theological truths of the Reformation RELIGIOUS NEWS SERVICE

faith was not altogether a spontaneous response of a people moved by an overwhelming spiritual concern. Their motives were mixed, and the path of progress the Reformers trod was not without its thorns.

Geneva had a complicated political and ecclesiastical history. For centuries the bishop had dominated the political affairs of the city and with the help of the House of Savoy overcame his only effective opposition, the counts of Geneva. But the bishop discovered that the House of Savoy was a far more formidable opponent. The count of Savoy turned the tables on the bishop by championing the rights of the burghers of the city. Thus in 1387 Bishop Adhémar Fabri was forced to grant a charter giving the burghers of the city the right to govern themselves, which they proceeded to do by forming a *council général* (General Assembly), which in turn elected annually the four syndics who administered the affairs of the city on a day-to-day basis. By the sixteenth century there were three councils: *Le Petit Couseil* (the Little

Council), numbering twenty-five members, the Council of Sixty, and the Council of Two Hundred. This meant that the governing of the city was a responsibility shared by the bishop, the *vicedominus* (his deputy for temporal affairs), and the citizens.[23]

Such a division of authority insured a balance of power as long as the bishop did not belong to the House of Savoy. However, in 1444 Amadeus VIII of Savoy, elected pope (Felix V) at the Council of Basel in competition with Pope Eugenius IV, became bishop, which gave the House of Savoy virtually complete control of Geneva. This turn of events provoked an increasingly hostile reaction from the citizens of Geneva, who in desperation turned for help to the neighboring Swiss cantons of Fribourg and Bern. The alliance thus formed in 1526 proved effective. In 1527 the Bishop Pierre de la Baume left Geneva, never to assume his role again. The authority of the *vicedominus* was abolished, and his responsibilities were taken over by the citizens.

In 1528 a new element entered into the struggle for the control of Geneva. In that year Bern formally embraced the Reformation and thus became an aggressive supporter of the Protestant cause, while Fribourg remained staunchly Roman Catholic. Soon the religious issue threatened the alliance that had won for the Genevese their freedom from the Savoyards. However, until 1532 Geneva considered itself a Catholic city and certainly seemed to be such, with its seven parishes and its churches, convents, and aggregate of three hundred clergy and nuns. Apparently there was no overt dissatisfaction with the religious situation or any manifestation of a desire to change until June 1532.

By that time, however, things were clearly beginning to change. Pope Clement VII had issued an indulgence within the city on the usual conditions. On the morning of June 9, the citizens of Geneva were startled to see huge printed posters on the doors of the churches proclaiming that a "plenary pardon would be granted to everyone for all their sins on the one condition of repentance, and a living faith in the promises of Jesus Christ."[24] A riot resulted as priests rushed to tear down the placards and some Genevese opposed them. Pierre Werley, one of the most militant canons of St. Peter's and a native of Fribourg, was wounded in the fracas.

Three or four months later, while the city was still buzzing with excitement over this event, William Farel and two companions arrived in Geneva. Even though the evangelicals worked quietly, they were discovered, and the city was once again in an uproar. The would-be Reformers were promptly arrested and banished. But Farel was not so easily turned aside. He had previously been associated with Lefèvre, Briconnet, and Marguerite d'Angoulême, queen of Navarre, around whom rallied "the group of Meaux." Farel's fearless preaching had led to his dismissal by Bishop Briçonnet. After leaving France for the second time, he had taken part in a disputation at Bern in 1528 and subsequently became its most successful agent in carrying the Reformation to the territory over which Bern exerted political control.

Upon being driven out of Geneva, Farel immediately turned for help to Antoine Froment, a fellow Frenchman and a trusted companion of previous years. Froment entered Geneva under the guise of a French teacher. Since many wives of prominent citizens wished to improve their ability to speak and write French, the new French teacher soon attracted a number of students. He "just happened" to choose the French New Testament as his textbook, which gave him a splendid opportunity to present the gospel. The result was predictable: his students became ardent supporters of the Reformation. Froment's teaching thus became a leavening agent in the growing agitation for reform. When a citizen who spoke disrespectfully of the mass was banished by the city council, the evangelical party

23. See Williston Walker, *John Calvin: The Organizer of Reformed Protestantism* (New York: Schocken Books, 1969), pp. 163-67.

24. Thomas Lindsay, *A History of the Reformation*, 2 vols. (New York: Scribner's, 1907, 1928), 2:64-65.

promptly appealed to Bern, thus providing just the opportunity the evangelicals had been waiting for. The council of Bern responded with a firm admonition to the council of Geneva regarding respect for the rights of evangelicals in their midst. Thus prodded, Geneva took a hesitant step toward the Reformation when its council issued the decree of March 30, 1533, which granted toleration to evangelicals while at the same time prohibiting attacks on Roman Catholic ceremonies. Preachers were ordered not to preach anything that could not be supported by Holy Scripture.

With this encouragement the evangelicals took heart and became more aggressive. On April 10 they held a communion service in a garden, which provoked the priests of the city to launch an armed attack upon a crowd of Protestants in front of St. Peter's Cathedral. The leader of the band, the militant priest Pierre Werley, was killed in the melee that followed. He was promptly proclaimed a martyr by the Roman Catholics of the city. Fribourg, a strong Catholic canton of which the slain priest was a native, called for the apprehension and punishment of the evangelicals involved in the fight. Once again the evangelicals appealed to Bern, and thus Geneva became the coveted prize in a tug-of-war between the Protestant canton of Bern and the Catholic canton of Fribourg.

Within the city of Geneva the conflict heated up. In December, Guy Furbiti, a monk and a champion of the Catholic cause, was brought to the city as the Advent preacher. His sermon constituted an attack on Reformation teachings and a personal attack on Froment. In concluding his sermon on December 2, he issued a challenge: "Where are those fine preachers of the fireside, who say the opposite? If they showed themselves here one could speak to them. Ha! Ha! they are well to hide themselves in corners to deceive poor women and others who know nothing." This was more than Froment could take. Immediately after the sermon he shouted, "Hear me! I am ready to give my life, and my body to be burned, to maintain that what that man has said is nothing but falsehood

and the words of Antichrist."[25] A mob almost succeeded in seizing Froment, but he managed to escape. Bern was immediately apprised of the situation, whereupon the Bernese demanded a public disputation in the wake of Geneva's equivocation and its failure to protect Froment.

Geneva capitulated, and Farel was sent to the city for the projected disputation. The council of Geneva found itself in a difficult situation. It did not want to offend the bishop or Bern, so it postponed taking action. When Bern threatened to end its alliance with Geneva if the council did not call Furbiti to give an account of himself in the presence of Farel and Pierre Viret, who had recently come from Bern, the council gave in. Furbiti admitted that he could not support his preaching from Scripture but cited as his authority Thomas Aquinas and the Pseudo-Isidorian Decretals.

A number of riots ensued that were apparently engineered by the bishop in hopes of turning the rising Protestant tide. But such violence had the opposite effect. When an evangelical was killed, the aroused citizens demanded an end to the anarchy fomented by Catholic zealots. In the wake of his failure to overcome the growing Protestant party, the bishop of Geneva formed an alliance with the duke of Savoy to organize an army to attack the city. This proved to be another strategic blunder on the bishop's part.

The preachers—Farel, Viret, and Froment—joined the citizens of Geneva in reinforcing the city's fortifications and taking their turns at standing watch in face of the threatened siege. A cook in the house where the three Reformers were staying attempted to poison them, and Roman Catholic priests were blamed for the near-fatal episode. This event marked the beginning of the end of Rome's domination of Geneva. Once again the tide turned decisively in favor of the Reformation. The council of Geneva itself now arranged to hold a disputation without further ado. Evangelical theses drawn up by

---

25. Lindsay, *History of the Reformation*, 2: 78–79.

the Reformers were posted in the city on May 1, 1535; copies were sent to all the priests and convents within the area. Safe conduct was guaranteed all participants, and an attempt was made to secure the most able defenders of the Catholic faith available. But the bishop of Geneva had forbidden the disputation, so no Roman defenders showed up for the opening session. In subsequent sessions, however, Jean Chapuis, prior of the Dominican monastery, and Jean Coci, confessor to the Sisters of St. Clara in the city, attempted to defend the Roman Catholic position. But these two were no match for Farel and Viret, and thus the people of Geneva were persuaded to close ranks behind the Reformers.

The disputation ended on June 24, 1535. Farel asked the council to declare itself in favor of the Reformation, but it hesitated. The fiery Reformer then took matters into his own hands. He took over the pulpit first in the Church of Madeleine, then in Saint-Gervais, and finally, on August 8, in St. Peter's itself. On the afternoon of the eighth an iconoclastic riot broke out during vespers. Images were seized, broken, and burned by the wrought-up crowd. The next day Farel was summoned to appear before the Small Council. Here he made an impassioned plea for anyone to prove him and his colleagues wrong by Scripture, closing the interview with a moving prayer he delivered on his knees. The next day the Council of Two Hundred met and resolved to temporarily abolish the mass and worship of the saints until the monks and priests of the city could appear before them and explain the Roman Catholic position.

When representatives of the Roman Church finally made their appearance on November 29, 1535—the monks in the morning and the parish priests (secular priests) in the afternoon—they advanced no substantive or convincing arguments for retaining the Roman Catholic faith. Instead, they pleaded ignorance and invoked tradition: they acknowledged that they were unlearned men and simply wished to follow in the footsteps of their fathers. The council was not impressed with either their learning or their piety. They were then informed that they must

cease saying mass until further notice. Thus the Reformation became legally established in Geneva.

Bern was moved to action by the fear that France would come to the aid of Geneva in the city's struggle with the duke of Savoy in alliance with the bishop of Geneva: Bern renounced its allegiance to the House of Savoy on the same day that Protestantism became official in Geneva (November 29, 1535). War was declared on January 16. Fribourg, whose fear of France proved greater than its fear of the Protestants, permitted the Bernese to march through its territories to attack the army of the duke and the bishop. The forces that had long threatened Geneva were dispersed, almost without a fight, and Geneva at last was free to become an independent republic under the protective arm of Bern. Along with Geneva and Lausanne, many a lesser town shared in the benefits of the armed intervention. By this action the threat of a French invasion was effectively thwarted. Few powers in Europe were willing to rush into combat against Swiss troops—and where could the French turn for mercenary soldiers if they attacked Switzerland?

The action of the Council of Two Hundred was officially confirmed by the citizens of Geneva on May 21, 1536. Even though it was official, however, the Reformation had only begun to capture the minds and hearts of the Genevese. With all the energy of his convictions, Farel attempted to build a truly evangelical church. He preached, taught, and founded schools and hospitals, but the godless undercurrent was too strong in this city so recently divorced from Roman Catholic traditions. Farel clearly needed help—and he found that help in the twenty-seven-year-old author of the *Institutes*.

CALVIN AND FAREL

After finishing the *Institutes* Calvin felt he needed a much-deserved rest. In search of a place to relax, he made a brief excursion into Italy to visit the duke and duchess of Farrara, but he was soon forced to leave when the authorities began to investigate the royal couple's guests. Clearly the attraction for Calvin was the duchess, who was Princess Renée, daughter of Louis XII: she was a patroness of the Reformers and a protector of evangelical refugees from France. Upon returning from Farrara, Calvin decided to make Strasbourg his home. It was one of the few cities where a French evangelical could feel secure within a culture that was not alien. According to his own account, he had intended to spend no more than one night in Geneva. But an old friend and recent traveling companion, Louis du Tillet, alerted Farel to the fact that the young man who called himself Charles d'Espeville was none other than John Calvin, the author of the *Institutes*.[26]

Farel was convinced that the hand of the Lord had brought Calvin to Geneva for just such a time. He promptly confronted the pale-faced Frenchman with Geneva's need for one possessing his gifts. Calvin protested, claiming that he needed rest, whereupon Farel exclaimed, "And may God curse your rest!" Calvin was shaken. Was that the voice of God he heard in the words of William Farel? He became convinced that it was. Later he wrote of the experience in the preface to his *Commentary on the Psalms*:

> A short time before, by the work of the same good man [Farel], and of Peter Viret, the papacy had been banished from the city; but things were still unsettled and the place was divided into evil and harmful factions. One man, who has since shamefully gone back to the papists, took immediate action to make me known. Then Farel, who was working with incredible zeal to promote the gospel, bent all his efforts to keep me in the city. And when he realized that I was determined to study in privacy in some obscure place, and saw that he gained nothing by entreaty, he descended to cursing, and said that God would surely curse my peace if I held back from giving help at a time of such great need. Terrified by his words, and conscious of my own timidity and cowardice, I gave up my journey and attempted to apply whatever gift I had in defense of my faith.[27]

On September 5, 1536, the minutes of the council of Geneva record, "Master William Farel stated the need for the lecture begun by this Frenchman in St. Peter's."[28] It was not long before "the professor in sacred learning to the church in Geneva" was no longer anonymous.

Lausanne was one of the cities "liberated" by Bern in the war against the House of Savoy. Not long afterwards Bern used a heavy hand to encourage its new ally to hold a disputation during the first week in October. Once again evangelical theses drawn up by Farel and Viret provided the agenda for debate. Of the 337 priests invited, only 174 appeared. Most of these were mute during the disputation; only four rose to defend the Roman cause. Farel launched the disputation with a stirring sermon on Sunday, October 1, and formally closed it in the same way on the following Sunday, October 8. Clearly Farel and Viret were the standard bearers of the evangelicals; Calvin was simply there for the experience. But on Thursday, when the doctrine of transubstantiation came under discussion, one of the priests read a well-prepared paper in which he claimed the Protestants neglected the ancient church fathers, believing that they did not support the Protestant position. Thereupon Farel turned to Calvin, who rose hesitantly, somewhat surprised. His opening remarks were caustic: "Those who attempt to quote the Fathers need to read them before they attempt to use them." Then he proceeded to quote from memory one patristic authority after another, citing edition, book, chapter, and paragraph in an amazing display of learning. It was a matchless performance, and the effect was electrifying. One monk was converted on the spot. In the weeks that followed, not only did Lausanne decide for the Reformation, but some two hundred priests and monks became Protestants. Calvin was no longer that anonymous Frenchman. He had proved his mettle.[29]

---

26. The use of pseudonyms was not an uncommon practice in the sixteenth century. Calvin had used this name before to protect his identity.

27. *Calvin: Commentaries*, p. 53.

---

28. Lindsay, *History of the Reformation*, 2: 102-5.

29. Lindsay, *History of the Reformation*, 2: 102-5.

Articles on the Church Order

Back in Geneva, Calvin attempted to bring order out of near chaos. For this purpose he and Farel drew up *Articles on the Organization of the Church and Its Worship at Geneva* and presented them to the council on January 6, 1537. Initially this "memorandum" included articles on the Lord's Supper, singing in public worship, religious instruction of children, marriage, and "discipline of excommunication." The articles were approved by both the Small Council and the Council of Two Hundred, but with certain changes. For example, Calvin had asked that the Lord's Supper be observed every month in each of the three churches where services were held; in fact, he really preferred a weekly observance. But the councils decided that once every three months was often enough. Further, the councils insisted that the announcement of a forthcoming marriage should be made three successive Sundays before celebration.

There is little indication that the members of the councils understood the implications of the document or took it seriously. But there is no question of the importance that Calvin and Farel attached to the *Articles*. Integral to the organization of the church in Geneva as envisioned by Calvin and Farel was discipline—discipline that they thought should be enforced by the magistracy. This was a serious blunder, as Thomas Lindsay suggests: "Calvin's mistake was that, while he believed that the membership and the pastorate should exercise discipline and excommunication, he also insisted that the secular power should enforce the censures of the

Calvin conferring with the Geneva City Council RELIGIOUS NEWS SERVICE

Church."[30] There was some ambiguity regarding its implementation, as T. H. L. Parker has shown. Whatever misgivings some members of the councils may have had were suppressed in the fervor of their enthusiasm for the new church order, an example of which is seen in the actions of January 16, 1537:

> When the *Two Hundred* met the same day they approved the decisions of the *Little Council* and further showed their zeal for the house of God by enacting that on Sundays during sermon time "neither brothers, nor tripe sellers, nor others, nor second hand dealers shall stay open beyond the last stroke of the great bell; that those who have idols at home break them up forth with; that there is to be no singing of idle songs and no playing of games of chance nor are the pastry cooks to cry their wares during the time of sermon."[31]

The *Articles* required that all the citizens and inhabitants of Geneva subscribe to a confession of faith. Such a confession had been drawn up and presented to the councils as early as November 10, 1536, but there had been considerable delay in implementing this provision with the new church order. Among the first to sign were members of the councils who complied, although not without protest. After further delay the Council of Two Hundred was prodded by the Reformers to implement a plan whereby the citizens, district by district, would take an oath in St. Peter's to live by the confession, "in order to recognize those in harmony with the Gospel and those longing rather to be of the kingdom of the pope than of the kingdom of Jesus Christ."[32] But resistance to such coercive measures mounted. Many were reluctant to subscribe, and some never did. Calvin and Farel were exasperated. Although words were exchanged, the ministers refused to back down. They appealed to Bern without success, an ill omen for the future. However, a catechism—*Instruction and Confession of Faith for Use of the Church of Geneva*—was ready by 1537. Similar in format to the *Institutes*, it explained the

meaning and significance of the Ten Commandments, the Apostles' Creed, the Lord's Prayer, and the sacraments. An appendix contained a discussion of the duties of pastors and magistrates. However, it proved too difficult for children to understand and was later replaced.

It was not long until the latent opposition to the attempts at discipline manifested itself. In February 1538 four syndics were chosen who were known opponents of the preachers. While the new leadership first seemed to be on the side of Calvin and Farel, they soon indicated otherwise. The new syndics were influenced by the fact that a majority of the people were becoming more and more hostile, chafing under the rather severe restrictions of the new church order.

The Easter Crisis of 1538

Bern, the defender of Geneva, became a party—perhaps unwittingly—to the rising tide of opposition to the preachers of Geneva. This powerful Protestant canton was intent on consolidating its control over its newly acquired territories. Its attempt to mandate uniformity of worship in Geneva and Lausanne may have been motivated by considerations more political than religious. At any rate, Geneva was pressured to adopt the Bernese practices, which meant that baptisms were to be performed at stone fonts, unleavened bread was to be used in observing the Lord's Supper, and four special days in the Christian year were to be observed—Christmas, Easter, Ascension Day, and Pentecost.[33]

The council of Geneva ordered immediate compliance with Bernese practices, but the ministers refused. They asked permission to postpone a decision until the forthcoming synod of the Reformed Church at Zürich. The preachers were in a precarious position, however. Farel and Calvin had been accused of har-

---

30. Lindsay, *History of the Reformation*, 2: 110.
31. Parker, *John Calvin*, p. 64.
32. Parker, *John Calvin*, p. 63.

33. Pentecost, also known as Whitsunday or Whitsuntide, was observed on the seventh Sunday or the fiftieth day after Easter.

boring desires to turn the city over to France, and thus had been dubbed Jacobites. Calvin had even referred to the council as "a council of the devil," and the blind preacher Courauld had called it "a council of drunkards," a slur for which he was promptly jailed. The situation became critical when the council demanded that the ministers use unleavened bread in the Lord's Supper on Easter Sunday. The preachers ignored the order: they preached but did not observe the Lord's Supper. The next day the council voted that the preachers should be dismissed as soon as suitable replacements could be found, but the following day it issued a new order asking them to leave Geneva within three days.

Calvin and Farel immediately went to Bern to protest the policies that had become the occasion for their dismissal. The Bernese repented and attempted to secure the reappointment of the ousted preachers, but to no avail. It appears that the underlying cause of discontent centered on Calvin's zeal for the strict application of discipline in the life of the church of Geneva, which happened to embrace the entire population. Thus ended Calvin's first attempt to serve the Reformed Church of Geneva.

THE STRASBOURG EXILE

Calvin, Farel, and Courauld now became ambassadors of Christ without portfolios. Where should they go—or rather, where *could* they go? They visited Zürich and then Basel. Farel returned to Neuchâtel to serve as pastor of the church that was to command his services for the remainder of his life. Calvin received an invitation to lead the French congregation in Strasbourg, an offer that Martin Bucer and Wolfgang Capito made possible. But after visiting the city to size up the situation, Calvin refused the invitation and returned to Basel. However, when Bucer would not take no for an answer and accused Calvin of being another Jonah whom God could not possibly bless, Calvin yielded. In September, after more than three months of wandering, he finally arrived in Strasbourg, his

destination two years before when his journey had been interrupted by Farel.

Calvin's duties in Strasbourg forced him back into an active ministry. He now found himself responsible for a congregation of about five hundred members. He preached or lectured twice on Sunday and once on every other day of the week. Here Calvin introduced both discipline and a Protestant version of auricular confession, taking pains to explain why he did so. The Psalms were sung in Geneva, but in Strasbourg they were sung with perhaps more understanding, because the church was composed of refugees from France who could give a reason for their faith. Only the melody was sung, however, because Calvin discouraged singing in parts. He even tried his hand at producing metrical versions of the Psalms in French.

In addition to his pastoral duties, Calvin took on a few students whom he instructed in theology and Greek. Though he augmented his meager income by teaching and practicing law, he was still poor. But poverty was not the only problem Calvin faced in Strasbourg. Two of his close friends—his cousin Olivétan and Courald, his blind colleague from his Geneva days—died in 1538, and more disappointments followed. For one thing, Louis du Tillet, Calvin's traveling companion in whose home he had once stayed, returned to France and to the Roman Catholic Church. In addition, Pierre Caroli, an erratic soul who had accused Calvin and Farel of Arianism in Geneva, turned up in Strasbourg. Caroli accused Calvin of heresy because he refused to accept the Athanasian Creed. Upon hearing Caroli's charges from Bucer, Calvin's temper flared. He called Caroli an impudent liar and blamed Farel for the whole episode because Farel had helped restore Caroli to the good graces of Bucer and Johannes Sturm after his lapse into Catholicism. An angry Calvin still refused to accept the Athanasian Creed. "I stated my resolution to die rather than subscribe [to these articles]," he exclaimed.[34]

---

34. Calvin, cited by Parker in *John Calvin,* p. 71.

Calvin's frequent explosions of temper, among other things, may have prompted his friends to suggest that he ought to get married. They reasoned that he was often lonely, ill-fed, and in need of the virtues of female companionship. Calvin was willing to go along with their plans if they could find him a "chaste, sensible, economical, patient wife [who] would look after his health."[35] Eventually Calvin found these attributes in Idelette de Bure, the widow of a former Anabaptist. She proved to be just the kind of wife he needed. His marriage to her marked the beginning of the happiest years of the Reformer's turbulent life.

Calvin's interlude in Strasbourg was a productive one. On August 1, 1539, he wrote the preface to the second edition of the *Institutes*, which was not only thoroughly revised but greatly enlarged, reflecting his growing maturity and understanding of the Scriptures and church history. Some scholars see the influence of Martin Bucer—an able biblical scholar in his own right—reflected in its pages, particularly in the doctrine of predestination. Two and a half months later Calvin wrote the dedication to his *Commentary on Romans*. Evidently he had been working on both books at the same time. He had actually begun preparing the commentary while delivering lectures on Romans in Geneva in 1536–37; the year and a half he spent in Basel and Strasbourg afforded him time to complete the work.

In the commentary Calvin was at his best. For him the Bible was God's Word to man. He recognized the historical nature of the documents that comprised Holy Scripture, and he felt that the exegete must seek to discover the plain, genuine, and literal meaning of Scripture. For Calvin the literal meaning constituted both the record and the key to the proper interpretation of God's revelation in Christ. Thus he undertook the painstaking work of translation and transcription in order to ascertain the correct text and thus hear the voice of God. Before leaving

Strasbourg Calvin was also to translate his *Institutes* into French (in 1541).

THE REFUGEE RETURNS

In March 1539 Cardinal Jacopo Sadoleto, archbishop of Carpentras, addressed a letter to the council of Geneva inviting the city to return to the mother church. He well knew that things had not gone well in Geneva since the expulsion of Calvin and his colleagues in 1538. However, he mistakenly thought that the city was ready to reject its commitment to the Reformation and return to the alleged peace and tranquility of Rome. His purpose was clear, and he stated his case well, but his judgment was flawed. No party in Geneva longed for a return to papal obedience. Even though the *Guillermins* (the followers of William [Guillaume] Farel) were winning out over the *Artichauds* (the Bernese party), the *Artichauds* had no intention of turning to Catholic France for support.

Since no minister in Geneva was capable of answering Sadoleto, the council turned to Viret, the Reformer of Lausanne, but he turned them down. In desperation the city fathers swallowed their pride and asked for help from the only man really capable of answering the cardinal archbishop on their behalf—Calvin. And answer him he did. That answer has become one of the classics of Reformation literature.

In *The Reply to Sadoleto*, Calvin followed the outline of Sadoleto's letter to the council, answering it point by point. The heart of the tract was concerned with the nature of the Catholic Church, from which Calvin claimed not to have separated, a claim he made in his dedicatory letter to Francis I in the first edition of the *Institutes*. He made the point that Rome had forsaken the Word of God and rejected the Holy Spirit and was therefore a shambles. Then he took the offensive:

> You know, Sadolet, and if you venture to deny, I will make it palpable to all that you knew, yet cunningly and craftily disguised the fact, not only that our agreement with antiquity is far closer than yours, but that all we have attempted has been to

35. Parker, *John Calvin*, pp. 71-72.

renew that ancient form of the Church, which, at first sullied and distorted by illiterate men of indifferent character, was afterwards flagitiously mangled and almost destroyed by the Roman Pontiff and his faction.[36]

Calvin proposed to compare the two forms of the church on the basis of doctrine, discipline, the sacraments, and ceremonies. On each of the points the Roman Church was weighed in the balance and found wanting. In the midst of delivering polemical barbs and a sharp critique of the medieval church, Calvin interjected a prayer in the Pauline vein, rich in autobiographical reflection, that recounted his own personal pilgrimage from Rome to Protestantism and from the attempts to find salvation through the sacraments and good works to belief in justification by faith alone. Throughout the work Calvin emphasized that meeting the ethical demands of the gospel is not a means of salvation but evidence of the new life in Christ Jesus. Rather than giving an individual license to sin, as Sadoleto had claimed, the new life in Christ manifests itself in holiness. "Wherever, therefore, that righteousness of faith which we maintain to be gratuitous, is," Calvin writes, "there too Christ is, and where Christ is, there too is the Spirit of holiness, who regenerates the soul to newness of life."[37]

Geneva was jubilant over Calvin's *Reply*. It was only a matter of time before the city council issued a new call to the deposed Reformer. The vocal opposition to him melted with the execution of one of the syndics and the accidental death of another, both of whom had belonged to the *Artichauds*. On September 21, 1540, the council made its first overtures, but Calvin rejected them. Next Farel interceded on behalf of Geneva, and once again Calvin heard the voice of God in that of William Farel. By the summer of 1541 Calvin had reached a decision. He agreed to return for a trial period of only six months—but providence was to rule otherwise.

On Tuesday, September 13, 1541, after considerable delay, Calvin and his family arrived in Geneva in a wagon that had been sent to Strasbourg to transport them. Calvin was provided with a furnished house and given a salary of five hundred florins in addition to an allotment of corn and wine. He dutifully paid his respects to the council and explained why he had delayed so long in coming. "That done, he asked that the church be set in order, and a memorandum was drawn up to this effect. And as for him, he offered himself to be always the servant of Geneva."[38]

THE YEARS OF STRUGGLE: 1541-1553

Doubtless Calvin had been planning a church order for Geneva ever since his abortive attempts to implement one during his first ministry in Geneva. By November 20 his newly proposed order, the *Ordonnances écclesiastiques* (*Ecclesiastical Ordinances*) had become law. The *Ordinances* called for a fourfold ministry to be carried out by pastors, teachers, elders, and deacons, as outlined in the *Institutes* of 1539. The plan also called for a weekly meeting of pastors and a quarterly meeting for mutual criticism; ministers were not to think of themselves as above the law. The ordinances even spelled out in detail the time and place as well as the nature of church services. Sermons were to be preached twice every Sunday at different hours in each of the three parishes. Catechetical classes were to be scheduled at noon in all three parish churches; additional sermons were to be scheduled at consecutive hours in each of the three churches on Mondays, Wednesdays, and Fridays. Provisions were made for schools, too—one school for the study of Bible and theology, and two elementary schools, one for boys and another for girls.

The new *Ordinances* also provided for a consistory to be formed in order to handle matters of discipline. In addition to the ministers of Geneva, it was to include twelve laymen: two from the Small Council, four from the Council of Sixty, and six from the Council of Two

---

36. *John Calvin: Selections from His Writings*, p. 92.
37. *John Calvin: Selections from His Writings*, p. 97.

38. Calvin, cited by Parker in *John Calvin*, p. 81.

Hundred. The president was to be the presiding syndic. Even though the consistory was a church court, its proposed organization and membership reflected how integrated church and state were in Calvin's Geneva. The consistory was to meet every Thursday to hear the cases of offenders sent to them by the Lords (*Seigneurie*). Those who listened to its admonitions were dismissed; the stubborn and unrepentant were excommunicated. But a distinction was made between a violation of church law and a violation of civil law. Offenders who violated civil law were to be turned over to the Lords (the Small Council) for punishment.

The organization of the consistory and a description of its functions reflect Calvin's training in law. Its proceedings were somewhat reminiscent of the Roman Inquisition, which is not surprising when Calvin's reasoning is taken into consideration: it was strictly medieval and Roman. In writing to Henry VIII, for example, Calvin recommended that the Anabaptists be burned as an example to other Englishmen. For, he wrote, "it is far better that two or three be burned than thousands perish in Hell."[39] For Calvin no less than for Rome, error had no rights. In Calvin's Geneva the affairs of church and state were just as enmeshed as they had been in Innocent's Holy Roman Empire of 1215. However, a number of test cases had to be faced and won before Calvin's authority became firmly established.

The first of these cases arose over Sebastian Castellio, who had studied with Calvin in Strasbourg. He had taken up the post of schoolmaster in Geneva, but the salary was insufficient for his needs. When he asked for a preaching post that would augment his meager income, it was refused him. It appears that Castellio had irritated Calvin by questioning the canonicity of the Song of Solomon. Calvin also took issue with Castellio over some passages in his French translation of the New Testament. Castellio retaliated by launching a verbal attack of his own against the chief minister of Geneva. Consequently, on Calvin's recommendation Castellio was removed from office and banished in 1544.

The second case involved Philippe de Ecclesia, a pastor in Vandoeuvres, a small village near Geneva. He was brought before the consistory for certain "absurdities" he had uttered, for which he apologized. Yet the next month he was back again, this time for slandering his colleagues. When the council attempted to resolve the problem by moving de Ecclesia to another parish, he refused to go. He was finally deposed.

The third case, that of Hieronymus Bolsec, was far more serious because it involved Calvin's doctrine of predestination, which was becoming more and more prominent in his theology. Bolsec was a former monk who held a doctor-of-theology degree from the University of Paris. Forced to leave France because of his evangelical faith, he had begun to practice medicine in Geneva, where he became the personal physician of M. de Falais, a prominent citizen. Bolsec's trouble began when he took exception to Calvin's doctrine of double predestination. He asked Calvin if God had a will other than that revealed in Scripture. He was willing to say that God had elected whom he pleased from among men, and that this election was in Jesus Christ, apart from whom no one is acceptable before God. Thus Bolsec believed that election was dependent on faith in Christ and that reprobation was the result of rejection of the gospel. This theological argument ended grimly for him: in 1551 he was arrested, imprisoned as a criminal, tried under civil law, and banished.

The "Libertines," as they were called, continually chafed under the yoke of church discipline enforced by the arm of the state. One of the most celebrated of numerous cases was that of Jacques Gruet. In a letter to the Lords of Geneva, Gruet protested what appeared to him to be the one-man rule of Geneva. In a bold challenge he called for a certain degree of freedom that had vanished. Obviously an intelligent layman, he wrote,

---

39. The reasons for Calvin's harsh attitude toward the Anabaptists are delineated by Willem Balke in *Calvin and the Anabaptist Radicals*, trans. William J. Heynen (Grand Rapids: Eerdmans, 1981), pp. 329–32.

Therefore it seems to me that a *seigneurie* (the magistracy) should establish a state in which there is no discord in making people subject to something against their nature. There is no king or government of a republic that allows a man to do what he does not wish to be done to himself. For example, one man murders another. He deserves punishment if the murder was deliberate. . . . In short, everyone who maliciously and voluntarily hurts another deserves to be punished. But suppose I am a man who wants to eat his meals as he pleases, what affair is that of others? Or if I want to dance, or have a good time, what is that to do with the Law? Nothing.[40]

After prolonged torture Gruet confessed to a number of unorthodox opinions. The court condemned him to death, and he was beheaded on July 26, 1547.

After a number of such setbacks, the Libertines were finally able to gain some ground. They even managed to achieve a majority in the Small Council, which meant that they were in a position to contest Calvin's control of Geneva. At this critical juncture, a longtime critic of Calvin, Michael Servetus, appeared on the scene. A brilliant but eccentric Spaniard, he had the poor judgment to show up in St. Peter's, Calvin's church, where he was promptly recognized.

MICHAEL SERVETUS

Even before Servetus arrived in Geneva on August 13, 1553, he was a marked man. Servetus was one of those erratic geniuses whom an age in intellectual and religious ferment appeared to set free from the shackles of tradition.

A Spaniard from Villeneuve, at one time secretary to the chaplain of Charles V, Servetus had studied law in Toulouse and medicine in Paris, but his preoccupation was theology. As early as 1531 he wrote a book entitled *Errors About the Trinity*. He soon made himself unwelcome in both Basel and Strasbourg. He was blacklisted by the Inquisition, whereupon he emerged in Paris as Michel de Villeneuve, lecturer in mathematics. While studying medicine he had dis-

---

40. Gruet, cited by Parker in *John Calvin*, p. 108.

Michael Servetus, who unsuccessfully challenged Calvin RELIGIOUS NEWS SERVICE

covered the pulmonary circulation of the blood; apparently he was the first to do so. He also wrote a book on the use of medical syrups. As a physician he had every promise of success, but he could not confine himself to the field of medicine.

His credentials and personal charm landed him the position of physician to the archbishop of Vienne in France. While in the service of the archbishop, Servetus published a second edition of Ptolemy's *Geography* in Latin (in 1541) and a new edition of Pagnini's Latin Bible (in 1542). In 1545 he made contact with Calvin through Jean Frellon, a bookseller in Lyons. He asked the bookseller to ask Calvin's opinion on three questions: "(1) Whether the crucified man Jesus was the Son of God and what was the manner or type of this Sonship? (2) Whether the kingdom of God is in men, when it begins, and when a man is regenerated? (3) Whether Baptism demands faith like the Supper, and why

Baptism was instituted in the new covenant?"[41] Calvin answered, but Servetus raised further questions. When Calvin sent a copy of his *Institutes* as a further reply, Servetus did a very tactless thing: he returned the book with his criticisms written in the margins. In this exchange the archbishop's physician displayed more arrogance than judgment. Servetus's response made Calvin's temper flare, and he wrote to Farel that if Servetus ever came to Geneva, "I will never let him depart alive, if I have any authority."[42]

In 1553 Servetus published his *Restoration of Christianity* (*Christianismi restitutio*). It was designed in part as a formal answer to Calvin's *Institutes,* an answer in which he called for a complete restoration of apostolic Christianity, including baptism. Servetus sent a copy of his latest book to Calvin, who revealed the true authorship to Guillaume de Trie, a citizen of Geneva. De Trie then sent the first page of Calvin's copy to a cousin of his, a Roman Catholic living in Vienne. (Although the book identified the author only as "MSV," Servetus's name was used in one of the dialogues. The book also included letters written to Calvin.) The upshot of it all was that Servetus was arrested and questioned about his true identity. He denied the accusations against him and disclaimed holding the heretical opinions with which he was charged. Before his true identity could be verified, he made good his escape. But Roman Catholic authorities sentenced him *in absentia* to die by burning. His books were also consigned to the flames.

Servetus's utter lack of judgment and his confidence in the rightness of his position, coupled with his serious misunderstanding of the situation in Geneva, made him unable to see the danger in a stopover in Geneva on his way to Italy. Perhaps out of curiosity, he attended St. Peter's, where Calvin was preaching. He was recognized and upon Calvin's insistence was arrested. The Libertines took advantage of the occasion, making a test case of Servetus in the hopes of embarrassing Calvin and gaining more freedom for themselves. But Servetus's views were so heretical that the Libertines soon realized that they had pinned their hopes on the wrong man. Calvin won out, and on October 27, 1553, Servetus was burned at the stake.

Servetus was put to death for his belief in two heretical doctrines: antitrinitarianism and antipedobaptism. Servetus did not deny that Christ was the Son of God, but he rejected the Athanasian formula that had dictated the Nicene Creed—a creed that Calvin himself had refused to accept when he had been confronted by Caroli and the ministers of Strasbourg a few years before. Servetus also questioned infant baptism and suggested that baptism be postponed until a believer was thirty years old. This doubtless raised the spectre of Anabaptist radicalism in Calvin's mind, although Servetus was not an Anabaptist. Before he died, Servetus asked Calvin to forgive him, and with his dying breath he prayed to the eternal Father and his Son.

As a careful reading of Willem Balke's *Calvin and the Anabaptist Radicals* will reveal, Calvin first wrote against the Anabaptists from hearsay. At the time—in 1534—he had no personal knowledge of Anabaptism, as he himself admitted: "They are said to circulate their follies in a kind of Tracts, which I have never happened to see."[43] He apparently wrote his *Psychopannychia* against the Lutherans and others who believed in "soul-sleep," but he attributed the belief to the Anabaptists in order to make the concept more abhorrent to his readers. While in Basel and Strasbourg he had adequate opportunities to learn about Anabaptist teachings firsthand, but he seems not to have bothered. His earlier impressions persisted, and with the failure of the Münster kingdom, he continually confused the Swiss Brethren, the South German Anabaptists, and the Mennonites with the Mün-

---

41. Parker, *John Calvin,* p. 118.

42. Calvin, cited by Roland Bainton in *Hunted Heretic* (Boston: Beacon Press, 1953), p. 145. For an account of the trial of Michael Servetus in Geneva, see pp. 168–201.

43. Calvin, cited by Balke in *Calvin and the Anabaptist Radicals,* p. 29.

sterites. He did, however, distinguish between
Anabaptists and Libertines, as Willem Balke indicates:

> Although Calvin frequently indicated his ability to
> distinguish sharply between the various Anabap-
> tist movements, he often in his polemic throws
> them all on one heap. Consequently it is some-
> times difficult to discern which Anabaptist or
> other radical group he had in mind when he
> referred to Fanatics. Generally he limited himself
> to his own distinction between Anabaptists and
> "*libertins spirituels.*"[44]

It is not surprising, therefore, that he identified Servetus with the despised radicals.[45] In his
attempt to exonerate Calvin, T. H. L. Parker reminds us that Servetus would have suffered the
same fate in Roman Catholic lands, which is
undoubtedly true.[46] This is an admission that
the situation for nonconformists in Calvin's Geneva was no different from what it had been
under the Roman Catholic bishops for centuries—except that during Calvin's ministry the
persecuting power of the state was dictated by
the Reformed Church of Geneva.[47] Perhaps Calvin's training in law blinded him to the possibility of religious freedom undergirded by the
separation of church and state. Roland Bainton's
assessment of Calvin's treatment of Servetus
seems well supported by the evidence:

> Nowhere does Calvin more clearly disclose him-
> self as one of the last great figures of the Middle
> Ages. To him it was all so perfectly clear that the
> majesty of God, the salvation of souls, and the
> stability of Christendom were at stake. Never for a
> moment did he suppose that he was acting simply
> on behalf of the laws of a single city. The law
> under which Servetus had first been imprisoned
> was that of the Holy Roman Empire; the law by
> which he was in the end condemned was that of
> the Codex of Justinian, which prescribes the pen-

alty of death for two ecclesiastical offenses—the
denial of the Trinity and the repetition of baptism.
Here again in variant form was a revival of the
ecclesiastical state in the sense of an entire society
operating under the law of God.[48]

With the Servetus episode the back of Calvin's opposition was finally broken. But the Libertines, unwilling to accept defeat, changed
their tactics. They attempted to arouse suspicions about Calvin's loyalty to Geneva and succeeded to some degree because he was a
Frenchman. So many French refugees were
flooding into the city that some Genevese imagined a conspiracy was afoot to turn the city over
to the French crown. This was an unlikely prospect in view of the growing persecution of Protestants in France, but apparently some of the
city's leaders actually believed such a preposter-
ous rumor. On March 16, 1555, the opponents
of Calvin lodged a sharp protest with the General Council against the fact that so many
Frenchmen were becoming citizens of Geneva.
That night a fight broke out involving Ami Perrin, Pierre Vandel, Balthasar Sept, and Froçois
Berthelier. These men were accused of foment-
ing an insurrection because Perrin reportedly
grabbed the baton (the symbol of the chief
syndic, or mayor) of the syndic Aubert. The
"insurrection" was actually little more than a
drunken brawl, but several of those involved in
the fracas were tortured and executed. Although
Perrin and Berthelier managed to escape, they
were tried *in absentia* and sentenced to death.
With this incident the Libertines were thoroughly discredited, and all organized opposition to Calvin ceased.[49]

THE YEARS OF TRIUMPH: 1555-1564

It is amazing that Calvin accomplished so much
considering the enormous difficulties he faced

---

44. Balke, *Calvin and the Anabaptist Radicals,* p. 330.

45. See Balke, *Calvin and the Anabaptist Radicals.*

46. Parker, *John Calvin,* p. 123.

47. For a delineation of Calvin's relationship to the
Anabaptists and their experiences in London, see the article
"John Calvin," in *The Mennonite Encyclopedia,* 4 vols., ed.
Harold S. Bender and C. Henry Smith (Scottdale, Pa.: Men-
nonite Publishing House, 1956-69), 1: 495-97.

48. Bainton, *Hunted Heretic,* p. 210.

49. Surely Calvin and Calvinism were not the blight on
the joy of life that Stefan Zweig insists they were; nevertheless, the indictment deserves careful scrutiny. See Stefan
Zweig, *The Right to Heresy: Castellio against Calvin,* trans.
Eden and Cedar Paul (New York: Viking Press, 1936).

and the manifold responsibilities he had. In addition to his preoccupation with discipline and his running battle with the Libertines, he continued to carry on a demanding pastoral ministry. At the same time, he maintained his enormous literary output.

The heart of his Genevan ministry, both before and after 1555, centered in his ministry from the pulpit. When he returned to Geneva in 1541, he began preaching again, continuing the exposition of Scripture that had been interrupted that fateful Easter Sunday in 1538. For Calvin, preaching was simply the exposition of Scripture. At first he preached in St. Peter's twice on Sundays and once on three other days during the week, but after a while this pattern varied. Eventually he was preaching twice on Sundays and once every day of alternate weeks. His custom was to preach from the Old Testament during the week and from the New Testament on Sundays. Sometimes he devoted Sunday afternoons to an exposition of the Psalms.

Calvin preached without notes and apparently from the Bible in the biblical languages. For all his erudition, his preaching was down-to-earth; he offered practical applications of his scriptural expositions. He repeatedly stressed what he perceived to be the two dominant themes of the Christian life, "the redemption of God in Christ and the believer's life of obedience":

> As often as we come to the sermon we are taught of the free promises of God, to show us that it is in his pure goodness and mercy that we must entirely repose, that we must not be grounded on our own merits or anything that we can bring on our side, but that God must hold out his hand to us, to commence and accomplish all. And this (as Scripture shows us) is applied to us by our Lord Jesus Christ; and that in such a way that we must seek him entirely . . . and that Jesus Christ alone must be our advocate. That, I say, is shewn us every day. It is also declared to us that God's service does not consist in imagining foolish devotions . . . and that we must serve God in obedience.[50]

One suspects that much of Calvin's preaching found its way into his numerous commentaries on books of the Bible. Beginning in 1549, a Frenchman by the name of Denis Raguenier began to take down Calvin's sermons word by word in shorthand. These sermons—which averaged six thousand words each—were subsequently transcribed, recorded, and bound in volumes.

Throughout his life Calvin kept up a lively correspondence with his friends; indeed, a biography of Calvin could well be written from his correspondence alone. Through his pen he became the spiritual counselor of the Protestant nobility and leading Reformers in half a dozen countries. It is in his letters that we get a glimpse of the more humane side of the Reformer of Geneva. True, the Calvin of the violent temper is in evidence—he took no pains to hide this part of himself, especially when he wrote to Farel, who probably received the lion's share of his letters—but there are also glimpses of a compassionate man who saw himself in quite a different light than did many of his critical contemporaries. The letters also reveal Calvin's frailty. He describes the extent and seriousness of his multitude of afflictions—tuberculosis, gout, a weak stomach, kidney stones—in rather gruesome detail.

His tenuous health made Calvin realize that his days were numbered, so in his last years he drove himself relentlessly. His day began at five or six, when, upon awakening, he would ask for his books. A secretary was then summoned to whom he would dictate his thoughts. Thus he devoted his best working hours—the mornings—to his studies. If his routine were interrupted by the responsibilities of the pulpit, he would fulfill them and promptly return to his writing, which he did lying upon his bed fully clothed.

After finishing his *Commentary on Romans* Calvin could not find time to return to Paul's letters right away, but when he did, he made impressive progress: by 1549, after only four years of work, he had written commentaries on all of the books attributed to Paul and on Hebrews as well. By 1555 he had completed com-

---

50. Calvin, cited by Parker in *John Calvin,* p. 94.

mentaries on the other books of the New Testament (though he wrote no commentary on Revelation). His Old Testament commentaries were often the verbatim record of his lectures on the Old Testament taken down by three stenographers; they compared notes and then read the record back to Calvin for his correction or alteration.

Calvin's first love, the *Institutes*, became a lifelong pursuit of excellence. By the seventh edition he had made numerous changes in the original edition, but he was still not satisfied with it. In 1558, despite severe illness, he forced himself to put everything else aside to make the final revisions of the Latin edition before his death. These he completed with the help of his brother Antoine by 1559.

Calvin's physical problems finally overcame him. Shortly before he died on May 27, 1564, he wrote Farel,

> Farewell, my most excellent and upright brother; and since it is the will of God that you should survive me in the world, live mindful of our intimacy, which, as it was useful to the church of God, so the fruits of it await us in heaven. I am unwilling that you should fatigue yourself for my sake. I draw my breath with difficulty, and every moment I am in expectation of breathing my last. It is enough that I live and die for Christ, who is to all his followers a gain both in life and death. Again I bid you and your brethren Farewell.[51]

In compliance with his request, Calvin was buried in an unmarked grave. His mantel fell on a trusted colleague, Theodore Beza (de Bèze), who was rector of the university.

CALVINISM IN FRANCE

Calvin's legacy was an expansive one that far exceeded the boundaries of Geneva. As Thomas Lindsay reminds us,

> Calvin did three things for Geneva, all of which went far beyond its walls. He gave its Church a trained and tested ministry, its homes an educated people who could give a reason for their faith,

and to the whole city an heroic soul which enabled the little town to stand forth as the Citadel and City of Refuge for the oppressed Protestants of Europe.[52]

Indeed, Geneva became a center of refuge for oppressed Protestants from many nations—including the Italians, Spanish, Flemish, Dutch, Scottish, and English—as well as numerous scholars, preachers, and students from France. In most instances the refugees returned to their native lands, carrying the principles of Calvinism with them. Thus Calvin's *Institutes* and commentaries, along with various translations of the Bible made in Geneva, found their way to the most unlikely places.

As has been noted, the year 1536 marked a new beginning for the Reformation in France. The following thirty-six years were years of growing strength for the Protestant movement despite the severe policy of repression adopted by Francis I. Among the victims of this monarch's capricious policies were the Waldenses of Durance, who according to an ancient agreement had enjoyed freedom of worship in thirty of their villages: they were almost completely exterminated. It has been estimated that as many as four thousand men and women were slaughtered and seven hundred were sent to the galleys. Their land was confiscated and parceled out to the nobility. Even Meaux, which had previously been immune to persecution because of Marguerite of Navarre, the king's sister, felt the heavy hand of oppression. In 1546 sixty-one persons were surprised at worship and arrested. Of these, fourteen were tortured, then condemned to death by burning; others—the less committed—were tortured but released after they were admonished and their books and Bibles were confiscated. By March 1547 Francis I was dead, but his legacy of persecution was kept alive by a tough corps of Catholic nobility led by the Guises. Yet despite this intermittent persecution, the Protestant movement, with help from Strasbourg and Geneva, continued to gather strength.

---

51. *John Calvin: Selections from His Writings*, p. 80.

52. Lindsay, *History of the Reformation*, 2: 131.

Calvin, a Frenchman who never forgot his roots, was the natural leader of these oppressed people. He possessed a French mentality shaped by a distinct French culture, and he had a burning desire to see France won for the Reformation. In spite of the stringent measures taken by Henry II, the successor of Francis I, to stem the swelling tide of Protestantism, the Geneva-led Reformation continued its advance in France.

By 1555 the first formally organized Reformed Churches began to appear in France. In fact, 1559—the year of Henry II's death—witnessed the formation of the first National Assembly of the Reformed Church in France. A number of churches—possibly as few as twelve or as many as sixty—represented in the assembly adopted a Calvinistic confession of faith. It is estimated that the French Protestants, now called Huguenots, numbered well over a hundred thousand. Allied with the Huguenots were some of the most influential individuals and families in France, such as Admiral Gaspard de Coligny; the Bourbons, led by Henry of Navarre; and the Chatillons, led by Cardinal Chatillon. Arrayed against them were the Guises and the Medicis, whose leading member was the queen regent, Catherine de Medici.

Thus, with the help of powerful friends and despite the opposition of the Guises, the Huguenots received legal recognition for the first time in 1562. The colloquy of Poissy led to the edict of January 17 (the Edict of Saint-Germain), which gave the Protestants the right to worship outside walled cities and allowed them to worship in private homes within walled cities and towns. Of course, these rights were highly restricted and never completely respected, but persecution did cease for about a year.[53]

Ten years later French Protestantism suffered its severest blow with the massacre of St. Bartholomew's Day. The occasion for the infamous massacre was the marriage of Catherine de Medici's daughter, Margaret of Valois, to Henry Navarre. Paris was filled with Huguenot gentlemen who had come to the capital for the auspicious occasion, certain that it meant victory for the Protestant cause. But Catherine de Medici had other thoughts. Out of her fear of a French alliance with the struggling Protestants of the Netherlands and her growing jealousy of Coligny's influence over her son, Charles IX, Catherine was persuaded by certain Roman Catholic conspirators to plan the assassination of Admiral Coligny and subsequently the extermination of the Protestant movement in France. The wedding took place on August 18, 1572. A few days later, on August 22, Coligny was shot from a house belonging to the Guises. He was only wounded, but two days later he was murdered by a band led by the duke of Guise. This slaying triggered the massacre. Few of the Huguenot gentlemen in Paris at the time escaped; at Orléans the slaughter went on for five days. It has been estimated that as many as seventy thousand Protestants perished in one fell swoop. Rome was jubilant, and a medal was struck to commemorate the event.

Eventually Henry of Navarre became Henry IV, but he was forced to become a Catholic in order to retain his throne. However, once crowned king of France, he did not forget his brethren. After a prolonged struggle he broke the power of the Catholic League. When this was an accomplished fact, he was in a position to issue the Edict of Nantes of 1598, which gave Protestants full civil rights and the protection of the crown with certain restrictions. Protestants could now enter universities and other schools as well as hospitals, and could hold public office. The Huguenots retained complete control of two hundred towns as well. That this toleration was severely limited is indicated by the following paraphrase of some of the edict's articles:

The construction of churches was permitted in the cult towns (article 16). Protestant burials were to be suitably provided for (articles 28 and 29). Protestants were expected to observe Church holidays, the degrees of consanguinity, and to pay Church dues. There was a new turn to the censorship laws, which had lost much of their impor-

---

53. For a summary of the provisions of this edict, see Sutherland, *The Huguenot Struggle for Recognition*, pp. 354–55.

tance. Protestant works might only be printed and publicly sold in the cult towns. Elsewhere religious works were subject to censorship (article 21).[54]

Despite such limitations, the Reformed Church of France at last enjoyed legal toleration. Thus, after the prolonged conflict that had thrown France into one armed conflict after another, it seemed that the sons of Rome and the sons of Calvin were prepared to accept a truce by which they could live together in peace, if not harmony. This, of course, only appeared to

be the case, as the subsequent history of the Huguenots in France was to show.[55]

By 1685, the year of the revocation of the Edict of Nantes under Louis XIV, Calvinism in its various forms had spread to most of the countries of Western Europe and to the American colonies as well. The revocation served to scatter and thus revive the influence of a most formidable expression of the Protestant faith. Thus the nation in the making—the English colonies in North America—became the greatest beneficiary of the Huguenot dispersal.

54. Sutherland, *The Huguenot Struggle for Recognition*, p. 370.

55. See Sutherland, *The Huguenot Struggle for Recognition.*

Chapter XIV

THE REFORMATION COMES TO ENGLAND

The Act of Supremacy passed by the English Parliament in 1534 separated the Church of England from Rome and made the king of England the head of the church. Thus Henry VIII (1491–1547), proclaimed "Defender of the Faith" by Pope Leo X for his polemical tract against Luther, became the defector of the faith. Some sympathetic historians have held that the Reformation in England was launched because of the amorous English monarch's desire to be free from Catherine, his aging spouse. But the truth of the matter is far more complicated than Henry's marital problems. While there is no denying that Henry VIII became infatuated with Anne Boleyn, a spirited young lady who wanted very much to be Henry's wife and England's queen, it is inaccurate to claim that Henry's adulterous affair caused a reformation of the English church. Such an observation is superficial if not malicious. If it hadn't been for extenuating circumstances and the support of loyal and capable men such as Thomas Cromwell and Thomas Cranmer, Henry's divorce from Catherine could have provoked a civil war, not a reformation. In the final analysis it produced not the English Reformation but only an opportunity for reform. The shape of the Reformation in England, therefore, was largely the result of a set of circumstances that had come to prevail in the island kingdom.

REFORMATION BEFORE 1534

Lollardy, the movement that owed its origin to the work of John Wycliffe, had not completely died out when the Reformation began to take root in English soil. Two distinctive emphases seem to have been basic to the movement from its inception: the authority of Scripture and the priority of preaching. These emphases were also dear to the Reformers; in fact, as A. G. Dickens suggests, "Perhaps the only major doctrine of the sixteenth century Reformers which Wycliffe cannot be said to have anticipated was that of Justification by Faith Alone."[1] The Lollards had much in common with other medieval anticlerical parties. They sowed the seeds of distrust and skepticism that were largely responsible for the anticlericalism of the fifteenth century. They often expressed their ideas crudely, but their meaning was unmistakable. Their list of griev-

---

1. Dickens, *The English Reformation* (New York: Schocken Books, 1964), p. 23.

249

ances included the ringing of church bells, relic worship, the use of images in worship, transubstantiation, purgatory, pilgrimages, indulgences (which they viewed as "payment for the forgiveness of sins"),[2] and the papacy itself.

Despite the heavy hand of persecution, the Lollards persisted. Their endurance was no doubt due in part to the fact that they possessed English translations of the Scriptures which were circulated in manuscript form. The opening decades of the sixteenth century witnessed the arrest and imprisonment of hundreds of Lollards. Most of them recanted; some were burned. But neither the recantations nor the executions succeeded in stamping out the movement. Apparently Lollardy did begin to fade as Luther's teachings found adherents throughout the country. But by that time the movement had done its work of preparation among the common people, who now began to embrace the more evangelical concepts of the Saxon Reformer.

RENAISSANCE HUMANISM

What Lollardy was doing for the disinherited masses, the Renaissance was doing for the educated. Even though Wycliffe was not unknown or unread in these circles, the urge to reform the church was also coming from other sources. The rediscovery of Greek and the appearance of Erasmus's Greek New Testament in 1516, as well as his and other calls for reform, were awakening the consciences of Cambridge and Oxford dons and students. Even Sir Thomas More, who refused to leave the Church of Rome, wrote in 1520 that if Pope Leo X should withdraw his approval of Erasmus's Greek New Testament, Luther's attacks on the papacy would be an act of piety compared to such a deed. William Tyndale, a student of Dean John Colet and a disciple of Erasmus, came out of humanist circles to produce the first translation of the New Testament printed in English.

---

2. This was a common understanding among the common people, as abundant evidence indicates.

By 1520 humanists at both Cambridge and Oxford were avidly reading Luther's works in clandestine meetings. In fact, Thomas Lindsay writes that most of the canons of Cardinal College, Cardinal Wolsey's new college, were suspected of having Lutheran sympathies. The White Horse Inn at Cambridge, dubbed "Little Germany" by the local clientele, became the favorite meeting place of Luther's English disciples, who by the same token were called "the Germans."

WILLIAM TYNDALE

Undoubtedly the most significant convert in the initial stages of the English Reformation was William Tyndale (ca. 1494-1536), a humanist turned Reformer. Tyndale was born in Gloucestershire in about 1494. A precocious youth, he had earned his bachelor-of-arts degree at Oxford by 1512 and his master's degree by 1515. Apparently, after a year of lecturing at Oxford, he went to Cambridge, which was more receptive to "the new church teaching" than was Oxford. Here Tyndale began to study Greek, and he soon showed promise as a gifted linguist.

In 1522, while the echoes of the Diet of Worms were still reverberating in Europe's halls of learning, Tyndale was charged with heresy but was acquitted. At some point during the course of his studies, he decided on his lifework: to translate Erasmus's Greek New Testament into English, just as Luther had translated it into German. After a fruitless attempt to undertake his work in England, Tyndale left for the Continent, convinced that he could never accomplish the task in his native land.

When he arrived in Germany, Tyndale and William Roye, his secretary and fellow Englishman, decided to visit Wittenberg to compare notes with Luther and Melanchthon. After spending about a year in Wittenberg, he and Roye moved to Cologne, where he intended to have his New Testament printed. However, the work had hardly begun in Peter Quentel's printshop when the project was accidentally discovered by Cochlaeus (John Dobneck), who reported it to the city council. The council ordered the printing stopped, and Tyndale fled. He next settled in Worms, a city far more congenial to his purposes. Here, by February 1526, he saw the first copies of his English New Testament through Peter Schoeffer's press. Within a few months six thousand bound copies in octavo were circulating in England.

Without the help of merchants dedicated to the cause, Tyndale's work would have been impossible. When other sources of income failed, Humphrey Monmouth, an English merchant, underwrote the entire enterprise; he also organized the means of distribution with the help of his colleagues. Producing and distributing the New Testament in English was still an illegal undertaking. The risks were high, and the opposition was formidable. Two of Tyndale's most relentless opponents were Bishop Cuthbert Tunstall and Sir Thomas More. In 1529 More wrote a *Dialogue* against Tyndale's New Testament (a criticism that Tyndale effectively answered in 1531). And in 1526 Tunstall bought up all available copies of Tyndale's New Testament for a Bible-burning spree at St. Paul's Cross.

Bishop Tunstall's desire to rid England of Tyndale's New Testament made it possible for Tyndale to bring out an improved version of it. An account of this interesting development is given in the *Chronicle* of Edward Halle. The bishop enlisted Augustine Packington to buy up copies of the work, no matter what the cost. Packington promptly went to Tyndale and made him an offer for his "heap of New Testaments":

"Who is the merchant?" said Tyndale. "The bishop of London," said Packington. "Oh, that is because he will burn them," said Tyndale. "Yea marry," quoth Packington. "I am the gladder," said Tyndale; "for these two benefits shall come thereof: I shall get money [from] him for these books, to bring myself out of debt, and the whole world shall cry out upon the burning of God's word. And the overplus of the money, that shall remain to me, shall make me more studious to correct the said New Testament, and so newly to imprint the same once again; and I trust the second will much better like you than ever did the first." And so forward went the bargain: the bishop had the

books, Packington had the thanks, and Tyndale had the money.[3]

But neither Tyndale nor the bishop counted on unauthorized editions. Copies of one such pirated reprint edition, produced in Antwerp, were selling in England by November 1526.

Perhaps the appearance of his New Testament in Antwerp caused Tyndale to move to that city. Both his polemical tracts, *The Parable of the Wicked Mamon* and *The Obedience of a Christian Man,* were published in Antwerp in 1528 by Jon Hoochstraten (Tyndale used the pseudonym Hans Lufft). Antwerp was an ideal city for Tyndale's purpose. It was the most important commercial center of Northern Europe. Well-known for its banking and shipping industries, it enjoyed the status of a free city, which made it almost immune from harrassment by heresy hunters. But an occasional flare-up of orthodox zeal would compel the Protestants to go easy every so often, and the year 1529 was such a time. Thus Tyndale thought it expedient to begin his translation of the Old Testament elsewhere. After considerable difficulty he finally reached Hamburg, where he and Miles Coverdale succeeded in translating the Pentateuch from the Hebrew into English. Since, by the time they were finished, the situation in Antwerp had improved considerably, the translators moved back to Antwerp, where Hoochstraten brought out the first five books of the Old Testament in five separate volumes. The work was completed by January 1530 and began circulating in England.

In 1530 Hoochstraten brought out another of Tyndale's polemical pamphlets, *The Practice of Prelates.* Unfortunately for Tyndale, he was now opposing the king's proposed divorce from Catherine in print. He took the position that the marriage of Catherine and Henry was valid and that divorce would invite a possible invasion or civil war. This work was immediately placed on a list of forbidden books in England. In spite of this work and his running paper battle with

3. Halle, cited by F. F. Bruce in *History of the Bible in English* (New York: Oxford University Press, 1978), p. 38.

The Gospell off S. Luke.

Or as moche as many have taken in hond to compyle a treates off thoo thyngs / which are surely knowen amonge vs / even as they declared them vnto vs / which from the begynynge sawe them with their eyes / and were misters at the doyng: J determined also / as sone as J had searched out diligently all things from the begynynge / that then J wolde wryte vnto the / goode Theophilus / that thou myghtest knowe the certente off thoo things / whereof thou arte informed.

The Fyrst. Chapter.

In the tyme of Herode kynge of iewry / there was a certayne prest named Zacarias / off the course of Abie. And his wyfe was of the doughters of Aaron: And her name was Elizabeth. Booth were perfect before god / and walked in all the lawes and ordinacions of the lorde that no man coulde fynde fawte with them. And they had no childe / because that Elisabeth was barren / And booth were wele stricken in age.

Hit cam to passe / as he executed the prestes office / before god as his course cam (accordinge to the custome of the prestes office) his lott was to bren odours / And went into the tempte of the

Thomas More, Cromwell longed to see Tyndale return to England under safe conduct and with a royal pardon. Stephen Vaughan was sent to Antwerp with the invitation and necessary guarantees of safe conduct. However, Vaughan could not promise the king would meet the one condition Tyndale laid down—namely, that the king permit "a bare text of the scripture to be put forth among his people." Thus the negotiations came to naught, and Tyndale turned once again to his first love: the translation of the New Testament into English.

Tyndale's completely revised edition of his New Testament came out in 1534. In this revision he had the help of Coverdale and John Rogers. Of the 1534 edition, F. F. Bruce writes, "It is not a superficial revision; the whole work has been gone over in scrupulous detail, and nearly always the changes are for the better, reflecting mature judgment and feeling."[4]

The following year Tyndale revised his New Testament once again, this time making only a few minor changes. He also translated the Old Testament books from Joshua to II Chronicles, which he never lived to see in print. His work was cut short by his arrest and imprisonment, a prelude to his execution. During much of his time in Antwerp, Tyndale lived in the home of an English merchant, Thomas Poyntz. He remained undisturbed until he was betrayed by a young Englishman named Henry Phillips, whom he had befriended and to whom he had disclosed the nature of his work. This led to his imprisonment in the Castle of Vilvorde near Brussels on May 21, 1535. In the fall of that year he wrote to the authorities, who had confiscated his possessions, in the hope of securing some relief from his suffering. His letter reveals not only the nature of his suffering but also his spirit:

> I believe, right worshipful, that you are not unaware of what may have been determined concerning me. Wherefore I beg your lordship, and that by the Lord Jesus, that if I am to remain here through the winter, you will request the commis-

sary to have the kindness to send me, from the goods of mine which he has, a warmer cap, for I suffer greatly from cold in the head, and am afflicted by a perpetual catarrh, which is much increased in this cell; a warmer coat also, for this which I have is very thin; a piece of cloth too to patch my leggings. My overcoat is worn out; my shirts are also worn out. He has a woollen shirt, if he will be good enough to send it. I have also with him leggings of thicker cloth to put on above; he has also warmer night caps. And I ask to be allowed to have a lamp in the evening; it is indeed wearisome sitting alone in the dark. But most of all I beg and beseech your clemency to be urgent with the commissary, that he will kindly permit me to have the Hebrew Bible, Hebrew grammar, and Hebrew dictionary, that I may pass the time in that study. In return may you obtain what you most desire, provided that it be consistent with the salvation of your soul. But if any other decision has been taken concerning me, to be carried out before winter, I will be patient, abiding the will of God, to the glory of the grace of my Lord Jesus Christ, whose Spirit (I pray) may ever direct your heart. Amen. W. Tindalus[5]

Tyndale's imprisonment lasted some sixteen months, during which time he was interrogated by doctors of divinity from the University of Louvain, tried, condemned, degraded by the Roman Church, and executed. He wrote out the answers to the questions addressed to him by his accusers, but these answers, including a work on justification, have been lost or, more probably, destroyed.

John Foxe in his *Book of Martyrs* gives an account of Tyndale's execution:

> At last after much reasoning, although he deserved no death, he was condemned by virtue of the emperor's decree, made in the assembly at Augsburgh, he was there brought forth to the place of execution; he was there tied to the stake, and then strangled by the hangman, and afterward consumed with fire in the town of Vilvorden, A.D. 1536; crying thus at the stake with a fervent zeal

---

4. Bruce, *History of the Bible in English*, p. 44.

5. Tyndale, cited by Bruce in *History of the Bible in English*, p. 52. For a fuller discussion of the letter, see J. F. Mozley, *William Tyndale* (New York: Macmillan, 1937), pp. 334-35.

and a loud voice, "Lord! open the King of England's eyes."[6]

Tyndale was cut down before he could complete the translation of the Old Testament, leaving the task for others to finish. But what he was able to accomplish has withstood the test of the centuries. Perhaps it is not too much to say that all English versions of the Bible reflect his influence to some degree—particularly the King James Version. (Mozley claims that ninety percent of Tyndale's work remains unaltered in the King James Version!)[7] Through his work as a Bible translator, Tyndale helped to shape the modern English language. But he was far more than a superb grammarian and a skilled linguist: he was above all else a man absolutely dedicated to the cause of reform, and his New Testament did more to bring the Reformation to England than anything else he did. A. G. Dickens puts Tyndale's work in perspective when he writes,

> Our own age can only by an effort of imagination grasp the full impact of the vernacular Bible upon a generation more ardent and narrow in its Christianity than our own, yet from which the private study of the Scriptures had been so rigorously withheld. It is hard indeed to recapture that blissful sense of release and new awakening. But it was a dawn made doubly poignant by tempest and sudden death.[8]

A FLICKERING FLAME

Tyndale's New Testament of 1526 was the spark that ignited a flame, although it was a flame that flickered with uncertain promise. A number of Englishmen attempted to fan the flame into fire with varying degrees of success. One of these was Simon Fish, an Oxford student who in 1525

transferred to Gray's Inn, the famous law school and alma mater of Thomas Cromwell. Soon afterwards, to escape Cardinal Wolsey's anger, he fled to the Netherlands, where he wrote a virulent anticlerical pamphlet, *A Supplication for the Beggars,* which was probably published in 1529. In this tract he articulated the grievances of many an Englishman against the clergy. Written in a popular style, it found a receptive audience that included Anne Boleyn, who brought the pamphlet to the attention of the king. Henry saw immediately that it could be used to serve his cause admirably, and he offered the author his protection. Among the other Protestant pamphleteers of the time were John Frith; George Joye, whom Tyndale criticized for altering his translation; and William Barlow, who wrote *A Dyaloge Describing the Orygynall Ground of These Lutheran Faceyons* (1531).[9] John Bale, later in exile on the Continent, and Henry Hart, more prominent during Edward's reign, also belong on this list. Altogether about forty Protestant books and tracts were published in England before 1534; perhaps half that many martyrs had died by that time, ten of them Dutch Anabaptists. Of the ten who were English, five were probably friends of Tyndale, including John Frith, who was burned at Smithfield in 1533. When William Poyntz, one of Cromwell's agents at Antwerp, tried to save Tyndale from execution, the Flemish reminded him that "there were those of their countrymen who were burned in England not long before."[10]

Thus the Reformation, still only a smoldering fire before the king of England separated the Church of England from Rome, soon burst into open flame. And with the king's authorization of the first legal English Bible, Tyndale's dying prayer was answered.

"THE KING'S GREAT MATTER"

The king's great matter was, of course, his interest in securing a divorce from Catherine of Ara-

---

6. *Foxe's Book of Martyrs: Acts and Monuments of the Christian Church,* ed. A. Clark (New York: London Printing and Publishing Co., n.d.), p. 233. As Foxe adds, Tyndale's prayer was answered. In 1538 the king issued a royal injunction making the Bible available in every parish church in England. The first translation of the entire Bible into English, the work of Miles Coverdale, was published in 1535.

7. Mozley, *William Tyndale,* p. 108.

8. Dickens, *The English Reformation,* p. 72.

9. See *the Reformation in England: To the Accession of Elizabeth I,* ed. A. G. Dickens and Dorothy Carr, Documents of Modern History Series (London: Edward Arnold, 1967), pp. 16-19.

10. Mozley, *William Tyndale,* pp. 252-53.

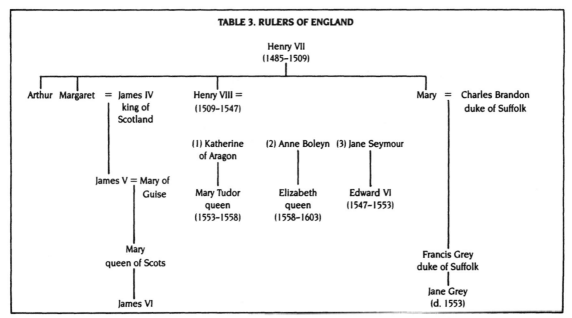

TABLE 3. RULERS OF ENGLAND

Henry VII (1485–1509); children: Arthur; Margaret = James IV king of Scotland; Henry VIII (1509–1547); Mary = Charles Brandon duke of Suffolk.

James IV and Margaret → James V = Mary of Guise → Mary queen of Scots → James VI.

Henry VIII married (1) Katherine of Aragon → Mary Tudor queen (1553–1558); (2) Anne Boleyn → Elizabeth queen (1558–1603); (3) Jane Seymour → Edward VI (1547–1553).

Mary and Charles Brandon → Francis Grey duke of Suffolk → Jane Grey (d. 1553).

gon so that he might marry Anne Boleyn and assure England of a male heir to the throne. Catherine had failed to give birth to a son, and since Henry had been able to father an illegitimate son, he reasoned that the fault was obviously Catherine's. He had apparently convinced himself that their son-less state was evidence that God was displeased with their union. Thus, after seventeen years of marriage, Henry informed his spouse that they had never been married in the eyes of God and were therefore not man and wife.

The basis for Henry's misgivings was real enough. Catherine was first married to Henry's older brother, Arthur, who died about five months later. Since neither Ferdinand nor Henry VII wished to lose the benefits of the marital ties thus provided, the monarchs of the two countries sought a special dispensation from Pope Julius II for Catherine to marry Henry. This was clearly against canon law based upon Leviticus 20:21 ("If a man takes his brother's wife, it is impurity; he has uncovered his brother's nakedness. They shall be childless"). But the pope was not one to let canon law stand in his way if by disregarding it he could ingratiate himself with two of the most powerful kings of Europe. Thus the necessary adjust-

ments were made, and Henry and Catherine dutifully married in 1509. Of the eight children Catherine bore during this marriage, only one survived, a girl whom Henry named Mary. England had never had a female monarch, and the idea was unthinkable to Henry. He was becoming desperate for a male heir to the English throne.

When confronted with Henry's request for an annulment of his marriage to Catherine, Clement VII found himself in a difficult position. He wanted to please Henry, but Charles V, Catherine's nephew and the master of Italy, was determined to support the cause of his beleaguered aunt. Since the pope could ill-afford to alienate Charles, he suggested alternatives to Henry. He told the king that he could take another wife without bothering to put away Catherine, or that he could declare his illegitimate son legitimate and thus the heir to the throne (although this option disappeared when the boy died). Cardinal Wolsey (ca. 1475–1530), the king's chancellor, didn't think that the divorce presented a great problem for Rome because similar cases had not created insurmountable difficulties before. But Wolsey had misread the Italian situation, and his failure spelled his downfall. In October 1529 he was indicted for violation of the statutes of praemunire because he had appealed to a foreign power, the pope. Stripped of his office as lord chancellor, Wolsey was succeeded by a man more set against the divorce than he: Sir Thomas More (1478–1535). But the king excused More from the case. Thus it was not More but two able although virtually unknown men who were to lead Henry and England to a final resolution of "the king's great matter." They were Thomas Cromwell, secretary to Wolsey, and Thomas Cranmer, a Cambridge professor.

Thomas Cranmer (1489–1556) came to the king's attention when he suggested that the solution to the king's problem might be found in the opinion of the great lawyer-teachers of the universities of Europe. They could examine Scripture to determine whether the papal dispensation granted by Julius II was valid; if they decided it was not, the pope's decision could be overturned. Henry responded enthusiastically—"Marry! I trow he has got the right sow by the ear!"—and Cranmer's scheme was followed. Although they did not deliver a unanimous opinion, the university faculties canvassed were overwhelmingly in favor of the divorce. It is not surprising that when Archbishop Warham died, Cranmer succeeded him and was consecrated archbishop of Canterbury on March 30, 1533.

A few days later the new archbishop presided over an ecclesiastical court that determined that Arthur and Catherine had consummated their marriage and that therefore the marriage of Catherine to Henry was invalid. The court further decided that the marriage between Henry and Anne Boleyn was valid. Anne was crowned queen on June 1, 1533. At last "the king's great matter" was satisfactorily resolved—at least in the eyes of the king and most of his loyal subjects.

THE REFORMATION, 1534-1547

Thomas Cromwell, a lawyer in the service of Thomas Wolsey, survived the fall of the cardinal to become Henry's chief minister and the architect of the Henrician statutes. By 1531 he had become a member of the King's Council and by 1533 the chief minister. The times demanded a man of Cromwell's genius, and he met the challenge. He possessed a rapier-like mind and the shrewdness of a veteran politician. An Erasmian and exponent of the teachings of Marsiglio of Padua, he was an ardent advocate of the king's supremacy over church as well as state. He made this clear in a critical piece of legislation he produced in 1533, the Act of Restraint in Appeals, in which England was referred to as an empire and Henry as the king "who owed no submission to any other human ruler."[11]

Not surprisingly, it was also Thomas Cromwell who set in motion the legal steps that separated the Church of England from Rome. In response to the pope's orders for Henry to undo what he had done upon threat of excommunication, a series of acts were passed by Parliament in 1534 under Cromwell's guidance that brought about complete separation. The most important of these was the Act of Supremacy, which declared that "the King is rightfully the Supreme Head of the Church of England, has been recognized as such by Convocation [the assembly of bishops and priests], and that it is within his powers to make ecclesiastical visitations and to redress ecclesiastical abuses."[12]

The Nature of the Establishment

Since after 1534 the king of England was the only head of the church in England, all ecclesiastical quarrels had to be settled in England; there could no longer be any appeals to Rome. To facilitate such matters, in January 1535 Henry appointed Thomas Cromwell his vicegerent and special commisary and in so doing gave Cromwell unlimited freedom to represent the king in all legal matters pertaining to the church. Apparently the only major difference in the Church of England before and after the Act of Supremacy was the locus of ultimate ecclesiastical authority.

---

11. Dickens, *The English Reformation*, p. 117.
12. Thomas Lindsay, *A History of the Reformation*, 2 vols. (New York: Scribner's, 1907, 1928), 2: 331.

However, other more profound differences were on the way, for the Reformation had already begun to make its impact in England and could not be ignored.

The Ten Articles

The attempt to draw up some basic theological guidelines for the new Church of England proved to be more difficult than it first appeared. While Cranmer, Cromwell, and Bishop Latimer harbored Lutheran sympathies, the older bishops were thoroughly Roman. The king, who was now taking his new responsibilities seriously, "was constrained to put his own pen to the book, and conceive certain articles which were agreed upon by Convocation as catholic and meet to be set forth by authority."[13] (No doubt he received substantial help from Cranmer.) Known as the Ten Articles, they were published in 1536. The Ten Articles were divided equally between doctrine and ceremonies. The Bible, the historic creeds (the Apostles' Creed, the Nicene Creed, and the Athanasian Creed), and the doctrinal decisions of the first four ecumenical councils were held to provide the indispensable foundation of faith. Infant baptism was declared necessary for salvation because newborns who died "shall undoubtedly be saved thereby, and *else not*." The sacrament of penance was retained. The "substantial, real, corporeal Presence of Christ's Body and Blood under the form of Bread and Wine in the Eucharist" was taught.[14] Faith and charity were held to be necessary for salvation. While images did not need to be destroyed, all offerings to them and worshiping and burning of incense before them was forbidden. The Virgin Mary and the saints were presented as intercessors. Prayers for the dead and belief in purgatory were both taught, but the articles maintained that it was vain superstition to believe any saint to be more merciful than Christ himself.

The Injunctions

Even though much of Roman Catholicism remained in these articles, progress was made toward the teaching of the Reformation. For example, although the "real presence" was taught, the doctrine of transubstantiation was not advocated, and four of the seven sacraments were not mentioned. The Injunctions of 1536 and 1538 were designed to interpret the articles in a "Protestant" sense.

Between the Injunctions of 1536 and 1538 there appeared the *Institution of the Christian Man,* which was designed to instruct the lower clergy and the common people regarding the changes made in the Church of England. Since the book was largely the product of a committee of bishops working under the king's command, it became popularly known as the Bishop's Book. It was published in July of 1537, shortly after the suppression of a series of rebellions against the policies of the king, including an ill-fated Roman Catholic uprising in the diocese of York known as the "Pilgrimage of Grace." The tenor of this book was decidedly more traditional than that of the Ten Articles or the Injunctions. Contrary to the Ten Articles, for example, it recognized all seven of the sacraments as valid (although three—baptism, penance, and the mass—were considered more significant than the others). This may have represented an attempt to placate the Roman Catholic North, from which the more severe of the anarchist movements had arisen. The Bishop's Book was to undergo further revision five years later, which made it even more compatible with medieval Roman Catholic teachings; in this form it included the advocacy of transubstantiation. This version was called the King's Book, and as A. G. Dickens so aptly remarks, "Though no doubt owing some of its literary merit to Thomas Cranmer, it might also be described as a monument to the defeat of the Archbishop in committee."[15] Apparently Cranmer, even though

---

13. Henry VIII, cited by Lindsay in *A History of the Reformation,* 2: 333.

14. Cited by Lindsay in *A History of the Reformation,* 2: 333.

15. Dickens, *The English Reformation,* p. 185.

the archbishop of Canterbury, was unable to overcome the persistent Roman Catholic position of the majority of the committee charged with the responsibility of revision.

The Injunction of 1538 called for Bibles to be made available to the people in every parish church: "one book of the whole Bible *of the largest volume,* in English, and the same set up in some convenient place within the said church that you have cure of, where your parishioners may most commodiously resort to the same, and read it. . . . " The clergy were warned not to discourage any person from reading or hearing the Bible read but rather to encourage its use, "for it is the lively word of God that every Christian man is bound to embrace, believe, and follow. . . . "[16] Thus Henry authorized Cranmer to employ a group of scholars to produce such a Bible under his direction.

A few years earlier, in October 1535, Miles Coverdale (1488–1569) had succeeded in publishing, with the backing of Cromwell, the first complete Bible in English. Although it was translated from German and Latin, not from the biblical languages, it read well. Coverdale had a way with words, and he, like Tyndale, was unusually sensitive to cadence and idiomatic usage. He also prefaced the edition with a flattering dedication to the king. Cromwell called the new Bible to Henry's attention; Henry liked it and provided the necessary license for its circulation. (Coverdale also edited the Great Bible of 1539 and contributed to the Geneva Bible of 1560. Although Coverdale was by no means the scholar that Tyndale was, Coverdale's work became a means by which Tyndale's work was preserved and utilized. The contribution of both men became foundational for the English Reformation.)

Thus, even before the Injunction of 1538 appeared, two different versions of the English Bible were in circulation: Coverdale's Bible in two editions and the new version known as Matthew's Bible. Matthew's Bible was edited by

John Rogers (ca. 1500–1555), who used the pen name of Thomas Matthew. He had previously worked with Tyndale. (Like his mentor, he died a martyr to his faith, one of the first to be burned at the stake during Mary's reign.) Cranmer much preferred Matthew's Bible, a copy of which he sent to Cromwell. The result was that this Bible as well as the two editions of Coverdale's Bible was licensed by the king.

Matthew's Bible was essentially Tyndale's work insofar as Tyndale had been able to complete it. Rogers also leaned heavily upon Coverdale's work and borrowed freely from Jacques Lefèvre's French Bible of 1534 and Pierre Olivétan's Bible of 1535. The significance of Roger's work lies in the fact that William Tyndale had been dead less than three years when his translation was being read in England, and that with the king's permission. Thus, while the Church of England reflected its Roman Catholic heritage in much of its liturgy and its teachings, the Bible and Reformational ideas from the Continent were beginning to penetrate its structure. But a reaction was not long in coming, and it was sparked by the king himself.

The King Reverses His Decision

After careful scrutiny Matthew's Bible was discovered to be too true to the biblical languages for the Tudor government—hence it was altered in 1538–39. The revised edition became known as the Great Bible. This was the version that finally made it to the lecterns of the churches for the Sunday morning Scripture lessons. In England even the Bible had to conform to the royal will.

With the death of Catherine on January 7, 1537, Henry began to breathe somewhat easier; now he no longer feared an invasion by Charles V. In the light of these circumstances the alliance with Saxony and the Lutherans did not appear nearly so advantageous as it once had. There is little doubt that Cromwell and Cranmer were always much more interested in pursuing such a policy than was Henry.

But Henry did find it to his advantage to act like a Protestant in the dissolution of the mon-

---

16. Cited in *Documents of the Christian Church,* 2nd ed., ed. Henry Bettenson (Oxford: Oxford University Press, 1982), pp. 231–32.

asteries. They were depositories of considerable wealth and, according to their enemies, cesspools of iniquity. After a visitation that revealed the widespread spiritual decadence of English monastic life, Parliament passed an act (in 1536) for the dissolution of the lesser monasteries.[17] A second visitation was followed by another act of Parliament that turned over all monastic property to the crown. Thus the king was able to replenish his depleted treasury and at the same time rid England of what many considered its ecclesiastical parasites. On this point Cranmer and the king had a difference of opinion. Cranmer wanted to use the proceeds for benevolent causes, but Henry and the nobles were determined to fill the royal coffers. Cranmer, however, was shrewd enough not to push his cause too far, and Henry had his way.

The Six Articles

At the same time that Henry was confiscating the property of the monasteries, he urged Parliament—against Cranmer's strenuous resistance—to pass the Six Articles' Act of 1539, which made obedience to the Six Articles, popularly referred to as "the Six Bloody Articles," the law of the land. The death penalty was prescribed for those who denied certain Roman Catholic teachings such as transubstantiation and celibacy for priests, monks, and nuns. Further, all clerical marriages were to be dissolved. (Thus Archbishop Cranmer, it was rumored, "carried his wife around in a box" until he sent her back to Germany for safekeeping.[18]) The Six Articles were not strictly enforced during Cromwell's lifetime because he was utterly against their provisions. But Cromwell's influence with the king was on the decline. Powerful enemies—Bishops Stephen Gardiner and Edmund Bonner, Roman Catholics at heart, had sown the

seeds of suspicion that led Henry to believe that he was not master in his own house. The immediate occasion that spelled the end for Henry's most trusted advisor and ablest chancellor was Cromwell's plan for Henry to marry Anne of Cleves, a German Protestant and sister-in-law of the elector of Saxony. The marriage took place on January 6, 1540, but it was a disaster, and Cromwell bore the brunt of Henry's disillusionment. He was summarily impeached and condemned without a trial. On July 28, 1540, the most powerful man in England next to the king—who claimed shortly before his death that he had never had any desire other than to faithfully serve his king—was executed.

Cromwell has often been depicted as a hard, even cruel man, but this was hardly the case. He was a realist, but he was not without feelings or principles. The reforms of church and state that took place during Henry's reign would have been impossible without him. If not a convinced Protestant himself, he revealed a certain sympathy for Protestant concepts. He used Parliament to accomplish his purposes and would doubtless have done much more if the king's unpredictable temper had not ended his career. G. R. Elton describes his capabilities in this way:

> Among the facts of social life in the 1530's was the demand for a moral rule which only the institutions of the Church could supply; and among the facts of political life were the services of Church lawyers, the power of bishops, and especially the convictions of the King. By his endeavours to turn the Church towards its tasks of preaching and moral suasion, Cromwell showed the essentially radical cast of his thinking; by his failure to put an axe to the root of the ecclesiastical organization and by his creation of the vicegerency, he showed his understanding of the practical possibilities.[19]

Shortly after the death of his chief minister, Henry moved to dramatize his ecclesiastical policy by approving the execution of three Protestants and three Roman Catholics. The Protestants—Robert Barnes, Thomas Garret, and William Jerome—were burned at the stake, and

---

17. Wolsey had initiated the suppression of twenty-nine monasteries in order to found colleges at Oxford and Ipswich. See Dickens, *English Reformation,* p. 111.

18. On a trip to the Continent, Cranmer had married a niece of Andreas Osiander, a Lutheran Reformer and professor at the University of Königsburg.

19. Elton, *Reform and Renewal* (Cambridge: Cambridge University Press, 1973), p. 161.

the Catholics were beheaded. That Cranmer escaped both the fall of Cromwell and the intrigues of his enemies who also accused him of heresy indicates both the special place the archbishop held in Henry's esteem and the fact that Cranmer was both shrewd and flexible.

The king—who, it is said, "never spared a man in his wrath or a woman in his lust"—died on January 28, 1547.[20] Though Henry died on a Friday, his death was concealed from the public until Monday. Less than a month before his death, Henry had nominated a council of regents to advise his young son Edward in ruling England. (Edward was Henry's son by his third wife, Jane Seymour.) The council was comprised of sixteen members, most of whom had Protestant leanings. Bishop Gardiner, who could have tipped the scales in the other direction, was left out. Thus Henry seems to have abandoned the *via media* at the very end of his rule.

When Henry died it was not clear what direction the Church of England would take. Cranmer, who had managed to weather many a storm that had proved disastrous to others, held the key to the future. But where did Cranmer stand? He had participated in the production of the King's Book of 1543, which affirmed transubstantiation, the offering of prayers for the dead, and the celibacy of the clergy. It also taught salvation by works, and rejected the Protestant teachings on the sacraments and justification by faith. As later developments clearly indicated, the King's Book surely did not reflect the archbishop's true position, but at the time this fact was not readily apparent.

EDWARD VI, 1547-1553

As it turned out, the council of regents that took over the reins of government was weighted in favor of the Reformation. Shortly after Edward's coronation, the new council moved swiftly to

compel all the bishops of the realm to take out new commissions in the name of the nine-year-old king. The Lord Chancellor Wriothesley, who under Henry had opposed further reforms, was forced to resign. Edward Seymour, earl of Hertford, a convinced Calvinist, was declared protector. It was soon clear that the Church of England would either voluntarily move toward or be pushed toward a more Protestant pattern of faith and order.

This Protestant emphasis was evident in the new series of injunctions published in July 1547, which were designed to encourage the reading of the Scriptures in English and further stifle Roman Catholic practices. A royal visitation also began in 1547 to determine the biblical knowledge of the clergy and the measure of their commitment to the Reformation. During Bishop Hooper's visitation of his diocese of Gloucester in 1551, 311 clergymen were examined. Of these, 168 were unable to repeat the Ten Commandments. Ten couldn't repeat the Lord's Prayer, thirty-four couldn't name its author, and thirty-nine couldn't tell where it was found. If this examination rendered a fair sample of the biblical literacy of the English clergy two years before the end of Edward's brief reign, the Church of England was far from being either informed or reformed.

However, Parliament did make some sweeping changes during Edward's reign. The first Parliament revoked the Act of the Six Articles and all acts concerning heresy that had been passed since the days of Richard II. Convocation also inaugurated significant changes: it ruled that participants in the Lord's Supper were to receive both bread and wine, and it declared null and void all ecclesiastical laws against married clergy. Parliament promptly passed acts approving the changes.

In 1549 the *Book of the Common Praier*, called *The First Prayer Book of King Edward VI*, was brought out in order to assure uniformity of worship throughout the Church of England. In the course of debate in the House of Lords, Cranmer admitted that he no longer held to transubstantiation, although the prayer book did not reflect this viewpoint. To the more ardent

---

20. This description may have come from Luther's vitriolic outburst against the king after he attacked Luther's teachings. See A. H. Newman, *A Manual of Church History*, 2 vols. (Philadelphia: American Baptist Publication Society, 1931), 2: 66-67.

Protestants the book appeared far more Catholic than Protestant.

The English Reformation suddenly found its forces greatly strengthened with the arrival of some able theologians from the Continent who were forced to leave Europe when the army of Charles V defeated the German Protestants in the Battle of Mühlberg in 1547. Subsequently the emperor imposed the Augsburg Interim upon the conquered Protestant territory, which in effect restored the Roman Catholic Church and its hierarchy, sacraments, and liturgy with only some insignificant concessions to the Protestants. With the exodus of four hundred or more Protestant preachers, South Germany was restored to the Roman Church. Among those who fled was Martin Bucer, the leading Reformer of Strasbourg, who was made Regius Professor of Divinity at Cambridge. After spending some time in Switzerland and Strasbourg, the Italian Reformers Peter Martyr Vermigli and Bernardino Ochino accepted Cranmer's invitation to take up residence in England. Martyr became the Regius Professor of Divinity at Oxford. In addition to these gifted theologians, many other earnest and dedicated Continental Protestants sought refuge in England under Cranmer's patronage. Among them were John à Lasco from Poland, Francisco de Enzinas from Spain, Paul Fagius from Germany, and the indomitable John Knox from Scotland. Of these, Bucer and Knox were probably the most influential in reshaping the theology and the liturgy of the Church of England.

A combination of circumstances now made further advance of the Reformation possible. Nicholas Ridley had become bishop of London, and almost immediately he ordered the altars removed from the churches and replaced by what he called "the Lord's board." He prohibited the clergy from counterfeiting the mass with traditional practices such as kissing the board and elevating the host. John Hooper, bishop of Gloucester, agitated for even more radical changes. In the meantime Cranmer asked Bucer to review *The First Prayer Book of King Edward VI*, intending to incorporate the criticisms he thought valid in a new edition. In the end Cranmer used about two-thirds of Bucer's suggestions in preparing the new prayer book, the use of which was made mandatory in April 1552 in a second act of uniformity.

This new version of the prayer book, properly called the *Book of Common Prayer*, expressly forbade the use of medieval vestments. The communion table was to be moved from the east end of the church to the chancel and placed with its ends facing east and west instead of alterwise. One of the most important changes made had to do with the liturgy of the Lord's Supper. In *The First Prayer Book* the words read, "The Body of our Lord Jesus Christ, which was given for thee, preserve thy body and soul unto everlasting life." In the new version the rubric was changed to "Take and eat this in remembrance that Christ died for thee, and feed on Him in thy heart by faith and with thanksgiving."[21] This change reflects a Zwinglian view of the Lord's Supper. The participant in communion was still required to kneel. John Knox objected to this practice, but Cranmer refused to change the prayer book to meet Knox's objections. Upon its own authority, however, the Council of Regents added what is known as the "Black Rubric," which stated that kneeling did not imply adoration of the elements or the bodily presence of Christ in the elements.

As significant as the accomplishments of Cranmer and his colleagues may have been, none were quite as important as the adoption of the Forty-two Articles. As early as 1549 Cranmer had compiled certain articles to be used in examining candidates for the ministry. These articles were revised in 1552 and discussed by the bishops, and the final version received the king's approval on June 2, 1553. The new articles enjoyed little circulation during Edward's reign because he died less than a month after approving them. But, with certain changes, additions, and deletions, they were destined to become the Thirty-nine Articles during the reign of Elizabeth.

---

21. Cited in Lindsay, *A History of the Reformation*, 2: 363.

THE MARIAN YEARS: 1553-1558

The death of King Edward VI made possible the reign of Mary Tudor, the daughter of Henry VIII and Catherine of Aragon. This had been the intention of the young king. Doubtless under the influence of Warwick, the duke of Northumberland, Edward had denied the succession to either of his two sisters; they had both been declared illegitimate in favor of Lady Jane Grey, the daughter of Henry's niece, Frances Brandon. To perpetuate himself in power, the duke of Northumberland arranged for his son, Guildford Dudley, to marry the sixteen-year-old Jane on May 21, 1553. But these carefully laid plans went awry. Northumberland failed to put Mary under lock and key because he thought the English people would never accept a Catholic queen. Nor did he count on the clamor of the people for a queen of Henry's flesh and blood. Mary's popularity with the English people, derived largely from the nostalgia surrounding her father's memory, was doubtless fed by the discontent of those for whom the sweeping changes in the English church had been too much. It soon became evident that the popular will was too strong to be resisted. After four days of attempting to muster support for Lady Jane Grey, Northumberland surrendered on July 20 and was promptly sent to the Tower.

Thus, just when Protestantism was facing its greatest opportunity in England, it met its downfall. The Roman Catholic bishops were soon back at their posts. Northumberland was executed, and Archbishop Cranmer and Lady Jane Grey, along with others, were imprisoned on charges of treason. The leading Protestant bishops—Hugh Latimer, Nicholas Ridley, John Hooper, Miles Coverdale, Thomas Becon, and John Rogers—and other prominent theologians and priests were charged with heresy and later executed. The "imported" theologians were allowed to leave along with hundreds of religious refugees who could manage to escape the ill-fated island.

Mary came to the throne with high expectations. Thirty-seven years old at the time, she was a very capable and determined person. She rightly perceived that much of the Reformation in England was a superficial facade. From the moment it appeared likely that the English throne would be hers, she launched a crusade to return the Church of England to the papacy and to guarantee its Roman character by marrying a Spaniard. She was a proud woman, and one of the sources of her pride was her Spanish ancestry. Doubtless the shabby way in which her father had dealt with her mother had conditioned her to emphasize the Spanish and Roman Catholic side of her heritage at the expense of her English and Tudor ancestry. The unpolitic way in which she assured everyone she was Spanish rather than English coupled with the growing influence of Spain in the English court soon disillusioned those who had so ardently supported her ascendency to the throne.

The growing resentment greatly increased when she announced her intention of marrying her cousin Philip II of Spain. Parliament sent a request that she reconsider and marry an Englishman instead, but she refused to change her course. The marriage was unpopular from the beginning, and Philip soon found it expedient to return to Spain, where he remained. Back in England Mary still pursued her purpose relentlessly. Uprisings with a mixture of political and religious motives were not long in coming. Nevertheless, Mary was right: she had not misread the English situation. Both Parliament and Convocation (the representative body of the clergy of the Church of England) were compliant if not enthusiastic.

The final step in bringing England back to Roman obedience came on November 27, 1554, when Cardinal Reginald Pole, an Englishman who was a papal legate, restored England to the Roman faith on behalf of the pope. Both houses of Parliament met in the palace and voted to return to papal obedience. Then the members of Parliament petitioned the queen "that they might receive absolution, and be received into the body of the Holy Catholic Church, under the Pope, the Supreme Head thereof." This supplication was made on November 30. In response, while the whole assembly knelt with the king and queen, Cardinal Pole "pronounced absolution and received the kingdom 'again into the unity of our Mother the Holy Church.'"[22] With this act Convocation as well as Parliament was absolved. To make the return to the Middle Ages all the more complete, Parliament revived all the old heresy laws designed to stamp out Lollardy. As a result, Protestants could be burned at the stake upon the authority of Parliament.

After these events came what was largely a "mopping up" operation. Bishop Stephen Gardiner received a special commission to try prisoners who had previously been arrested for heresy. John Rogers, Tyndale's trusted colleague and the compiler of Matthew's Bible, was the first to suffer martyrdom. Thousands applauded him as he was led to the site of execution, a sign that the renewed allegiance to Rome was more appearance than fact. This was an ominous sign of the beginning of the end of Mary's crusade—but the burnings continued. Nicholas Ridley and Hugh Latimer had been prisoners at Oxford for a year and a half before they were burned at the stake on October 16. When a lighted fagot was placed at Ridley's feet, Latimer encouraged his comrade: "Be of good comfort, brother Ridley, and play the man; we shall this day light such a candle by God's grace in England, as I trust shall never be put out."[23] Cranmer witnessed their execution from the tower in which he was confined.

Because Cranmer was an archbishop, his case called for special treatment. His trial took place in St. Mary's Church in Oxford. The major charges brought against him were those of adultery (since he was married), perjury, and heresy. He defended himself admirably in two letters that he addressed to the queen, but his pleas fell on deaf ears. Mary and her Spanish advisors, Bartolomé de Carranza and Alfonso y Castro, were determined to subject the deposed archbishop to the greatest indignities possible. For this purpose a series of recantations were pre-

pared for Cranmer to sign. The first four were ambiguous statements that could be interpreted in different ways, but the last two were far more damaging. A copy of the final recantation is preserved in John Foxe's *Book of Martyrs: Acts and Monuments of the Christian Church.* In it Cranmer claimed to have forsaken all the Protestant teachings he had ever taught and reaffirmed all the Roman Catholic doctrines he had long ago repudiated. It is difficult to imagine a more damaging recantation; the archbishop had thoroughly compromised his faith, and all to no avail. Mary ordered that Cranmer's recantation be published and distributed throughout the kingdom. Casting all pretense aside, the feeble old man determined in his hour of humiliation to undo the damage his act of cowardice had done.

On March 21, 1556, after he had spent three years in prison, the archbishop was led in a procession between two monks to St. Mary's Church in Oxford. Here he was compelled to stand on a platform constructed for the occasion and to listen to a sermon explaining why it was necessary for him to die. The preacher reasoned that Cranmer must die in order to pay for the death of Fisher of Rochester, just as the death of the duke of Northumberland had paid for the martyrdom of Sir Thomas More. Throughout the sermon Cranmer wept openly. Finally the condemned man was allowed to speak. Instead of delivering the expected recantation of his Protestant errors, he withdrew his earlier recantation in deep humility and repentance. He confessed his sorrow, saying,

> And now I come to the great thing which so much troubleth my conscience, more than anything that ever I did or said in my whole life, and that is the setting abroad of a writing contrary to the truth, which now here I renounce and refuse, as things written with my hand contrary to the truth which I thought in my heart, and written for fear of death, and to save my life if it might be, and that is, all such bills and papers which I have written or signed with my hand since my degradation, wherein I have written many things untrue. And forasmuch as my hand offended, writing contrary to my heart, my hand shall first be punished for

22. Lindsay, *A History of the Reformation,* 2: 373.
23. Latimer, cited in *Foxe's Book of Martyrs,* p. 623.

it; for when I come to the fire it shall be first burned.

And as for the Pope, I refuse him, as Christ's enemy and antichrist, with all his false doctrine.

And as for the sacrament, I believe as I have taught in my book against the bishop of Winchester, which book teacheth so true a doctrine of the sacrament, that it shall stand at the last day before the judgment of God, where the papistical doctrine shall be ashamed to shew her face.[24]

Cranmer's accusers were hardly prepared for this confession. When they recovered their senses, they pulled him off the platform and took him to the site of execution, where he was chained to the stake. True to his word, he thrust his right arm into the fire and held it there, often repeating, "This unworthy right hand!" and crying out, in the words of Stephen, "Lord, Jesus, receive my spirit!" until he died. Little did Mary realize that in burning the archbishop she was kindling the fire that would eventually consume the cause that she so fervently championed.

Equally damaging to Mary's influence was the vindictive execution of Lady Jane Grey in the wake of Sir Thomas Wyatt's rebellion. Made of sterner stuff than some of the more illustrious martyrs, she deserves to be widely recognized. The story of her martyrdom reveals not only the brilliant defense of a young girl under the most difficult of circumstances but also the deep convictions that the new faith was capable of nurturing in so young a heart.

Four days before she was beheaded at the Tower of London, the sixteen-year-old girl wrote out her dialogue with a staunch Roman Catholic, Master Feckenham, who had been sent to obtain a recantation and win a convert. The account (excerpts of which are given here with the spelling modernized) reveals the remarkable strength of her faith:

Feckenham speaks first.
What thing is required in a Christian?
JANE: To believe in God the Father, in God the Son, in God the Holy Ghost, three persons and one God.

FECKENHAM: Is there nothing else required in a Christian but to believe in God?
JANE: Yes, we must believe in Him, we must love Him with all our heart, with all our soul and all our mind, and our neighbor as ourself.
FECKENHAM: Why then faith justifies not, nor saves not.
JANE: Yes, verily, faith (as St. Paul says) only [alone] justifies.
FECKENHAM: Why St. Paul says: If I have all faith without love, it is nothing.
JANE: True it is, for how can I love him in whom I trust not? Or how can I trust in him whom I love not? Faith and love agree both together, and yet love is comprehended in faith.[25]

After another exchange on the same subject, Feckenham moved on to the subject of the sacraments. When Jane stated that there were two sacraments, those of baptism and the Lord's Supper, Feckenham corrected her, claiming there were seven. Her challenge was simple but intelligent: "By what scripture find you that?" She went on to give definitions of the two sacraments, offering a cogent argument against transubstantiation:

FECKENHAM: Why, doth not Christ speak these words: "Take, eat, this is my body?" Require we any plainer words? Doth not He say that it is His body?
JANE: I grant He says so, and so He says: "I am the vine, I am the door," but yet He is never the more the vine nor the door. Doth not St. Paul say that He calleth those things that are not as though they were? God forbid that I should say that I eat the very natural body and blood of Christ, for then either I should pluck away my redemption, either else there were two bodies, or two Christs or else two bodies? The one body, was tormented on the cross; . . . then, if they did eat another body, . . . either He had two bodies, [or] else, if His body [was] eaten, it was not broken upon the cross; . . . if it were broken upon the cross, it was not eaten [by] His disciples.[26]

---

24. Cranmer, cited in *Foxe's Book of Martyrs*, p. 736.

25. Cited by Lewis W. Spitz in *The Protestant Reformation* (Englewood Cliffs, N.J.: Prentice-Hall, 1966), p. 170.
26. Cited by Spitz in *The Protestant Reformation*, p. 171.

Jane further argued that Christ was present at the table when he said "This is my body," and therefore these words could not lend themselves to a literal interpretation. Feckenham then questioned Jane's sources:

> FECKENHAM: You ground your faith upon such authors as say and unsay, both with [one] breath, and not upon the church to whom you ought to give credit.
>
> JANE: No, I ground my faith upon God's Word and not upon the church. For if the church be a good church, the faith of the church must be tried by God's Word, and not God's Word by the church, neither yet my faith.[27]

When one considers Jane's age and the situation in which she found herself, her testimony is all the more amazing. It indicates how deeply the cardinal principles of the Reformation had taken hold of an obviously brilliant and articulate young girl.

In her desire to exterminate the Reformation in England, Mary went to extreme lengths. She condemned to the flames and smoke of burning fagots not only the high and mighty but also the simple, humble artisans—often nameless—from among the Protestant underground. Of the 273 known martyrs during Mary's five-year reign of terror, 201 were laypersons. Of these, 78 (men) belonged to the artisan class, and 60 were women. One English historian suggests that two-thirds of the Marian martyrs would have met their fate at Edward's hand if only he had lived longer. But this is difficult to believe because during his six-year reign Edward sentenced only two people to die for their faith. What this statement implies is that two-thirds of the martyrs during Mary's reign were probably Anabaptists or members of similar radical groups. An examination of the accounts of many of these humbler sorts as given by John Foxe suggests that they could have been Anabaptists.

Of these, two of the more prominent individuals—Humphrey Middleton and Cuthbert Sympson—were undoubtedly Anabaptists. Sympson, whom Foxe identifies as a deacon of

the Christian congregation at London, was burned in March 1558. Humphrey Middleton was executed in July 1555. While it is difficult to pin down with absolute certainty the religious complexion of these laymen, it appears that they posed no great threat to the queen's authority or religion. But this obviously made no difference to Mary. It was enough that they existed and worshiped outside the Roman Church.

While Mary was eminently successful at burning martyrs, she was an abysmal failure at everything else. She failed to address herself to the problems of restructuring the Church of England for the future. The Spanish entourage was suspicious of English ecclesiastics, particularly Archbishop Pole, and they began to undermine his authority. In a war with France, Mary lost Calais, England's last foothold in France, and English pride suffered a severe blow that, curiously enough, made the man in the street question the validity of Catholicism. In addition to all this, Mary's marriage to Philip II was troubled. She did not become pregnant, and consequently there were no prospects of a Catholic heir—male or female—to the English throne. The restlessness of the people was mounting, and civil war threatened. Mary's increasing disappointment was suddenly relieved by death. She died a disillusioned and embittered woman on November 17, 1558. Perhaps to most Englishmen her death was a welcome relief from a terrible nightmare. A day later Cardinal Pole also lay dead, and thus closed a baffling chapter in England's turbulent history.

ELIZABETH AND THE ELIZABETHAN SETTLEMENT, 1558-1603

When the news of Mary Tudor's death reached the streets of London on the afternoon of November 17, 1558, there was great jubilation. Church bells were rung, and bonfires were set by feasting celebrants. Elizabeth's accession to the throne was a foregone conclusion. She too was a daughter of Henry VIII. At the time she began her reign she was only twenty-five but wise beyond her years. Her mother, whom she

---

27. Cited by Spitz in *The Protestant Reformation*, p. 171.

had hardly known, had honored the Protestant cause. And even though she had been compelled to worship as a Roman Catholic during the latter years of Mary's intolerant reign, she was by education and inclination a Protestant. Most Englishmen did not doubt this, but some devotees of the Roman Church in England and abroad—particularly the pope and the Catholic sovereigns of Europe—held out the vain hope that she would continue the religious policies of her sister. England was still at war with France and allied with Spain. It was thus to Elizabeth's advantage and that of the nation that she not reveal her intentions prematurely, so she made no immediate declarations.

Her contemporaries testified to the fact that she succeeded in this bit of political chicanery. One bit of evidence of her success in this regard is found in a letter that a foreign diplomat wrote to Ferdinand: "From the very beginning of her reign she has treated all religious questions with so much caution and incredible prudence that she seems both to protect the Catholic religion and at the same time not entirely to condemn or outwardly reject the new Reformation."[28] Elizabeth didn't need to employ such strategy for long. Within six months England was at peace with France and Scotland. While the Catholic powers used every opportunity to influence the queen to retain ties with Rome, there were strong signs that she would not. As late as 1560, the papal nuncio attempted to persuade her to remain Catholic. But by then it was too late—if, indeed, Catholicism had ever been a live option for her.

Not only did Elizabeth have to contend with the Roman Catholic party, but she was also forced to come to terms with the Marian exiles, who, like so many homing pigeons, began to flock back to England in droves. Foxe gives the names of 888 refugees who sought and found refuge on the Continent during Mary's reign; doubtless there were others. Many had become ardent followers of Calvin and returned to their homeland determined to implement the Genevan pattern of church life wherever possible. These zealous advocates of a more militant Protestantism were growing restless at the queen's apparent lack of action. For her part, Elizabeth determined to avoid the extremes. Every cautious step she took was deliberate.

Before Elizabeth was crowned, her actions had given those watching her conflicting signals. On Christmas Day 1558 she walked out of mass celebrated by a bishop who refused her request not to elevate the host. Two days later she issued a proclamation forbidding all preaching, Protestant and Catholic alike. At her coronation, however, mass was said, and all the ancient rites of the church were followed. The lone deviation from the traditional ritual came with the reading of the epistle and the gospel. The lessons were also given in English as well as Latin. But the Sunday after her coronation Elizabeth received the Lord's Supper, partaking of both the bread and the wine. By the time her first Parliament convened, most astute observers were beginning to detect that a new direction would be followed.

The religious question was paramount, yet religion and politics were so intricately related that the two could hardly be separated. Even though Elizabeth was not deeply religious, she found herself forced to make decisions that affected the very nature of the religious establishment. She realized that before a religious settlement could be achieved, the structure of the government had to be overhauled. She began this delicate task by reorganizing the privy council. Six members who had served under Mary were dismissed, and ten were retained. The Lord Chancellor Nicholas Heath, archbishop of York, was relieved of his positions and imprisoned for a short time. He was replaced as lord chancellor by Nicholas Bacon, a brother-in-law of William Cecil. Among the new council members were a number of able men and convinced Protestants. Elizabeth was exceedingly fortunate in her choice of William Cecil, her chief secretary and advisor on the council. His integrity and competence go far in explaining Elizabeth's remarkable success. (He

---

28. Cited by Carl S. Meyer in *Elizabeth I and the Religious Settlement of 1559* (St. Louis: Concordia Publishing House, 1960), p. 13.

served faithfully and well until the day of his death, August 8, 1598.) Under Cecil's guidance the privy council became the queen's most effective instrument in accomplishing her goals both in determining foreign policy and in settling the religious question. The council in effect became the queen's lobby in securing the necessary legislation for her policies in Parliament.

Parliament met on January 23, 1559. Mass was said, but Elizabeth did not make her appearance until afterwards. Hymns were sung in English, and the queen was met by the abbot of Westminster "with the usual candles sputtering in the hands of his clergy, whereupon Elizabeth shouted, 'Away with these torches, we have light enough.'"[29] A Protestant sermon was preached by Dr. Cox, who had only recently returned from Frankfurt full of zeal for the restoration of Anglicanism. It was now increasingly evident, as the Spanish ambassador wrote his government, that "the queen is every day standing up against religion more openly" and that "all the heretics who had escaped are beginning to flock back again from Germany."[30]

Roman Catholicism was still the dominant force within Convocation, however. When it convened, the clergy declared themselves against royal supremacy and for the concept of transubstantiation, affirming that the mass was indeed a sacrifice. It now became abundantly clear that if the Church of England was going to return to the Protestantism of Edward's reign, the necessary changes would have to come by parliamentary action, a secular process. The House of Commons was unquestionably weighted in favor of Protestantism, but the House of Lords was another question. A majority of the lords were under the influence of the Marian bishops and reportedly had resolved never to agree to a restoration of the Act of Supremacy.

The first two attempts to pass a new act of supremacy failed. Apparently the first bill was withdrawn, and the second was rejected by the queen, who took exception to the wording proclaiming her the "Supreme head of the Church."[31] This was a clever move. The bill had been so altered by the House of Lords that the Commons refused to agree to the revision that had nullified its original provisions. By refusing to give her consent, Elizabeth pleased both the Romanists and the Calvinists. In fact, both parties took credit for her action. This put the question of the religious settlement back where it had begun, and Cecil and Elizabeth were given a new opportunity to rethink their strategy.

The provisions of the bill were separated and finally successfully passed in separate bills. The first, a new act of supremacy that declared the queen "the only supreme governor of this realm . . . as well as in all spiritual or ecclesiastical things or causes as temporal," was passed on April 29.[32] Despite the use of the humbler term "governor," all the powers given to Henry VIII by Parliament were assigned to Elizabeth. The Act of Uniformity was introduced eight days after the Act of Supremacy but was passed one day earlier. It restored the Church of England to the position it had enjoyed in the last year of King Edward's reign as set forth in *The Book of Common Prayer and Administration of the Sacraments and Other Rites and Ceremonies in the Church of England.* Thus the acts of Mary's Parliament were repealed, and, as Thomas Lindsay writes, "All Englishmen, of whatever creed, were to be compelled by law to join in one common public worship according to the ritual prescribed."[33] The Act of Uniformity also contained a provision for yet another revision of the *Book of Common Prayer.*

Elizabeth was anxious that the new prayer book accommodate the more moderate Catholics. Her suggestion that Roman Catholic vestments and practices might be retained unaltered

---

29. Cited by Lindsay in *A History of the Reformation,* 2: 390.

30. Cited by Lindsay in *A History of the Reformation,* 2: 390.

31. Cited by Lindsay in *A History of the Reformation,* 2: 393.

32. Cited by Lindsay in *A History of the Reformation,* 2: 393.

33. Lindsay, *A History of the Reformation,* 2: 395.

was rejected, but Anglo-Catholics were accommodated by a rewording of certain crucial passages. The formula for the celebration of the Lord's Supper, for example, was changed from a strictly Zwinglian phrasing to a more sacramental wording that permitted those who believed in the real presence of Christ to partake by interpreting the revised statement as they chose. The Zwinglian phrasing read, "Take and eat this, in remembrance that Christ died for thee, and feed on Him in thy heart by faith with thanksgiving. . . . Drink this in remembrance that Christ's blood was shed for thee, and be thankful." It was revised to read as follows:

> The Body of our Lord Jesus Christ, which was given for thee, preserve thy body and soul unto everlasting life. Take and eat this in remembrance that Christ died for thee, and feed on Him in thy heart by faith with thanksgiving.
>
> The Blood of our Lord Jesus Christ, which was shed for thee, preserve thy body and soul unto everlasting life. Drink this in remembrance that Christ's Blood was shed for thee, and be thankful.[34]

The revised prayer book was also less anti-Catholic than that of 1552. A condemnatory prayer—"from all sedition and privy conspiracy, from the tyranny of the bishop of Rome and all his detestable enormities . . . good Lord deliver us"—was omitted.[35] Clearly Elizabeth intended to follow the *via media* as far as possible.

The next task was to apply the law. Cecil was convinced that it would be possible to enforce uniformity without stirring up rebellion. The "extremists" on either side, he felt sure, could be handled without too much difficulty. He also believed that pliant Catholics and most Protestants could be counted on to conform— and he was right. In the end only 183 of the 900 Catholic priests refused to swear their allegiance. Fifteen of the sixteen bishops from Mary's reign refused and consequently were forced to retire. It is significant that none of the retired bishops

were executed, not even Archbishop Nicholas Heath of York, who had issued the orders of execution for Archbishop Thomas Cranmer. Matthew Parker, a champion of the *via media,* was consecrated archbishop of Canterbury by three bishops whom Mary had banished; he then consecrated the newly appointed bishops. Thus the apostolic succession was preserved.[36]

The Forty-two Articles, which had been drawn up shortly before Edward's death, were restored as the doctrinal affirmation of the Church of England. They were revised by Convocation in 1563 and reduced to thirty-nine in number. However, only thirty-eight of the thirty-nine articles were published in 1563; Elizabeth omitted one that she feared might offend the Lutherans, whose good graces she wished to retain in order to enjoy the protection that the Diet of Augsburg (1555) had provided. But by 1571 her throne was more secure, and all thirty-nine articles were published in English under the title "The Thirty-Nine Articles of Religion of the Church of England." The omitted article (number 29) reads, "The Wicked, and such as be void of a lively faith, although they do carnally and visibly press with their teeth (as Saint Augustine saith) the Sacrament of the Body and Blood of Christ; yet in no wise are they partakers of Christ: but rather, to their condemnation, do eat and drink the sign or Sacrament of so great a thing."[37] Article 20 reflects Elizabeth's opinion in its declaration that the church has the right to establish ceremonies and the authority to settle controversies arising over matters of faith.

According to a letter that Archbishop Parker sent to Elizabeth on December 24, 1566, there were four reasons for enforcing the Thirty-nine Articles: (1) they advanced true religion; (2) they agreed with God's Word; (3) they condemned error; and (4) they would establish

---

34. Cited by Lindsay in *A History of the Reformation,* 2: 401.

35. Cited by Newman in *A Manual of Church History,* 2: 268.

36. Although this ceremony meant nothing to Puritans, it was important to Anglo-Catholics to preserve apostolic succession. In their minds the validity of a bishop's consecration depended on the line of bishops (going back to Simon Peter) remaining unbroken.

37. Cited in *The Evangelical Protestant Creeds, with Translations,* vol. 3 of Philip Schaff's *Creeds of Christendom* (Grand Rapids: Baker Book House, 1966), pp. 506–7.

unity. The Thirty-nine Articles also condemned Roman Catholicism as well as the Anabaptists and their teachings. In fact, as Charles Hardwick points out, eighteen of the Forty-two Articles were directed against Anabaptist teachings. Irvin B. Horst agrees that this is the case with the exception of article 4, which condemns those who deny the resurrection. The influence of the Marian exiles may be detected in the revised Thirty-nine Articles of 1563 and 1571, which reflect a Calvinist understanding of the Christian faith.

Elizabeth's policy of moderation was a difficult achievement. Upon her ascension to the throne, both Convocation and the universities were clearly committed to Catholicism, and the returning Marian exiles were, for the most part, ardent Protestants with Calvinist convictions. They were often dogmatic and averse to compromise, and their enthusiasm for a Reformation along Genevan lines was not acceptable to Elizabeth. John Knox, the Reformer of Scotland, did not help to endear the Calvinist cause to her by unleashing his attack against the rule of women. Frustrated in his attempts to return to his native Scotland, while awaiting some favorable word at Dieppe, he wrote *The First Blast of the Trumpet Against the Monstrous Regiment of Women* in October 1557. The objects of his wrath were three Marys: Mary of Lorraine, queen mother and regent of Scotland; Mary Tudor; and Mary Stuart. Even though the fiery Scot had no way of knowing that Elizabeth would come to rule England before the echo of his blast had faded, she did, and she resented the implications of the tract. While she had little sympathy for the Calvinists, she was driven closer to them by the international Catholic intrigue set in motion against her and a Protestant England.

A series of attempts to overthrow Elizabeth were rumored abroad. Secret agreements between Philip II, the pope, and other sovereigns of Europe to overthrow Elizabeth were afoot as early as 1560 and an open secret by 1565. Mary Stuart's aspirations to the English throne were supported by France and Spain as well as by Roman sympathizers among the English noblemen. The recently organized Society of Jesus (the Jesuits) founded English colleges in France at Douai and Rheims, and also in Rome for the training of English priests in the hopes of sending them back to England as underground missionaries. By 1585 it is estimated that three hundred priests had been sent secretly to England in an attempt to overthrow the queen and subvert her Protestant regime. Pope Pius V declared Elizabeth illegitimate and excommunicated her in 1570 for holding to impious constitutions and the "atrocious mysteries of Calvin," and for demanding that her subjects observe them.[38] An abortive attempt on Elizabeth's life was popularly believed to have been the work of the Jesuits. For her part, Elizabeth secretly sent aid to the beleaguered Huguenots, the Dutch Calvinists, and the Scottish Presbyterians through John Knox. Eventually English troops helped to secure Scotland for Knox and the Presbyterians. It was only a matter of time before her enemies played their trump card: the invasion of England by Spain. The successful massacre of St. Bartholomew's Day encouraged the conspirators to believe that God was without question on their side and that such a scheme could not fail.

In 1588 the greatest navy ever assembled up until that time was sent against England by the Spanish monarch with the express purpose of invading the island kingdom on behalf of the true faith. But the storms off the coast of England and the clever use the English made of the forces of nature to set fire to the Spanish galleons spelled doom to the proud pretensions of Spain and Philip II's great design. It also sealed the fate of Roman Catholicism in England and signaled the rising maritime power of a powerful Protestant nation. Two things became abundantly clear: England was Protestant, albeit with reservations; and Elizabeth's throne was secure. The Elizabethan settlement had come to stay.

---

38. Meyer, *Elizabeth I and the Religious Settlement of 1559,* p. 124.

Chapter XV

THE CATHOLIC REVIVAL

n this ecumenical age it has become increasingly unpopular to speak of the revival of the Roman Catholic Church in Europe in the sixteenth century as the Counter-Reformation, although some historians still do. "The Catholic Reformation" has become the more acceptable designation. In a sense the movement was both a revival of medieval piety and a reaction to the Protestant Reformation that eventually brought about certain reforms. That which is beyond dispute, as August Franzen and other Catholic historians have shown, is that a revival of medieval Catholicism, without which Rome would have been ill-equipped to face either the future or the Protestant challenge, was already in progress when Luther launched his attack on the indulgence traffic.[1]

That the revival antedates the Protestant Reformation is also beyond question because its beginnings lay within the same *devotio moderna* and the Christian humanism that helped to precipitate the Reformation. The widespread influence of Erasmus, as well as the earlier im-

pact of the *devotio moderna* of the Brethren of the Common Life, brought the best in medieval piety and humanist learning to bear upon the ills of a church that seemed incapable of mounting any effective reform. The need for reform was evident everywhere. Some of those most acutely aware of that need were the Erasmians, who, like Erasmus himself, never broke with the Roman Church but continued to work within its structure.

Although many aspects of the Catholic revival such as the founding of new orders and the reforming of older ones had little if anything to do with the Protestants, it soon became quite evident that the Reformation was exerting a stimulating influence upon the Roman Catholic Church and its more thoughtful prelates. Thus movements within the church that arose out of deep spiritual longings and personal pilgrimages were in the end shaped by the plight of a church caught in a struggle for its very life. "Reactionary" may be too strong a word to describe some of these developments, but it appropriately defines much of what occurred during this revival. Initially attempts were made to renew the spiritual and moral life of the church; in the end these aspirations became subservient to the acute needs of the papacy

---

1. See August Franzen and John Dolan, *A History of the Church* (New York: Herder & Herder, 1969), pp. 316–20.

and the chastened church to erect a defense against the Protestant menace. Thus there was both renewal and reaction—reformation and counter-reformation.

ATTEMPTS AT REFORM

In addition to North Europeans like Erasmus, John Colet, Thomas More, John Standonck, Guillaume Briçonnet, Jacques Lefèvre, John Fisher, and those lesser known, there were both Italian and Spanish scholars and prelates who longed for a cleansing and renewal of the church. Among these were Cardinal Gasparo Contarini, the ambassador of Venice; Bishop Gian Matteo Giberti of Verona; Cardinal Jacopo Sadoleto, whom Calvin answered so effectively; Cardinal Giovanni Morone, papal nuncio to Germany; Cardinal Giovanni Pietro Caraffa, later to become Pope Paul IV; and Cardinal Francisco Jiménez (Ximénez) de Cisneros, archbishop of Toledo and founder of the University of Alcalá. This is an impressive list, particularly because these names represent the highest echelons of the Roman Catholic Church, including the papacy itself. Most if not all of these prelates were identified with Erasmus until the renowned Dutchman and his writings began to fall into disrepute. It is evident that the spirit of the *devotio moderna* and evangelical humanism motivated these churchmen to become advocates of reform as it had motivated Erasmus himself. None was to reflect these influences more than Francisco Jiménez.

Francisco Jiménez de Cisneros (ca. 1436-1517)

After graduating from the University of Salamanca in 1456, Jiménez spent some time in Rome and later served as a secular priest in Spain. When he was suddenly seized by a desire to live a life of discipleship completely devoted to Christ, he abandoned his parish to become an Observantine Franciscan. His austerities and sacrificial life so impressed Queen Isabella that she made him her confessor in 1492. Three years later he was awarded the archbishopric of

Toledo, the most prestigious archbishopric in Spain and the wealthiest in Europe. Jiménez used his position to further the new learning and to reform the monastic orders of the country. He founded three universities, the most famous of which was Alcalá, near Madrid. It was here that he used his own funds to sponsor the publication of the *Complutensian Polyglot*. This was a superb achievement. Because Jiménez was interested in correcting the numerous errors in the Vulgate, he put the Vulgate in parallel columns with the Hebrew and the Septuagint in the Old Testament and alongside the Aramaic and a critical Greek text in the New Testament. A Latin translation of the Septuagint and the Targumim was also included. This ambitious project, undertaken in 1502, was not completed until 1517, and was not licensed by Leo X until 1520. The Greek text was completed by 1514, two years before that of Erasmus, but it was not in general circulation until 1522. Some thirty scholars, including some eminent Jewish converts, put forth their best efforts in producing this monumental work.

Jiménez also sponsored the publication of the *Imitation of Christ* and the *Life of Christ* by Ludolf the Saxon, both of which were to have a profound influence upon Ignatius Loyola. The archbishop also encouraged the teaching of the Bible along with the theology of Thomas Aquinas in the universities. His herculean efforts to reform monastic life and educate the Spanish clergy were highly successful, and as a consequence the Spanish clergy achieved a standard of competence unequaled elsewhere. Jiménez was no obscurantist. Neither was he a subservient supporter of Rome nor a slavish follower of Erasmus. In both his administration of his archbishopric and his service to the crown, he clearly demonstrated his own version of the Christian faith; he saw no conflict in serving both his church and his country.

Although Jiménez did not inaugurate the work of the Inquisition in Spain, he supported it. In 1502 he was made both a cardinal and the grand inquisitor of Castile and Leon. At times he found his attempts to provide the tools for a more enlightened and better-educated clergy

Haec tibi pentadecas tetragonon respicit illud.
Hospitium petri τ pauli ter quinqz dierum.
Ramus instrumentum vetus hebdoas sumit octe.
Et nova sicnatur.ter quinqz recepat vtrunqz.

Flouum testamentum
grece τ latine in academia
complurensi nouiter
impressum.

Title page of Volume IV of the *Complutensian Polyglot*

frustrated by agents of the Inquisition. Yet he seems to have enjoyed "the smell of gunpowder" and to have entertained no second thoughts about launching a crusade against the Moors in North Africa. In 1509–10 he personally led armies against Oran, Algiers, and Tripoli. By this time, however, he had in effect become an earthly prince and the ruler of Castile, a responsibility that he exercised from the time of Queen Isabella's death in 1504 until the arrival of Charles V in 1517, the year of his own death.

Although Jiménez achieved a certain working synthesis of traditional Spanish orthodoxy and an awakened spiritual life characteristic of Christian humanism, he had no way of knowing that it would not last. The Erasmian features of

his synthesis were soon suspect and then discredited, and in the end only the intransigent policy of Spanish Catholicism remained. The spirit of Philip II, not that of Erasmus, was destined to survive and conquer.

Gasparo Contarini (1483-1542)

Contarini was an uncommon cardinal. Even though he was made a cardinal by Paul III, he was never in orders but remained a layman. He was no ordinary layman, however. He was educated at the University of Padua, and in 1521 he became an ambassador of the republic of Venice to Charles V. He traveled to England as well as to Spain and Rome. In the course of his spiritual pilgrimage he suffered a personal crisis of faith in 1511 that resulted in his becoming a patron of the new learning. Not long afterwards, in 1516, he demonstrated his competence as a theologian by authoring a treatise on the immortality of the soul; he even wrote against Luther in 1530, although later he was to adopt a variation of Luther's teaching on justification by faith. In the meantime he had become an ardent advocate of reform within the church, and in this he was not alone.

In Rome Contarini became a member of the Oratory of Divine Love, a group of devout priests and laymen concerned about the moral decadence within the church and convinced of the need for reform. They emphasized personal holiness and works of charity. (The first such society apparently formed in Vicenza as early as 1494.)[2] By 1517 an oratory that had been organized in Genoa began to meet in a suburb of Rome, and more oratories were formed in other Italian cities. The movement numbered among its devotees such notables as Cardinal Contarini, Cardinal Morone, and Cardinal Caraffa. It was just such reform-minded men that Paul III chose for his new cardinals.

Before his death in 1542, however, Contarini came under the suspicion of heresy. Appointed

---

2. A. G. Dickens, *The Counter Reformation* (London: Thames & Hudson, 1968), p. 69.

to the cardinalate by Paul III, he was further commissioned—along with Cardinals Giovanni Pietro Caraffa, Jacopo Pole, Sadoleto, and others, including the traditionalist Cardinal Aleander—to survey the religious situation in order to pinpoint the needs for reform. The commission did as directed. The resulting report, *The Council on Reforming the Church (Consilium delectorum cardinalium et allorum praelatorum de emendanda ecclesia)*, was a candid and at times severe indictment of a church in disarray. The report was leaked, and Luther published it in Germany, much to the consternation of the Holy See. The Protestants were elated because it highlighted the abuses that had prompted Luther's attack. Both Contarini and Caraffa had a hand in writing the final report of 1537. However, when Caraffa was made Paul IV and came to reject the policy of conciliation, he put his former friend under papal censure. Their concepts of reform were at variance: Contarini was

open to the Protestant critique, but Caraffa, as pope, obviously rejected this approach.

The Colloquy of Regensburg, 1541-42

In spite of the growing suspicions about his orthodoxy, it was Contarini who kept alive on the Catholic side Charles V's hope for reunion with the Protestants. The initial conversations between Protestant theologians—Melanchthon, Bucer, and Calvin— and their Catholic counterparts—Johannes Gropper, Julius Pflug, Johann Eck, and Contarini, who was the papal legate—looked promising. Meeting first in Hagenau and later in Worms in 1540, the conference was moved to Regensburg (Ratisbon) in April 1541. In addition to some initial agreements on original sin and freedom of the will, the conferees formulated a version of the concept of justification by faith suggested by Erasmus's *Repair of Christian Unity* (1533). Yet the bright hopes of

CONSILIVM

DELECTORVM CARDI-

NALIVM ET ALIORVM

PRÆLATORVM,

De emendanda Ecclesia, S. D. N D. PAVLO III.
ipso iubente, conscriptum & exhi·
bitum, Anno.1538.

EATISSIME pater, tantum abest vt verbis explicare possimus, quin magnas gratias Respub. Christiana Deo Opt. Max. agere debeat, q te Pontificem hisce temporibus ac pastorem gregi suo presecerit, eamq quã habes mentê dederit: vt minimê speremus, cogitatione eas quas Deo gratias debet, cōsequi posse. nam spiritus ille Dei, quo virtus cęlorũ firmata est, vt ait Propheta, labantem, imò ferè collapsam, in preceps Ecclesiam Christi per te restaurare, & huic ruinę manum, vt videmus, supponere decreuit. eamq erigere

Psal. 32. b

Title page of the *Consilium*

the colloquy turned to disillusionment and disappointment because of both dogmatic and political issues. Contarini was insistent upon the concept of transubstantiation and papal authority, but the Protestants rejected both. For his part, the intransigent Paul IV felt Contarini had betrayed the faith. From afar Luther rejected outright the modified concept of justification by faith. Among the princes of Europe the reaction was mixed. Charles V was encouraged by the progress made, but neither the elector of Saxony nor Francis I was happy with the proposed justification-by-faith concept—the elector for theological reasons and Francis for political reasons. Francis feared a reunited German church under the emperor's control, and thus sought every means possible to sabotage the colloquy. In this he had the support of numerous Catholics and quite a few Protestants, though for widely different reasons.

Episcopal Reform

The Catholic revival also brought with it a new dedication to the pastoral calling on the part of many prelates. Absenteeism was one of the major problems of the church, because numerous bishops never resided in their sees during their period of tenure. They much preferred cities like Rome and its familiar haunts. An early exception to this pattern was Gian Matteo Giberti, the bishop of Verona. After serving in the Curia under the pontificates of Leo X and Clement VII, he finally received permission from Clement to return to his diocese. Here he carried out a thoroughgoing reform of ecclesiastical and social life. Following the pattern of the Oratory of Divine Love, he formed a group called the Confraternity of the Blessed Sacrament, the first of many such societies. He also effectively stamped out concubinage, nonresidency, and immorality among the secular priests, and established orphanages and almshouses. His life was as exemplary as his deeds, and his influence was widespread. Charles Borromeo and Cardinal Jacopo Sadoleto were two among many who drew their inspiration for reform from Giberti's example. A. G. Dickens

also points out that Giberti's printed instructions for his parish priests reappear in certain decrees of the Council of Trent.[3]

MONASTICISM

The resurgence of religious devotion within sixteenth-century Catholicism precipitated a revival of monastic life. New orders were formed, and old orders were reformed. This in itself was no innovation, because this pattern of renewal and reform had been a characteristic of the medieval monastic movement for centuries. At the time of this resurgence it was widely admitted on all sides that monasticism was experiencing problems. Despite the fact that there were some who strove mightily to live in accordance with the best traditions of their orders, the movement was in disrepute and under heavy attack. The dissolution of the monasteries in England came in the wake of all kinds of charges (though some of them were undoubtedly false). Even the Council of Trent considered suppressing the movement that had brought both glory and shame to the church. However, as in times of previous crises, the orders were neither suppressed nor dissolved but reformed, and with reformation new orders were established.

The Theatines

In 1524, Giovanni Pietro Caraffa, at the time archbishop of Brindisi, and Factavo Thiene, who resigned his position with the Curia in order to promote reform among the secular clergy, formed the Theatines, a new order of secular priests. They envisioned priests bound together by a common rule but not sequestered in a cloister. Even though they took the vow of poverty, the Theatines were forbidden to beg. Instead they devoted themselves to work in the world.[4] This was a new direction that the Jesuits were eventually to implement more effectively.

---

3. Dickens, *The Counter Reformation*, p. 54.
4. Franciscus Ragonesi, "Theatines," in *The Catholic Encyclopedia*, 15 vols. (New York: Encyclopedia Press, 1913), 14: 557–58.

Other orders such as the Barnabites of Milan and the Somaschi were similar, having been inspired by the Theatines. Among the new orders, the Somaschi distinguished themselves through their work with orphans and in their establishment of hospitals.

The Capuchins

The Franciscans, who had enjoyed a number of revivals since the death of Saint Francis, experienced still another that led to the formation of the Capuchins. This new expression of Franciscan devotion received its name from the pointed cowl that Matteo da Bascio, a member of the Observantine branch of the order, adopted to distinguish his stricter followers from the Conventuals. He sought to recover the vision of the founder in every way, and instituted the wearing of the pointed cowl (*capuche*) because he claimed Saint Francis had always worn it. The Capuchins received the approval of Clement VII in 1528, but they did not gain independent status as an order in their own right until 1619. By that date they had so prospered that they could count fifteen hundred houses under their rule. They barely escaped suppression when a general of the order, Bernardino Ochino, forsook the Catholics for the Protestants, but they survived to serve the cause of Catholicism with marked success in the years that followed. Their survival was in part due to a reform-minded noblewoman named Vittoria Colonna, the confidante of Michelangelo and a friend of Juan de Valdés. She was only one of a remarkable group of highly respected noblewomen who exerted far-reaching influence on behalf of the reform of sixteenth-century Catholicism.

Saint Teresa of Ávila and the Discalced Carmelite Nuns

Teresa of Ávila was one of those deeply devout and capable women who sparked a revival among nuns of various orders. In 1555, when she was forty years old, her spiritual pilgrimage, like that of Jiménez almost half a century before,

took an abrupt turn. This "second conversion," as it is often called, was marked by "mental prayer" and ecstatic visions. Some of her friends suggested that her visions were diabolical, but her father confessor, a Jesuit named Baltasar Alvarez, gave her the necessary support and the assurance that she was indeed a vessel of the Lord chosen for a great purpose. Her mystical contemplation soon found practical expression in a movement she launched to reform the Carmelite Order of Nuns to which she belonged. On August 24, 1562, the resolute nun founded the Convent of Discalced (barefoot) Carmelite Nuns of the Primitive Rule of St. Joseph. The order was recognized by Paul IV, and after it was visited by the general of the Carmelites, Saint Teresa was encouraged to continue her work. Like Ignatius, she came under the scrutiny of the Inquisition, but with the help of Philip II she escaped imprisonment, remaining free to form houses of the new order for the remainder of her life.

This unusual woman succeeded in combining mystical contemplation with a vigorous activism. It was her conviction that the devotional life should lead to action, not lethargy. She authored four books in which her teachings became enshrined for posterity. Her prodigious efforts, which she persisted in although she was frail and frequently ill, made her one of the heroines of the Catholic Reformation. It is not surprising that in 1622, only forty years after her death, she was canonized by Gregory XV.

The Society of Jesus

Of all the orders that the sixteenth century spawned, none was to prove as influential as that of the Jesuits. The Society of Jesus was founded by a Basque of noble lineage named Ignatius Loyola (1491–1556). Although not ostensibly formed to combat the Protestants, it soon proved to be Rome's most effective instrument in bringing many of the disenchanted back into the Roman fold. Thus the history of the Jesuits is to a considerable extent the history of the Counter-Reformation.

Although the Society of Jesus was not recognized as such by Paul III until September 1540, the order traced its beginnings to August 15, 1534. On that memorable day six young men accompanied their mentor to the chapel of Saint Denis on Montmartre, took the vows of poverty, chastity, and absolute obedience to the pope, and resolved to go to Palestine to convert the Moslems to the Catholic faith. If this proved impossible, however, they agreed to offer their services to the church at the command of the pope. Although they had hoped to launch a mission to Jerusalem, they expressed a willingness to go anywhere the pope should send them. A few characteristics of the embryonic organization stand out. Like many monastic movements before it, the Jesuit order began in the vision of one man. It was also largely a lay movement in the beginning: only one of the original company, Pierre Favre (Faber), was a priest. It was he who conducted mass on that eventful day.

The original little band of six soon grew to ten. It consisted of Loyola, Simon Rodriguez from Portugal, four Frenchmen—Paschaius Bronet, Jean Codure, and Pierre Favre and Claude Le Jay from Savoy—and four Spaniards: Francis Xavier, Diego Laynez, Alfonso Salmeron, and Nicholas Alfonso of Bobadilla. Together they possessed little else besides their vision and dedication. But from the beginning they envisioned themselves as an international order with a world mission.

Meager as this beginning may have appeared, it represented a dream come true for the one-time Spanish patriot. Loyola first entertained thoughts of conquest in the name of Christ in 1521 while recuperating from a war injury: a cannonball shot had shattered his leg in the Battle of Pamplona near the French border. During his enforced rest he read the *Life of Christ* by Ludolph of Saxony, and he was moved to dedicate his life to the service of Christ and the Virgin Mary. Later this former page in the court of King Ferdinand confessed that since his crippled leg had forced him to give up his earlier plans to win fame as an officer in the Spanish army, he had decided to become a soldier who would fight the battles of the Lord. Whatever his

motivation, his new goals plunged him into a spiritual struggle during which he sought release from his burden of sin. Forgiveness finally came when he decided to throw himself upon the mercy of God.

In the course of his search he began to read other devotional works, including the *Imitation of Christ,* which introduced him to the rich mystical tradition of the Brethren of the Common Life. For almost a year he practiced the most austere asceticism at Manresa, a Dominican monastery near Montserrat. It was here that he discovered much about fasting and the life of mystical experience. He recorded these insights, which appeared later in his *Spiritual Exercises,* a volume that bears some resemblance to *Exercises of the Spiritual Life* (attributed to Garcia de Cisneros, the nephew of Cardinal Francisco Jiménez). But in Loyola's hands the older guides to meditation underwent a transformation. He systematized the entire meditative process, giving specific instructions for inducing certain graphic visions of heaven and hell, Adam and Eve, Christ, the passion of the cross, and the resurrection. He prescribed the necessary exercises in specific detail, exercises that the initiate was expected to follow under the guidance of a director during twenty-five consecutive days in solitude. Every participant could expect to be changed. The purpose of the exercises in meditation and contemplation was to bring every member of the proposed "Company of Jesus" into complete submission to the will of God as Ignatius envisioned it, which meant being reduced to a state of absolute obedience to one's immediate superior. Ignatius formulated the major concepts of the *Spiritual Exercises* before he left Manresa, before he had studied either Latin or theology, yet he never changed them significantly.

After he made a pilgrimage to Jerusalem, Ignatius got into trouble with the Inquisition when he attempted to gain converts to his particular version of the Christian life. Twice imprisoned, he was finally released due to the intervention of some influential women whom he had counseled along the way. But he was prohibited from distinguishing between mortal and venial sins until he had studied theology for at least four years. Latin was the key to theology, and Ignatius knew no Latin. So at thirty years of age he began to acquire this necessary tool, learning along with students less than half his age. After spending some years at Spain's two great university centers, Alcalá and Salamanca, he entered the Collège de Montaigu in 1528, the very same year in which Calvin left the University of Paris for Orléans. But this new student had come to teach as well as to learn. His system lacked a few refinements, but it was already essentially complete. He was there to attain the necessary credentials to establish his credibility in the service of the church.

Six years later, with his master-of-arts degree in hand, Ignatius was well on his way to forming the most influential order in the history of the Roman Catholic Church. While in Paris he had added a final section to the *Spiritual Exercises* entitled "Rules for Thinking with the Church," which was comprised of eighteen articles that indicated the mind-set of Ignatius and his new order. These articles were intended to cultivate complete support for the traditional teachings of the Roman Catholic Church and unquestioning obedience to its hierarchy. Articles eleven through thirteen made it clear that the challenge of Luther and the Protestant critique were categorically rejected. In summary, Ignatius wrote,

> If we wish to proceed securely in all things, we must hold fast to the following principle: What seems to me white, I will believe black if the hierarchical Church so defines. For I must be convinced that in Christ our Lord, the bridegroom, and in His spouse the Church, only one Spirit holds sway, which governs and rules for the salvation of souls. For it is by the same Spirit and Lord who gave the Ten Commandments that our holy Mother Church is ruled and governed.[5]

By 1537 Ignatius and his disciples were in Venice, preparing to embark on their mission to convert Moslems in Jerusalem. It was here that Ignatius and five others were ordained to the priesthood. Frustrated in their efforts to launch their missionary enterprise because of the outbreak of war, they went to Rome to place themselves at the command of the papacy. They did not anticipate the suspicions their presence in the Holy City would provoke. However, with the help of Cardinal Contarini they soon won the confidence of Paul III, who gave them permission to engage in preaching and works of mercy among the poor and the destitute. On September 27, 1540, the pope formally recognized the order in the bull *Regimini militantis ecclesiae*. Although he initially limited membership in the order to sixty, he lifted this limitation three years later. In the few years of their existence the Jesuits had proved just how valuable their services could be in the interest of reform.

Requests soon began to pour in from princes and bishops on the firing lines who were struggling to regain lost Catholic territory. The Jesuits responded with what appeared to be a never-ending supply of able and dedicated priests. It soon became evident that their unquestioning loyalty to the papacy and the traditional teachings of the church made them perfectly suited to be teachers and preachers able to hold their own with the better-educated Protestant clergy. Jesuit schools were soon established from Rome to Douai. The first Jesuit college was founded in Bologna in 1546. In Rome, Loyola founded two colleges, the Collegium Romanum in 1550 and the Collegium Germanicum in 1552. The latter became exceedingly important in training missionaries for reclaiming lost territory in Germany, especially after the Council of Trent. At first France was reluctant to admit the "Spanish fanatics," but by 1570 Clermont had become one of the most successful of the Jesuit colleges. Ignatius, now general of the order, wrote from Rome to Manuel Lopez on June 17, 1555,

> Here in Rome we have become very numerous, for although some have been sent away these days to various places, the number in the college is higher than 112, and in this house we are between 60 and 70.
>
> Services are held in our church as usual, especially sermons and confessions. The Spiritual Exercises are given outside, enemies are reconciled,

5. Ignatius, cited by John C. Olin in *The Catholic Reformation: Savonarola to Ignatius Loyola* (New York: Harper & Row, 1969), p. 210.

old and obstinate sinners recalled, catechism taught, and other works of mercy, corporal and spiritual, practiced. It would take too long to go into particulars.[6]

Even before the Society of Jesus was formally recognized, Paul III was using its members in numerous confidential missions on behalf of the papacy. Such missions steadily increased after 1540. While members of the order found themselves involved in a variety of missionary and educational enterprises, they proved most effective in reclaiming lost territory for the church. Their success in this endeavor was little short of phenomenal. Perhaps the most able advocate of Catholicism in newly won and disputed territory was Peter Canisius (1521-1597).

Canisius, a German, had been recruited for the order by Pierre Favre. Educated at the Universities of Cologne and Louvain, two strongholds of Catholic orthodoxy, he brought no meager talent to the cause. He successfully opposed Archbishop Hermann von Wied's attempt to introduce the Reformation in his archdiocese. He helped the South German and Austrian Catholic forces to regroup in the face of the Lutheran challenge. He published three catechisms that sought to counteract those of Luther. These were reprinted numerous times and proved exceedingly popular and effective in setting forth Catholic teachings. He also established schools to provide better education for the parish priests and monks. He became the father confessor to Emperor Ferdinand of Austria and in this capacity reinforced Ferdinand's own Catholic convictions at a time when it appeared that, like his brother Charles V, he would insist upon giving the cup to the laity and approving clerical marriage as concessions to the Protestants.

With such stalwarts as Canisius, Alfonso Salmeron, Diego Laynez, and Saint Francis Xavier, the Jesuits attracted the best talent Catholic youth had to offer in the service of the church and provided its most able champions at the time of its greatest need. The order was formally

recognized on the eve of the Council of Trent. Paul III now saw no reason to further delay holding a general council, as his predecessors had done.

THE COUNCIL OF TRENT, 1545-1563

Luther had called for a general council as early as 1519 in Leipzig and had repeatedly asked to be heard at a council of competent representatives of the whole church, by which he meant a general council that would include Protestant as well as Catholic theologians. Emperor Charles V had attempted upon his own authority to achieve such a meeting of the minds, first at the Diet of Augsburg in 1530 and later at Regensburg in 1542. A council was finally called, but the emperor had little input in its deliberations, and he became quite disillusioned with its lack of progress toward any rapprochement with the Protestants.

Back in Rome many popes had talked of a general council, but no plans had been made to hold one. There was a growing feeling that if a council were convened, its findings might cause problems. At best, the findings would ultimately militate against papal aspirations and even threaten papal authority; at worst, the council might also seek reconciliation with the Protestants at the expense of the faith and cause further division within the church. Thus one pope after another had successfully forestalled the calling of a council until Paul III.

The pope who finally succeeded in calling a general council was an unlikely prospect for such an undertaking. A member of a prominent Italian family, the Farneses of Canino, he had been made a cardinal by Alexander VI in 1493. However, although he was a prince of the church, he seems to have been a man of indifferent morals. During his earlier years he fathered three, possibly four illegitimate children. Once elected to the papacy, he used his position to further the interests of his family. He made two of his young grandsons cardinals, and through intrigue—of which he was apparently a master—he enabled his son Pierluigi to become

---

6. *Letters of St. Ignatius of Loyola,* ed. William J. Young (Chicago: Loyola University Press, 1959), p. 394.

the duke of Parma and Piacenze. But later on, despite his advanced age and his somewhat checkered career, he became committed to reform. In addition to his grandsons he appointed a number of Catholic Reformers to the cardinalate, including Contarini, Caraffa, Morone, Pole, and Sadoleto.

The pope took the first open step toward a council by appointing a commission to draw up a report on conditions of the church that called for reform. The commission was made up entirely of the reform-minded cardinals. The report, *The Council on Reforming the Church,* was ready by 1537 and published in 1538. It not only delineated abuses in need of reform from the papacy on down, but called for the abolition of unreformed Franciscan and Augustinian monasteries. The report further questioned the use of Erasmus's *Colloquies* by schoolboys. Paul received the report but did nothing immediately, despite the urging of such high-minded supporters as Contarini and Vittoria Colonna. Realizing that the reforms they urged would deprive the papacy of much-needed revenues, he made only a few gestures toward reform, and nothing significant came of these actions.

In the meantime Contarini and Caraffa pursued reform in keeping with their own insights. Contarini sought reconciliation with the Protestants at Worms and Regensburg but, as we have seen, to no avail. Caraffa, on the other hand, pursued quite a different course. While in Spain he was impressed with the efficiency of the Inquisition, and he later asked papal permission to reform the Papal Inquisition in Italy after the Spanish model. He even equipped his own house with cells in which to imprison the accused. The reorganized Inquisition inaugurated a reign of terror in the land, driving liberal Catholics underground and Protestants into exile. Which kind of reform would the Catholic Reformation follow? Only the forthcoming council could answer that question. Contarini died in 1542, however, and at that time the Jesuits were rapidly becoming the most powerful force on the horizon. And Caraffa and the Jesuits appeared to be of one mind.

After a number of fruitless attempts, Paul III called for the council to meet at Trent on November 1, 1542. But war broke out once again between Charles V and Francis I, and each forbade his bishops to attend. Quarrels over the Farnese family and the dukedom of Parma further delayed the much-anticipated council. It finally convened on December 13, 1545 in Trent, Austria, an imperial city and therefore to some degree neutral territory that enjoyed certain rights and freedoms protected by the Holy Roman Empire. From the beginning it was evident that the council would be largely an Italian affair. Nevertheless, its accomplishments were indisputably significant.

When at long last the council convened, its opening session was neither well-attended nor representative of the entire church. There were only thirty-one bishops and less than fifty theologians and canonists present. Even though Trent was in Austria, the Germanic peoples were hardly in evidence; the Italian prelates dominated the sessions from beginning to end. A. G. Dickens provides the figures that tell the story: "Of the 270 bishops attending at one time or another, 187 were Italians, 31 Spaniards, 26 French and 2 German."[7] The makeup of the council had a great deal to do with its decisions. At the first session it was decided that instead of having nations vote, which had been the procedure at Constance, the bishops and a few generals of specific monastic orders would vote. This decision immediately gave the Italians the advantage, which meant the ultimate defeat of the emperor's party and the emperor's conviction that it was incumbent upon the council to make certain reforms in order to effect a reconciliation with the Protestants. It also assured the eventual triumph of papal policies within the council.

The Council of Trent consisted of twenty-five sessions held in three periods over a span of eighteen years. In some respects the first period—from December 1545 to March 1547—was the most decisive one. The tenor of the council was decidedly traditional and anti-Prot-

---

7. Dickens, *The Counter Reformation,* p. 109.

estant. The problem presented by the conflicting interests of pope and emperor was solved
by the decision to consider simultaneously both
doctrinal concerns—the papacy's chief desire—
and disciplinary reforms, which Charles longed
to see adopted. But in this approach actual reformatory measures lost out. Among the dogmatic decisions the conciliar fathers made was
the determination that Scripture and Tradition
were equally valid as sources of dogma. The
conciliar fathers ascribed the sole right of interpreting Scripture to the church, and the Vulgate
was given priority over all other Latin texts.

The longest of the decrees of Trent was that
devoted to the doctrine of justification by faith:
it consisted of sixteen chapters and thirty-three
canons. The purpose of the decree was to condemn Luther's teachings on the subject while
affirming those of Augustine. The Tridentine
fathers also effectively closed the door on Bible
study when they rejected the appeal of certain
reform-minded prelates to urge the study of
Scripture at the expense of Scholasticism. The
bishops and canonists not only rejected this
approach to the education of priests but failed
to encourage Bible study by laymen as well.

War broke out again—this time between the
elector of Saxony and Charles V—and the work
of the council was suspended after its eighth
session. In the meantime the emperor successfully overran Elector John Frederick of Saxony
at Mühlberg. The pope then withdrew his soldiers from the emperor's army, and in retaliation
Charles used the Interim of Augsburg to come
to terms with the Protestants, a tactic that in the
end had disastrous consequences for Protestantism.

The second period of the council's meeting—from May 1551 to April 1552—began
with session nine, which was called by Pope
Julius III; he had succeeded Paul III upon the
latter's death in November 1549. In order to
please the emperor, the council invited the Protestants to send their representatives. But those
who did manage to attend soon recognized the
futility of expecting any genuine concessions
from the conciliar fathers and left after making
no new proposals themselves. However, before

the council was forced to bring its deliberations
to a close with its fourteenth session, the fathers
did make a few things quite clear. They reaffirmed the doctrine of transubstantiation and
condemned the teachings of Luther, Zwingli,
and Calvin on the subject. They also reaffirmed
the sacraments of penance and extreme unction. Thus the conservative trend that had
marked the first period of Trent continued until
the council was suspended once again—this
time due to the threat of an invasion by Maurice
of Saxony, the renegade Lutheran prince who
had once been an ally of the emperor. Now
allied with France, he drove the emperor and
his army out of Western Europe. The interrupted
council would not reconvene for another ten
years.

The third and last period of deliberations,
which opened with session fifteen, began in
January 1562 and closed two years later in December 1563. The council doubtless would
have concluded its work sooner if it had not
been for Paul IV (1555-1559), who ascended
the papal throne in May 1555 determined not to
reconvene the council. He saw no need for one;
he felt the papacy was quite capable of handling
the affairs of the church without such help. To
him the procedures of the council were a waste
of time and energy. He was, however, a reforming pope who worked with a vengeance to abolish perceived abuses among the clergy. He
employed the Papal Inquisition to rid the
church of heretics, real and imagined, and those
with whom he was displeased. He even imprisoned Cardinal Morone, without whom the
Council of Trent could hardly function. He summoned Cardinal Pole to Rome for trial while the
cardinal was in the midst of his own work of
reconverting England to Catholicism. In 1559
he brought out the first *Index of Prohibited
Books*, which condemned all the works of Erasmus and all translations of the Bible in vernacular tongues. When the council did reconvene
in 1562 under the pontificate of Pius IV, the
Jesuits had forged to the forefront, and the legacy of Paul IV had created a new atmosphere
within which the council now carried on its
work. After a few initial debates over safe con-

duct for whatever Protestants might show up, the fathers no longer attempted to talk with the Protestant world or even maintain the pretense of doing so. Instead they talked to themselves, reasserting traditional Catholic beliefs more forcibly and clearly than ever before.

Under the guidance of the new pontiff, Giovanni Angelo Medici, who took the name Pius IV (1559–65), the council came under complete papal control. Charles had abdicated, and his brother Ferdinand, even though he still pressed for some of the reforms that Charles had sought, was more easily manipulated than his more sensitive and astute brother had been. In the end he was won over by promises that proved empty. In addition, France now sought papal favor and support in dealing with the Huguenots and thus proved more subservient to papal wishes than it had been previously. As a result, theological questions were answered and troublesome issues were settled not by the fathers on the floor of the council hall but by papal nuncios employing diplomatic tactics in the courts of the princes of Europe. The question of the equality of all bishops with the bishop of Rome was ultimately referred to the pope for a definitive answer. Upon the insistence of the Jesuit theologians Alfonso Salmeron and Diego Laynez, the mass was declared a propitiatory sacrifice for the living and the dead. It was to be offered to the laity in one kind only and said in Latin. Although indulgences were not prohibited in the closing sessions of the council, as some had wished and others had feared they would be, the office of the indulgence seller was eliminated, and an attempt was made to reform the indulgence traffic.

The last session of the council began at 10 A.M. in the cathedral. Tasks left undone—such as preparation of the Breviary, Missal, *Index,* and Catechism—were referred to the pope. A decree was also adopted confirming all previous actions taken under the pontificates of Paul III and Julius III and the decisions made during the sessions of the third period. Now that the church spoke with only one voice—that of the papacy—Pope Pius IV had no difficulty in confirming all decrees and canons of the council in

January 1564. Trent demonstrated among other things that the exaggerated fears entertained by the papacy before the council convened were largely unfounded. The conciliar movement that had given rise to the Council of Constance and had perpetuated itself in the Councils of Basel and Ferrara had clearly run its course. Evidence of the triumph of the papacy over the conciliar movement was most obvious in the fact that for three hundred and six years after Trent no council met, and when one finally did, a schism resulted because of the attempt to make explicit what had been implicit at Trent: papal infallibility.

Even though the more moderate forces seeking a new direction in the education of the priests and more thoroughgoing reforms were ultimately defeated, it must be admitted that Trent did achieve its major goals. Instead of seeking reconciliation with the Protestants, the council delineated the orthodox position so as to eliminate any closet Protestants and their sympathizers. Like the Jesuits, the church now stood closer to the church of Thomas Aquinas and Innocent III than to that of John XXIII or Pope Paul VI. Certain reforms were implemented, but most important, plans were projected for the establishment of seminaries in every diocese. The priesthood was exalted and challenged to attain a higher level of intellectual and moral achievement. The era of uncertainty and self-reproach was replaced by one of confidence and determination to seize the initiative.

INQUISITION AND *INDEX*

Although approved by the pope in the bull *Benedictus Deus* (1564), the decrees of Trent met with a mixed response. The Protestants, understandably enough, were not impressed. What they had previously seen as a serious cleavage between the two confessional camps now seemed to them an unbridgeable gulf. The Holy Roman Empire withheld its approval, divided as it was between Catholic and Protestant princes. In France, Gallicanism was still very much alive, and the attempt to work out a *modus vivendi* with the Huguenots forestalled approval. Spain accepted the doctrinal decrees but rejected any actions of the council that would diminish the authority of their monarch, Philip II. Only in Italy and Poland did the authority of the council and the Tridentine faith hold full sway.

Papal Authority

Even before the council had come to a close, Pius IV flaunted his authority by making cardinals of young boys—one an eleven-year-old Medici, the other an eighteen-year-old. The Council of Trent had moved somewhat half-heartedly to deal with the problem of young cardinals by prohibiting the bestowal of the office on boys below the age of fourteen. Pius was in effect saying that the pope was above the rule of the council, and while some were outraged by this suggestion, the prelates had become so subservient to the pope that they offered no concerted opposition to it. This could be seen as a signal that any genuine reformation had ended and the Counter-Reformation had begun.

Pius V (1566–1572), Michele Ghislieri, was motivated by the ideals of Caraffa, his close friend. With a fierce zeal characteristic of Caraffa he gave his support to the Roman Inquisition, which succeeded in crushing the Protestant movement in Italy. He imposed severe discipline on the monastic orders and the prelates in every land in which his authority was recognized. He did what Paul III had been hesitant to attempt and what even Paul IV had failed to do: he launched radical reforms of the Curia's financial system, eliminating the preaching of indulgences and reducing the papal court from a force of a thousand to five hundred.

Pius V was also bitterly antagonistic toward the Protestants. He congratulated the duke of Alva in his campaign to exterminate Protestantism in the Netherlands. He sent a contingent of troops to Charles IX in France to help destroy the Huguenots, instructing the men to take no prisoners but to execute on the spot all those unfortunate enough to fall into their hands. He lent his support to those who fomented rebellion in England and sent priests into the country with the explicit purpose of undermining the

government and overthrowing Elizabeth. In fact, in the bull *Regnans in excelsis,* issued in 1570, he excommunicated Elizabeth and attempted to incite her subjects to rebellion.

The spirit of Pius V lived on in his successors, particularly Gregory XIII (1572–1585) and Sixtus V (1585–1590). In the very year that Gregory ascended the papal throne the Massacre of St. Bartholomew's Day occurred. Gregory celebrated the event by singing the *Te Deum* in the Sistine Chapel and ordering a medallion struck commemorating the occasion. Gregory also lent his support to the Catholic League of France, led by the Guises, and sowed the seeds of rebellion in Ireland, hoping to attack Elizabeth's rear guard. Sixtus became even more involved in international intrigue and sedition than Gregory had been. It was he who envisioned both the possibility and the necessity of winning Henry IV of France, a Huguenot, for the Catholic Church. He did not live to see the fulfillment of his grand design, but Clement VIII (1592–1605) did, and once again Rome possessed a means by which the papacy could checkmate Spain and Philip II.

With the papacy firmly in control and the Council of Trent behind it, the Roman Catholic Church was poised for decisive action on a number of fronts. This situation has been carefully evaluated by the Catholic historian Henri Daniel-Rops:

> The Church then was not indifferent and resigned in face of Protestantism and its impressive achievements. She did not shut herself up in the fortress of dogma and disciplinary canons built by the Council of Trent, though it must be admitted that her first care hence forward was her own defence. Never before had she been obliged to meet an attack that threatened her very existence and that of the faith whereby she lives. She was still a besieged city, courageously sending out the best of her troops to recover lost ground; but she had also to think of repelling the enemy's assaults. We must not overlook these facts if we wish to understand some of the steps we shall see her take, certain of her judgments in the field of ideas. Even during their own lifetimes Luther, Calvin and other Reformers found themselves and their theories assailed by opponents who, though formi-

dable, were never their equals. But the situation had now altered. There were theologians and exegetes qualified to deal with Protestant attacks; the counteroffensive of Catholic orthodoxy was conducted no less vigorously at the intellectual than at the military level.[8]

The Literary Front

While one may question the accuracy of the last assertion of Daniel-Rops, there is no question that the "counteroffensive" was launched on the literary front as well as the military front. The inventions of printing, a rotary press with movable type, and a relatively inexpensive paper had occurred just in time to make possible the flowering of the Renaissance and the birth of the Reformation. The rapid expansion of small presses in the cities as well as the amazing output of the great printers such as Johann Froben of Basel, Christoph Froschauer of Zürich, and Aldus Manutius of Venice had flooded Europe with an avalanche of humanist and Reformational books and tracts that sent the Roman Church reeling. Although Rome was a little tardy in fully exploiting the new medium, it began to return the fire in kind. Although the *Complutensian Polyglot* was a monument to the printer's art and in itself a magnificent achievement of Catholic scholarship, it was an almost negligible factor in the manuscript warfare that now ensued. The gifted Jesuit convert Peter Canisius led the way with his *Catechism*. Robert Bellarmine and Cesare Baronius were quick to follow with impressive and effective tomes of their own.

To Robert Bellarmine (1542–1621) goes the credit for encapsulating within the covers of a single volume Roman Catholic theology as defined by the Council of Trent. Educated at the Universities of Padua and Louvain, Bellarmine taught at Louvain for seven years before becoming "Professor of Controversies" at the New Roman College (Gregorian University). It was

here that he wrote his well-known *Disputationes de controversiis Christianae fidei (Controversies)*, which was a studied attempt to set forth the teachings of Protestant and other heresies for a thoroughgoing refutation in the light of the decisions made at Trent. Its usefulness in countering the Reformation was immediately recognized, and it was soon translated into the vernacular tongues of Europe. Bellarmine barely escaped the clutches of the Inquisition led by Sixtus V for foolishly denying the temporal authority of the pope over all the earth; he was saved by some wiser than he. Later he participated in still another revision of the Vulgate, which all knowledgeable scholars, Catholic and Protestant alike, recognized as riddled with errors. Through his writings and lectures he helped to fortify many a young priest against evangelical propaganda. He was rewarded for his efforts by being made a cardinal as well as archbishop of Capua. In 1930 he was canonized and declared a "Doctor of the Church" by Pius XI.

Cesare Baronius (1538–1607), although not the recipient of the honors that were heaped on Bellarmine, made an honest attempt to write and document church history in such a way as to refute Protestant works such as Sebastian Franck's *Chronica (Chronicle)* and Flacius Illyricus's *Centuries of Magdeburg*. For thirty years he labored to produce his *Ecclesiastical Annals (Annals of the Church)*. He attempted to base his work upon relevant historical documents and spent years doing intensive research in the Vatican Archives. The product was actually not so much a work about the history of the church as an apologetical work that attempted to use certain historical data on behalf of Rome in its struggle with the heretics. However effective it may have been for the times in which it was written, it has failed to withstand the test of time.

The Inquisition

In its conflict with Protestantism, the church also discovered more weapons in its arsenal. The most ancient of these was that of the Inquisi-

8. Daniel-Rops, *The Catholic Reformation*, trans. John Warrington (New York: Dutton, 1962), p. 338.

tion. In the ninth century the responsibility of seeking out heretics and punishing them was placed in the hands of the bishops. But the episcopal Inquisition proved too haphazard in its attempt to stamp out heresy, and it was reorganized. From the thirteenth century onward it was more closely supervised and regulated by the papacy. Consequently, the center of the entire operation was moved to Rome. The bishops were still responsible for the suppression of heresy in their respective dioceses, but the process was now systematized and supervised by Rome. The Inquisition operated as the Papal Inquisition but with limited success. In 1478 Sixtus IV issued a papal bull giving Ferdinand and Isabella sweeping authority to establish a Spanish Inquisition. In a short time this new Inquisition became the most efficient instrument for the suppression of dissent yet developed.

In its initial stages the Spanish Inquisition sought out heretics other than Protestants, since at that time there were no Protestants in Spain (or anywhere else, for that matter). Its purpose was to rid the church of those converts from Judaism and Mohammedanism who were suspected of holding on to their old beliefs and secretly practicing their former religion. Spain's long and arduous struggle with the Moors and the jealousy of the Iberians toward the successful and wealthy Jews and Moors within their midst undoubtedly accounted for the racial overtones of the early stages of the Spanish Inquisition. The first victims were six Jews who were burned to death in an auto-da-fé in Seville on February 6, 1481. When Protestantism did appear, the machinery already existed for its efficient annihilation.

The operations of the Spanish Inquisition were marked by secrecy and torture. The belief that it was possible to purify the church and save multitudes by making an example of relatively few heretics was embraced by the Catholic monarchs and the Inquisitor General Tomás de Torquemada with a fervor not matched elsewhere. Torquemada directed the Inquisition in Spain for eighteen years, during which time, according to Ilorente (who was at

one time its secretary), an estimated 114,000 victims were accused of heresy. Of these, 10,220 were burned to death, and 97,000 were sentenced to life imprisonment or to performing acts of public penance. Of course, the church did not punish those declared guilty but turned them over to civil authorities for punishment. The examination and torture of those suspected of heresy was carried out by the Dominicans and at times by the Franciscans. The Spanish Inquisition was thorough, and few charismatic leaders escaped suspicion. Even Ignatius Loyola and Saint Teresa of Ávila were among the accused.

When Caraffa visited Spain, he was so impressed with the effectiveness of the Spanish version of the Inquisition that he decided to reorganize the Papal Inquisition after its pattern. The Congregation of the Holy Office, as the revamped Papal Inquisition was called, was established by Paul III in 1542. Six cardinals, including Caraffa, were appointed inquisitor generals and given the authority to try all cases of heresy in Europe, to arrest and imprison suspects, and to set up inquisitorial courts to do the same. The targets of its immediate activities were Rome and the States of the Church, but its zealous work soon reached into every part of Italy. Caraffa was determined to stamp out Protestantism, which had found a following in nine or ten Italian cities, including Ferrara, Lucca, Naples, Siena, and Venice. The Holy Office accomplished its purpose in short order, even driving Renée, the duchess of Ferrara, from her little province. Caraffa (as Pope Paul IV) became so paranoid that he even had Cardinal Morone imprisoned. Henri Daniel-Rops gives a brief but revealing glimpse into the work of the Holy Office in Italy as it extended into the early decades of the seventeenth century:

> What steps did the Church take when confronted with such grave perils? In the most flagrant cases of impiety and atheism she was still too strong not to react by way of violence and the argument of authority. At such times she wore a grim and threatening look, as indeed she was obliged to do amid the terrible dangers that beset her; at such times the Inquisition struck. Giordano Bruno, who foolishly allowed himself to be arrested at

Venice, was condemned and burned in the Campo dei Fiori at Rome (1600) for his heretical views on Transubstantiation and the Trinity, as well as for his theory of a plurality of worlds. Campanella just managed to escape with his life; after spending twenty-seven years in prison he died peacefully in the convent of Rue Saint-Honore at Paris. Galileo was denounced to the Holy Office and condemned in 1616, less no doubt on account of his strictly scientific ideas than because of the tenacity with which he applied them to Scripture. His submission saved him from the worst, but did not protect him from a second trial in 1633. Vanini had his tongue torn out by the executioner and was burned alive. Théophile de Viau was thrown into prison when the government of Louis XIII, by request of the Church, decided to inflict severe penalties on atheists and blasphemers (1617).[9]

Although the revamped Roman Inquisition was never as severe or as thorough as the Spanish Inquisition, it did strike terror in the hearts of many, and it did accomplish its purpose. A whole series of popes used the newly sharpened tool to weed heresy from the land. Even the Waldenses in Cambria near Cosenza were not spared. As Daniel-Rops admits, the church did not hesitate to use every means at its command, including the stake and the sword, to combat the Protestants. One of those means that it used more or less successfully was the *Index of Prohibited Books.*

The *Index*

Paul IV, who drafted the first papal *Index* in 1559, did not give birth to the idea of thought control through censorship. It had existed for a long time. The medieval church had sought to destroy "pernicious books" through various means but with little success. With the advent of the printing press the task had become increasingly difficult if not impossible. To attempt to stem the tide of heretical literature, Torquemada had committed about six thousand volumes to the flames at Salamanca in 1490.

Beginning with Alexander VI, the popes began to take a lively interest in throttling the press. In 1501 the Borgia pope sent orders to the archbishops of Cologne (Köln), Mainz, Trier, and Magdeburg that no books were to be printed without previous license. Leo X made the prohibition more explicit, and in 1547 Sixtus IV sent orders to the University of Cologne repeating the prohibitions of Alexander VI. When the Papal Inquisition was reorganized, censorship of suspected books became a part of its responsibility. Despite mushrooming *Indexes* in Catholic Europe, however, the task of suppressing heretical literature remained formidable. Paul IV attempted to make the prohibitions universal with his *Index librorum prohibitorum.* As Peter Klassen indicates, Paul's *Index* censored several kinds of publications:

> (1) all works by authors who were guilty or suspected of heresy, even though individual volumes might be inoffensive (all works of Erasmus were included in this category); (2) selected works of otherwise orthodox authors, since these specific books might undermine the faith of some; and (3) various books which contained heretical teachings, many of them of anonymous authorship. The *Index* also prohibited the reading of vernacular translations of the New Testament. All publications coming from some sixty-one presses were condemned.[10]

The Council of Trent wrestled with the problem of determining principles whereby the *Index* would suppress heresy without prohibiting the writing and printing of legitimate and necessary books. But the conciliar fathers were not very successful in this endeavor. The ten rules upon which they finally agreed and that they recommended to the pope dealt a death blow to genuine scholarship. In addition to forbidding the works of the Reformers, the rules declared the Vulgate the only authorized version of Scripture. It alone was authoritative; vernacular versions could not be quoted. Because of the rules, commentaries and other books were scrupulously examined for references or

9. Daniel-Rops, *The Catholic Reformation,* p. 351.

10. Klassen, *Europe in the Reformation* (Englewood Cliffs, N.J.: Prentice-Hall, 1979), p. 227.

footnotes that might possibly "mislead" any reader. Censors were not above harassing authors, suppressing their books for reasons other than acceptable content, and attempting to collect blackmail from booksellers. Thomas M. Lindsay writes,

> So effectually was learning slain in Italy, that when the Popes at the close of the sixteenth century strove to revive the scholarship of the Church and to gather together at Rome a band of men able to defend the Papacy with their pens, these scholars had to work under immense disabilities. Baronius wrote his *Annals*, and Latini edited the Latin Fathers, both of them ignorant of Greek, and both harassed by the censorship.[11]

Lindsay is not alone in his indictment of the *Index*. Peter Canisius, the German Jesuit, protested in vain against the severity of the *Index* as published by Pius IV in 1564. Paul Sarpi, a Roman Catholic author, dubbed it "the finest secret which has ever been discovered for applying religion to the purpose of making men idiots."[12] There is little doubt that the *Index*

---

11. Lindsay, *A History of the Reformation*, 2 vols. (New York: Scribner's, 1907, 1928), 2: 605.

12. Sarpi, cited by Lindsay in *A History of the Reformation*, 2: 604.

inflicted a severe blow upon the church's intellectual life; indeed, it took the church centuries to recover from it. Only Vatican Council II (1962–1966) revealed to what extent the Roman Catholic Church has thrown off the shackles of Trent and its strictures on Scripture and scholarship.

Resort to the Sword

The cold war that the revival of Catholicism in its medieval grandeur fought turned hot as papal armies carried out orders to exterminate Huguenots, Waldenses, and Hussites. As Rome grew more militant, so did the Protestants. That there were religious wars before the Council of Trent ended is a well-known fact, but the enormous scale of the conflict between rival Protestant and Catholic armies is sometimes minimized when and if it is recalled at all. Both tension and military action escalated and continued to increase until the stalemate marked by the Peace of Westphalia in 1648. Before that pivotal date the religious situation in Europe became increasingly volatile, politicized, and confusing. It constitutes one of the saddest chapters in Reformation history, but dark as it is, it cannot be avoided.

Chapter XVI

CONFLICT AND CHANGE

uring the eighteen-year span of the Council of Trent, the religious configuration of Northern Europe was undergoing a rapid change. An occasional setback notwithstanding, the march of Protestantism in the Holy Roman Empire seemed irresistible. When Albert of Mainz died in September 1545, he was succeeded by one who owed his office to the support of Protestant princes, whom he soon repaid by opening his territory to evangelical preaching. He also permitted clerical marriage and communion in both kinds. The elector of the Palatinate also received communion in both kinds in January 1546 and joined the Schmalkaldic League, a military alliance made up of Lutheran territories and cities. Consequently, by the outbreak of the Schmalkaldic War, the majority of the electors of the Holy Roman Empire were casting their lots with the Protestants.

CHARLES V AND THE SCHMALKALDIC WAR

After still another conference at Regensburg failed to achieve reconciliation between Protestants and Catholics, the emperor decided to resort to arms. In July he denounced as outlaws Landgrave Philip of Hesse, Elector John Freder-

ick of Saxony, and the leaders of the Schmalkaldic League. Charles V was now surer than ever of a military victory over the German princes because of the defection of Maurice of Saxony. Maurice had a sizable army and ambition to match. He allied himself with Charles V in the hopes of defeating the Schmalkaldic League and gaining for himself John Frederick's position as elector. In a very short time he overran the land and with the aid of the emperor and his Spanish army secured the coveted position for himself. He was made elector in October 1546. John Frederick was defeated by Charles and his army at Mühlberg and taken captive on April 24, 1547. Philip of Hesse, Maurice's father-in-law, surrendered to the emperor at Halle on June 19 and was imprisoned. The archbishop elector of Cologne was forced to retire to his ancestral estate. Spanish troops occupied every major Protestant center in Germany. Thus the Schmalkaldic League was destroyed and with it Lutheran religious life and political influence in much of Germany.

But Charles was astute enough to realize that peace would not come to his troubled empire without compromise. For this reason he drew up a confession of faith known as the Augsburg Interim, to which some of the leading Protestant theologians subscribed, including Melanch-thon. It made a few concessions to the Lu-therans, but once again, as at the Second Diet of Speyer, the Lutheran princes—notably John Frederick, who was a prisoner of Charles V at the time—refused to compromise. The wisdom of John Frederick's courageous action soon be-came apparent as the triumphant emperor de-termined to use every means at his command to coerce conformity to the Catholic faith. The displacement of Lutheran worship by Catholic liturgy proved much more successful in south-ern Germany than in the North. Magdeburg be-came the last stronghold of the Lutherans, but it too fell in November 1551. The military defeat of the Protestant cause by the emperor and his allies seemed total until Maurice once again turned the tables.

Henry II of France—apparently out of the same kind of greed that had motivated Maurice in 1546—entered into a secret agreement with Maurice to wage war against Charles on a num-ber of fronts. Maurice had become increasingly dissatisfied because of the continued imprison-ment of Philip of Hesse, his father-in-law. The German princes who still had the capacity to wage war joined Maurice's army as he laid siege to Innsbruck. Charles barely escaped. In the meantime a French army fought against the Spanish in the Netherlands, and Henry II won a significant victory in Lorraine. Albert of Bran-denburg, a Catholic, successfully waged war against the imperial cities of Nuremberg, Bam-berg, and Würzburg, and then turned to assist the French on the Rhine. Maurice and his army won the Battle of Sieverhausen in July 1553, but two losses accompanied the victory: Maurice lost his life, and Charles lost his throne.

The aged emperor, having suffered embar-rassment and defeat, now found himself op-posed by his old enemies, the papacy and France. Betrayed and defeated by his new ally, he determined to abdicate in favor of his son Philip II, leaving it to his brother Ferdinand, archduke of Austria, to come to grips with the problems of an empire in turmoil. The result was the Peace of Augsburg, spelled out in a treaty drawn up on September 25, 1555. The

following year the frustrated and disheartened monarch retired to a monastery to live out his remaining days in religious devotion. The Peace of Augsburg applied only to the Lutherans be-cause it recognized only those who were party to the Augsburg Confession of 1530. In essence it followed the guidelines of the First Diet of Speyer. The princes, Catholic or Lutheran, were to have full authority over the religious life of their territories (*cujus regio, ejus religio*). If there were those who lived in an area ruled by a prince who did not share their faith, they could move out of the territory without loss of honor or worldly goods. However, the Eccle-siastical Reservation stated that if a Catholic prel-ate changed his faith, he would be obliged to resign and give his position to one recognized by the Roman Church. Although the Augsburg treaty carried within it the seeds of future con-flict, at that time it appeared to be the best possible solution to an increasingly complex religious conflict. What neither party counted on was the development of a vastly more ag-gressive and militant form of the Protestant faith: Calvinism.

THE SPAIN OF PHILIP II

"Most of the political and religious history of Europe during the latter half of the sixteenth century was determined by the ambitions of Philip II (1556-1598) of Spain, whom the dying Pope Paul IV had recognized as the strongest pillar of Catholicism." Thus begins Harold Grimm's evaluation of Philip II and his influ-ence upon the history of Christianity in Spain and Europe.[1] Although a Hapsburg and an ad-mirer of his father, Charles V, Philip considered himself a Spaniard. He was born in 1527 in Valladolid. By the time he was eighteen, he had married a Portuguese princess; she gave him a son but she died in childbirth. When he was not quite thirty, he became king of Spain and the ruler of its far-flung possessions. The most pow-

---

1. Grimm, *The Reformation Era, 1500-1650* (New York: Macmillan, 1954), p. 419.

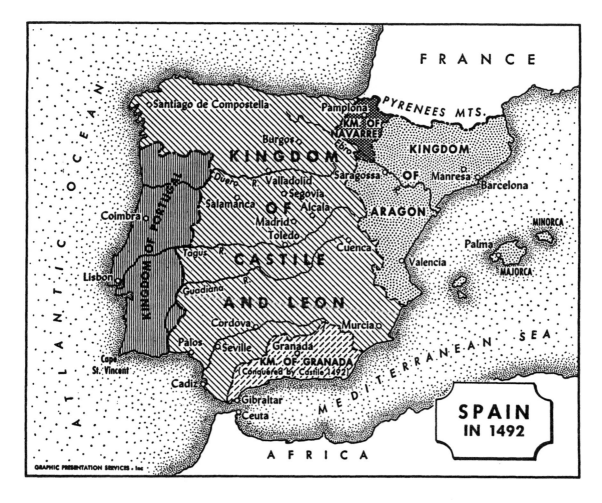

erful nation in Europe faced the last half of her "Golden Century" with confidence and pride— and Philip was almost equal to the task.

The young king personified the Spanish ideal of the Catholic Reformation. In addition to his mother tongue, he was fluent in French, Latin, and Italian. He was also a patron of the arts and literature. He turned the Escorial Palace, itself a splendid example of Spanish architecture, into a museum housing his collection of art objects that had few rivals in Europe. Because of his love of books he built up a library of more than four thousand volumes. He was also a lover of music and a competent musician in his own right. Above everything else, the gifted young monarch was a devout Catholic. He attended mass every day, and he provided for a monastery

in his palace. He supported the work of the Inquisition, giving its courts free rein to stamp out the Protestant heresy and to keep the *moriscos* and *conversos* under surveillance and control. In fact, the Inquisition began hounding "good Catholics" so relentlessly that Pope Pius V launched a protest against its unscrupulous severity.

In Spain it was said that there was no pope, only a king. More than one pope accused the Spanish monarchs of usurping papal prerogatives for themselves. That there was some substance to these charges is undeniable. Philip, for example, waited more than a year to publish the decrees of the Council of Trent, realizing that they would interfere with royal revenues. When he finally did publish them on July 19,

1564, he added certain royal reservations that nullified some of the decrees. Three years later Pius V issued an edict against bullfights that Philip ignored; it was Philip's stated policy that no papal bulls could be published in Spain without his approval. It became very clear early in his reign that the young monarch, like his father, would serve the church only on his own terms, and it was increasingly evident that in his eyes Rome's interests were second to those of Spain.

The rule of Philip was absolute. Eventually he had twelve councils to which he turned for information and advice, and two able personal advisors, Ruy Gomez de Silva, the prince of Eboli, and Ferdinando Alvarez de Toledo, the duke of Alva, but he alone made the final decisions of government. He took seriously his father's advice—to depend upon no one but himself. As a consequence, the pace of government was painfully slow, and Philip frequently got bogged down in details and seemed unable to distinguish between the trivial and the important. Yet he was his own man, and even when his final decisions were disastrous for his country, as his grand designs frequently were, he remained undaunted, "bloody but unbowed."

Philip dealt with military matters differently than his father. He did not attempt to give orders to the Spanish troops in the field, leaving that chore to Don Juan, his half brother, and the duke of Alva. Neither does he seem to have realized, as his father did, the depth of earnest conviction that motivated many Protestants. Philip was apparently gentle by nature and treated his family and the members of his court with kindness, but he was relentless in his determination to stamp out heresy, whether Protestant or Moorish. The few exceptions he made—such as the case of Elizabeth—seem to have been motivated by personal and political considerations rather than religious reasons. Such a devotee of the Roman Church proved a mixed blessing to the Counter-Reformation, but he did succeed in stamping out the last vestige of the Reformation in Spain.

PROTESTANTISM IN SPAIN

The art of printing in Spain lagged behind that in other European countries. The first book apparently was a small grammar printed in Barcelona in October 1468. The most ambitious printing project was that of Cardinal Jiménez, who imported German printers to set up the presses and cast the type for the *Complutensian Polyglot*. The works of Luther and other Reformers were printed elsewhere and smuggled into the country by Spaniards who had traveled abroad and by foreigners as well. In 1520 Luther's *Commentary on Galatians* was printed in Spanish, and other tracts from his facile pen soon followed. About the same time, books by Erasmus such as his *Adages, The Enchiridion*, and *The Praise of Folly*, which had been available in Latin editions, were also translated into Spanish. However, the Inquisition banned almost all of Erasmus's works as well as those of Luther. Despite this prohibition, the books did manage to trickle in, but the flow hardly resembled an unchecked stream. Foreign and Spanish ships sailing from foreign ports were subjected to systematic searches, and any Protestant books discovered were seized and burned. Spanish priests, university students, soldiers, and members of the entourage of Charles V frequently traveled outside of Spain, so contact with Reformation ideas and writings was unavoidable. But Spain was as effectively protected against the Lutheran heresy as the agents of the Inquisition could make it.

Indeed, the Inquisition was so pervasive and thorough that even the hint of heresy fired by the slightest animosity or jealously on the part of an inquisitor became the occasion for investigation and, not infrequently, condemnation. Consequently, many a promising Reformer was driven from his homeland. According to R. Trevor Davies, the Reformation was crushed in Spain within a decade, and hence all subsequent Protestant activity within Spain was instigated by outsiders.[2] Whether or not this was

---

2. Davies, *The Golden Century of Spain* (New York: Harper & Row, 1937), p. 141.

actually the case is difficult to ascertain, but what became all too obvious for the comfort of the inquisitors was the widespread influence of Spanish Reformers living in exile. Thus the history of the Spanish Reformation cannot be confined to the Iberian peninsula.

From the beginning the Spanish Reformation attracted the elite from among the high born and the hierarchy of the Roman Church. Among these were Alfonso and Juan de Valdés.

Alfonso and Juan de Valdés

Alfonso and Juan de Valdés were twin sons born to the Spanish nobleman, the mayor of Cuença, about the turn of the century. They received an excellent education through a private tutor named Pedro Martis de Angleria, an Italian who had come to Spain as an ambassador extraordinaire. Martis taught the Valdés brothers more than grammar and an eloquent Latin style; he imbued them with an openness to the truth and a respect for the convictions of others.

In addition, Martis had the necessary connections to place Alfonso in the service of Charles V. Alfonso was with the Spanish entourage at Aix-la-Chapelle (Aachen) in 1520 when Charles V was crowned emperor of the Holy Roman Empire. He was with the emperor again at Worms and was convinced that the Edict of Worms was not the end of Luther's rebellion (which he referred to as a "tragedy"), but "the beginning of it."[3]

Alfonso was an ardent disciple of Erasmus and favorably inclined toward the Reformation, but he was also a Roman Catholic and in the service of the emperor. On Charles's behalf he wrote a defense of the Spanish sack of Rome. After Clement VII and Charles were reconciled, the emperor was crowned a second time, this time by the pope at Bologna. Alfonso was there, and later in the same year he attended the Diet of Augsburg. There he sought to influence the emperor to adopt a more tolerant attitude toward the Lutherans. It is not likely that he was a closet Lutheran, but he did join Luther's call for a general council. While still in the service of the emperor, he died at Vienna of the plague on October 5, 1532.

Much more is known about Juan's religious convictions than those of Alfonso. In the fall of 1527 Juan was enrolled in the University of Alcalá to study the humanities. The famous *Complutensian Polyglot* had been published just five years before. Although well educated, Juan longed to learn Greek, probably because of his theological interest. His fascination with theological concerns is indicated by his first published work, *Dialogue on Christian Doctrine,* published by Miguel de Equía in 1529. It immediately came under fire by hostile critics. The Inquisition was alerted, but by August 1531 Juan had fled to Rome. Through a friend's help he was employed by the emperor, in whose service he remained for a short time. For another brief period he was a chamberlain of Pope Clement VII. After the death of Clement he moved to Naples, where he lived the last six years of his life. These years proved the most fruitful of his brief career.

Juan had never been physically strong, and when he sensed that his days were numbered, he devoted himself with feverish energy to prayer, Bible study, and writing. On Sundays a group of friends gathered in his home for worship. Because of these gatherings and his personal friendships with numerous like-minded persons, his influence knew no national barriers. His reformatory efforts had a profound effect upon a number of people, including Cardinal Pietro Carnesecchi, member of the Curia and secretary of Clement VII; Bernardino Ochino de Siena, general of the Capuchins; Peter Martyr Vermigli, gifted Greek scholar and able theologian; Vittoria Colonna, a noblewoman and personal friend of Cardinal Contarini; Marquesa di Pescara; and Giulia Gonzaga, countess of Fondi, who guarded the unpublished manuscripts of Valdés. Several members of the Valdensian congregation in Naples were martyred for their faith; others fled the country.

---

3. Edward Boehmer, *Spanish Reformers of Two Centuries from 1520,* 2 vols. (Strasbourg: Trübner, 1874, 1883), 1: 5.

Valdés is known today because of the discovery and publication of the writings left unpublished during his lifetime. Pier Pado Vergerio, bishop of Capo d'Istria, was papal nuncio and a member of the Council of Trent. He thought so much of Valdés's *One Hundred and Ten Considerations* that he had it published in Basel in 1550. (*The Christian Alphabet,* which ranks along with *One Hundred and Ten Considerations* and which marked the beginning of a deeper spiritual life for Valdés, was not published until much later.) A few years after his death, Spanish translations of his commentaries on Romans and First Corinthians were published in Geneva (in 1556 and 1557 respectively). Valdés also wrote commentaries on the Psalms and the Gospel of Matthew.

In the final analysis, what was the religious affiliation of Juan de Valdés? This is not an easy question to answer. Some recent authors have claimed him for the Catholic Church, and indeed his closest friend, Giulia Gonzaga, wrote that Valdés died in the faith in which he lived. But Angel Mergal suggests that Valdés was not a Catholic,[4] and Catholic historians such as Menéndez y Pelayo and Ludwig Pastor as well as Protestant historians such as Griffen and Edward Boehmer agree. Yet if he was neither a Calvinist nor a Lutheran, as Boehmer contends, then what was he? Mergal insists that he was a Spanish Reformer in the tradition of Spanish mysticism, and surely there is some truth in this. But it is also evident that there was a progression in Valdés's thought. He was first an Erasmian, but under the influence of the *devotio moderna,* his own study of the Scriptures, and a variety of influences both Catholic and Protestant, he developed his own concepts of justification by faith, regeneration, general atonement, and freedom of the will. There are some striking parallels between his thought and that of Luther and even Hubmaier, yet he rejected Scholastic categories and developed his own theology in a

conscious attempt to bring his mind into conformity with that of Christ. Mergal summarizes Valdés well when he writes,

> Self-knowledge and knowledge of God, the inquiry into the image of man as he is and the image of man as he ought to be according to the image of God as revealed by Jesus Christ—this is his point of departure from which he approaches all reality. He finds evil in man as a whole, body and mind. The capacity for discriminating good from evil is the essence of human personality, yet even that is the consequence of original sin. To get beyond the limitations that evil places upon man's judgment, a restitution of the original image of God is necessary. This is done by the acceptance of the gospel as a personal experience of pardon. Only then is truth unveiled to man, even if not fully.[5]

Juan de Valdés may not have been "the greatest of the Spanish Reformers," as Mergal claims, but he certainly was the first of a number of able and devout Spaniards to give themselves to the work of reformation in Spain and beyond. Juan never attacked the errors of Catholicism but chose rather to present his understanding of the evangel in a positive and biblical fashion. However, this did not prevent the *Index* from prohibiting the reading and possession of many of his works.

Lutherans with a Spanish Accent

Although Lutheran influence is discernable in the later works of Juan de Valdés, he was not a doctrinaire Lutheran. But a number of zealous Spanish converts to the Reformation were indeed Lutherans. The first of these, Juan Díaz, was also one of the most gifted and noble of the converts. Like Valdés, he was from Cuença. For thirteen years or more he was at the University of Paris, where he applied himself to the study of theology and the biblical languages. Here he met a convinced Protestant and fellow countryman, Jaime de Enzinas, who was responsible for turning his religious quest in a new direction. Shortly after experiencing this

---

4. Mergal, "Evangelical Catholicism as Represented by Juan de Valdes," in *Spiritual and Anabaptist Writers,* ed. Mergal and G. H. Williams, vol. 25 of the Library of Christian Classics (Philadelphia: Westminster Press, 1957), p. 318.

5. Mergal, "Evangelical Catholicism," pp. 318-19.

change, Diaz left Paris for Geneva. After spending some time in Geneva he made a public profession of his faith in the church under Martin Bucer's leadership at Strasbourg, professing in the presence of another Spaniard by the name of Pedro Maluenda. Maluenda never forgave Diaz for his apostasy, his rejection of the Roman Church, and from this time on sought to reconvert him.

Diaz became a close friend of Bucer, who recognized the value of Diaz's superb intellectual and spiritual gifts. Bucer thus invited him to become one of the Protestant delegation to that last abortive colloquy between Protestant and Catholic theologians at Regensburg. Such prominence brought Diaz to the attention of his brother Alfonso, who promptly left Rome for Regensburg on a mission for the Curia: to reclaim Juan or kill him. The two met and had many an earnest conversation, but Alfonso failed to bring his erring brother back into the fold. A final tearful farewell took place at Neuburg. Early the next morning Alfonso and his traveling companion slipped back into the town and managed to gain entrance to the pastor's home where Juan was staying with his friend Senarcleus. Swiftly the deed was done, and Juan Diaz lay dying with a hatchet buried in his skull. The news of the treachery that ended the life of one of Spain's most devout sons was soon being told in Spain itself. Even 450 years later the event finds its way into almost every book that relates the history of the Spanish Reformation.[6]

Jaime de Enzinas, who first bore witness to Juan Diaz, was himself martyred in Rome the following year (1546-47). Against his better judgment he had returned to Italy at his parents' insistence. When he was apprehended and interrogated by the Inquisition, he remained steadfast in the faith and consequently was burned at the stake near the bridge of St. Angelo.[7] His older brother, Francisco de Enzinas, also known as Dryander (the Greek equivalent), became a fervent evangelical and lived to make the greater contribution.

Francisco and Jaime were from a wealthy family of Burgos in northern Spain. Both brothers apparently studied for a while in Louvain, which in 1540 was rapidly turning away from the openness that had characterized it when Erasmus taught there, although a few professors remained sympathetic toward evangelical reform. Jaime left Louvain for Paris, later returning before going to Antwerp to publish his Spanish catechism. Francisco stayed about a year but longed to study with Melanchthon, so he left Louvain for Germany and enrolled in the University of Wittenberg on October 27, 1541. Fired with the determination to translate the Greek New Testament into Spanish, Francisco spent every waking moment on his beloved project with Melanchthon as his consultant. Early in 1543 he completed the project and left Germany for the Netherlands to seek a printer.

Francisco Enzinas now made several attempts to have his translation examined by competent Roman Catholic theologians. After repeated attempts he secured the approval of some anonymous Franciscans, who pronounced it without serious error. Friends advised him to wait until the emperor's arrival in Brussels to obtain permission for its publication. Although he rejected this advice and had his New Testament printed in Antwerp, he did wait to distribute it until a copy was presented to the aging monarch. What Enzinas didn't know was that when Charles V had heard that a Castilian translation was being printed, he had issued an order prohibiting its sale. However, when Charles finally granted Enzinas an audi-

---

6. R. Trevor Davies's *The Golden Century of Spain* is an exception. Menéndez y Pelayo in his *Historia de los Heterodoxos Españoles*, 4 vols. (Buenos Aires: Editorial Glem, 1945), 1: 586-96, relates the tragic story in as much detail as does Edward Boehmer in his *Spanish Reformers of Two Centuries*, 1: 187-99. However, Boehmer adds that although Alfonso was never indicted for the crime or called before any tribunal, he hanged himself at the Council of Trent in 1551. Both authors apparently base their accounts on those of Senarcleus and Sepúlveda, the imperial historiographer. There are also references to Diaz's murder in Bucer's account of the colloquy.

7. John Stoughton, *The Spanish Reformers: Their Memories and Dwelling Places* (London: Religious Tract Society, 1883), p. 84.

ence, he pretended to receive the translator with respect and to respond to his New Testament graciously. But the emperor's confessor, a Dominican by the name of Pedro Soto, declared the translation an act of heresy. After his last interview with Soto on December 13, 1543, Francisco was seized by waiting soldiers and imprisoned.

The harshness of prison life was made more tolerable by fellowship with other prisoners who were also serving time for their heretical views. But in January martyrdom became the fate of two of the prisoners. Just van Ousberghen from Louvain was beheaded on January 7, and Aegidius Tielmans, his close friend, was tortured before being burned to death on January 27. In February, however, Enzinas benefitted from a fortuitous error. Leaning against a door one day, he discovered that it was unlocked— as was the next one and the outside door as well. He fled, and with the help of friends he made his way back to Wittenberg. Returning to the home of Melanchthon, he drew up a narrative of his experiences entitled *On the State of the Netherlands and on Religion in Spain.* (This has become the source that many writers have used to learn the essential facts of Enzinas's narrow escape.) Soon afterwards he was to write the tragic story of Juan Diaz's murder, based upon details supplied by Senarcleus, Diaz's close friend and traveling companion.

Although he was never allowed to return to his homeland, Enzinas made his impact upon the Protestant Reformation not only in Northern Europe but also in his native Spain as well. Like Calvin, whose thoughts were always directed toward France, Enzinas never forgot his native land. Shortly before his death he wrote to a friend, "I am working with good conscience, God be my witness. If the people of this time will not thank me, I hope there will come others in the future of better judgment, to whom our studies shall not be useless."[8] Like so many Spanish evangelicals after him, Enzinas became

a vagabond. In his journeys he met and was befriended by the leading Reformers of Europe, with whom he carried on a lengthy correspondence. Calvin was the single exception; Enzinas felt little sympathy with him. Cranmer even gave Enzinas a professorship of Greek at Cambridge, a position that he held until just two years before his death. Spain did not escape the impact of so prolific a writer, but this did not become evident until later, after Enzinas had died of the pestilence in Strasbourg on December 30, 1552.

The Reformation Centers in Spain

During the sixteenth century the Protestant Reformation was not nearly as pervasive in Spain as certain reports suggest. This was due partly to the fact that overzealous inquisitors saw heresy where there was none and partly to the fact that they did their work so effectively that they stifled the Reformation in its Spanish cradle. Then too, some who were reported to have been Protestants—including "Crazy Jane," mother of Charles V; Don Carlos, the afflicted son of Philip II and his first wife; and Archbishop Bartholomé Carranza—were by any impartial standard of judgment not Protestants. Others like Alfonso de Valdés, although sympathetic to certain aspects of the Reformation, could hardly be accurately identified as Lutheran. In some respects, then, John E. Longhurst's title of his work on the Reformation in Spain, *Luther's Ghost in Spain (1517-1546),* is as appropriate as it is suggestive. However, Longhurst does maintain that there was something more than a Lutheran apparition in the Iberian peninsula. He gives a list of accused "Lutherans" that consists of slightly more than fifty names.

While here and there a bona fide Protestant showed up in some small town or hamlet, apparently there were only two major centers of the Reformation in Spain—Seville and Valladolid. What makes the whole situation so confusing, as Longhurst points out, is that in the period under study a suspected heretic did not have to be a Lutheran or even know Luther's name to be accused of Lutheranism. Quite frequently the accused were condemned because

---

8. Enzinas, cited by Boehmer in *Spanish Reformers of Two Centuries,* 1: 155.

of an inquisitor's ignorance about the nature of Luther's teaching or malice toward the accused—indeed, this was generally true of the accusations of Protestant heresy brought against many.

Seville

Although the Protestants in Spain did not form churches after any recognizable Reformational pattern, apparently in both Seville and Valladolid there were informal conventicles where like-minded persons met for prayer, fellowship, and Bible study. In Seville the monastery of San Isidro del Campo, not far from the Castle of Triena, the inquisitorial prison, became the cradle of the newborn evangelical movement. Its leader was an abbot by the name of Garcia de Arias, also known as Dr. Blanco. Under his direction the entire monastery was radically changed, and its influence spread among Seville's elite, including both the nobility and some of the leading cathedral preachers.

The Protestants of Seville met in the homes of the believers. One that became known to the Inquisition was that of Doña Isabella de Baena, and in 1560 the inquisitors ordered that the house be destroyed and the ground be salted down. A marble column was erected on the spot to serve as a perennial reminder of the disgrace.

Apparently Seville was also a distribution center for Protestant books smuggled into the country. In fact, the Protestant underground was uncovered when a book (*Images of the Antichrist* by Calvin) intended for a sympathetic priest was delivered to another priest by the same name, who then turned the volume over to the Inquisition. This led to the first auto-da-fé in which Protestants were put to death; it occurred on September 25, 1559.

R. Trevor Davies offers this description of the Protestant congregation of Seville in 1557: "It had grown to number over a hundred persons—mostly clergy, monks and nuns, but also persons of such different social levels as a kinsman of the Duke of Arcos and a couple of ragpickers."[9] But in fact, the Protestant community

there, which may have included as many as three hundred at one time, was made up almost exclusively of the upper classes of Sevillian society. Indeed, the evangelical movement in Spain was essentially an upper-class movement. Perhaps this phenomenon helps to explain why Protestantism there was so easily suppressed. Although there were notable exceptions, most martyrs in Spain seem to have lacked the fortitude of martyrs elsewhere. And there never was a popular ground swell to embrace Reformational teachings. Doubtless the common people had not forgotten the bloody repression of the *comuneros* or the continued harassment of both the *conversos* (converted Jews) and the *moriscos* (Moors). Certainly the reign of terror that the Inquisition maintained in Spain for more than three centuries helped to create an atmosphere in which duplicity and recantation became fairly common among would be converts.

But there were those who sacrificed their lives for the Protestant cause in Spain. Rodrigo de Valer, a wealthy nobleman, died while in custody of the Inquisition; he had been held since 1541. Dr. Juan Gil (Egidio), an eloquent cathedral preacher and able scholar, had also been imprisoned. Released in 1555, he became gravely ill upon his return from Valladolid and died in 1556. Dr. Constantino de la Fuente, his successor, was imprisoned in the Castle of Triena in 1558 and died two years later of dysentery; it was falsely reported that he committed suicide.[10]

Don Rodrigo de Valer was thought to be an idiot or at best insane. Thus, after confiscating his property, the Inquisition let him go. During this period of relative immunity, Valer continued to confront priests with the need to reform the Catholic Church, even disrupting services to openly argue with the preacher of the hour. His *sambenito* (the outer shirt of a heretic, which every individual convicted of heresy was required to wear) did not keep him from advising

9. Davies, *Golden Century of Spain*, p. 141.

10. Boehmer, *Spanish Reformers of Two Centuries*, 2: 18.

priests, whether in public or in private. He became the counselor of the renowned scholar Dr. Juan Gil when Gil's first efforts at preaching appeared to fail completely. It was he who influenced Gil to embrace evangelical truth, a commitment that transformed the cathedral canon into a most effective preacher.

In fact, Gil so impressed Charles V with his eloquence that the emperor appointed him to the bishopric of Tortosa in 1550. But the Inquisition kept him from occupying his see by trapping him into admitting heretical ideas and imprisoning him on charges of heresy. (Menéndez y Pelayo claims that the Inquisition treated Gil leniently. This may be true in the light of the severe treatment of others, but one must remember that Gil was the cathedral preacher with the approval and support of Charles V and a canon of the cathedral.) Gil was arrested in 1550, and he recanted on August 21, 1552. In the eyes of the inquisitors a recantation was far better than a burning at the stake because a recantation would discredit the heretic before the people and the community. But during a trip to Valladolid Gil reaffirmed his previous evangelical commitment. When he returned to Seville he became ill and died in 1556. Although several of his manuscripts, some written in prison, survived him, none were printed, and none are extant. Gil was succeeded as cathedral preacher by the greatest Spanish preacher of the age, Dr. Constantino de la Fuente.

Like Gil, Constantino had studied at the University of Alcalá. His services to the Catholic Church in Seville were interrupted when he responded to a call of duty on behalf of the emperor and his court. He traveled with Prince Philip through Italy, Germany, and the Netherlands and was with him in England. Charles V made him his confessor and chaplain, and he was with the emperor at the Diet of Augsburg in 1550. When he returned to Seville shortly before Gil's death, he was immediately sought out by the chapter of the cathedral to replace Gil. Despite the fact that the canons elected Constantino by a unanimous vote on May 12, 1556, the provisor (the representative of the archbishop) nominated a rival candidate, a Dr.

Zumel. When Zumel lost to Constantino, the provisor had Constantino arrested and jailed, whereupon the accused preacher appealed to Rome. While the appeal was pending, the Inquisition, which had been behind the objections raised against the cathedral preacher in the first place, accused him of heresy and imprisoned him in the Castle of Triena. But the charges lacked real substance until a manuscript that had been hidden in the wall of a house was turned over to the inquisitors. When confronted with the new evidence, Constantino confessed, "I wrote it all, and it represents my real convictions. Seek no further proofs against me, and do with me what seems good to you."[11]

When Charles V heard that his former confessor had been charged with heresy, he is reported to have said, "If Constantino is a heretic, he is a great one."[12] (One of the thirty books that the emperor had with him when he died was Constantino's *Christian Doctrine.*) After two years in prison Constantino fell victim to dysentery, which was brought on by the extreme heat and unsanitary conditions under which he had been forced to live. A monk who shared his cell reported the circumstances of his death, and Sepúlveda, the imperial historiographer, indicated that both Gil and Constantino died of disease. (The Inquisition later reported that Constantino committed suicide by using the broken glass of a wine canister, but Edward Boehmer, who made a thorough investigation of the records, rejects this allegation.[13]) Constantino died in the summer of 1560, and the following December his bones were exhumed along with those of Dr. Juan Gil and committed to the flames. Dr. Zumel was now elected to the vacant magisterial canonry.

With the death of Constantino the Reformation was effectively suppressed in Seville, but the Protestant movement was not crushed. The

---

11. Constantino, cited by Boehmer in *Spanish Reformers of Two Centuries,* 2: 17.

12. Charles V, cited by Boehmer in *Spanish Reformers of Two Centuries,* 2: 17.

13. Boehmer, *Spanish Reformers of Two Centuries,* 2: 18.

evangelical community that had at one time claimed such champions as Vargas, Gil, and Constantino appeared to die out with only a whimper, but it was not as readily squelched as it might first appear. It continued to win Spanish converts both inside and outside the borders of the country.

The Inquisition, meanwhile, continued its deadly work at its usual snail's pace. An auto-da-fé was finally held on September 24, 1559, with the fanfare of a fiesta and the pomp and ceremony of a high holy day. The condemned, wearing their *sambenitos*, sat in bleachers on either side of the altar where they could witness the mass and hear the sermon preached by a representative of the Inquisition. The dignitaries—Philip II, canons of the cathedral, noblemen, and ladies—filled the seats reserved for them. This auto-da-fé took place in the Plaza Constitucional near the cathedral, where the first Jews had been condemned by the Inquisition more than seventy-five years before. The actual executions followed at the *quemadero,* just outside the walls at the site of El Prado de Sanbastián.

This first auto-da-fé of Protestants in Seville was marked by understandable weakness but also by examples of admirable courage. Juan De Leon from the monastery of San Isidro de Campo and Juan Gonzalez, a man of Moorish descent, and two of his sisters died witnessing to their faith to the very end. Dr. Blanco, abbot of San Isidro, leaned on his staff as he ascended the scaffold where he was burned alive. Cristobal Losada, a medical doctor, continued to defend his faith until his voice was silenced by the flames. Doña Maria de Bohorques encouraged the weaker brethren as she was led to her death.

The most memorable testimony among the martyrs of Seville was given by Julián Hernández, a man of humble birth but deep conviction, at the second auto-da-fé of Protestants in December 1560. For some time Hernández had brought evangelical books and tracts into Seville, secretly conveying them to those with open minds and hungry hearts. He had finally been apprehended and condemned. As he faced the stake, he cried out,

Courage, comrades! . . . this is the hour in which we must show ourselves valiant soldiers for Jesus Christ. Let us now bear faithful testimony to His truth before men, and within a few hours we shall receive the testimony of His approbation before angels, and triumph with Him in heaven.[14]

Two Englishmen and a Frenchman were also consumed in the flames. It was at this auto-da-fé that the bones of Gil and Constantino were burned; in addition, Gil, Constantino, and Juan Pérez de Pineda, who had escaped, were burned in effigy.

Juan Pérez de Pineda became the connecting link between the Spanish Reformation in Seville and the later Spanish Protestant movement that was more strongly identified with Calvin than with Luther. In the meantime, the fires of the auto-da-fé increasingly became the Spanish Catholic answer to the Protestant challenge.

Valladolid

The evangelical community of Valladolid was second in importance to Seville. At this time it served as the capital of Spain. The beginnings of Protestantism in the city are somewhat obscure. It is thought that Domingo de Roxas, a Dominican and the son of the first Marquis de Posa, sowed the first evangelical seeds there. Eventually the Protestant community in Valladolid, like that in Seville, counted among its members some of the most prominent families and ecclesiastics of the city.

One of these was Dr. Augustino Cazalla, Valladolid's most famous preacher, who became the leader of the city's evangelicals. He had come to Valladolid as court preacher for Charles V. He had accompanied the emperor on some of his journeys into Northern Europe, and was highly regarded by both the emperor and the citizens of Valladolid. The change in his beliefs began when he debated with Protestant leaders in Germany and could not counter their arguments to his own satisfaction. This experience led him to further examine Scripture and to

---

14. Hernández, cited by Stoughton in *Spanish Reformers*, p. 164.

accept much of what the Protestants taught. Such belief was not atypical in his family. His younger brother Pedro, parish priest in the diocese of Zomara, was an outspoken Lutheran, and several other members of the Vibero-Cazalla family were identified with the evangelicals of the city.

The Inquisition sought out such believers with a vengeance. Dr. Cazalla tried to be very cautious, but a house owned by the Cazalla family became the meeting place of the harassed group, and this raised suspicions. In fact, all of the Cazallas were suspect because they were of Jewish extraction. The inquisitors also singled out Don Carlos de Seso, an Italian nobleman employed by the emperor, because he was a staunch Protestant. Quite a few other socially prominent men and women were also numbered among those accused of heresy in this stronghold of Spanish patriotism.

The inquisitors' work resulted in two macabre autos-da-fé in 1559 in which "Lutherans" were put to death. At the first auto-da-fé, held on May 21, sixteen accused heretics were imprisoned, fourteen were strangled before burning, and two—Antonio Herezuelo and Francisco de Vibero Cazalla—were burned alive. The behavior of Dr. Cazalla, among others, suggested that the evangelicals in Valladolid lacked both intellectual leaders of the caliber of those in Seville as well as the constancy and fortitude of the martyrs there. Facing death by fire, Dr. Cazalla, who had been broken on the rack, wavered and confessed, and therefore was strangled before he was burned.

But the second auto-da-fé, held on October 29, told a different story. One of the thirty victims was Don Carlos de Seso, and Philip II, whom he had faithfully served, was present. After his trial and condemnation De Seso called for a pen and wrote, "This is the true faith of the Gospel as opposed to the Church of Rome, which has been corrupted for ages. In this faith I wish to die, and in remembrance and lively belief of the passion of Jesus Christ, to offer to God my body now, reduced so low." When he was at the stake and his gag was removed, instead of confessing he exclaimed, "I could dem-

onstrate to you that you ruin yourselves by not imitating my example; but there is no time. Executioners, light the pile that is to consume me."[15] This uncommon courage of martyrs like De Seso at the second auto-da-fé may explain why the Inquisition was still having trouble with Protestantism in Valladolid ten years later.

When the inquisitors ran out of Protestants or those whom they suspected of holding to certain concepts that could conceivably be identified as Lutheran, they again focused their attention upon Catholics of Jewish and Moorish descent and a stray ecclesiastic here and there. Hence it was that Dr. Bartholomé de Carranza, the archbishop of Toledo, became a victim of the Inquisition. De Carranza's last words to the dying Charles V were cited as providing the reason to take action against this Catholic prelate who had been so intent on exhuming the bones of Reformers and persecuting Protestants while in England in the service of Philip II. He was reported to have admonished the monarch to turn to Christ, something that another priest present considered a Protestant heresy. But the real reasons for the indictment seem to have been the envy of Melchior Cano and the jealousy of the inquisitors Fernando de Valdes and Domingo de Soto. The case dragged on for seventeen years, during the course of which De Carranza appealed to Rome. When his case was finally heard, Pope Gregory XIII declared that "*por lo cual vehementemente sospechoso de herejia.*" Because De Carranza was strongly suspected of heresy, the pope demanded that he abjure sixteen propositions containing his errors. De Carranza did so in Gregory's presence on April 14, 1576, and was sentenced to five years' confinement in a monastery. Sixteen days later he died.[16]

---

15. De Seso, cited by Stoughton in *Spanish Reformers,* pp. 220–21.

16. See Menéndez y Pelayo, *Historia de los Heterodoxos Españoles,* 3: 7-53, for a thorough account of the Inquisition's handling of the case of the archbishop of Toledo. It is Pelayo's opinion that De Carranza did hold to the doctrine of justification by faith and other Lutheran teachings, but that the way in which the case was handled by the Inquisition with the support of Philip II was a disgrace. He claims that the only redeeming features of the tragic affair were the actions of Pius V and Gregory XIII.

Thus, by fair means or foul, the Inquisition managed to rid Spain of every known or suspected Protestant. In the process it also succeeded in driving from Spain some of the most gifted Reformers the Spanish Reformation produced. But these ardent advocates of reform were not easily deterred. They created an evangelical literature in Spanish that continued to sow the seeds of reform for centuries to come.

SPANISH REFORMERS OUTSIDE OF SPAIN

The first of the Spanish Reformers who escaped the snares of the Inquisition to carry on the work of reform elsewhere had come to embrace Reformational teachings under the influence of the Reformation in Spain. Later, as Spanish New Testaments and Bibles as well as Protestant tracts began to filter back into the peninsula, others came to commit their lives to carry on the evangelical witness wherever they might find the freedom necessary to work. Thus the "Spanish Protestant Church" became the church of a *diaspora*. Scattered abroad, committed Spanish evangelicals went everywhere proclaiming the gospel. The first city to which Spanish exiles began to gravitate was Geneva.

Geneva became the city of refuge not only for French, English, and Scottish refugees but for Italian and Spanish exiles as well. In fact, the Spanish, who lacked a church of their own, worshiped with the Italian congregation that was led by Bernardino Ochino, the former general of the Capuchins, who had come under the influence of Juan de Valdés in Naples and subsequently had fled Italy. His successor in Geneva was another from the Valdensian circle, Peter Martyr Vermigli. Geneva was also the city in which Juan Pérez, formerly director of the Colegio de Doctrina in Seville, and a few other Spanish exiles worshiped. Pérez was a close friend of Dr. Juan Gil. When Gil was seized and imprisoned by the Inquisition, Pérez fled.

By 1556 Pérez had succeeded in translating the Greek New Testament and the Hebrew Psalms into Spanish. Julián Hernández became his collaborator in smuggling the recently printed New Testaments into Spain, an alliance

that cost him his life. Despite such setbacks, Pérez never forgot his native land or ceased to work to convert its people to the Protestant faith. For a few years he served as pastor of a small congregation—about fifteen families—of Spanish exiles in Geneva. Although he was later pastor in Blois and chaplain of the court of the duchess of Ferrara, his most significant work remained his translation of the New Testament into Spanish. He died in Paris in 1567.

During the time that Pérez worked as a Reformer, two significant changes occurred in the Spanish Reformation. First, it became a movement that operated mostly outside of the country, even though a few Protestants continued to be discovered in Spain from time to time throughout the sixteenth century. Second, up to this time the Spanish Reformation had been largely Lutheran, but from 1555 onward it came increasingly under the influence of Calvin and the Calvinists.[17]

Geneva became the center of Spanish reformatory activities. The Spanish Protestants were generally on the move, of course, but most were initially residents of Geneva. Eventually Spanish Reformers were found in half a dozen European cities, including Frankfurt, Amsterdam, and London. In fact, a Spanish congregation is known to have existed in London in the sixteenth century with the knowledge and support of the Church of England. In defense of their faith this congregation published a confession of faith that reflected the influence of Calvin and the Reformed Church. Their theology of the Lord's Supper was clearly Reformed, not Lutheran. In the face of Philip's indignant protests, John Jewel wrote in defense of England's kind treatment of Spanish heretics in England, "Thanks be to God, this realm is able to receive them. Why may not Queen Elizabeth receive a few afflicted members of Christ which are compelled to carry His cross, whom, when He thought good to bring safely by the dangers of the sea, and to set in at our havens, should

17. See John E. Longhurst, *Luther's Ghost in Spain (1517-1546)* (Lawrence, Kans.: Coronado Press, 1969), pp. 297-363.

we cruelly have driven them back again, or drowned them, or hanged them or starved them."[18] Both Casiodoro de Reina and Cipriano Valera were the beneficiaries of English hospitality, as were many other Spanish refugees.

For some reason Juan Pérez had not translated the entire Bible into Spanish; perhaps he had felt himself unequal to the task. Casiodoro de Reina finished what Pérez had started. After twelve years of hard work, he finally succeeded in seeing through the press the first complete Spanish Bible translated by a Protestant. It appeared considerably later than similar efforts in the German and English languages, but it was a remarkable accomplishment. It was beautifully printed and bound in leather; the figure of a bear robbing a beehive hanging in a tree was stamped in gold on the front cover and also appeared on the title page. Thus this Bible became known as "The Bible of the Bear" (*Biblia del Oso*). This first edition, which numbered 2,603 copies, was published in Basel in September 1569. Its style has hardly been surpassed by more modern versions, something acknowledged even by Menéndez y Pelayo, the renowned Catholic historian. De Reina, who fled Seville in 1557, died on March 15, 1594.

Cipriano de Valera, another native of Seville, also translated the Bible into Spanish using work previously completed by his countrymen. His New Testament was published in 1596 and his complete Bible in 1602. De Valera spent considerable time in England attending Cambridge University, from which he received both a bachelor-of-arts degree and a master's degree. His Bible, however, was published in Amsterdam, with two editions appearing in the same year. He was perhaps the most able polemicist the Spanish Reformation produced. He wrote numerous tracts against the Roman Church; he also translated Calvin's *Catechism* into Spanish in 1596 and translated the entire *Institutes* into his native tongue the following year. James Arminius befriended him, making it possible for

De Valera and his wife to return to England. Within a few months of their return De Valera died at the age of seventy.

For three and a half centuries Spanish-speaking people have been using the De Valera edition of the Bible, to which only minor revisions have been made. By dedicating themselves to the publication of the Bible in Spanish, Casiodoro de Reina and Cipriano de Valera undoubtedly did more for the cause of the Reformation in Spain than they would have done had they become—like so many others—martyrs at an auto-da-fé in Seville. As it was, the worst the Inquisition could do was to condemn them *in absentia* and burn them in effigy. Unfortunately, the Spanish Inquisition did much more than that in the Netherlands.

THE NETHERLANDS IN REVOLT

When Charles V appeared before the States General in Brussels to abdicate his throne, he walked in leaning upon the arm of one of his favorites, William of Orange (1533–1584). Charles did abdicate, but his policies of repression and persecution lived on, and the one upon whom he leaned withdrew his support from his son, Philip II. The result was that William of Orange became the means by which the seven northern provinces of the seventeen provinces making up the Spanish Lowlands gained their independence. In the real-life chess game that ensued, Philip found himself checkmated by a handful of sailors, derisively called "Sea Beggars," and a united people under the leadership of William, also known as "William the Silent." While Philip, with the aid of the Inquisition and the Jesuits, effectively suppressed all forms of dissent in Spain, including Protestantism, he and the Spanish troops more than met their match in the Lowlands.

Even though the Netherlands, like Spain, was officially Roman Catholic, there was a spirit of independence in the air. This spirit was due partly to the successful commercial enterprises of the port cities like Antwerp, and partly to the Protestant Reformation. Since the seven provinces of the north were German-speaking, the

---

18. Jewel, cited by Stoughton in *Spanish Reformers*, pp. 296–97.

THE LOW COUNTRIES
IN THE AGE OF
THE REFORMATION

NORTH

SEA

GRONINGEN

Groningen

Leeuwarden

FRIESLAND

Alkmaar

Zuider Zee

Zwolle

OVERYSSEL

UNITED NETHERLANDS

Haarlem

Amsterdam

Naarden

Deventer

HOLLAND

Leiden

Zutphen

GUELDERS

The Hague

Delft

Utrecht

Rotterdam

UTRECHT

Brill

Nijmegen

Dort

Grave

Mook

ZEELAND

Hertogenbosch

Bergen - op - Zoom

UPPER GUELDERS

Breda

Venloo

Flushing

Goes

Rhine

Ostend

Sluis

Antwerp

Bruges

BRABANT

Dunkirk

Ghent

Mechelen

Meuse

Gravelines

FLANDERS

LIMBURG

Ypres

Scheldt

Brussels

Maastricht

GERMANY

SPANISH

Liege

LIEGE

NETHERLANDS

NAMUR

Mons

Namur

Hesdin

HAINAULT

Arras

Valenciennes

LUXEMBURG

Cambray

Cateau - Cambresis

PICARDY

Luxemburg

Aisne R.

FRANCE

GRAPHIC PRESENTATION SERVICES · Inc

early treatises of Luther and other Reformers found a ready audience and, not surprisingly, a number of converts. But the early successes of the Lutherans were overshadowed by those of the Anabaptists, who at one time constituted the largest evangelical party in the Netherlands. However, since the Anabaptists were generally nonresistant and apolitical, it was a militant form of Calvinism that supplanted Anabaptism and that provided the religious fervor that undergirded the independence movement.

In a sense Charles was responsible for this shift in the evangelical balance in the Netherlands because his policies of oppression helped to create the situation in which the Calvinists became the dominant party. In 1521 he issued the "Placards" prohibiting the printing and reading of Lutheran books; he also attempted to enforce the Edict of Worms, which called for the death penalty for anyone buying or selling Luther's books or writing in support of Luther or against Rome. The immediate result was that two Augustinian monks, Henrik Voes and Jan Loch, were burned to death in Brussels on July 1, 1523, becoming the first martyrs of the Reformation in the Low Countries.

Zwingli's reformatory work became known in the Netherlands at an early date. His teachings on the Lord's Supper held a particular attraction for the Dutch, which may have been due to the fact that his ideas were not new to them. Karlstadt's similar views were already known, and the Dutch theologian Cornelius van Hoen (Honius) not only anticipated Zwingli but was responsible for bringing to Zwingli's attention that in the institution of the Lord's Supper, Christ's phrase "This *is* my body" can only mean "This *signifies* my body." Zwingli's familiarity with the Greek text made it possible for him to work out his new theology of the Lord's Supper, of which commemoration and thanksgiving were integral parts.[19] Zwingli and those who adopted the position that he articulated became known as Zwinglians or Sacramentarians. The

Sacramentarian movement became pervasive in the Netherlands, replacing Lutheran views and preparing the way for Anabaptism.

The success of Anabaptism was phenomenal. It attracted adherents primarily from the lower classes.[20] Charles' reaction to this popular movement was predictable: he used every means at his command to eradicate "the pestilence." The result was that Anabaptism suffered irreparable losses. The Venetian ambassador reported that thirty thousand people, mostly Anabaptists, were executed. There were few incidents in which Anabaptists resorted to armed rebellion, because they had strong scruples against war and the use of the sword. The Calvinists, on the other hand, entertained no such resistance to an appeal to arms.

Although forces were at work that would inevitably create out of the seven provinces an independent nation, it is not at all certain that the chronology would have been the same without the provocation of a monarch determined, for the sake of his religion, "to rule or ruin." Philip II was a Spaniard. His father had been born in Flanders, but he had been born in Valladolid. He built the Escorial Palace in the foothills of the Guadarrama Mountains, about thirty miles from Madrid. Here he lived and worshiped with an ardent devotion to the interests of both his country and his church, leaving trusted lieutenants to carry out his policies in the vast territories over which he reigned. This pattern of rule succeeded quite well at home and abroad—with the single exception of the Netherlands.

Although the Netherlands seemed united when Philip took the reins from his father, appearances were deceiving. Strong resentment of Spain's rule and its policy of persecution had grown steadily. From 1555 on the unrest mounted. Philip's appointment of his half-sister, Margaret of Parma, as his regent did not help matters. What made the situation intolerable to the States General and impossible for Margaret

19. See G. R. Potter, *Zwingli* (Cambridge: Cambridge University Press, 1977), pp. 290–301, for a brief but incisive discussion of Zwingli's position.

20. See Cornelius Krahn, *Dutch Anabaptism*, 2nd ed. (Scottdale, Pa.: Herald Press, 1981), p. 262.

was the fact that she had no real authority. Of the three councils with which she attempted to rule, the Council of State, made up of five councilors, was the most important. Cardinal Granvelle along with two other members of the council attempted to carry out the king's policies in the reorganization of the church and the centralization of government. These three men constituted a secret council that attempted to railroad their program of repression through the government against the wishes and the better judgment of the two other council members, Count Egmont and William of Orange.

Granvelle's repressive measures were resisted by Margaret and the people, and Philip II finally recalled Granvelle at Margaret's insistence. But whatever relief from oppression this action may have provided the nobility and the people was short-lived. In 1564 Philip ordered that the decrees of the Council of Trent be enforced in the Low Countries. The order caused widespread consternation and was immediately opposed by the Council of State, the nobility, and the guilds. Lutherans, Calvinists, and Catholics took steps to consolidate their position by gathering hundreds of signatures on a document called "the Compromise." This action was spearheaded by Philip of Marnix and Louis of Nassau, a younger brother of William of Orange. The opposition crossed confessional lines: Louis was a Lutheran, and Philip was a Calvinist. The *noble compagnie,* as the protesters were known, pledged themselves to protect the persecuted and to resist the Inquisition.

The protest mounted. On March 28, 1566, some two hundred young noblemen appeared before the palace in Brussels to request that Margaret abolish the Inquisition, refuse to enforce the decrees of the Council of Trent, and call a meeting of the States General. Margaret asked her councilors what she should do, to which Baron de Barlaymont is reported to have replied, "Madame, is your Highness afraid of these beggars (*ces guex*)?"[21] After the petition-

ers were assured of leniency until the will of the king was known, they left. They reassembled and celebrated their cause. They called themselves "Beggars," adopting the beggar's sack as their symbol, and the movement caught fire. The people, inspired and spurred on by stirring Calvinistic preaching, armed themselves and held their services out-of-doors. Iconoclastic riots broke out in city after city: images and statues were smashed, and Catholic books and manuscripts were burned. Two thousand assembled at Liège in July 1566. The nobles were appalled. Anticipating the worst from a vengeful monarch, Louis of Nassau began negotiating with French Huguenots and German Lutheran princes for military assistance. Margaret reported the outrage to Philip, who reacted in the only way he knew how—by overreacting. He sent an army of ten thousand veteran Spanish troops, headed by his very able but merciless military leader, the duke of Alva, to punish the rebels. After failing to convince the Counts Egmont and Hoorn that it was time to resist the Spanish, William of Orange sold all his movable possessions and left the Netherlands for his ancestral home in Dillingsberg, Germany.

The duke of Alva, determined to carry out the mandate of his sovereign, launched a reign of terror that knew no mercy. He created a new court of law, the Council of Tumults, the decisions of which were to take precedence over those of all other courts in the land. It was soon dubbed "the Council of Blood." The council's pursuit of heretics was relentless. The Counts Egmont and Hoorn and a number of other nobles were arrested even though they had refused to join William of Orange in mounting a defense strategy and remained loyal to Philip. On a single day in March 1568 five hundred new arrests were made. On July 1 eighteen noblemen were beheaded in Zavel Square in Brussels, and four days later Egmont and Hoorn were executed in the Great Market Square. The previous January the duke of Alva had written to his king rejecting the idea of a general amnesty, which was rumored to be in the works: "Everyone must be made to live in constant fear of the roof falling down over his head," he declared.

---

21. Barlaymont, cited by Thomas Lindsay in *A History of the Reformation,* 2 vols. (New York: Scribner's, 1907, 1928), 2: 250.

The words may have been the duke's, but the spirit was that of the Inquisition and the mentality reflected was Philip's. At this juncture William of Orange, who had been reared a Lutheran and educated in Brussels as a Catholic, announced that he had become a Calvinist—a shrewd move. During the Spanish occupation the Calvinists had rapidly gained the ascendency over all other Reformation parties. Thus, like Constantine of old, William cast his lot with the confessional group that showed the greatest promise of success—in this case, the best chance of freeing the Low Countries from the yoke of Spain and the tyranny of Alva. As it turned out, he was able to command the support of Catholics as well as Protestants to a remarkable degree. The coalition lasted long enough for William's combined forces to loosen Spain's grip upon the country.

Alva was recalled in 1573 at his own request, but Luis de Requeséns y Zúñiga, although not as insensitive as Alva, continued the purge, which only served to harden the opposition. As early as 1570 William and a miscellaneous collection of sailors, who managed to acquire some ships, began to harass the Spanish fleet, even defeating it in the Zuider Zee. But the Massacre of St. Bartholomew's Day destroyed all chances of the Netherlands' receiving the fifteen thousand French reinforcements that Admiral Coligny had promised the Dutch. William was forced to disband his army. Although the Dutch seemed incapable of besting the Spanish on land, the battle on the sea was a different story.

Admiral Coligny pointed out to the Prince of Orange that the Dutch might well defeat the Spanish by using their sailors and fishermen. William took his advice and authorized eighteen small ships to cruise the waterways of the Lowlands and attack the Spanish. The Sea-Beggars, as they became known, soon proved their worth. The Spanish garrison that commanded the entrance to Antwerp fell to the combined forces of the local populace and the Sea-Beggars, and in 1574 the Sea-Beggars utterly routed the Spanish fleet in the battle to free Middleburg at the mouth of the Scheldt. But the battle in

Leiden was almost lost before the city was saved.

Leiden was under seige by the Spanish. Louis of Nassau led an army to Leiden's rescue, but he met with disaster at Hookerheide: he and his younger brother Henry were both killed in the battle with the Spanish. The situation seemed hopeless when William asked the Estates of Holland to cut the dykes and let the sea in. They agreed, having spent four months sealed off from the rest of the Netherlands and from help and food. When the sea rolled in, the Sea-Beggars came with it, shouting their battle cry, "Sooner Turks than Papists."[22] Leiden was saved, and with it the War of Independence took a new turn. Once again Requeséns attempted to negotiate a peace, but William refused even to talk until three conditions were met. He demanded "freedom of conscience, and liberty to preach the Gospel according to the Word of God; the restoration of all the ancient charters; and the withdrawal of all Spaniards from all posts military and civil."[23] However, neither Requeséns nor Philip II was inclined to meet these conditions. The only concession Philip offered was time for all Protestants to leave the Netherlands. He felt confident that his troops were invincible, and thus believed that victory was only a matter of time. But the sudden death of Requeséns in March 1575 gave the northern and southern provinces an opportunity to draw up a treaty that would unite their efforts. Such a movement was afoot when the news of the "Spanish Fury" let loose at Antwerp reached Brussels.

Spanish soldiers mutinied for lack of pay and went on a rampage, raping and pillaging. They turned Antwerp into a wasteland. The reaction to the news of this destruction unified the provinces as never before. The treaty drawn up at Ghent in October was signed in November by both the States General (southern provinces) and the Council of State. Known as the Pacification of Ghent, this treaty formed a federation. It gave William the authority of a sovereign head-

---

22. Lindsay, *History of the Reformation*, 2: 264.
23. Lindsay, *History of the Reformation*, 2: 263.

of-state. The prince of Orange was declared the governor of the seventeen provinces and the admiral-general of Holland and Zeeland. Until the new regent, Don John of Austria, arrived, an uneasy truce prevailed. The Estates General finally allowed Don John to assume his office on May 7, 1577, after agreeing to certain conditions. In the meantime, Philip gathered an army of twenty thousand Spanish and Italian troops and placed them under the command of the duke of Parma, the son of Margaret of Parma. He defeated the Dutch at Gemblours on January 31, 1578, a victory that was the beginning of the end of the federation formed by the Pacification of Ghent. Foreign armies now converged on the Netherlands to protect their interests against the designs of Spain.

William tried valiantly to hold his fragile union together with a broad policy of religious toleration, but he was not successful. Three Roman Catholic provinces—Hainaut, Dounai, and Artois—met at Arras on January 5, 1579, to form a league to attempt a reconciliation with Spain. In response to this action, Holland, Zeeland, Utrecht, Gelderland, and Zutphen met on January 29, 1579, to form the Union of Utrecht to defend their independence against all foreign threats, particularly Philip II. But William of Orange, holding out until the very last in hopes of a united country, did not sign the Treaty of Utrecht until the third of May. The struggle was to continue off and on, with each league pursuing its own policies, until the Peace of Westphalia. But independence was virtually achieved by the northern provinces by 1581.

Philip made a last desperate attempt to destroy this new nation by calling for the assassination of William of Orange. He denounced William as a traitor and an enemy of the human race, and offered twenty-five crowns and the rank of nobility to anyone who would turn him over to the king dead or alive. William then published the *Apology,* a recounting of his life with an indictment of Philip II for his crimes against the Dutch people. The *Apology* was translated into several languages and sent to the heads of every nation in Europe. In answer to Philip's action, the provinces of Brabant, Flan-

ders, Utrecht, Gelderland, Holland, and Zeeland celebrated an Act of Abjuration on July 26, 1581, in which they formally renounced their allegiance to the king of Spain and constituted themselves into an independent republic.

Doubtless William was made acutely aware of his own vulnerability when Admiral Coligny, the courageous leader of the French Huguenots, was assassinated. On July 10, 1584, William met his fate. A Catholic who had posed as a Calvinist in order to gain admittance to William's home shot him in front of his family. Despite William's death, the new nation survived, although initially its prospects were not at all promising.

At first it looked as if an assassin's bullet had put an end to a courageous struggle for freedom, but William's son Maurice (1567–1625) and Johan van Oldenbarnevelt (1547–1619) fielded an increasingly effective fighting force that finally drove the Spanish army out of the northern provinces. The duke of Parma (Alexander Farnese), the brilliant general, was deprived of reinforcements because of Philip's grand design to invade England, reestablish Catholicism there, and add the English dominions to his own. Nevertheless, with the Union of Arras, the duke of Parma successfully separated the southern provinces of the Netherlands from the United Provinces and proceeded to reestablish the Roman Catholic religion there. The Reformed Church was established in the northern provinces. The borders of Belgium and the Netherlands thus established have remained essentially the same from 1581 to the present.

By 1609 Spain had had enough of war with the stubborn Dutch, and Calvinism triumphed. A twelve-year truce brought an end to almost half a century of warfare in the Low Countries. The Peace of Westphalia in 1648 confirmed the status achieved by 1609 and brought peace to Europe after more than a hundred years of sectarian conflict.

Calvinism: A House Divided

The first Reformed churches were established in 1563, but no national structure was formed until 1569. It was essentially a presbyterian system that was adopted. The work of the national church was to be carried on through consistories, classes, and synods in ascending order. The Reformed Church needed an educated ministry but had no university. During the war with the Spanish the little city of Leiden had defended itself against the Spanish tide so courageously that William of Orange had decided that it should be the site of such a center of learning. This university soon became the strongest center of Calvinistic theology in the Netherlands. In 1603 James Arminius (1560–1609) was called from Amsterdam to the chair of theology there. He immediately came into conflict with Francis Gomarus, a rigid supralapsarian Calvinist who felt constrained to present his form of Calvinism in a most offensive way.

The inspiration for many supralapsarian Calvinists in the Netherlands was Calvin's successor, Theodore Beza. Beza carried Calvin's concept of double predestination to its logical extreme and defended it with a highly developed Scholasticism. He taught that the "eternal decree of God concerning the manifestation of his glory in saving some whom it has seemed fit to him to save through his mercy and in destroying some by just judgment, precedes in the order of causes not only the determination of man's corruption, but also that of his integrity, and so that of his creation itself."[24] Beza's thought in Gomarus's formulation appeared even more extreme. His concepts included the belief that "God moves the tongues of men to blaspheme," and the idea that "as God predestined man to death, so he predestined him to sin as the only means of death." Gomarus thus concluded that the decree of reprobation (damnation) preceded even that of creation.[25] His extremism stirred the mild-mannered Arminius to counter with an alternate form of Calvinism that his opponents quickly branded "Arminian-

ism."[26] The controversy spread from the faculty to the student body and from Leiden to the entire Reformed Church of the Netherlands.

John Piscator, professor at Herborn, is an example of Gomarus's influence. In the midst of controversy in 1613, Piscator stated his theology in such extreme form that it returned to haunt him—in fact, in the end he rejected it completely and became an Arminian. But before his conversion to Arminianism he drew up a series of propositions that reflected an understanding of Calvinism similar to that of Gomarus. The eighth proposition stated, "God justly wills that sins be committed by us, and indeed absolutely wills that they be committed; nay procures in time these sins themselves."[27]

Eventually Arminius, who had never enjoyed controversy, was called to defend himself before the States General at the Hague. The strain was too much for his delicate health, and he became violently ill and died in 1609. After his death his doctrines were vigorously defended by his followers, who were mainly former students of his, although throughout the Netherlands there was a ground swell of opposition to the more extreme forms of Calvinism.

The followers of Arminius were soon known as Remonstrants because in 1610 they presented their position in a document entitled *The Remonstrance (Articuli Arminiani sire remonstrantia)*. Addressed to the government with a plea for toleration, it contained the following five points:

> I. That God, by an eternal and immutable decree in Jesus Christ his son, before the world was founded, determined to save in Christ for Christ's sake and through Christ those who, through the grace of the Holy Spirit, shall believe on his Son Jesus and shall persevere in this faith in faithful obedience, through this grace, even to the end; and, on the other hand, to leave the unbelieving

24. Beza, cited by A. H. Newman in *A Manual of Church History,* 2 vols. (Philadelphia: American Baptist Publication Society, 1931), 2: 337–38.

25. Beza, cited by Newman in *A Manual of Church History,* 2: 239.

26. For a description of Arminius's first public presentation of his form of Calvinism, see Carl Bangs, *Arminius: A Study in the Dutch Reformation* (New York: Abingdon, 1971), pp. 262ff.

27. Piscator, cited by Newman in *A Manual of Church History,* 2: 338.

in sin and to condemn them as alienated from Christ according to the gospel in John 3:36.

II. That Jesus Christ the Saviour of the world, died for all men and for every man, so that he has obtained for them all, by his death on the cross, reconciliation and the forgiveness of sins; yet that no one actually enjoys this forgiveness of sin except the believer, according to the word of the Gospel of John 3:16. . . .

III. That man does not have of himself saving grace nor the strength of a free will. Man can of and by himself neither think, will, nor do anything that is truly good (such as saving faith evidently is); but that it is necessary that he be born again of God in Christ, through his Holy Spirit, and renewed in understanding, inclination, will, and all his powers, in order that he may rightly understand, think, will, and do what is truly good, according to the Scripture in John 15:5.

IV. That this grace of God is the beginning, continuance, and accomplishment of all good, even to the extent that the regenerate man himself, without prevenient or assisting, awakening, following, and co-operative grace, can neither think, will, nor do good, nor withstand any temptations to evil; . . . but regarding the mode of the operation, this grace is not irresistible. Many have resisted the Holy Spirit. Acts 7 and other places.

V. That those who are incorporated into Christ by a true faith, have thereby become partakers of his life-giving Spirit, have thereby full power to strive against Satan, sin, the world, and their own flesh, and to win the victory; it being well understood that it is ever through the assisting grace of the Holy Spirit; and that Jesus Christ assists them through his Spirit in all temptation, extends to them his hand, and if only they are ready for the conflict, and desire his help, and are not inactive, keeps them from falling so that they, by no craft or power of Satan, can be misled or plucked out of Christ's hands, according to the word of Christ, John 10:28.[28]

---

28. This is basically a modern translation in English of the Latin text. The Dutch, Latin, and English versions are given in *The Evangelical Protestant Creeds, with Translations,* vol. 3 of Philip Schaff's *Creeds of Christendom* (Grand Rapids: Baker Book House, 1966), pp. 545–49. For Arminius's views, see *The Writings of James Arminius,* 3 vols., trans. James Nichols and W. R. Bagnall (Grand Rapids: Baker Book House, 1956).

The Synod of Dort (November 13, 1618–May 9, 1619) was called to deal with controversy revolving around the Remonstrants. Consequently their teachings were condemned, and two hundred Remonstrants were banished. Some leaders were imprisoned and others were executed. However, sanity returned to the Netherlands by 1625, when toleration was granted them. All restrictions were removed in 1630.

CALVINISM COMES TO SCOTLAND

While Luther captured the imagination of Europe and ignited hope for a genuine reform within the church, his protest, though it inaugurated a new church structure, remained confined largely to the German-speaking world. Calvinism, on the other hand, became the most formidable and international of the Reformation movements. Although Denmark and the Scandinavian countries became Lutheran, it was Calvinism that dominated Protestant life in Western Europe. Scotland was no exception.

Early Reformatory Efforts

Pre-Reformation Scotland was a barbarous country made up of warring tribes. The humanist scholarship that characterized the circles of John Colet, Sir Thomas More, and Erasmus was virtually unknown in the land of kilts and bagpipes. However, the teachings of Wycliffe and Huss were disseminated quite early by students who traveled back and forth from Scotland to the universities in England. Thus Lollardy was introduced relatively early and by 1455 provided a martyr for the cause. Paul Craw was a physician from Bohemia who had been sent to Scotland to sow the seeds of the Hussite gospel among the Scots. But the Highlanders did not take kindly to such missionary endeavors. As a consequence, Craw was arrested on July 23, 1433, tried for heresy, condemned, and burned at the stake at St. Andrews. John Knox wrote that he was put to death because he denied transubstantiation, auricular confession, and prayers to the saints. Nevertheless, Lollardy caught on and continued to command a following in Scotland until the end of the Reformation. In 1494, for example, thirty Lollards were brought before King James IV at Glasgow. (Because some of them, men of prestige and wealth, were friends of the king, all of the accused received a royal pardon.)

Soon after Tyndale's New Testament was published, copies were smuggled into Scotland, where they found their way into the hands of priests and monks. One of these was Patrick Hamilton, the abbot of Ferne. Hamilton (ca. 1500–1528) was the son of Sir Patrick Hamilton of Kincavil and Catherine Stewart, the daughter of the duke of Albany. He studied extensively, first at Louvain and later at the University of Paris, from which he received his master's degree in 1520. In 1524 he joined the faculty of arts at St. Andrew's University, where he was soon suspected of heresy. When he was summoned to appear before the archbishop, Cardinal David Beaton, he sought refuge on the Continent.

Hamilton first made his way to Wittenberg to consult Melanchthon and Luther, who urged him to enroll in the new University of Marburg, founded by Philip of Hesse. He was there for the opening of the university on May 30, 1527. While there he drew up theses in Latin for the first academic disputation, theses that later became the basis for a small book in English entitled *Patrick's Places.* The selection reproduced by John Foxe in his *Book of Martyrs* set forth clearly and straightforwardly a strong evangelical theology with a heavy emphasis on justification by faith. Against the advice of his Marburg friends, Hamilton decided to return to Scotland to preach the gospel. After only a few weeks of freedom in his native land, he was arrested on February 27, 1528, and tried and condemned the next day. At noon he was burned at the stake outside the gates of the university while holding his beloved Bible in his arms. The fagots with which the fire was kindled were damp and burned sluggishly, causing the courageous Scot to die a slow and excruciating death. As his clothes were stripped from his body, he bequeathed them to his ser-

vant, explaining that they were all he could leave him besides "the example of his death."[29]

Alexander Alane (Alesius) was the Augustinian monk who attempted to persuade Hamilton to recant and save his life. He failed in his efforts. Instead, he was persuaded to embrace the gospel by the courageous witness of Hamilton's death. Thus what Hamilton's arguments may have failed to do, his martyrdom did. Alesius wrote of Hamilton's death, "[He] never gave one sign of impatience or anger, nor ever called to heaven for vengeance on his persecutors, so great was his faith, so strong his confidence in God."[30] John Lindsay, a friend of Cardinal Beaton, warned Beaton of the adverse effect of such executions: "My Lord, if ye burn any more, except ye follow my counsel, ye will destroy yourselves. If ye will burn them, let them be burnt in [low] cellars; for the reik (i.e. smoke) of Maister Patrik Hammylton has infected as many as it blew upon."[31]

The persecution, although severe, was not thorough enough—as it was in Spain—to stamp out the new faith; in fact, it had just the opposite effect. A number of the new believers were committed to sowing the seeds of the Reformation in Scotland. Although they enjoyed the protection of sympathetic barons and prelates, they were not entirely safe: Patrick Hamilton was only the first of a number of martyrs to die for the Protestant faith in Scotland. Both his brother James and his sister Catherine were accused of heresy, but because of the intervention of the king they escaped Patrick's fate. Others, however, were not so fortunate. Among these were Dean Thomas Forrest (1553), David Stratton and Gourlay (1554), and a number of other priests and monks as well as laymen. The records indicate that as many as twenty people were executed for their faith before 1560. Oth-

---

29. Accounts differ regarding the exact chronology. Some say that Hamilton was executed on the day of his trial.

30. Alesius, cited by A. M. Renwick in *The Story of the Scottish Reformation* (Grand Rapids: Eerdmans, 1960), p. 26.

31. Lindsay, cited by Renwick in *The Story of the Scottish Reformation,* p. 26.

ers, including George Buchanan, escaped to the Continent. One of those who joined the exodus but returned to die a martyr's death was George Wishart (1513–1546).

Wishart was the son of Sir James Wishart of Pitarrow in the Mearns. He became the connecting link between the early reformatory efforts of Patrick Hamilton and the Reformation led by John Knox. Although he met the same fate as Hamilton, he managed to preach for about two years with the protection of powerful noblemen before he was executed. He was first suspected of heresy in 1538 because he taught his students at Montrose to read the Greek New Testament. At this point he fled to England and later visited the Reformation centers on the Continent. When he returned to his homeland, he introduced the First Helvetic Confession to Scotland. He concentrated his evangelistic efforts in the towns of Dundee, Ayr, and Montrose, where he had previously taught. The Earl of Bothwell betrayed Wishart into the hands of Beaton, who confined him in the "Bottle Dungeon" at the cardinal's castle. On February 28 he was tried and condemned for heresy, and on March 1 he was led out to receive his punishment. John Knox, who had become Wishart's constant companion and his self-appointed bodyguard during the last months of his life, accompanied his mentor with a two-edged sword in hand, determined to die for his faith also. But Wishart told him, "Nay, return to your bairns (i.e. his pupils), and God bless you! One is sufficient for a sacrifice."[32] Wishart was burned at the stake just outside the gates of the castle.

It was perhaps in Scotland that the ancient adage attributed to Tertullian—"The blood of the martyr becometh the seed of the church"— was graphically demonstrated. Among the martyrs who drew many to the Protestant cause was Walter Myln, a former priest at Forfar. He was eighty-two years old when he was tried and condemned by the ecclesiastical court. As he was led to his death, his great age and faltering step filled those who watched with a swelling tide of pity and contempt—pity that one so old and weak was to be put to death in so cruel a fashion, and contempt for the church that felt compelled to so act. Despite his frailty, Myln declared, "I am fourscore and two years old, and could not live long by the course of nature; but a hundred better shall arise out of the ashes of my bones."[33]

The Reformation in Scotland

Although Reformation teachings seem to have reached the inhospitable valleys of the Highlands rather late, when they came they took firm root in the minds and hearts of a people through whose veins flowed the blood of the Vikings. With the publication of Tyndale's New Testament came the first departures from the traditional teachings of Catholicism. The change in church alignment occurring in England seemed to have had little influence in Scotland, apparently for two reasons. First, Scotland had closer cultural and religious ties with France than with England, and France was still largely committed to Rome. And second, the English Reformation appeared more political than religious and consequently held very little interest for the Scottish people. The same was not true of England's attitude toward Scotland. The Tudors had always been interested in tying Scotland closer to the English throne. So, when James V died on December 14, 1542, leaving an infant daughter named Mary, Henry entertained the dream of arranging a premarital treaty between the queen regent and himself that would stipulate that his son Edward would marry the young queen of Scots. In this way he could bring the child to England, where she would receive an English and a Protestant education. The treaty was actually signed with this provision, but Cardinal Beaton, who represented the French and papal interests in Scotland, had other ideas. (As archbishop he had previously

---

32. Wishart, cited by Renwick in *The Story of the Scottish Reformation*, p. 29.

33. Myln, cited by Renwick in *The Story of the Scottish Reformation*, p. 30.

published the papal bull excommunicating Henry when the king married Anne Boleyn, and the pope had rewarded him with a cardinal's hat.) Consequently, Mary was reared and educated in France by the Guises.

Henry was thus outmaneuvered, and he was not one to accept such a defeat gracefully. In retaliation he put a price on the cardinal's head that implicated some "Protestants." Beaton

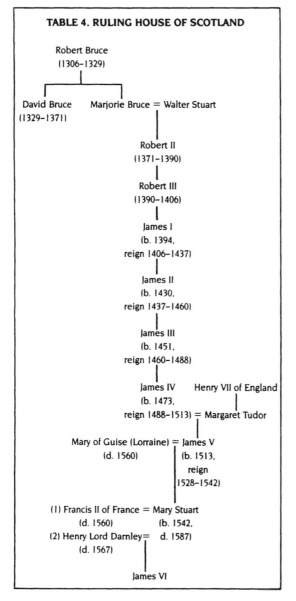

TABLE 4. RULING HOUSE OF SCOTLAND

claimed that he was convinced that Wishart was a part of the conspiracy—hence his alleged reason, besides all the usual accusations of heresy, for the arrest, trial, and execution of Wishart. This execution, however, proved to be the cardinal's undoing, because vengeance lay in store for him. In fact, on May 29, 1546, only three months after Wishart's death, Norman Lesley, Kirkcalday of Grange, and a small band of men slipped inside the gate of the cardinal's castle when the cardinal's mistress was leaving early in the morning. They stealthily crept to the cardinal's bedroom and stabbed him to death, then threw his body to the ground below. Murdering the cardinal allowed the small band to take over the castle. Ten months later John Knox agreed, against his better judgment, to serve the conspirators in the castle as chaplain. By that time the castle had become a refuge for those fleeing from Rome and the queen regent.

After all early efforts to retake the castle failed, a French fleet arrived in the bay just below St. Andrews to lay siege to the Protestant bastion. The castle finally fell, and contrary to the terms of the surrender, Knox and the others were chained night and day to benches on French ships and made to serve as galley slaves. Knox was a prisoner of war for nineteen months before the English were able to secure his release. Doubtless this experience gave him time to reflect upon the situation in Scotland and to resolve to never again be a party to an adventure doomed to failure.

When Mary Tudor came to the throne, Knox found himself a refugee once again, this time from England. The homeless preacher, now without church or country, made his way to Switzerland. While there he visited Zürich and Geneva, remaining in Geneva until November 1554, when he departed for Frankfurt to assume the leadership of a congregation of English refugees in that city. His work was disrupted by the arrival of Dr. Richard Cox, formerly of Oxford, and a large influx of Englishmen. Cox demanded conformity to the *Prayer Book,* and when Knox and the church were slow to cooperate, he accused Knox of treason. Cox reported that Knox had spoken disrespectfully of

Charles V while in England, and the city council of Frankfurt (which was an imperial city) considered this such a serious matter that they asked Knox to leave. Thus by the autumn of 1555 he had returned to Geneva, where he became a trusted colleague of Calvin and pastor of a congregation of English refugees. In the midst of his pastoral work, he decided to take advantage of a more tranquil situation in Scotland and returned there for a preaching tour that lasted ten months.

In 1555–56 Knox realized that the time was not yet ripe to inaugurate the Reformation in Scotland. A number of factors led him to this conclusion. He felt that Mary of Lorraine, queen regent, could not be trusted, and she was an ardent defender of Catholicism. The French connection was still very strong, and French troops were everywhere. Some Scottish nobles supported the queen regent, and some, like John Erskine, tried to maintain a neutral position. The Roman Church, backed by the government, continued to deal harshly with dissent. Despite all this, Protestant sentiment was growing, and Protestants, encouraged by the backing of powerful Scottish noblemen, were increasingly impatient to bring an end to the "false and idolatrous worship" of the Roman Church and put in its place the preaching of the gospel as proclaimed by John Knox.[34]

The brief visit Knox made to Scotland in 1555 served to stimulate the clamor for reform throughout the little country. When he was comfortably settled back in Geneva with his new wife, Marjory Bowes, and his mother-in-law, he received an encouraging letter, dated March 1556, from some of "the faithful" at Stirling, asking him to come back: "We will heartily desire you, in the name of the Lord, that ye will return again in these parts, where ye shall find all faithful that ye left behind you, not only glad to hear your doctrine, but will be ready to jeopard lives and goods in the forward setting of the glory of God, as he will permit time."[35] Calvin and other ministers in Geneva urged Knox to answer the call, and he did. However, when he reached Dieppe on October 28, 1557, he found letters waiting for him requesting that he delay his return until a more opportune time. The frustrated Reformer sat down and wrote a sharp rebuke to the brethren in Scotland in which he revealed he was not only determined to preach the gospel for the reform of the church in Scotland but also determined to free Scotland from the "slavery of strangers."[36] (Knox always considered the Guises and the French enemies of the gospel and the Scottish people.) His letter was not without its effect.

Before the end of the year the indomitable Scot received a reply signed by six noblemen. They informed him that they had drawn up a covenant (*Band*) for mutual support in the "true preaching of Christ's Evangel." Further, they pledged "to strive in our Master's cause, even to the death."[37] In a sense, an evangelical community already existed even if it was not formally organized. This much is indicated in the heart of the letter as revealed by Knox:

> We do promise before the Majesty of God, and his congregation, that we (by his grace) shall with all diligence continually apply our whole power, substance, and our very lives, to maintain, set forward, and establish the most blessed word of God and his Congregation; and shall labour at our possibility to have faithful Ministers purely and truly to minister Christ's Evangel and Sacraments to his people.[38]

In the meantime Knox wrote a caustic little pamphlet against Mary of Lorraine (Guise), queen mother and regent of Scotland; her daughter, Mary Stuart, queen of Scots; and Mary Tudor, the disheartened queen of England. But by the time the tract was known in England,

34. See *John Knox's History of the Reformation in Scotland*, 2 vols., ed. William Croft Dickinson (New York: Philosophical Library, 1950), 2: 132.

35. Cited in *John Knox's History of the Reformation*, 1: 132.

36. *John Knox's History of the Reformation*, 1: 134.

37. Cited in *John Knox's History of the Reformation*, 1: 136.

38. Cited in *John Knox's History of the Reformation*, 1: 136.

John Knox reprimands the ladies of the court of Mary Queen of Scots for their immorality. When the Scottish Parliament formally espoused the Reformation in 1560, Knox led in organizing the Church of Scotland in the face of the determined opposition of Queen Mary. RELIGIOUS NEWS SERVICE

Mary Tudor was dead, and Elizabeth had come to the throne. Elizabeth had a difficult time believing that the polemical treatise was not directed against her. Coupled with this suspicion was her lack of appreciation for Calvin, which in time would make her reluctant to support the Knox-led Reformation in Scotland.

Knox finally returned to Scotland early in the spring of 1559. After the collapse of his plans to return to his native land in 1557, he had gone back to Geneva. The seventeen-month interlude witnessed the growing strength of the Protestants in Scotland. It was largely a movement led by laypersons. In 1558 two significant events occurred: a church was organized at Dundee, and the aged priest Walter Myln was executed at St. Andrews on April 28. Myln's martyrdom evoked much sympathy and widespread support for the Reformation. Mary Lorraine immediately summoned the evangelical preachers to

appear before her, but the Protestant lords would not permit them to go alone. In the confrontation that ensued, the queen regent declared the preachers rebels, and the Protestants vowed never to return to the superstitions and abominations of Rome but to continue on the course they had chosen.[39] The preachers appeared on May 10, and on May 11 an iconoclastic riot broke out at Saint Johnston (Perth).

Scotland now became the focal point of a violent struggle between Protestant and Catholic forces. While the lords were consolidating their position and strengthening their hand against the French troops and the crown, Knox was leading the spiritual battle at St. Giles, lecturing daily on the Scriptures. The Reformer fared better in his spiritual struggle than the

---

39. *John Knox's History of the Reformation*, 1: 158–63.

untrained soldiers of the Protestants did in battle against the French troops. Without England's belated reinforcements, the prospects of a Protestant victory would have been bleak indeed. On January 27, 1560, the English and Scottish entered into an agreement and by April 4 fielded an army of nine thousand Englishmen and ten thousand Scots. This was the beginning of the end of the French presence in Scotland. The queen regent died on June 10, 1560. Peace came on July 6 when both French and English agreed to leave Scotland.

At the request of Parliament, Knox and five other ministers—John Spottiswood, John Willock, John Row, John Douglas, and John Winram—prepared *The Confession of Faith Professed and Believed by the Protestants within the Realm of Scotland.* Parliament approved the confession on August 11, and on August 24, 1560, Parliament decreed that the bishop of Rome no longer had jurisdiction or authority in Scotland. It also rescinded all previous acts contrary to the new confession and forbade saying or hearing the mass. The scene was a dramatic one. As the articles of faith were presented one by one, the lords spoke with deep feeling and conviction. The English ambassador, Randolph, reported to William Cecil "that the lords gave their consent with 'as glad a will as ever I heard men speak.' "[40] This confession served the Church of Scotland until the Westminster Confession replaced it in 1647.

Parliament asked the preachers to produce a document showing how they proposed to govern their church. The result was the *Book of Discipline, or the Policie and Discipline of the Church.* It reflected—although it did not duplicate—the ideas that Calvin set forth in his *Institutes* and the *Ecclesiastical Ordinances of the French Church.* It provided the guidelines for the Reformed (Presbyterian) Church of Scotland. Knox and his fellow ministers also authored other documents to meet the needs of the young church, which still faced an uncertain future.

Upon the death of Francis II, Mary Stuart, his young widowed queen, returned to her native Scotland in August 1561 to rule. Her Protestant subjects were very apprehensive, and with good reason, because she symbolized France and the Roman Church. She was determined to do in Scotland what Mary Tudor had attempted to do in England. But Mary Stuart's ambitions were seriously flawed by both her character and her claim to the English throne. She was really a stranger to Scotland, and this led her to make two serious miscalculations: she underestimated the appeal of the Protestant faith to her subjects, and she also failed to reckon with the character of John Knox. In him the Scottish Protestants had a champion who could be neither deceived nor seduced. The long and bitter struggle between Mary and her Protestant subjects was not over until she was imprisoned on June 16, 1567, in Loch Leven Castle, and she abdicated in favor of her infant son. Thus began the reign of James VI, and with his reign Protestantism was victorious over the resurgent Catholicism. Only then were the Confession of Faith and the Acts of Parliament made the law of the land. Lord James Stewart, the regent acting for the boy king, signed the Acts of 1560, which were introduced to Parliament and passed once again for good measure.[41] At last Protestantism

40. Randolph, cited by Renwick in *The Story of the Scottish Reformation*, p. 91.

41. In addition to adopting the Confession of Faith and the *Book of Discipline,* Parliament passed three more acts on August 24, 1560, as A. M. Renwick notes: "1. *An Act repealing all former Acts of Parliament contrary to the Word of God and the Confession of Faith recently adopted.* This decreed that all previous statutes regarding the censures of Church or the worshipping of saints should be annulled. 2. *An Act for abolishing of the pope and his usurped authority in Scotland.* The pope was to have no jurisdiction nor authority within the realm in the time coming. 3. *An Act against the Mass and the sayers and the bearers thereof.* This act laid down that as the Roman Church has corrupted the Sacraments of Baptism and the Lord's Supper, no person shall administer the sacraments unless he is admitted and have power to that effect; nor say Mass, nor hear Mass, nor be present thereat under the pain of confiscation of goods for the first offence, banishment for the second, and death for the third" (*Story of the Scottish Reformation,* p. 93). For the most important documents related to the Reformation in Scotland, see *John Knox's History of the Reformation in Scotland,* pp. 219-333.

had triumphed in Scotland with the help of the English and the dauntless courage of John Knox. However, without the vigorous support of both the nobility and the common people, neither the English nor Knox could have made the religious settlement a lasting one.

The transformation of Scotland—from a barbaric land of lawless tribes and a decadent Catholicism marked by immorality and ignorance to one of the most enlightened, moral, and devout lands on earth—was miraculous. Here the Protestant Reformation scored one of its most notable triumphs. By the same token, the Counter-Reformation—despite the vigorous support of the Guises, France, Philip II, and the papacy—suffered one of its more severe setbacks.

REFORMATION AS REVOLUTION

In the end Charles V did not bring about a reconciliation between the Protestants and the Catholics, partly because he feared the strength and appeal of the Protestant movement and the political implications of its revolutionary concepts. In the wake of this failure, war broke out. The Catholic armies were eminently successful in the early years of the conflict. Before the cessation of hostilities sealed by the Peace of Westphalia (on October 24, 1648), the Protestant movement had been virtually wiped out in such countries as Bohemia. By the time the fighting stopped, the struggle between the warring factions had reached a stalemate, but the revolution would go on. The Magisterial Reformers were no more successful in harnessing the irrepressible force than Rome had been in its attempt to crush it. It could be that these architects of the Protestant state churches failed to understand the nature of the movement of which they were a part or to reject its more radical aspects when they did understand them. Thus, much in Protestantism was simply a replay of the religious life of the Middle Ages. Nevertheless, the revolutionary aspects of the Reformation, once unfettered from both Protestant and Catholic forces of repression, were destined to create new forms of the

Christian faith that in turn helped to build new and democratic societies upon the ruins of the *corpus christianum.*

The Reformation called sixteenth-century man to a re-examination of the gospel itself as basic to all else. From this new understanding of the revelation of God in Christ emanated a new concept of freedom, and the principle of voluntarism was born. This discovery held enormous implications for church and state alike. For one thing, the state's role in religious matters became severely limited. To provide a free society, free from coercion in religious concerns, became its new and revolutionary goal— a complete reversal of its role in suppressing every form of dissent that had characterized the medieval church from the Constantinian era into the sixteenth century.

In the light of this new understanding, a state-sponsored church that could at its own discretion tolerate a certain degree of dissent was no longer tenable. Recognition of this fact (and consequent change) was a long time in coming, and in the sixteenth century it was not apparent except to a very few. In fact, modern man still struggles with the problems of creating a responsible society without the broken reed of an established church or a national creed.

Perhaps most Christians view the Radical Reformation's concept of a free church in a free state as the ideal, but its very limited implementation has often consigned it to theory rather than fact.

Coupled with the new and dynamic concept of the church was a closer scrutiny of the sacraments, an attempt to rediscover their nature and meaning according to Christ. Eventually most evangelicals were to discard all but two sacraments—baptism and the Lord's Supper—as lacking scriptural support. While the Magisterial Reformers retained infant baptism as the sign of continuity with the true church, the Anabaptists insisted upon believer's baptism. This became the hallmark of the most revolutionary aspects of the Radical Reformation because it constituted a direct rejection of infant baptism and an implied repudiation of the Erastianism of the Protestants (their support of state churches) as well as the *corpus christianum* of Roman Catholic creation.

It must be admitted that these concepts found relatively few adherents in the sixteenth century, but the seventeenth century witnessed a breakthrough. The English climate gave rise to the rapid growth of an evangelical reformation within the official Reformation and the migration of revolutionary ideas to the shores of the North American continent. Here they took firm root and helped to forge a government that recognized both the limitations of the state and its essentially secular nature. For these bold pioneers the state was secular. For them this did not mean that God did not exist or that he did not care, but rather that God in his providence had determined that governments would serve secular ends. The rejection of the Massachusetts Bay theocracy as a prototype for the new nation made this point emphatically clear. Thus the church was free to be the church, and the state could no longer commandeer religion for its own ends or suppress dissent among the ranks of an established church and faith. With this development the implications of the revolutionary aspects of the Reformation were evident, albeit imperfectly realized. Revolution in this sense did not mean the introduction of a new

tyranny—that of the totalitarian state—but liberation.

Nicolas Berdyaev could have been writing about the liberating effect of the Reformation when he wrote in 1936,

> The greatest contribution of Christianity, although it is not fully recognized by the Christian world, consisted in that it liberated man from the power of the baser elemental nature and demons. It did so through the agency of Christ and the mystery of Redemption. It rescued man forcibly from his immersion in elemental nature and revived his spirituality. It distinguished him from baser nature and set him up as an independent spiritual being, freeing him from submission to the natural world and exalting him to the heavens. Christianity alone restored the spiritual freedom of which man had been deprived by the power of the demons, the natural spirits and elemental forces in the pre-Christian world. The essential contribution of Christianity therefore lay in that it liberated man and offered a free solution for human destiny.[1]

To a remarkable degree the Reformation did uncover layers of debris that had obscured authentic Christianity for centuries and robbed it of its redemptive power. Both Vatican Council II and various forms of Marxist socialism reflect how pervasive and lasting certain Reformation emphases have become. At the same time, some modern evangelicals seem quite willing to abandon the "freedom with which Christ has set us free" for some form of religious establishment in an attempt to counteract the forces of disintegration that threaten to destroy contemporary society. It is apparently always a temptation, when the wellsprings of spiritual vitality begin to run dry, to resort to the arm of flesh to fight the battles of the Lord. The history of the Reformation should teach us that this is a temptation that can only end in dashed hopes. The character of an age and the shape of any society depend largely upon the ideology with the greatest vitality. This remains both the perennial challenge of the Reformation and the church's hope for the future.

------

1. Berdyaev, *The Meaning of History*, trans. George Reavey (London: Centenary Press, 1936), pp. 113–14.

SELECTED BIBLIOGRAPHY

THE RENAISSANCE

General

Hulme, Edward Maslin. *The Renaissance, the Protestant Revolution and the Catholic Reformation in Continental Europe.* New York: Century, 1915.

Molho, Anthony, and John A. Tedeschi, eds. *Renaissance: Studies in Honor of Hans Baron.* DeKalb: Northern Illinois University Press, 1971.

Paetow, Louis J. *A Guide to the Study of Medieval History.* New York: Appleton-Century-Crofts, 1959.

Ross, James Bruce, and Mary Martin McLaughlin, eds. *The Portable Renaissance Reader.* 2 vols. New York: Viking Press, 1977.

Spitz, Lewis W. *The Renaissance and Reformation Movements.* Chicago: Rand McNally, 1971.

Thompson, Karl F. *Middle Ages, Renaissance and Reformation.* Vol. 2 of *Classics of Western Thought.* Ed. Thomas H. Greer. New York: Harcourt Brace Jovanovich, 1973.

The Southern Renaissance

Burckhardt, Jacob. *The Civilization of the Renaissance in Italy.* Trans. S. G. C. Middlemore. New York: Albert & Charles Boni, 1935.

Chapman, John Jay. *Lucian, Plato and Greek Morals.* New York: Houghton Mifflin, 1931.

Ferguson, Wallace K. *The Renaissance in Historical Thought.* New York: Houghton Mifflin, 1948.

Mattingly, Garrett, et al. *Renaissance Profiles.* Ed. J. H. Plumb. New York: Harper & Row, 1965.

O'Malley, John W. *Praise and Blame in Renaissance Rome.* Durham, N.C.: Duke University Press, 1979.

Pater, Walter. *The Renaissance Studies in Art and Poetry.* London: Macmillan, 1914.

Sellery, George Clarke. *The Renaissance: Its Nature and Origins.* Madison: University of Wisconsin Press, 1962.

Wold, Milo, and Edmund Cykler. *An Introduction to Music and Art in the Western World.* Dubuque, Iowa: William C. Brown, 1959.

The Northern Renaissance

Allen, P. S. *The Age of Erasmus.* New York: Russell & Russell, 1963.

———. *Erasmus: Lectures and Wayfaring Sketches.* Oxford: Clarendon Press, 1934.

Bainton, Roland H. *Erasmus of Christendom.* Scribner's, 1969.

Boyle, Marjorie O'Rourk. *Erasmus on Language and Method in Theology.* Toronto: University of Toronto Press, 1977.

Erasmus, Desiderius. *Christian Humanism and the Reformation: Selected Writings of Erasmus.* Ed. John C. Olin. New York: Harper & Row, 1965.

———. *The Correspondence of Erasmus.* 6 vols. Trans. R. A. B. Mynors and D. F. S. Thomson. Ed. Beatrice Corrigan. Toronto: University of Toronto Press, 1974–81.

———. *The "Enchiridion" of Erasmus.* Trans. and ed. Raymond Himelick. Bloomington: Indiana University Press, 1963.

———. *"The Praise of Folly" and "Letter to Martin Dorp, 1515."* Trans. Betty Radice. New York: Penguin Books, 1971.

Froude, J. A. *Life and Letters of Erasmus.* New York: Scribner's, 1895.

Huizinga, Johan. *Erasmus and the Age of Reformation.* New York: Harper & Row, 1957.

———. *The Waning of the Middle Ages.* Garden City, N.Y.: Doubleday, 1924.

Hyma, Albert. *The Brethren of the Common Life.* Grand Rapids: Eerdmans, 1950.

———. *The Christian Renaissance: A History of the "Devotio Moderna."* Hamden, Conn.: Shoe String Press–Archon Books, 1965.

Miller, Edward Waite, ed. *Wessel Gansfort: Life and Writings.* 2 vols. Trans. Jared W. Scudder. New York: Knickerbocker Press, 1917.

Payne, John B. *Erasmus: His Theology of the Sacraments.* Richmond: John Knox Press, 1970.

Phillips, Margaret Mann. *The "Adages" of Erasmus: A Study with Translations.* Cambridge: Cambridge University Press, 1964.

———. *Erasmus and the Northern Renaissance.* London: English Universities Press, 1949.

Post, R. R. *The Modern Devotion: Confrontation with Reformation and Humanism.* Leiden: E. J. Brill, 1968.

Rabil, Albert, Jr. *Erasmus and the New Testament: The Mind of a Christian Humanist.* San Antonio: Trinity University Press, 1972.

Spitz, Lewis W. *The Religious Renaissance of the German Humanists.* Cambridge: Harvard University Press, 1963.

Thompson, Sister Geraldine. *Under Pretext of Praise: Satiric Mode in Erasmus' Fiction.* Toronto: University of Toronto Press, 1973.

Tracy, James D. *The Politics of Erasmus: A Pacifist Intellectual and His Political Milieu.* Toronto: University of Toronto Press, 1978.

PRE-REFORMATION MOVEMENTS

Betts, Reginald Robert. *Essays in Czech History.* Ed. G. H. Bolsover et al. London: University of London–Athlone Press, 1969.

Brock, Peter. *The Political and Social Doctrines of the Unity of Czech Brethren in the Fifteenth and Early Sixteenth Centuries.* The Hague: Mouton, 1957.

De Schweinitz, Edmund. *The History of the Church Known as the Unitas Fratrum.* Bethlehem, Pa.: Moravian Publication Concern, 1901.

Heath, Peter. *The English Parish Clergy on the Eve of the Reformation.* Studies in Social History Series. Toronto: University of Toronto Press, 1969.

Hutton, J. E. *A History of the Moravian Church.* London: Moravian Publication Office, 1909.

Hyma, Albert. *Renaissance to Reformation.* Grand Rapids: Eerdmans, 1951.

Kaminsky, Howard. *A History of the Hussite Revolution.* Los Angeles: University of California Press, 1967.

Kepler, Thomas S., ed. *Theologia Germanica.* New York: World Publishing Co., 1952.

Loserth, Johann. *Hus und Wyclif: zur Genesis der Husitischen Lehre.* Munich, 1925.

Oberman, Heiko Augustinus. *The Harvest of Medieval Theology: Gabriel Biel and Late Medieval Nominalism.* Cambridge: Harvard University Press, 1963.

Ozment, Steven. *The Age of Reform, 1250-1550: An Intellectual and Religious History of Late Medieval and Reformation Europe.* New Haven: Yale University Press, 1980.

———. *Mysticism and Dissent: Religious Ideology and Social Protest in the Sixteenth Century.* New Haven: Yale University Press, 1973.

Spinka, Matthew. *John Hus: A Biography.* Princeton: Princeton University Press, 1968.

———. *John Hus' Concept of the Church.* Princeton: Princeton University Press, 1966.

Strand, Kenneth A. *German Bibles before Luther: The Story of Fourteen High German Bibles, 1466-1518.* Grand Rapids: Eerdmans, 1966.

Thomas à Kempis. *The Imitation of Christ.* Milwaukee: Bruce Publishing Co., 1940.

Workman, Herbert B. *John Wyclif: A Study of the English Medieval Church.* 2 vols. Oxford: Clarendon Press, 1926.

Zeman, Jarold Knox. *The Anabaptists and the Czech Brethren in Moravia, 1526-1628: A Study of Origins and Contacts.* Paris: Mouton, 1969.

———. *The Hussite Movement: A Bibliographical Study Guide.* Ann Arbor, Mich.: Michigan Slavic Publications, 1977.

THE REFORMATION

General

Estep, W. R., ed. *The Reformation: Luther and the Anabaptists.* Nashville: Broadman Press, 1979.

Grimm, Harold J. *The Reformation Era, 1500-1650.* New York: Macmillan, 1954.

Hillerbrand, Hans J. *The Protestant Reformation.* New York: Harper & Row, 1968.

———. *The Reformation: A Narrative History Related by Contemporary Observers and Participants.* New York: Harper & Row, 1964.

———. *The World of the Reformation.* New York: Scribner's, 1973.

Kidd, B. J., ed. *Documents Illustrative of the Continental Reformation.* Oxford: Clarendon Press, 1911.

Klassen, Peter J. *Europe in the Reformation.* Englewood Cliffs, N.J.: Prentice-Hall, 1979.

———. *The Reformation: Change and Stability.* Problems in Civilization Series. St. Louis: Forum Press, 1980.

Lindsay, Thomas M. *A History of the Reformation.* 2 vols. New York: Scribner's, 1907, 1928.

Lortz, Joseph. *Die Reformation in Deutschland.* 2nd ed. Freiburg: Herder, 1941.

Luck, William. *Reformation Documents.* Wittenberg, n.d.

Moeller, Bernd. *Imperial Cities and the Reformation.* Trans. and ed. H. C. Erik Middelfort and Mark U. Edwards, Jr. Philadelphia: Fortress Press, 1972.

Montgomery, W. *Protestantism and Progress.* Boston: Beacon Press, 1958.

Ozment, Steven. *The Reformation in the Cities.* New Haven: Yale University Press, 1975.

———, ed. *Reformation Europe: A Guide to Research.* St. Louis: Center for Reformation Research, 1982.

Smith, Preserved. *The Age of the Reformation.* New York: Henry Holt, 1920.

Spitz, Lewis W., ed. *The Protestant Reformation.* Englewood Cliffs, N.J.: Prentice-Hall, 1966.

The Magisterial Reform

Arminius, James. *The Writings of James Arminius.* 3 vols. Trans. James Nichols and W. R. Bagnall. Grand Rapids: Baker Book House, 1956.

Atkinson, James. *The Trial of Luther.* London: B. T. Batsford, 1971.

Bainton, Roland. *Here I Stand: A Life of Martin Luther.* New York: Abingdon Press, 1959.

Balke, Willem. *Calvin and the Anabaptist Radicals.* Trans. William Heynen. Grand Rapids: Eerdmans, 1981.

Bangs, Carl. *Arminius: A Study in the Dutch Reformation.* New York: Abingdon Press, 1971.

Battles, Ford Lewis, and John Walchenbach. *An Analysis of "The Institutes of the Christian Religion" of John Calvin.* Grand Rapids: Baker Book House, 1980.

Boehmer, Heinrich. *Der junge Luther.* Stuttgart: R. J. Koehler Verlag, 1951.

———. *Martin Luther: Road to Reformation.* Trans. John W. Doberstein and Theodore G. Tappert. New York: Meridian Books, 1957.

Bornkamm, Heinrich. *The Heart of Reformation Faith: The Fundamental Axioms of Evangelical Belief.* Trans. John W. Doberstein. New York: Harper & Row, 1965.

Bromiley, G. W., trans. and ed. *Zwingli and Bullinger.* Vol. 24 of the Library of Christian Classics. Philadelphia: Westminster Press, 1953.

Calvin, John. *Calvin: Commentaries.* Trans. and ed. Joseph Haroutunian. Vol. 23 of the Library of Christian Classics. Philadelphia: Westminster Press, 1958.

———. *Calvin's Calvinism: A Treatise on the Eternal Predestination of God.* Trans. Henry Cole. Grand Rapids: Eerdmans, 1950.

———. *Institutes of the Christian Religion.* 2 vols. Trans. Henry Beveridge. Grand Rapids: Eerdmans, 1958.

———. *Johannis Calvini Opera quae supersunt omnia.* Ed. Guilielmus Baum et al. 59 vols. Corpus Reformatorum series. Braunschweig: C. A. Schwetschke & Son, 1863–1900.

———. *John Calvin: Selections from His Writings.* Ed. John Dillenberger. Garden City, N.Y.: Doubleday, 1971.

———. *Tracts and Treatises.* 3 vols. Trans. Henry Beveridge. Grand Rapids: Eerdmans, 1953.

Chrisman, Miriam Usher, and Otto Gründler, eds. *Social Groups and Religious Ideas in the Sixteenth Century.* Studies in Medieval Culture, no. 13. Kalamazoo: Medieval Institute of Western Michigan University, 1978.

Crew, Phyllis Mack. *Calvinist Preaching and Iconoclasm in the Netherlands, 1544–1569.* London: Cambridge University Press, 1978.

Dickens, A. G. *The English Reformation.* New York: Schocken Books, 1964.

———, and Dorothy Carr, eds. *The Reformation in England: To the Accession of Elizabeth I.* Documents of Modern History series. London: Edward Arnold, 1967.

Donaldson, Gordon. *The Scottish Reformation.* Cambridge: Cambridge University Press, 1960.

Ebeling, Gerhard. *Luther: An Introduction to His Thought.* Trans. R. A. Wilson. Philadelphia: Fortress Press, 1970.

Edwards, Mark U. *Luther and the False Brethren.* Stanford, Calif.: Stanford University Press, 1975.

Elton, G. R. *Reform and Renewal.* Cambridge: Cambridge University Press, 1973.

———. *Reformation Europe, 1517–1559.* London: Collins–Fontana, 1963.

Farner, Oskar. *Zwingli the Reformer.* Trans. D. G. Sear. London: Lutterworth Press, 1952.

Fast, Heinold, ed. *Ostschweiz.* Vol. 2 of *Quellen zur Geschichte der Täufer in der Schweiz.* Zürich: Theologischer Verlag, 1973.

Foxe, John. *Foxe's Book of Martyrs: Acts and Monuments of the Christian Church.* Ed. A. Clark. New York: London Printing and Publishing Co., n.d.

Friedenthal, Richard. *Luther: His Life and Times.* Trans. John Nowell. New York: Harcourt Brace Jovanovich, 1967.

Gäbler, Ulrich. *Huldrych Zwingli.* Zürich: Theologischer Verlag, 1975.

Garrett, James Leo, Jr. *Calvin and the Reformed Tradition.* Nashville: Broadman Press, 1980.

Gollwitzer, Helmut, ed. *Luther.* Frankfurt: Fischer Bücherei, 1955.

Grimm, Harold J., and Helmut T. Lehmann. *Career of the Reformer: I.* Vol. 31 of *Luther's Works.* Philadelphia: Muhlenberg Press, 1957.

Hutchinson, F. E. *Cranmer and the English Reformation.* New York: Collier Books, 1962.

Jackson, Samuel Macauley. *Huldreich Zwingli: The Reformer of German Switzerland, 1484–1531.* New York: Putnam, 1901.

Knox, John. *John Knox's History of the Reformation in Scotland.* 2 vols. Ed. William Croft Dickinson. New York: Philosophical Library, 1950.

Locher, Gottfried W. *Huldrych Zwingli in neuer Sicht.* Zürich: Zwingli-Verlag, 1969.

Luther, Martin. *D. Martin Luthers Werke* (Weimar Ausgabe). Ed. Hermann Böhlau. Weimar: n.p., 1883.

———. *Luther: Early Theological Works.* Trans. and ed. James Atkinson. Philadelphia: Westminster Press, 1962.

———. *Reformation Writings of Martin Luther.* Ed. Bertram Lee Woolf. London: Lutterworth Press, 1956.

———. *Three Treatises.* Philadelphia: Muhlenberg Press, 1960.

McDonnell, Kilian. *John Calvin, the Church, and the Eucharist.* Princeton: Princeton University Press, 1967.

McGoldrick, James Edward. *Luther's English Connection.* Milwaukee: Northwestern Publishing House, 1979.

McNeill, John T. *The History and Character of Calvinism.* New York: Oxford University Press, 1954.

Melanchthon, Philipp. *Melanchthon: Selected Writings.* Trans. Charles Leander Hill. Ed. Elmer Ellsworth Flack and Lowell J. Satre. Minneapolis: Augsburg, 1962.

Meyer, Carl S. *Elizabeth I and the Religious Settlement of 1559.* St. Louis: Concordia, 1960.

Mueller, William A. *Church and State in Luther and Calvin: A Comparative Study.* Nashville: Broadman Press, 1954.

Parker, T. H. L. *John Calvin: A Biography.* Philadelphia: Westminster Press, 1975.

Potter, G. R. *Zwingli.* London: Cambridge University Press, 1977.

Renwick, A. M. *The Story of the Scottish Reformation.* Grand Rapids: Eerdmans, 1960.

Riedel, Johannes. *The Lutheran Chorale: Its Basic Tradition.* Minneapolis: Augsburg, 1967.

Rilliet, Jean. *Zwingli: Third Man of the Reformation.* Trans. Harold Knight. Philadelphia: Westminster Press, 1964.

Ritter, Gerhard. *Luther: His Life and Work.* Trans. John Riches. New York: Harper & Row, 1963.

Rupp, Gordon. *Luther's Progress to the Diet of Worms.* New York: Harper & Row, 1964.

———, and Benjamin Drewery, eds. *Martin Luther.* New York: St. Martin's Press, 1970.

Schwiebert, E. G. *Luther and His Times: The Reformation from a New Perspective.* St. Louis: Concordia, 1950.

Strand, Kenneth A. *Luther's "September Bible" in Facsimile.* Ann Arbor, Mich.: Ann Arbor Publishers, 1972.

Tappert, Theodore G., trans. and ed. *The Book of Concord.* Philadelphia: Muhlenberg Press, 1959.

Vatja, Vilmos. *Luther and Melanchthon: In the History and Theology of the Reformation.* Philadelphia: Muhlenberg Press, 1961.

Walker, Williston. *John Calvin: The Organizer of Reformed Protestantism.* New York: Schocken Books, 1969.

Wendel, François. *Calvin: The Origins and Development of His Religious Thought.* Trans. Philip Mairet. New York: Harper & Row, 1963.

Wood, A. Skevington. *Captive to the Word: Martin Luther, Doctor of Sacred Scripture.* Grand Rapids: Eerdmans, 1969.

Zwingli, Ulrich. *Huldreich Zwinglis Sämtliche Werke.* 12 vols. Ed. Emil Egli and Georg Finsler. Munich: Kraus Reprint, 1981.

———. *Huldreich Zwinglis Werke.* 8 vols. Ed. Melchior Schuler and Johann Schulthess. Zürich: Friedrich Schulthess, 1828.

———. *Ulrich Zwingli (1484-1531): Selected Works.* Ed. Samuel Macauley Jackson. Philadelphia: University of Pennsylvania Press, 1901.

———. *Zwingli Hauptschriften.* 9 vols. Ed. Fritz Blanke, Oskar Farner, and Rudolf Pfister. Zürich: Zwingli-Verlag, 1947.

The Radical Reformation

Bainton, Roland H. *Hunted Heretic.* Boston: Beacon Press, 1953.

Behrends, Ernst. *Der Ketzerbischof: Leben und Ringen des Reformators Menno Simons, 1561.* Basel: Agape-Verlag, 1966.

Bender, Harold S. *Conrad Grebel, c. 1498–1526: The Founder of the Swiss Brethren, Sometimes Called Anabaptists*. Goshen, Ind.: Mennonite Historical Society, 1950.

Bergsten, Torsten. *Balthasar Hubmaier: Anabaptist Theologian and Martyr*. Ed. W. R. Estep, Jr. Valley Forge, Pa.: Judson Press, 1978.

———. *Balthasar Hubmaier: Seine Stellung zu Reformation und Täufertum, 1521–1528*. Kassel: J. G. Oncken Verlag, 1961.

Blanke, Fritz. *Brothers in Christ*. Trans. Joseph Nordenhaug. Scottdale, Pa.: Herald Press, 1961.

Brandsma, J. A. *Menno Simons von Witmarsum*. Kassel: J. G. Oncken Verlag, 1962.

Clasen, Claus-Peter. *Anabaptism: A Social History, 1525–1618*. Ithaca: Cornell University Press, 1972.

Estep, William R., ed. *Anabaptist Beginnings (1523–1533): A Source Book*. Nieuwkoop: B. de Graaf, 1976.

———. *The Anabaptist Story*. Grand Rapids: Eerdmans, 1975.

Franck, Sebastian. *Chronica*. Darmstadt: Wissenschaftliche Buchgesellschaft, 1969.

Gross, Leonard. *The Golden Years of the Hutterites*. Scottdale, Pa.: Herald Press, 1980.

Hershberger, Guy F., ed. *The Recovery of the Anabaptist Vision: A Sixtieth Anniversary Tribute to Harold S. Bender*. Scottdale, Pa.: Herald Press, 1957.

Hillerbrand, Hans J. *A Fellowship of Discontent*. New York: Harper & Row, 1967.

Horsh, John. *The Hutterian Brethren, 1528–1931*. Goshen, Ind.: Mennonite Historical Society, 1931.

Hubmaier, Balthasar. *Balthasar Hubmaier: Schriften*. Ed. Gunnar Westin and Torsten Bergsten. Vol. 9 of *Quellen zur Geschichte der Täufer*. Gütersloh: Verlagshaus Gerd Mohn, 1962.

Jones, Rufus M. *Spiritual Reformers in the Sixteenth and Seventeenth Centuries*. Boston: Beacon Press, 1914.

Kiwiet, Jan J. *Pilgram Marbeck*. Kassel: J. G. Oncken Verlag, 1957.

Klassen, William. *Covenant and Community: The Life, Writings and Hermeneutics of Pilgram Marpeck*. Grand Rapids: Eerdmans, 1968.

Krahn, Cornelius. *Dutch Anabaptism*. 2nd ed. Scottdale, Pa.: Herald Press, 1981.

Krajewski, Ekkehard. *Leben und Sterben des Zürcher Täuferführers, Felix Mantz*. Kassel: J. G. Oncken Verlag, 1957.

Littell, Franklin H. *A Tribute to Menno Simons*. Scottdale, Pa.: Herald Press, 1961.

Lumpkin, William. *Baptist Confessions of Faith*. Valley Forge, Pa.: Judson Press, 1959.

Marpeck, Pilgram. *The Writings of Pilgram Marpeck*. Trans. and ed. William Klassen and Walter Klaasen. Scottdale, Pa.: Herald Press, 1978.

Muralt, Leonhard von, and Walter Schmid, eds. *Zürich*. Vol. 1 of *Quellen zur Geschichte der Täufer in der Schweiz*. Zürich: S. Hirzel Verlag, 1952.

Rideman, Peter. *Confession of Faith*. Rifton, N.Y.: Plough Publishing House, 1970.

Ruth, John L. *Conrad Grebel: Son of Zurich*. Scottdale, Pa.: Herald Press, 1975.

Sider, Ronald J. *Andreas Bodenstein von Karlstadt: The Development of His Thought, 1517–1525*. Leiden: E. J. Brill, 1974.

———. *Karlstadt's Battle with Luther*. Philadelphia: Fortress Press, 1978.

Simons, Menno. *The Complete Writings of Menno Simons, c. 1496–1561*. Trans. Leonard Verduin. Ed. John C. Wenger. Scottdale, Pa.: Herald Press, 1956.

Stayer, James M. *Anabaptists and the Sword*. Lawrence, Kans.: Coronado Press, 1972.

Vedder, Henry C. *Balthasar Hubmaier: The Leader of the Anabaptists*. New York: Putnam, 1905.

Verduin, Leonard. *The Anatomy of a Hybrid: A Study in Church-State Relationships*. Grand Rapids: Eerdmans, 1976.

———. *The Reformers and Their Stepchildren*. Grand Rapids: Eerdmans, 1964.

Wenger, J. C. *Conrad Grebel's Programmatic Letters: 1524*. Scottdale, Pa.: Herald Press, 1970.

Williams, George Hunston. *The Radical Reformation*. Philadelphia: Westminster Press, 1962.

———, and Angel M. Mergal, eds. *Spiritual and Anabaptist Writers*. Vol. 25 of the Library of Christian Classics. Philadelphia: Westminster Press, 1957.

Windhorst, Christof. *Täuferisches Taufverständnis: Balthasar Hubmaiers Lehre zwischen traditioneller und Reformatorischer Theologie*. Leiden: E. J. Brill, 1976.

Yoder, John H., ed. *The Legacy of Michael Sattler*. Vol. 1 of the Classics of the Radical Reformation series. Scottdale, Pa.: Herald Press, 1973.

Attempts at Reform

Artús, Wilfrido. *Los Reformadores Españoles del Siglo XVI*. Mexico: Casa Unida de Publicaciones, n.d.

Boehmer, Edward. *Spanish Reformers of Two Centuries from 1520*. 2 vols. Strasbourg: Trübner, 1874, 1883.

Longhurst, John E. *Luther's Ghost in Spain (1517–1546)*. Lawrence, Kans.: Coronado Press, 1969.

Menéndez y Pelayo, Marcelino. *Historia de los Heterodoxos Españoles*. 4 vols. Buenos Aires: Editorial Glem, 1945.

Stoughton, John. *The Spanish Reformers: Their Memories and Dwelling Places.* London: Religious Tract Society, 1883.

Sutherland, N. M. *The Huguenot Struggle for Recognition.* New Haven: Yale University Press, 1980.

Valdés, Juan de. *Dialogo de Doctrina Christiana.* 1529; rpt. Madrid: Libreria Nacional y Extranjera, 1929.

Catholic Reform

Broderick, James. *The Origin of the Jesuits.* New York: Longmans, Green, 1940.

———. *Saint Ignatius Loyola.* New York: Farrar, Straus & Cudahy, 1956.

Christian, William A., Jr. *Local Religion in Sixteenth-Century Spain.* Princeton: Princeton University Press, 1981.

Daniel-Rops, Henri. *The Catholic Reformation.* Trans. John Warrington. New York: Dutton, 1962.

Davies, R. Trevor. *The Golden Century of Spain, 1501–1621.* Rev. ed. New York: Harper & Row, 1965.

Dickens, A. G. *The Counter Reformation.* London: Thames & Hudson, 1968.

Eck, John. *Enchiridion of Commonplaces: Against Luther and Other Enemies of the Church.* Trans. Ford Lewis Battles. Grand Rapids: Baker Book House, 1979.

Fleming, David L. *The Spiritual Exercises of St. Ignatius.* Ed. George G. Ganss. St. Louis: Institute of Jesuit Sources, 1978.

Fremantle, Anne, ed. *The Papal Encyclicals in Their Historical Context.* New York: Mentor–Omega, 1956.

Ignatius of Loyola, Saint. *Letters of Saint Ignatius of Loyola.* Trans. and ed. William J. Young. Chicago: Loyola University Press, 1959.

Janelle, Pierre. *The Catholic Reformation.* Milwaukee: Bruce Publishing Co., 1963.

Olin, John C. *The Catholic Reformation: Savonarola to Ignatius Loyola.* New York: Harper & Row, 1969.

Wulf, Friedrich, ed. *Ignatius of Loyola: His Personality and Spiritual Heritage, 1556–1956.* St. Louis: Institute of Jesuit Sources, 1956.

Young, William J., ed. *Finding God in All Living Things: Essays in Ignatian Spirituality Selected from Christus.* Chicago: Henry Regnery Co., 1958.

ADDITIONAL REFERENCE WORKS

Abrahams, Israel. *Jewish Life in the Middle Ages.* New York: Meridian Books, 1958.

Apel, Willi, ed. *Harvard Dictionary of Music.* Cambridge: Belknap Press of Harvard University Press, 1969.

Bainton, Roland H. *Early and Medieval Christianity.* Boston: Beacon Press, 1962.

———. *Studies on the Reformation.* Boston: Beacon Press, 1963.

———, and Eric W. Gritsch. *Bibliography of the Continental Reformation: Materials Available in English.* Hamden, Conn.: Shoe String Press–Archon Books, 1972.

Berdyaev, Nicolas. *The Meaning of History.* Trans. George Reavey. London: Centenary Press, 1936.

Bettenson, Henry, ed. *Documents of the Christian Church.* 2nd ed. Oxford: Oxford University Press, 1982.

Cannon, William Ragsdale. *History of Christianity in the Middle Ages.* Nashville: Abingdon Press, 1960.

Coulton, G. G. *Medieval Panorama.* New York: World Publishing Co., 1955.

Daly, Lowrie J. *The Medieval University, 1200–1400.* New York: Sheed & Ward, 1961.

Eisenstein, Elizabeth L. *The Printing Press as an Agent of Change: Communications and Cultural Transformations in Early-Modern Europe.* 2 vols. New York: Cambridge University Press, 1979.

Elton, G. R. *England Under the Tudors.* New York: Harper & Row, 1974.

Fairweather, Eugene R., ed. and trans. *A Scholastic Miscellany: Anselm to Ockham.* Vol. 10 of the Library of Christian Classics. Philadelphia: Westminster Press, 1956.

Franzen, August, and John P. Dolan. *A History of the Church.* New York: Herder & Herder, 1969.

Grout, Donald J. *A History of Western Music.* New York: Norton, 1960.

Gutierrez-Marin, C. L. *Misticos Españoles del Siglo-16.* Mexico: Casa Unida de Publicaciones, 1946.

Janson, H. W. *History of Art.* Englewood Cliffs, N.J.: Prentice-Hall, 1969.

Kingdon, Robert M., ed. *The Sixteenth-Century Journal.* Kirksville, Mo.: n.p., 1985.

Latourette, Kenneth Scott. *A History of Christianity.* New York: Harper, 1953.

Leith, John H., ed. *Creeds of the Churches: A Reader in Christian Doctrine from the Bible to the Present.* Garden City, N.Y.: Doubleday, 1963.

Lucas, Henry S. *The Renaissance and the Reformation.* 2nd ed. New York: Harper & Row, 1960.

Newman, Albert Henry. *Modern Church History (A.D. 1517–1932).* Vol. 2 of *A Manual of Church History.* Philadelphia: American Baptist Publication Society, 1931.

Runciman, Steven. *A History of the Crusades.* 3 vols. Cambridge: Cambridge University Press, 1951–54.

Schaff, Philip. *The Evangelical Protestant Creeds, with Translations.* Vol. 3 of *Creeds of Christendom.* Grand Rapids: Baker Book House, 1966.

Index

Printed in the United States
99715LV00003B/43-90/A